FAMILIES UNDER CONSTRUCTION: PARENTAGE, ADOPTION, AND ASSISTED REPRODUCTION

ASPEN COURSEBOOK SERIES

FAMILIES UNDER CONSTRUCTION: PARENTAGE, ADOPTION, AND ASSISTED REPRODUCTION

Second Edition

Susan Frelich Appleton
Lemma Barkeloo & Phoebe Couzins
Professor of Law
Washington University in St. Louis

D. Kelly Weisberg
Professor of Law
Hastings College of the Law
University of California

Wolters Kluwer

Printed in the United States of America.

1 2 3 4 5 6 7 8 9 0

ISBN 978-1-5438-2052-2

Library of Congress Cataloging-in-Publication Data

Names: Appleton, Susan Frelich, 1948- author. | Weisberg, D. Kelly, author.
Title: Families under construction : parentage, adoption, and assisted reproduction / Susan Frelich Appleton, Lemma Barkeloo & Phoebe Couzins, Professor of Law, Washington University in St. Louis; D. Kelly Weisberg, Professor of Law, Hastings College of the Law, University of California.
Description: Second edition. | New York : Wolters Kluwer, [2021] | Series: Families under construction | Includes bibliographical references and index. | Summary: "Coursebook offering in-depth exploration of the issues emerging out of biotechnology and society's expanding understanding of family identity" —Provided by publisher.
Identifiers: LCCN 2020045072 (print) | LCCN 2020045073 (ebook) | ISBN 9781543820522 (paperback) | ISBN 9781543820539 (ebook)
Subjects: LCSH: Adoption — Law and legislation — United States. | Human reproductive technology — Law and legislation — United States.
Classification: LCC KF545 .A97 2021 (print) | LCC KF545 (ebook) | DDC 346.7301/78 — dc23
LC record available at https://lccn.loc.gov/2020045072
LC ebook record available at https://lccn.loc.gov/2020045073

SUSTAINABLE FORESTRY INITIATIVE   Certified Sourcing
www.sfiprogram.org
SFI-00756

About Wolters Kluwer Legal & Regulatory U.S.

Wolters Kluwer Legal & Regulatory U.S. delivers expert content and solutions in the areas of law, corporate compliance, health compliance, reimbursement, and legal education. Its practical solutions help customers successfully navigate the demands of a changing environment to drive their daily activities, enhance decision quality and inspire confident outcomes.

Serving customers worldwide, its legal and regulatory portfolio includes products under the Aspen Publishers, CCH Incorporated, Kluwer Law International, ftwilliam.com and MediRegs names. They are regarded as exceptional and trusted resources for general legal and practice-specific knowledge, compliance and risk management, dynamic workflow solutions, and expert commentary.

To the next generations.

SUMMARY OF CONTENTS

CONTENTS

PREFACE

Who is a child's parent? When do adults and minors constitute a family? According to the idea that animates this book, political or policy choices shape the answers to these questions. Understanding these choices, in turn, requires consulting constitutional doctrine, state family law, bioethical and religious considerations, social norms, economic and other inequalities, and assumptions about dependency — all sites of continuing flux.

Once, these choices produced legal parentage rules that relied on gestation, marriage to the child's mother, and adoption. Now, such familiar connections merely provide a starting point for more expansive and often more contested approaches that look to behaviors, functions, and intentions. These new approaches also defy conventional constructions reflected in gendered terms such as "mother" and "father" and in the traditional idea that a given child can have no more than two parents. Even these contemporary criteria for parentage, however, require decisions about what conduct and mental states count and what fails to meet the chosen test.

Scientific advancements, such as more accurate genetic testing and assisted reproductive technologies (or ARTs), account for some of the transformations in the law of parentage. Shifts in society have played at least an equally consequential role. The long list of pertinent twentieth and twenty-first century developments includes the largely class-based retreat from marriage, evolving sexual norms, the emergence of families headed by LGBTQ adults (married or not), a decreasing number of white infants available for adoptive placement, a child welfare and foster care system always under fire, a growing number of older children with special needs but without permanent homes, the decline of secrecy in adoption, fluctuating attitudes about transracial and intercountry adoption, and a burgeoning market — domestic and international — for infertility treatments.

In situating law in its larger cultural context and emphasizing change over time, these materials challenge the common intuition that parentage is "natural" or rests on "nature." Of course, adoption — one route to parentage examined here — has long provided a means of establishing an officially recognized parent-child relationship based on law rather than biology. Yet the legal fiction that adoption is said to create does not stand alone, and this book is designed to expose similarities in longstanding rules for determining who is a parent as well as in contemporary responses to ARTs.

Part I introduces foundational principles of parentage derived from common law, the United States Constitution, state and federal statutes and policies, and law reform projects, including model legislation. This Part begins with the history of adoption, the paradigm case of legally and socially constructed parentage. This history sets the stage for cases about traditional doctrines that, like adoption, subordinate biological connections to variables law has chosen to prioritize in determining parentage, such as marriage and gender as well as parental support duties, which help maintain dependency as a private responsibility. This Part also explores newer doctrines that emphasize performance, bonding, and intent. The focus then turns to why parentage matters, highlighting the autonomy ordinarily accorded to parental decisionmaking.

Building on these foundations, the book's Parts II and III delve more deeply into adoption and assisted reproduction, respectively. For each, the materials examine the individual and societal interests at stake; existing legal regimes and processes, including applicable constitutional considerations and the consequences of failed arrangements; and practices across state and international boundaries. To the extent that the governing law is still emerging, the materials necessarily pose normative questions about the purposes of regulation and the best way to achieve such ends.

Investigating parentage, adoption, and ARTs together offers several payoffs. First, juxtaposing these topics underscores that there are multiple ways to create a family. For those who face reproductive challenges (from infertility or the absence of a different-sex partner), adoption, increasingly, has become only one option among many. Indeed, millions of babies now have been born as a result of ARTs. Two principal interventions, alternative insemination (once called "artificial insemination") and in vitro fertilization (commonly called "IVF") permit a range of collaborations, including use of donated genetic material (ova, sperm, or both) or the outsourcing of gestational services (surrogacy). Such collaborations require rethinking traditional parentage rules and also complicate the concept of adoption.

Second, the laws governing all three contexts are entwined because the resolution of familiar legal problems often provides models for grappling with more novel issues, although not without controversy. Sometimes traditional principles of parentage apply to ARTs. Yet, sometimes, modernization of such principles in the ARTs setting prompts reforms applicable to children brought into being in more conventional ways. Similarly, law's familiarity with adoption has provided one ready guidepost for addressing questions presented by ARTs, with popular locutions, such as "embryo adoption," illustrating the pervasiveness of this analogical reasoning.

Third, the laws of parentage, adoption, and ARTs all exemplify a deep-seated tension between procreative liberty or parental autonomy, on the one hand, and state intervention in family decisionmaking, on the other. Despite the oft-acknowledged privacy of procreative and childrearing choices, some children become available for adoption after state child-protective efforts result in involuntary termination of parental rights. Although contemporary constitutional doctrine presumptively shields sexual reproduction from state interference, such rights are purely negative with no guarantee of government support if needed. At the other end of the regulatory continuum, parentage by adoption requires successful navigation of a state-controlled system that supervises acquisition of the original parents' consent and criteria for child placement, professes to center the best interests of the child, and culminates in a judicial decree. Increased use of independent placements, in which birth parents select adoptive parents, however, reveals a movement toward greater autonomy and private ordering. The changing nature of adoption regulation surfaces elsewhere too, for example, in the push for opening once sealed birth records, with both opponents and proponents of secrecy invoking privacy. Locating the various ARTs collaborations on this dynamic regulatory continuum remains a work in progress in many U.S. jurisdictions and abroad.

Finally, this book's topics and themes — which raise issues of identity, ancestral roots, and family secrets — touch deep emotions and provide engaging fodder for literature, media, and popular culture. For example, several contemporary television series have featured these matters, including *Life Unexpected* (2010-2011), *Generation Cryo* (2013), *The Fosters* (2013-2018), *This is Us* (2016-), and *Little Fires Everywhere* (2020), to name a few. Although these shows often take poetic license with governing law, they help bring the legal issues to life. These depictions also contribute to the public understanding of parentage, adoption, and ARTs and, in turn, the personal and political choices at work. To take advantage of the reciprocal relationship among law, life, and culture, this book incorporates sidebars about selected films and novels in the hope that they will pique curiosity, provoke discussion, and require consideration of lived experience, even if only in fiction.

Teaching Notes

This casebook is designed for law school seminars and courses, including first-year electives, as well as undergraduate courses in legal studies or other departments. Supplementary activities for the class might include visiting a local family court (for example, to observe annual "National Adoption Day" proceedings), hosting a reproductive endocrinologist as a guest speaker, or showing and then analyzing a pertinent film, whether one included in the sidebars or a different one.

In this edition, almost all citations of authority appear in footnotes to give curious teachers and students alike access to a robust set of sources without the distractions of a cluttered text.

Editorial Matters

Cases and excerpts have all been edited, often quite extensively. Most deletions are indicated by ellipses, with some exceptions: Some concurring and dissenting opinions have been eliminated; citations have been modified or eliminated; many footnotes and references have been omitted; and paragraphs have been modified, and sometimes combined, to save space and to make the selections more coherent. Brackets are used at times to indicate substantial changes and deletions. Original footnotes in cases and excerpts are reprinted nonconsecutively throughout the book. The editors' footnotes are numbered consecutively in each chapter and appear in brackets to differentiate them from original footnotes. References follow A Uniform System of Citation (20th ed. 2015), except when that style conflicts with the publisher's style. In addition, statutory citations were checked on Lexis or Westlaw.

Susan Frelich Appleton
D. Kelly Weisberg

August, 2020

ACKNOWLEDGMENTS

This project initially grew out of our earlier efforts on the casebook Modern Family Law: Cases and Materials, published by Wolters Kluwer. The first edition, entitled Adoption and Assisted Reproduction: Families Under Construction, was published in 2009. Much has changed in the more than a decade since. This second edition has a new title, revised framing, organizational changes, and expanded coverage. For this edition, we appreciate the outstanding research assistance of Kylee Mattoon, Rebecca McDonald, Shelby Saxon, and Meredith Stone (all from Washington University School of Law). We also thank Jordan Jepsen and Lynn Churchill at Wolters Kluwer and Kathy Langone, Nick Walther, and Frannie Ruch at The Froebe Group for welcome encouragement, valuable guidance, and helpful editorial support—all during a period in which COVID-19 disrupted familiar ways of working.

We thank the publishers and copyright holders listed here for their permission to reprint the various excerpts indicated.

Andrews, Lori. Between Strangers: Surrogate Mothers, Expectant Father and Brave New Babies (1989). Harper & Row. Copyright © 1989.

Bartholet, Elizabeth, Where Do Black Children Belong? The Politics of Race Matching in Adoption. 139 University of Pennsylvania Law Review (1991). University of Pennsylvania. Copyright © 1991. Reprinted by permission.

Berebitsky, Julie. Like Our Very Own: Adoptions and the Changing Culture of Motherhood, 1851-1950 (2001). University Press of Kansas. Copyright © 2001.

Fessler, Ann, The Girls Who Went Away (The Penguin Press 2006). Copyright © 2006 by Ann Fessler. Used by permission of The Penguin Press, a division of Penguin Group (USA) Inc.

Perry, Twila L., Transracial and International Adoption: Mothers, Hierarchy, Race, and Feminist Legal Theory. 10 Yale Journal of Law & Feminism (1998). Yale Law School. Copyright © 1998.

Presser, Stephen, The Historical Background of the American Law of Adoption. 11 Journal of Family Law (1971). University of Louisville, Louis D. Brandeis School of Law. Reprinted by permission of the author.

Roberts, Dorothy. Shattered Bonds: The Color of Child Welfare (1998). Basic Books. Copyright © 1998 by Dorothy Roberts. Reprinted by permission of the author.

Savage, Dan, Two Moments of Transcendent Bliss, adapted from The Commitment, Copyright © 2005 by Dan Savage. Used by permission of Dutton, a division of Penguin Group (USA) Inc.

Spar, Debora L., The Baby Business: How Money, Science, and Politics Drive the Commerce of Conception (Harvard Business School Publishing Corp. 2006). Copyright © 2006 by Harvard Business School Publishing Corporation; all rights reserved. Reprinted by permission of Harvard Business School Press.

Uniform Adoption Act, Comment, UAA §14 (1999). Reprinted by permission of the Uniform Law Commission.

Uniform Nonparent and Visitation Act, Section 4 (2018). Reprinted by permission of the Uniform Law Commission.

Uniform Parentage Act, Section 607, Section 706, Section 708, Sections 702-704, Section 802, Section 804, Section 809, Sections 811-812 (2017). Reprinted by permission of the Uniform Law Commission.

Walbert, Meghan Moravcik, After Losing A Foster Child, Contemplating Another, The New York Times, Jan. 19, 2017. The New York Times Company. All rights reserved. Used under license.

Wooten, Colton, A Father's Day Plea to Sperm Donors, The New York Times, June 19, 2011. The New York Times Company. All rights reserved. Used under license.

Whitehead, Mary Beth & Loretta Schwartz-Nobel. A Mother's Story (1989). St. Martin's Press. Copyright © 1989.

Witt, April, About Isabella, Washington Post, Feb. 4, 2007, at W14. From The Washington Post, February 4, 2007 © 2007 The Washington Post. All rights reserved. Used by permission.

We also appreciate the ability to use 325 words or more from the following:

Michael Boucai, Is Assisted Procreation an LGBT Right? 2016 Wisconsin Law Review (2016).

Lisa C. Ikemoto, Reproductive Tourism: Equality Concerns in the Global Market for Fertility Services. 27 Law & Inequality: A Journal of Theory and Practice (2009).

Jody Lyneé Madeira, Taking Baby Steps: How Patients and Fertility Clinics Collaborate in Conception (2018).

FAMILIES UNDER CONSTRUCTION: PARENTAGE, ADOPTION, AND ASSISTED REPRODUCTION

PART I

PARENTAGE

FOUNDATIONS: PARENTAGE THEN AND NOW

A. ADOPTION'S HISTORY AND PURPOSE

Adoption provides a lens for examining the role of law in creating parent-child relationships. Characterizing adoption as a "fiction" or describing it as "artificial," as in the excerpt below, suggests a contrast with real or genuine versions of such relationships. Yet, the state assigns parents to children even when it chooses to rely on biological connections[1] or on criteria like marriage and gender.

What do adoption and its history teach us about parentage more generally? Is adoption designed to serve primarily the interests of adults, of children, or of society? In an ideal world, would adoption exist at all?

STEPHEN B. PRESSER, THE HISTORICAL BACKGROUND
OF THE AMERICAN LAW OF ADOPTION

11 J. Fam. L. 443, 445-489 (1971)

Sir Henry Maine, in his *Ancient Law*, takes the position that the early patriarchal civilizations would not have been able to grow out of their "swaddling clothes" without the custom of adoption. It is Maine's contention that without the fiction of adoption, primitive tribes could not have absorbed each other, or could not have combined except on terms of "absolute superiority on one side and absolute subjection on the other." Primitive peoples also found a strong motive for the artificial extension of the family in their desire for male issue to perpetuate the family rites of ancestor worship.

We can document the practice of adoption among the ancient Babylonians, Egyptians, and Hebrews, as well as the Greeks, but the most advanced early law on adoption which we have is from the Romans. In contrast with current adoption law, which has as its purpose the "best interests" of the child, it appears that ancient adoption law, and particularly the Roman example, was clearly designed to benefit the *adopter*, and any benefits to

---

[1] James G. Dwyer, The Relationship Rights of Children 26, 135 (2006).

the adoptee were secondary. There were two broad purposes that Roman adoption law served: (1) to avoid extinction of the family, and (2) to perpetuate rites of family religious worship. . . .

[Adoption was not known at common law.] The usual explanation for the absence of a legal recognition of adoption in the English common law is the inordinately high regard for blood lineage of the English. [Another possible reason was xenophobia.]

The purpose of the American adoption statutes passed in the middle of the nineteenth century was to provide for the welfare of dependent children, a purpose quite different from that of the old Roman laws. [On the other hand, in England] there were mechanisms for the care of children, dependent and otherwise, that made adoption for social welfare purposes unnecessary. These mechanisms, which were instituted early and which were very well developed by the seventeenth century, were the institutions of "putting out" and "apprenticeship." In a very real sense these institutions were a form of "adoption," although the purpose was neither inheritance nor the perpetuation of the adopter's family, but the temporary training of the child. [T]he customs of "apprenticeship" and "service" were brought to America by the New England Puritans. . . .

The first comprehensive adoption statute was passed in 1851 in Massachusetts. Among its key provisions were requirements 1) that written consent be given by the natural parents . . . ; 2) that the child himself must consent if he is fourteen years of age or older; 3) that the adopter's [spouse] must join in the petition for adoption; 4) that the probate judge . . . must be satisfied that the petitioner(s) were "of sufficient ability to bring up the child . . . and that it is fit and proper that such adoption should take effect" . . . ; 5) that once the adoption was approved by the probate court, the adopted child would become "to all intents and purposes" the legal child of the petitioner(s); [and] 6) that the natural parents would be deprived by the decree of adoption of all legal rights and obligations respecting the adopted child . . . .

[The purpose of the Massachusetts law and others like it remains unclear. One theory says that an increase in adoptions arranged by foundling societies prompted these statutes.] It is naive to attribute the passage of adoption statutes in so many states solely to the activities of "foundling societies." The activity of these societies *is* demonstrative of a larger movement for child welfare of which the passage of the adoption statutes also represents a part. This movement came about as a result of the economic changes which made the stop-gap institutions of apprenticeship, service, and indenture quite unable to cope with the great numbers of children who had been neglected by their families and also were neglected, until about the middle of the nineteenth century in most cases, by the society and the state. In order to understand better the motives that lay behind the passage of the adoption statutes, it is important to understand some of these other developments in child welfare work. . . .

[F]rom philanthropic motives most probably inspired by the continuing plight of dependent children in the hands of public authorities, private agencies for the care of such children were founded. . . . In the first half of the nineteenth century, at least seventy-seven such agencies were founded . . . . After 1850 the increase in the number of such agencies was even more rapid. . . . Before 1850, the private agencies sought to teach their charges to read and write. . . . Prior to the establishment of the public school systems and compulsory attendance, the agencies felt their primary service should be to give to their children the rudiments of an education before they were placed out in indenture or service.

Around 1850, however, private agencies began to be founded with the avowed purpose of placing younger children in a suitable family atmosphere. The work of some of the "infant's hospitals," "foundling asylums," and "maternity hospitals" in New York and Boston stands out in this regard, as does the work of the Children's Aid Societies started in those cities in 1853 and 1865, respectively. . . . The Children's Aid Societies made efforts to place children in suitable homes, usually homes far from the city, in the expanding states and territories of the West. [T]he Children's Aid Society of New York [] placed over twenty thousand children in homes out of New York City in the twenty years after it was founded. . . .

[Many of] the children placed by such agencies as the New York Children's Aid Society found themselves in situations which not only resembled "adoption" as we know it today but which was called by the same name. As the phenomenon of children in adopted homes became more common, there was increased pressure not only to pass laws regulating and insuring the legal relations between adopted children and their natural and adoptive parents, but to guarantee that some benefits of heirship were conferred on the adopted child. This pressure, which originated with the activities of the charitable associations working in child welfare, led to passage of the general adoption statutes in the third quarter of the nineteenth century. . . .

NOTES AND QUESTIONS

1. *Adoption's roots.* Professor Presser offers several reasons why English law did not develop adoption before it emerged in the United States. Not only did the British hostility reflect xenophobia and strict adherence to a common law of inheritance based on blood ties, but the British practices of indenture, placing (or putting) out, and apprenticeship (both voluntary and involuntary) offered ways to provide care for children who could not remain in their original families. Similarly, neither traditional Jewish law nor Islamic law recognizes formal adoption because of the importance of biological lineage, although informal arrangements to care for orphans and to facilitate inheritance appear in ancient texts.[2]

2. *Early adoption statutes.* Because adoption remained unknown at common law, it is a purely statutory institution. Although many statutes enacted in the mid-nineteenth century reflected the old civil law of adoption, the Massachusetts statute transformed the earlier understanding by making adoption "a legal procedure" and "creat[ing] a means of establishing an

---

[2] See Mark Goldfeder, The Adoption of Children in Judaism and in Israel; A Conceptual and Practical Review, 22 Cardozo J. Int'l. & Comp. L. 321 (2014); Daniel Pollack et al., Classical Religious Perspectives on Adoption, 79 Notre Dame L. Rev. 693 (2004).

artificial bond between a parent and child that closely approximated the legal ideal of republican domestic relations."[3] More significantly, however, the Massachusetts statute and others modeled on it portrayed adoption as a child-welfare measure, in contrast to the emphasis on adult interests reflected in earlier approaches.[4]

3. *Adoption in the Progressive Era.* The child-centered understanding of adoption gained strength in the Progressive Era of the late nineteenth and early twentieth centuries. During this period, a broad reformist movement embraced child welfare and provided a focus for the then-new profession of social work; the resulting "childsaving" project saw adoption as the goal for children removed from their homes because of poverty, neglect, and abuse.[5] Despite the primary emphasis on "adoption as rescue" during this time, the practice served to achieve other objectives as well. An examination of California "trial court records, orphanage reports, appellate court decisions, and other sources" revealed three types of adoptions from this period:

> *Family preservation* adoption, which reflected a tie to past, informal "adoption" practices, enabled adopters to keep already-established families and family money together.
> *Family creation* adoption, which emerged as the dominant type of adoption in the late nineteenth and early twentieth centuries, gave childless couples a way to approximate the biological parent-child relationship.
> And *family re-creation* adoption, a precursor to the modal practice of adoption in the mid-to-late twentieth century, enabled stepfathers to remake families previously disrupted by divorce or death.[6]

Family creation adoptions accounted for approximately two-thirds of the adoptions during this period.[7]

4. *Orphan trains.* The Progressive Era's childsaving initiatives included "orphan trains," developed by Charles Loring Brace (founder of the New York Children's Aid Society in 1853) to send poor children from large East Coast urban areas, where they might land in almshouses or other institutional settings, to live and work in Midwest farm families. Despite the nomenclature, the practice was not limited to orphans. Although Brace's supporters lauded his child-welfare motives, critics claim that the shipment of child labor westward constituted exploitation, removed children from parental care without valid consent, and disregarded the best interests of the child principle.[8] The sharply contrasting views of the orphan trains

---

[3] Michael Grossberg, Governing the Hearth: Law and the Family in Nineteenth Century America 271 (1985). See generally Jamil S. Zainaldin, The Emergence of a Modern American Family Law: Child Custody, Adoption, and the Courts, 1796-1851, 73 Nw. U. L. Rev. 1038 (1979).

[4] Grossberg, supra note [3], at 271-272.

[5] See id. at 278-280; Mary Ann Mason, From Father's Property to Children's Rights: A History of Child Custody in the United States 87-92, 189 (1994).

[6] Chris Guthrie & Joanna L. Grossman, Adoption in the Progressive Era: Preserving, Creating, and Re-Creating Families, 43 Am. J. Legal Hist. 235, 236 (1999).

[7] Id. at 245.

[8] See generally Marilyn Irvin Holt, The Orphan Trains: Placing Out in America (1992); Stephen O'Connor, Orphan Trains: The Story of Charles Loring Brace and the Children He Saved and Failed (2001).

evoke questions about the Progressive Era's child-centered understanding of adoption and presage more modern controversies, including debates about transracial and international adoptions. See Chapter 4, section A1a; Chapter 6, section C.

Depictions in Popular Culture: John Irving, The Cider House Rules (1985)

In this novel, a sprawling Dickensian tale that begins during the Progressive Era at St. Cloud's, a remote Maine orphanage, Dr. Wilbur Larch provides a choice to his many clients facing unwanted pregnancies: to give birth to an orphan (to await adoption) or have an abortion (illegal at the time). As the story progresses, Homer Wells, an orphan who returns to St. Cloud's after several foster placements fail, grows up there — emerging as the protagonist who struggles with the moral issues posed by abortion, by his love for Candy, who is betrothed to a close friend serving far away in World War II, and by his obligations to St. Cloud's mission after Dr. Larch's demise. When Candy and Homer secretly have a child, they present him as an orphan whom Homer has adopted.

What reflections of the way we think about adoption and its purposes appear in *The Cider House Rules*? How is adoption regarded at St. Cloud's? Consider the verbal ritual, after each adoptive placement, in which Dr. Larch informs the orphans that one of their number "has found a family" and he urges them "to be happy" for the child. Consider also Homer's preference for staying at the orphanage, rather than joining an adoptive family. What can one learn about the secrecy traditionally associated with adoption from Candy's and Homer's secret (which turns on its head the traditional practice of presenting adopted children as if they had been born to the family)? What insights come from Dr. Larch's even-handed willingness to offer women with unwanted pregnancies the choice of the delivery of an orphan, on the one hand, or an abortion, on the other?

More generally, what is the relationship between abortion and adoption? Several observers agree that the number of white infants available for adoption dramatically declined with the legalization of abortion in Roe v. Wade, 410 U.S. 113 (1973). Note, too, that many opponents of abortion advocate adoption instead, although *Roe* — in listing the postbirth detriments suffered by women who were denied legal abortions — implied that surrendering a child for adoption does not sufficiently avoid such detriments. See id. at 153. Why? What reasoning underlies the Court's rejection of adoption as an adequate way for a woman to extricate herself at least from the problems that she would face after the child's birth? What burdens might continued pregnancy and adoption surrender impose that legally permissible abortion might avoid?[9] What other considerations should inform an analysis of the connections between adoption and abortion law? See Chapter 2, section A.

B. THE TRADITIONAL LAW OF PARENTAGE: CONSTRUCTING LEGAL FATHERHOOD

Because adoption replaces one parent-child relationship with another, the practice presupposes a determination of a child's original parents. What is the basis of original parentage?

Law long relied on gestation, marriage, and gender for this purpose. Historically, a child born out of wedlock was treated as "filius nullius" (a child of no one) without a father and in some jurisdictions with questionable maternal ties, too.[10] Beginning in the late 1960s, the United States Supreme Court struck down many laws discriminating against such children as an "illogical and unjust" means of deterring adults' extramarital sexual conduct.[11] These cases, extending the rights of nonmarital children under the Fourteenth Amendment's Equal Protection Clause, raised two related issues: how law determines the father of such children (whose mother is identified through birth) and whether the prevailing inequalities violate the constitutional rights not only of the children but also of the unmarried adults themselves.

Some significant contextual factors require emphasis in an examination of law's evolving approach to parentage. First, the move toward equal treatment of nonmarital children began before the advent of today's sophisticated and largely accurate methods of genetic testing. Second, sex outside of marriage violated not only social norms but also criminal laws against fornication and adultery.

Third, a double standard and gender stereotypes prevailed, so that women typically bore the brunt of the stigma of nonmarital pregnancy and birth while the notion of fatherhood, especially outside marriage, included no expectation that a man would perform a parental role. A racial and class-based hierarchy governed as well, so that nonmarital childbearing in poor minority communities was understood as the predictable deviancy of an entire population; among middle- and upper-class white women, however, it was a sign of personal and scandalous transgression.[12]

Against this background, this section focuses on the construction of paternity or legal fatherhood, both in state law and under the United States Constitution. To what extent do these traditional approaches remain operative today? How would you reform them to meet contemporary needs, such

---

[9] See Sherry F. Colb, "Never Having Loved at All": An Overlooked Interest That Grounds the Abortion Right, 48 Conn. L. Rev. 933 (2016).

[10] See, e.g., Levy v. Louisiana, 391 U.S. 68 (1968); Grossberg, supra note [3], at 197, 207.

[11] E.g., Weber v. Aetna Casualty & Surety Co., 406 U.S. 164, 175 (1972).

[12] See, e.g., Rickie Solinger, Beggars and Choosers: How the Politics of Choice Shapes Adoption, Abortion, and Welfare in the United States 69-70 (2001).

as those reflected in the decline in marriage[13] and the rise of families headed by same-sex couples?

STANLEY V. ILLINOIS

405 U.S. 645 (1972)

Mr. Justice WHITE delivered the opinion of the Court.

Joan Stanley lived with Peter Stanley intermittently for 18 years during which time they had three children. When Joan Stanley died, Peter Stanley lost not only her but also his children. Under Illinois law the children of unwed fathers become wards of the State upon the death of the mother. Accordingly, upon Joan Stanley's death, in a dependency proceeding instituted by the State of Illinois, Stanley's children were declared wards of the State and placed with court-appointed guardians. Stanley appealed, claiming that he had never been shown to be an unfit parent and that since married fathers and unwed mothers could not be deprived of their children without such a showing, he had been deprived of the equal protection of the laws guaranteed him by the Fourteenth Amendment. . . .

Stanley presses his equal protection claim here. The State continues to respond that unwed fathers are presumed unfit to raise their children . . . . We granted certiorari to determine whether this method of procedure by presumption could be allowed to stand in light of the fact that Illinois allows married fathers — whether divorced, widowed, or separated — and mothers — even if unwed — the benefit of the presumption that they are fit to raise their children. . . .

We must [examine this question]: Is a presumption that distinguishes and burdens all unwed fathers constitutionally repugnant? We conclude that, as a matter of due process of law, Stanley was entitled to a hearing on his fitness as a parent before his children were taken from him and that by denying him a hearing and extending it to all other parents whose custody of their children is challenged, the State denied Stanley the equal protection of the laws guaranteed by the Fourteenth Amendment. . . .

Illinois has two principal methods of removing nondelinquent children from the homes of their parents. In a dependency proceeding it may demonstrate that the children are wards of the State because they have no surviving parent or guardian. Ill. Rev. Stat., c. 37, §§702-1, 702-5. In a neglect proceeding it may show that children should be wards of the State because the present parent(s) or guardian does not provide suitable care. Ill. Rev. Stat., c. 37, §§702-1, 702-4.

The State's right — indeed duty — to protect minor children through a judicial determination of their interests in a neglect proceeding is not challenged here. Rather, we are faced with a dependency statute that empowers state officials to circumvent neglect proceedings on the theory that an unwed father is not a "parent" whose existing relationship with his children

---

[13] See June Carbone & Naomi Cahn, Marriage Markets: How Inequality is Remaking the American Family (2014); Shelly Lundberg & Robert A. Pollak, Cohabitation and the Uneven Retreat from Marriage in the United States, 1950-2010, in Human Capital in History: The American Record 241 (Leah Platt Boustan et al. eds., 2014).

must be considered. "Parents," says the State, "means the father and mother of a legitimate child, or the survivor of them, or the natural mother of an illegitimate child, and includes any adoptive parent," Ill. Rev. Stat., c. 37, §701-14, but the term does not include unwed fathers.

Under Illinois law, therefore, while the children of all parents can be taken from them in neglect proceedings, that is only after notice, hearing, and proof of such unfitness as a parent as amounts to neglect, an unwed father is uniquely subject to the more simplistic dependency proceeding. By use of this proceeding, the State, on showing that the father was not married to the mother, need not prove unfitness in fact, because it is presumed at law. Thus, the unwed father's claim of parental qualification is avoided as "irrelevant."

In considering this procedure under the Due Process Clause, we recognize, as we have in other cases, that due process of law does not require a hearing "in every conceivable case of government impairment of private interest." Cafeteria Workers v. McElroy, 367 U.S. 886 (1961). [That case] firmly established that "what procedures due process may require under any given set of circumstances must begin with a determination of the precise nature of the government function involved as well as of the private interest that has been affected by governmental action." . . .

The private interest here, that of a man in the children he has sired and raised, undeniably warrants deference and, absent a powerful countervailing interest, protection. . . . The Court has frequently emphasized the importance of the family. The rights to conceive and to raise one's children have been deemed "essential," Meyer v. Nebraska, 262 U.S. 390, 399 (1923), "basic civil rights of man," Skinner v. Oklahoma, 316 U.S. 535, 541 (1942), and "[r]ights far more precious . . . than property rights," May v. Anderson, 345 U.S. 528, 533 (1953). . . .

Nor has the law refused to recognize those family relationships unlegitimized by a marriage ceremony. The Court has declared unconstitutional a state statute denying natural, but illegitimate, children a wrongful-death action for the death of their mother, emphasizing that such children cannot be denied the right of other children because familial bonds in such cases were often as warm, enduring, and important as those arising within a more formally organized family unit. Levy v. Louisiana, 391 U.S. 68, 71-72 (1968). "To say that the test of equal protection should be the 'legal' rather than the biological relationship is to avoid the issue. For the Equal Protection Clause necessarily limits the authority of a State to draw such 'legal' lines as it chooses." Glona v. American Guarantee Co., 391 U.S. 73, 75-76 (1968). These authorities make it clear that, at the least, Stanley's interest in retaining custody of his children is cognizable and substantial.

For its part, the State has made its interest quite plain: Illinois has declared that the aim of the Juvenile Court Act is to protect "the moral, emotional, mental, and physical welfare of the minor and the best interests of the community" and to "strengthen the minor's family ties whenever possible, removing him from the custody of his parents only when his welfare or safety or the protection of the public cannot be adequately safeguarded without removal . . ." Ill. Rev. Stat., c. 37, §701-2. These are legitimate interests well within the power of the State to implement. We do not question the assertion that neglectful parents may be separated from their children.

But we are here not asked to evaluate the legitimacy of the state ends, rather, to determine whether the means used to achieve these ends are constitutionally defensible. What is the state interest in separating children from fathers without a hearing designed to determine whether the father is unfit in a particular disputed case? We observe that the State registers no gain towards its declared goals when it separates children from the custody of fit parents. Indeed, if Stanley is a fit father, the State spites its own articulated goals when it needlessly separates him from his family.

[I]t may be, as the State insists, that most unmarried fathers are unsuitable and neglectful parents. It may also be that Stanley is such a parent and that his children should be placed in other hands. But all unmarried fathers are not in this category; some are wholly suited to have custody of their children. This much the State readily concedes, and nothing in this record indicates that Stanley is or has been a neglectful father who has not cared for his children. Given the opportunity to make his case, Stanley may have been seen to be deserving of custody of his offspring. Had this been so, the State's statutory policy would have been furthered by leaving custody in him....

[I]t may be argued that unmarried fathers are so seldom fit that Illinois need not undergo the administrative inconvenience of inquiry in any case, including Stanley's.... But the Constitution recognizes higher values than speed and efficiency.... Procedure by presumption is always cheaper and easier than individualized determination. But when, as here, the procedure forecloses the determinative issues of competence and care, when it explicitly disdains present realities in deference to past formalities, it needlessly risks running roughshod over the important interests of both parent and child. It therefore cannot stand.

... The State's interest in caring for Stanley's children is *de minimis* if Stanley is shown to be a fit father. It insists on presuming rather than proving Stanley's unfitness solely because it is more convenient to presume than to prove. Under the Due Process Clause that advantage is insufficient to justify refusing a father a hearing when the issue at stake is the dismemberment of his family....

The State of Illinois assumes custody of the children of married parents, divorced parents, and unmarried mothers only after a hearing and proof of neglect. The children of unmarried fathers, however, are declared dependent children without a hearing on parental fitness and without proof of neglect. Stanley's claim in the state courts and here is that failure to afford him a hearing on his parental qualifications while extending it to other parents denied him equal protection of the laws. We have concluded that all Illinois parents are constitutionally entitled to a hearing on their fitness before their children are removed from their custody. It follows that denying such a hearing to Stanley and those like him while granting it to other Illinois parents is inescapably contrary to the Equal Protection Clause....

Michael H. v. Gerald D.

---

491 U.S. 110 (1989)

Justice Scalia announced the judgment of the Court and delivered an opinion, in which The Chief Justice joins, and in all but note 6 of which Justice O'Connor and Justice Kennedy join.

Under California law, a child born to a married woman living with her husband is presumed to be a child of the marriage. Cal. Evid. Code Ann. §621 (West Supp. 1989). The presumption of legitimacy may be rebutted only by the husband or wife, and then only in limited circumstances. The instant appeal presents the claim that this presumption infringes upon the due process rights of a man who wishes to establish his paternity of a child born to the wife of another man, and the claim that it infringes upon the constitutional right of the child to maintain a relationship with her natural father.....

The facts of this case are, we must hope, extraordinary. On May 9, 1976, in Las Vegas, Nevada, Carole D., an international model, and Gerald D., a top executive in a French oil company, were married. The couple established a home in Playa del Rey, California, in which they resided as husband and wife when one or the other was not out of the country on business. In the summer of 1978, Carole became involved in an adulterous affair with a neighbor, Michael H. In September 1980, she conceived a child, Victoria D., who was born on May 11, 1981. Gerald was listed as father on the birth certificate and has always held Victoria out to the world as his daughter. Soon after delivery of the child, however, Carole informed Michael that she believed he might be the father.

In the first three years of her life, Victoria remained always with Carole, but found herself within a variety of quasi-family units. In October 1981, Gerald moved to New York City to pursue his business interests, but Carole chose to remain in California. At the end of that month, Carole and Michael had blood tests of themselves and Victoria, which showed a 98.07% probability that Michael was Victoria's father. In January 1982, Carole visited Michael in St. Thomas, where his primary business interests were based. There Michael held Victoria out as his child. In March, however, Carole left Michael and returned to California, where she took up residence with yet another man, Scott K. Later that spring, and again in the summer, Carole and Victoria spent time with Gerald in New York City, as well as on vacation in Europe. In the fall, they returned to Scott in California.

In November 1982, rebuffed in his attempts to visit Victoria, Michael filed a filiation action in California Superior Court to establish his paternity and right to visitation. In March 1983, the court appointed an attorney and guardian ad litem to represent Victoria's interests. Victoria then filed a cross-complaint asserting that if she had more than one psychological or de facto father, she was entitled to maintain her filial relationship, with all of the attendant rights, duties, and obligations, with both. In May 1983, Carole filed a motion for summary judgment. During this period, from March through July 1983, Carole was again living with Gerald in New York. In August, however, she returned to California, became involved once again with Michael, and instructed her attorneys to remove the summary judgment motion from the calendar.

For the ensuing eight months, when Michael was not in St. Thomas he lived with Carole and Victoria in Carole's apartment in Los Angeles and held Victoria out as his daughter. In April 1984, Carole and Michael signed a stipulation that Michael was Victoria's natural father. Carole left Michael the next month, however, and instructed her attorneys not to file the stipulation. In June 1984, Carole reconciled with Gerald and joined him in New York, where they now live with Victoria and two other children since born into the marriage.

In May 1984, Michael and Victoria, through her guardian ad litem, sought visitation rights for Michael *pendente lite*. To assist in determining whether visitation would be in Victoria's best interests, the Superior Court appointed a psychologist to evaluate Victoria, Gerald, Michael, and Carole. The psychologist recommended that Carole retain sole custody, but that Michael be allowed continued contact with Victoria pursuant to a restricted visitation schedule. The court concurred and ordered that Michael be provided with limited visitation privileges *pendente lite*.

On October 19, 1984, Gerald, who had intervened in the action, moved for summary judgment on the ground that under Cal. Evid. Code §621 there were no triable issues of fact as to Victoria's paternity. This law provides that "the issue of a wife cohabiting with her husband, who is not impotent or sterile, is conclusively presumed to be a child of the marriage." The presumption may be rebutted by blood tests, but only if a motion for such tests is made, within two years from the date of the child's birth, either by the husband or, if the natural father has filed an affidavit acknowledging paternity, by the wife.

On January 28, 1985, having found that affidavits submitted by Carole and Gerald sufficed to demonstrate that the two were cohabiting at conception and birth and that Gerald was neither sterile nor impotent, the Superior Court granted Gerald's motion for summary judgment, rejecting Michael's and Victoria's challenges to the constitutionality of §621. The court also denied their motions for continued visitation pending the appeal under Cal. Civ. Code §4601, which provides that a court may, in its discretion, grant "reasonable visitation rights . . . to any . . . person having an interest in the welfare of the child." Cal. Civ. Code Ann. §4601 (West Supp. 1989). It found that allowing such visitation would "violate the intention of the Legislature by impugning the integrity of the family unit." [Michael and Victoria appeal.]

Before us, Michael and Victoria both raise [constitutional] challenges. . . . We address first the [due process] claims of Michael. At the outset, it is necessary to clarify what he sought and what he was denied. California law, like nature itself, makes no provision for dual fatherhood. Michael was seeking to be declared the father of Victoria. The immediate benefit he evidently sought to obtain from that status was visitation rights. But if Michael were successful in being declared the father, other rights would follow — most importantly, the right to be considered as the parent who should have custody . . . . All parental rights, including visitation, were automatically denied by denying Michael status as the father. . . .

Michael contends as a matter of substantive due process that, because he has established a parental relationship with Victoria, protection of Gerald's and Carole's marital union is an insufficient state interest to support termination of that relationship. This argument is, of course, predicated on the assertion that Michael has a constitutionally protected liberty interest in his relationship with Victoria. . . .

In an attempt to limit and guide interpretation of the [Due Process] Clause, we have insisted not merely that the interest denominated as a "liberty" be "fundamental" (a concept that, in isolation, is hard to objectify), but also that it be an interest traditionally protected by our society. . . . This insistence that the asserted liberty interest be rooted in history and tradition is evident, as elsewhere, in our cases according constitutional protection to certain parental rights. Michael reads the landmark case of Stanley v. Illinois, 405 U.S. 645 (1972), and the subsequent cases of Quilloin v. Walcott, 434 U.S. 246 (1978), Caban v. Mohammed, 441 U.S. 380 (1979), and Lehr v. Robertson, 463 U.S. 248 (1983), as establishing that a liberty interest is created by biological fatherhood plus an established parental relationship — factors that exist in the present case as well. We think that distorts the rationale of those cases. As we view them, they rest not upon such isolated factors but upon the historic respect — indeed, sanctity would not be too strong a term — traditionally accorded to the relationships that develop within the unitary family.[3] . . .

Thus, the legal issue in the present case reduces to whether the relationship between persons in the situation of Michael and Victoria has been treated as a protected family unit under the historic practices of our society, or whether on any other basis it has been accorded special protection. We think it impossible to find that it has. In fact, quite to the contrary, our traditions have protected the marital family (Gerald, Carole, and the child they acknowledge to be theirs) against the sort of claim Michael asserts.[4]

The presumption of legitimacy was a fundamental principle of the common law. H. Nicholas, Adulturine Bastardy 1 (1836). Traditionally, that presumption could be rebutted only by proof that a husband was incapable of procreation or had had no access to his wife during the relevant period. As explained by Blackstone, nonaccess could only be proved "if the husband be out of the kingdom of England (or, as the law somewhat loosely phrases it, *extra quatuor maria* [beyond the four seas]) for above nine months. . . ." 1 Blackstone's Commentaries 456 (J. Chitty ed. 1826). And, under the common law both in England and here, [neither parent could testify to bastardize the child]. The primary policy rationale underlying the common law's severe restrictions on rebuttal of the presumption appears to have been an aversion to declaring children illegitimate, thereby depriving them of rights of inheritance and succession, and likely making them wards of the state. A secondary policy concern was the interest in promoting the "peace and tranquillity of

---

3. Justice Brennan asserts that only "a pinched conception of 'the family' "would exclude Michael, Carole, and Victoria from protection. We disagree. The family unit accorded traditional respect in our society, which we have referred to as the "unitary family," is typified, of course, by the marital family, but also includes the household of unmarried parents and their children. Perhaps the concept can be expanded even beyond this, but it will bear no resemblance to traditionally respected relationships — and will thus cease to have any constitutional significance — if it is stretched so far as to include the relationship established between a married woman, her lover, and their child, during a 3-month sojourn in St. Thomas, or during a subsequent 8-month period when, if he happened to be in Los Angeles, he stayed with her and the child.

4. Justice Brennan insists that in determining whether a liberty interest exists we must look at Michael's relationship with Victoria in isolation, without reference to the circumstance that Victoria's mother was married to someone else when the child was conceived, and that that woman and her husband wish to raise the child as their own. We cannot imagine what compels this strange procedure of looking at the act which is assertedly the subject of a liberty interest in isolation from its effect upon other people — rather like inquiring whether there is a liberty interest in firing a gun where the case at hand happens to involve its discharge into another person's body. The logic of Justice Brennan's position leads to the conclusion that if Michael had begotten Victoria by rape, that fact would in no way affect his possession of a liberty interest in his relationship with her.

States and families," a goal that is obviously impaired by facilitating suits against husband and wife asserting that their children are illegitimate. . . .

We have found nothing in the older sources, nor in the older cases, addressing specifically the power of the natural father to assert parental rights over a child born into a woman's existing marriage with another man. Since it is Michael's burden to establish that such a power (at least where the natural father has established a relationship with the child) is so deeply embedded within our traditions as to be a fundamental right, the lack of evidence alone might defeat his case. But the evidence shows that even in modern times — when, as we have noted, the rigid protection of the marital family has in other respects been relaxed — the ability of a person in Michael's position to claim paternity has not been generally acknowledged. . . .

Moreover, even if it were clear that one in Michael's position generally possesses, and has generally always possessed, standing to challenge the marital child's legitimacy, that would still not establish Michael's case. As noted earlier, what is at issue here is not entitlement to a state pronouncement that Victoria was begotten by Michael. It is no conceivable denial of constitutional right for a State to decline to declare facts unless some legal consequence hinges upon the requested declaration. What Michael asserts here is a right to have himself declared the natural father and *thereby to obtain parental prerogatives.* What he must establish, therefore, is not that our society has traditionally allowed a natural father in his circumstances to establish paternity, but that it has traditionally accorded such a father parental rights, or at least has not traditionally denied them. . . . What counts is whether the States in fact award substantive parental rights to the natural father of a child conceived within, and born into, an extant marital union that wishes to embrace the child. We are not aware of a single case, old or new, that has done so. This is not the stuff of which fundamental rights qualifying as liberty interests are made.[6] . . .

We do not accept Justice Brennan's criticism that this result "squashes" the liberty that consists of "the freedom not to conform." It seems to us that reflects the erroneous view that there is only one side to this controversy — that one disposition can expand a "liberty" of sorts without contracting an equivalent "liberty" on the other side. Such a happy choice is rarely available. Here, to provide protection to an adulterous natural father is to deny protection to a marital father, and vice versa. If Michael has a "freedom not to conform" (whatever that means), Gerald must equivalently have a "freedom to conform." One of them will pay a price for asserting that "freedom." . . . Our

---

6. Justice Brennan criticizes our methodology in using historical traditions specifically relating to the rights of an adulterous natural father, rather than inquiring more generally "whether parenthood is an interest that historically has received our attention and protection." . . . We do not understand why, having rejected our focus upon the societal tradition regarding the natural father's rights vis-à-vis a child whose mother is married to another man, Justice Brennan would choose to focus instead upon "parenthood." Why should the relevant category not be even more general — perhaps "family relationships"; or "personal relationships"; or even "emotional attachments in general"? Though the dissent has no basis for the level of generality it would select, we do: We refer to the most specific level at which a relevant tradition protecting, or denying protection to, the asserted right can be identified. If, for example, there were no societal tradition, either way, regarding the rights of the natural father of a child adulterously conceived, we would have to consult, and (if possible) reason from, the traditions regarding natural fathers in general. But there is such a more specific tradition, and it unqualifiedly denies protection to such a parent. . . .

disposition does not choose between these two "freedoms," but leaves that to the people of California. Justice Brennan's approach chooses one of them as the constitutional imperative, on no apparent basis except that the unconventional is to be preferred. . . .

We have never had occasion to decide whether a child has a liberty interest, symmetrical with that of her parent, in maintaining her filial relationship. We need not do so here because, even assuming that such a right exists, Victoria's claim must fail. Victoria's due process challenge is, if anything, weaker than Michael's. Her basic claim is not that California has erred in preventing her from establishing that Michael, not Gerald, should stand as her legal father. Rather, she claims a due process right to maintain filial relationships with both Michael and Gerald. This assertion merits little discussion, for, whatever the merits of the guardian ad litem's belief that such an arrangement can be of great psychological benefit to a child, the claim that a State must recognize multiple fatherhood has no support in the history or traditions of this country. Moreover, even if we were to construe Victoria's argument as forwarding the lesser proposition that, whatever her status vis-à-vis Gerald, she has a liberty interest in maintaining a filial relationship with her natural father, Michael, we find that, at best, her claim is the obverse of Michael's and fails for the same reasons.

Victoria claims in addition that her equal protection rights have been violated because, unlike her mother and presumed father, she had no opportunity to rebut the presumption of her legitimacy. We find this argument wholly without merit. We reject, at the outset, Victoria's suggestion that her equal protection challenge must be assessed under a standard of strict scrutiny because, in denying her the right to maintain a filial relationship with Michael, the State is discriminating against her on the basis of her illegitimacy. See Gomez v. Perez, 409 U.S. 535, 538 (1973). Illegitimacy is a legal construct, not a natural trait. Under California law, Victoria is not illegitimate, and she is treated in the same manner as all other legitimate children: she is entitled to maintain a filial relationship with her legal parents. . . . Since it pursues a legitimate end [protecting the integrity of the marital family] by rational means, California's decision to treat Victoria differently from her parents is not a denial of equal protection. . . .

Justice O'CONNOR, with whom Justice KENNEDY joins, concurring in part.

I concur in all but footnote 6 of Justice Scalia's opinion. This footnote sketches a mode of historical analysis to be used when identifying liberty interests protected by the Due Process Clause of the Fourteenth Amendment that may be somewhat inconsistent with our past decisions in this area. See Griswold v. Connecticut, 381 U.S. 479 (1965); Eisenstadt v. Baird, 405 U.S. 438 (1972) [(protecting right to use and have access to birth control)]. On occasion the Court has characterized relevant traditions protecting asserted rights at levels of generality that might not be "the most specific level" available [(as specified in the plurality's footnote 6)]. See Loving v. Virginia, 388 U.S. 1, 12 (1967) [(holding unconstitutional ban on interracial marriage)]. I would not foreclose the unanticipated by the prior imposition of a single mode of historical analysis.

Justice STEVENS, concurring in the judgment.

. . . I do not agree with Justice Scalia's analysis. He seems to reject the possibility that a natural father might ever have a constitutionally protected interest in his relationship with a child whose mother was married to, and cohabiting with, another man at the time of the child's conception and birth. I think cases like Stanley v. Illinois, 405 U.S. 645 (1972), and Caban v. Mohammed, 441 U.S. 380 (1979), demonstrate that enduring "family" relationships may develop in unconventional settings. I therefore would not foreclose the possibility that a constitutionally protected relationship between a natural father and his child might exist in a case like this. Indeed, I am willing to assume for the purpose of deciding this case that Michael's relationship with Victoria is strong enough to give him a constitutional right to try to convince a trial judge that Victoria's best interest would be served by granting him visitation rights. I am satisfied, however, that the California statute, as applied in this case, gave him that opportunity.

Section 4601 of the California Civil Code Annotated (West Supp. 1989) provides:

> "[R]easonable visitation rights [shall be awarded] to a parent unless it is shown that the visitation would be detrimental to the best interests of the child. In the discretion of the court, reasonable visitation rights may be granted *to any other person having an interest in the welfare of the child."* (Emphasis added.)

The presumption established by §621 denied Michael the benefit of the first sentence of §4601 because, as a matter of law, he is not a "parent." It does not, however, prevent him from proving that he is an "other person having an interest in the welfare of the child." On its face, therefore, the statute plainly gave the trial judge the authority to grant Michael "reasonable visitation rights." . . .

Under the circumstances of the case before us, Michael was given a fair opportunity to show that he is Victoria's natural father, that he had developed a relationship with her, and that her interests would be served by granting him visitation rights. On the other hand, the record also shows that after its rather shaky start, the marriage between Carole and Gerald developed a stability that now provides Victoria with a loving and harmonious family home. In the circumstances of this case, I find nothing fundamentally unfair about the exercise of a judge's discretion that, in the end, allows the mother to decide whether her child's best interests would be served by allowing the natural father visitation privileges. . . . I am satisfied that the California statutory scheme is consistent with the Due Process Clause of the Fourteenth Amendment. . . .

Justice BRENNAN, with whom Justice MARSHALL and Justice BLACKMUN join, dissenting. . . .

Today's plurality . . . does not ask whether parenthood is an interest that historically has received our attention and protection; the answer to that question is too clear for dispute. Instead, the plurality asks whether the specific variety of parenthood under consideration — a natural father's relationship with a child whose mother is married to another man — has enjoyed such protection. . . .

In construing the Fourteenth Amendment to offer shelter only to those interests specifically protected by historical practice, moreover, the plurality ignores the kind of society in which our Constitution exists. We are not an assimilative, homogeneous society, but a facilitative, pluralistic one, in which

we must be willing to abide someone else's unfamiliar or even repellant practice because the same tolerant impulse protects our own idiosyncracies. Even
if we can agree, therefore, that "family" and "parenthood" are part of the
good life, it is absurd to assume that we can agree on the content of those
terms and destructive to pretend that we do. In a community such as ours,
"liberty" must include the freedom not to conform. The plurality today
squashes this freedom by requiring specific approval from history before protecting anything in the name of liberty. . . . [Here,] we confront an interest —
that of a parent and child in their relationship with each other — that was
among the first that this Court acknowledged in its cases defining the
"liberty" protected by the Constitution. . . .

The evidence is undisputed that Michael, Victoria, and Carole did live
together as a family; that is, they shared the same household, Victoria called
Michael "Daddy," Michael contributed to Victoria's support, and he is eager
to continue his relationship with her. Yet they are not, in the plurality's view,
a "unitary family," whereas Gerald, Carole, and Victoria do compose such a
family. The only difference between these two sets of relationships, however,
is the fact of marriage. . . . However, the very premise of *Stanley* and the cases
following it is that marriage is not decisive in answering the question
whether the Constitution protects the parental relationship under
consideration. . . .

The plurality's exclusive rather than inclusive definition of the "unitary
family" is out of step with other decisions as well. This pinched conception
of "the family," crucial as it is in rejecting Michael's and Victoria's claims of
a liberty interest, is jarring in light of our many cases preventing the States
from denying important interests or statuses to those whose situations do
not fit the government's narrow view of the family. From Loving v. Virginia,
388 U.S. 1 (1967), to Levy v. Louisiana, 391 U.S. 68 (1968), and Glona v. American Guarantee & Liability Ins. Co., 391 U.S. 73 (1968), and from Gomez v.
Perez, 409 U.S. 535 (1973), to Moore v. East Cleveland, 431 U.S. 494 (1977), we
have declined to respect a State's notion, as manifested in its allocation of
privileges and burdens, of what the family should be. Today's rhapsody on
the "unitary family" is out of tune with such decisions. . . .

NOTES AND QUESTIONS ON *STANLEY* AND *MICHAEL H.*

1. Stanley's *rationale.* Why did the Court invoke the Due Process Clause
to resolve a claim that Stanley pressed under the Equal Protection Clause?
On what bases did the Illinois classify? Why might the Court have avoided
a broad holding based on equal protection? The Court's emphasis on due
process to resolve claims of discrimination surfaced in several cases decided
contemporaneously and became known as the "irrebuttable presumption
doctrine."[14] To what extent does *Stanley* recognize substantive, as distinguished from procedural, rights for unwed fathers? Whose rights are being
vindicated? The father's? The children's?

---

[14] See, e.g., Cleveland Bd. of Educ. v. LaFleur, 414 U.S. 632 (1974); Note, The
Irrebuttable Presumption Doctrine in the Supreme Court, 87 Harv. L. Rev. 1534 (1974).

2. State interests in Stanley. Today, the legal regime challenged in *Stanley* seems surprising, if not perverse. As Professor Nancy Polikoff writes:

> The rule disregarding as a parent the father of children born outside marriage was consistent with centuries of law that such children were not legally his, but it was clearly not good for these children.... The outcome ... may seem obvious today — how could it possibly be in children's best interests to lose their father after they have lost their mother? But it was extraordinary in 1972. The Supreme Court found that Peter Stanley's right to raise his children had been violated, and the decision required *every* state to revise its laws.[15]

Why did Illinois enact the statute challenged in *Stanley*? Consider and evaluate the following possibilities: (a) The state assumed that unmarried fathers, unlike unmarried mothers and married fathers, have no interest in a relationship with their children. (b) The state sought to facilitate adoptions of children born to and surrendered by unmarried mothers, and requiring unmarried fathers to consent would slow down or obstruct the process. (See Chapter 3, section B2.) (c) The state sought to encourage marriage by making it a precondition for men to acquire parental rights in children conceived sexually.

3. Stanley's scope. Stanley suggests that not all genetic fathers are entitled to the protections afforded to those men who, like Stanley, have both "sired and raised" their children. Precisely what degree of parental involvement is necessary to trigger constitutional protection? If *Stanley* guarantees only notice and a hearing, how can a particular man's involvement with his child be assessed *before* the hearing?

How do the following facts, presented in an omitted dissenting opinion, affect the understanding of Stanley's involvement with the children and the scope of the holding?

> The position that Stanley took at the dependency proceeding was not without ambiguity. Shortly after the mother's death, he placed the children in the care of Mr. and Mrs. Ness, who took the children into their home. The record is silent as to whether the Ness household was an approved foster home. Through Stanley's act, then, the Nesses were already the actual custodians of the children. At the dependency proceeding, he resisted only the court's designation of the Nesses as the legal custodians; he did not challenge their suitability for that role, nor did he seek for himself either that role or any other role that would have imposed legal responsibility upon him. Had he prevailed, of course, the status quo would have obtained: the Nesses would have continued to play the role of actual custodians until either they or Stanley acted to alter the informal arrangement, and there would still have been no living adult with any legally enforceable obligation for the care and support of the infant children.

405 U.S. at 663 n.2 (Burger, C.J., dissenting).[16]

---

[15] Nancy D. Polikoff, Beyond (Straight and Gay) Marriage: Valuing All Families Under the Law 130 (2008).

[16] See also Josh Gupta-Kagan, Stanley v. Illinois's Untold Story, 24 Wm. & Mary Bill Rts. J. 773 (2016) (using archival evidence to flesh out the facts, litigation strategies, and Justices'

4. *"Biology plus."* In later cases, a majority of the Court elaborated on the requirement of paternal involvement, sometimes finding a father's conduct sufficient to trigger constitutional protection and sometimes finding it insufficient. As the Court summarized in one of these cases, Lehr v. Robertson, 463 U.S. 248 (1983):

> The significance of the biological connection is that it offers the natural father an opportunity that no other male possesses to develop a relationship with his offspring. If he grasps that opportunity and accepts some measure of responsibility for the child's future, he may enjoy the blessings of the parent-child relationship and make uniquely valuable contributions to the child's development.

Id. at 262.[17] Commentators have discerned in this approach a "biology plus" test.[18] In an omitted dissent in *Michael H.,* Justice White refers to the quoted summary from *Lehr.* "It is as if this passage was addressed to Michael. Yet the plurality today recants."[19] Do you agree that the *Michael H.* plurality conflicts with this reading of the earlier cases? Can you reconcile them? What role do the children's interests play in the cases?

Notwithstanding the plurality opinion, does a majority in *Michael H.* reject the "biology plus" test? Note that a sharply divided Court decided the case. In an omitted portion of the dissenting opinion, Justice Brennan (joined by Justices Marshall and Blackmun) highlighted the divisions, pointing out that five Justices refused to foreclose the possibility that a biological father in Michael's position might ever have a constitutionally protected interest, four Justices agreed that Michael has a liberty interest, and five Justices believed that the flaw is procedural. Indeed, a majority of the Justices agreed that Michael is entitled to some procedural protections; however, Justice Stevens, providing the fifth vote on this point, concurred in the result because he found that Michael received the process that was due.

5. *Relationship to the mother.* Professor Janet L. Dolgin sees familial relationships as the determinative variables in the cases:

> [T]he unwed father cases, from *Stanley* through *Michael H.,* delineate three factors that make an unwed man a father. These are the man's biological relation to the child, his social relation to the child, and his relation to the child's mother. . . . In this regard, *Michael H.* clarifies the earlier cases. A biological father does protect his paternity by developing a social relationship with his child, but this step demands the creation of a family, a step itself depending upon an appropriate relationship between the man and his child's mother.[20]

---

evolving positions); Serena Mayeri, Foundling Fathers: (Non-)Marriage and Parental Rights in the Age of Equality, 125 Yale L.J. 2292 (2016) (tracing history and limits of rights of unmarried fathers).
   [17] The other cases include Caban v. Mohammed, 441 U.S. 380 (1979) (finding father's conduct sufficient), and Quilloin v. Walcott, 434 U.S. 246 (1978) (finding father's conduct insufficient).
   [18] E.g., Melanie B. Jacobs, My Two Dads: Disaggregating Biological and Social Paternity, 38 Ariz. St. L.J. 809, 827-828 (2006); Lacey Johnson, Comment, Low-Income Fathers, Adoption, and the Biology-Plus Test for Paternal Rights, 70 Ark. L. Rev. 1113 (2018).
   [19] 491 U.S. at 163 (White, J., dissenting).
   [20] Janet L. Dolgin, Just A Gene: Judicial Assumptions About Parenthood, 40 UCLA L. Rev. 637, 671 (1993).

According to Professor Gary Spitko, the mother's consent is critical, and biological paternity becomes important to the extent that it usually signals "the implicit consent of the biological mother to allow the biological father to co-parent her child."[21]

6. *Definitions.* In Moore v. City of East Cleveland, 431 U.S. 494 (1997), the Court overturned the city zoning law's definition of "family" because it prohibited a grandmother from living with her two grandsons, who were cousins, not brothers. A plurality condemned the law for "slicing deeply into the family itself," thereby suggesting a constitutionally protected definition of family that exists apart from any legislative definition; this plurality found that the law thus violated Inez Moore's substantive due process rights. See id. at 498 (plurality opinion). Like *Moore, Stanley* and *Michael H.* test the government's power to write its own definition of certain terms: "parent" in *Stanley* and "father" in *Michael H.* Can you reconcile the *Michael H.* plurality's approach to the definitional question with the approach of the two earlier cases? Is footnote 3 in the *Michael H.* plurality opinion persuasive?

7. *Interplay of parentage rules and sex equality doctrine.* As the Supreme Court was developing the "biology-plus" case law in the 1970s, it was also beginning to transform family law from a field constructed from traditional gender-based role assignments to a site committed to formal equality for women and men. In striking down gender-based family role assignments, the Court explicitly rejected reliance on gender stereotypes.[22] The Court announced that, to survive constitutional challenge, gender-based classifications must meet an intermediate standard of review, which requires that the classification must serve important governmental objectives and must have a substantial relationship to achieving such objectives;[23] later the Court ratcheted up the standard for this heightened level of scrutiny, requiring an "exceedingly persuasive justification" for gender classifications.[24]

At the same time, however, the Court has indicated that gender-based classifications reflecting "real differences" would survive constitutional review. For example, in Michael M. v. Superior Court, 450 U.S. 464 (1981), the Court upheld a statutory rape law applicable only to male perpetrators because only females can become pregnant; thus, the statute, purportedly designed to combat teen pregnancy, "realistically reflects the fact that the sexes are not similarly situated." Id. at 469 (plurality opinion).[25] Do parentage laws like those examined in *Stanley, Michael H.,* and the intervening cases rest on "real differences," given distinct sex-based roles in reproduction, or on gender stereotypes, particularly contrasting gender norms and expectations for family care work?[26] The Justices have not answered this question

---

[21] E. Gary Spitko, The Constitutional Function of Biological Paternity: Evidence of the Biological Mother's Consent to the Biological Father's Co-Parenting of Her Child, 48 Ariz. L. Rev. 97, 100 (2006).

[22] See generally Susan Frelich Appleton, How Feminism Remade American Family Law (and How It Did Not), in Research Handbook on Feminist Jurisprudence 426, 430-431 (Robin West & Cynthia Grant Bowman eds., 2019); Allison Anna Tait, A Tale of Three Families: Historical Households, Earned Belonging, and Natural Connections, 63 Hastings L.J. 1345 (2012).

[23] Craig v. Boren, 429 U.S. 190 (1976).

[24] United States v. Virginia, 518 U.S. 515, 531 (1996).

[25] But see Sylvia A. Law, Rethinking Sex and the Constitution, 132 U. Pa. L. Rev. 955, 999 (1984) (critiquing opinion for mistaking "stereotype for biology").

[26] See, e.g., Nev. Dept. of Hum. Resources v. Hibbs, 538 U.S. 721 (2003).

with one voice, issuing conflicting decisions in cases challenging disparate rules of derivative citizenship for nonmarital children born outside the U.S. depending on whether the citizen-parent is the mother or the father. For example, in Nguyen v. INS, 533 U.S. 53, 73 (2001), a majority wrote: "The difference between men and women in relation to the birth process is a real one, and the principle of equal protection does not forbid Congress to address the problem at hand in a manner specific to each gender," rejecting an analysis by the four dissenters who saw "overbroad sex-based generalizations" at work. Id. at 86 (O'Connor, J., dissenting). More recently, in Sessions v. Morales-Santana, 137 S. Ct. 1678 (2017), the Supreme Court struck down a different federal statute that privileged a foreign-born child's ties to an unmarried citizen mother over such ties to an unmarried citizen father. Justice Ginsburg's opinion for the Court determined that the differential treatment rested on stereotypes about women's domestic roles, in violation of equal protection. Id. at 1692-1693.[27] See Chapter 9, section B1. On what grounds other than stereotyping might one challenge laws that treat mothers and fathers differently?[28]

Finally, how does the analysis of these issues change with the contemporary visibility of pregnancies and births by individuals who have uteruses but do not identify as women, such as transmen and those who reject the traditional gender binary?[29] What is the relevance, if any, of the Supreme Court's rulings that Title VII's ban on sex discrimination in employment covers discrimination based on sexual orientation or transgender identity?[30]

Depictions in Popular Culture: Evelyn (2002)

This film tells the true story from the 1950s of Desmond Doyle, an unemployed Irish housepainter with three children whose wife deserts him for another man, prompting the National Society for the Prevention of Cruelty to Children to take custody of his children, daughter Evelyn and her two younger brothers. Ireland's Children Act of 1908 authorizes a judge to send a destitute child under the age of 15 to an industrial school. A subsequent amendment (the Children Act of 1941 §10) mandates the consent of both parents for the child's detention unless the child is an orphan. Additional exceptions to the two-parent consent requirement exist if one parent is mentally disabled, imprisoned, or has deserted the family. Based on a peculiarity in the amended statute, a sole parent's consent suffices to justify a child's detention but not to justify the child's discharge

---

[27] For extensive analysis of such issues, see Kristin A. Collins, Illegitimate Borders: Jus Sanguinis Citizenship and the Legal Construction of Family, Race, and Nation, 123 Yale L.J. 2134 (2014).

[28] See Courtney Megan Cahill, The New Maternity, 133 Harv. L. Rev. 2221 (2020).

[29] See, e.g., Jessica A. Clarke, They, Them, and Theirs, 132 Harv. L. Rev. 894, 954-57 (2019); David Fontana & Naomi Schoenbaum, Unsexing Pregnancy, 119 Colum. L. Rev. 309 (2019); Sonia K. Katyal & Ilona M. Turner, Transparenthood, 117 Mich. L. Rev. 1593 (2019); Laura Nixon, The Right to (Trans)Parent: A Reproductive Justice Approach to Reproductive Rights, Fertility, and Family-Building Issues Facing Transgender People, 20 Wm. & Mary J. Women & L. 73 (2013).

[30] Bostock v. Clayton Cty., Ga., 140 S. Ct. 1731 (2020).

(for which both parents must consent). Because the mother fled without leaving contact information, Doyle cannot obtain her consent for the state to discharge the children even after his financial situation improves. First, Doyle unsuccessfully petitions the Minister of Education to discharge the children. He then challenges the statute's constitutionality.

The struggle reflects the tension evident in Stanley v. Illinois. While the legal establishment's position reflects gendered assumptions about the inability of a father to rear children without a mother or mother figure, Doyle (Pierce Brosnan) and his legal team (including Stephen Rea, Aidan Quinn, and Alan Bates) contend that §10 of the Children Act of 1941 violates the Irish Constitution's protections for family matters. Specifically, Doyle's challenge invokes constitutional provisions guaranteeing "inalienable and imprescriptible rights, antecedent and superior to all positive law"; "[the] inalienable right and duty of parents to provide, according to their means, for the . . . education of their children"; and a provision stating that "The State shall not oblige parents . . . to send their children to schools established by the State."[31] The courtroom scenes include one of young Evelyn on the witness stand.

Despite the odds, including warnings that a father's removal of his children from protective custody would undermine the fundamental principles of Irish family law, Doyle persists and ultimately prevails in a case that the film portrays as the first in which the Irish Supreme Court set aside a statute as unconstitutional. As the film ends, Bernadette (Julianna Margulies), to whom Doyle develops a romantic attachment, moves in to help him care for the children upon their return. Do the gendered assumptions underlying the controversy thus prevail as well?

One reviewer points out that, with divorce unavailable in Ireland, Doyle and the Bernadette character cannot marry.[32] But does the unavailability of divorce perhaps explain the mother's desertion? Was it her only opportunity for exit?

---

8. *Presumption of legitimacy.* The presumption of legitimacy (or marital presumption) has a long history in British common law, which included Lord Mansfield's rule barring spousal testimony that might show another man's paternity. Professor Michael Grossberg traces American adherence to such principles to the strong reluctance to stigmatize nonmarital children in the post-Revolutionary period. He adds that this reluctance ultimately found expression in the creation of common law marriage, the exclusion

---

[31] Michael Asimow, Evelyn — The Best Legal Movie of 2002?, Picturing Justice, The On-Line Journal of Law & Popular Culture, Jan. 21, 2003, http://www.usfca.edu/pj/evelyn_asimow.htm (quoting Articles 41.1, 42.1, and 42.3.1 of the Irish Constitution of 1937). For Evelyn's autobiographical account, see Evelyn Doyle, Tea and Green Ribbons: Evelyn's Story (2004).

[32] Asimow, supra note [31].

of evidence that would bastardize the child of a married woman, the recognition of the offspring of annulled marriages as legitimate, and the development of the doctrine of putative marriage. As Grossberg elaborates:

> In the agonizing conflict between a man's right to limit his paternity only to his actual offspring and the right of a child born to a married woman to claim family membership, the common law, first in England and then in America, generally made paternal rights defer to the larger goal of preserving family integrity.[33]

9. *Additional paternity presumptions.* While children born to married women acquired legal fathers by presumption, judicial proceedings to establish paternity provided the traditional way to identify the father of nonmarital children and to impose support duties upon them, if the law made them financially responsible at all. Such proceedings took the form of criminal "bastardy" prosecutions or civil suits often brought by the child's mother.[34]

The legal disadvantages imposed on nonmarital children caught the critical attention of the Supreme Court and scholars alike, beginning in the late 1960s. The Supreme Court struck down under the Equal Protection Clause several laws that targeted nonmarital children, settling on intermediate scrutiny (the same test applied to gender classifications) as the proper standard of review.[35] Professor Harry Krause's classic book, *Illegitimacy: Law and Social Policy* (1971), called for an end to discrimination against nonmarital children, while others have observed how the official use of illegitimacy subordinated, often purposely, people of color and women.[36] Indeed, the legal erasure of unmarried fathers was critical to the economics of slavery because it meant that the offspring of enslaved mothers (often forcibly conceived by the enslaver) took her status, not his.[37]

Such inequities prompted the development of a model statute designed to equalize treatment for nonmarital children by making the presumption of legitimacy just one of several presumptions that would identify a child's legal father. Under the auspices of the National Conference of Commissioners on Uniform State Laws (now called the Uniform Law Commission or ULC), Professor Krause served as Reporter for the Uniform Parentage Act (UPA), promulgated in 1973; revised versions followed in 2000-2002 and 2017.

a. UPA (1973). Recognizing that according treatment to nonmarital children equal to that enjoyed by their marital counterparts first requires identifying the fathers of the former, the UPA (1973) developed a network

---

[33] Grossberg, supra note [3], at 201-202.

[34] Compare, e.g., State v. Camp, 209 S.E.2d 754 (N.C. 1974), and Miller v. State, 20 So. 392 (Ala. 1895), with, e.g., Berry v. Chaplin, 169 P.2d 442 (Cal. Dist. Ct. App. 1946).

[35] E.g., Clark v. Jeter, 486 U.S. 456 (1988); Mathews v. Lucas, 427 U.S. 495, 504-506 (1976); see also *Levy*, 391 U.S. 68.

[36] E.g., Anders Walker, The Ghost of Jim Crow: How Southern Moderates Used Brown v. Board of Education to Stall Civil Rights (2009); Martha F. Davis, Male Coverture: Law and the Illegitimate Family, 56 Rutgers L. Rev. 73, 107-109 (2003); Serena Mayeri, Marital Supremacy and the Constitution of the Nonmarital Family, 103 Calif. L. Rev. 1277 (2015). See also Zanita E. Fenton, Bastards! . . . and the Welfare Plantation, 17 J. Gender, Race & Just. 9 (2014) (exploring connections between illegitimacy and slavery).

[37] Dorothy Roberts, Killing the Black Body: Race, Reproduction, and the Meaning of Liberty 24-31 (1997).

of presumptions for identifying fathers. These presumptions rested on marriage (including attempted marriage and invalid marriage); a man's receiving a child into his home and holding the child out as his own before the child's majority; and the filing of a written acknowledgment of paternity. UPA §4 (1973).

Suppose more than one of these presumptions applies, as in *Michael H.* The statute says: "If two or more presumptions arise which conflict with each other, the presumption which on the facts is founded on the weightier considerations of policy and logic controls." Id. §4(a)(5). Further, a presumption can be rebutted by clear and convincing evidence. Id.

b. UPA (2002). In 2000, NCCUSL promulgated a new UPA, which it revised in 2002. Although the drafters determined that technological advances — including ARTs (assisted reproductive technologies) and increasingly accurate genetic testing — called for an updated statute, this version of the UPA reaffirms the original policy of equal treatment of children regardless of their parents' marital status and continues to tie equality to means of identifying legal parents. UPA §202 (2002). This statutory scheme provides for the establishment of both the mother-child relationship and the father-child relationship. Id. §201. Like its predecessor, the UPA (2002) rests paternity presumptions on marriage (including attempted and invalid marriage) and on "holding out." Specifically, a presumption of paternity applies to a man if "for the first two years of the child's life, he resided in the same household with the child and openly held out the child as his own." Id. §204(a)(5). A presumption of paternity can be rebutted only by an adjudication in a paternity proceeding, covered in Article 6. Id. §204(b). Article 6, in turn, authorizes paternity proceedings, including genetic testing. For children with no presumed father, a paternity proceeding can be brought at any time. Id. §606. The following limitations apply to a child with a presumed father:

Section 607. Limitation: Child Having Presumed Father.

(a) Except as otherwise provided in subsection (b), a proceeding brought by a presumed father, the mother, or another individual to adjudicate the parentage of a child having a presumed father must be commenced not later than two years after the birth of the child.

(b) A proceeding seeking to disprove the father-child relationship between a child and the child's presumed father may be maintained at any time if the court determines that:

(1) the presumed father and the mother of the child neither cohabited nor engaged in sexual intercourse with each other during the probable time of conception; and

(2) the presumed father never openly held out the child as his own.

UPA §607 (2002).

When initially drafted in 2000, this UPA omitted a presumption based on "holding out" a child as one's own, on the theory that accurate genetic evidence made conduct-based rules unnecessary. See id. §204 cmt. In 2002, however, the drafters inserted §204(a)(5), quoted supra. Why? What is the reason for the two-year requirement in the presumption based on "holding out" and the two-year limitation period for adjudicating parentage for a child with a presumed father? How would a court following this version of the UPA, as amended in 2002, decide the controversy in the *Michael H.* case?

Eleven states enacted this version of the UPA between 2001 and 2015.[38]

c. *UPA (2017).* While the 1973 and 2000-2002 versions of the UPA build on traditional, gendered understandings of parentage, the advent of nation-wide marriage equality and claims for recognition by members of nontraditional families prompted more thoroughgoing revisions in 2017. The UPA (2017) retains the substance of the presumptions in the earlier versions but "revises them so that they apply equally to men and women." UPA §204 cmt. (2017). As of 2020, four states have enacted the UPA (2017), and legislators have introduced it in six others.[39] For additional analysis of the changes made by the UPA (2017), see section C.

10. *Purpose of presumptions.* What is the purpose of the presumption of legitimacy and the other paternity presumptions? *Michael H.* suggests that the presumption of legitimacy was designed to preserve marital harmony and establish the marital family as the norm. Commentators have seen such presumptions as a crude way of determining biological paternity before proof of such relationships became scientifically possible, as a reflection of the belief that a marital family best serves children, and as a means of securing support for children.[40]

11. *Weight of genetic evidence.* At one time, the presumption of legitimacy was conclusive when the spouses were cohabiting at the time of conception and the husband was not sterile, impotent, or racially different in appearance from the child.[41] What explains the exceptions? Under federal child support legislation, states have the option of making the presumption rebuttable or conclusive, depending on genetic test results indicating a threshold probability that the alleged father is the father of the child.[42] What advantages and disadvantages does each alternative present? Today, the conclusive common law presumption of legitimacy has largely given way to a rebuttable presumption.[43]

Given modern scientific determinations of parentage, what role *should* genetic evidence play? Should genetic evidence always trump presumptions resting on social factors, such as marriage or "holding out" the child as one's own? At least for the children of different-sex couples, to what extent would a regime of fatherhood resting exclusively on genetics best achieve equal

---

[38] Uniform Law Commission, Parentage Act (2002), https://www.uniformlaws.org/committees/community-home?CommunityKey=5d5c48d6-623f-4d01-9994-6933ca8af315.

[39] Uniform Law Commission, Parentage Act (2017), https://www.uniformlaws.org/committees/community-home?CommunityKey=c4f37d2d-4d20-4be0-8256-22dd73af068f.

[40] See, e.g., Katharine K. Baker, Bargaining or Biology? The History and Future of Paternity Law and Parental Status, 14 Cornell J.L. & Pub. Pol'y 1 (2004); June Carbone & Naomi Cahn, Which Ties Bind? Redefining the Parent-Child Relationship in an Age of Genetic Certainty, 11 Wm. & Mary Bill Rts. J. 1011 (2003); Theresa Glennon, Somebody's Child: Evaluating the Erosion of the Marital Presumption of Paternity, 102 W. Va. L. Rev. 547, 590-591 (2000); Marjorie Maguire Shultz, Reproductive Technology and Intent-Based Parenthood: An Opportunity for Gender Neutrality, 1990 Wis. L. Rev. 297, 317.

[41] See, e.g., Kusior v. Silver, 354 P.2d 657, 668 (Cal. 1960); In re Estate of Jones, 8 A.2d 631, 635-636 (Vt. 1939).

[42] 42 U.S.C. §666(a)(5)(G).

[43] See, e.g., Simmonds v. Perkins, 247 So. 3d 397 (Fla. 2018) (examining history and purposes, but allowing rebuttal by biological father on facts similar to *Michael H.*); J.A.S. v. Bushelman, 342 S.W.2d 850 (Ky. 2011) (recounting history and modern developments).

treatment of all children, regardless of the marital status or living arrangements of their mothers? What disadvantages come with basing parentage on genetics?[44] Alternatively, when genetic evidence conflicts with the presumption of legitimacy or one of the other paternity presumptions, should courts consider a child's best interests in resolving the conflict? What factors do "best interests" include in this context?[45]

12. *Paternity disestablishment.* Increasingly, jurisdictions are permitting, by case law or statute, the disestablishment of paternity, generally on the basis of paternity fraud. Typically, a former husband or nonmarital father will attempt to invalidate a support obligation after genetic evidence shows that the children are not biologically his offspring. Some states require that the man act within a prescribed time, and some allow recovery in tort for paternity fraud. Does disestablishment constitute sound policy? Should all children undergo genetic testing at birth to avoid such situations? Why?[46]

Should a man be permitted to disestablish paternity once he has already assumed the role of the child's father? Courts sometimes deny disestablishment claims based on principles of equitable estoppel, while others bar paternity disestablishment based on res judicata principles, treating as a final judgment the divorce decree or child support order establishing paternity.[47]

13. *How many fathers? Michael H.* rests on the assumption that a child may have only one father. What is the basis for this assumption? Given modern sexual mores and the high divorce rate, does this assumption continue to make sense? If the dissenters would afford constitutional protection to Michael's interests because he, Carole, and Victoria lived together as a family for a time, would they afford similar protection to any interests asserted by Scott, another man with whom Carole and Victoria lived? Why or why not?

Louisiana has allowed dual paternity since the 1970s.[48] According to one account, that state predicted that the Supreme Court would eventually require legal protection of biological fathers, even for children born to married women. Dual paternity was designed to afford parental status to the mother's husband in the face of such constitutional interpretation. Is the concept of dual paternity a workable solution to *Michael H.*? For

---

[44] See Katharine K. Baker, The DNA Default and its Discontents: Establishing Modern Parenthood, 96 B.U. L. Rev. 2037 (2016). See also Katharine K. Baker, Legitimate Families and Equal Protection, 56 B.C. L. Rev. 1647 (2015) (urging tempered reading of illegitimacy cases to avoid genetic essentialism).

[45] For authorities grappling with such questions, see, e.g., In re Nicholas H., 46 P.3d 932 (Cal. 2002); K.E.M. v. P.C.S., 38 A.3d 798 (Pa. 2012); In re T.K.Y., 205 S.W.3d 343 (Tenn. 2006); Kerry Abrams & Brandon L. Garrett, DNA and Distrust, 91 Notre Dame L. Rev. 757, 790-802 (2015); Katharine K. Baker, Bionormativity and the Construction of Parenthood, 42 Ga. L. Rev. 649 (2008). See also B.E.B. v. R.L.B., 979 P.2d 514 (Alaska 1999) (application of paternity by estoppel rests only on risk of financial harm, not emotional harm to child).

[46] See generally Susan Ayres, Paternity (Un)Certainty: How the Law Surrounding Paternity Challenges Negatively Impacts Family Relationships and Women's Sexuality, 20 J. Gender, Race & Just. 237 (2017); Vanessa S. Browne-Barbour, "Mama's Baby, Papa's Maybe": Disestablishment of Paternity, 48 Akron L. Rev. 263 (2015); Melanie B. Jacobs, When Daddy Doesn't Want to Be Daddy Anymore: An Argument Against Paternity Fraud Claims, 16 Yale J.L. & Feminism 193 (2004).

[47] Compare, e.g., Kamp v. Dept. of Hum. Resources, 980 A.2d 448 (Md. 2009), and Shondel J. v. Mark D., 853 N.E.2d 610 (N.Y. 2006), with e.g., State v. R.L.C., 47 P.3d 327 (Colo. 2002), and Betty L.W. v. William E.W., 569 S.E.2d 77, 88 (W.Va. 2002).

[48] See, e.g., Warren v. Richard, 296 So.2d 813 (La. 1974); Glennon, supra note [40], at 577.

contemporary authorities recognizing more than two legal parents for a given child, see section C & Chapter 8, section B.

A different form of plural fatherhood is "partible paternity" found in some South American societies. It assumes that pregnancy comes from multiple inseminations, so that several men might be the biological fathers of a single child.[49]

14. *Response to* Michael H. Legislative and judicial responses to *Michael H.* reveal discomfort with the plurality's decision. The state legislature in California (the site of *Michael H.*) amended the conclusive presumption of legitimacy to allow a challenge, based on genetic evidence, by one who is a presumed parent (for example, by taking the child into his home and holding the child out as his own), so long the action is brought within two years of the child's birth. See Cal. Fam. Code §§7541, 7611.

The UPA (2002) incorporates California's two-year limitation on the putative father's ability to request blood tests,[50] subject to estoppel principles (regarding the conduct of the parties, the equities of disproving the father-child relationship between the child and the presumed or acknowledged father, or the best interests of the child). UPA §§607-608 (2002). The UPA (2017) also adheres to the two-year limit for overcoming a presumption of parentage, while recognizing exceptions if the presumed parent is not a genetic parent, never resided with the child, and never held the child out as the presumed parent's child or the child has more than one presumed parent. UPA §608 (2017).

15. *Child's role.* Given the goal of equal treatment for children regardless of their parents' behavior, what role should children play in paternity and/ or disestablishment proceedings? What does the plurality opinion suggest in addressing Victoria's claims in *Michael H.*? Should children be bound by suits that others bring or fail to bring? Why? Under both the UPA (2002) and the UPA (2017), a determination of parentage does not generally bind the child, with exceptions that include determinations based on genetic testing or the child's participation in a previous proceeding. UPA §623(b) & cmt. (2017) (noting that this provision follows the approach of the UPA (2002)).

PROBLEMS

1. DeAndre, born out of wedlock, is killed in an auto accident at age 20. Although a judicial proceeding established his biological father's paternity years before, his father never openly acknowledged his son. After DeAndre's death, the young man's mother sues to sever any inheritance rights that his father might claim. State law precludes the father of a nonmarital child from inheriting from the child if the father either failed or refused to provide support or openly acknowledge the child as his own. The father challenges the statute as an unconstitutional gender-based classification because unmarried

---

[49] See Stephen Beckerman & Paul Valentine, The Concept of Partible Paternity Among Native South Americans, in Cultures of Multiple Fathers: The Theory and Practice of Partible Paternity in Lowland South America 1 (Beckerman & Valentine eds., 2002).

[50] Cf. In re J.C., 594 S.W.3d 466 (Tex. App. 2019) (applying Texas statute, which gives biological fathers four years to challenge presumption); Castro v. Lemus, 456 P.3d 750 (Utah 2019) (reading the statute to give alleged biological fathers standing to challenge presumption).

mothers need not meet any requirements before inheriting from their children. DeAndre's mother and the state argue that the statute differentiates not on the basis of gender but rather distinguishes fathers who openly acknowledge their nonmarital children from those who do not. They also argue that the statute advances the state interest in encouraging fathers to take responsibility for their nonmarital children by precluding an uninvolved father from profiting from the child's death. What result and why?[51]

2. Nina Viola Montepagani, a 59-year-old retired schoolteacher in New York, sues there to remove from her birth certificate the name of her father, Giuseppe Viola. According to letters she has discovered, she was born eight months after her mother came from Italy to New York and married Viola, who raised Montepagani and in every way treated her as his daughter until he died. The letters indicate that her mother believed Montepagani's genetic father to be an Italian doctor, Sebastiano Raeli, a belief that Viola himself might have shared as well. Raeli recently died in Italy, officially childless and leaving an estate worth $100 million. Under Italian law, a decedent's child can claim up to half of a parent's estate, but a birth certificate naming a different man as father would stand in the way. How should the New York court rule on Montepagani's petition to remove Viola's name? To the extent the court is open to granting the requested relief, what sort of evidence should it require?[52]

3. Some scholars recommend abolishing the presumption of legitimacy because they claim: (1) it exacerbates inequalities among families, (2) it gives undue power to the biological mother, and (3) it is unnecessary given the availability and accuracy of genetic testing.[53] Would you support this recommendation? Why? Why not? Which of the arguments cited do you find most compelling? How do the materials in the next section contribute to your answers?

C. KEEPING DEPENDENCY PRIVATE

Stanley and *Michael H.*, supra, reveal how underlying state policies based on gender and marriage shape the traditional principles that identify a child's parents. An additional, powerful government interest lies in ensuring a private source of support for dependent children. Expanding the understanding of who is a parent provides a way to advance this increasingly salient objective, as the following case shows. What other objectives do contemporary approaches to parentage serve?

---

[51] See Rainey v. Chever, 510 S.E.2d 823 (Ga. 1999); Linda Kelly Hill, Equal Protection Misapplied: The Politics of Gender and Legitimacy and the Denial of Inheritance, 13 Wm. & Mary J. Women & L. 129 (2006); Eleanor Mixon, Note, Deadbeat Dads: Undeserving of the Right to Inherit from the Illegitimate Children and Undeserving of Equal Protection, 34 Ga. L. Rev. 1773, 1775-1776 (2000). See also In re Rogiers, 933 A.2d 971 (N.J. Super. Ct. App. Div. 2007).

[52] See William Glaberson & Elisabetta Povoledo, A Question of Paternity, N.Y. Times, Apr. 17, 2011, at MB1; Montepagani v. New York City Dept. of Health, 47 Misc. 3d 1228(A) (N.Y. Sup. Ct. 2015).

[53] See Carbone & Cahn, supra note [13], 134 (2014); Veronica Sue Gunderson, Personal Responsibility in Parentage: An Argument Against the Marital Presumption, 11 U.C. Davis J. Juv. L. & Pol'y 335 (2007); Clare Huntington, Postmarital Family Law: A Legal Structure for Nonmarital Families, 67 Stan. L. Rev. 167, 225 (2015).

ELISA B. v. SUPERIOR COURT

117 P.3d 660 (Cal. 2005)

MORENO, J. . . .

On June 7, 2001, the El Dorado County District Attorney filed a complaint in superior court to establish that Elisa B. is a parent of two-year-old twins Kaia B. and Ry B., who were born to Emily B., and to order Elisa to pay child support. [Elisa denied being the twins' parent.] Elisa testified that she entered into a lesbian relationship with Emily in 1993. They began living together six months later. Elisa obtained a tattoo that read "Emily, por vida," which in Spanish means Emily, for life. They introduced each other to friends as their "partner," exchanged rings, opened a joint bank account, and believed they were in a committed relationship.

Elisa and Emily discussed having children and decided that they both wished to give birth. Because Elisa earned more than twice as much money as Emily, they decided that Emily "would be the stay-at-home mother" and Elisa "would be the primary breadwinner for the family." At a sperm bank, they chose a donor they both would use so the children would "be biological brothers and sisters." [Each attended the other's insemination procedures, prenatal medical appointments, labor, and delivery.] Elisa gave birth to Chance in November, 1997, and Emily gave birth to Ry and Kaia prematurely in March, 1998. Ry had medical problems; he suffered from Down's Syndrome, and required heart surgery.

They jointly selected the children's names, joining their surnames with a hyphen to form the children's surname. They each breast fed all of the children. Elisa claimed all three children as her dependents on her tax returns and obtained a life insurance policy on herself naming Emily as the beneficiary so that if "anything happened" to her, all three children would be "cared for." Elisa believed the children would be considered both of their children.

Elisa's parents referred to the twins as their grandchildren and her sister referred to the twins as part of their family and referred to Elisa as their mother. Elisa treated all of the children as hers and told a prospective employer that she had triplets. Elisa and Emily identified themselves as coparents of Ry at an organization arranging care for his Down's Syndrome.

Elisa supported the household financially. Emily was not working. Emily testified that she would not have become pregnant if Elisa had not promised to support her financially, but Elisa denied that any financial arrangements were discussed before the birth of the children. Elisa later acknowledged in her testimony, however, that Emily "was going to be an at-home mom for maybe a couple of years and then the kids were going to go into day care and she was going to return to work."

They consulted an attorney regarding adopting "each other's child," but never did so. Nor did they register as domestic partners or execute a written agreement concerning the children. Elisa stated she later reconsidered adoption because she had misgivings about Emily adopting Chance.

Elisa and Emily separated in November, 1999. Elisa promised to support Emily and the twins "as much as I possibly could" and initially paid the mortgage payments [and later the rent for Emily and the twins. Then she stopped providing such support.] At the time of trial, Elisa was earning $95,000 a year.

[The superior court found that Elisa and Emily had rejected the option of using a private sperm donor because "[t]hey wanted the child to be raised *exclusively* by them as a couple"; that they intended to create a child and "acted in all respects as a family"; that Elisa was obligated to support the twins under the doctrine of equitable estoppel. The superior court concluded:] "The need for the application of [equitable estoppel] is underscored by the fact that the decision of Respondent to create a family and desert them has caused the remaining family members to seek county assistance. One child that was created has special needs that will require the remaining parent or the County to be financially responsible of those needs. The child was deprived of the right to have a traditional father to take care of the financial needs of this child. Respondent chose to step in those shoes and assume the role and responsibility of the 'other' parent. This should be her responsibility and not the responsibility of the taxpayer." Elisa was subsequently ordered to pay child support in the amount of $907.50 per child for a total of $1815 per month. . . .

We must determine whether the Court of Appeal erred [in reversing, ruling under California's version of the original Uniform Parentage Act (UPA), Cal. Fam. Code §7600 et seq.] that Elisa could not be a parent of the twins born to her lesbian partner, and thus had no obligation to support them. . . . The UPA defines the " '[p]arent and child relationship' " as "the legal relationship existing between a child and the child's natural or adoptive parents. . . . The term includes the mother and child relationship and the father and child relationship." (§7601). One purpose of the UPA was to eliminate distinctions based upon whether a child was born into a marriage, and thus was "legitimate," or was born to unmarried parents, and thus was "illegitimate." Thus, the UPA provides that . . . : "The parent and child relationship extends equally to every child and to every parent, regardless of the marital status of the parents." (§7602.) . . .

Section 7611 provides several circumstances in which "[a] man is presumed to be the natural father of a child," including: if he is the husband of the child's mother, is not impotent or sterile, and was cohabiting with her (§7540); if he signs a voluntary declaration of paternity stating he is the "biological father of the child" (§7574, subd. (b)(6)); and if "[h]e receives the child into his home and openly holds out the child as his natural child" (§7611, subd. (d)). [Although] the UPA contains separate provisions defining who is a mother and who is a father, it expressly provides that in determining the existence of a mother and child relationship, "[i]nsofar as practicable, the provisions of this part applicable to the father and child relationship apply." (§7650.)

The Court of Appeal correctly recognized that, under the UPA, Emily has a parent and child relationship with each of the twins because she gave birth to them. (§7610, subd. (a)). . . . Relying upon our statement in Johnson v. Calvert, [851 P.2d 776 (Cal. 1993)], that "for any child California law recognizes only one natural mother," the Court of Appeal reasoned that Elisa, therefore, could not also be the natural mother of the twins and thus "has no legal maternal relationship with the children under the UPA."

The Attorney General, appearing pursuant to section 17406 to "represent the public interest in establishing, modifying, and enforcing support obligations," argues that the Court of Appeal erred, stating: "*Johnson's* one-natural-mother comment cannot be thoughtlessly interpreted to deprive the child of same-sex couples the same opportunity as other children to two parents and to two sources of child support when only two parties are eligible for parentage." As we shall explain, the Attorney General is correct that our statement in *Johnson* that a child can have "only one natural mother" does not mean that both Elisa and Emily cannot be parents of the twins [because this case is distinguishable.]

In *Johnson,* [a dispute arising from a gestational surrogacy arrangement], we addressed the situation in which three people claimed to be the child's parents: the husband, who undoubtedly was the child's father, and two women [the biological mother versus surrogate mother], who presented conflicting claims to being the child's mother. We rejected the suggestion of amicus curiae that both the wife and the surrogate could be the child's mother, stating that a child can have only one mother, but what we considered and rejected in *Johnson* was the argument that a child could have three parents: a father and two mothers.[4] . . . The Court of Appeal in the present case erred, therefore, in concluding that our statement in *Johnson* that a child can have only one mother under California law resolved the issue presented in this case. . . .

We perceive no reason why both parents of a child cannot be women. That result now is possible under the current version of the domestic partnership statutes [providing that: "The rights and obligations of registered domestic partners with respect to a child of either of them shall be the same as those of spouses." Cal. Fam. Code §297.5(d).] Prior to the effective date of the current domestic partnership statutes, we recognized in an adoption case that a child can have two parents, both of whom are women. [Sharon S. v. Superior Court, 73 P.3d 554 (Cal. 2003).] If both parents of an adopted child can be women, we see no reason why the twins in the present case cannot have two parents, both of whom are women.

[W]e proceed to examine the UPA to determine whether Elisa is a parent to the twins in addition to Emily. . . . Subdivision (d) of section 7611 states that a man is presumed to be the natural father of a child if "([h]e receives the child into his home and openly holds out the child as his natural child." The Court of Appeal in [In re Karen C., 124 Cal. Rptr. 2d 677 (Ct. App. 2002)], held that subdivision (d) of section 7611 "should apply equally to women."[W]e must determine whether Elisa received the twins into her home and openly held them out as her natural children [pursuant to Cal. Fam. Code §7611]. There is no doubt that Elisa satisfied the first part of this test. . . . Our inquiry focuses, therefore, on whether she openly held out the twins as her natural children.

---

4. We have not yet decided "(whether there exists an overriding legislative policy limiting a child to two parents." [Sharon S. v. Superior Court, 73 P.3d 554, 561 (Cal. 2003)].

The circumstance that Elisa has no genetic connection to the twins does not necessarily mean that she did not hold out the twins as her "natural" children under section 7611. We held in [In re Nicholas H., 46 P.3d 932 (Cal. 2002)] that the presumption under section 7611, subdivision (d), that a man who receives a child into his home and openly holds the child out as his natural child is not necessarily rebutted when he admits he is not the child's biological father. The presumed father [Thomas, who was *not* the biological father] in *Nicholas H.*, [was] named as the child's father on his birth certificate and provided a home for the child and his mother for several years [and subsequently sought custody when the court removed the child from the mother's care].

We held in *Nicholas H.* that Thomas was presumed to be Nicholas's father despite his admission that he was not Nicholas's biological father. . . . We noted, however, that the UPA does not state that the presumption under section 7611, subdivision (d), *is* rebutted by evidence that the presumed father is not the child's biological father, but rather that it *may* be rebutted in an appropriate action by such evidence. We held that *Nicholas H.* was not an appropriate action in which to rebut the presumption because no one had raised a conflicting claim to being the child's father. Applying the presumption, therefore, would produce the "harsh result" of leaving the child fatherless. . . .

The Court of Appeal in In re Karen C., [124 Cal. Rptr. 2d 677 (Ct. App. 2002)], applied the principles discussed in *Nicholas H.* regarding presumed fathers and concluded that a woman with no biological connection to a child [but who had raised a child from birth] could be a presumed mother under section 7611, subdivision (d). . . .

We conclude that the present case, like *Nicholas H.* . . . , is not "an appropriate action" in which to rebut the presumption of presumed parenthood with proof that Elisa is not the twins' biological parent. . . . It is undisputed that Elisa actively consented to, and participated in, the artificial insemination of her partner with the understanding that the resulting child or children would be raised by Emily and her as coparents, and they did act as coparents for a substantial period of time. Elisa received the twins into her home and held them out to the world as her natural children. . . .

Declaring that Elisa cannot be the twins' parent and, thus, has no obligation to support them because she is not biologically related to them would produce a result similar to the situation we sought to avoid in *Nicholas H.* of leaving the child fatherless. . . . Rebutting the presumption that Elisa is the twin's parent would leave them with only one parent and would deprive them of the support of their second parent. Because Emily is financially unable to support the twins, the financial burden of supporting the twins would be borne by the county, rather than Elisa.

In establishing a system for a voluntary declaration of paternity in section 7570, the Legislature declared: "There is a compelling state interest in establishing paternity for all children. Establishing paternity is the first step toward a child support award, which, in turn, provides children with equal rights and access to benefits, including, but not limited to, social security, health insurance, survivors' benefits, military benefits, and inheritance rights. . . ." By recognizing the value of determining paternity, the Legislature implicitly recognized the value of having two parents, rather than one, as a source of both emotional and financial support, especially when the obligation to support the child would otherwise fall to the public. . . .

We observed in dicta in *Nicholas H.* that it would be appropriate to rebut the section 7611 presumption of parentage if "a court decides that the legal rights and obligations of parenthood should devolve upon an unwilling candidate." But we decline to apply our dicta in *Nicholas H.* here, because we did not consider in *Nicholas H.* a situation like that in the present case.

Although Elisa presently is unwilling to accept the obligations of parenthood, this was not always so. . . . We conclude, therefore, that Elisa is a presumed mother of the twins under section 7611, subdivision (d). . . .

NOTES AND QUESTIONS

1. *Rationale.* Why must Elisa B. pay child support for the twins born to Emily? According to the American Law Institute, "Once legal parentage is established, a legal parent owes a duty of reasonable economic support."[54] Could the court have required Elisa to support the twins without recognizing her as their parent?[55] What theory makes parents financially responsible for their children? Blackstone described the duty of parents to support their children as "a principle of natural law."[56]

2. *Privatizing dependency.* Starting with Professor Martha Fineman, who focused on marriage, several scholars conceptualize the "privatization of dependency" as the animating purpose of family law generally.[57] From this perspective, "family law rules that establish financial relationships and liability between individuals constitute a form of social insurance."[58] How does *Elisa B.* illustrate this theory? Note that the litigation in *Elisa B.* began when the state sought to collect private child support so that the twins would not be dependent on public assistance. To what extent does this theory also explain the presumption of legitimacy, as in *Michael H.,* supra?[59] If only parents have support responsibilities, how might such support responsibilities play a role in determining who is a parent?

3. *Alternative visions.* What alternatives to private parental support can you imagine? To the extent that children constitute community assets — the next generation of citizens — why shouldn't taxpayers assume responsibility — as they do for public education, for example?[60] Indeed, in colonial America, care for children who could not remain at home was

---

[54] See Restatement of Children and the Law §2.10 cmt. a (Am. Law Inst. Tent. Draft No. 1 2018).

[55] See id. cmt. h.

[56] 1 William Blackstone, Commentaries *447-448. See Ira Mark Ellman & Tara O'Toole Ellman, The Theory of Child Support, 45 Harv. J. on Legis. 107, 129 (2008) (articulating "principle of the primacy of the parents' support obligation").

[57] Martha Albertson Fineman, The Autonomy Myth: A Theory of Dependency 44, 108-109, 208 (2004). See also, e.g., Joanna L. Grossman & Lawrence M. Friedman, Inside the Castle: Law and the Family in 20th Century America 262 (2011); Laura A. Rosenbury, Federal Visions of Private Family Support, 67 Vand. L. Rev. 1835, 1866 (2014).

[58] Anne L. Alstott, Private Tragedies? Family Law as Social Insurance, 4 Harv. L. & Pol'y Rev. 3, 4 (2010).

[59] See, e.g., Baker, supra note [40]; Jana Singer, Marriage, Biology, and Paternity: The Case for Revitalizing the Marital Presumption, 65 Md. L. Rev. 246 (2006).

[60] See, e.g., Scott Altman, A Theory of Child Support, 17 Int'l J. L. Pol'y & Fam. 173 (2003).

regarded as a community responsibility necessary to produce good citizens for the future.[61]

Fineman offers a different justification for public support: The state should subsidize mothers so that they can care for their children, because childcare constitutes valuable labor.[62] This approach rejects current welfare measures, which require single custodial parents of young children to work outside the home (with states permitted to have some exemptions).[63] Evaluate Fineman's proposal.[64]

4. *Estoppel.* What role, if any, does the doctrine of estoppel play in the court's analysis? What facts give rise to estoppel? In a companion case, Kristine H. v. Lisa R., 117 P.3d 690 (Cal. 2005), the California Supreme Court invoked estoppel more explicitly. Having participated in a prebirth judicial proceeding that stipulated that Kristine and Lisa were both parents of the child whom Kristine, seven months pregnant, was expecting, Kristine was estopped from questioning the stipulation later, after the women's relationship dissolved. The court limited its decision, however, declining to decide the validity of the stipulated judgment for other purposes. Id. at 695. Similarly, in McLaughlin v. Jones, 401 P.3d 492, 501 (Ariz. 2017), the court ruled that a joint parenting agreement estopped Kimberly, the child's mother, from challenging the presumptive parental status of Suzan, her spouse.[65] The American Law Institute's Principles of the Law of Family Dissolution (ALI Principles) recognize "parents by estoppel." They have the same rights and responsibilities as legal parents, but parental status by estoppel arises only in the context of dissolution of the family relationship. Principles of the Law of Family Dissolution: Analysis and Recommendations §2.03 (Am. Law Inst. 2002). Parentage by estoppel arises when a man has lived with the child for two years (or since birth) and believed that he was the biological father and continued assuming parental responsibilities even after the belief no longer existed; alternatively, the status arises when one has lived with the child since birth or for two years, accepting full and permanent responsibilities and holding the child out as one's own, pursuant to a co-parenting agreement with the parent or parents, and recognition as a parent would serve the child's best interests. Id. §2.03(b)(ii)-(iv). In addition, parentage by estoppel can arise when one is ordered to pay child support. Id. §203(b)(i).

On what basis would the ALI Principles recognize Elisa B. as a parent by estoppel? Do you agree a man who truly but erroneously believed that he was the biological father should be estopped from denying paternity when

---

[61] See Elaine Tyler May, Barren in the Promised Land: Childless Americans and the Pursuit of Happiness 24-31 (1997); Mary Ann Mason, From Father's Property to Children's Rights: A History of Child Custody in the United States 73 (1994).

[62] See generally Fineman, supra note [57]. See also Anne L. Alstott, No Exit: What Parents Owe Children and What Society Owes Parents (2004).

[63] See 42 U.S.C. §607(b)(5).

[64] See generally, e.g., Lee Anne Fennell, Relative Burdens: Family Ties and the Safety Net, 45 Wm. & Mary L. Rev. 1453 (2004); Matthew B. Lawrence, Against the "Safety Net," 72 Fla. L. Rev. 49 (2020); Symposium, The Structures of Care Work, 76 Chi.-Kent L. Rev. 1389-1786 (2001).

[65] See also In re Paternity of H.H., 879 N.E.2d 1175 (Ind. Ct. App. 2008) (estopping mother from denying ex-boyfriend's paternity); K.E.M., 38 A.3d 798 (limiting doctrine of paternity by estoppel to cases when it serves the child's best interests and finding it should have a larger role than the marital presumption).

he later learns the truth?[66] Why should parental status follow from support duties?[67] Note that the ALI's latest approach to such issues, the Restatement of Children and the Law, does not follow the Principles, but instead relies on the UPA (2017), which omits parentage by estoppel but includes more robust protections for de facto parents. Restatement of Children and the Law, Part I Introductory Note (Am. Law Inst. Tent. Draft No. 2 2019). On de facto parents, see infra Note 7c.

5. *Parentage by contract.* Cases like *McLaughlin*, supra, rest estoppel on a pre-birth agreement, and the ALI Principles refer to agreements as one trigger for parentage by estoppel. Should courts simply treat such co-parenting agreements as contracts judicially enforceable on their own terms? Why? Courts have split.[68] To the extent agreements reflect the parties' intentions, they provide evidence relevant for establishing parentage based on intent, examined infra Note 7d.

6. *The federal role and "voluntary acknowledgments of paternity."* Considerable impetus for modern state efforts to keep dependency private originated with Congress, which sought to curb growing use of public dollars to support needy families. Starting in the 1960s, Congress enacted legislation conditioning states' receipt of federal welfare funds on the enforcement of child support obligations. Over the years, conditional federal funding has required states to adopt ever more aggressive enforcement mechanisms, while also requiring states to set child support awards according to numerical guidelines, rather than relying on judicial discretion. Data documenting the "feminization of poverty" along with underlying heteronormative assumptions meant that these efforts focused on fathers.[69]

The voluntary acknowledgment of paternity (VAP) has emerged as one of the most frequently used devices for securing child support. In 1993, Congress conditioned state eligibility for federal welfare funds on adoption of such programs, imposing additional requirements in later years.[70] Professor Leslie Harris provides this summary:

---

[66] Compare San Diego County v. Arzaga, 62 Cal. Rptr. 3d 329 (Ct. App. 2007), with *Shondel J.*, 853 N.E.2d 610.

[67] In re J.B., 953 A.2d 1186 (N.H. 2008). But see A.H. v. M.P., 857 N.E.2d 1061 (Mass. 2006) (financial contribution to family, although a parenting function, does not make one a parent by estoppel); Heatzig v. MacLean, 664 S.E.2d 347 (N.C. Ct. App. 2008) (rejecting theory of "parent by estoppel"). See generally Katharine K. Baker, Asymmetric Parenthood, in Reconceiving the Family: Critique on the American Law Institute's Principles of the Law of Family Dissolution 121 (Robin Fretwell Wilson ed., 2006) (contrasting Principles' expansive approach to child custody rights with narrow approach to child support obligations).

[68] Compare Frazier v. Goudschaal, 295 P.3d 542 (Kan. 2013) (holding co-parenting agreement enforceable), and In re T.P.S., 978 N.E.2d 1070, 1075 (Ill. App. Ct. 2012) (allowing common law contract and promissory estoppel causes of action for custody and visitation brought by the nonbiological parent), with Wakeman v. Dixon, 921 So. 2d 669 (Fla. Dist. Ct. App. 2006) (holding partners' co-parenting agreement unenforceable), and T.F. v. B.L., 813 N.E.2d 1244 (Mass. 2004) (rejecting parentage by contract between former lesbian partners). See also In re Adoption of T.M.M.H., 416 P.3d 999, 1008 (Kan. 2018) (opining that a grandparent could be co-parent, based on agreement); Brooke S.B. v. Elizabeth A.C.C., 61 N.E.3d 488 (N.Y. 2016) (according standing as a parent to seek custody and visitation to birth mother's former partner, based on agreement to conceive and raise a child together).

[69] See, e.g., Andrea H. Beller & John W. Graham, Small Change: The Economics of Child Support (1993); Fathers Under Fire: The Revolution in Child Support Enforcement (Irwin Garfinkel et al. eds., 1998).

[70] See 42 U.S.C. §666(a)(5)(C).

A voluntary acknowledgment of paternity (VAP) is a document signed by a child's mother and the putative father that identifies the man as the father. When the document is filed with the state office of vital statistics, it establishes legal paternity. The VAP is a creature of federal child support law, but its use and social impact extend beyond the child support arena. . . .

[Under federal law] states must authorize VAPs. . . . Federal law imposes additional rules to govern VAPs. States may not require blood testing as a precondition to signing a VAP. The law must treat a VAP as if it resolves a legal dispute; when a VAP is filed with the state office of vital statistics, it has the legal effect of a judicial determination of paternity. The state cannot condition the validity of the acknowledgment on any kind of proceeding. States must give full faith and credit to acknowledgments signed in other states if they contain the information required by federal standards and have been executed in compliance with the procedures required by the state in which they were signed.

Voluntary acknowledgment forms must be offered to all parents at all birthing facilities and birth records offices in the state. Each party must be given oral and written notice of the alternatives to, legal consequences of, and rights and responsibilities arising from the signed acknowledgment. Either party must be able to rescind the acknowledgment within sixty days of the child's birth or the date of any judicial or administrative proceeding relating to the child, whichever occurs first. After that, an acknowledgment can be challenged only on the ground of fraud, duress, or material mistake of fact.[71]

Note that a VAP goes beyond presumptions, constituting an establishment of paternity with the effect of a judicial determination.

7. *Beyond fathers: gender-neutralizing paternity laws.* Writing before *Elisa B.*, Professor Susan Dalton criticized law's asymmetrical treatment of parentage for males and females and the underlying incapacity for "imagining a gender-free subject" in this context.[72] While law has recognized a man's parental status based on social factors such as marriage to the child's mother or holding out a child as his own, biological ties remained essential for a woman to achieve such status.[73]

To what extent does *Elisa B.* address Dalton's critique? Which particular provision(s) of the UPA does the court apply? Why? Is the court's reasoning persuasive that the UPA's paternity provisions should apply to women?[74] What other paternity provisions might apply in such cases? While the court applied then-applicable provisions of the UPA (1973), California has now enacted the UPA (2017). The newer legislation continues to make clear that a court should, when practicable, apply in a gender-neutral

[71] Leslie Joan Harris, Voluntary Acknowledgments of Parentage for Same-Sex Couples, 20 Am. U. J. Gender Soc. Pol'y & L. 467, 475-476 (2012). See Tianna N. Gibbs, Paper Courts and Parental Rights: Balancing Access, Agency, and Due Process, 54 Harv. Civ. Rts. Civ. Lib. L. Rev. 549 (2019) (noting that such measures increase access to determinations of parental rights, but criticizing the absence of procedural protections that should accompany matters of such consequence); Caroline Rogus, Fighting the Establishment: The Need for Procedural Reform of Our Paternity Laws, 21 Mich. J. Gender & L. 67 (2014).

[72] Susan E. Dalton, From Presumed Fathers to Lesbian Mothers: Sex Discrimination and the Legal Construction of Parenthood, 9 Mich. J. Gender & L. 261, 266 (2003).

[73] Id. at 289. See Cahill, supra note [28].

[74] For similar analysis, see, e.g., Partanen v. Gallagher, 59 N.E.3d 1133 (Mass. 2016).

way provisions expressed in gendered terms. UPA §107 (2017); Cal. Fam. Code §7650. The UPA (2017) goes farther still, expressly seeking "to ensure the equal treatment of child born to same-sex couples." UPA (2017) (prefatory note). What measures might accomplish that goal? How do such measures help maintain dependency as private?

a. *Gender-neutral VAPs.* Harris, supra, cites empirical data showing that unmarried parents are using VAPs, not for support, but "to identify themselves as a child's co-parents and to memorialize that relationship."[75] What are the arguments for and against making this approach available to same-sex couples, like the family in *Elisa B.*? Should Congress expand the conditions for federal funding to require states to authorize voluntary acknowledgments of parentage on a gender-neutral basis?[76] The UPA (2017) explicitly extends VAPs — now short for "voluntary acknowledgments of parentage" — so that they can be signed by the woman who gave birth and a second party who need not be the alleged genetic father. UPA §301 (2017).

b. *Extending traditional presumptions.* Although not addressing paternity presumptions directly, after its landmark marriage-equality decision in Obergefell v. Hodges, 135 S.Ct. 2584 (2015), the Supreme Court ruled in Pavan v. Smith, 137 S.Ct. 2075 (2017), that state laws entering the name of a mother's male spouse on her child's birth certificate must apply equally when the mother's spouse is female. Relying on such precedents, authorities have extended the traditional presumption of legitimacy to a mother's wife. For example, in *McLaughlin*, supra, the court reasoned that this presumption falls within the "constellation of benefits the States have linked to marriage" to be enjoyed equally by married same-sex couples.[77] The court went on to state: "A primary purpose of the marital paternity presumption is to ensure children have financial support from two parents."[78] The UPA (2017) follows this approach, carrying over the substance of presumptions from earlier versions but revising them to apply equally to men and women. UPA §204 cmt. (2017).

c. *De facto parentage.* The UPA (2017) also advances gender neutrality by permitting adjudication of a claim of de facto parentage. To prevail, the individual must show by clear and convincing evidence that the individual resided with the child as a regular member of the family, engaged in consistent caretaking of the child, undertook full and permanent parental responsibilities without expecting compensation, held the child out as the individual's own, established "a bonded and dependent relationship with the child which is permanent in nature," and had that relationship fostered or supported by another parent of the child; in addition, one must show that

---

[75] Harris, supra note [71], at 477.

[76] See id.; Jessica Feinberg, A Logical Step Forward: Extending Voluntary Acknowledgments of Parentage to Female Same-Sex Couples, 30 Yale J.L. & Feminism 99 (2018).

[77] 401 P.3d at 494. See generally Susan Frelich Appleton, Presuming Women: Revisiting the Presumption of Legitimacy in the Same-Sex Couples Era, 86 B.U. L. Rev. 227 (2006); June Carbone & Naomi Cahn, Marriage and the Marital Presumption Post-*Obergefell*, 84 UMKC L. Rev. 663 (2016).

[78] *McLaughlin*, 401 P.3d at 499. See also LC v. MG & Child Support Enf't Agency, 430 P.3d 400 (Haw. 2018) (applying parentage presumption to secure child support following mother's divorce from her wife); Boquet v. Boquet, 269 So. 3d 895 (La. Ct. App. 2019) (holding in child support proceeding that "the female spouse of a birth mother [must have] the same 'constellation of benefits' and obligations as those of a male spouse of a birth mother").

continuing the relationship between the child and the individual serves the child's best interests. UPA §609 (2017). Note the irrelevance of not only gender and marriage but also genetic ties.[79] In contrast to the UPA (2017), under which de facto parents can get full parental rights and responsibilities, the Principles of the Law of Family Dissolution accord only visitation opportunities to de facto parents, while recognizing parents by estoppel as full legal parents. Principles of the Law of Family Dissolution: Analysis and Recommendations §2.03 (Am. Law Inst. 2002).

d. *Intent-based parentage.* The UPA (2017) includes as well several provisions designed to facilitate recognition of "intended parents"—with intent to assume parental status disconnected from gender, marriage, and genetic ties. E.g., UPA §§301, 612 (2017). The behaviors that make one a de facto parent often grow out of an earlier plan or intent to create and rear a child, making co-parenting agreement important evidence and estoppel a relevant equitable doctrine. See supra Notes 4 & 5. Intent-based parentage originally arose in the specific context of assisted reproduction, examined in Chapters 7 and 8.

e. *Function over formalities.* De facto and intent-based parentage exemplify family law's functional turn, which purports to reflect "the reality of family life," even if individuals do not comply with formal criteria for recognition, such as marriage.[80] In the context of parentage, this approach emphasizes the performance of parental functions and roles, rather than marriage, gender, or biology.[81] Although not all jurisdictions follow this approach,[82] those that do use several different terms, such as "psychological parent," "de facto parent," or "in loco parentis."[83] As demonstrated by *Elisa B.*, California uses the term "natural parent" even for those who acquire their status functionally. For more on such approaches, see Chapter 2, section B2. What are the advantages of a functional approach? The disadvantages?[84]

Professor Douglas NeJaime contends that the rationale for recognition of functional parent-child relationships in state family law provides a firm basis for taking the next step, namely according constitutional protection to such relationships:

> What exactly is the Constitution protecting when it approaches parenthood in light of insights from family law? As we have seen, the functional turn in family law prioritized actual parent-child relationships. Recognizing that limiting parentage by marriage or blood would

---

[79] See, e.g., Pitts v. Moore, 90 A.3d 1169 (Me. 2014) (applying to mother's male lover, who was not the child's genetic father, criteria for de facto parentage similar to those in the UPA (2017)).

[80] Braschi v. Stahl Associates Co., 543 N.E.2d 49, 54 (N.Y. 1989) (applying functional approach to anti-eviction provisions of New York's rent control law). See also Nikita Stewart, Seen as Family, Aide Wins $283-a-Month Home, N.Y. Times, Feb. 4, 2020, at A1 (same).

[81] See generally, e.g., Douglas NeJaime, The Nature of Parenthood, 126 Yale L.J. 2260 (2017).

[82] See, e.g., Russell v. Pasik, 178 So. 3d 55 (Fla. Dist. Ct. App. 2015); C.G. v. J.H., 193 A.3d 891 (Pa. 2018); Hawkins v. Grese, 809 S.E.2d 441 (Va. Ct. App. 2018).

[83] See Susan Frelich Appleton, Gender and Parentage: Family Law's Equality Project in Our Empirical Age, in What Is Parenthood? Contemporary Debates about the Family 237, 240 (Linda C. McClain & Daniel Cere eds., 2013).

[84] For a critique, see Katharine K. Baker, Quacking Like a Duck? Functional Parenthood Doctrine and Same-Sex Parents, 92 Chi.-Kent L. Rev. 135 (2017). See also Moreau v. Sylvester, 95 A.3d 416, 423 (Vt. 2014) (rejecting broad de facto parent doctrine).

exclude relationships that exist in fact, courts and legislatures acted to protect the developed relationships between parents and children.

Such protection serves many important ends. It recognizes the difficult work of parenting that individuals undertake in a range of family configurations. It values care work and parental responsibility. Protection of actual parent-child relationships also promotes children's interests by safeguarding their relationships with their psychological parents. Internalizing insights about child development, family-law authorities endeavored to protect children from the trauma that severing a parental bond would inflict.

Protection of actual parent-child relationships also serves important equality interests.[85]

8. *Limits to gender neutrality?* How far can law go in gender-neutralizing parentage laws? Can a genetic father's wife invoke the presumption of legitimacy in her claim to establish that she is a child's legal mother?[86] Must some ways of presuming or establishing parentage remain unavailable to gay male couples? Why? In an early marriage equality case, one judge expressed concerns about "troubling anomalies":

> [A]pplied literally, the [marital] presumption would mean very different things based on whether the same-sex couple was comprised of two women as opposed to two men. For the women, despite the necessary involvement of a third party, the law would recognize the rights of the "mother" who bore the child and presume that the mother's female spouse was the child's "father" or legal "parent." For the men, the necessary involvement of a third party would produce the exact opposite result — the biological mother of the child would retain all her rights, while one (but not both) of the male spouses could claim parental rights as the child's father. . . .[87]

Is the judge correct? Why does the UPA (2017), for example, refer in each of its presumptions of parentage to "the woman who gave birth" or say that one party who signs a VAP must be "the woman who gave birth"? UPA §§204, 301 (2017). How would you respond to the challenges of achieving parity and equality for different-sex and same-sex couples?[88] For the law applicable to surrogacy arrangements, see Chapter 8, section A.

9. *Rebuttal.* If genetic evidence is increasingly permitted to rebut parentage presumptions, what will this development signify for same-sex couples? What limitations on rebuttal does the *Elisa B.* court's reasoning suggest? Is the case governed by the reasoning in *Nicholas H.*, as the court asserts? Would the analysis of the rebuttal of presumed parentage differ if Elisa and Emily had been spouses? If genetic evidence controls, what good are parentage presumptions for same-sex couples, who must always use some donated genetic

---

[85] Douglas NeJaime, The Constitution of Parenthood, 72 Stan. L. Rev. 261, 355 (2020). But see, e.g., Sheardown v. Guastella, 920 N.W.2d 172 (Mich. Ct. App. 2018).

[86] Compare In re S.N.V., 284 P.3d 147 (Colo. Ct. App. 2011) (allowing claim), with Amy G. v. M.W., 47 Cal. Rptr. 3d 297 (Ct. App. 2006) (disallowing claim when child would have more than two parents).

[87] Opinions of the Justices to the Senate, 802 N.E.2d 565, 577 n.3 (Mass. 2004) (Sosman, J., dissenting).

[88] See Appleton, supra note [77]; Joanna L. Grossman, Parentage Without Gender, 17 Cardozo J. Conflict Res. 717 (2016).

material? What do these questions suggest about rebuttal in more traditional contexts?[89] The UPA (2017) avoids the term "rebuttal" while recognizing ways to "overcome" parentage presumptions, explaining that the new language "better captures the concept that the determination as to whether a presumed parent is a legal parent is a policy choice based on equitable considerations." See UPA §201 cmt. (2017).

10. *Numerical limits.* Does *Elisa B.* suggest that two parents are always better than one? To what extent does *Elisa B.*'s preference for two parents rest on economic issues alone? Might more than two parents be better still? Contrast *Michael H.,* supra, which declined to recognize dual paternity, with footnote 4 in *Elisa B.,* where the court cautions that it has not decided "whether there exists an overriding legislative policy limiting a child to two parents" (citing a case permitting a woman's second-parent adoption of the biological child of her partner). Should the law fix a specific number of parents as the maximum for all children? Today, a few states allow recognition of more than two legal parents.[90] The UPA (2017) offers alternative provisions, depending on whether the enacting state allows recognition of more than two parents. See UPA §613 (2017) (adjudicating competing claims of parentage). See Chapter 8, section B.

---

[89] See Jessica Feinberg, Restructuring Rebuttal of the Marital Presumption for the Modern Era, 104 Minn. L. Rev. 243 (2019).

[90] E.g., Cal. Fam. Code §7612(c) (permitting a child to have more than two parents when failure to do so would result in detriment to the child); Me. Rev. Stat. tit. 19-a, §1853(2) (allowing court to determine that a child has more than two parents).

2

PARENTAL AUTONOMY

A. THE DECISION WHETHER TO BECOME A PARENT

Law has long accorded parents wide freedom to rear their children as they see fit, locating such decisions in "the private realm of family life which the state cannot enter."[1] More recently, such notions of liberty and privacy have become part of the judicial rhetoric about the decision whether to become a parent in the first place.

EISENSTADT V. BAIRD

405 U.S. 438 (1972)

Mr. Justice BRENNAN delivered the opinion of the Court.

Appellee William Baird was convicted at a bench trial in the Massachusetts Superior Court under Massachusetts General Laws Ann., c. 272, §21, first, for exhibiting contraceptive articles in the course of delivering a lecture on contraception to a group of students at Boston University and, second, for giving a young woman a package of Emko vaginal foam at the close of his address. The Massachusetts Supreme Judicial Court unanimously set aside the conviction for exhibiting contraceptives on the ground that it violated Baird's First Amendment rights, but by a four-to-three vote sustained the conviction for giving away the foam. Commonwealth v. Baird, 247 N.E.2d 574 [(Mass. 1969)]. . . .

Massachusetts General Laws Ann., c. 272, §21 [provides] a maximum five-year term of imprisonment for "whoever . . . gives away . . . any drug, medicine, instrument, or article whatever for the prevention of conception," except as authorized in §21A. . . . As interpreted by the State Supreme Judicial Court, these provisions make it a felony for anyone, other than a registered physician or pharmacist acting in accordance with the terms of §21A, to dispense any article with the intention that it be used for the prevention of conception. [M]arried persons may obtain contraceptives to prevent pregnancy, but only from doctors or druggists on prescription; . . . single persons may not obtain contraceptives from anyone to prevent pregnancy. . . .

---

[1] Prince v. Massachusetts, 321 U.S. 158, 166 (1944).

The question for our determination in this case is whether there is some ground of difference that rationally explains the different treatment accorded married and unmarried persons under Massachusetts General Laws Ann., c. 272, §§21 and 21A.[7] ...

First. [W]e cannot agree that the deterrence of premarital sex may reasonably be regarded as the purpose of the Massachusetts law.

It would be plainly unreasonable to assume that Massachusetts has prescribed pregnancy and the birth of an unwanted child as punishment for fornication, which is a misdemeanor under Massachusetts General Laws Ann., c. 272, §18. Aside from the scheme of values that assumption would attribute to the State, it is abundantly clear that the effect of the ban on distribution of contraceptives to unmarried persons has at best a marginal relation to the proffered objective. ... Like Connecticut's laws [in *Griswold*], §§21 and 21A do not at all regulate the distribution of contraceptives when they are to be used to prevent, not pregnancy, but the spread of disease. Nor, in making contraceptives available to married persons without regard to their intended use, does Massachusetts attempt to deter married persons from engaging in illicit sexual relations with unmarried persons. Even on the assumption that the fear of pregnancy operates as a deterrent to fornication, the Massachusetts statute is thus so riddled with exceptions that deterrence of premarital sex cannot reasonably be regarded as its aim. ...

Second. ... If health were the rationale of §21A, the statute would be both discriminatory and overbroad. ... The Court of Appeals [stated]: "If the prohibition (on distribution to unmarried persons) ... is to be taken to mean that the same physician who can prescribe for married patients does not have sufficient skill to protect the health of patients who lack a marriage certificate, or who may be currently divorced, it is illogical to the point of irrationality." 429 F.2d, at 1401. Furthermore, we must join the Court of Appeals in noting that not all contraceptives are potentially dangerous. ... ["If health] was the Legislature's goal, §21 is not required" in view of the federal and state laws *already* regulating the distribution of harmful drugs. ...

Third. If the Massachusetts statute cannot be upheld as a deterrent to fornication or as a health measure, may it, nevertheless, be sustained simply as a prohibition on contraception? ... We need not and do not, however, decide that important question in this case because, whatever the rights of the individual to access to contraceptives may be, the rights must be the same for the unmarried and the married alike.

If under *Griswold* the distribution of contraceptives to married persons cannot be prohibited, a ban on distribution to unmarried persons would be equally impermissible. It is true that in *Griswold* the right of privacy in question inhered in the marital relationship. Yet the marital couple is not an independent entity with a mind and heart of its own, but an association of two individuals, each with a separate intellectual and emotional makeup. If

---

7. Of course, if we were to conclude that the Massachusetts statute impinges upon fundamental freedoms under *Griswold*, the statutory classification would have to be not merely *rationally* related to a valid public purpose but *necessary* to the achievement of a *compelling* state interest. E.g., Loving v. Virginia, 388 U.S. 1 (1967). But ... we do not have to address the statute's validity under that test because the law fails to satisfy even the more lenient equal protection standard.

the right of privacy means anything, it is the right of the *individual,* married or single, to be free from unwarranted governmental intrusion into matters so fundamentally affecting a person as the decision whether to bear or beget a child. See Stanley v. Georgia, 394 U.S. 557 (1969). See also Skinner v. Oklahoma ex rel. Williamson, 316 U.S. 535 (1942); Jacobson v. Massachusetts, 197 U.S. 11, 29 (1905).

On the other hand, if *Griswold* is no bar to a prohibition on the distribution of contraceptives, the State could not, consistently with the Equal Protection Clause, outlaw distribution to unmarried but not married persons. In each case the evil, as perceived by the State, would be identical, and the underinclusion would be invidious.

... We hold that by providing dissimilar treatment for married and unmarried persons who are similarly situated, Massachusetts General Laws Ann., c. 272, §§21 and 21A, violate the Equal Protection Clause. The judgment of the Court of Appeals is affirmed.

NOTES AND QUESTIONS

1. *History.* Spurred by the crusade of Anthony Comstock, in the late nineteenth century Congress and state legislatures enacted restrictions on birth control, abortion, and information about both.[2] "Comstock laws" claimed to focus on morality. Yet, historians have shown how these measures responded to physicians' efforts to halt competition by midwives in providing women's health care and to fears of "race suicide," prompted by rising immigration rates along with non-immigrant mothers' efforts to limit family size.[3] The radical birth control movement in the United States emerged as part of the Socialist Party's agenda in the early 1900s. Margaret Sanger, a leader in the movement, appreciated the revolutionary potential for women and for sexual liberation more generally. Sanger founded the American Birth Control League, which later became Planned Parenthood.[4]

Many Comstock Laws fell in the 1950s, through legislative repeal or judicial limitation.[5] Two such laws became the focus of landmark cases in the U.S. Supreme Court, Griswold v. Connecticut, 381 U.S. 479 (1965), and *Eisenstadt,* the principal case here.

2. *Building on* Griswold. *Eisenstadt* relies heavily on *Griswold,* a successful challenge to a Connecticut statute prohibiting the use of contraceptives even by married couples. The *Griswold* majority found that the law violated an unarticulated constitutional right of privacy discernable in the "penumbras" of several parts of the Bill of Rights, specifically, the First, Third, Fourth, Fifth, and Ninth Amendments, along with the Fourteenth. The opinion's

[2] Michael Grossberg, Governing the Hearth: Law and the Family in Nineteenth Century America 156-193 (1985).

[3] Id.; Kristin Luker, Abortion and the Politics of Motherhood 20-29 (1984).

[4] Linda Gordon, The Moral Property of Women: A History of Birth Control Politics in American 145 (2002). See generally Jonathan Eig, The Birth of the Pill: How Four Crusaders Reinvented Sex and Launched a Revolution (2014). In 2020, Planned Parenthood removed Sanger's name from its New York health clinic because of her ties to the eugenics movement. Nikita Stewart, Planned Parenthood in N.Y. Disavows a Founder, N.Y. Times, July 22, 2020, at A15.

[5] See Catherine G. Roraback, Griswold v. Connecticut: A Brief Case History, 16 Ohio N.U. L. Rev. 395, 395 (1989).

concerns about privacy centered on the inference that a ban on use would require enforcement in the "sacred precincts of marital bedrooms." 381 U.S. at 485. Along the way, the majority emphasized the special features of marriage, which it called "an association for as noble a purpose as any involved in our prior decisions." Id. at 486. Dissenting opinions expressed disapproval of the law but found no constitutional warrant for overturning it; instead, they said, such decisions belong to the people of Connecticut and their elected representatives.

3. *Contrasts.* How does *Eisenstadt* differ from *Griswold?* Consider each of the following: the scope of the statute, the place of enforcement, the constitutional provisions invoked, the right-holder, and the meaning of "privacy." Which case emerges as the stronger precedent for future litigation? Why?

4. *State interests.* While *Griswold* says almost nothing about what Connecticut interests might support its law, *Eisenstadt* engages with several alleged justifications for the Massachusetts statute. Why do none of these survive even rational-basis review? If you were a Massachusetts lawmaker seeking to ban birth control to the extent permitted by the Constitution, what would your law say in light of *Griswold?*[6] Note that the prohibitions in both *Griswold* and *Eisenstadt* exempted condoms, based on the theory that this type of "birth control" prevents disease.[7] What other rationales might underlie these exemptions?

5. *Language.* Why does *Eisenstadt* accord hypothetical and alternative meanings to "the right of privacy"? Why does the Court suggest that "the right of privacy" might not mean anything? Some observers read *Eisenstadt's* "bear or beget" language to anticipate how the Court might rule in constitutional challenges to abortion restrictions, which were then pending.[8] To what extent does the Court's language suggest a broad commitment to equal treatment regardless of marital status?

6. *Abortion and beyond.* The next year, the Court's majority cited *Eisenstadt* in holding that the right of privacy, which it located in the liberty protected by the Fourteenth Amendment's Due Process Clause, includes the decision whether to terminate a pregnancy, to be limited only when necessary to serve compelling state interests. Roe v. Wade, 410 U.S. 113, 152-154 (1973). The Court's later abortion jurisprudence has shown more deference to state regulation by replacing strict scrutiny with an undue burden standard. See Planned Parenthood of Southeastern Pa. v. Casey, 505 U.S. 833 (1992); Whole Woman's Health v. Hellerstedt, 136 S. Ct. 2292 (2016). Abortion rights remain under attack and could weaken or even disappear. See June Medical Servs. L.L.C. v. Russo, 140 S. Ct. 2103 (2020). Nonetheless, *Eisenstadt* has continued to serve as influential precedent for other facets of liberty, for example, in cases invalidating both prohibitions on LGBTQ sex and bans on same-sex marriage. Lawrence v. Texas, 539 U.S. 558, 565-566 (2003); Obergefell v. Hodges, 135 S. Ct. 2584, 2598-2599, 2604 (2015). For what point

---

[6] See Susan Frelich Appleton, The Forgotten Family Law of Eisenstadt v. Baird, 28 Yale J.L. & Feminism 1, 6-7 (2017).

[7] See id. at 21-22.

[8] David J. Garrow, Liberty and Sexuality: The Right to Privacy and the Making of Roe v. Wade 541-544 (updated ed. 1998).

does Justice O'Connor cite *Griswold* and *Eisenstadt* in her concurring opinion in *Michael H.*, Chapter 1, section B?

7. *Parenthood*. What implications do *Eisenstadt* and its progeny have for our understanding of parenthood — and, in turn, the law of parentage? What does "the decision whether to bear or beget a child" include? What state interests can overcome it?

Does it create protection against "compulsory motherhood"?[9] Do men have a parallel right to avoid legal fatherhood and its financial responsibilities, especially if the pregnancy resulted from contraceptive fraud and/or the man offered to pay for an abortion? Courts have rejected such claims, emphasizing the resulting child's need for support (and, by inference, the assumption that the state should not provide such support).[10] What ramifications does *Eisenstadt* have for a right to procreate or to become a parent? Note how *Eisenstadt* and *Stanley*, Chapter 1, section B, both cite Skinner v. Oklahoma, 316 U.S. 535 (1942), which used the Equal Protection Clause to overturn a law that punished certain crimes with sterilization. The *Skinner* Court explained:

> We are dealing here with legislation which involves one of the basic civil rights of man. Marriage and procreation are fundamental to the very existence and survival of the race. The power to sterilize, if exercised, may have subtle, farreaching and devastating effects. In evil or reckless hands it can cause races or types which are inimical to the dominant group to wither and disappear. There is no redemption for the individual whom the law touches. Any experiment which the State conducts is to his irreparable injury. He is forever deprived of a basic liberty. We mention these matters not to reexamine the scope of the police power of the States. We advert to them merely in emphasis of our view that strict scrutiny of the classification which a State makes in a sterilization law is essential, lest unwittingly or otherwise invidious discriminations are made against groups or types of individuals in violation of the constitutional guaranty of just and equal laws.

Id. at 541.[11] What do such precedents mean for state or federal restrictions on fertility treatments or various forms of assisted reproduction? See Chapter 7, section A.

8. *Access and class*. Although the laws struck down in *Griswold* and *Eisenstadt* appear class-neutral, they operated to limit access by those unable to afford care by private physicians, who had long provided contraception to their patients. By allowing clinics to remain open and by lifting restrictions on distribution, these cases implicitly took account of poor families'

---

[9] See, e.g., Reva B. Siegel, Reasoning from the Body: A Historical Perspective on Abortion Regulation and Questions of Equal Protection, 44 Stan. L. Rev. 261, 263-266 (1992); Mary Ziegler, Abortion and the Constitutional Right (Not) to Procreate, 48 U. Richmond L. Rev. 1263, 1314-1315 (2014).

[10] See Dubay v. Wells, 506 F.3d 422 (6th Cir. 2007) (unsuccessful challenge in case dubbed "Roe v. Wade for men"); Wallis v. Smith, 22 P.3d 682 (N.M. Ct. App. 2001). Compare Shari Motro, The Price of Pleasure, 104 Nw. U. L. Rev. 917 (2010) (urging additional financial obligations for men who conceive), with Lisa Lucile Owens, Coerced Parenthood as Family Policy: Feminism, the Moral Agency of Women, and Men's "Right to Choose," 5 Ala. C.R. & C.L. L. Rev. 1, 33 (2013) (urging a "new reproductive policy that gives men a meaningful opportunity to choose whether to become legal and social fathers" even after pregnancy).

[11] But see Buck v. Bell, 274 U.S. 200 (1927) (upholding involuntary sterilization to achieve eugenic goals).

needs for access.[12] Similar sensitivity to class during the era can be found in Congress's enactment of the Family Planning and Population Research Act of 1970, legislation that encouraged, inter alia, the development of accessible family planning services and gave rise to the Title X program, which provides federal support for family planning services for low-income and uninsured individuals.[13]

More recently, the Affordable Care Act (ACA), which Congress enacted in 2010, expands access to birth control. It requires large employers to furnish group health insurance for their employees, and regulations require that coverage must provide free preventive care and screenings, including prescription contraceptive methods, sterilization procedures, and patient education and counseling. This "contraceptive mandate" recognizes that women pay more for preventive care, that cost barriers thwart their access to contraception, and that access problems result in unintended pregnancies, with personal and economic effects.[14]

Note that statutory supports for access, like the Title X program and the ACA's contraceptive mandate, are subject to legislative and administrative changes, including repeal. Thus, they differ from a constitutional right to access or to assistance from the government, which would be resistant to such changes. With respect to the constitutional guarantees, the Supreme Court has made clear that its rulings protect only "negative rights," rejecting arguments that the Constitution guarantees government aid for those who cannot afford to execute reproductive decisions on their own.[15] Indeed, new limits on the Title X program have forced out some service providers, decreasing access, and new exemptions to the contraceptive mandate based on employers' religious and moral objections shrink the number of workers covered.[16]

9. *Reproductive justice.* Just as class bias and fears of "race suicide" underlay restrictions on birth control and abortion, class and race have continued to inform understandings of reproductive self-determination. Led by women of color, the movement for reproductive justice widens the lens beyond abortion and contraception to include also the ability to choose parenthood, to have healthy pregnancies and births, and to rear one's children in a safe

---

[12] See Cary Franklin, The New Class Blindness, 128 Yale L.J. 2, 10-13 (2018).

[13] See 42 U.S.C. §300.

[14] Id. §18001; see Nora V. Becker & Daniel Polsky, Women Saw Large Decrease in Out-of-Pocket Spending for Contraceptives After ACA Mandate Removed Cost Sharing, 34 Health Affairs 1204 (2015).

[15] See Harris v. McRae, 448 U.S. 297 (1980) (upholding ban on financial assistance even for therapeutic abortions); Dandridge v. Williams, 397 U.S. 471 (1970) (upholding caps on welfare funds to large families even if such limits constrain personal decisions about how many children to have).

[16] See, e.g., Little Sisters of the Poor Sts. Peter & Paul Home v. Pa., 140 S. Ct. 2367 (2020) (upholding administrative authority to grant morality-based exceptions to contraceptive mandate, regardless of availability of coverage); Burwell v. Hobby Lobby Stores, 573 U.S. 682 (2014) (allowing religion-based exemption by small employer on the assumption that employees could still obtain coverage without cost); Pam Belluck, Planned Parenthood Opts Out Over Trump Rule, N.Y. Times, Aug. 20, 2019, at A1; Mary Ziegler, Sexing *Harris*: The Law and Politics of the Movement to Defund Planned Parenthood, 60 Buff. L. Rev. 701, 729-730 (2012).

environment with, at minimum, decent housing and acceptable educational opportunities.[17]

From a reproductive-justice perspective, might the Family Planning and Population Research Act of 1970 merit a second look? What inferences should we draw from its enactment at a time when states were beginning to cap assistance to poor families and involuntary sterilization of poor women of color was a common, albeit illegal, practice?[18] How should we understand contemporary proposals to supply long-acting reversible contraception to young people not ready financially for parenthood? What of the arguments of those who would limit reproductive freedom today by invoking the now reviled eugenics movement?[19] How, if at all, would you distinguish government subsidized family planning services from involuntary sterilization and other eugenic limits on reproduction?

B. PARENTS, THIRD PARTIES, AND THE STATE

Parentage matters not only because of the responsibilities it entails but also because of the authority it grants. Traditionally, these responsibilities and rights constituted an indivisible set based on a legal understanding of parentage as complete and exclusive.[20] Under this approach, adults falling outside the definition of "parent" remain legal strangers or third parties even if they have performed a parental role for many years. This section examines what it means to be recognized as a child's legal parent and whether assumptions underlying the all-or-nothing approach need rethinking.

1. DIRECTING A CHILD'S UPBRINGING

TROXEL V. GRANVILLE

530 U.S. 57 (2000)

Justice O'CONNOR announced the judgment of the Court and delivered an opinion, in which the CHIEF JUSTICE, Justice GINSBURG, and Justice BREYER join. . . .

---

[17] See generally Dorothy Roberts, Killing the Black Body: Race, Reproduction, and the Meaning of Liberty (1999); Loretta Ross & Rickie Solinger, Reproductive Justice: An Introduction (2017).

[18] See, e.g., Laura T. Kessler, "A Sordid Case": Stump v. Sparkman, Judicial Immunity, and the Other Side of Reproductive Rights, 74 Md. L. Rev. 833, 893 (2015) (citing, among the "shifting justifications" for family planning, "racism; concerns about hereditary degeneracy; controlling women's sexuality; channeling sex and reproduction into the marital family and maintaining the gendered marital family more generally; social and economic efficiency; population control; and theological determinism").

[19] Compare Isabel V. Sawhill, Generation Unbound: Drifting into Sex and Parenthood without Marriage (2014) (recommending increased access to long-acting reversible contraceptives for unmarried youth who cannot afford to be parents), with Box v. Planned Parenthood of Ind. & Ky., Inc., 139 S. Ct. 1780, 1782-1791 (2019) (Thomas, J., concurring) (citing eugenics movement in support of specific abortion restrictions).

[20] See Katharine T. Bartlett, Rethinking Parenthood as an Exclusive Status: The Need for Legal Alternatives When the Premise of the Nuclear Family Has Failed, 70 Va. L. Rev. 879 (1984). See also Emily Buss, Essay, "Parental" Rights, 88 Va. L. Rev. 635, 640 (2002) (distinguishing parental identity from parental authority); Joanna L. Grossman, Constitutional Parentage, 32 Const. Comment. 307, 314 (2017) (distinguishing parental status from parental rights).

Tommie Granville and Brad Troxel shared a relationship that ended in June 1991. The two never married, but they had two daughters, Isabelle and Natalie. Jenifer and Gary Troxel are Brad's parents, and thus the paternal grandparents of Isabelle and Natalie. After Tommie and Brad separated in 1991, Brad lived with his parents and regularly brought his daughters to his parents' home for weekend visitation. Brad committed suicide in May 1993. Although the Troxels at first continued to see Isabelle and Natalie on a regular basis after their son's death, Tommie Granville informed the Troxels in October 1993 that she wished to limit their visitation with her daughters to one short visit per month.

[Two months later, the Troxels filed this petition for visitation.] At trial, the Troxels requested two weekends of overnight visitation per month and two weeks of visitation each summer. Granville did not oppose visitation altogether, but instead asked the court to order one day of visitation per month with no overnight stay. [T]he Superior Court [ordered] visitation one weekend per month, one week during the summer, and four hours on both of the petitioning grandparents' birthdays.

[The Court of Appeals reversed the visitation order based on their statutory interpretation that nonparents lack standing unless a custody action is pending. The state supreme court held that the state statute granting visitation rights to "any person" at "any time" (Wash. Rev. Code §26.10.160 (3) (1994)) infringed on parents' fundamental right to rear their children. While the appeal was pending, the mother remarried, and her husband adopted the children.]

The demographic changes of the past century make it difficult to speak of an average American family. The composition of families varies greatly from household to household. While many children may have two married parents and grandparents who visit regularly, many other children are raised in single-parent households. In 1996, children living with only one parent accounted for 28 percent of all children under age 18 in the United States. Understandably, in these single-parent households, persons outside the nuclear family are called upon with increasing frequency to assist in the everyday tasks of child rearing. In many cases, grandparents play an important role. For example, in 1998, approximately 4 million children — or 5.6 percent of all children under age 18 — lived in the household of their grandparents.

The nationwide enactment of nonparental visitation statutes is assuredly due, in some part, to the States' recognition of these changing realities of the American family. Because grandparents and other relatives undertake duties of a parental nature in many households, States have sought to ensure the welfare of the children therein by protecting the relationships those children form with such third parties. The States' nonparental visitation statutes are further supported by a recognition, which varies from State to State, that children should have the opportunity to benefit from relationships with statutorily specified persons — for example, their grandparents. The extension of statutory rights in this area to persons other than a child's parents, however, comes with an obvious cost. For example, the State's recognition of an independent third-party interest in a child can place a substantial burden on the traditional parent-child relationship. . . .

The liberty interest at issue in this case — the interest of parents in the care, custody, and control of their children — is perhaps the oldest of the fundamental liberty interests recognized by this Court. More than 75 years ago, in Meyer v. Nebraska, 262 U.S. 390, 399, 401 (1923), we held that the "liberty" protected by the Due Process Clause includes the right of parents to "establish a home and bring up children" and "to control the education of their own." Two years later, in Pierce v. Society of Sisters, 268 U.S. 510, 534-535 (1925), we again held that the "liberty of parents and guardians" includes the right "to direct the upbringing and education of children under their control." We explained in *Pierce* that "the child is not the mere creature of the State; those who nurture him and direct his destiny have the right, coupled with the high duty, to recognize and prepare him for additional obligations." 268 U.S. at 535. We returned to the subject in Prince v. Massachusetts, 321 U.S. 158 (1944), and again confirmed that there is a constitutional dimension to the right of parents to direct the upbringing of their children. "It is cardinal with us that the custody, care and nurture of the child reside first in the parents, whose primary function and freedom include preparation for obligations the state can neither supply nor hinder." 321 U.S. at 166. . . . In light of this extensive precedent, it cannot now be doubted that the Due Process Clause of the Fourteenth Amendment protects the fundamental right of parents to make decisions concerning the care, custody, and control of their children.

Section 26.10.160(3), as applied to Granville and her family in this case, unconstitutionally infringes on that fundamental parental right. The Washington nonparental visitation statute is breathtakingly broad. According to the statute's text, *[a]ny person* may petition the court for visitation rights *at any time*, and the court may grant such visitation rights whenever "visitation may serve *the best interest of the child.*" §§26.10.160(3) (emphases added). That language effectively permits any third party seeking visitation to subject any decision by a parent concerning visitation of the parent's children to state-court review. Once the visitation petition has been filed in court and the matter is placed before a judge, a parent's decision that visitation would not be in the child's best interest is accorded no deference. Section 26.10.160(3) contains no requirement that a court accord the parent's decision any presumption of validity or any weight whatsoever. Instead, the Washington statute places the best-interest determination solely in the hands of the judge. Should the judge disagree with the parent's estimation of the child's best interests, the judge's view necessarily prevails. Thus, in practical effect, in the State of Washington a court can disregard and overturn any decision by a fit custodial parent concerning visitation whenever a third party affected by the decision files a visitation petition, based solely on the judge's determination of the child's best interests. . . .

Turning to the facts of this case, the record reveals that the Superior Court's order was based on precisely the type of mere disagreement we have just described and nothing more. The Superior Court's order was not founded on any special factors that might justify the State's interference with Granville's fundamental right to make decisions concerning the rearing of her two daughters. [T]he combination of several factors here compels our conclusion that §26.10.160(3), as applied, exceeded the bounds of the Due Process Clause.

First, the Troxels did not allege, and no court has found, that Granville was an unfit parent. That aspect of the case is important, for there is a presumption that fit parents act in the best interests of their children. [S]o long as a parent adequately cares for his or her children (i.e., is fit), there will normally be no reason for the State to inject itself into the private realm of the family to further question the ability of that parent to make the best decisions concerning the rearing of that parent's children.

The problem here is not that the Washington Superior Court intervened, but that when it did so, it gave no special weight at all to Granville's determination of her daughters' best interests. More importantly, it appears that the Superior Court [adopted "a commonsensical approach [that] it is normally in the best interest of the children to spend quality time with the grandparent" and placed] on Granville, the fit custodial parent, the burden of *disproving* that visitation would be in the best interest of her daughters. . . .

The decisional framework employed by the Superior Court directly contravened the traditional presumption that a fit parent will act in the best interest of his or her child. In that respect, the court's presumption failed to provide any protection for Granville's fundamental constitutional right to make decisions concerning the rearing of her own daughters. In an ideal world, parents might always seek to cultivate the bonds between grandparents and their grandchildren. Needless to say, however, our world is far from perfect, and in it the decision whether such an intergenerational relationship would be beneficial in any specific case is for the parent to make in the first instance. And, if a fit parent's decision of the kind at issue here becomes subject to judicial review, the court must accord at least some special weight to the parent's own determination.

Finally, we note that there is no allegation that Granville ever sought to cut off visitation entirely. Rather, the present dispute originated when Granville informed the Troxels that she would prefer to restrict their visitation with Isabelle and Natalie to one short visit per month and special holidays. . . . The Superior Court gave no weight to Granville's having assented to visitation even before the filing of any visitation petition or subsequent court intervention. . . . Significantly, many other States expressly provide by statute that courts may not award visitation unless a parent has denied (or unreasonably denied) visitation to the concerned third party.

Considered together with the Superior Court's reasons for awarding visitation to the Troxels, the combination of these factors demonstrates that the visitation order in this case was an unconstitutional infringement on Granville's fundamental right to make decisions concerning the care, custody, and control of her two daughters. The Washington Superior Court failed to accord the determination of Granville, a fit custodial parent, any material weight. In fact, the Superior Court made only two formal findings in support of its visitation order. First, the Troxels "are part of a large, central, loving family, all located in this area, and the [Troxels] can provide opportunities for the children in the areas of cousins and music." Second, "[t]he children would be benefitted from spending quality time with the [Troxels], provided that that time is balanced with time with the childrens' *[sic]* nuclear family." These slender findings, in combination with the court's announced presumption in favor of grandparent visitation and its failure to accord significant weight to Granville's already having offered meaningful visitation to the Troxels, show that this case involves nothing more than a simple disagreement between the Washington Superior Court and Granville concerning her children's best interests. The Superior Court's announced reason for ordering one week of visitation in the summer demonstrates our conclusion well: "I look back on some personal experiences. . . . We always spen[t] as kids a week with one set of grandparents and another set of grandparents, [and] it happened to work out in our family that [it] turned out to be an enjoyable experience. Maybe that can, in this family, if that is how it works out." [T]he Due Process Clause does not permit a State to infringe on the fundamental right of parents to make childrearing decisions simply because a state judge believes a "better" decision could be made. [W]e hold that §26.10.160(3), as applied in this case, is unconstitutional.

Because we rest our decision on the sweeping breadth of §26.10.160(3) and the application of that broad, unlimited power in this case, we do not consider the primary constitutional question passed on by the Washington Supreme Court — whether the Due Process Clause requires all nonparental visitation statutes to include a showing of harm or potential harm to the child as a condition precedent to granting visitation. We do not, and need not, define today the precise scope of the parental due process right in the visitation context. [T]he constitutionality of any standard for awarding visitation turns on the specific manner in which that standard is applied . . . . Because much state-court adjudication in this context occurs on a case-by-case basis, we would be hesitant to hold that specific nonparental visitation statutes violate the Due Process Clause as a *per se* matter. . . .

[In separate omitted concurring opinions, Justice Souter would uphold the state court's determination of the statute's facial unconstitutionality, and Justice Thomas asserted that strict scrutiny ought to apply.]

Justice STEVENS, dissenting.

. . . While, as the Court recognizes, the Federal Constitution certainly protects the parent-child relationship from arbitrary impairment by the State, we have never held that the parent's liberty interest in this relationship is so inflexible as to establish a rigid constitutional shield, protecting every arbitrary parental decision from any challenge absent a threshold finding of harm. The presumption that parental decisions generally serve the best interests of their children is sound, and clearly in the normal case the parent's interest is paramount. But even a fit parent is capable of treating a child like a mere possession.

Cases like this do not present a bipolar struggle between the parents and the State over who has final authority to determine what is in a child's best interests. There is at a minimum a third individual, whose interests are implicated in every case to which the statute applies — the child. . . . A parent's rights with respect to her child have thus never been regarded as absolute, but rather are limited by the existence of an actual, developed relationship with a child, and are tied to the presence or absence of some embodiment of family. These limitations have arisen, not simply out of the definition of parenthood itself, but because of this Court's assumption that a parent's interests in a child must be balanced against the State's long-recognized interests as parens patriae, and, critically, the child's own complementary interest in preserving relationships that serve her welfare and protection.

While this Court has not yet had occasion to elucidate the nature of a child's liberty interests in preserving established familial or family-like bonds, it seems to me extremely likely that, to the extent parents and families have fundamental liberty interests in preserving such intimate relationships, so, too, do children have these interests, and so, too, must their interests be balanced in the equation. At a minimum, our prior cases recognizing that children are, generally speaking, constitutionally protected actors require that this Court reject any suggestion that when it comes to parental rights, children are so much chattel. The constitutional protection against arbitrary state interference with parental rights should not be extended to prevent the States from protecting children against the arbitrary exercise of parental authority that is not in fact motivated by an interest in the welfare of the child.

This is not, of course, to suggest that a child's liberty interest in maintaining contact with a particular individual is to be treated invariably as on a par with that child's parents' contrary interests. Because our substantive due process case law includes a strong presumption that a parent will act in the best interest of her child, it would be necessary, were the state appellate courts actually to confront a challenge to the statute as applied, to consider whether the trial court's assessment of the "best interest of the child" incorporated that presumption.... But presumptions notwithstanding, we should recognize that there may be circumstances in which a child has a stronger interest at stake than mere protection from serious harm caused by the termination of visitation by a "person" other than a parent. The almost infinite variety of family relationships that pervade our ever-changing society strongly counsel against the creation by this Court of a constitutional rule that treats a biological parent's liberty interest in the care and supervision of her child as an isolated right that may be exercised arbitrarily. It is indisputably the business of the States, rather than a federal court employing a national standard, to assess in the first instance the relative importance of the conflicting interests that give rise to disputes such as this....

[In separate omitted dissenting opinions, Justice Scalia declined to recognize unenumerated constitutional rights, and Justice Kennedy reasoned that the best interest doctrine is not always an unconstitutional standard in visitation cases.]

NOTES AND QUESTIONS

1. *Constitutional liberty.* As *Troxel* explains, the Court has long recognized that parents have the authority to direct the upbringing of their children, as a substantive "liberty" protected by the Fourteenth Amendment's Due Process Clause. Earlier, in Meyer v. Nebraska, 262 U.S. 390 (1923), the Court struck down a law barring the teaching of German to children, on the ground that parents, not the state, should decide what their children may learn. Similarly, in Pierce v. Society of Sisters, 268 U.S. 510 (1925), the Court invalidated a law requiring all children to attend public school and disallowing private schooling. In Parham v. J.R., 442 U.S. 584 (1979), the Court invoked the principle of parental autonomy in the context of decisionmaking about a child's medical care, specifically the decision to commit a minor to a state mental health institution. The particular parental prerogative at

stake in *Troxel* concerns choosing those with whom the child will spend time, often called visitation.

What reasons justify investing parents with such authority? *Troxel* embraces a presumption that fit parents act in their children's best interests.[21] *Parham* attributes the presumption to "natural bonds of affection," while conceding that the presumption does not always prove true. Id. at 602-603. Is this rationale the same as, or different from, a theory that parental control advances child wellbeing?[22] Does parental control makes sense as a quid pro quo in exchange for child support?[23] To what extent does the doctrine stem from what *Pierce*, supra, describes as the rejection of "of any general power of the state to standardize its children" and thus a preference for decentralization and pluralism? 268 U.S. at 535.[24] Compare the rights articulated in *Eisenstadt*, supra, and *Troxel*. What connections do you see? What differences?[25]

What downsides do you see in investing parents with such authority over children? Do parental autonomy and privatized dependency necessarily mean unequal life chances for children?[26]

2. *Children as property.* Although revered as "liberal icons" that protect privacy and promote pluralism, *Meyer* and *Pierce* express a conservative attachment to the patriarchal family and a view of children as property owned by their parents, according to Professor Barbara Bennett Woodhouse. After examining the historical context of the cases, she concludes:

> By constitutionalizing a patriarchal notion of parental rights, *Meyer* and *Pierce* interrupted the trend of family law moving toward children's rights and revitalized the notion of rights of possession.... Patriarchal notions of ownership do not lend themselves to a child-centered theory of custody or parenthood....
>
> [O]ur legal system fails to respect children. Children are often used as instruments, as in *Meyer* and *Pierce*. The child is denied her own voice and identity and becomes a conduit for the parents' religious expression, cultural identity, and class aspirations. The parents' authority to speak for and through the child is explicit in *Meyer*'s "right of control" and *Pierce*'s "high duty" of the parent to direct his child's destiny....[27]

---

[21] See, e.g., In re C.J.C., 603 S.W.3d 804 (Tex. 2020) (applying *Troxel*'s presumption).

[22] See Clare Huntington & Elizabeth S. Scott, Conceptualizing Legal Childhood in the Twenty-First Century, 118 Mich. L. Rev. 1371 (2020).

[23] See, e.g., Katharine T. Bartlett, Re-Expressing Parenthood, 98 Yale L.J. 293, 298 (1988) (theorizing "exchange view" of parenthood).

[24] See Peggy Cooper Davis, Contested Images of Family Values: The Role of the State, 107 Harv. L. Rev. 1348, 1371-1372 (1994). See also Jeffrey Shulman, *Meyer, Pierce,* and the History of the Entire Human Race: Barbarism, Social Progress, and (the Fall and Rise of) Parental Rights, 43 Hastings Const. L.Q. 337, 377 (2016) (contextualizing *Meyer* and *Pierce* in the era's fears of the "socialist menace").

[25] See Jamie R. Abrams, The Polarization of Reproductive and Parental Decision-Making, 44 Fla. St. U. L. Rev. 1281 (2017) (criticizing inaccurate framing of reproductive rights as focused solely on woman's interests and parental rights as focused solely on children's best interests).

[26] Anne L. Alstott, Is the Family at Odds with Equality? The Legal Implications of Equality for Children, 82 S. Cal. L. Rev. 1 (2008).

[27] Barbara Bennett Woodhouse, "Who Owns the Child?": *Meyer* and *Pierce* and the Child as Property, 33 Wm. & Mary L. Rev. 995, 996, 1113-1114 (1992). See also Dara E. Purvis, The Origin of Parental Rights: Labor, Intent, and Fathers, 41 Fla. St. U. L. Rev. 645 (2014) (invoking labor-based theory of property to explain parental rights).

How does the presumption of legitimacy reinforce the notion of children as property?[28]

If property ownership provides the wrong legal model for the parent-child relationship, what alternatives might prove more helpful? Parenting as creative expression, protected by the First Amendment?[29] Caregiving as preparation of children for democratic citizenship?[30] An understanding of parents as stewards or fiduciaries?[31] If law made children's interests paramount, according children equal moral consideration and valuing their present interests as children rather than as future adults, how would it treat parentage and parental autonomy?[32]

3. *Scope of parental autonomy.* How far does the principle of parental autonomy extend? Despite constitutional protection, parental rights are not unlimited, as the *Troxel* opinions note. First, when married parents divorce, courts routinely make orders of child support, custody, and visitation, including often grandparent visitation, pursuant to explicit statutory provisions.[33] How does the family in *Troxel* resemble a divorcing family? How does it differ?[34] Note that in *Troxel,* the mother decided to reduce (but not eliminate) the grandparents' visitation after she married a man with children and found that unpredictable visits undercut her effort to "nurture her new blended family."[35] On what basis did the trial court order grandparent visitation?

Second, when parental conduct or decisionmaking subjects the child to harm or the risk of harm, the state may intervene, according to Prince v. Massachusetts, 321 U.S. 158 (1944). *Prince* relied on this principle to uphold, under child labor laws, the conviction of a guardian whose ward had accompanied her to distribute copies of "Watchtower" and "Consolation," as required for the Jehovah's Witnesses. What does *Troxel* say about the harm standard?

4. *Standard of review.* By holding the statute unconstitutional as applied, the *Troxel* plurality avoided deciding that the statute was facially unconstitutional. The Court also evaded identifying the appropriate standard of review. What standard of review should courts apply to third-party visitation statutes? Should courts be especially protective of parental interests and apply strict scrutiny (as Justice Thomas reasons in an omitted concurrence)? Should

---

[28] See Kevin Noble Maillard, Rethinking Children as Property: The Transitive Family, 32 Cardozo L. Rev. 225 (2010).

[29] See Merry Jean Chan, Note, The Authorial Parent: An Intellectual Property Model of Parental Rights, 78 N.Y.U. L. Rev. 1186 (2003).

[30] See Anne C. Dailey, Developing Citizens, 91 Iowa L. Rev. 431 (2006) (examining developmental approach, with focus on caregiving as a precondition for preparing children for democratic citizenship).

[31] See Elizabeth S. Scott & Robert E. Scott, Parents as Fiduciaries, 81 Va. L. Rev. 2401 (1995).

[32] See generally James G. Dwyer, The Relationship Rights of Children (2006); Anne C. Dailey & Laura A. Rosenbury, The New Law of the Child, 127 Yale L.J. 1448 (2018); Samantha Godwin, Against Parental Rights, 47 Colum. Hum. Rts. L. Rev. 1 (2015); Pamela Laufer-Ukeles, The Relational Rights of Children, 48 Conn. L. Rev. 741 (2016).

[33] See, e.g., N.M. Stat. Ann. §40-9-2.

[34] See D.P. v. G.J.P., 146 A.3d 204 (Pa. 2016) (distinguishing divorcing parents from merely separated parents, for whom court-ordered grandparent visitation over joint parental objection violates due process). See also Bazen v. Bazen, 837 S.E.2d 23 (S.C. 2019) (applying *Troxel* in visitation dispute between mother and paternal grandparents after father's death).

[35] Brief for Respondents at 10, Troxel v. Granville, 530 U.S. 57 (2000), available at 1999 WL 1146868.

they apply an undue burden standard (i.e., whether visitation unduly burdens the parents' constitutional rights)? Courts have split.[36]

If strict scrutiny governs, what sort of showing would satisfy it? The best interests of the child (as Justice Stevens and, in an omitted concurrence, Justice Kennedy assert)? Or would it require showing potential harm to the child if visitation is not granted, as suggested by *Prince*, supra?[37]

5. *Beyond visitation.* Parental autonomy looms large in several contemporary disputes in politics and the "culture wars." For example, parents have challenged state bans on "reparative therapy," which purports to "convert" children with nonnormative sexual orientations to heterosexuality, arguing that such bans (enacted because the "treatment" has been shown to be harmful and ineffective) unconstitutionally interfere with their right to control their children's upbringing. How should a court decide the parents' challenge?[38] What of state laws that would prohibit either gender-confirming surgery or hormone treatment for minors asserting a different gender identity than the one assigned at birth?[39] What standard of review applies in such cases?[40]

What role should parents' culture or religion play in the analysis? Critics have observed how cultural biases shape the doctrine of parental autonomy. For example, a federal statute criminalizes genital surgeries on female minors (usually called "female genital mutilation," a traditional practice in some cultures)[41] "while the law ignores mainstream practices where parents invade the bodily integrity of their children for nonmedical reasons. . . ."[42] What other examples might support this argument?

Depictions in Popular Culture: Captain Fantastic (2016)

Family autonomy comes to life in *Captain Fantastic* as Ben Cash (Viggo Mortensen) rears his six children (roughly ages six to eighteen) in the wilderness, teaching them to reject mainstream society, to

---

[36] Compare, e.g., In re Visitation of A.A.L., 927 N.W.2d 486 (Wis. 2019) (applying strict scrutiny to hold grandparent visitation statute unconstitutional as applied), with Blakely v. Blakely, 83 S.W.3d 537 (Mo. 2002) (finding no undue burden imposed by visitation order under statute).

[37] Compare Doe v. Doe, 172 P.3d 1067 (Haw. 2007) (requiring harm standard), with Hiller v. Fausey, 904 A.2d 875 (Pa. 2006) (finding unnecessary a showing of harm). See Blixt v. Blixt, 774 N.E.2d 1052, 1060 (Mass. 2002) (requiring significant harm that adversely affects health, safety, or welfare plus a significant preexisting relationship). See Jeff Atkinson & Barbara Atwood, Moving Beyond *Troxel*: The Uniform Nonparent Custody and Visitation Act, 52 Fam. L.Q. 479, 481-482 (2018) (noting inconsistencies among lower courts).

[38] See Doe ex rel. Doe v. Governor of New Jersey, 783 F.3d 150 (3d Cir. 2015).

[39] See Zein Murib, A New Kind of Anti-Trans Legislation is Hitting the Red States, Wash. Post (Feb. 25, 2020), https://www.washingtonpost.com/politics/2020/02/25/new-kind-anti-trans-legislation-is-hitting-red-states/.

[40] See generally Margaret Ryznar, A Curious Parental Right, 71 S.M.U. L. Rev. 127 (2018) (suggesting varying levels of scrutiny depending on specific issue presented).

[41] 18 U.S.C. §116. But see United States v. Nagarwala, 350 F. Supp. 3d 613 (E.D. Mich. 2018) (holding Congress lacked power to enact the statute).

[42] Elaine M. Chiu, The Cultural Differential in Parental Autonomy, 41 U.C. Davis L. Rev. 1773, 1780 (2008). See Stephen R. Munzer, Examining Nontherapeutic Circumcision, 28 Health Matrix 1 (2018).

hunt for their own food, and to hone their physical strength and agility. With Ben's left-wing ideology, demanding teaching style, and always-truthful responses to their questions, the children are clearly educated and engaged with ideas, well beyond others in their age group living more typical American lives. Recently, Ben has been acting as a single parent while his wife and the children's mother, Leslie, has been hospitalized with bipolar disorder. When they receive word that she has committed suicide, their seemingly idyllic world begins to crack.

Although Leslie's parents attempt to bar Ben from attending her funeral, the family sets out in their bus to stop her burial in order to honor her written preference for cremation, with her ashes to be flushed down a toilet. A stop along the way at the home of Ben's more conventional sister showcases contrasting childrearing styles and the pluralism that parental autonomy supports. Viewers also begin to see the complete absence of social skills the children have developed in their isolated existence. Upon their arrival at Leslie's parents' home, the children receive a warm welcome but Ben faces accusations that he caused Leslie's death.

Ambiguity emerges. Did Leslie love the family's "off the grid" existence? Was she unhappy? Are the children happy? Or, do they want a different life? Does Ben deserve the deference accorded to a "fit" parent? Leslie's father insists that Ben's childrearing constitutes abuse and threatens to ask a court to remove the children from Ben's care and award custody to the grandparents. All of these developments unfold in what remains an essentially private dispute, even though one of the children suffers a serious injury. In the end, viewers see Ben and the children savor a meaningful victory but also compromise on a less extreme way of life.

The film implicitly calls attention to the value judgments that pervade the doctrine of parental autonomy and its limits. Ben is a hero, albeit a complicated one, and his father-in-law is the villain. Suppose Ben were indoctrinating his children with right-wing or religious values, as some reviewers hypothesized.[43] Suppose an African-American family had deviated from standard expectations of childrearing. Would they have escaped the long arm of the state and enjoyed the second chance accorded to Ben and his family?

6. *"Extraordinary" families?* Professor Ariela Dubler notes the contrasting judicial portrayals of the families in *Michael H.*, Chapter 1, section B, on the one hand, and *Troxel*, on the other. Of the former, Justice Scalia writes: "[t]he facts of this case are, we must hope, extraordinary." Some might

---

[43] See Richard Brody, The Counter-Superhero Calibrations of "Captain Fantastic," New Yorker (Aug. 5, 2016), https://www.newyorker.com/culture/richard-brody/the-counter-superhero-calibrations-of-captain-fantastic; Sheila O'Malley, Captain Fantastic, RogerEbert.com (July 8, 2016), https://www.rogerebert.com/reviews/captain-fantastic-2016.

regard the family in the latter as unusual, too — with a couple who never married, their two children, the woman's three children from her first marriage, her two stepchildren from her new marriage, one child from the new marriage, her new husband's adoption of the two children from the nonmarital relationship, assorted grandparents, and a suicide. How do you explain the "narrative normalization of family fissure and reconstitution" that Professor Dubler discerns in *Troxel*?[44] How do the opinions accomplish this normalization? Justice O'Connor's plurality opinion cites demographic data to challenge the notion of "an average American family." Similarly, Justice Stevens's dissent invokes the "almost infinite variety of family relationships that pervade our ever-changing society." Why are these observations relevant to the constitutionality of the Washington statute? What of the trial court's approach? On what basis did it decide to order visitation?

7. *Parents versus third parties.* Note that *Troxel* assumes a classification that makes an adult either a child's parent or a third party. Parents, in turn, presumptively have authority to decide what relationships, if any, their children have with such third parties or "legal strangers."[45] To what extent does *Troxel* and its binary reflect "a dominant White, middle-class, nuclear family model in which parents alone raise their children"?[46] Two responses to this binary have emerged:

First, courts and law reform projects, while adhering to the binary, have expanded criteria to bring more individuals into the "parent" category. *Elisa B.*, family law's reliance on functional approaches, and the development of constructs such as "de facto parents" with full parental status all illustrate this move. See Chapter 1, section C. Courts have increasingly rejected challenges that claim such moves are unconstitutional and inconsistent with *Troxel*.[47]

Second, inroads on the binary itself have increased. For example, every state has enacted grandparent-visitation statutes,[48] reflecting an appreciation that many children have important relationships with such family members — and perhaps exposing the power of grandparents in state legislatures. After *Troxel*, states with expansive grandparent visitation statutes narrowed them to require a specific triggering event, such as divorce, parental death, or adoption of the child, as well as something more than a showing of the child's best interests.[49] Despite these statutes, however, grandparents ordinarily remain distinct from parents.[50]

---

[44] Ariela R. Dubler, Constructing the Modern American Family: The Stories of Troxel v. Granville, in Family Law Stories 95, 109 (Carol Sanger ed., 2008).

[45] See generally Family Boundaries: Symposium on Third-Party Rights and Obligations with Respect to Children, 40 Fam. L. Q. 1-147 (2006).

[46] Solangel Maldonado, When Father (or Mother) Doesn't Know Best: Quasi-Parents and Parental Deference after Troxel v. Granville, 88 Iowa L. Rev. 865, 897 (2003). See Michael J. Higdon, The Quasi-Parent Conundrum, 90 U. Colo. L. Rev. 941 (2019) (criticizing as outdated *Troxel*'s assumptions about the nuclear family and the impact on children).

[47] E.g., A.A. v. B.B., 384 P.3d 878 (Haw. 2016); Smith v. Guest, 16 A.3d 920 (Del. 2010) (analyzing statute). But see, e.g., LP v. LF, 338 P.3d 908 (Wyo. 2014) (leaving issue of de facto parentage for legislative resolution). See generally Douglas NeJaime, The Constitution of Parenthood, 72 Stan. L. Rev. 261, 355 (2020).

[48] See, e.g., Tenn. Code Ann. §36-6-306.

[49] E.g., Mo. Stat. Ann. §452.402.

[50] See Philbrook v. Theriault, 957 A.2d 74 (Me. 2008) (holding that intermittent care by grandparents does not make them de facto parents).

A more thoroughgoing effort appears in the Uniform Nonparent Custody and Visitation Act (UNCVA), promulgated by the ULC in 2018. Acknowledging that *Troxel* provides insufficient guidance to the states about when courts can order either custody or visitation with a nonparent, the UNCVA §4 allows relief in two types of cases:

Section 4. Requirements for Order of Custody or Visitation.

(a) A court may order custody or visitation to a nonparent if the nonparent proves that:

(1) the nonparent:

(A) is a consistent caretaker; or

(B) has a substantial relationship with the child and the denial of custody or visitation would result in harm to the child; and

(2) an order of custody or visitation to the nonparent is in the best interest of the child.

(b) A nonparent is a consistent caretaker if the nonparent without expectation of compensation:

(1) lived with the child for not less than 12 months, unless the court finds good cause to accept a shorter period;

(2) regularly exercised care of the child;

(3) made day-to-day decisions regarding the child solely or in cooperation with an individual having physical custody of the child; and

(4) established a bonded and dependent relationship with the child with the express or implied consent of a parent of the child, or without the consent of a parent if no parent has been able or willing to perform parenting functions.

(c) A nonparent has a substantial relationship with the child if:

(1) the nonparent:

(A) is an individual with a familial relationship with the child by blood or law; or

(B) formed a relationship with the child without expectation of compensation; and

(2) a significant emotional bond exists between the nonparent and the child.

How does a "consistent caretaker" differ from a de facto parent?[51] Could Michael in *Michael H*, Chapter 1, section B, have received relief under this provision? Did he have a "substantial relationship" with Victoria? (Recall that Justice Stevens would have recognized Michael as someone entitled to an opportunity for a hearing on visitation, not as a "parent" but instead as "any other person having an interest in the welfare of the child.")

North Dakota has enacted the UNCVA.[52] Why do you think other states have not done so? More generally, how would you evaluate this approach? Does it go far enough in recognizing that adults who do not act as parents provide care and perform childrearing functions?[53] Too far? Note that

---

[51] See Atkinson & Atwood, supra note [37], at 497.

[52] Uniform Law Commission, Nonparent Custody and Visitation Act (2018), https://www.uniformlaws.org/committees/community-home?CommunityKey=e33c7569-9eb3-48ef-b998-cb2e558fa2de.

[53] See, e.g., Melissa Murray, The Networked Family: Reframing the Legal Understanding of Caregiving and Caregivers, 94 Va. L. Rev. 385 (2008); Laura A. Rosenbury, Between Home and School, 155 U. Pa. L. Rev. 833 (2007).

the statute does not address child support awards by or to a nonparent. UNCVA §19.

8. *Deconstructing parenthood?* How might orders for nonparent custody and visitation challenge the traditional understanding of parenthood as comprehensive, indivisible, and exclusive?[54] Under a functional approach, can parenthood instead be conceptualized as a bundle of rights and responsibilities that might be fragmented and exercised by multiple individuals?[55] Consider, for example, the "parenting plan" that many statutes now require each divorcing parent to submit—a blueprint that informs, but does not bind, the court in adjudicating child custody. Such plans cover specific allocations of time with a child over every day of the year; details of decisionmaking authority in different areas of the child's life, from education to health care; and responsibility for particular expenses.[56] How does such disaggregation of parental functions inform the understanding of what parentage and parenthood mean?

PROBLEMS

1. Consider the following scenario:

For four years, Mike had known that the girl he had rocked to sleep and danced with across the living-room floor was not, as they say, "his." The revelation from a DNA test was devastating and prompted him to leave his wife — but he had not renounced their child. He continued to feel that in all the ways that mattered, she was still his daughter, and he faithfully paid her child support. It was only when he learned that his ex-wife was about to marry the man who she said actually *was* the girl's biological father that Mike flipped. Supporting another man's child suddenly became unbearable.[57]

Mike seeks to maintain his relationship with the child through regular visitation, but he insists that he should have no obligation to pay support now that she will be living with both her biological parents. Mike consults you for legal advice. Assuming that this is a case of first impression in your jurisdiction, what would you tell him? What additional facts, if any, would you try to elicit? What constitutional interests, if any, are at stake?[58]

2. The United States Congress enacted the Rape Survivor Child Custody Act (RSCCA), which became effective in 2017. By promising them additional federal funding, the RSCCA encourages states to enact laws terminating the parental rights of a father shown by clear and convincing evidence to have conceived the child by rape; per the following language, the RSCCA allows states to continue to collect child support from such men, however:

Nothing in this paragraph shall be construed to require a State, in order to receive an increase in the amount provided to the State under the covered formula grants under this chapter, to have in place a law that terminates any obligation of a person who fathered a child through rape to support the child.

[54] See Bartlett, supra note [20].
[55] See Melanie B. Jacobs, Why Just Two? Disaggregating Traditional Parental Rights and Responsibilities to Recognize Multiple Parents, 9 J.L. & Fam. Stud. 309 (2007).
[56] See, e.g., Mo. Stat. Ann. §452.310(8); 23 Pa. Cons. Stat. §5331; Susan Frelich Appleton, Parents by the Numbers, 37 Hofstra L. Rev. 11, 23-26 (2008).
[57] Ruth Padawer, Losing Fatherhood, N.Y. Times Mag., Nov. 17, 2009, at 38.
[58] See id.; see also Stacy M. v. Jason M., 858 N.W.2d 852 (Neb. 2015); NeJaime, supra note [47].

34 U.S.C. §21301.The RSCCA also includes the following Congressional findings:

> (1) Men who father children through rape should be prohibited from visiting or having custody of those children.
>
> (2) Thousands of rape-related pregnancies occur annually in the United States.
>
> (3) A substantial number of women choose to raise their child conceived through rape and, as a result, may face custody battles with their rapists.
>
> (4) Rape is one of the most under-prosecuted serious crimes, with estimates of criminal conviction occurring in less than 5 percent of rapes.
>
> (5) The clear and convincing evidence standard is the most common standard for termination of parental rights among the 50 States, territories, and the District of Columbia.
>
> (6) The Supreme Court established that the clear and convincing evidence standard satisfies due process for allegations to terminate or restrict parental rights in Santosky v. Kramer (455 U.S. 745 (1982)).[59]
>
> (7) Currently only 10 States have statutes allowing rape survivors to petition for the termination of parental rights of the rapist based on clear and convincing evidence that the child was conceived through rape.
>
> (8) A rapist pursuing parental or custody rights causes the survivor to have continued interaction with the rapist, which can have traumatic psychological effects on the survivor, and can make it more difficult for her to recover.
>
> (9) These traumatic effects on the mother can severely negatively impact her ability to raise a healthy child.
>
> (10) Rapists may use the threat of pursuing custody or parental rights to coerce survivors into not prosecuting rape, or otherwise harass, intimidate, or manipulate them.

Id. §21302. You are a legislative assistant in a state considering whether to enact a statute that would meet the requirements of the RSCCA and thus make the state eligible to receive additional federal funds. What would you recommend? What problems, if any, do you see?[60]

2. LIMITS ON PARENTAL AUTONOMY: THE CASE OF FOSTER CARE

In exercising its authority to infringe parental autonomy in response to harm or the risk of harm, the state often invokes the jurisdiction of the juvenile or family court over abused, neglected, and dependent children. If this court decides that the problem requires removal of the child from the home, the court's disposition often entails placement in a foster family. As the following case shows, foster parents exercise some but not all of the usual parental prerogatives, thus challenging the traditional understanding of an indivisible and comprehensive set of parental rights and responsibilities.

Who benefits from the state's reliance on foster care? This hybrid arrangement, which gives roles to parents, the state, and foster parents, is often justified by its ability to offer the advantages of a family-like setting

---

[59] Reprinted Chapter 3, section A.

[60] See Jennifer S. Hendricks, The Wages of Genetic Entitlement: The Good, the Bad, and the Ugly in the Rape Survivor Child Custody Act, 112 Nw. U. L. Rev. Online 75 (2017).

for children in need while maintaining state supervision and promoting reunification with the family of origin. Yet, sometimes foster care constitutes a transitional arrangement, if termination of the original parents' rights and adoption ultimately follow. Consider whether foster care's simulation of the parent-child relationship and its occasional connection to adoption also might create disadvantages and ambiguities — for children and adults alike.

SMITH V. ORGANIZATION OF FOSTER FAMILIES FOR EQUALITY AND REFORM (OFFER)

431 U.S. 816 (1977)

Mr. Justice BRENNAN delivered the opinion of the Court.

Appellees, individual foster parents[1] and an organization of foster parents, brought this civil rights class action pursuant to 42 U.S.C. §1983 . . . on their own behalf and on behalf of children for whom they have provided homes for a year or more. They sought declaratory and injunctive relief [alleging] that the procedures governing the removal of foster children from foster homes [N.Y. Soc. Serv. Law §§383(2), 400, and 18 N.Y.C.R.R. §450.14] violated the Due Process and Equal Protection Clauses. . . . A group of natural mothers of children in foster care[5] were granted leave to intervene on behalf of themselves and others similarly situated. [The district court determined that the preremoval procedures worked an unconstitutional deprivation of due process by denying the foster child a hearing before transfer to another foster home or return to the natural parents. 418 F. Supp. 277, 282 (S.D.N.Y. 1976).]

The expressed central policy of the New York system is that "it is generally desirable for the child to remain with or be returned to the natural parent because the child's need for a normal family life will usually best be met in the natural home, and . . . parents are entitled to bring up their own children unless the best interests of the child would be thereby endangered," Soc. Serv. Law §384-b(1)(a)(ii). But the State has opted for foster care as one response to those situations where the natural parents are unable to provide

---

1. Appellee Madeleine Smith is the foster parent with whom Eric and Danielle Gandy have been placed since 1970. The Gandy children, who are now 12 and 9 years old respectively, were voluntarily placed in foster care by their natural mother in 1968, and have had no contact with her at least since being placed with Mrs. Smith. The foster-care agency has sought to remove the children from Mrs. Smith's care because her arthritis, in the agency's judgment, makes it difficult for her to continue to provide adequate care. . . . Appellees Ralph and Christiane Goldberg were the foster parents of Rafael Serrano, now 14. His parents placed him in foster care voluntarily in 1969 after an abuse complaint was filed against them. [The Goldbergs eventually separated, placing Rafael in residential care.] Appellees Walter and Dorothy Lhoton were foster parents of the Wallace sisters, who were voluntarily placed in foster care by their mother in 1970. The two older girls were placed with the Lhotons in that year, their two younger sisters in 1972. In June 1974, the Lhotans were informed that the agency had decided to return the two younger girls to their mother and transfer the two older girls to another foster home. The agency apparently felt that the Lhotans were too emotionally involved with the girls and were damaging the agency's efforts to prepare them to return to their mother. [The children eventually were returned to their mother.]

5. Intervenor Naomi Rodriguez, who is blind, placed her newborn son Edwin in foster care in 1973 because of marital difficulties. When Mrs. Rodriguez separated from her husband three months later, she sought return of her child. Her efforts over the next nine months to obtain return of the child were resisted by the agency, apparently because it felt her handicap prevented her from providing adequate care. [She] finally prevailed, three years after she first sought return of the child. . . .

the "positive, nurturing family relationships" and "normal family life in a permanent home" that offer "the best opportunity for children to develop and thrive." §§384-b(1)(b), (1)(a)(i). [T]he distinctive features of foster care are, first, "that it is care in a *family,* it is noninstitutional substitute care," and, second, that it is for a *planned* period — either temporary or extended. This is unlike adoptive placement, which implies a *permanent* substitution of one home for another.

Under the New York scheme children may be placed in foster care either by voluntary placement or by court order. Most foster care placements are voluntary. They occur when physical or mental illness, economic problems, or other family crises make it impossible for natural parents, particularly single parents, to provide a stable home life for their children for some limited period. [Under voluntary placements, a written agreement between the parent and agency may provide for the child's return at a specified date, but if not, the child must be returned within 20 days of notice from the parent.]

The agency . . . commonly acts under its authority to "place out and board out" children in foster homes. Foster parents, who are licensed by the State or an authorized foster-care agency, provide care under a contractual arrangement with the agency, and are compensated for their services. The typical contract expressly reserves the right of the agency to remove the child on request. . . .

The New York system divides parental functions among agency, foster parents, and natural parents, and the definitions of the respective roles are often complex and often unclear. The law transfers "care and custody" to the agency, but day-to-day supervision of the child and his activities, and most of the functions ordinarily associated with legal custody, are the responsibility of the foster parent. Nevertheless, agency supervision of the performance of the foster parents takes forms indicating that the foster parent does not have the full authority of a legal custodian. Moreover, the natural parent's placement of the child with the agency does not surrender legal guardianship; the parent retains authority to act with respect to the child in certain circumstances [e.g., consent to surgery, etc.]. The natural parent has not only the right but the obligation to visit the foster child and plan for his future; failure of a parent with capacity to fulfill the obligation for more than a year can result in a court order terminating the parent's rights on the ground of neglect.

Children may also enter foster care by court order. . . . The consequences of foster-care placement by court order do not differ substantially from those for children voluntarily placed, except that the parent is not entitled to return of the child on demand . . . ; termination of foster care must then be consented to by the court. . . .

The provisions of the scheme specifically at issue in this litigation come into play when the agency having legal custody determines to remove the foster child from the foster home, either because it has determined that it would be in the child's best interests to transfer him to some other foster home, or to return the child to his natural parents in accordance with the statute or placement agreement. Most children are removed in order to be transferred to another foster home. The procedures by which foster parents may challenge a removal made for that purpose differ somewhat from those where the removal is made to return the child to his natural parent.

Section 383(2), n.3, supra, provides that the "authorized agency placing out or boarding (a foster) child . . . may in its discretion remove such child from the home where placed or boarded." Administrative regulations implement this provision. The agency is required, except in emergencies, to notify the foster parents in writing 10 days in advance of any removal. The notice advises the foster parents that if they object to the child's removal, they may request a "conference" with the Social Services Department. The department schedules requested conferences within 10 days of the receipt of the request. The foster parent may appear with counsel at the conference, where he will "be advised of the reasons (for the removal of the child), and be afforded an opportunity to submit reasons why the child should not be removed."§450.10(a). The official must render a decision in writing within five days after the close of the conference, and send notice of his decision to the foster parents and the agency. The proposed removal is stayed pending the outcome of the conference.

If the child is removed after the conference, the foster parent may appeal to the Department of Social Services for a [full adversary administrative hearing which is subject to judicial review]; however, the removal is not automatically stayed pending the hearing and judicial review.

This statutory and regulatory scheme applies statewide.[28] In addition, regulations [applicable to New York City] provide even greater procedural safeguards [in the form of a *preremoval* trial, upon request of the foster parents, if a child is being transferred to another foster home]. One further preremoval procedural safeguard is available. [Soc. Serv. Law §392] provides a mechanism whereby a foster parent may obtain preremoval judicial review of an agency's decision to remove a child who has been in foster care for 18 months or more. . . .

Foster care of children is a sensitive and emotion-laden subject, and foster-care programs consequently stir strong controversy. [F]oster care has been condemned as a class-based intrusion into the family life of the poor. See, e.g., Jenkins, Child Welfare as a Class System, in Children and Decent People 3 (A. Schorr ed. 1974). It is certainly true that the poor resort to foster care more often than other citizens. . . .

The extent to which supposedly "voluntary" placements are in fact voluntary has been questioned on other grounds as well. For example, it has been said that many "voluntary" placements are in fact coerced by threat of neglect proceedings and are not in fact voluntary in the sense of the product of an informed consent. Mnookin, [Foster Care: In Whose Best Interests?, 43 Harv. Educ. Rev. 599, 601 (1973)]. Studies also suggest that social workers of middle-class backgrounds, perhaps unconsciously, incline to favor continued placement in foster care with a generally higher-status family rather than return the child to his natural family, thus reflecting a bias that treats the natural parents' poverty and lifestyle as prejudicial to the best

---

28. There is some dispute whether the procedures set out in 18 N.Y.C.R.R. §450.10 and Soc. Serv. Law §400 apply in the case of a foster child being removed from his foster home to be returned to his natural parents. [N]othing in either the statute or the regulations limits the availability of these procedures to transfers within the foster-care system. Each refers to the decision to remove a child from the foster family home, and thus on its face each would seem to cover removal for the purpose of returning the child to its parents. . . .

interests of the child. This accounts, it has been said, for the hostility of agencies to the efforts of natural parents to obtain the return of their children.

Appellee foster parents as well as natural parents [note] that children often stay in "temporary" foster care for much longer than contemplated by the theory of the system. The District Court found as a fact that the median time spent in foster care in New York was over four years. Indeed, many children apparently remain in this "limbo" indefinitely. Mnookin, [Child-Custody Adjudication: Judicial Functions in the Face of Indeterminacy, 39 Law & Contemp. Probs., Summer 1975, at 226, 273]. The District Court also found that the longer a child remains in foster care, the more likely it is that he will never leave . . . . It is not surprising then that many children, particularly those that enter foster care at a very early age and have little or no contact with their natural parents during extended stays in foster care, often develop deep emotional ties with their foster parents.[40]

Yet such ties do not seem to be regarded as obstacles to transfer of the child from one foster placement to another. The record in this case indicates that nearly 60% of the children in foster care in New York City have experienced more than one placement, and about 28% have experienced three or more. [E]ven when it is clear that a foster child will not be returned to his natural parents, it is rare that he achieves a stable home life through final termination of parental ties and adoption into a new permanent family.

[W]e present this summary in the view that some understanding of those criticisms is necessary for a full appreciation of the complex and controversial system with which this lawsuit is concerned. [But, our] task is only to determine whether the District Court correctly held that the present procedures preceding the removal from a foster home of children resident there a year or more are constitutionally inadequate. . . .

Our first inquiry is whether appellees have asserted interests within the Fourteenth Amendment's protection of "liberty." . . . The appellees' basic contention is that when a child has lived in a foster home for a year or more, a psychological tie is created between the child and the foster parents which constitutes the foster family the true "psychological family" of the child. That family, they argue, has a "liberty interest" in its survival as a family protected by the Fourteenth Amendment. Upon this premise they conclude that the foster child cannot be removed without a prior hearing satisfying due process. Appointed counsel for the children, . . . however, disagrees, and has consistently argued that the foster parents have no such liberty interest independent of the interests of the foster children, and that the best interests of the children would not be served by procedural protections beyond those already provided by New York law. The intervening natural parents of children in foster care . . . also oppose the foster parents, arguing that recognition of the procedural right claimed would undercut both the substantive family

---

40. The development of such ties points up an intrinsic ambiguity of foster care that is central to this case. The warmer and more homelike environment of foster care is intended to be its main advantage over institutional child care, yet because in theory foster care is intended to be only temporary, foster parents are urged not to become too attached to the children in their care. Mnookin, [43 Harv. Educ. Rev.,] at 613. Indeed, the New York courts have upheld removal from a foster home for the very reason that the foster parents had become too emotionally involved with the child. In re Jewish Child Care Assn. (Sanders), 5 N.Y.2d 222, 183 N.Y.S.2d 65, 156 N.E.2d 700 (1959). See also the case of the Lhotans, named appellees in this case. . . .

law of New York, which favors the return of children to their natural parents as expeditiously as possible, and their constitutionally protected right of family privacy, by forcing them to submit to a hearing and defend their rights to their children before the children could be returned to them.

[We] turn to appellees' assertion that they have a constitutionally protected liberty interest . . . in the integrity of their family unit. This assertion clearly presents difficulties. . . . There does exist a "private realm of family life which the state cannot enter," Prince v. Massachusetts, 321 U.S. 158, 166 (1944), that has been afforded both substantive and procedural protection. But is the relation of foster parent to foster child sufficiently akin to the concept of "family" recognized in our precedents to merit similar protection? [W]e are not without guides to some of the elements that define the concept of "family" and contribute to its place in our society.

First, the usual understanding of "family" implies biological relationships, and most decisions treating the relation between parent and child have stressed this element. Stanley v. Illinois, 405 U.S. 645, 651 (1972), for example, spoke of "(t)he rights to conceive and to raise one's children" as essential rights. . . . A biological relationship is not present in the case of the usual foster family. But biological relationships are not exclusive determination of the existence of a family. . . . No one would seriously dispute that a deeply loving and interdependent relationship between an adult and a child in his or her care may exist even in the absence of blood relationship. At least where a child has been placed in foster care as an infant, has never known his natural parents, and has remained continuously for several years in the care of the same foster parents, it is natural that the foster family should hold the same place in the emotional life of the foster child, and fulfill the same socializing functions, as a natural family. For this reason, we cannot dismiss the foster family as a mere collection of unrelated individuals.

But there are also important distinctions between the foster family and the natural family. First, unlike the earlier cases recognizing a right to family privacy, the State here seeks to interfere, not with a relationship having its origins entirely apart from the power of the State, but rather with a foster family which has its source in state law and contractual arrangements. . . . Here, however, whatever emotional ties may develop between foster parent and foster child have their origins in an arrangement in which the State has been a partner from the outset. . . .

A second consideration related to this is that ordinarily procedural protection may be afforded to a liberty interest of one person without derogating from the substantive liberty of another. Here, however, such a tension is virtually unavoidable. Under New York law, the natural parent of a foster child in voluntary placement has an absolute right to the return of his child in the absence of a court order obtainable only upon compliance with rigorous substantive and procedural standards, which reflect the constitutional protection accorded the natural family. Moreover, the natural parent initially gave up his child to the State only on the express understanding that the child would be returned in those circumstances. These rights are difficult to reconcile with the liberty interest in the foster family relationship claimed by appellees. It is one thing to say that individuals may acquire a liberty interest against arbitrary governmental interference in the family-like associations into which they have freely entered, even in the absence of biological connection or state-law recognition of the relationship. It is quite another to say that one may acquire such an interest in the face of another's constitutionally recognized liberty interest that derives from blood relationship, state-law sanction, and basic human right — an interest the foster parent has recognized by contract from the outset. Whatever liberty interest might otherwise exist in the foster family as an institution, that interest must be substantially attenuated where the proposed removal from the foster family is to return the child to his natural parents.

As this discussion suggests, appellees' claim to a constitutionally protected liberty interest raises complex and novel questions. It is unnecessary for us to resolve those questions definitively in this case, however, for like the District Court, we conclude that "narrower grounds exist to support" our reversal. We are persuaded that, even on the assumption that appellees have a protected "liberty interest," the District Court erred in holding that the preremoval procedures presently employed by the State are constitutionally defective. . . .

Where procedural due process must be afforded because a "liberty" or "property" interest is within the Fourteenth Amendment's protection, there must be determined "what process is due" in the particular context. . . . Consideration of the procedures employed by the State and New York City [in light of the factors in Mathews v. Eldridge, 414 U.S. 319 (1976), i.e., the private interest affected; the risk of an erroneous deprivation of such interest by the procedures; and, the government's interest, including avoiding fiscal or administrative burdens that additional or substitute procedural requirements would entail] requires the conclusion that those procedures satisfy constitutional standards.

Turning first to the procedure applicable in New York City, [SSC Procedure No. 5] provides that before a child is removed from a foster home for transfer to another foster home, the foster parents may request an "independent review." . . . Such a procedure would appear to give a more elaborate trial-type hearing to foster families than this Court has found required in other contexts of administrative determinations. The District Court found the procedure inadequate on four grounds, none of which we find sufficient to justify the holding that the procedure violates due process.

First, the court held that the "independent review" administrative proceeding was insufficient because it was only available on the request of the foster parents. [That is,] the proceeding should be provided as a matter of course, because the interests of the foster parents and those of the child would not necessarily be coextensive, and it could not be assumed that the foster parents would invoke the hearing procedure in every case in which it was in the child's interest to have a hearing. . . . We disagree. As previously noted, the constitutional liberty, if any, sought to be protected by the New York procedures is a right of *family* privacy or autonomy, and the basis for recognition of any such interest in the foster family must be that close emotional ties analogous to those between parent and child are established when a child resides for a lengthy period with a foster family. If this is so, necessarily we should expect that the foster parents will seek to continue the relationship to preserve the stability of the family; if they do not request a hearing, it is difficult to see what right or interest of the foster child is protected by holding a hearing . . . .

Second, the District Court faulted the city procedure on the ground that participation is limited to the foster parents and the agency and the natural parent and the child are not made parties to the hearing. This is not fatal in light of the nature of the alleged constitutional interests at stake. When the child's transfer from one foster home to another is pending, the interest arguably requiring protection is that of the foster family, not that of the natural parents. Moreover, . . . nothing in the New York City procedure prevents consultation of the child's wishes . . . . Such consultation, however, does not require that the child or an appointed representative must be a party with full adversary powers in all preremoval hearings.

The other two defects in the city procedure found by the District Court must also be rejected. One is that the procedure does not extend to the removal of a child from foster care to be returned to his natural parent. But as we have already held, whatever liberty interest may be argued to exist in the foster family is significantly weaker in the case of removals preceding return to the natural parent, and the balance of due process interests must accordingly be different. . . . Similarly, the District Court pointed out that the New York City procedure coincided with the informal "conference" and postremoval hearings provided as a matter of state law. This overlap in procedures may be unnecessary or even to some degree unwise, but a State does not violate the Due Process Clause by providing alternative or additional procedures beyond what the Constitution requires.

Outside New York City, where only the statewide procedures apply, foster parents are provided not only with the procedures of a preremoval conference and postremoval hearing provided by 18 N.Y.C.R.R. §450.10 and Soc. Serv. Law §400, but also with the preremoval *judicial* hearing available on request to foster parents who have in their care children who have been in foster care for 18 months or more, Soc. Serv. Law §392. [A] foster parent in such case may obtain an order that the child remain in his care.

The District Court found . . . defects in this full judicial process. First, a §392 proceeding is available only to those foster children who have been in foster care for 18 months or more. . . . We do not think that the 18-month limitation [renders] the New York scheme constitutionally inadequate. The assumed liberty interest to be protected in this case is one rooted in the emotional attachments that develop over time between a child and the adults who care for him. But there is no reason to assume that those attachments ripen at less than 18 months or indeed at any precise point. . . . Finally, the §392 hearing is available to foster parents, both in and outside New York City, even where the removal sought is for the purpose of returning the child to his natural parents. Since this remedy provides a sufficient constitutional preremoval hearing to protect whatever liberty interest might exist in the continued existence of the foster family when the State seeks to transfer the child to another foster home, a fortiori the procedure is adequate to protect the lesser interest of the foster family in remaining together at the expense of the disruption of the natural family.

. . . Since we hold that the procedures provided by New York State in §392 and by New York City's SSC Procedure No. 5 are adequate to protect whatever liberty interest appellees may have, the judgment of the District Court is [r]eversed.

Mr. Justice STEWART, with whom the CHIEF JUSTICE and Mr. Justice REHNQUIST join, concurring in the judgment.

. . . I cannot understand why the Court thinks itself obliged to decide these cases on the assumption that either foster parents or foster children in New York have some sort of "liberty" interest in the continuation of their relationship. Rather than tiptoeing around this central issue, I would squarely hold that the interests asserted by the appellees are not of a kind that the Due Process Clause of the Fourteenth Amendment protects.

[T]he predicate for invoking the Due Process Clause — the existence of state-created liberty or property — [is] missing here. New York confers no right on foster families to remain intact, defeasible only upon proof of specific acts or circumstances. . . . Similarly, New York law provides no basis for a justifiable expectation on the part of foster families that their relationship will continue indefinitely. . . .

What remains of the appellees' argument is the theory that the relation of the foster parent to the foster child may generate emotional attachments similar to those found in natural families. The Court surmises that foster families who share these attachments might enjoy the same constitutional interest in "family privacy" as natural families. . . .

But under New York's foster-care laws, any case where the foster parents had assumed the emotional role of the child's natural parents would represent not a triumph of the system, to be constitutionally safeguarded from state intrusion, but a failure. The goal of foster care, at least in New York, is not to provide a permanent substitute for the natural or adoptive home, but to prepare the child for his return to his real parents or placement in a permanent adoptive home by giving him temporary shelter in a family setting. . . . Perhaps it is to be expected that children who spend unduly long stays in what should have been temporary foster care will develop strong emotional ties with their foster parents. But this does not mean, and I cannot believe, that such breakdowns of the New York system must be protected or forever frozen in their existence by the Due Process Clause of the Fourteenth Amendment.

One of the liberties protected by the Due Process Clause, the Court has held, is the freedom to "establish a home and bring up children." Meyer v. Nebraska, supra, 262 U.S., at 399. . . . But this constitutional concept is simply not in point when we deal with foster families as New York law has defined them. The family life upon which the State "intrudes" is simply a temporary status which the State itself has created. It is a "family life" defined and controlled by the law of New York, for which New York pays, and the goals of which New York is entitled to and does set for itself. . . .

MEGHAN MORAVCIK WALBERT, AFTER LOSING
A FOSTER CHILD, CONTEMPLATING ANOTHER

N.Y. Times, Jan. 19, 2017[61]

He's sitting on a couch with his brothers, presumably in the home in which he's now growing up. The photo has a graininess to it that is

---

[61] https://www.nytimes.com/2017/01/19/well/family/after-losing-a-foster-child-contemplating-another.html?searchResultPosition=8.

reminiscent of photos from the 1980s, but this picture is much more recent than that. It's the first visual I've had of my former foster son since I hugged him goodbye.

The boy we nicknamed "BlueJay" lived with us for almost a year when extended family members stepped forward to take custody of him and his two brothers back in March. . . . I wrote about the experience of loving and losing him. Now, I zoom in and out of this photo, studying every blurry detail. I know he was 4 years old when the photo was taken, the same age he was when he left our home, but he looks so much older. I can see how his legs are longer, his shoulders broader.

His biological mother sent me the picture. She and I have remained in contact since he left. As far as I know, it is the only photo she has received since her son went to live in a home several hours away from her. The updates she gets and passes along to me are sporadic and superficial. I'm not sure even she really knows how he is doing. I dream about him. . . .

My son, Ryan, who is now 6 years old, recently asked me if we could call his former foster brother one day to talk to him, to tell him we miss him.

"I'm sorry, buddy, we can't," I said.

"But why?"

But why. It is the central question I have struggled with over the past 10 months. Why couldn't we stay in his life? Why couldn't we send him a new outfit for school or call him to wish him a happy birthday when he recently turned 5? Why couldn't we continue to offer him our love from afar?

We couldn't because his relatives didn't want us to. They didn't see the point of it, the value in it. They wanted a clean break.

A lot of time has passed since our foster son left. We talk about him more with smiles now than with tears. We've given ourselves the time and space needed to figure out whether the hole in our lives is one that only he was meant to fill or whether our family is still incomplete.

Finally, we are starting to feel ready. My husband, Mike, and I are preparing, once again, for foster care adoption.

We're being more cautious and more deliberate this time. This time, we are moving slowly. This time, we are more educated and less exuberant.

We are setting new parameters. We will consider only children who are legally free for adoption or as close to it as possible. We will not be called one day and asked to pick up a child in need of an immediate, temporary home. This time, we will be matched with a child who may have been waiting for a permanent family for as long as we've been waiting to complete ours. Realistically, that probably means a child Ryan's age or older. There will be fliers with pictures and stacks of files and the child's own opinions to consider.

Caring for a child for almost a year and then being given less than 24 hours to pack him up and say a permanent goodbye changes a person. It strips you of your naïveté. It inflicts a sense of loss that cuts deep. It can harden you with cynicism, sadness and fear, if you let it. . . .

[Yet, we] can acknowledge our own heartache for what it was: The inevitable result of fully loving a child who was never really ours. There was no mistake in that.

We can let go of our worry and instead, believe in him. Believe that he's strong enough to overcome the hardships of his early life, strong enough to thrive.

We can allow ourselves to hope the final piece of our family's puzzle is still out there. We can close our eyes, take a deep breath, center ourselves. And then we can go in search of that piece.

NOTES AND QUESTIONS

1. *A protected liberty interest?* *OFFER* holds that the preremoval hearing regulations afforded by New York City and the state accorded sufficient due process protection to foster parents. Must a hearing be provided before removal, or can a social services agency rely on less formal interviews? In other words, how should the Court decide the issue that Justice Stewart accuses the majority of "tiptoeing around"? Post-*OFFER*, several courts have refused to recognize the liberty interests of foster families, even after long-term care and plans for adoption.[62]

2. OFFER *and parentage.* What does *OFFER* contribute to the understanding of legal parentage and the autonomy that the Constitution protects for parents? On the one hand, *OFFER* rejects the approach of *Stanley* and *Elisa B.*, refusing to recognize as parents caregiving adults whom the law traditionally excluded. To that extent, *OFFER* is compatible with the plurality opinion of *Michael H.* Indeed, does *OFFER* remain good law, given later developments that increasingly recognize bonds between children and adult caregivers, regardless of marriage or biology?[63] On the other hand, *OFFER* complicates the traditional understanding of parental prerogatives, as depicted in *Troxel*, because the "natural parents" retain their status but with significant limitations on their authority to direct the child's upbringing. The role recognized for foster parents in *OFFER* thus presages some newer approaches, by defying both the conventional parent/third party binary and the usual exclusion of the state from the day-to-day upbringing of children. What does the state's participation in foster care mean for the analysis?

3. *The payment problem.* Consider Walbert's reflection. Should she and her family be able to maintain contact with "BlueJay" for whom they had provided a foster home, despite the objections of his current caregivers? Why? Because foster parents receive payment from the state for their services, some expansive approaches to parentage exclude foster parents for this reason alone. For example, the Restatement of Children and the Law's definition of "de facto parent" explicitly requires that the individual "assumed significant obligations of parenthood without expectation of financial

[62] E.g., Rodriguez v. McLoughlin, 214 F.3d 328 (2d Cir. 2000); M.S. v. People, 303 P.3d 102 (Colo. 2013). But see Elwell v. Byers, 699 F.3d 1208, 1215-1218 (10th Cir. 2012) (recognizing a liberty interest in preadoptive foster parents who had cared for the child for a significant period when the state had terminated biological parents' rights).

[63] See NeJaime, supra note [47], at 267-268; id. at 277 n.73 ("*OFFER* has been cited in Supreme Court opinions in only three cases since 2000.").

compensation." Restatement of Children and the Law §1.82 (Am. Law Inst. Tent. Draft No. 2 2019).[64]

Recognizing the disagreements among the states on this issue and the additional bonds that kinship foster parents have with a child, the UNCVA, supra, takes a more nuanced approach.[65] It gives states the option whether to disallow custody or visitation proceedings by nonparents "solely because the nonparent served as a foster parent of the child." UNCVA §3(c).

Continued contact with a paid nanny, over parental objection, presents similar issues. Here, the UNCVA hews more closely to the Restatement and ALI Principles, stating that nonrelatives seeking relief under the "substantial relationship" category must have "formed a relationship with the child without expectation of compensation." UNCVA §4(c)(1)(B).

How should law treat paid caregivers? Critics have noted that the restrictive approach to paid caregivers reflects class bias and subordinates a child's emotional bonds to other factors.[66] How would you reconcile the restrictive approach with the federal subsidies that states can provide to adults who adopt children with special needs?[67] See Chapter 4, section A2.

4. *Kinship care.* Some legal authorities offer greater protection to foster families composed of relatives.[68] Although most foster children are placed in unrelated family homes, as in *OFFER*, an increasing number are placed with close relatives (a practice known as "kinship care").[69] Federal law now provides financial incentives to encourage the development of kinship foster care programs and services to help kinship foster families.[70] Why?

The benefits of kinship care include family continuity, reduced trauma from separation from biological parents, and — according to evolutionary biology — better treatment than that from unrelated caregivers.[71] Yet, data show that children in kinship care are more likely to live in poverty and also to have caregivers who are older, less financially stable, less well educated, and burdened with more health problems than nonkin caregivers. In addition, the child's parents are more likely to have access to a child in kinship

---

[64] See also ALI Principles §2.03(1)(c). But see In re Custody of A.F.J., 314 P.3d 373 (Wash. 2013) (holding that one's status as a foster parent does not necessarily bar recognition as a de facto parent).

[65] See Atkinson & Atwood, supra note [37], at 492-493.

[66] See, e.g., Pamela Laufer-Ukeles, Money, Caregiving, and Kinship: Should Paid Caregivers Be Allowed to Obtain De Facto Parental Status?, 74 Mo. L. Rev. 25 (2009); Dorothy E. Roberts, Spiritual and Menial Housework, 9 Yale J.L. & Feminism 51 (1997).

[67] See 42 U.S.C. §673b.

[68] See Gabrielle A. Paupeck, Note, When Grandma Becomes Mom: The Liberty Interests of Kinship Foster Parents, 70 Fordham L. Rev. 527 (2001) (arguing that kinship foster parents and their foster children enjoy a due process right of family association).

[69] See U.S. Dept. of Health & Hum. Servs., Admin. for Child. & Fam., The AFCARS Report No. 26: Preliminary FY 2018 Estimates as of Aug. 22, 2019, Child. Bureau 1, 1, https://www.acf.hhs.gov/sites/default/files/cb/afcarsreport26.pdf (showing 46 percent of most recent foster placements in non-related homes and 32 percent in related homes).

[70] See, e.g., 42 U.S.C. §627 (kinship navigator program); id. §5106 (a)(4) (grants for implementing "procedures using adult relatives as the preferred placement for children removed from their home"); id. §5113 (b)(6) (requiring Secretary of HHS to "support the placement of children in kinship care arrangements, pre-adoptive, or adoptive homes"). See also id. §671(a)(28) (allowing states to enter "kinship guardianship assistance agreements").

[71] See David J. Herring, Kinship Foster Care: Implications of Behavioral Biology Research, 56 Buff. L. Rev. 495 (2008).

care — a particularly problematic situation when placement results from parental abuse.[72]

Advocates of permanence oppose treating kinship care, often used for African-American children, as a reason to deviate from the usual preference for adoption.[73] Finally, kinship placements often operate as part of a "hidden foster care system" that lacks the usual oversight and procedural protections because agency workers pressure parents to entrust their children to relatives "voluntarily" to avoid being taken to court.[74] Yet sometimes a parent cannot succeed in getting the child returned.[75]

To the extent that foster care is designed to serve as a transitional step to permanent outcomes, either family reunification or adoption, how does the rise of kinship care complicate the goal of permanence?[76]

5. *Grandparent caregivers.* Frequently, kinship caregivers are grandparents. When a mother is incarcerated, her own mother often provides foster care, despite frequent health and financial challenges, especially in African-American families.[77] According to Census Bureau figures, over 6 million grandchildren under 18 are living with a grandparent householder. Roughly 40 percent are white, 20 percent African American, and 30 percent Hispanic or Latinx (of any race). Almost 20 percent are reported to live below the poverty level, and in 18 percent of the households none of the child's own parents is present.[78] The number of grandparents and other relatives caring for children has risen with the increase in opioid addition.[79] In 2018 the "Supporting Grandparents Raising Children Act" became law, establishing a federal advisory council to support such families. P.L. 115-196, 132 Stat. 1511 (2018). Should such programs require a formal foster care arrangement, or should informal grandparent care arrangements suffice?[80] Why?

The Supreme Court considered an informal grandparent caregiving arrangement in Moore v. City of East Cleveland, 431 U.S. 494 (1977). By sharing her home with a son, his son, and another grandson, who was the cousin of the first grandson, Inez Moore violated a local zoning ordinance limiting

---

[72] See Cynthia G. Hawkins-Leon & Carla Bradley, Race and Transracial Adoption: The Answer is Neither Simply Black or White Nor Right or Wrong, 51 Cath. U. L. Rev. 1227, 1278 (2002).

[73] See Margaret F. Brinig & Steven L. Nock, How Much Does Legal Status Matter? Adoptions by Kin Caregivers, 36 Fam. L.Q. 449, 462 (2002) (finding "foster care does not compare favorably with adoption for any children").

[74] For an excellent critique, see Josh Gupta-Kagan, America's Hidden Foster Care System, 72 Stan. L. Rev. 841 (2020).

[75] See In re Custody of S.M., 444 P.3d 637 (Wash. Ct. App. 2019).

[76] See Sacha Coupet, Swimming Upstream Against the Great Adoption Tide: Making the Case for "Impermanence," 34 Cap. U. L. Rev. 405 (2005); Josh Gupta-Kagan, The New Permanency, 19 U.C. Davis J. Juv. L. & Pol'y 1 (2015).

[77] Jessica Dixon Weaver, African-American Grandmothers: Does the Gender Entrapment Theory Apply? Essay Response to Professor Beth Richie, 37 Wash. U. J.L. & Pol'y 153, 157 (2011).

[78] U.S. Census Bureau, United States, S1001, Grandchildren Characteristics (2018 American Community Survey 1-Year Estimates), https://data.census.gov/cedsci/table?q=grandchildren&hidePreview=false&tid=ACSST1Y2018.S1001&t=Grandparents%20and%20Grandchildren&vintage=2018.

[79] See Lydia Anderson, The Opioid Prescribing Rate and Grandparents Raising Grandchildren: State and County Level Analysis, U.S. Census Bureau Working Paper No. SEHSD-WP2019-04 (Apr. 11, 2019), https://www.census.gov/library/working-papers/2019/demo/SEHSD-WP2019-04.html; Dan Levin, Removed From Addicts, Children Find Hope in 'Kinship' Homes, N.Y. Times, Dec. 27, 2019, at A9.

[80] For the downsides of informal kinship care arrangements, see Gupta-Kagan, supra note [74].

the area to single "family" occupancy. In her constitutional challenge to the ordinance, a plurality along with a fifth vote in a concurring opinion determined that substantive rights protected by the Due Process Clause include a grandmother's decision to share her home with her grandchildren, despite the ordinance's narrower definition of "family." *Moore* not only signals that the grandparent-grandchild relationship merits constitutional protection but also promotes the policy of keeping dependency private by affirming the extended family as a source of support.[81] What changes in the principles and assumptions of *Troxel*, supra, might follow from the co-residence of grandparents and grandchildren?[82]

6. *"Voluntary" surrender.* As *OFFER* explains, a parent often initiates foster placement. Given *OFFER*'s depiction of the foster care system, what factors complicate the distinction between such "voluntary" surrenders and those imposed by the state?[83]

7. *Psychological parent doctrine.* Appellees' argument in *OFFER* that legally cognizable emotional bonds develop within foster families relies on the concept of "psychological parent" formulated by Joseph Goldstein, Anna Freud, and Albert Solnit in Beyond the Best Interests of the Child (1973). Their theory asserts that children often begin to regard a caregiving adult as a parent and might suffer traumatic loss from the disruption of such relationships, even if they were meant to be temporary. This theory proved influential with courts in their efforts to apply the indeterminate standard of "best interests of the child." Although some states have legislated a preference for biological parents over nonparents in custody disputes,[84] the psychological parent theory took on new importance as same-sex couples began openly to rear children biologically related only to one of them and then brought custody disputes to court when the adults' relationship dissolved.[85] The theory, which above all emphasizes the child's point of view, later became absorbed into broader doctrines, like "de facto" parentage and the UNCVA's categories for relief. See Chapter 1, section C.

Does *OFFER* adequately protect the interests of children who see their foster parents as parents? Can the foster parents assert these interests? Note that the foster parents suing in *OFFER* did so on their own behalf and on behalf of the children. In an omitted footnote 44, the Court addressed the

---

[81] See, e.g., June Carbone & Naomi Cahn, *Moore*'s Potential, 85 Fordham L. Rev. 2589, 2597 (2017).

[82] See, e.g., Maldonado, supra note [46]; Sonia Gipson Rankin, Note, Why They Won't Take the Money: Black Grandparents and the Success of Informal Kinship Care, 10 Elder L.J. 153 (2002).

[83] Compare, e.g., Dupuy v. Samuels, 465 F.3d 757, 760-762 (7th Cir. 2006) (deeming consent to a "safety plan" voluntary), with Croft v. Westmoreland Cty. Child. & Youth Servs., 103 F.3d 1123, 1125 & n.1 (3d Cir. 1997) (finding ultimatum that father leave home or state would place child in foster care to be "blatantly coercive"). See Dorothy Roberts, Shattered Bonds: The Color of Child Welfare 82-89 (2002) (citing various pressures and power imbalances faced by poor parents and families of color); Gupta-Kagan, supra note [74]; Kathleen B. Simon, Catalyzing the Separation of Black Families: A Critique of Foster Care Placements without Judicial Review, 51 Colum. J.L. & Soc. Probs. 347 (2018) (focusing on emergency removals from home).

[84] E.g., Okla. Stat. tit. 43 §112.5.

[85] See Nancy Polikoff, From Third Parties to Parents: The Case of Lesbian Couples and Their Children, 77 L. & Contemp. Probs. 195 (2014). See also Michelle M. Gros, In the Case of Biology v. Psychology: Where Did My "Parent" Go?, 52 Fam. L.Q. 147 (2018).

argument that the foster parents lacked standing to raise the children's interests:

> Ordinarily, it is true, a party would not have standing to assert the rights of another, himself a party in the litigation; the third party himself can decide how best to protect his interests. But children usually lack the capacity to make that sort of decision, and thus their interest is ordinarily represented in litigation by parents or guardians. In this case, however, the State, the natural parents, and the foster parents, all of whom share some portion of the responsibility for guardianship of the child, are parties, and all contend that the position they advocate is most in accord with the rights and interests of the children. In this situation, the District Court properly appointed independent counsel to represent the children, so that the court could have the benefit of an independent advocate for the welfare of the children, unprejudiced by the possibly conflicting interests and desires of the other parties. It does not follow, however, that that independent counsel, who is not a guardian *ad litem* of the children, is solely authorized to determine the children's best interest.
>
> [The foster parents'] standing to raise the rights of the children in their attack on those procedures is a prudential question. We believe it would be most imprudent to leave entirely to court-appointed counsel the choices that neither the named foster children nor the class they represent are capable of making for themselves, especially in litigation in which all parties have sufficient attributes of guardianship that their views on the rights of the children should at least be heard.

431 U.S. at 842 n.44. Does that solve the problem?[86]

Evaluate dissenting Justice Stewart's assertion that the child's emotional ties to the foster parents constitute "breakdowns" of the system that the Due Process Clause should not protect. What does Walbert's reflection add to your evaluation? Does it follow that a child should be moved to a new foster home once such ties begin to develop?[87] Why?

8. *Foster Care Population.*

a. *Entry into foster care.* When *OFFER* was decided, the typical parent who placed a child in foster care was a divorced spouse with financial problems, a single mother, or a mother on public assistance who was unable temporarily to care for a child because of illness or financial problems. A leading authority identified family disruption, financial difficulties, and medical reasons as the primary factors.[88] Neglect, abuse, and abandonment also accounted for many children's entry into foster care. Beginning in the mid 1980s, significant changes occurred in the numbers of children in foster care, their characteristics, and the reasons for their entrance into care. In 1980 approximately 300,000 children were in foster care. That number practically doubled by

---

[86] See Annette Ruth Appell, Representing Children Representing What? Critical Reflections on Lawyering for Children, 39 Colum. Hum. Rts. L. Rev. 573 (2008); Jane Spinak, When Did Lawyers for Children Stop Reading Goldstein, Freud and Solnit? Lessons from the Twentieth Century on Best Interests and the Role of the Child Advocate, 41 Fam. L. Q. 393 (2007); see also Dailey & Rosenbury, supra note [32], at 1513-1514 (advocating more recognition of relationships developed between children and foster parents).

[87] See In re Jewish Child Care Ass'n of N.Y. (Sanders), 156 N.E.2d 700 (N.Y. 1959).

[88] Alfred Kadushin, Child Welfare Services 402 (1974).

1998.[89] More African-American, Hispanic, and Native American children entered foster care, and more sibling groups needed to be placed together. A considerable number of children entered foster care because their families lacked adequate housing. Substance abuse was another contributing factor, with the increase in use of crack cocaine leading to the placement of more infants in foster care, based on drug toxicity at birth, substance-related abandonment, or parenting that fell short of standards used by child welfare workers. Children with HIV or whose parents died of AIDS further enlarged the foster care population. As a result of these factors, many children entered foster care with special needs.

b. *Current characteristics.* According to a 2019 report reflecting data from 2018, an estimated 437,283 children were in foster care. Of these children, 46 percent were in nonrelative foster family homes, 32 percent were in kinship foster homes, 10 percent were in group homes or institutions, and 4 percent were in pre-adoptive homes. The median age of children in foster care was 7.6 years. In terms of racial characteristics, 44 percent of children in foster care were white, 23 percent were Black/African American, and 21 percent were Hispanic. Slightly more than half of the children in foster care were identified as male. The mean time spent in foster care was 19.7 months; however, over one quarter who left foster care had been in care for more than 2 years, and 5 percent had been in care for 5 or more years. Of 250,000 children who exited foster care in 2018, 49 percent were reunited with parent(s) or primary caretaker(s), 25 percent were adopted, 18 percent went to live with a relative or guardian, and 7 percent were emancipated.[90]

Some critics note that the family setting contemplated by foster care does not serve all children equally well, especially "unaccompanied youth" who often end up homeless or in juvenile detention.[91] Other critics note how criteria for foster parents tend to favor the less affluent, by disqualifying, for example, adults whose work includes travel.[92]

9. *Epilogue.* Although the Supreme Court reversed the district court's finding of unconstitutionality in *OFFER*, the case had an impact. First, the Gandy children (see footnote 1) were permitted to remain with their foster mother Mrs. Smith. Eventually, she adopted them. Second, the litigation put on notice those states without any preremoval conferences that their procedures might have constitutional flaws. Third, the litigation resulted in new procedural protections in New York City (although not statewide) regarding the formal hearings prior to intrafoster care transfers. Foster parents (who must request these hearings) may appear with counsel; witnesses are sworn and subject to cross-examination; and expert testimony is often taken.

---

[89] Sandra Bass et al., Children, Families, and Foster Care: Analysis and Recommendations, in 14 The Future of Children 5, 8 (2004).

[90] U.S. Dept. of Health & Hum. Servs., supra note [69].

[91] See Jordan Blair Woods, Unaccompanied Youth and Private-Public Order Failures, 103 Iowa L. Rev. 1639 (2018).

[92] See Ginia Bellafante, Hurdles to a Broader Pool of Foster Parents, N.Y. Times, Jan. 19, 2020, at MB3.

Although only a small number of such hearings are held, the reversal rate for these contested decisions is quite high.[93]

10. *Foster care reform.* Foster care was envisioned as a temporary solution to family dysfunction or disruption. However, in the 1970s, public attention began focusing on the problem of "foster care drift" or "foster care limbo." The terms signify the experience of foster care children who undergo multiple foster care placements, moving continuously from foster home to foster home without hope of family reunification or adoption.[94] Many commentators criticized the practice and highlighted its psychological harm to children.[95] *OFFER* reinforced this critique.

A succession of federal laws, offering funds to states that meet specified standards, reveals continuously changing priorities.[96] What does the following summary reveal about official understandings of foster care? Which of the approaches summarized below do you find most supportable as a matter of policy? Why?

a. *Adoption Assistance and Child Welfare Act.* In 1980 Congress enacted the Adoption Assistance and Child Welfare Act (AACWA), Pub. L. No. 96-272, 94 Stat. 500 (1980). The primary objective of the AACWA was to facilitate finding permanent homes for children (by preventing the need for removal, returning children to their families, or placing them for adoption). The AACWA provides federal matching funds to states for administering foster care and adoption services (emphasizing preventive and rehabilitative services) subject to certain requirements, including the formulation of state case plans ("permanency planning") designed to achieve placement in the least restrictive setting possible and focused on family reunification, with "reasonable efforts" to prevent the need to remove a child from the home and to facilitate the child's return as soon as possible.

b. *Adoption and Safe Families Act.* AACWA's emphasis on family preservation and reunification ultimately evoked criticism. According to critics, these policies exposed children to unnecessary risks (by leaving children in or returning them to dangerous homes) and perpetuated foster care drift and foster care limbo (by delaying adoption). In 1997, Congress enacted the Adoption and Safe Families Act (ASFA), Pub. L. No. 105-89, 111 Stat. 2115 (1997). ASFA recognized that reunification is not possible or advisable in all cases and provided for speedier termination of parental rights with a goal of promoting adoption, as discussed in more detail Chapter 3, section A. Accordingly, ASFA authorized concurrent planning so that plans for

---

[93] David L. Chambers & Michael S. Wald, Smith v. OFFER, in In the Interest of Children: Advocacy, Law Reform, and Public Policy 114-116 (Robert H. Mnookin ed. 1985).

[94] See, e.g., Cris Beam, To the End of June: The Intimate Life of American Foster Care (2013); Nina Bernstein, The Lost Children of Wilder: The Epic Struggle to Change Foster Care (2001).

[95] See, e.g., Joseph Goldstein, Anna Freud, and Albert J. Solnit, Beyond the Best Interests of the Child (1973); Robert H. Mnookin, Foster Care — In Whose Best Interest?, 43 Harv. Educ. Rev. 599 (1973); Michael S. Wald, State Intervention on Behalf of "Neglected" Children: Standards for Removal of Children From Their Homes, Monitoring the Status of Children in Foster Care, and Termination of Parental Rights, 28 Stan. L. Rev. 623 (1976).

[96] See, e.g., Claire Houston, What Ever Happened to the "Child Maltreatment Revolution"?, 19 Geo. J. Gender & L. 1, 30-37 (2017) (noting how "family preservation" in child maltreatment law "flows then ebbs then flows").

adoption could begin even while reunification efforts are pending and prospective adopters could serve as foster parents.[97]

c. *Fostering Connections to Success and Increasing Adoptions Act.* This statute, Pub. L. 110-351, 122 Stat. 3949 (2008), became law in October 2008. In providing funds to the states, it gives them the option of subsidizing kinship care and otherwise promoting kinship connections; the law also permits states to receive funding while continuing to provide foster care for those up to 21 years of age, in contrast to the traditional and often criticized approach under which youths "age out" of foster care upon turning 18.

d. *Preventing Sex Trafficking and Strengthening Families Act.* This 2014 law, Pub. L. 113-183, 128 Stat. 1919 (2014), requires collection of information about children who run away from foster care and are at risk of sex trafficking. It also improves adoption incentives and calls for states to implement a "reasonable and prudent parent standard" for foster parents or officials at a child care institution.[98]

e. *Family First Prevention Services Act.* While the 1997 and 2008 reforms, supra, sought to increase adoptions and, for older youth, to extend foster care, the Family First Prevention Services Act, Pub. L. No. 15-271, 132 Stat. 3294 (2018), tilts the other way. It allows federal funds previously available for foster care and adoption assistance to be used for prevention services that would enable "candidates for foster care" to stay with their parents or relatives. Such services include in-home parenting classes, mental health counseling, and substance abuse treatment. For those who cannot stay with family members, it favors foster homes, seeking to limit "congregate care" or group homes.[99] Note that by treating parents and relatives as equally favored for candidates for foster care, the statute promotes "hidden foster care."[100]

PROBLEM

Ernest and Regina Twigg sought discovery to determine the paternity of Kimberly Mays. They allege that Kimberly, who was reared by Robert Mays and his wife (now deceased), was actually the Twiggs' daughter, who had been switched at birth at the hospital. (The daughter reared by the Twiggs, born on the same date at the same hospital, had died of a heart ailment; during the course of her medical treatment, the Twiggs first learned that she was not their biological daughter.) Can a court order the blood tests over Mays's objection? Must it do so? Why?

---

[97] See Maggie Wong Cockayne, Foster to Adopt: Pipeline to Failure and the Need for Concurrent Planning Reform, 60 Santa Clara L. Rev. 151 (2020).

[98] See Children's Defense Fund, Preventing Sex Trafficking and Strengthening Families Act (H.R. 4980) (Oct. 2014), https://www.childrensdefense.org/wp-content/uploads/2018/08/fact-sheet-on-hr-4980.pdf [https://perma.cc/W3HU-QZ4S].

[99] See Asheley Pankratz, What About Florida's Children? Analyzing the Implications of the Family First Prevention Services Act of 2018, 44 Nova L. Rev. 63, 73 (2019); Teresa Wiltz, This New Federal Law Will Change Foster Care as We Know It, Pew Stateline, May 2, 2018, https://www.pewtrusts.org/en/research-and-analysis/blogs/stateline/2018/05/02/this-new-federal-law-will-change-foster-care-as-we-know-it. For an example of the programs supported by funding under the Act, see Leah Thorsen, Local Program Places Kids in Crisis with Relatives, St. Louis Post-Dispatch, Apr. 20, 2020, at A1.

[100] See Gupta-Kagan, supra note [74], at 894-896.

Suppose blood tests take place and corroborate the Twiggs' claim. They sue for visits with Kimberly (now age 15), who wants to remain with Mays as the only family she has ever known. What result and why? Alternatively, suppose Kimberly prefers to live with the Twiggs.[101]

How, if at all, would your analysis of the custody dispute change if Kimberly were age seven and had come to live with Mays three years earlier, after her biological parents, the Twiggs, had temporarily entrusted her to his care during a particularly difficult time? Suppose that, thereafter, Kimberly began to regard Mays as her father and expert testimony established that she was thriving in his care. Then, when the Twiggs seek her return, Mays refuses to send her back. Now, what result and why?[102]

Suppose Kimberly were age seven when her biological parents, the Twiggs, discover that the daughter they thought had been killed in a fire as an infant had, in fact, been kidnapped by Mays and reared as his own. Would Kimberly's desire to remain with Mays, even if expert testimony showed her to be thriving, carry any weight at all? Why?[103]

Depictions in Popular Culture: Antwone Fisher (2002)

Antwone Fisher, a Hollywood film based on a memoir, unfolds in the aftermath of a childhood spent in foster care. The eponymous anger-prone seaman in the U.S. Navy (Derek Luke) reflects on his past, with the firm but caring support of psychiatrist Dr. Jerome Davenport (Denzel Washington, also in his directorial debut). It is a childhood marked by abandonment, crime, and all manner of abuse — physical, emotional, and sexual — in his foster home, replayed in flashback with vivid and horrifying detail, including repeated racial epithets and vicious corporal punishment. Indeed, Antwone's connection to his foster family turns *OFFER*'s focus on attachment into a cruel fantasy.

As Antwone learns to trust Dr. Davenport, he develops the confidence to explore a relationship with Cheryl, another member of the Navy, and Dr. Davenport persuades a reluctant Atwone to search for his birth family to fill in missing knowledge and achieve closure regarding possible sources of his anger.

Despite the obstacles, Antwone's quest succeeds. He must first confront his foster family, to gain valuable information in his

---

[101] See Twigg v. Mays, 1993 WL 330624 (Fla. Cir. Ct. Aug. 18,1993); Lauren Effron & Peri Muldofsky, Kim Mays, Biological Family Involved in Switched-at-Birth Scandal, Custody Battle Describe Navigating Troubled Times, ABC News (Nov. 27, 2019), https://abcnews.go.com/US/kim-mays-biological-family-involved-switched-birth-scandal/story?id=67303922. See generally Cynthia R. Mabry, The Tragic and Chaotic Aftermath of a Baby Switch: Should Policy and Common Law, Blood Ties, or Psychological Bonds Prevail?, 6 Wm. & Mary J. Women & L. 1 (1999).

[102] See Painter v. Bannister, 140 N.W.2d 152 (Iowa 1966).

[103] See Jacqueline Soteropoulos, Woman Sentenced for Kidnapping Infant in 1997, Phil. Inquirer, Sept. 24, 2005, at domestic news. For other "baby-switch" stories, see, e.g., Susan Dominus, The Mixed-Up Brothers of Bogotá, N.Y Times Mag., July 12, 2015, at 34; Switched at Birth, This American Life, July 25, 2008, https://www.thisamericanlife.org/360/switched-at-birth.

search. He then meets the welcoming family of his birth father (who was murdered before he was born) and confronts but forgives his largely silent mother (Viola Davis), who gave birth to him in prison and never returned to claim him after her release. When Antwone returns to thank Dr. Davenport for urging him to find his family, Dr. Davenport thanks Antwone for serving as a catalyst in his struggle with own problems.

Although Antwone's experiences with his foster family stand out, the abandonment that Antwone feels plays an even more important role in shaping his conduct and sense of self. The film thus highlights how loss infuses both foster care and adoption, regardless of the success or failure of a particular placement.[104]

The film generated positive commentary about its treatment of race and racism. As one reviewer explains a brief scene:

> Early in Antwone's therapy the doctor gives him John W. Blassingame's book "The Slave Community," which theorizes that the harsh discipline Antwone (like countless children like him) endured as a foster child growing up in Cleveland was an internalized reflection of the abuse his ancestors suffered at the hands of slave owners. Those slave owners, it suggests, loomed as punishing surrogate parents, wielding far more authority than the slaves' own biological parents.
>
> To any child, the behavior of an ultimate authority figure, no matter how oppressive, tends to define how that child wields parental power later in life. According to the theory, that pattern of instilled self-loathing established in the days of slavery has been passed down from generation to generation.[105]

A more scholarly examination observes:

> What is particularly notable about the 2002 film *Antwone Fisher*, then, particularly within historical cinematic interactions between therapists and black patients, is the way that the film acknowledges, rather than obscures or obliterates, race and racism as constitutive aspects of identity even within its rather traditional approach to psychoanalytic treatment.[106]

With the professed willingness of many members of the general public to grapple with systemic and structural racism in 2020, almost two decades after *Antwone Fisher* was released, what messages does the film offer? What should these contemporary conversations about American law and society say about foster care and adoption, in particular?

---

[104] See also, e.g., Kacey Vu Shap, Why Did She Leave Me There?, N.Y. Times, July 26, 2020, at ST5 (recounting author's visit to Vietnamese orphanage where his grandmother had left him years before).
[105] Stephen Holden, Film Review: A Director and His Hero Find Answers in the Details, N.Y. Times, Dec. 19, 2002, at E1.
[106] Badia Sahar Ahad, The New Normal: Black Psychic Subjectivity in *Antwone Fisher*, 13 New Centennial Rev. 139, 140 (2013).

PART II

ADOPTION

3

ENDING THE ORIGINAL PARENT-CHILD RELATIONSHIP

Adoption creates a new legal relationship of parent and child. With traditional rules limiting a child to no more than two parents and making parentage a comprehensive, exclusive, and indivisible status, the ordinary prerequisites for adoption include bringing to an end any existing parent-child relationship. Two primary tracks lead to this result: the state's termination of parental rights (TPR), even over the objection of the parents, and parental decisions to surrender or relinquish a child for adoption.

A. INVOLUNTARY TERMINATION OF PARENTAL RIGHTS

SANTOSKY v. KRAMER

---

455 U.S. 745 (1982)

Justice BLACKMUN delivered the opinion of the Court.

Under New York law, the State may terminate, over parental objection, the rights of parents in their natural child upon a finding that the child is "permanently neglected." The New York Family Court Act §622 requires that only a "fair preponderance of the evidence" support that finding. Thus, in New York, the factual certainty required to extinguish the parent-child relationship is no greater than that necessary to award money damages in an ordinary civil action. . . . The question here is whether New York's "fair preponderance of the evidence" standard is constitutionally sufficient.

Petitioners John Santosky II and Annie Santosky are the natural parents of Tina and John III. In November 1973, after incidents reflecting parental neglect, respondent Kramer, Commissioner of the Ulster County Department of Social Services, initiated a neglect proceeding under Fam. Ct. Act §1022 and removed Tina from her natural home. About 10 months later, he removed John III and placed him with foster parents. On the day John was taken, Annie Santosky gave birth to a third child, Jed. When Jed was only three days old, respondent transferred him to a foster home on the ground that immediate removal was necessary to avoid imminent danger to his life or health.

In October 1978, respondent petitioned the Ulster County Family Court to terminate petitioners' parental rights in the three children. [When petitioners challenged the "preponderance" standard,][t]he Family Court Judge rejected this constitutional challenge, and weighed the evidence under the statutory standard. While acknowledging that the Santoskys had maintained contact with their children, the judge found those visits "at best superficial and devoid of any real emotional content." After deciding that the agency had made "'diligent efforts' to encourage and strengthen the parental relationship," he concluded that the Santoskys were incapable, even with public assistance, of planning for the future of their children. The judge later held a dispositional hearing and ruled that the best interests of the three children required permanent termination of the Santoskys' custody. [Petitioners unsuccessfully appealed.]

Last Term in Lassiter v. Department of Social Services, 452 U.S. 18 (1981), this Court [held] that the Fourteenth Amendment's Due Process Clause does not require the appointment of counsel for indigent parents in every parental status termination proceeding. The case casts light, however, on the two central questions here — whether process is constitutionally due a natural parent at a State's parental rights termination proceeding, and, if so, what process is due....

The fundamental liberty interest of natural parents in the care, custody, and management of their child does not evaporate simply because they have not been model parents or have lost temporary custody of their child to the State. Even when blood relationships are strained, parents retain a vital interest in preventing the irretrievable destruction of their family life. If anything, persons faced with forced dissolution of their parental rights have a more critical need for procedural protections than do those resisting state intervention into ongoing family affairs. When the State moves to destroy weakened familial bonds, it must provide the parents with fundamentally fair procedures.

In Lassiter, the Court and three dissenters agreed that the nature of the process due in parental rights termination proceedings turns on a balancing of the "three distinct factors" specified in Mathews v. Eldridge, 424 U.S. 319, 335 (1976): the private interests affected by the proceeding; the risk of error created by the State's chosen procedure; and the countervailing governmental interest supporting use of the challenged procedure.... Evaluation of the three Eldridge factors compels the conclusion that use of a "fair preponderance of the evidence" standard in [termination] proceedings is inconsistent with due process....

"The extent to which procedural due process must be afforded the recipient is influenced by the extent to which he may be 'condemned to suffer grievous loss.'" Whether the loss threatened by a particular type of proceeding is sufficiently grave to warrant more than average certainty on the part of the factfinder turns on both the nature of the private interest threatened and the permanency of the threatened loss.

Lassiter declared it "plain beyond the need for multiple citation" that a natural parent's "desire for and right to 'the companionship, care, custody, and management of his or her children'" is an interest far more precious than any property right. 452 U.S., at 27 quoting Stanley v. Illinois, 405 U.S., at 651. When the State initiates a parental rights termination proceeding, it seeks not merely to infringe that fundamental liberty interest, but to end it.... Thus, the first *Eldridge* factor — the private interest affected — weighs heavily against use of the preponderance standard at a state-initiated permanent neglect proceeding....

[T]he factfinding hearing pits the State directly against the parents. The State alleges that the natural parents are at fault. The questions disputed and decided are what the State did — "made diligent efforts," — and what the natural parents did not do — "maintain contact with or plan for the future of the child." The State marshals an array of public resources to prove its case and disprove the parents' case. Victory by the State not only makes termination of parental rights possible; it entails a judicial determination that the parents are unfit to raise their own children.[10]

[U]ntil the State proves parental unfitness, the child and his parents share a vital interest in preventing erroneous termination of their natural relationship. Thus, at the factfinding, the interests of the child and his natural parents coincide to favor use of error-reducing procedures....

Under Mathews v. Eldridge, we next must consider both the risk of erroneous deprivation of private interests resulting from use of a "fair preponderance" standard and the likelihood that a higher evidentiary standard would reduce that risk.... In New York, the factfinding stage of a state-initiated permanent neglect proceeding bears many of the indicia of a criminal trial.... The State, the parents, and the child are all represented by counsel. The State seeks to establish a series of historical facts about the intensity of its agency's efforts to reunite the family, the infrequency and insubstantiality of the parents' contacts with their child, and the parents' inability or unwillingness to formulate a plan for the child's future. The attorneys submit documentary evidence, and call witnesses who are subject to cross-examination. [T]he judge then determines whether the State has proved the statutory elements of permanent neglect by a fair preponderance of the evidence.

At such a proceeding, numerous factors combine to magnify the risk of erroneous factfinding. Permanent neglect proceedings employ imprecise substantive standards that leave determinations unusually open to the subjective values of the judge. [T]he court possesses unusual discretion to underweigh probative facts that might favor the parent. Because parents subject to termination proceedings are often poor, uneducated, or members of minority groups, such proceedings are often vulnerable to judgments based on cultural or class bias.

The State's ability to assemble its case almost inevitably dwarfs the parents' ability to mount a defense. No predetermined limits restrict the sums an agency may spend in prosecuting a given termination proceeding. The State's attorney usually will be expert on the issues contested and the procedures employed at the factfinding hearing, and enjoys full access to all public records concerning the family. The State may call on experts in family

---

10. The Family Court judge in the present case expressly refused to terminate petitioners' parental rights on a "non-statutory, no-fault basis." Nor is it clear that the State constitutionally could terminate a parent's rights without showing parental unfitness. See Quilloin v. Walcott, 434 U.S. 246, 255 (1978) ("We have little doubt that the Due Process Clause would be offended '[i]f a State were to attempt to force the breakup of a natural family, over the objections of the parents and their children, without some showing of unfitness and for the sole reason that to do so was thought to be in the children's best interest,'" quoting Smith v. Organization of Foster Families, 431 U.S. 816, 862-863 (1977) (Stewart, J., concurring in judgment)).

relations, psychology, and medicine to bolster its case. Furthermore, the primary witnesses at the hearing will be the agency's own professional caseworkers whom the State has empowered both to investigate the family situation and to testify against the parents. Indeed, because the child is already in agency custody, the State even has the power to shape the historical events that form the basis for termination.[13]

The disparity between the adversaries' litigation resources is matched by a striking asymmetry in their litigation options. Unlike criminal defendants, natural parents have no "double jeopardy" defense against repeated state termination efforts. If the State initially fails to win termination, as New York did here, it always can try once again to cut off the parents' rights after gathering more or better evidence. Yet even when the parents have attained the level of fitness required by the State, they have no similar means by which they can forestall future termination efforts.

Coupled with a "fair preponderance of the evidence" standard, these factors create a significant prospect of erroneous termination. A standard of proof that by its very terms demands consideration of the quantity, rather than the quality, of the evidence may misdirect the factfinder in the marginal case....

Raising the standard of proof would have both practical and symbolic consequences.... An elevated standard of proof in a parental rights termination proceeding would alleviate "the possible risk that a factfinder might decide to [deprive] an individual based solely on a few isolated instances of unusual conduct [or] . . . idiosyncratic behavior." Addington v. Texas, 441 U.S., at 427. "Increasing the burden of proof is one way to impress the factfinder with the importance of the decision and thereby perhaps to reduce the chances that inappropriate" terminations will be ordered. Ibid.

The Appellate Division approved New York's preponderance standard on the ground that it properly "balanced rights possessed by the child . . . with those of the natural parents. . . ." 427 N.Y.S.2d, at 320. By so saying, the court suggested that a preponderance standard properly allocates the risk of error *between* the parents and the child. That view is fundamentally mistaken.

The court's theory assumes that termination of the natural parents' rights invariably will benefit the child.[15] Yet we have noted above that the parents and the child share an interest in avoiding erroneous termination. Even accepting the court's assumption, we cannot agree with its conclusion that a preponderance standard fairly distributes the risk of error between parent and child. Use of that standard reflects the judgment that society is nearly neutral between erroneous termination of parental rights and

---

13. In this case, for example, the parents claim that the State sought court orders denying them the right to visit their children, which would have prevented them from maintaining the contact required by Fam. Ct. Act §614.1.(d). The parents further claim that the State cited their rejection of social services they found offensive or superfluous as proof of the agency's "diligent efforts" and their own "failure to plan" for the children's future....

15. This is a hazardous assumption at best. Even when a child's natural home is imperfect, permanent removal from that home will not necessarily improve his welfare. See, e.g., Wald, State Intervention on Behalf of "Neglected" Children: A Search for Realistic Standards, 27 Stan. L. Rev. 985, 993 (1975) ("In fact, under current practice, coercive intervention frequently results in placing a child in a more detrimental situation than he would be in without intervention"). Nor does termination of parental rights necessarily ensure adoption. Even when a child eventually finds an adoptive family, he may spend years moving between state institutions and "temporary" foster placements after his ties to his natural parents have been severed.

erroneous failure to terminate those rights. For the child, the likely consequence of an erroneous failure to terminate is preservation of an uneasy status quo. For the natural parents, however, the consequence of an erroneous
termination is the unnecessary destruction of their natural family. A standard that allocates the risk of error nearly equally between those two outcomes does not reflect properly their relative severity....

Two state interests are at stake in parental rights termination
proceedings — a parens patriae interest in preserving and promoting the welfare of the child and a fiscal and administrative interest in reducing the cost
and burden of such proceedings. A standard of proof more strict than preponderance of the evidence is consistent with both interests.

... As parens patriae, the State's goal is to provide the child with a permanent home. Yet while there is still reason to believe that positive, nurturing
parent-child relationships exist, the parens patriae interest favors preservation, not severance, of natural familial bonds.... We cannot believe that it
would burden the State unduly to require that its factfinders have the same
factual certainty when terminating the parent-child relationship as they
must have to suspend a driver's license. [Without deciding the outcome
under a constitutionally proper standard], we vacate the judgment of the
Appellate Division and remand the case for further proceedings not inconsistent with this opinion....

Justice REHNQUIST, with whom the CHIEF JUSTICE, Justice WHITE, and Justice
O'CONNOR join, dissenting.

... New York has created an exhaustive program to assist parents in
regaining the custody of their children and to protect parents from the
unfair deprivation of their parental rights. And yet the majority's myopic
scrutiny of the standard of proof blinds it to the very considerations and procedures which make the New York scheme "fundamentally fair." ...

The three children to which this case relates were removed from petitioners' custody [pursuant to New York's procedures] and in response to what
can only be described as shockingly abusive treatment.[10]

[P]etitioners received training by a mother's aide, a nutritional aide, and a
public health nurse, and counseling at a family planning clinic. In addition,
the plan provided psychiatric treatment and vocational training for the
father, and counseling at a family service center for the mother. Between
early 1976 and the final termination decision in April 1979, the State spent
more than $15,000 in these efforts to rehabilitate petitioners as parents.

Petitioners' response to the State's effort was marginal at best. They
wholly disregarded some of the available services and participated only

---

10. Tina Apel, the oldest of petitioners' five children, was removed from their custody by
court order in November 1973 when she was two years old. Removal proceedings were commenced in response to complaints by neighbors and reports from a local hospital that Tina had
suffered injuries in petitioners' home including a fractured left femur, treated with a home-
made splint; bruises on the upper arms, forehead, flank, and spine; and abrasions of the upper
leg. The following summer, John Santosky III, petitioners' second oldest child, was also removed
from petitioner's custody. John, who was less than one year old at the time, was admitted to the
hospital suffering malnutrition, bruises on the eye and forehead, cuts on the foot, blisters on
the hand, and multiple pin pricks on the back. Jed Santosky, the third oldest of petitioners' children, was removed from his parents' custody when only three days old as a result of the abusive
treatment of the two older children.

sporadically in the others. As a result, and out of growing concern over the length of the children's stay in foster care, the Department petitioned in September 1976 for permanent termination of petitioners' parental rights so that the children could be adopted by other families. Although the Family Court recognized that petitioners' reaction to the State's efforts was generally "non-responsive, even hostile," the fact that they were "at least superficially cooperative" led it to conclude that there was yet hope of further improvement and an eventual reuniting of the family. Accordingly, the petition for permanent termination was dismissed. [In October 1978, the agency again filed a termination proceeding because petitioners had made few efforts to take advantage of social services or to visit their children.]

[T]he State's extraordinary 4-year effort to reunite petitioners' family was not just unsuccessful, it was altogether rebuffed by parents unwilling to improve their circumstances sufficiently to permit a return of their children. At every step of this protracted process petitioners were accorded those procedures and protections which traditionally have been required by due process of law. . . . It is inconceivable to me that these procedures were "fundamentally unfair" to petitioners. . . . The interests at stake in this case demonstrate that New York has selected a constitutionally permissible standard of proof.

On one side is the interest of parents in a continuation of the family unit and the raising of their own children. The importance of this interest cannot easily be overstated. Few consequences of judicial action are so grave as the severance of natural family ties. . . . On the other side of the termination proceeding are the often countervailing interests of the child. A stable, loving homelife is essential to a child's physical, emotional, and spiritual well-being. . . .

In addition to the child's interest in a normal homelife, "the State has an urgent interest in the welfare of the child." Lassiter v. Department of Social Services, 452 U.S., at 27. Few could doubt that the most valuable resource of a self-governing society is its population of children who will one day become adults and themselves assume the responsibility of self-governance. . . .

When, in the context of a permanent neglect termination proceeding, the interests of the child and the State in a stable, nurturing homelife are balanced against the interests of the parents in the rearing of their child, it cannot be said that either set of interests is so clearly paramount as to require that the risk of error be allocated to one side or the other. Accordingly, a State constitutionally may conclude that the risk of error should be borne in roughly equal fashion by use of the preponderance-of-the-evidence standard of proof. . . .

NOTES AND QUESTIONS

1. *Context.* When parental conduct creates harm or a risk of harm to a child, the state can intervene, according to Prince v. Massachusetts, 321 U.S. 158 (1944). Termination of parental rights (TPR) proceedings represent the culmination of such interventions, generally evolving over several stages. Initially, state child welfare workers ask a family court or juvenile court to assert jurisdiction over the child. (In an emergency, the state might use summary seizure to remove the child from the home, followed by a jurisdictional

proceeding.) For the state to exercise its authority, the court must find by a preponderance of the evidence that the child meets statutory criteria, which typically provide for jurisdiction over abused, neglected, and dependent children. Because of the constitutional status of family integrity as a fundamental right, some authorities require such initial intervention to meet the requirements of strict scrutiny (especially if temporary custody of the child is to follow).[1] Assuming satisfaction of this jurisdictional threshold, the court then selects a disposition. Dispositional alternatives include, inter alia, educational sessions for parents, ongoing home visits, or placement of the child in foster care, with efforts to address the problem and reunify the family. The dissenting opinion in *Santosky* discusses several of these options.

As *Santosky* explains, if the problem requiring removal of the child from home persists, the state may seek TPR. Such proceedings, in turn, entail an initial stage at which the court makes a determination of unfitness (the "unfitness stage") and a subsequent stage at which the court determines whether TPR would serve the child's best interests (sometimes called "the best interests stage"). (*Santosky* refers somewhat differently to the stages of a child neglect proceeding, pursuant to New York statute, as "the fact-finding hearing" at which the state is required to prove permanent neglect and "the dispositional hearing" at which the court determines which placement serves the child's best interests.) These stages may occur in a single hearing.

All of these decisions take place against a backdrop of laws designed to be expansive in the name of child protection, thus inviting value judgments about proper parenting that might well reflect bias based on race, culture, and class.[2]

2. *Standard.* What do the various participants in TPR proceedings have at stake in the distribution of the risk of error? Why does the majority reject neutrality as the appropriate stance toward erroneous terminations of parental rights and erroneous failures to terminate those rights? What are the consequences of each type of erroneous decision? Does the clear-and-convincing standard, required in *Santosky*, adequately protect family autonomy? Adequately protect the interests of children? Ensure that children spend lengthy periods in foster care? States may require a higher standard still. Should they do so?[3]

Although *Santosky* requires the clear and convincing evidence standard before TPR, several states reason that *Santosky* applies only to the

---

[1] See, e.g., In re Juvenile Appeal (83-CD), 455 A.2d 1313, 1318 (Conn. 1983) (requiring a compelling state interest and narrow tailoring of legislation to serve only such legitimate interests); In re Welfare of Child of R.D.L., 853 N.W.2d 127, 133 (Minn. 2014) (deeming strict scrutiny applicable to statutes interfering with parent's fundamental right to make decisions concerning care, custody, and control of children); see generally John Thomas Halloran, Families First: Reframing Parental Rights as Familial Rights in Termination of Parental Rights Proceedings, 18 U.C. Davis J. Juv. L. & Pol'y 51 (2014).

[2] See Dorothy Roberts, Shattered Bonds: The Color of Child Welfare (2002); Shani King, The Family Law Canon in a (Post?) Racial Era, 72 Ohio St. L.J. 575 (2011); Janet L. Wallace & Lisa R. Pruitt, Judging Parents, Judging Place: Poverty, Rurality, and Termination of Parental Rights, 77 Mo. L. Rev. 95 (2012).

[3] Compare, e.g., Sharon B. Hershkowitz, Due Process and the Termination of Parental Rights, 19 Fam. L.Q. 245, 292-295 (1985) (criticizing heightened standard for jeopardizing child welfare by guaranteeing greater protection of family autonomy), with In re KMO, 280 P.3d 1203, 1214 (Wyo. 2012) (noting the requirement of proof beyond a reasonable doubt for Native American parents under the Indian Child Welfare Act).

determination of unfitness, with a lower standard of proof governing the best-interests stage.[4] What implications does *Santosky* have for such matters?

3. *Establishing parentage compared.* Should the same standard govern termination of parental rights and the establishment of parentage? How does the risk of error cut in this context? In Rivera v. Minnich, 483 U.S. 574 (1987), Jean Marie Minnich, an unmarried woman, sought child support for her three-week-old son, alleging that Gregory Rivera was the father. Rivera argued that due process required clear and convincing evidence, relying on *Santosky*. Rejecting the higher standard, the Court held that due process requires only the preponderance of the evidence standard of proof in paternity proceedings. The Court distinguished the state's imposition of parent-child obligations from the termination of those obligations because of the latter's severe consequences (that is, the elimination of preexisting rights). Justice Brennan, dissenting, argued that paternity proceedings result in "the imposition of a lifelong relationship with significant financial, legal, and moral dimensions." Id. at 583. Is neutrality with respect to erroneous decisions more appropriate for establishing paternity than for terminating parental rights? Is it more problematic for the "wrong" father to be recognized or for no father at all to meet the test? For whom?

4. *Substantive implications.* Although *Santosky* resolves an issue of procedural due process, what implications does it have for constitutionally required substantive standards? In theory, TPR occurs in response to parental failure to correct the situation that required removal of the child, even after the state's reasonable efforts to assist the parent in remedying the problem. Would a law that based TPR exclusively on a showing of the child's best interest survive constitutional review? Why? What inferences do you draw from the majority's footnote 10? In an omitted passage, the dissent responds:

> By holding that due process requires proof by clear and convincing evidence the majority surely cannot mean that any state scheme passes constitutional muster so long as it applies that standard of proof. A state law permitting termination of parental rights upon a showing of neglect by clear and convincing evidence certainly would not be acceptable to the majority if it provided no procedures other than one 30-minute hearing. Similarly, the majority probably would balk at a state scheme that permitted termination of parental rights on a clear and convincing showing merely that such action would be in the best interests of the child.

455 U.S. at 772-773 (Rehnquist, J., dissenting). Does the Constitution permit "no-fault" terminations if they serve the child's interests? Suppose the parent has had trouble caring for the child because of limited cognitive abilities or mental illness.[5] Suppose the child has bonded with foster parents who want

---

[4] Compare In re B.H., 348 S.W.3d 770 (Mo. 2011), with KC v. State, 351 P.3d 236 (Wyo. 2015). See also Josh Gupta-Kagan, Filling the Due Process Donut Hole: Abuse and Neglect Cases Between Disposition and Permanency, 10 Conn. Pub. Int. L.J. 13, 14 (2010) (criticizing absence of safeguards "in the middle of abuse and neglect cases").

[5] See In re D.A., 862 N.E.2d 829 (Ohio 2007) (holding limited cognitive abilities are not alone sufficient); In re Adoption of S.L.D., 437 P.3d 205 (Okla. Civ. App. 2018) (holding involuntary commitment for mental illness interrupted the time period of no contact for determining whether the mother's consent was necessary for the adoption of her child).

to adopt.[6] Suppose parents are incarcerated.[7] If the child's current place-ment meets her needs, is TPR justified solely to allow adoption?[8] What weight should the court give to the bond between the (original) parent and the child in the best interests determination for TPR?[9] Is each birth parent entitled to an individual adjudication, or may adjudication for one suffice for TPR for both? Why?[10]

5. *ASFA.* In response to criticisms that children were too often languish-ing in foster care because of an overemphasis on parents' rights, Congress in 1997 enacted the Adoption and Safe Families Act (ASFA), Pub. L. No. 105-89, 111 Stat. 2115 (codified as amended in scattered sections of 42 U.S.C. and amended subsequently). See Chapter 2, section B2. Under current provisions, ASFA eliminates the usual requirement that the state undertake reasonable efforts to reunify the family in certain severe cases (i.e., torture, sexual abuse, parental murder of another child, or loss of parental rights to a sibling) (42 U.S.C. §671(a)(15)(D)). In addition, ASFA aims to facilitate adoption by reducing the amount of time that children spend in foster care. ASFA short-ens the period triggering permanency hearings to no later than 12 months after the child's entry into foster care and also requires states to seek termina-tion of parental rights for children who have been in foster care for 15 of the last 22 months (Id. §675(5)(C) & (E)). States need not file such petitions if (a) a relative cares for the child, (b) a state agency has documented a compelling reason that termination would not serve the best interests of the child, or (c) a state agency has failed to provide the family with reunification services.

Critics claim that these reforms undervalue minority families and encour-age transfer of African-American children to Caucasian families — serving the needs of adopters rather than children.[11] What constitutional issues do ASFA's time triggers (12 months and 15 of the last 22 months) raise?[12]

Under ASFA, the child welfare system (including foster care and TPR) pro-duces large numbers of children to be adopted, with data from 2018 showing 437,263 children in foster care, of whom 125,422 were awaiting adoption and 71,254 were awaiting adoption after TPR.[13]

6. *Parent's right to counsel.* Is *Santosky* consistent with Lassiter v. Dept. of Soc. Servs., 452 U.S. 18 (1981), discussed in *Santosky*? Which procedural protec-tion, a right to counsel or a heightened standard of proof, is more valuable to parents fighting TPR? Which offers better protection of children's interests?

[6] See, e.g., In re Nevaeh W., 120 A.3d 1177 (Conn. 2015).

[7] See, e.g., People ex rel. M.S., 845 N.W.2d 366 (S.D. 2014). See also In re M.D., 921 N.W.2d 229 (Iowa 2018) (holding that allowing imprisoned mother to participate in TPR hearing by phone violates due process).

[8] Compare Demetrius L. v. Joshlynn F., 365 P3d 353, 356 (Ariz. 2016) (stating that TPR to allow adoption serves child's best interests), with In re Welfare of Children of R.W., 678 N.W.2d 49, 54-55 (Minn. 2004) (finding error in TPR solely based on child's best interests).

[9] See, e.g., Joy B. v. State, 382 P.3d 1154, 1167 (Alaska 2016) (noting that "the existence of a bond between a parent and a child is not dispositive in the best-interests inquiry").

[10] See In re Sanders, 852 N.W.2d 524 (Mich. 2014); Josh Gupta-Kagan, In re Sanders and the Resurrection of Stanley v. Illinois, 5 Calif. L. Rev. Circuit 383 (2014).

[11] See Roberts, supra note [2], at 165-172; Cynthia Godsoe, Parsing Parenthood, 17 Lewis & Clark L. Rev. 113 (2013).

[12] In re H.G., 757 N.E.2d 864 (Ill. 2001) (finding violation of substantive due process).

[13] U.S. Dept. of Health & Human Servs., Admin. for Child. & Fam., The AFCARS Report No. 26: Preliminary FY2018 Estimates as of Aug. 22, 2019, Child. Bureau 1, 1, https://www.acf.hhs.gov/sites/default/files/cb/afcarsreport26.pdf.

Which imposes greater costs on the state? Despite the Supreme Court's holding in *Lassiter*, many states guarantee indigent parents the right to counsel in TPR proceedings.[14]

7. *Alternatives to termination*. Even if the state decides that parents are unfit to rear their children, must TPR follow? What lessons might come from the modern law of child custody after divorce, which emphasizes the importance of maintaining the child's ties to both parents?[15] Consider the following alternatives to TPR, all of which challenge the conventional view that parentage must be complete and exclusive.[16]

a. *Guardianship*. Traditionally, parents serve as a child's "natural guardians," but courts appoint a guardian for a minor (or incompetent person) when parental care is unavailable or inadequate to serve a particular need of the child. For example, absence for military service might prompt a parent to name a guardian. Most courts hold that, even after seeking guardianship, fit parents enjoy the constitutionally based presumption that they act in the child's best interest, including when petitioning to terminate the guardianship.[17]

Critics of the push for TPR in the name of permanency say such policies fail to appreciate the psychological understanding of permanency as a sense of belonging, which guardianship can often successfully achieve.[18] Guardianship has emerged as especially important in the context of kinship care because relatives frequently choose not to pursue adoption in order to maintain the official status of the child's "parent," regardless who is performing day-to-day parental functions. Under such arrangements, a parent might continue to reside with the child even while other relatives who share the home serve as the child's guardians.[19]

The HIV/AIDS epidemic prompted the development of a new type of guardianship, standby guardianship, enabling parents suffering from what was then seen as a terminal illness to plan for the future of their children before death or incapacitation. This approach responds to the particular needs of ill single mothers by allowing for a "backup" guardian without requiring the mother to relinquish parental rights.[20] Might this device prove useful for front-line workers in the age of COVID-19?

b. *Other alternatives*. Compare guardianship with other arrangements that permit the retention of ties with biological families, such as long-term

---

[14] E.g., J.B. v. Florida Department of Children & Families, 170 So. 3d 780 (Fla. 2015) (requiring effective assistance of counsel); In re Adoption of J.E.V., 141 A.3d 254 (N.J. 2016) (requiring appointed counsel for indigent parent in TPR proceedings).

[15] See, e.g., Sacha Coupet, Swimming Upstream Against the Great Adoption Tide: Making the Case for "Impermanence," 34 Cap. U. L. Rev. 405 (2005); Marsha Garrison, Parents' Rights v. Children's Interests: The Case of the Foster Child, 22 N.Y.U. Rev. L. & Soc. Change 371 (1996); Josh Gupta-Kagan, The New Permanency, 19 U.C. Davis J. Juv. L. & Pol'y 1 (2015).

[16] See Katharine T. Bartlett, Rethinking Parenthood as an Exclusive Status: The Need for Legal Alternatives When the Premise of the Nuclear Family Has Failed, 70 Va. L. Rev. 879 (1984).

[17] See, e.g., Morris v. Clark, 572 S.W.3d 366 (Ark. 2019). But see Adoption of Riahleigh M., 202 A.3d 1174 (Me. 2019) (upholding involuntary TPR in private adoption following guardianship).

[18] E.g., Cynthia Godsoe, Permanency Puzzle, 2013 Mich. St. L. Rev. 1113, 1114 (2013).

[19] In re Guardianship of Patrick D., 280 P.3d 909, 916-917 (N.M. 2012).

[20] E.g., Va. Code Ann. §§16.1-349 to -355. But see In re Richard P., 708 S.E.2d 479 (W. Va. 2010) (in the absence of standby statute, holding that a healthy parent cannot name friend as co-guardian).

foster care (Chapter 2, section B2) and open adoption with visitation (Chapter 5, section C2). What are the advantages of each? The disadvantages?

c. *Post-termination custody.* After TPR, suppose the child, who has not been adopted, continues to have behavioral problems and lacks a stable placement, while her mother completes her prison sentence and overcomes her substance abuse. May the mother now petition for custody? Why?[21]

PROBLEMS

1. Bobby B. is placed in foster care at age two because of his single mother's repeated drug use and her chronic liver disease. She will need a transplant for long-term survival, and her substance abuse has placed her near the bottom of those awaiting donor organs. Bobby's mother wants him to return home so that she can spend her remaining time with him. To achieve this goal, she completes parenting classes and a drug rehabilitation program, as ordered by the Juvenile Court. She has not yet found employment, as directed by the court, but is participating in a job-training program to achieve that goal. All of these efforts require more time than usual because of frequent interruptions caused by her health difficulties.

The governing statute requires "reasonable efforts" to reunite biological families. You are Bobby's court-appointed guardian ad litem. You have learned that, although Bobby had regular supervised visits with his mother, he has bonded with his foster mother and father whom he regards as his psychological parents. The foster parents seek to adopt Bobby, and the state Department of Family Welfare supports this outcome because of Bobby's mother's poor prognosis. In deciding how to handle Bobby's case, you must address the following questions posed by the judge: Should a child in a loving foster home be put through a wrenching separation when the parent seeking return is likely to die or become seriously ill? Alternatively, is time with a parent so important to a child's identity that it should override other considerations? What result and why?[22]

2. The Commissioner of Children and Families seeks to terminate Anthony M.'s and Jessica C.'s parental rights to their three minor children. The commissioner alleges that the parents, who had neglected the children, cannot benefit from the reunification efforts of the Department of Children and Families. The trial court appoints separate counsel for the respondent mother and father and their children, as required by state statute. During the three-day evidentiary hearing, the attorney representing the children supports the commissioner's position that TPR would serve the best interests of the children. At the end of the trial, the court acknowledges the mutual love between the parents and their children, but it finds that the commissioner had proven the allegations and, accordingly, it terminates the parents' rights.

---

[21] See LaShanda Taylor Adams, (Re-)Grasping the Opportunity Interest: Lehr v. Robertson and the Terminated Parent, 25 Kan. J.L. & Pub. Pol'y 31 (2015).

[22] See Felicia R. Lee, Difficult Custody Decisions Being Complicated by AIDS, N.Y. Times, Mar. 4, 1995, at 1, 16.

In their appeal, the parents fault the trial court for having failed to appoint, along with an attorney to represent the children's best interests, a guardian ad litem to advocate for their expressed wishes. In particular, they contend that children subject to a TPR petition have a constitutional right to effective assistance of counsel. They also argue that the trial court had an obligation, sua sponte, to ensure that there was no conflict between the children's legal interests and their best interests, given evidence in the record that the children's attorney was not advocating for the expressed wishes of the children. In response, the commissioner contends that the parents in TPR proceedings lack standing to assert the constitutional rights of their children and that the children themselves lack standing. The commissioner also contends that children have no constitutional right to representation by counsel in TPR proceedings or to a guardian ad litem. Assuming an adequate record, how should the court decide the parents' appeal? Why?[23]

B. PARENTAL SURRENDER

1. VALIDITY AND REVOCABILITY

Although American adoption statutes long have reflected a child-centered policy (see Chapter 1, section A), historians have observed that, following World War II, adoption practice shifted its focus to the needs of infertile couples, who faced stigma in an era of "compulsory parenthood."[24] Nevertheless, adoption's traditional child-welfare rhetoric remained strong because white unmarried mothers were regarded as deviant and unfit to parent — so their children needed to be "saved" from such dysfunctional families.[25] Thus, such birth mothers faced enormous pressure to surrender, both because of the perceived dangers that their deviance posed to their children and because of the valuable resources (babies) they could provide for married infertile couples. Further, according to the conventional wisdom, adoption also "saved" these birth mothers, who could forget about their sexual transgressions and reconstitute their lives as if nothing had happened — all under a shroud of secrecy, maintained through sealed records, in order to protect their own reputations and their families'. Birth mothers' own experiences, as reported in their own words later, cast doubt on the premises and effectiveness of this approach, as the excerpt from Ann Fessler's book, infra, shows.

The phenomenon distinctively targeted white mothers and infants. Unmarried African-American mothers typically reared their children, often

---

[23] See In re Christina M., 908 A.2d 1073 (Conn. 2006); In re K.C., 99 N.E.3d 1061 (Ohio Ct. App. 2017). See also Farthing v. McGee, 158 So. 3d 1223 (Miss. Ct. App. 2015) (applying Mississippi requirement for guardian ad litem in TPR proceedings); Matter of Dependency of E.H., 427 P.3d 587 (Wash. 2018) (rejecting constitutional right to counsel for child in dependency proceeding). See generally Barbara Atwood, Representing Children Who Can't or Won't Direct Counsel: Best Interests Lawyering or No Lawyer at All?, 53 Ariz. L. Rev. 381 (2011).

[24] See Elaine Tyler May, Barren in the Promised Land: Childless Americans and the Pursuit of Happiness 127-149 (1997).

[25] Rickie Solinger, Beggars and Choosers: How the Politics of Choice Shapes Adoption, Abortion, and Welfare in the United States 69-70 (2001).

in an extended family setting and sometimes with public funding. The race-specific nature of such practices stemmed from the relative absence of a "market" for babies of color, compared to white babies, and the assumption that African-American women as a class were deviant and beyond redemption.[26]

SCARPETTA V. SPENCE-CHAPIN ADOPTION SERVICE

269 N.E.2d 787 (N.Y. 1971)

JASEN, J.

This appeal involves the return of an out-of-wedlock infant to its natural mother after she had executed a purported surrender of the child to an authorized adoption agency....

The infant child was born on May 18, 1970, to Olga Scarpetta, who was unmarried and 32 years old. She had become pregnant in her native Colombia by a married Colombian in the summer of 1969. Seeking to minimize the shame of an out-of-wedlock child to herself and her family, Miss Scarpetta came to New York for the purpose of having her child. She was well acquainted with this country and its language. She had had her early schooling in New Jersey and her college education in California. Indeed, she had been trained in the social sciences.

Four days after the birth of the child, she placed the infant for boarding care with Spence-Chapin Adoption Service, an agency authorized by statute to receive children for adoption. Ten days later, a surrender document was executed by Miss Scarpetta to the agency, and on June 18, 1970, the baby was placed with a family for adoption. Five days later, on June 23, 1970, the mother repented her actions and requested that the child be returned to her.

After several unsuccessful attempts to regain her child from the agency, the mother commenced this habeas corpus proceeding. Before the surrender, the mother had had a number of interviews with representatives of the adoption agency. On the other hand, shortly before or after the birth of the child, her family in Colombia, well-to-do, and devout in their religion, were shocked that she should put out her child for adoption by strangers. They assured her of their support and backing and urged her to raise her own child. [The courts below ruled in favor of Scarpetta. This court affirms.]

The resolution of the issue of whether or not a mother, who has surrendered her child to an authorized adoption agency, may regain the child's custody, has received various treatment by the legislatures and courts in the United States. At one extreme, several jurisdictions adhere to the rule that the parent has an absolute right to regain custody of her child prior to the final adoption decree. On the other hand, some jurisdictions adhere to the rule that the parent's surrender is final, absent fraud or duress. The majority of the jurisdictions, however, place the parent's right to regain custody within the discretion of the court — the position which, of course, our Legislature has taken. The discretionary rule allows the court leeway to approve a revocation of the surrender when the facts of the individual case

---

[26] See id.

warrant it and avoids the obvious dangers posed by the rigidity of the extreme positions.

In New York, a surrender executed by a mother, in which she voluntarily consents to a change of guardianship and custody to an authorized agency for the purpose of adoption, is expressly sanctioned by law. (Social Services Law, §384.) The statute nowhere endows a surrender with irrevocability foreclosing a mother from applying to the court to restore custody of the child to her. In fact, the legislation is clear that, until there has been an actual adoption, or the agency has met the requirements of the Social Services Law [requiring agency or court approval of surrender following notice], the surrender remains under, and subject to, judicial supervision.

Inherent to judicial supervision of surrenders is the recognition that documents of surrender are unilateral, not contracts or deeds, and are almost always executed under circumstances which may cast doubt upon their voluntariness or on understanding of the consequences of their execution. . . . Of necessity, therefore, there is always an issue about the fact of surrender, document or no document. On the other hand, the courts have the strongest obligation not to permit surrenders to be undone except for the weightiest reasons. . . .

Having the power to direct a change of custody from the agency back to the natural parent, notwithstanding the document of surrender, the court should exercise it only when it determines "that the interest of such child will be promoted thereby and that such parent is fit, competent and able to duly maintain, support and educate such child." (Social Services Law, §383, subd. 1.) . . . It has repeatedly been determined, insofar as the best interests of the child are concerned, that "[the] mother or father has a right to the care and custody of a child, superior to that of all others, unless he or she has abandoned that right or is proved unfit to assume the duties and privileges of parenthood." [Citations omitted.]

The primacy of status thus accorded the natural parent is not materially altered or diminished by the mere fact of surrender under the statute, although it is a factor to be considered by the court. To hold, as the agency suggests — that a surrender to an authorized adoption agency constitutes, as a matter of law, an abandonment — would frustrate the policy underlying our legislation, which allows a mother to regain custody of her child, notwithstanding the surrender to the agency, provided, of course, that there is some showing of improvidence in the making of the surrender, that the interest of such child will be promoted and "that such parent is fit, competent and able to duly maintain, support and educate such child." . . .

In no case, however, may a contest between a parent and nonparent resolve itself into a simple factual issue as to which affords the better surroundings, or as to which party is better equipped to raise the child. It may well be that the prospective adoptive parents would afford a child some material advantages over and beyond what the natural mother may be able to furnish, but these advantages, passing and transient as they are, cannot outweigh a mother's tender care and love unless it is clearly established that she is unfit to assume the duties and privileges of parenthood.

We conclude that the record before us supports the finding by the courts below that the surrender was improvident and that the child's best interests — moral and temporal — will be best served by its return to the natural mother.

Within 23 days after the child had been given over to the agency, and only 5 days after the prospective adoptive parents had gained provisional custody of the child, the mother sought its return. If the matter had been resolved at that time, much heartache and distress would have been avoided....

[The court rejects the prospective adoptive parents' petition to intervene on the ground that intervention would necessarily lead to disclosure of the names of the natural parents and prospective adoptive parents to each other in violation of the policy of secrecy, which relies on the adoption agency to serve as intermediary.] Similarly, we find no merit to the contention that the failure to allow the prospective adoptive parents to intervene in the instant proceeding deprived them of due process of law so as to render the court's determination awarding custody of the child to the mother, constitutionally invalid. The prospective adoptive parents do not have legal custody of the baby. Spence-Chapin, the adoption agency, by virtue of the mother's surrender, was vested with legal custody. The agency, in turn, had placed the baby with the prospective adoptive parents pursuant to an arrangement reached between them, for the purpose of prospective adoption of the child. This arrangement is, of course, subject to our adoption statutes, and in no way conveys any vested rights in the child to the prospective adoptive parents....

ANN FESSLER, THE GIRLS WHO WENT AWAY: THE HIDDEN
HISTORY OF WOMEN WHO SURRENDERED CHILDREN FOR
ADOPTION IN THE DECADES BEFORE ROE V. WADE

207-210 (2006)

I guess once I got married I felt more normal but still, it's kind of like being in a black hole somewhere. It's as if part of you went away when that happened. A really big part of you went away and you pretend that it didn't. You don't know who you are anymore. It's like suddenly you got cut in half. So what you really end up being is half a person who pretends she's whole. Even though I got married twice, I had two kids, and I have a very successful business, nothing takes away that black hole. Because you're always lying, you're always pretending. You're not true to who you really are.

-Ann

Surrendering a child for adoption has been described by many of the women I interviewed as the event that defined their identity and therefore influenced every major decision they made thereafter. Since most of these women surrendered when they were between the ages of sixteen and twenty-three, the event shaped their entire adult lives. It affected the timing of, or ability to pursue, their educational goals, their choice of a career, their decision about having subsequent children, their parenting style, and their relationships with parents, friends, and partners.

Women who said they never entertained the idea of parenting at the time of their surrender often described the same lifelong grief as those who fought to bring their baby home. Their grief has been exacerbated, and in some cases become chronic, because they were not permitted to talk about or properly grieve their loss. Not only was the surrender of their child not recognized as a loss; the implication was they should be grateful that others had taken care of their problem.

> It was never to be mentioned, it was never to be grieved, it was just to be denied. Then little by little, I started picking up with life, but I think I was filled with rage. I have to say, it was the most altering event of my whole life — a defining moment, a defining time. I believe that the way that I led my life, let's say the first ten years after, was reckless, was without regard for myself, my health, well-being, anything, because I had no value. And it was probably without regard for other people as well, because it was difficult for me to respect other people, it was difficult for me to trust.
>
> I'm sure people looked at my life and thought I had everything all together. I have a lot of aunts and uncles and I can remember being called nice little Kathi and thinking, "If you only knew." I felt like I was a demon. It wasn't until I went into therapy that I ever reached the point of feeling I deserved to be valued; it was all about deserving. People do not have a clue what people's lives are like from appearances. Appearances are just the greatest illusion. I think if somebody feels they're all alone, that's one of the worst feelings.
>
> *-Kathi*

Studies that have examined the grief of relinquishing mothers have identified a sense of loss that is unique and often prolonged. In one such study, the grief was likened to the separation loss experienced by a parent whose child is missing, or by a person who is told their loved one is missing in action. Unlike the grief over the death of a child, which is permanent and for which there is an established grieving process, the loss of a child through adoption has no clear end and no social affirmation that grief is even an appropriate response.

> Afterward I was very introverted. I could not have a close friend because I felt like such a fraud. How could I consider myself a close friend without them knowing about this? And, of course, I wasn't supposed to tell anyone. I was a good girl and was going to do what I was told. It just makes you feel like a lesser person, because you've done this horrible thing, this unspeakable thing. I just kind of withdrew. It's like the person that you are was put on hold and you're somebody else, you're flawed.
>
> *-Connie III*

Anger, guilt, and depression are normal grief responses to a major loss. And though grief may never go away, it generally subsides with time. For relinquishing mothers, however, the grief may actually intensify over time. One study has shown that high levels of unresolved grief in women were found to correlate with the "lack of opportunity to express feelings about the loss, the lack of finality of the loss (the child continues to exist), the perception of coercion, and the resulting guilt and shame over the surrender."

> Before I went into that place [a home for unmarried expectant mothers] I was always very happy, liked everybody, would talk to everybody, was a class officer in high school, a cheerleader. I was *that* kind of a person. I came out of there a different person. It changed me. It really changed my personality. I got very sad. I was very withdrawn.
>
> I went back to school after that happened and everybody would say to me, "What's your problem? What's the matter with you? Did someone die in your

family?" Well, having a child, giving it up for adoption is like having a death in the family. The only difference is you can't publicly be sad; you gotta be sad by yourself. I think it hardened me. I was really nasty to people. I was mad at the world. I was mad at my parents, I was mad at everybody, even if they had nothing to do with it.

—Cathy II

The National Mental Health Association has issued a list of the best ways to cope with a major loss, like the death of a loved one. The list suggests that the grieving person should "seek out people who understand your feelings of loss; tell others how you feel; take care of your physical health and be aware of the danger of developing a dependence on medication or alcohol; make an effort to live in the present and not dwell on the past; try to take time to adjust to your loss by waiting to make major changes such as moving, remarrying, changing jobs or having another child; seek outside help when grief seems like it is too much to bear; and be patient because it can take months or years to absorb a major loss." Without proper guidance or counseling, most of the women I interviewed took action that was precisely the opposite of these recommendations, some of it on the advice of professionals.

I got married. I thought, "I better get myself off the streets. This is not going well." I was just living this lie, this lie, this lie. "Do you have children?" "No." It's like being Judas every time. You're denouncing who you are, who they are. You just feel terrible. I married this man under false pretenses. Did he ever know I had children? Absolutely not. I didn't tell him.

I had a wedding, the wedding that my sister wanted. Everything was a lie. I didn't want a wedding, but he was Italian and Catholic, and you had to have a wedding. Oh, God. Then he says, "We can have children." I looked at him, like, "Are you insane?" The last thing I ever wanted to be was pregnant. I said, "I'm too young to get pregnant." That's what I told him. I was twenty, twenty-one at the time. He was an airline pilot, I was a stewardess. I said, "Well, maybe in five years, I don't know." But the whole idea was so repellent to me. It was all mixed up with this grief and this guilt. No, I just couldn't.

So I'm married and everything is so perfect. We go on a Hawaiian honeymoon — everything is just so, so, nice. We lived on forty acres of land, we built this beautiful house, we had so much money. Every weekend we were going over to my parents' house and having steak dinners and barbecues. I remember one of these Sundays as we pulled into my parents' suburban neighborhood I just started hitting my head against the seat of the car. I was just going a little crazy. It was all the things I couldn't say. It was July. The birth month. So July was always horrible, horrible, horrible. Even if my mind didn't remember, my body remembered. This really lives in your body.

—Diane IV

NOTES AND QUESTIONS

1. *Epilogue.* After the court's decision in *Scarpetta*, the adoptive family (the DiMartinos) fled with "Baby Lenore" to Florida. Scarpetta filed a habeas corpus action there, claiming full faith and credit for the New York decision. The DiMartinos successfully argued that they should not be bound by litigation in which they were not permitted to participate. At the ensuing trial, the court focused on the child's best interests. Experts testified about her

development with the DiMartinos and the trauma separation would cause. The Florida court ruled the DiMartinos should retain custody.[27] The U.S. Supreme Court denied certiorari, DiMartino v. Scarpetta, 404 U.S. 805 (1971). For exploration of the problems that can arise when adoption cases involve more than one jurisdiction, see Chapter 6.

In response to the case, New York amended the statute. It now provides that in contested revocation cases parents who surrendered "have no right to the custody of the child superior to that of the adoptive parents" and custody "shall be awarded solely on the basis of the best interests of the child," with no presumption favoring any particular disposition. N.Y. Dom. Rel. Law §115-b(6)(d)(v).[28] Evaluate this approach.

2. *Agency placement.* The adoption process can begin, as *Scarpetta* illustrates, when the birth parent voluntarily surrenders the child to an agency, which takes legal custody and selects an adoptive family. After a residential period under the agency's supervision, a court issues an adoption decree. Under traditional practice, neither the birth parents nor the adopters learn the others' identities. Moreover, if the placement fails during the trial period, the child returns to the agency's care, not to the birth parent whose rights are terminated by the surrender. Advocates claim that only agency adoptions serve the birth parents' needs for counseling and support, the child's needs for placement with capable and prepared adopters, and the adopters' needs for a full range of services.[29] Agencies may be state-licensed private entities, like the Spence-Chapin Adoption Service in *Scarpetta,* or public social services departments, like those that manage children in foster care, as in *Santosky,* supra. In recent years, public agency adoptions have increased, while private agency adoptions have decreased.[30]

3. *The surrender experience.* According to *Scarpetta,* why did the birth mother surrender her child? Why did she change her mind? What does the excerpt from Ann Fessler's book add to your understanding of Scarpetta's experience? To your evaluation of the *Scarpetta* case and the legal treatment of surrender? Consider the thesis of historian Rickie Solinger, developed from communications with birth mothers:

> Based on what I've learned about the experiences of birthmothers in the United States, I want to suggest that the conventional understanding of adoption should be turned on its head. Almost everybody believes that on some level, birthmothers *make a choice to give their babies away.* . . . I argue that adoption is rarely about mothers' choices; it is, instead, about the abject choicelessness of some resourceless women.[31]

---

[27] Henry H. Foster, Jr., Adoption and Child Custody: Best Interests of the Child?, 22 Buff. L. Rev. 1, 8 (1972).

[28] See, e.g., Matter of Baby Girl XX, 99 N.Y.S.3d 485 (App. Div. 2019) (disallowing revocation because adoption would serve child's best interests).

[29] See L. Jean Emery, Agency Versus Independent Adoption: The Case for Agency Adoption, The Future of Children, Spring 1993, at 139, 140-142.

[30] Jo Jones & Paul Placek, Adoption by the Numbers: A Comprehensive Report of U.S. Adoption Statistics 7 (National Council for Adoption 2017), https://www.adoptioncouncil.org/files/large/249e5e967173624 [https://perma.cc/5XAZ-7DWK]. But see id. at iv (noting difficulty in determining whether private or public entity facilitated each adoption reported).

[31] Solinger, supra note [25], at 67.

Calling for additional studies, experts have noted that the surrender experience has a life-long impact.[32] How might the insights provided by the narratives in Fessler's book support the right to abortion?[33]

Today, most unmarried women rear their children.[34] What social constraints shape such choices? Should birth parents have a tort remedy against adoption agencies for "wrongful family separation" in cases of surrenders procured by fraud, duress, or undue influence?[35]

4. *Stolen babies.* Beyond the pressures described by Fessler and Solinger, the history of adoption includes stories of babies stolen at birth, given falsified birth certificates, and placed with new parents, typically for a significant price. The U.S. lore includes the practices of Georgia Tann and Gertrude Pitkanen Van Orden, both running large-scale baby-selling operations from the mid-1920s until about 1950.[36]

When the military junta controlled Argentina, 1976-1980, thousands of young Argentines were "disappeared" (imprisoned as subversives and eventually murdered), including pregnant women and new mothers, whose babies were given to junta loyalists to rear. Years later, persistent protests by the biological grandparents of the stolen children have resulted reunions for a fraction of them.[37]

5. *Revocation of consent.* Of the different approaches to revocation surveyed by *Scarpetta*, which is most sound? What should be the legal significance of Scarpetta's regret about her decision to surrender the baby?[38] What can states do to improve the consent process and minimize attempted revocations?[39]

a. *Time period.* One approach makes determinative the timing of consent or revocation. For example, Illinois law provides that consent may be signed no sooner than 72 hours after the child's birth and that actions to revoke consent, when permitted, must commence within 12 months. 750 Ill. Comp. Stat. Ann. 50/9; id. 50/11. In some jurisdictions, consent is effective immediately.[40] Another approach allows withdrawal of consent any time before

---

[32] See Priscilla K. Coleman & Debbie Garratt, From Birth Mothers to First Mothers: Toward Compassionate Understanding of the Life-Long Act of Adoption Placement, 31 Issues L. & Med. 139 (2016).

[33] See Sherry F. Colb, "Never Having Loved at All": An Overlooked Interest that Grounds the Abortion Right, 48 Conn. L. Rev. 933 (2016).

[34] See Jones & Placek, supra note [30], at 5-6 (noting that about one percent of unmarried mothers choose adoption for their infants).

[35] See Malinda L. Seymore: Adopting Civil Damages: Wrongful Family Separation in Adoption, 76 Wash. & Lee L. Rev. 895 (2019).

[36] See Barbara Bisantz Raymond, The Baby Thief: The Untold Story of Georgia Tann, the Baby Seller Who Corrupted Adoption (2008); Kirk Johnson, "Gertie's Babies," Sold at Birth, Use DNA to Unlock Secret Past, N.Y. Times, Apr. 5, 2015, at A1; Hannah Noll-Wilensky, Note, Black-Market Adoptions in Tennessee: A Call for Reparations, 30 Hastings Women's L.J. 287 (2019).

[37] See, e.g., Clyde Haberman, Children of Argentina's "Disappeared" Reclaim Past, With Help, N.Y. Times (Oct. 11, 2015), https://www.nytimes.com/2015/10/12/us/children-of-argentinas-disappeared-reclaim-past-with-help.html [https://perma.cc/VMS2-TS7J]; Matthew Wills, The Stolen Children of Argentina, JSTOR Daily, Aug. 22, 2018, https://daily.jstor.org/stolen-children-of-argentina.

[38] See Susan Frelich Appleton, Reproduction and Regret, 23 Yale J.L. & Feminism 255 (2011).

[39] See Elizabeth J. Samuels, Time to Decide? The Laws Governing Mothers' Consents to the Adoption of Their Newborn Infants, 72 Tenn. L. Rev. 509 (2005).

[40] See, e.g., McCann v. Doe, 660 S.E.2d 500, 506 (S.C. 2008).

the final decree of termination of parental rights or adoption.[41] Should pre-birth consents be binding?[42]

b. *Fraud or duress.* Many states allow revocation of consent procured by fraud or duress.[43] Should confusion, mistake, or change of heart suffice? What about "emotional stressors"?[44]

6. *Consent substitutes.* Can a state constitutionally grant an adoption *without* valid parental consent? Involuntary termination of parental rights comporting with all procedural and substantive requirements dispenses with the need for parental consent. See *Santosky,* supra. Can a state replace consent or the usual grounds for TPR with a showing that adoption serves the child's best interests?[45] Failure to communicate with or to support a child out of custody for a statutory period of time, sometimes termed abandonment, typically suffices.[46] Suppose the reason for the failure to communicate is the mother's effort to overcome drug addiction.[47] Can a court find abandonment despite frequent contacts and visits by the parent if it deems the relationship to be "merely superficial or tenuous"?[48] Can the commission of three felonies before the child's birth suffice?[49]

If the state can dispense with parental consent, can it do so in a way that treats birth fathers and mothers differently? The next section explores this question.

PROBLEM

Encarnación, approximately six months pregnant, comes to the United States from Guatemala. She initially lives with roommates in southwest Missouri. Although she has no prenatal care, she receives services through home visits from a parent-educator representing Parents as Teachers, including advice about nutrition and preparation for the baby's arrival. Such services continue after her son, Carlos, is born and she moves with him to the nearby home of her brother, his wife, and their three children. Reports from the visiting educator indicate that the living conditions in both residences are crowded and "poor" and that Carlos is underweight, has not had all his immunizations, and exhibits some developmental delays.

Encarnación, who speaks little English, finds work in a local poultry processing plant, which the Department of Homeland Security raids because of

[41] See, e.g., 25 U.S.C. §1913(c) (Indian Child Welfare Act).

[42] Compare, e.g., K.L.R. v. K.G.S., 264 So.3d 65 (Ala. Civ. App. 2018) (finding no violation of due process in prebirth consent without counsel), with In re Adoption of N.J.G., 891 N.E.2d 60 (Ind. Ct. App. 2008) (holding prebirth consent invalid).

[43] E.g., Va. Code Ann. §63.2-1234(2); Ex Parte Carter, 813 S.E.2d 686 (S.C 2018).

[44] Compare In re S.K.L.H., 204 P.3d 320, 327 (Alaska 2009) (holding confusion, mistake, and change of heart do not suffice), with *McCann,* 660 S.E.2d at 508 (holding "emotional stressors" support revocation of consent).

[45] See, e.g., Mass. Gen. Laws Ann. ch. 210, §3(a)(ii) & (c) (so permitting).

[46] See, e.g., Ga. Code Ann. §19.8.10; Wyo. Stat. Ann. §1-22-110.

[47] Compare E.B.F. v. D.F., 93 N.E.3d 759 (Ind. 2018), with In re L.C.C., 114 N.E.3d 448 (Ohio Ct. App. 2018).

[48] See S.S.S. v. C.V.S., 529 S.W.3d 811, 817 (Mo. 2017).

[49] See In re N.G., 115 N.E.3d 102 (Ill. 2018).

the employment of undocumented immigrants, including Encarnación, who is arrested and jailed. Carlos is seven months old at the time. Relatives make various caregiving arrangements for Carlos, and one clergy couple who help with babysitting know of a local family seeking a child to adopt, Melinda and Seth Moser. Encarnación finds these developments surprising when the Parents as Teachers educator informs her during a visit to the jail because Encarnación has assumed her relatives are caring for Carlos, as they had agreed to do. She makes clear she will not consent to Carlos's adoption. The Mosers, licensed foster parents, begin visiting with Carlos, including having him stay at their home overnight. Eventually, he is living with them full time. They file a petition to adopt him just before he turns a year old. In the meantime, Encarnación, charged with identity theft, pleads guilty. She is sentenced to two years of incarceration, to be served at a federal penitentiary in West Virginia, to be followed by deportation.

During Encarnación's incarceration, adoption proceedings continue. At first Encarnación receives no notice, but later the Mosers agree to pay for an attorney who can speak Spanish to represent her. Carlos, whom the Mosers call Jamison, is two years old when the court terminates Encarnación's parental rights, based on abandonment, which it finds from her incarceration and her failure to contact the child or those caring for him; it also grants the Mosers' adoption petition, based the child's best interests. In particular, the court notes that he has bonded with the Mosers and that he has overcome the malnourishment and developmental delays he exhibited before his mother's arrest.

Encarnación now appeals. She contends that incarceration alone cannot constitute abandonment, that she made clear she would not consent to adoption, and that her limited English skills and lack of notice prevented her from taking a more active role in the proceedings. She raises several due process arguments, including her representation by an attorney hired by the Mosers and the court's combining the TPR and adoption proceedings, which in turn allowed it to rely improperly on best interest factors — such as her immigration status and resulting criminal record — in terminating her parental rights. What should the court of appeals decide? Why?[50]

2. UNMARRIED BIRTH FATHERS' RIGHTS IN NEWBORN ADOPTIONS

The Supreme Court has recognized constitutional protections for the interests of some unmarried fathers who have developed a relationship with their children. Compare Stanley v. Illinois with Michael H. v. Gerald D., Chapter 1, section B. What does this doctrine mean for the interests of an unmarried father when a newborn's mother decides to surrender the child for adoption?

---

[50] See In re Adoption of C.M.B.R., 332 S.W.3d 793 (Mo. 2011), abrogated on other grounds, *S.S.S.,* 529 S.W.3d 811; In re Adoption of C.M., 414 S.W.3d 622 (Mo. 2013) (on remand), cert. denied, 573 U.S. 955 (2014); Kelly McGee, What's So Exceptional About Immigration and Family Law Exceptionalism? An Analysis of Canonical Family and Immigration Law as Reflective of American Nationalism, 20 Geo. J. Gender & L. 699 (2019). See also C.J. v. M.S., 572 S.W.3d 492, 497 (Ky. Ct. App. 2019); Adoption of Yadira, 68 N.E.3d 1175 (Mass. 2017).

ADOPTION OF KELSEY S.

---

823 P.2d 1216 (Cal. 1992)

BAXTER, J.

The primary question in this case is whether the father of a child born out of wedlock may properly be denied the right to withhold his consent to his child's adoption by third parties despite his diligent and legal attempts to obtain custody of his child and to rear it himself, and absent any showing of the father's unfitness as a parent. . . .

Kari S. gave birth to Kelsey, a boy, on May 18, 1988. The child's undisputed natural father is petitioner Rickie M. He and Kari S. were not married to one another. At that time, he was married to another woman but was separated from her and apparently was in divorce proceedings. He was aware that Kari planned to place their child for adoption, and he objected to her decision because he wanted to rear the child.

Two days after the child's birth, petitioner filed an action in superior court under Civil Code section 7006 to establish his parental relationship with the child and to obtain custody of the child. [The court awarded petitioner temporary custody, stayed all adoption proceedings, and prohibited contact with the prospective adopters.] On May 24, 1988, Steven and Suzanne A., the prospective adoptive parents, filed an adoption petition under Civil Code section 226[, alleging] that only the mother's consent to the adoption was required because there was no presumed father under section 7004, subdivision (a). [The court modified its order and awarded the birth mother temporary custody.] The court ordered the mother to live with the child in a shelter for unwed mothers. [T]he trial court prohibited visitation by either the prospective adoptive parents or petitioner. [The prospective adopters then petitioned under §7017 to terminate petitioner's parental rights.] The superior court consolidated that proceeding with the adoption proceeding. The court allowed petitioner to have supervised visitation with the child at the women's shelter where the child was living with his mother. The court also allowed the prospective adoptive parents to have unsupervised visitation at the shelter.

[Despite a stipulation of petitioner's biological paternity, the court below held that he was not a "presumed father" under the controlling statute. After four days of hearings, including arguments by the child's attorney that petitioner should retain parental rights, the court held that the child's best interests required termination of his parental rights, by a bare preponderance of the evidence.] Petitioner appealed. He contended the superior court erred by: (1) concluding that he was not the child's presumed father; (2) not granting him a parental placement preference; and (3) applying a preponderance-of-the-evidence standard of proof. The Court of Appeal rejected each of his contentions. . . .

Section 7004 states, "A man is presumed to be the natural father of a child . . ." if the man meets any of several conditions set forth in the statute. Whether a biological father is a "presumed father" under section 7004 is critical to his parental rights. If the mother of a child . . . consents to the child's adoption, [t]he child's best interest is the sole criterion where there is no presumed father. As in the present case, the trial court's determination is frequently that the child's interests are better served by a third party adoption than by granting custody to the unwed natural father. [The relevant statutes are now Cal. Fam. Code §§7611, 7611.5, & 7612 (2008).]

Mothers and *presumed* fathers have far greater rights. [A] mother or a presumed father must consent to an adoption absent a showing by clear and convincing evidence of that parent's unfitness....

A man becomes a "presumed father" under section 7004, subdivision (a) (4) if *"[h]e receives the child into his home* and openly holds out the child as his natural child." (Italics added.) It is undisputed in this case that petitioner openly held out the child as being his own. Petitioner, however, did not physically receive the child into his home. He was prevented from doing so by the mother, by court order, and allegedly also by the prospective adoptive parents....

There remains ... the question of whether a natural father's federal constitutional rights are violated if his child's mother is allowed to unilaterally preclude him from obtaining the same legal right as a presumed father to withhold his consent to his child's adoption by third parties. [This question] has not been addressed by the United States Supreme Court. We are guided, however, by a series of high court decisions dealing with the rights of unwed fathers. [The court then analyzed three Supreme Court precedents: Stanley v. Illinois, 405 U.S. 645 (1972); Quilloin v. Walcott, 434 U.S. 246 (1978); and Caban v. Mohammed, 441 U.S. 380 (1979). These cases are noted in Chapter 1, section B.]

The high court again considered the rights of biological fathers only four years later in Lehr v. Robertson (1983) 463 U.S. 248. The father and mother lived together before the child's birth, and he visited the child in the hospital when the child was born. He did not, however, live with either the mother or child after its birth, and he did not provide them with any financial support. Nor did he offer to marry the mother. Eight months after the child's birth, the mother married another man. When the child was two years old, the mother and her new husband began adoption proceedings. One month later, the biological father filed an action seeking a determination of his paternity, an order of support, and visitation with the child. Shortly thereafter, the biological father learned of the pending adoption proceeding, and almost immediately he sought to have it stayed pending the determination of his paternity petition. The state court informed him that it had already signed the adoption order earlier that day, and then dismissed his paternity action.... The *Lehr* court held that, "because appellant, like the father in *Quilloin*, has never established a substantial relationship with his daughter ... the New York statutes at issue in this case did not operate to deny appellant equal protection [in treating him differently from other fathers]."

[*Lehr*] did not purport to decide the legal question in the present case, that is, whether the mother may constitutionally prevent the father from establishing the relationship that gives rise to his right to equal protection. The *Lehr* court, however, recognized the uniqueness of the biological connection between parent and child. "The significance of the biological connection is that it offers the natural father an opportunity that no other male possesses to develop a relationship with his offspring. If he grasps that opportunity and accepts some measure of responsibility for the child's future, he may enjoy the blessings of the parent-child relationship and make uniquely valuable contributions to the child's development." (Id., at p. 262.) *Lehr* can fairly be read to mean that a father need only make a reasonable and meaningful attempt to establish a relationship, not that he must be successful against all obstacles. [The court then considered Michael H. v. Gerald D., 491 U.S. 110 (1989), reprinted Chapter 1, section B.]

[O]ne unifying and transcendent theme emerges. The biological connection between father and child is unique and worthy of constitutional protection if the father grasps the opportunity to develop that biological connection into a full and enduring relationship. . . .

Petitioner asserts a violation of equal protection and due process under the federal Constitution; more specifically, that he should not be treated differently from his child's mother. . . . Respondents do not adequately explain how an unwed mother's control over a biological father's rights [substantially furthers the state's important] interest in the well-being of the child. The linchpin of their position, however, is clear although largely implicit: Allowing the biological father to have the same rights as the mother would make adoptions more difficult because the consent of both parents is more difficult to obtain than the consent of the mother alone. This reasoning is flawed in several respects.

A. Respondents' view too narrowly assumes that the proper governmental objective is adoption. [T]he constitutionally valid objective is the protection of the child's well-being. . . . If the possible benefit of adoption were by itself sufficient to justify terminating a parent's rights, the state could terminate an unwed *mother's* parental rights based on nothing more than a showing that her child's best interest would be served by adoption. . . .

B. Nor is there evidence before us that the statutory provisions allowing the mother to determine the father's rights are, in general, substantially related to protecting the child's best interest. [Respondent] assumes an unwed mother's decision to permit an immediate adoption of her newborn is always preferable to custody by the natural father, even when he is a demonstrably fit parent. . . .

C. The lack of any substantial relationship between the state's interest in protecting a child and allowing the mother sole control over its destiny is best demonstrated by the results that can arise when a mother prevents the father from obtaining presumed status under section 7004, subdivision (a). . . . Under the statute, the father has basically two ways in which to achieve that status: he can either marry the mother, or he can receive the child into his home and hold it out as his natural child. Of course, the first alternative is entirely within the mother's control. . . . The system also leads to irrational distinctions between fathers. Based solely on the mother's wishes, a model father can be denied presumed father status, whereas a father of dubious ability and intent can achieve such status by the fortuitous circumstance of the mother allowing him to come into her home, even if only briefly — perhaps a single day. . . .

D. We must not lose sight of the way in which the present case and others like it come before the courts. A mother's decision to place her newborn child for adoption may be excruciating and altogether altruistic. Doing so may reflect the extreme of selflessness and maternal love. As a legal matter, however, the mother seeks to sever all ties with her child. [Yet even if] the mother somehow has a greater connection than the father with their child and thus should have greater rights in the child, the same result need not obtain when she seeks to relinquish custody and to sever her legal ties with the child and the father seeks to assume his legal burdens....

E. In summary, we hold that section 7004, subdivision (a) and the related statutory scheme [are unconstitutional]. If an unwed father promptly comes forward and demonstrates a full commitment to his parental responsibilities — emotional, financial, and otherwise — his federal constitutional right to due process prohibits the termination of his parental relationship absent a showing of his unfitness as a parent. Absent such a showing, the child's well-being is presumptively best served by continuation of the father's parental relationship. Similarly, when the father has come forward to grasp his parental responsibilities, his parental rights are entitled to equal protection as those of the mother.

A court should consider all factors relevant to that determination. The father's conduct both before and after the child's birth must be considered. Once he knows or reasonably should know of the pregnancy, he must promptly attempt to assume his parental responsibilities as fully as the mother will allow and his circumstances permit. In particular, the father must demonstrate "a willingness himself to assume full custody of the child — not merely to block adoption by others." [In Matter of Raquel Marie, 559 N.E.2d 418, 428 (N.Y. 1990).] A court should also consider the father's public acknowledgement of paternity, payment of pregnancy and birth expenses commensurate with his ability to do so, and prompt legal action to seek custody of the child....

[I]f (but only if) the trial court finds petitioner demonstrated the necessary commitment to his parental responsibilities, there will arise the further question of whether he can be deprived of the right to withhold his consent to the adoption.... For purposes of remand, ... any finding of petitioner's unfitness must be supported by clear and convincing evidence. Absent such evidence, he shall be permitted to withhold his consent to the adoption.

[If] the trial court concludes that petitioner has a right to withhold consent, that decision will bear only on the question of whether the adoption will proceed. Even if petitioner has a right to withhold his consent (and chooses to prevent the adoption), there will remain the question of the child's custody. That question is not before us, and we express no view on it....

NOTES AND QUESTIONS

1. *Independent placement.* The independent adoption in *Kelsey S.* contrasts with the agency placement in *Scarpetta,* supra. Generally, in independent adoptions the birth parents select the adopters themselves, often with the assistance of an intermediary such as an attorney, and place the child directly with the adopters, pending the issuance of a final adoption decree.[51] A few states prohibit or strictly limit independent placements.[52] Critics claim

---

[51] For the extensive regulatory scheme for independent adoptions in California, the site of *Kelsey S.,* see Cal. Fam. Code Div. 13, Pt. 2, Ch. 3, §§8800 et seq.

[52] See, e.g., Del. Code Ann. tit. 13 §904.

independent adoptions primarily help adults seeking a child to adopt, at the expense of child welfare, while supporters assert: (a) birth parents prefer independent adoption because it allows them to select the adopters; (b) adopters avoid long waiting lists and play an active role in the process; and (c) children avoid the necessity of spending a transitional period in foster care.[53] Because adoptive parents often pay birth parents' expenses in independent placements, some call these "gray market" adoptions.[54]

2. *Thwarted fathers. Kelsey S.* considers the rights of a "thwarted father" to veto an infant's adoption planned by the birth mother. In deciding in favor of the father, the *Kelsey S.* court considers a series of Supreme Court precedents: Stanley v. Illinois, 405 U.S. 645 (1972); Quilloin v. Walcott, 434 U.S. 246 (1978); Caban v. Mohammed, 441 U.S. 380 (1979); Lehr v. Robertson, 463 U.S. 248 (1983); and Michael H. v. Gerald D., 491 U.S. 110 (1989) (all examined or noted Chapter 1, section B). Compare in particular the *Kelsey S.* court's portrayal of the facts in *Lehr* with the version presented by Justice White's dissent in *Lehr*. See Lehr v. Robertson, 463 U.S. 248, 268-269 (1983) (White, J., dissenting). Justice White describes how Lehr and the mother had cohabited, how he had visited her and the infant in the hospital upon birth, and how later he "never ceased his efforts to locate" them (even hiring a detective), despite the mother's concealment of their whereabouts. Lehr also offered financial support. What implications follow? If Justice White's recitation of the facts in *Lehr* is accurate, then the Supreme Court had already rejected the equal protection claims of a father who tried to maintain a relationship with his child but was thwarted by the mother's unilateral actions. Do the two cases warrant different approaches because *Lehr*, unlike *Kelsey S.*, concerned a stepparent adoption in which the birth mother would continue to rear the child? The Supreme Court had a subsequent opportunity to address the rights of biological fathers to block an adoption arranged by the mother in 2013 in Adoptive Couple v. Baby Girl, reprinted in Chapter 4, section A1a.

Are there constitutionally acceptable reasons for giving biological mothers greater authority than fathers to determine placement of a nonmarital infant?[55] How does recognizing rights for fathers in such cases amount to "genetic entitlement" that feminists should find troubling — or, alternatively, how does it advance feminist goals?[56] More generally, what is the appropriate balance of power between unmarried birth mothers and fathers, when they have different plans for the infant's future?

3. *Competing interpretations.* Writing before *Adoptive Couple* (noted supra), Professor David Meyer identifies two different ways to interpret the

---

[53] Compare Emery, supra note [29], at 139, 143, with Mark T. McDermott, Agency Versus Independent Adoption: The Case for Independent Adoption, The Future of Children, Spring 1993, at 146, 147.

[54] See, e.g., Melinda Lucas, Adoption: Distinguishing Between Gray Market and Black Market Activities, 34 Fam. L.Q. 553 (2000).

[55] See generally Mary L. Shanley, Unwed Fathers' Rights, Adoption, and Sex Equality: Gender-Neutrality and the Preservation of Patriarchy, 95 Colum. L. Rev. 60 (1995).

[56] Jennifer S. Hendricks, Fathers and Feminism: The Case Against Genetic Entitlement, 91 Tul. L. Rev. 473 (2017). But see Michael J. Higdon, Marginalized Fathers and Demonized Mothers: A Feminist Look at the Reproductive Freedom of Unmarried Men, 66 Ala. L. Rev. 507, 523-539 (2015).

Supreme Court precedents. Under the "child centered" view, only an actual parent-child relationship matters, not the efforts of a father whom the mother successfully thwarts. Under a second reading, "the Supreme Court is concerned not simply with the existence or non-existence of a meaningful father-child relationship, but ultimately also with the strength of the father's moral claim [, that is,] whether the claimant has acted in a way deserving of protection."[57] Which view do you discern in the Supreme Court cases, including the opinions in *Michael H.*, in Chapter 1, section B? In *Kelsey S.*?

Under the second reading, how does a father show he is deserving? Does setting aside money for the child suffice?[58] If a state requires the father to make reasonable efforts to communicate with or support the child, does his initiating a paternity action suffice?[59] Can the father's prebirth conduct toward the mother be determinative?[60] Should the mother have the duty to notify the father of the birth (or pregnancy), or is it his responsibility to determine whether their sexual activity resulted in conception?[61] Does the father's criminal conduct prevent a finding that he is deserving, for purposes of halting an adoption?[62] If the child is conceived as the result of a sexual assault, is the biological father's consent required? Do you agree with an omitted footnote in *Kelsey S.* (823 P.2d at 1237 n.14) stating that the constitutional protections do not apply in such circumstances?[63] See Chapter 2, section B1 (Problem 2).

4. *Maternal deception.* Suppose the mother purposely misidentifies the father when surrendering the child or falsely tells him that she had a miscarriage or abortion or does not plan to surrender the child. Courts have divided on the consequences of such deception for the father's efforts to block an adoption. For example, in In re Adoption of B.Y., 356 P.3d 1215 (Utah 2015), the Utah Supreme Court required strict adherence to statutory requirements for the father to preserve his right to overcome the mother's choice to have the child adopted, reasoning that he has only himself to blame if he believes her promises not to surrender the child. By contrast, in In re Adoption of Baby Girl P., 242 P.3d 1168 (Kan. 2010), the Kansas Supreme Court invoked

---

[57] David D. Meyer, Family Ties: Solving the Constitutional Dilemma of the Faultless Father, 41 Ariz. L. Rev. 753, 764 (1999).

[58] In re Adoption of C.H.M., 812 S.E.2d 804 (N.C. 2018) (no). See also In re Adoption of Anderson, 624 S.E.2d 626 (N.C. 2006) (holding unaccepted offer to provide support does not suffice).

[59] See In re Adoption of C.L., 427 P.3d 951 (Kan. 2018) (holding paternity action sufficient). See also Jeremiah J. v. Dakota D., 843 N.W.2d 820 (Neb. 2014) (holding failure to provide assistance alone is insufficient to eliminate father's consent if he otherwise made his interest clear).

[60] Compare In re Adoption of Baby E.A.W., 658 So. 2d 961 (Fla. 1995) (father's prebirth "abandonment" of mother suffices to free child for adoption), with Ex parte F.P., 857 So. 2d 125 (Ala. 2003) (limiting application of prebirth abandonment statute). See C.H.M., 812 S.E.2d at 808 (requiring "reasonable and consistent payments for the support of the biological mother or minor child before . . . the date the adoption petition is filed"); Mary M. Beck, Prenatal Abandonment: "Horton Hatches the Egg" in the Supreme Court and Thirty-Four States, 24 Mich. J. Gender & L. 53 (2017).

[61] See In re Adoption of S.D.W., 758 S.E.2d 374 (N.C. 2014) (placing responsibility on father).

[62] Compare In re Adoption of C.D.M., 39 P.3d 802 (Okla. 2001) (stalker-father could not invoke protective order, which prohibited contact with child, as excuse for abandonment), with In re Adoption of TLC, 46 P.3d 863 (Wyo. 2002) (rejecting reliance on father's incarceration to show willful failure to support).

[63] Cf. In re Kyle F., 5 Cal. Rptr. 3d 190 (Ct. App. 2003) (distinguishing statutory rape from forcible rape to allow father to demonstrate a basis to withhold consent to adoption). But see LeClair v. Reed ex rel. Reed, 939 A.2d 466 (Vt. 2007) (holding that conception by sexual assault does not preclude standing to establish parentage).

the preference for maintaining "the rights of natural parents" to hold that deception about the father's identity and a miscarriage together with the father's prompt action once he knew about the child require a transfer of custody to him, despite the trauma for the child who had been living with the adoptive family for two years. Id. at 1174.[64]

In two highly publicized cases of maternal deception (purposely misidentifying the father and lying that the child had died), the birth mothers subsequently used the absence of paternal consent to halt or undo the adoptions that they had unilaterally arranged.[65] As a result, in each case, the birth mother, who then married the birth father, was able to regain custody despite her earlier surrender. How would you decide such cases? Why?

Will recognition of the biological father's rights raise the "specter of newly named genetic fathers, upsetting adoptions, perhaps years later"?[66] Should (could) a state require a woman to identify the father correctly or to notify him of her pregnancy as a precondition to adoption?[67] What time limits should govern the right to challenge an adoption for defective parental consent? When a birth father claims that the birth mother practiced deception but the state imposes time limits on challenging adoptions, should the limitations period begin to run only once he has discovered the fraud?[68]

5. *The child's rights.* How should a court balance the rights of biological parents against the child's asserted liberty interest in remaining with "psychological parents"? Put differently, should a court allow the child's best interests in staying with an adoptive family, especially after several years there, trump a thwarted father's rights?[69]

If a court makes the child's best interests determinative, should it focus on short-term or long-term interests? What weight should a court accord to potential trauma from separation from the psychological family? According to psychological theory, disrupted early attachment jeopardizes the formation of later intimate relationships.[70] Do long-term interests favor return to the birth parents? Why?

6. *Statutory reforms.*

a. Expanded definitions. In the wake of high-profile challenges to adoptive placements by the thwarted fathers, several states expanded the grounds for terminating parental rights, broadening definitions of "abandonment"

---

[64] See also, e.g., In re Adoption of Baby Boy B., 394 S.W.3d 837 (Ark. 2012) (holding that father's consent was necessary because he did everything he could to establish a relationship, which mother thwarted.

[65] See In re B.G.C., 496 N.W.2d 239 (Iowa 1992) ("Baby Jessica" case, reprinted in Chapter 6, section A); In re Doe, 638 N.E.2d 181 (Ill. 1994); In re Kirchner, 649 N.E.2d 324 (Ill. 1995) ("Baby Richard" case), abrogated by In re R.L.S. 844 N.E.2d 22 (Ill. 2006) (interpreting guardianship statute).

[66] *B.G.C.,* 496 N.W.2d at 247 (Snell, J., dissenting).

[67] Cf. In re Baby Boy W., 988 P.2d 1270, 1274 (Okla. 1999).

[68] See McCallum v. Salazar, 636 S.E.2d 486 (Va. Ct. App. 2006) (holding discovery rule does not apply). See also In re Marquette S., 734 N.W.2d 81 (Wis. 2007) (holding that court must consider unmarried father's efforts after he discovers child's existence and before termination of his rights).

[69] The case law favors the father. See *Doe,* 638 N.E.2d 181; In re Adoption of Baby Girl P., 242 P.3d 1168 (Kan. 2010); *B.G.C.,* 496 N.W.2d 239.

[70] See Marcus T. Boccaccini & Eleanor Willemsen, Contested Adoption and the Liberty Interest of the Child, 10 St. Thomas L. Rev. 211, 219 (1998). Cf. Gregory A. Kelson, In the Best Interest of the Child: What Have We Learned from Baby Jessica and Baby Richard?, 33 J. Marshall L. Rev. 353, 362, 370-371 (2000) (reporting aftermath of cases).

and "unfitness." Most of these laws, however, have not been interpreted to allow "no-fault" terminations.[71]

b. *Registries.* Several states use "putative father registries," which eliminate the need for adoption notification or consent for a man who failed to take the initiative by registering.[72] The Supreme Court approved reliance on a registry system in *Lehr,* supra. Both the 2002 and 2017 versions of the UPA follow this approach to facilitate and expedite infant adoptions, while requiring notification for genetic fathers of children older than one year, regardless of registration, and exempting fathers of infants who initiate timely proceedings to establish paternity or have established a parent-child relationship. UPA Art. 4 cmt., §402 (2002) (requiring registration no later than 30 days after birth or commencement of paternity proceedings before termination of his parental rights). The UPA (2017) states that it makes no substantive changes to UPA (2002)'s registry provisions except that it replaces "gendered terms with gender-neutral ones where appropriate." UPA Art. 4 cmt. (2017). Where would it be appropriate? Why does Article 4 still bear the gendered title "Registry of Paternity" and refer to "a man who desires to be notified of a proceeding for adoption"? Id. §402. Note that registration does not establish parentage, but only triggers notification and an opportunity to oppose an adoption. Id. Art. 4 cmt. Consistent with this view, some courts have allowed putative fathers to file paternity actions even if they failed to register, but others construe the statutory requirements strictly.[73]

How far does the reliance on registries in the newer versions of the UPA go in solving the problem presented in *Kelsey S.* and the Supreme Court's "biology plus" cases cited in *Kelsey S.*? Note that the original UPA from 1973, the basis of the California statutes applicable in *Kelsey S.,* did not contain registry provisions — so the court had to turn to the paternity presumption based on receiving a child into one's home and holding the child out as one's own, actions that the birth mother thwarted. Given that the decision whether to register belongs to the putative father alone, do these new laws effectively prevent "thwarting"?

In some states, failure to register obviates notification even in cases of maternal deception, as when the mother falsely assures the man that he is not the father.[74] Because only a tiny fraction of men register and many lack knowledge of the requirement, do these laws simply create a means to bar most unmarried fathers from the adoption process? What information must the risk-averse man provide if he registers before he knows of a pregnancy? What problems do you see in this approach?[75]

---

[71] See Meyer, supra note [57], at 770-792.

[72] See id. at 756-757.

[73] Compare David C. v. Alexis S., 375 P.3d 945 (Ariz. 2016), and J.S.A. v. M.H., 863 N.E.2d 236 (Ill. 2007), with In re Adoption of J.S., 358 P.3d 1009 (Utah 2014).

[74] See Frank R. v. Mother Goose Adoptions, 402 P.3d 996 (Ariz. 2017).

[75] See Tamar Lewin, Unwed Fathers Fight for Babies Placed for Adoption by Mothers, N.Y. Times, Mar. 19, 2006, §1, at 1; Kevin Noble Maillard, A Father's Struggle to Stop His Daughter's Adoption, The Atlantic (July 7, 2015), https://www.theatlantic.com/politics/archive/2015/07/paternity-registry/396044/ [https://perma.cc/6H66-WZ4X]; Ivy Waisbord, Note, Amending State Putative Father Registries: Affording More Rights and Protections to America's Unwed Fathers, 44 Hofstra L. Rev. 565 (2015).

c. *Publication.* Another approach entails notifying unidentified fathers of adoption proceedings by posting or publication. Often, such notices exclude the mother's name to protect her privacy, thus compromising their ability to convey information to a putative father.[76] Would it violate the birth mother's constitutional rights to require, as Florida did, that preadoption publication must include the minor's birth name, each city in which conception might have occurred, and the name of the mother and any man she reasonably believes might be the father? Does the measure violate the right to privacy by interfering with both a woman's autonomy in choosing adoption and her interest in protecting intimate personal information from disclosure, without satisfying strict scrutiny?[77]

7. *Adoption versus custody. Kelsey S.* explicitly distinguishes adoption from custody, stating that — even if the biological father can block the adoption — custody remains a separate issue. Does the court suggest that the prospective adoptive parents might retain custody even without an adoption decree?[78] Yet if custody might remain with the adopters, why does the court say that to prevail in blocking an adoption a birth father must demonstrate a willingness to assume *full custody?*[79] Would a better "solution" be adoption with visitation rights for biological parents, in other words, "non-consensual open adoption"?[80] Recall the similar dilemmas posed by children who have spent years in foster care, Chapter 2, section B2.

The Utah Supreme Court, for one, has rejected the separate consideration of long-term custody in failed adoptions. In In re Adoption of P.N., 148 P.3d 927 (Utah 2006), the mother had contractually agreed to be inseminated, to bear a child for the biological father, and to surrender the child to his care. When the biological father landed in prison, the mother surrendered the child to a prospective adoptive couple but later changed her mind. The trial court decided that, despite the failed adoption, the prospective adopters should get custody based on a best-interests analysis. The supreme court reversed, holding that the statute on contested adoptions

> cannot be used to permanently cut off custody and visitation to parents who have not been found unfit and who have not consented to such placement. It cannot be used to give permanent custody of a child to legal strangers, which

---

[76] See, e.g., Jones v. S.C. Dept. of Soc. Servs., 534 S.E.2d 713 (S.C. Ct. App. 2000).

[77] G.P. v. State, 842 So. 2d 1059 (Fla. Dist. Ct. App. 2003) (holding statutory requirements violate the state constitutional right to privacy). See Alison S. Pally, Father by Newspaper Ad: The Impact of In re the Adoption of a Minor Child on the Definition of Fatherhood, 13 Colum. J. Gender & L. 169 (2004) (critiquing Florida's "biology only" test for fathers); Claire L. McKenna, Note, To Unknown Male: Notice of Plan for Adoption in the Florida 2001 Adoption Act, 79 Notre Dame L. Rev. 789 (2004) (analyzing Florida requirements under compelled speech doctrine). See generally Laurence C. Nolan, Preventing Fatherlessness Through Adoption While Protecting the Parental Rights of Unwed Fathers: How Effective Are Paternity Registries?, 4 Whittier J. Child & Fam. Advoc. 289, 319-320 (2005) (citing advantages of registries over publication).

[78] See also Adoption of Daniele G., 105 Cal. Rptr. 2d 341 (Ct. App. 2001) (applying *Kelsey S.* to award guardianship to would-be adopters because removal would be detrimental); People ex rel. A.J.C., 88 P.3d 599 (Colo. 2004) (ruling child's best interests determine custody after failed adoption). Cf. In re Baby Girl L., 51 P.3d 544 (Okla. 2002) (interpreting "best interests" to require showing of severe psychological harm to justify continued custody with would-be adopters).

[79] See Adoption of Baby Boy W., 181 Cal. Rptr. 3d 130 (Ct. App. 2014) (applying *Kelsey S.* and finding father met the requirements to block adoption arranged by mother).

[80] Meyer, supra note [57], 792-812, 833-845.

is what the [prospective adopters] became once the court dismissed their petition for adoption.

Id. at 930. This result follows, said the court, even "where a custody battle between two biological parents looms once the adoption fails." Id.[81] If the separate issue of custody does concern the birth mother versus the birth father, what role should the mother's decision to surrender the child play in the best interests analysis?

9. *Empirical evidence.* The evidence is scant:

> Birth mothers' emotions have historically been obscured by the primary focus on the practical and psychological needs of adoptive parents and adoptees; however birth fathers in contrast have been utterly ignored. Research is needed to examine all facets of the paternal experience (before, during, and after the decision to place for adoption).[82]

An early classic study reveals that surrender of a child for adoption long remains an emotional issue for birth fathers, with many reporting negative views of the surrender and obsessions with finding the child.[83] More recent analysis finds that birth fathers in closed adoptions continue to feel connected to their children and, increasingly, are searching to make contact with them.[84] Despite such data, other studies reveal negative community attitudes about birth fathers, associating them with failure to take responsibility.[85]

3. WHEN THE BIRTH PARENT IS A MINOR

What difference does the birth parent's age make for the validity of the surrender? For any attempt to revoke consent for adoption? May the actions of a minor birth parent's own parent control? Should special procedural protections apply in such cases? Consider the controversy in the following case.

In re Adoption of D.N.T.

843 So. 2d 690 (Miss. 2003) (en banc)

Carlson, Justice, for the Court. . . .

D.N.T. (Diane), born September 8, 1999, is the daughter of C.M.T. (Camille), born August 26, 1983. In January 1999, Camille, who was hardly unaccustomed

---

[81] See also Barnes v. Solomon, 158 P.3d 1097 (Utah 2007) (rejecting order for permanent physical custody to prospective adopters, with joint legal custody and visitation to birth father).

[82] Coleman & Garratt, supra note [32], at 159.

[83] See Eva Y. Deykin et al., Fathers of Adopted Children: A Study of the Impact of Child Surrender on Birthfathers, 58 Am. J. Orthopsychiatry 240, 244, 246-247 (1988).

[84] Gary Clapton, Against All Odds? Birth Fathers and Enduring Thoughts of the Child Lost to Adoption, 3 Genealogy, no. 2, 2019, at 13, https://doi.org/10.3390/genealogy3020013 [https://perma.cc/Z4U8-HZQ8]. See also Malinda L. Seymore, Grasping Fatherhood in Abortion and Adoption, 68 Hastings L.J. 817, 847-850 (2017).

[85] Older studies include: Charlene Miall & Karen March, Community Attitudes Toward Birth Fathers' Motives for Adoption Placement and Single Parenting, 54 Family Relations, Oct. 2005, at 535; Paul Sachdev, The Birth Father: A Neglected Element in the Adoption Equation, 72 Fam. Soc'y: J. Contemp. Hum. Servs. 131 (1991).

to living in various places for short periods of time,[3] became pregnant while living with D.W.P. (Dan) in Lufkin, Texas.[4] After Camille became pregnant, she moved back to Yuma, Arizona, to live with her mother, S.T. (Sally); however, Camille soon returned to Texas in an effort to make amends with Dan and to stay with her father, C.R.T. (Curt). Within a few days after her sixteenth birthday, Camille gave birth to Diane in Llano, Texas, where she had been living with her father for about five months prior to Diane's birth. When Diane was born, her father (Dan) was living in Llano. Camille and Diane remained in Texas with Camille's father, for about two and a half months after Diane's birth, at which time Camille and Diane returned to Yuma, Arizona, on approximately November 17, 1999, to resume living with Sally.

Camille had received prenatal care in both Arizona and Texas, and she had relied on her mother for support during the pregnancy and after the birth of the child. Diane's father (Dan) never supported Diane and rarely called to check on the child. Dan and Camille never married, and Dan never took legal action to be recognized as Diane's father.

By going to a store in Yuma, Arizona, and purchasing a packet, Sally, Diane's maternal grandmother, established a "do-it-yourself" guardianship in Arizona, whereby Sally became the "guardian" of Diane. This guardianship, was established so that Diane could benefit from Sally's insurance coverage. These "do-it-yourself papers" were filed by Sally and Camille with the Yuma County Clerk's Office in October 2000. This guardianship was established without consultation with an attorney. Camille testified that she took this action because "I wanted a responsible adult to have guardianship of Diane and my mother could put her (Diane) on her insurance if she was listed as a dependent." [W]e are able to conclude that a judge entered an order appointing Sally as Diane's guardian though no documentation appears in the record regarding the guardianship papers. This "guardianship" was still in effect when Camille and Diane came to Mississippi.

Camille and Diane left Arizona for Mississippi approximately one week before Christmas 2000, for the purpose of visiting Camille's father (Curt), who had by that time moved from Texas to Wesson, Mississippi. Camille stated that she wanted her father to "get to know his granddaughter." Camille testified that at the time she left Arizona, she planned to return Diane to Sally's home in Yuma, Arizona, in mid-January 2001, and that although she came to visit in Mississippi, she felt like she would "end up back in Arizona."

Camille stayed with her father for one week, but then she met C.A.H. and R.D.H. (Carol and Rick), on Christmas Day 2000, and Camille and Diane promptly moved in with Rick and Carol in Stonewall, Clarke County, Mississippi. Camille lived with Rick and Carol from Christmas 2000, through the time the adoption petition was filed in March 2001, and Camille relied on

---

3. The record reveals that Camille had a history of living for awhile with her mother in Arizona, then living with her father in whatever city or state he happened to be living at the time, as well as living with different men for short periods of time.

4. This was Camille's second pregnancy. Camille's mother (Sally) testified that Camille became sexually active at age 12, became pregnant at age 13, and had an abortion in Arizona.

Carol for support. In addition, Carol's mother and Camille's father (Curt) lived together.[6] ... Camille testified that she did not always stay with Rick and Carol at night, but that she was there during the day.[7] While Camille was away at night, Carol would keep Diane. At the time of the chancery court hearing, Diane had lived continuously with Rick and Carol for several months, and Rick and Carol had fully supported her.

Around January 10, 2001, Carol helped Camille write a letter to a judge in Arizona to terminate the guardianship Sally and Camille had established. Camille testified she took efforts to terminate the guardianship "so Carol could adopt Diane." On the other hand, Sally testified she never intended to relinquish any rights over Diane when Camille went to Mississippi. The Arizona guardianship over Diane was judicially terminated on or about February 14, 2001.

On March 8, 2001, Rick and Carol filed in the Chancery Court of Clarke County, Mississippi, a sworn Complaint for Adoption, also signed under oath by Camille; however, on March 23, 2001, Camille [decided she did not wish to relinquish Diane, so she] filed an Objection to Proceedings, requesting the chancery court to "set aside, cancel and hold for naught any documents [she] signed or executed in anticipation of the [adoption] matter." Notwithstanding the objection filed by Camille, the chancellor entered a temporary judgment of custody in favor of Rick and Carol on April 2, 2001. On April 6, 2001, Camille and Sally, through counsel, filed a Complaint to Revoke Consent and For Custody of Minor Child [challenging, inter alia, the court's jurisdiction and Camille's capacity to consent].

[The chancellor held that the case was a contested adoption and that a guardian ad litem must be appointed. After a hearing, the chancellor concluded, inter alia, that Camille was not the victim of undue influence or fraud and ruled in favor of Carol and Rick. Camille and Sally appealed.] [W]henever reviewing adoption proceedings, we must always remember that the best interests of the child are paramount. ...

Miss. Code Ann. §93-15-103(2) (Supp. 2002) states:

> (2) The rights of a parent with reference to a child, including parental rights to control or withhold consent to an adoption, and the right to receive notice of a hearing on a petition for adoption, *may be relinquished and the relationship of the parent and child terminated by the execution of a written voluntary release, signed by the parent, regardless of the age of the parent.*

(Emphasis added).

Camille originally joined in the adoption complaint, as evidenced by her signature on the document. [Invoking Mississippi authority for the principle that abandonment may result from a single decision of a parent at a particular point in time, the] chancellor found this act on the part of Camille

---

6. Additionally, Camille's father (Curt) and mother (Sally), though having lived separately for some nine years, were still married.

7. Camille admitted under oath that for the first two weeks after moving in with Rick and Carol, she was there "day and night," but then she began to only stay with Carol and Diane during the day, spending her nights with C.M. (Calvin), having sex and smoking marihuana, and returning to Rick and Carol's home each morning around 7:00 a.m., about the time that Diane was waking up.

constituted an abandonment by her of Diane and found that the appropriate
Mississippi court had jurisdiction . . . .

Miss. Code Ann. §93-17-7 states in pertinent part:

> No infant shall be adopted to any person if either parent, after having been
> summoned, shall appear and object thereto before the making of a decree
> for adoption, unless it shall be made to appear to the court from evidence
> touching such matters that the parent so objecting had abandoned or
> deserted such infant or is mentally, or morally, or otherwise unfit to rear and
> train it . . . .

[W]e must next determine whether the consent was voluntary and abandonment was both physical and legal. C.C.I. v. Natural Parents, 398 So. 2d 220
(Miss. 1981). "Absent a showing by the parent(s) establishing either fraud,
duress, or undue influence by clear and convincing evidence, surrenders executed in strict compliance with the safeguard provision of §93-17-9, supra
[applicable to relinquishments to adoption agencies], are irrevocable." Id. at
226. . . . In C.C.I., we also stated:

> Undue influence is one of several grounds demonstrating a lack of voluntary
> consent on the part of the parents. Several of the means which may constitute
> undue influence include over-persuasion, threat of economic detriment or
> promise of economic benefit, the invoking of extreme family hostility both
> to the child and mother, and undue moral persuasion. Because undue influ-
> ence is such a broad concept, cases must be resolved upon their particular
> facts. [The party asserting undue influence has the burden of establishing it
> by clear and convincing evidence.]

C.C.I., 398 So. 2d at 222-223.

Turning to the facts of this case, Carol testified that she helped Camille
word a letter to have Sally's guardianship in Arizona terminated, and the
guardianship was in fact terminated by an Arizona judge in February 2001.
Sally testified that she was not able to afford a lawyer to contest the termination of the guardianship. Carol also testified that the "ideas" in the letter to
the Arizona judge were both hers and Camille's. On the other hand, Camille
testified that she had no intention of putting Diane up for adoption until
Carol brought it up "jokingly"; that she never initiated any conversations
about adoption; that Carol also confided in her that she had considered
"cheating on Rick to get pregnant"; that the idea of writing the letter to terminate the guardianship was Carol's idea; that Carol actually wrote the letter; that Rick and Carol were providing food and shelter and spending
money for her and that she was not working at all; that when she told her
mother (Sally) of her second thoughts about the adoption on March 18 or
19, Sally immediately left Arizona to come for Camille in Mississippi; that
she was afraid to tell Rick and Carol of her change of heart until her mother
was close by; that as soon as she told Carol she wanted to withdraw her consent to the adoption, Carol began crying; and, that when Rick found out, he
told Camille to get the "f — out of his house" and that "no one was going to
take this baby from them — that he would hurt anyone that tried."

At the close of the case-in-chief as presented by Sally and Camille, Rick and Carol, through counsel, made an ore tenus motion to dismiss pursuant to Miss. R. Civ. P. 41(b), which was granted by the chancellor, but only after a detailed finding of fact which consumed approximately seven pages of the trial record. The chancellor found:

> [Camille] knew for a substantial amount of time prior to the time that the adoption papers were drawn up that the adoption was in the works. She knew when Rick and Carol went to the attorney's office; she knew that the adoption papers were being drawn up, and she went without Rick and Carol to the lawyer's office.
>
> She could have called her father or her mother at any time during the time that she remained with Rick and Carol. She was not under Rick and Carol's direct control at all times. She spent substantial periods of time with her boyfriend, Calvin, and could have called either parent at any time.
>
> She had a contemporary with her when she went to the lawyer's office to sign the papers and that contemporary told her she wouldn't sign adoption papers, she wouldn't give up her child, and yet Camille made the decision to go in to the lawyer's office and complete the process of signing the consent forms.
>
> At the time that she signed the consent forms she was in a relationship with her boyfriend who had asked her to marry [him] and even offered to raise the minor child as his own.

The chancellor's findings of fact are amply supported by the record. . . . The record clearly reveals that Camille signed the original complaint for adoption, though she later changed her mind and attempted to withdraw her consent. Under Miss. Code Ann. §93-15-103(2) . . . , the chancellor was eminently correct in finding that upon joining in the sworn complaint for adoption and requesting, inter alia, that Diane be permanently adopted to Rick and Carol, Camille had in effect relinquished her parental rights to Diane. The record likewise clearly supports the chancellor's finding that Camille (and Sally) failed to prove by clear and convincing evidence that Camille's consent to the adoption was procured by Rick and Carol's exercise of "undue influence or fraud." *C.C.I.*, 398 So. 2d at 222-23.

The record is replete with bad decisions Camille has made her entire life. She has proven herself immature beyond understanding, as evidenced adequately by her own testimony of leaving Diane with almost strangers (Rick and Carol) while she spent the nights at her new boyfriend's house having sex and smoking marihuana with him.

The brief of Camille and Sally lists a litany of things minors may not do including voting, entering into binding contracts, etc. Likewise, Camille and Sally discuss in their brief the Mississippi statutory requirement for consent by the parents or legal guardian of an unemancipated minor before that minor may have an abortion, as opposed to no such requirement of parental or guardian consent before an unmarried minor gives her child up for adoption. After all, argue Camille and Sally, both a consent to an abortion and a consent to an adoption result in the minor mother being forever deprived of her child. With this, the Court cannot argue. On the other hand, perhaps the learned chancellor in this case said it best when responding to the abortion vs. adoption argument propounded by Camille and Sally:

> [The attorney for Camille and Sally] asks the Court to compare allowing a minor to consent to an adoption with not allowing a minor to consent to an abortion. A minor who is contemplating an abortion has not yet become a parent and there is a clear distinction in the law between the way a minor child contemplating an abortion is treated and the way that a minor child contemplating an adoption is considered and it's the fact of that child's parenthood that makes that decision different.
>
> There comes a point when a child must become responsible for his or her decisions and our Legislature has set out that a child who has given birth has the capacity to consent to an adoption.

Our adoption statutes state specifically that age does not matter when it comes to voluntarily releasing the child for adoption . . . . Camille was competent to waive process and has, under our case law and statutes, effectively done so. Additionally her actions, under Mississippi law, constituted an abandonment of Diane, and the chancellor was eminently correct in so ruling.

[The court then decides that failure to join Sally as a party was not fatal to the adoption.] The statute makes no mention of a requirement that the guardian of a minor parent be joined. Camille and Sally assert that "No minor in Mississippi may sue or be sued in his or her own right." That is the case in nearly all civil settings, but we have express exceptions to this rule through our adoption statutes. . . .

Though the testimony of Camille and Sally suggests at least an inference of undue influence, the chancellor was there on the scene and not only heard the testimony of the witnesses, but also had the opportunity to observe their manner and demeanor and ultimately make findings of fact based on the record before the court. Accordingly, the chancellor did not manifestly err by finding Camille had failed to meet her burden of proof. As such, the chancellor did not err in granting the dismissal . . . .

CobB, Justice, Concurring:

I agree with the majority's application of existing law to all issues presented in this case, and I strongly support the very important and valid public policy of encouraging, facilitating, and promptly finalizing adoptions. However, I believe that this Court has moved too far away from protecting vulnerable minor parents in the adoption process. Thus I write separately to express this concern, with the hope that either by case law or by statute, some protection might be made available in certain circumstances.

Here, an unmarried 17-year-old mother was taken in by a childless couple who had expressed an interest in her 15 month old daughter from the moment the couple met her. By taking the mother and child into their home and effectively supporting them, the couple applies strong emotional pressure on the mother to let them adopt her daughter, promising, inter alia, that the mother will be allowed ample contact with the child afterwards. Without independent legal counsel, the young mother goes to the couple's lawyer and signs away her full legal rights to the child. Only three weeks later, the mother realizes the gravity of what she has done, regrets her decision, and asks for her child back. But she is virtually thrown out of the couple's house and denied any future contact with her child. Going to court, she finds that she has no recourse, and learns, too late, that the moment she signed the document consenting to the adoption was her last moment as her baby's legal parent, as established by prior decisions of this state.

In addition to the interests of the infant child D.N.T., there are also the interests of the other minor in this case, C.M.T., which should not be forgotten. I question the analysis of the trial court and the majority which concludes that the physical act of giving birth automatically bestows upon a minor mother, however young and vulnerable, the capacity to consent to an adoption without any advice or counsel from lawyer or layman, regarding the law and the consequences of signing a consent form. I am not at all convinced that the Legislature, when it enacted Miss. Code Ann. §93-15-103(2), contemplated this Court's pronouncement that the single act of signing a consent to adoption could forever remove the child from its parent without counsel, especially with regard to a minor mother.

I am mindful of the fact that it is not the place of this Court to rewrite the statutes. That should not end the issue, however, because this Court [under its equity powers] does have a constitutional *duty* to protect children — be they 15 months old or 17 years old — insofar as that is consistent with the law....

Where the minor parent's own parent or guardian is not involved with the adoption, the minimum safeguard for protecting the minor parent's rights is independent legal counsel. A guardian ad litem should be appointed by the court where the minor is unable to secure such counsel. The relatively insignificant delay and expense involved in appointing a guardian ad litem should not outweigh the importance of ensuring that the minor parent understands the irrevocable nature of the proceedings....

[T]here is no conflict between a minor parent's having the power to consent to an adoption and her being provided adequate legal advice as to the nature and consequences of her act.... It is time for this Court to seriously consider adopting the practice of our neighboring states. Alabama and Arkansas specifically provide for independent legal counsel for minor parents in adoption proceedings.... Many other states also have some requirement that the minor parent be provided counsel before entering into a momentous and irreversible surrender of her precious parental rights.

Further, in all equity, providing a guardian ad litem to a minor parent presents no impediment to legitimate adoptions (and even should make them all the more secure from challenge), whereas it offers literally the only chance under our rigorous statutory and case law to protect a minor parent from unjust and unfair pressures and misrepresentations.

Our case law has evolved, almost heartlessly, and it now says that once the paper is signed, the child is considered "abandoned," and any hope of reversing the proceeding is effectively lost, unless the minor can meet an extraordinarily high burden of proof to show undue influence.[17] This is true

---

17. It is disconcerting to contrast our case law on wills, where a confidential relationship creates the presumption of undue influence, with our case law on adoption. Had it been a question of C.M.T. bequeathing them something of monetary value, the adoptive parents surely would have been found to be in a confidential relationship with C.M.T., and she would have been entitled to the presumption. But since she was only giving them her child, the law says otherwise. This is contrary to logic, reason, and common sense.

no matter whether the change of heart occurs within a day or two, a week or two, or a year or two. How can this be considered equitable? It is crucial, in my opinion, that the court of equity should be completely satisfied that the minor parent has been advised as to what signing the document to consent to the adoption of her child really means. Adoptive parents and their legal counsel cannot be relied upon to protect the minor parent's interest. Only independent legal counsel, if necessary a guardian ad litem, can fulfill the court's duty to the minor parent.

In any event, these arguments come too late for C.M.T. Her daughter has been living with the adoptive parents for three years, thinking of them as her parents, and it is unlikely that her best interests would be served by disrupting her life further. However, this Court has the opportunity, from this day forward, to implement a simple and adequate safeguard to uphold the most sacred and fundamental of rights in the field of family law, a parent's right regarding her child. . . .

McRae, Presiding Justice (joined by Diaz, J.,), Dissenting:

I dissent . . . . The facts show that the adoptive parents all but held the mother's hand while she signed the papers. They used every manipulative tactic available to convince the mother, a seventeen-year-old child herself, that she should allow them to adopt her child. Their coercion and underhandedness are obvious; therefore the majority's abandonment argument is without merit since the totality of the circumstances does not evidence voluntary abandonment.

Second, the adopted child's father was not given adequate notice of the adoption proceeding. . . . I believe that under the circumstances of this case, the natural father was entitled to notice. Had the parties to the adoption been unaware of the natural father's name and location, the failure to serve him with notice of the proceedings may have been justified. . . . The record shows that the father has had very little contact with the adoptive child since her birth, but some contact is more than none. . . .

Third, the minor mother did not have capacity to execute the papers to relinquish her rights. It is well-established law in Mississippi that minors have limited contract rights and are not able to waive constitutionally protected rights even in civil litigation. In civil and criminal litigation, a minor's right to waive the protection of certain liberties and constitutional rights are so too limited. . . . Yet, here this Court allows a seventeen-year-old girl to consent to an adoption without the advice of counsel or her guardian; i.e. her mother. Furthermore, when the minor mother went to sign the adoption papers she was told she could not leave the lawyer's office with the papers to look them over and the attorney who prepared the papers was not available for questions regarding their content. Could it be any clearer that this girl was being taken advantage of and did not have had the mental capacity and knowledge to consent to the adoption? . . .

. . . After reviewing the facts of this action, it is apparent that the adoptive parents exerted undue influence over the mother. The majority omits many facts regarding this action. In December 2000, the mother brought the child with her to Mississippi to visit her father and his live-in girlfriend who is the mother of the adopting mother. During their visit, the adopting parents began showing a great deal of affection toward both the mother and child. They suggested that the girls move in with them for a while until they returned to Arizona. During the first week of her living with them, the adoptive parents began making comments about how they were unable to have children and were trying desperately to adopt. The adoptive mother often came to the mother crying about her inability to have a child or adopt. They treated the mother and child like daughters and often encouraged the mother to go out with friends. In fact they began giving the mother spending money for that very purpose. Less than one month after meeting them, the adoptive parents encouraged the mother to end the guardianship of the child by her maternal grandmother. They drafted the paperwork and paid for the proceedings to end guardianship. Then the adoptive parents took their final step only after three (3) months of knowing the mother and child. Through coercion and manipulation, they convinced the mother that she should sign papers allowing the child to be adopted by them. They even promised her that she had six months to change her mind and that if the adoption went through she would be able to spend as much time with the child as she liked. Their attorney drew up the paperwork and had the mother sign the documents without even explaining their significance or advising her to get counsel. Less than a week after the papers were signed the mother realized their significance. She went to the adoptive mother and told her that she did not want to give her child up for adoption. There could not be a more clear cut case of undue influence and coercion. The adoptive parents preyed on an innocent and uneducated teenager. They even had an inside track. The mother of the adoptive mother was the live-in girlfriend of the child's mother's father who undoubtedly played a role in convincing the child's mother that adoption was the right thing to do. . . .

Fourth, the majority fails to give appropriate consideration for the best interest of the child. Mississippi has consistently and repeatedly held that "the best interest of the child is a polestar consideration in the granting of any adoption." . . . Here, the child was one year and four months (16 months) old when she and her mother came to Mississippi to visit her grandfather. Children at this age are very attached to their parents. Their only security in life are those who have cared for them since birth. The child only knew the adoptive parents for three months before they filed their complaint for adoption. Only ten months after the child met the adoptive parents, the Chancery Court of Clarke County, Mississippi entered an order granting the adoption. There is no way the child could have known the adoptive parents well enough to be emotionally stable with her adoption and placement with them. The child had only two persons close to her: her mother and her maternal grandmother. It can not be in the best interest of this child to allow this adoption. Furthermore, the majority seems to emphasize on the mother's personal life as a reason why it would be in the best interest of the child to be adopted, but her personal decisions do not justify its findings. After all, this Court has always ruled that a parent's personal choices which are not in view of their child and that have no negative impact on their child rearing are not sufficient for a finding that it would not be in the child's best interest to be placed [or] remain with the parent. . . .

NOTES AND QUESTIONS

1. *Minors' surrenders.* Ordinarily, parents bear the responsibility of supporting minors, minors remain subject to parental control, and the contracts that minors enter are voidable. Emancipation, however, confers adult status on children for many legal purposes.[86] The criteria for emancipation vary from jurisdiction to jurisdiction. While marriage emancipates a minor, in some states pregnancy and parenthood also trigger emancipation; in others, they do not, if the minor has not become self-supporting.[87] Against this background, how should the law approach the surrender for adoption of a minor's child? Evaluate the Mississippi statute, applied in *D.N.T.*, which makes the birth parent's age irrelevant. How should the tendency of adolescents to make impulsive decisions influence the analysis when minors seek to revoke consent to adoption?[88] Must courts appoint a guardian ad litem for minor birth parents for the surrender to be valid? Or should court-appointed counsel be required?[89] Should courts require the consent of the minor birth parent's parents?[90] Can a minor birth parent who subsequently seeks to revoke consent be bound by her own parents' consent?

Should the same rules govern minor parents' consent to adoption regardless of gender? Evaluate the dissenting judge's assertion that the rights of Diane's father were not properly terminated.

2. *Minors' abortions. D.N.T.* contrasts the law governing minors' abortions. According to the U.S. Supreme Court's abortion jurisprudence, the Constitution permits greater state regulation of minors' abortion rights compared to those of adults. Why? In Bellotti v. Baird, 443 U.S. 622, 634 (1979), a plurality of the Supreme Court invoked the vulnerability of youth; their inability to make mature, informed decisions; and the need to foster the parental role in childrearing. While these reasons support parental-involvement requirements for minors' abortions, *Bellotti* went on to say that states with such laws must also provide an alternative to allow some minors to proceed without their parents, specifically when they are sufficiently mature to make their own abortion decisions or when terminating the pregnancy will serve their best interests. A number of states with abortion restrictions responded, creating procedures for a minor to appear before a judge in order to "bypass" the parental consent or notification otherwise required; the judge, in turn evaluates the minor's maturity and best interests.[91]

---

[86] See, e.g., State v. C.R., 797 P.2d 459 (Utah Ct. App. 1990); Cal. Fam. Code §7050.

[87] Compare LaBrecque v. Parsons, 910 N.E.2d 947 (Mass. App. Ct. 2009) (rejecting emancipation based on status as an unmarried mother), with Caldwell v. Caldwell, 823 So. 2d 1216, 1221 (Miss. Ct. App. 2002) (child's "adult decisions," such as becoming pregnant, help show emancipation).

[88] See K.F. v. B.B., 145 N.E.3d 813 (Ind. Ct. App. 2020).

[89] See In re Adoption of A.L.O., 132 P.3d 543 (Mont. 2006).

[90] Compare, e.g., Minn. Stat. §259.24(2) (requiring the consent of minor birth parent's parent or guardian and an opportunity for the minor to consult an attorney, member of the clergy, or medical professional), with Mo. Stat. §453.050(3) (validating waiver of consent even if parent is under age 18).

[91] See, e.g., Hodgson v. Minnesota, 497 U.S. 417 (1990); Lambert v. Wiklund, 520 U.S. 292 (1997).

Should the law require a similar assessment of maturity and best interests before a minor carries her pregnancy to term and gives birth?[92] Before a minor surrenders a baby for adoption, as in *D.N.T.*? Critics of parental involvement laws and bypass proceedings for abortions cite studies that have examined the decisionmaking processes of adolescents and adults and that find few, if any, differences in cognitive abilities, at least for those adolescents who are age 14 and older.[93] To what extent do these analyses of abortion laws have implications for the issue of minors' consent to adoption, as in *D.N.T.*?

Professor Maya Manian recommends increased access to professional advice for minors like Camille — for example, required consultation with legal counsel and/or a mental health counselor prior to surrender.[94] Evaluate this proposal. How would *D.N.T.* have played out if Camille had had access to such professional advice?

3. *Teen sexuality.* What value judgments and attitudes about Camille's sexuality appear in the majority opinion? What bearing do (should) Camille's sexuality have on the issue presented?

a. Information and education. What role should the state play in educating young persons (or even their parents) about sexuality and ways to communicate about it?[95]

Many of those depicted in Fessler's book, supra, gave birth as teenagers. They had little understanding of heterosexual activity and its consequences. One of those depicted in the book, "Nancy I," reminisces about the conversation she had with her mother just before "going away" to continue her pregnancy in secret, give birth, and surrender the child:

> The night before I was scheduled to leave, . . . I had the very first, possibly the only, honest conversation I'd ever had with [my mother]. I felt safe enough . . . to ask her this question: "How do they get rid of the mark when they take the baby out?" I'd seen people in bathing suits and I could never tell if they'd had children. She stood there, three feet from me, with a look of horror on her face and said, "My God, Nancy, that baby comes out the same way it went in." I said, "You have got to be kidding me." She said, "No."
>
> I mean, it's borderline child abuse not to share this kind of information. How can anyone think that we will just absorb it naturally, or that it's our responsibility as children to figure it out? It just mystifies me. I had no idea. I mean, we never had pets. I didn't live on a farm. We had a very puritanical, Beaver Cleaver lifestyle, and it just wasn't anything that was ever discussed.

---

[92] See Planned Parenthood of Cent. N.J. v. Farmer, 762 A.2d 620 (N.J. 2000); see also Nanette Dembitz, The Supreme Court and a Minor's Abortion Decision, 80 Colum. L. Rev. 1251, 1255-1256 (1980).

[93] See J. Shoshanna Ehrlich, Who Decides? The Abortion Rights of Teens 61-62, 93-95 (2006) (asserting few differences in cognitive abilities of adults and adolescents, in terms of decisionmaking processes). See also Richard J. Bonnie & Elizabeth S. Scott, The Teenage Brain: Adolescent Brain Research and the Law, 22 Current Directions in Psych. Science 158 (2013) (noting how maturity varies by context and emphasizing developmental view of teen risk taking and criminal activity). See generally Emily Buss, What the Law Should (and Should Not) Learn from Child Development Research, 38 Hofstra L. Rev. 13 (2009).

[94] Maya Manian, Minors, Parents, and Minor Parents, 81 Mo. L. Rev. 127, 198-204 (2016). See also Guttmacher Institute, Minors' Rights as Parents (May 1, 2020), https://www.guttmacher.org/state-policy/explore/minors-rights-parents (summarizing states' approaches).

[95] See Susan Frelich Appleton, Toward a "Culturally Cliterate" Family Law?, 23 Berkeley J. Gender L. & Just. 267, 313-315 (2008).

> I mean, as amazing as it sounds, I was sixteen and pregnant and I did not know how babies were born. It's pathetic, but it's true.[96]

Should we presume that Camille, in the principal case, had more knowledge because she had been pregnant before (see footnote 4)?

The federal government currently provides two different funding streams for sex education. One supports programs that meet the criteria for "sexual risk avoidance education," formerly known as "abstinence-only" sex education.[97] The other supports what Congress calls "personal responsibility education," which covers abstinence, contraception, and sexually transmitted infections.[98] Sex education has long been a flashpoint in the "culture wars," with more conservative voices urging that such learning should take place exclusively in the home or, if not, then it should promote abstinence until marriage. Critics of that approach point to the ineffectiveness of abstinence education in preventing pregnancy and STIs and the gender stereotypes and anti-LGBTQ bias typically embodied in such lessons; instead, they advocate comprehensive curricula that include medically accurate information about contraception and, increasingly, healthy relationships and sexual pleasure.[99]

b. *Sexual activity.* Forty percent of adolescents aged 15- to 19-years old in the United States have had penile-vaginal sex at least once; by age 15 only about 20 percent have so engaged, but by age 18, two thirds have done so.[100] Young persons aged 15-24 account for half the 20 million new cases of STIs reported each year in the U.S.[101] Adolescent brain development influences decisionmaking about sexual activity.[102]

Gender is salient. First, data have shown that the contemporary "hook up" culture on college campuses offers more advantages for young men than young women.[103] Second, the rise of the #MeToo movement and activism surrounding the application of Title IX of the Education Amendments Act

---

[96] Ann Fessler, The Girls Who Went Away: The Hidden History of Women Who Surrendered Children for Adoption in the Decades before Roe v. Wade 49 (2006).

[97] 42 U.S.C. §710.

[98] 42 U.S.C. §713.

[99] See, e.g., Judith Levine, Harmful to Minors: The Perils of Protecting Children from Sex (2002); Kristin Luker, When Sex Goes to School (2006); Leslie M. Kantor & Laura Lindberg, Pleasure and Sex Education: The Need for Broadening Both Content and Measurement, 110 Am. J. Pub. Health 145 (2020); Leah H. Keller & Laura D. Lindberg, Expanding the Scope of Sex Education and the Teen Pregnancy Prevention Program: A Work in Progress, Guttmacher Inst. (Feb. 2020), https://www.guttmacher.org/article/2020/02/expanding-scope-sex-education-and-teen-pregnancy-prevention-program-work-progress; Clifford Rosky, Anti-Gay Curriculum Laws, 117 Colum. L. Rev. 1461 (2017). For the expansive approach developed by the World Health Organization, which defines access to sexuality education as a basic human right and includes curricular objectives for different age groups beginning with 5-8 years, see United Nations Educational, Scientific and Cultural Organization (UNESCO), International Technical Guidance on Sexuality Education: An Evidence-Informed Approach 16, 34 (2018), https://unesdoc.unesco.org/ark:/48223/pf0000260770/PDF/260770eng.pdf.multi.

[100] Guttmacher Institute, Fact Sheet: Adolescent Sexual and Reproductive Health in the United States (Sept. 2019), https://www.guttmacher.org/fact-sheet/american-teens-sexual-and-reproductive-health [https://perma.cc/TFT4-QQYT].

[101] Id.

[102] See Ahna Ballonoff Suleiman et al., Becoming a Sexual Being: The "Elephant in the Room" of Adolescent Brain Development, 25 Dev. Cognitive Neuroscience, 209 (2017).

[103] Paula England et al., Hooking Up and Forming Romantic Relationships on Today's College Campuses, in The Gendered Society Reader 531 (Michael S. Kimmel & Amy Aronson eds., 3d ed. 2008).

of 1972, 20 U.S.C. §§1681 et seq., to sexual misconduct on campus have high-lighted the pivotal role of consent — while also raising questions why young persons, especially young women, engage in sexual activity they describe as unwelcome.[104]

c. *Pregnancy and birth rates.* Although the U.S. long had the highest rates of teen pregnancies and births among developed countries, recent years have witnessed steady declines, attributed to improved access to contraception.[105] With this decline, women aged 15-19 had a total of 194,377 births in 2017, for a birth rate of 18.8 per 1000 women in this group.[106] The numbers vary by race and ethnicity, with the birth rates for Hispanic and non-Hispanic Black teens twice as high than that for non-Hispanic white teens.[107] Despite the mainstream view of teen motherhood's devastating consequences (educational, economic, and psychological), some challenge this conventional wisdom for African-American teens, asserting that considerations of health, kinship support, and insurance networks make youthful childbearing rational, as a collective or cultural matter. This argument has gained new attention with increased publicity about the disproportionate maternal and infant mortality rates for African-Americans and the thesis that years of exposure to the stress of a racist society causes "weathering," which in turn produces poor pregnancy outcomes.[108]

d. *Abortion.* Data from 2013 show a declining rate for teen abortions. For that year, for every 1,000 women aged 15-19 there were 10.6 abortions, with the rate for African Americans almost four times that for Caucasians.[109]

4. *Independent placement redux.* While *Scarpetta*, supra, depicts an agency placement and *Kelsey S.*, supra, illustrates one form of independent placement, consider the variation of this process illustrated in *D.N.T.* In particular, consider the arrangement under which Diane and Camille resided with Carol and Rick for a period preceding the relinquishment. What are the advantages of this increasingly common practice? The risks?

5. *Abandonment.* Note how the *D.N.T.* court's treatment of Camille's initial consent as abandonment blurs the distinction between children who

[104] See, e.g., Jessica Bennett, When "Yes" is Easier than "No," N.Y. Times, Dec. 17, 2017, at SR 8; Deborah Tuerkheimer, Rape On and Off Campus, 65 Emory L.J. 1 (2015); Robin West, Consensual Sexual Dysphoria: A Challenge for Campus Life, 66 J. Legal Educ. 804 (2017).

[105] Laura D. Lindberg et al., Changing Patterns of Contraceptive Use and the Decline in Rates of Pregnancy and Birth Among U.S. Adolescents, 2007-2014, 63 J. Adolescent Health 251 (2018).

[106] Centers for Disease Control and Prevention (CDC), Reproductive Health: Teen Pregnancy (Mar. 1, 2019), https://www.cdc.gov/teenpregnancy/about/index.htm [https://perma.cc/WC69-24Q2].

[107] Id. See also Rachel H. Scott et al., Adolescent Sexual Activity, Contraceptive Use, and Pregnancy in Britain and the U.S.: A Multidecade Comparison, 66 J. Adolescent Health 582 (2020).

[108] Arline T. Geronimus, Teenage Childbearing and Social and Reproductive Disadvantage: The Evolution of Complex Questions and the Demise of Simple Answers, 40 Fam. Relations 463 (1991). Dr. Geronimus also developed the "weathering" theory, which has been featured in the publicity about the connections between race and infant and maternal mortality rates. See, e.g., Linda Villarosa, Why America's Black Mothers and Babies Are in a Life-or-Death Crisis, N.Y. Times Mag. (April 11, 2018), https://www.nytimes.com/2018/04/11/magazine/black-mothers-babies-death-maternal-mortality.html.

[109] Kathryn Kost, Pregnancies, Births and Abortions Among Adolescents and Young Women in the United States, 2013: National and State Trends by Age, Race and Ethnicity, Guttmacher Institute Report, (Sept. 2017), https://www.guttmacher.org/report/us-adolescent-pregnancy-trends-2013 [https://perma.cc/3PQY-DNAB].

have become available for adoption as the result of involuntary termination of parental rights, as in *Santosky,* supra, versus those available by parental surrender. This analysis also makes initial consent to adoption irrevocable.

6. *"Safe haven" laws.* In response to highly publicized cases of abandonment and infanticide by teen parents, several states have enacted statutes that provide anonymity and immunity from prosecution for parents who leave their babies at designated safe sites. Although the majority of states have enacted such laws, their effectiveness has been limited. An empirical study of neonaticidal mothers finds a mismatch between the stated purposes of such laws and their impact, concluding with several unanswered questions:

> [D]o either the mental health or legal system truly understand the neonaticide phenomenon? Both systems analyze neonaticide differently because both are informed by opposing operational values. The mental health system places high value on therapeutic treatments to enable people to achieve their human potential. The legal system places high value on human accountability to punish people for conduct that is illegal and harmful to others. While the mental health system seeks insight and behavioral awareness, the legal system seeks control. Is the mental health system, which places a premium on helping people without judging them, correct in its diagnosis that Neonaticidal Mothers are so threatened by an unwanted pregnancy that they are incapable of acknowledging its existence? Or, is the legal system, which places a premium on judging people without helping them, correct in its high conviction rates and low acceptance rates of neonaticide syndrome defenses? Do defense attorneys understand that neonaticide syndrome defenses are a direct route to conviction because the Mother is inevitably impeached by evidence that she knew of and concealed her pregnancy? Do politicians understand that Safe Haven laws may not be saving infants' lives if the women who need them don't know about them and the women who use them would not otherwise kill or abandon their infants? Do state governments understand that without tracking systems there is no way to know if the laws are reaching their intended population and that Safe Haven information can be publicized with little cost on social network sites, in churches in Hispanic parishes, high school locker rooms, college dorms, grocery stores, at bus stops, on local television and radio news programs? Are they all in denial, blinded by their own perspectives?[110]

Critics contend that safe haven laws, properly understood, constitute efforts to promote a "culture of life" and to eliminate legal abortion;[111] that they target mothers and ignore the rights and roles of fathers;[112] and that they fail to provide the social and economic support that pregnant teens and others need to avoid feeling so desperate.[113]

---

[110] Diane S. Kaplan, Who Are the Mothers Who Need Safe Haven Laws? An Empirical Investigation of Mothers Who Kill, Abandon, or Safely Surrender Their Newborns, 29 Wis. J.L. Gender & Soc'y 447, 510-511 (2014).

[111] See Carol Sanger, Infant Safe Haven Laws: Legislating in the Culture of Life, 106 Colum. L. Rev. 753 (2006).

[112] See Jeffrey A. Parness, Lost Paternity in the Culture of Motherhood: A Different View of Safe Haven Laws, 42 Val. U. L. Rev. 81 (2007). See also In re Miller, 912 N.W.2d 872 (Mich. Ct. App. 2018) (holding that mother's surrender at safe haven ends her husband's parental rights too).

[113] See Laury Oaks, Giving Up Baby: Safe Haven Laws, Motherhood, and Reproductive Justice (2015).

Nebraska's safe haven law received extensive publicity when its failure to limit application to infants prompted parents from several different states to leave older children, often teens, at hospitals and other designated safe sites, prompting legislative change. Observers discerned in the response to the original version of the law evidence of the inadequate services available for families with troubled children.[114]

Depictions in Popular Culture: Juno (2007)

This film, reviewed as a comedy, presents a lighthearted look at a teen's unplanned pregnancy. Wisecracking Juno tries out sexual intercourse once with her nerdy friend, Paulie; rejects abortion; confesses her pregnancy to her blue-collar and supportive father and stepmother; opts "to kick it out old school," choosing a "yuppie" childless couple to adopt her baby — while remaining in high school throughout these developments. Although the adoptive couple's own story turns out to be less ideal than Juno first imagines, she follows through on the planned surrender, remains close to Paulie, and never looks back.

Some observers detect in *Juno* and contemporaneous films (e.g., *Knocked Up* (2007) and *Waitress* (2007)) a positive attitude toward unplanned pregnancy, perhaps reflected in data showing a recent increase in the teen birth rate at that time.[115] Others see a "fairy tale" that ignores the lifelong effects of surrendering a child and minimizes the very different consequences of sexual activity for girls and boys.[116] Still others disagree whether *Juno* assumes a conservative stance in the "culture wars" or challenges the views of both warring factions.[117]

How do you interpret the film's portrayal of teen pregnancy and the decision to surrender a baby? A contrasting portrayal, centered on a teen who decides to terminate her pregnancy and the challenges she faces in doing so, appears in the film *Never Rarely Sometimes Always* (2020).[118]

---

[114] Id. at 150-161; Erik Eckholm, Nebraska Limits Safe Haven Law to Infants, N.Y. Times, Nov. 22, 2008, at A10.

[115] See Meghan Daum, Knocked Up but Not Out: Why Has the Teenage Birthrate Increased After Years of Decline?, L.A. Times (Dec. 15, 2007), https://www.latimes.com/news/la-oe-daum15dec15-column.html (opinion column) (wondering whether the increased birth rate results not from a lack of education but "a lack of mortification").

[116] See Caitlin Flanagan, Sex and the Teenage Girl, N.Y. Times, Jan. 13, 2008, at WK13 (op-ed).

[117] Compare Melissa Fletcher Stoeltje, Hollywood's New Family Values?, San Antonio Express-News, Jan. 28, 2008, at 1D, with Ann Hulbert, *Juno* and the Culture Wars: How the Movie Disarms the Family Values Debate, Slate (Dec. 18, 2007), http://www.slate.com/id/2180275/ [https://perma.cc/YG7Q-JV4N].

[118] See Manohla Dargis, A Woman's Modern Heroic Journey, N.Y. Times, Mar. 13, 2020, at C6.

PROBLEMS

1. Circe and Kelly, two women who share a romantic relationship, agree to adopt a child from Ethiopia and rear the child together. Because Ethiopia does not permit same-sex couples to adopt, the international adoption application identifies Circe as the prospective adoptive parent and Kelly as a household member. When the couple breaks up and executes a separation agreement, no specific child had yet been identified for Circe to adopt. Circe decides to proceed with the adoption on her own.

Circe and Kelly remain close after the breakup. When Circe travels to Ethiopia to take custody of the 15-month-old child, Abush, Kelly meets them in London and accompanies them to New York. Although Circe alone completes adoption proceedings, Kelly helps regularly with babysitting, including overnight stays, and all three of them occasionally occupy a house the two women had once jointly owned on Fire Island. Kelly identifies herself as the Abush's godmother.

Suppose Circe marries and she and her new spouse seek to complete a stepparent adoption. Kelly then seeks to intervene, claiming she is a parent to Abush and that consent or termination of her parental rights would be required before a stepparent adoption. In support of her position, Kelly says her situation resembles that of a couple who broke up during the gestation of a jointly conceived child. She asserts that Abush would not have come into their lives without her, and she describes Abush as "a product of our mutual intention, our mutual efforts." How should the court rule on Kelly's petition to intervene and the merits of her claim to be a parent who can block the stepparent adoption?[119]

2. T.W. gives birth to twin daughters in Missouri. While the premature twins are hospitalized, T.W. brings them breast milk. Because T.W. is rearing three other children, she explores the possibility of placing the twins for adoption. Seeking an open adoption (which Missouri does not permit), she chooses a California couple whom she finds with help from an adoption professional and an Internet search. Later, she reclaims the twins, within the permissible time period for revocation, because she concludes that the couple would not respect her preference for continuing contact. Next, she chooses a British couple, and an Arkansas court issues the adoption decrees. After British social service workers find this couple unfit and the Arkansas adoption is set aside for lack of jurisdiction, the twins are placed in foster care in Missouri. T.W., who by then changes her mind about adoption, seeks the twins' return to her custody.

---

[119] The Problem is based on K.G. v. C.H., 79 N.Y.S.3d 166 (App. Div. 2018); Kelly G. v. Circe H., 117 N.Y.S.3d 171 (App. Div. 2019). The case received considerable publicity, which also appears in the Problem, including Sharon Otterman, A Complicated Case Tests the State's Expanded Definition of Parenthood, N.Y. Times, Oct. 19, 2016, at A17; Ian Parker, What Makes a Parent, New Yorker (May 15, 2017), https://www.newyorker.com/magazine/2017/05/22/what-makes-a-parent [https://perma.cc/2HTR-9LFG]; Nancy Polikoff, NY Appellate Court Gets Gunn v. Hamilton Wrong, Beyond (Straight and Gay) Marriage (July 9, 2018), https://www.newyorker.com/magazine/2017/05/22/what-makes-a-parent [https://perma.cc/2HTR-9LFG]. In this case, the litigation (initiated by Kelly) seeking recognition as a parent was prompted by the decision of the mother (Circe) to move back to her original home in London with Abush (without Kelly). For a case in which a marriage and stepparent adoption prompt similar litigation, see A.H. v. W.R.L., 482 S.W.3d 372 (Ky. 2016).

The family court terminates T.W.'s parental rights on the ground that she abandoned the twins and emotionally abused them by surrendering them twice for adoption. T.W. appeals, contending that she neither abandoned nor abused the twins and asserting that no other permissible basis for TPR exists. What result and why?[120] Of what relevance is T.W.'s use of the Internet to find a placement?[121] If the foster parents now wish to adopt the children, should the court resolve the dispute by deciding whether adoption or their return to T.W. will serve their best interests? Put differently, did T.W. waive the preference usually given to birth parents once she first surrendered the twins for adoption?[122]

---

[120] See In re K.A.W., 133 S.W.3d 1 (Mo. 2004); Robert Patrick, Mom Set to See 'Net Twins,' Now 5, St. Louis Post-Dispatch, Mar. 21, 2006, at A1.

[121] See generally Michelle M. Hughes, Internet Promises, Scares, and Surprises: New Realities of Adoption, 41 Cap. U. L. Rev.279 (2013).

[122] See Moore v. Asente, 110 S.W.3d 336 (Ky. 2003).

CHAPTER 4

CHOOSING AN ADOPTIVE FAMILY

A. THE REGULATION AND PROFESSIONALIZATION OF CHILD PLACEMENT

Imagine a child available for adoption and many families applying to have a child placed with them. How does the selection take place? What characteristics of the prospective adopters and the child are important? Who should decide the relevance of such characteristics? Legislators? Judges? Social workers at adoption agencies? Lawyers or other intermediaries? The birth parents themselves? What standard should be used?

Historian Julie Berebitsky, in the excerpt below, shows how adoption began to enjoy popular acceptance in the United States, how adoption assumed an influential role in defining the normative family, and how adoptive placement came within the special jurisdiction of social workers. As you read the materials that follow the excerpt, consider the extent to which Berebitsky's observations about the past remain apt today.

JULIE BEREBITSKY, LIKE OUR VERY OWN: ADOPTION AND THE
CHANGING CULTURE OF MOTHERHOOD, 1851-1950

52-56, 62, 103-104, 113-117, 121-127, 129-138 (2000)

In October 1907, the *Delineator* [a popular women's magazine] published "The Child without a Home," which told of the 25,000 poor, primarily immigrant children who lived without a mother's love in institutions throughout New York. [In the months thereafter, the magazine's "Child Rescue Campaign"] would feature the photos and life stories of dependent children who were available to any interested reader who wanted to take them out of an institution and into her home. [The campaign, which emphasized how adoption would save homeless children, save marriages, and save the nation from the social threat of those reared without a mother's love,] generated a tremendous amount of reader response. ... The first letters the *Delineator* published expressed the intense longing for children felt by childless women and women whose children had died; they all hoped to adopt the children to "fill the vacancy in [their] home[s] and still the ache in [their] heart[s]." The *Delineator* had urged women to adopt the children by appealing to their sense of patriotic and civic duty, in addition to their motherly

133

instinct. Yet these letters suggest that women responded on a personal level; they needed the children as much as the children needed them. Nonetheless, adoption at the turn of the century was uncommon enough, and fears about bad heredity prevalent enough[, as reflected in the eugenics movement], that many women needed assurance, encouragement, and a place to voice their fears before they could comfortably adopt a child. . . .

The series also articulated a definition of motherhood based on a woman's capacity to love and nurture a child, not on blood ties. . . . If motherhood was a spiritual state, an attitude, and not the result of a physical experience, then a woman's marital status also bore no relation to her maternal instincts. Consequently, the *Delineator* sometimes advocated that single women adopt. Motherhood was woman's highest calling, . . . so shouldn't single women also have the opportunity to experience it, especially since countless children suffered for lack of mothering? . . . Physicians and others doing private adoption placement who were interviewed for these stories agreed that it was natural for unmarried women to find an outlet for their maternal longings through adoption. . . . As long as the culture understood single adoptive mothers as "mother-women," they were acceptable, because they posed no challenge to traditional gender roles; in fact, they seemed to celebrate them. . . .

In the 1920s, [however,] an array of voices, which included social workers, sociologists, psychologists, members of the legal profession, and married adoptive parents, began to inveigh against allowing single women to adopt. . . . By the 1920s, children had become a "priceless commodity," fathers had become vital to a child's healthy psychological development, and women had become sexual beings. An assortment of social scientists and other professionals defined the best "family" as one in which husband and wife enjoyed emotional intimacy and sexual pleasure and nurtured a few children, to the personal fulfillment of all involved. . . .

It appears that by the 1920s, adoption was becoming more popular among married childless couples and that virtually all healthy, adoptable young children could find homes in such families. Given that demand far exceeded supply, many felt that it was only natural that childless couples should be given first choice. Yet a close examination of the reservations expressed by those set against allowing single women to adopt shows more than just concern for the well-being of the child. These critiques of single adoptive mothers are as much about cultural fears surrounding lesbianism, the maintenance of distinct male-female gender roles, and the stability of the traditional family as they are about the best interests of children. They also reflect the growing influence of psychology, not only in adoption but also in the definition of appropriate adult emotional adjustment and the determination of child-development practices. . . . As this study argues throughout, adoption serves as a site on which the culture plays out its fears about the stability of the family and, more broadly, its anxieties about the ever-changing, unknowable future. . . .

The first two decades of the twentieth century [also] witnessed efforts by social workers to establish their occupation as a profession distinct from the sentimental philanthropy of volunteers. The principle underlying social work held that those dispensing aid should be guided not by social class, the rich helping the poor, but by science, the expert assisting the uninformed. A six-week summer training course for charity workers held in

New York in 1898 marked the beginning of social work education; by 1920, seventeen schools of social work existed. . . .

Social workers, however, came to adoption slowly. The idea of adoption conflicted with their efforts toward family preservation and their belief in the primacy of the blood tie. Social workers thought that unwed mothers should keep their infants, a philosophy that continued unchallenged within the profession through the 1930s. In addition, beginning in the 1910s, social workers, influenced by the findings of the new intelligence tests, felt that a definite link existed between illegitimacy and inherited feeblemindedness — a link that they believed made most illegitimate children unadoptable. Consequently, social workers focused their efforts on issues other than adoption.

Meanwhile, in the 1910s, individuals, generally well-to-do women, began to establish private adoption agencies. Imbued with a philanthropic spirit, they strongly disagreed with social workers, especially regarding the disposition of illegitimate infants. They believed that these children were adoptable and that an unwed mother and her child did not make a real family. . . . In Chicago, Florence Walrath found herself in the adoption business after locating an infant for her sister, whose firstborn child had died shortly after birth. Soon word of Walrath's success spread, and friends and acquaintances began to approach her to find infants for them. Walrath officially opened the Cradle, Chicago's first formal adoption agency, in 1923. The Cradle quickly achieved a national reputation as such Hollywood stars as George Burns and Gracie Allen flew to Chicago to claim their own bundles of joy. . . .

As a result, social workers had an uphill battle in the 1920s when they began to look at child placing and tried to bring adoption under their professional jurisdiction. They had to both assert their unique qualifications to be in charge and convince the public that the current practices were dangerous to the child, the adoptive parent, the biological parent, *and* society at large. . . . Changing popular opinion and behavior was a daunting task. Legislative efforts focused on establishing laws that required an investigation into the circumstances surrounding the placement by a child welfare professional or the state welfare department and a six-month trial period of residence in the prospective home before any adoption could be finalized. In 1917, Minnesota passed the first such law, and by the end of 1941, thirty-four states required an investigation before the court issued an adoption decree. [I]n placements made by public agencies, social workers had almost complete authority; the court was in no way involved with an agency's initial decision to reject or approve an applicant and virtually always granted an adoption that a public agency recommended. Still, despite social workers' increased involvement, even in states that required an investigation, judges had the ultimate power to deny or approve a petition. . . .

. . . Social workers argued that child placing was a "most exacting" science that required "careful preparation and study." . . . As social workers developed adoption policy and refined the practice in the 1920s, 1930s, and 1940s, they claimed expertise in three areas of special concern to prospective adopters. First, social workers spoke to adopters' fear of a child's heredity. Social workers promised to evaluate a child's heritage thoroughly by extensive interviewing and testing. Second, and directly related to the first, social workers maintained that through the extensive evaluation of a child and his or her biological parents, they could "match" a child to the adoptive parents. Social workers asserted that they could find a child "who might have been born to you." Children would "fit" their adoptive homes in physical characteristics, intellectual capacities, temperament, and religious and ethnic affiliation. The policy of matching assumed that this affinity would lead to easier assimilation. And finally, responding to the adoptive parents' fear of biological parents changing their minds, social workers maintained that their procedures ensured that the child was really free to be adopted and that the biological parents would stick to their decision. . . .

1. PLACEMENT CRITERIA

a. Matching

CRUMP V. MONTGOMERY

---

154 A.2d 802 (Md. 1959)

PRESCOTT, J.

This is an appeal by the petitioners below, Lloyd R. and Dorothy V. Crump, (the Crumps) from a decree entered by the Circuit Court for Wicomico County, dismissing the petition of the Crumps for the adoption of a minor child and decreeing the adoption of said child by Arthur P. and Blanche P. Montgomery, (the Montgomerys), who had also petitioned the court for the adoption of the child.

The child, Johnnie, was born in May of 1957 to an unwed mother. When he was seven days old, he was placed by the Montgomery County Welfare Board (Montgomery Board), which later received from his mother a written right to consent to his adoption, in the home of the Crumps, in Montgomery County, for foster care and pre-adoptive study. The Crumps had received five other foster children from the Montgomery Board and cared for them satisfactorily — not more than two being in their home at any one time. When first placed with the Crumps, it was thought Johnnie would be placed for adoption within three to six months. However, they were notified in a few months by a welfare worker that he was not adoptable, because of his showing in his early psychological tests. In later psychological tests, the child showed such improvement (his rating was then slightly below average) that he was rated as eligible for adoption and the Crumps were informed of this fact in September of 1958. During the intervening months (about 15) that Johnnie had been in their home, the Crumps had become very much attached to him and strongly desired him to be their adopted son. Oral requests concerning the adoption of Johnnie were frequently made by the Crumps to the Montgomery Board worker, but they were told, as they had been before, that they were not eligible as adoptive parents, due to the fact that they were foster parents, and also because the Montgomery Board had "closed its adoption list."

Following the determination that Johnnie was adoptable, his name was placed on the roll of children in that category with the State Welfare Department in Baltimore, which roll is designated as a child "Pool." The testimony does not make the method of operation of this "Pool" certain, but it seems that the children's names (probably minus their surnames), together with their backgrounds, are sent to Baltimore, where they are, in turn, sent to the various Welfare Boards throughout the state to be considered for adoption by prospective adoptive parents who have made application to them. Johnnie's name came to the attention of the Wicomico County Welfare Board (Wicomico Board), which had such an application from the Montgomerys, who had already adopted one child through that Board. The Wicomico Board notified the Montgomerys, who, after consultation with the Board, consideration of Johnnie's background and an interview with him in Montgomery County, decided they would like to have him as their adopted son. . . .

The Montgomery Board, over the protests of the Crumps, placed the custody of the child in the Wicomico Board for adoption, and thereafter, without any independent investigation of their own of the Montgomerys and without investigating the Crumps as possible *adoptive* parents, joined the Wicomico Board in consenting to the adoption of Johnnie by the Montgomerys. . . .

[At trial, the] testimony disclosed that Mr. and Mrs. Crump were 34 and 32 years of age, respectively, and had been married 12 years; they had one natural daughter, aged eleven, who was living with them; Mr. Crump had been an orphan himself and stated he desired to give some of the things that he had missed as a child to Johnnie; for the last six years they had lived in a modern brick bungalow in a desirable residential neighborhood in Silver Spring, Maryland; that Mr. Crump had been employed by the United States Government for nine years and was a scientist and engineer, receiving a salary of $7,200 per year, which was supplemented by approximately $5,000 per year, from his publications, inventions and private enterprises; one witness said that he was a "brilliant scientist"; that he was a steady, reliable and industrious worker; that Mrs. Crump was unemployed and spent her time in the care of the home, her child and the foster children; that neither Mr. nor Mrs. Crump indulged in alcoholic beverages and they were a compatible and congenial couple; and that the children in their home were receiving proper religious instructions.

In summary, the learned Chancellors below found that the testimony of "all of the witnesses who were familiar with the situation shows the Crump home to be an excellent one, the care given to little Johnnie was all that could be desired, and no one, certainly not this Court, offers the slightest criticism of their conduct while the little boy was in their custody," but "[o]n the contrary, we wholeheartedly commend their conduct and what they have done for this little boy."

The testimony also disclosed that the Montgomerys are splendid people and maintain a nice home. Mr. Montgomery was 41 years of age — his wife 31 — and they had been married about 15 years. They were living in a "comfortable, modest and attractive" home in a wholesome residential community on the outskirts of Salisbury, with one daughter — 4 years of age — whom they had previously adopted. His home and automobile were fully paid for and he had money in the bank. The wife was a high school graduate, while the husband had stopped his formal education when through the eleventh grade, but had taken several vocational courses when in the armed services during the war. Mr. Montgomery had been employed by the Eastern

Shore Public Service Company since 1948, starting as a member of a line crew and his "job," at the time of the hearing below, was "maintenance and utility." He received $2.18, per hour, from which he derived about $5,000 yearly. He and Mrs. Montgomery were, also, a compatible couple, who were attentive to, and mindful of, their children's welfare. She was unemployed and spent her time in the care of her home where she saw that the children were receiving proper religious training. The Chancellors expressed their "complete approval and satisfaction with Mr. and Mrs. Montgomery as well as with the home they maintain."

The Montgomery Board objected to the Crumps as adoptive parents for Johnnie on two grounds: first, that in their opinion the child would be "over-placed"; and, second, it had not investigated their home for adoptive purposes *in accordance with their policies*. The Montgomery Board, while it advocated the wisdom of its established policy (not consistently applied) of not considering foster-care parents as eligible to become adoptive parents, concedes that this policy is not binding upon a court, which has the final authority to approve or disapprove a proposed adoption.

The "over-placed" objection was based upon the fact that Mr. Crump was a well-educated, highly intelligent young man, who might, because Johnnie was slightly "below average" in his psychological tests, become dissatisfied with the boy and exert "pressure" upon him if the child were unable to exhibit a very high degree of intellectual ability.[3] The Chancellors expressed serious doubt upon this point, stating: "We are not altogether in agreement with the position that an intelligent man should be penalized by being prohibited from adopting a child whose home and background is not apparently up to his standard, and especially is this so when the child is only 18 or 20 months old, and any determination of the capacity of the child to grow in intelligence must be speculative at this [stage] of his life. . . . *We would be inclined to say that such a home would be more beneficial to him.*" (Emphasis supplied.) . . .

Had the matter of alleged over-placing been fully explored, it may have satisfied the Chancellors that their opinion, quoted above, was sound. . . . The results of Johnnie's early psychological tests would possibly be a matter of real concern as to his "over-placement" if they disclosed some serious impediment in his mentality, or if they could be correlated to his mental potential at any time in the future. . . . In considering further the relative intellectual powers of the prospective adoptive father, Mr. Crump, and the boy, . . . it should be noted that the intellectual feature of matching is only one of many factors, such as race, religion, physical likeness, etc., that should be considered under the general heading of "matching adoptive parents with adoptive children." . . .

Schapiro, op. cit., Vol. 1, p. 84, recognizes that matching is an important part of agency practice in adoptions, but points out there is "no one rule for appraising the qualitative contributions that any single factor can make

---

3. This objection is based on one of the elements that comes under a general heading usually termed "matching." Rule 517.1 of the Board of Public Welfare calls for "likeness in temperament, intelligence and racial heritage." 1 Schapiro, A Study of Adoption Practice, p. 84, lists ten factors considered as important in "matching."

to the general atmosphere of a home, as [t]here is no unanimity of opinion on what constitutes sound matching," and "matching has become more flexible because agencies have begun to recognize that some adoptive parents are frequently able to accept differences." See also, Child Welfare League of America Standards for Adoption Service, p. 23, par. 4.3, "Matching."

Thus, we have two families that have been passed as eligible for adoptive purposes — both desiring to adopt the same child. The Child Welfare League of America Standards for Adoption Service, p. 23, says the selection of a family for an adoptive child should be made on the basis of an appraisal of their suitability for each other, and suitability "should be appraised in terms of the capacity of adoptive parents to meet the individual needs of the particular child, and of the child to benefit by placement with them and to bring them the satisfaction of parenthood." It will be noticed the emphasis here is on the benefit to the child . . . .

In making short qualitative analyses of the two families involved herein, we make no reference to the qualifications where they seem to be equal, but only to those that differ. The Crumps have the better educational-occupational status (unless it is ultimately determined that the mental attainments of Mr. Crump will probably interfere with his accepting the child, or that he is likely to exert undue pressure upon the child to attain a level of mental development of which the child is incapable); they have a larger income, $12,200, per year, as compared to $5,000; they have a slightly better residence; and Mr. Montgomery demonstrated in his testimony that he does not speak grammatically in simple, ordinary statements of speech. On the other hand, the daughter of the Montgomerys was nearer the age of Johnnie than the daughter of the Crumps (4 years as compared to 11), and Mr. Montgomery's mental development is not such as to raise any question about his accepting the child. Another matter that the Chancellors should have thoroughly considered and weighed is that the adoption of Johnnie by the Montgomerys involved a change from the home, locality and environment in which he had been, practically, since birth. . . .

[I]t is plainly seen that the Chancellors adopted the decision and judgment of the Montgomery Board as to which family would better subserve the welfare and best interests of Johnnie by his adoption, and made no actual finding of their own upon the subject, although clearly intimating that their conclusion was contrary to the Board's. [The statute] places the responsibility for the granting of adoptions in the counties of this State upon the Circuit Courts, and, in granting adoptions, it is the duty of said courts to determine what will best promote the welfare and interests of the child. . . . In view of the fact that the Chancellors failed to make a definite finding of their own with reference to the welfare and best interests of the child, and the testimony in regards to certain aspects of the case is not so complete as it might be, as previously indicated in this opinion, we have decided . . . to remand the case without affirmance or reversal so that the court below may take such additional testimony as it desires, have an independent investigation made of the prospective adoptive parents and the infant if it deems the same necessary or desirable, and render a final and definitive finding, insofar as that court is concerned, as to what will best serve the welfare and best interests of Johnnie. . . .

NOTES AND QUESTIONS

1. *Epilogue.* After remand, the attorneys for the two families and the Welfare Board of Montgomery County met with the judges and appointed a committee charged with making a "complete study of, and report to the court on, the 'home situations' of the potential adoptive couples." Crump v. Montgomery, 168 A.2d 355, 356 (Md. 1961). Psychiatrists and psychologists examined the individuals, most of whom recommended that Johnnie stay with the Montgomerys, where he had lived since being removed from the Crumps' home. Finding sufficient support for this conclusion, the court affirmed while observing that the transfer from the Crumps' home was handled poorly and opining that tact and diplomacy in dealing with the Crumps might have avoided the litigation. Id. Does the outcome mean that the court believes the Montgomerys' home was always a better placement for Johnnie, or only that it became so with the passage of time?

2. *Adoption process.* In this classic case illustrating matching practices in adoption, what is the division of authority between the agency, on the one hand, and the court, on the other? Note that the adoption process usually includes a close evaluation of the prospective adopters, often called a "home study" or a "placement investigation," including visits both before and after placement.[1] What explains such regulation of adoptive placements, compared to the absence of regulation (or "privacy") for those who become parents by sexual conception? Evaluate the criticism that such regulation of adoption reflects a preference for biological relationships and signals distrust of those who would raise a "child born to another" or who seek to parent "someone else's child."[2]

3. *Placement preferences.* State statutes often list preferences for adoptive placement, such as with relatives or in a home with a sibling, and some allow birth parents themselves to choose the placement.[3] Over the years, case law has raised numerous questions about the factors that agencies and the state can (and cannot) consider in choosing an adoptive placement. Which of the following should disqualify prospective adopters and why? Deafness? Undisclosed pregnancy of prospective adoptive mother? Age? Obesity? Adoptive parents' divorce? Status as a single woman? As a single man? A divorcing couple? A nonmarital couple? Two individuals who are simply friends?[4]

---

[1] See, e.g., Iowa Code §600.8; 23 Pa. Cons. Stat. §2530.

[2] Elizabeth Bartholet, Family Bonds: Adoption, Infertility, and the New World of Child Production 69 (rev. ed. 1999). See id. at 34, 93.

[3] E.g., Minn. Stat. Ann. §259.29 (first with a relative and then with a friend); Nev. Rev. Stat. §127.2825 (in the adoptive family of a sibling); Va. Code Ann. §63.2-1230 ("The birth parent, legal guardian, or adoptive parent of a child may place his child for adoption directly with the adoptive parents of his choice.").

[4] See, e.g., In re Adoption of Richardson, 59 Cal. Rptr. 323 (Ct. App. 1967) (deafness); Brett M. ex rel. Children's Home Soc'y v. Vesely, 757 N.W.2d 360 (Neb. 2008) (undisclosed pregnancy); McClement v. Beaudoin, 700 N.Y.S.2d 570 (App. Div. 1999) (age); Lanai Scarr, Couples Told: You're Too Fat to Adopt Kids, Advertiser (Australia), Sept. 3, 2017, 2017 WLNR 27057579; In re Adoption of M.C.D., 42 P.3d 873 (Okla. Civ. App. 2001) (couple's divorce); Jessica R. Feinberg, Friends as Co-Parents, 43 U.S.F. L. Rev. 799 (2009); Cynthia R. Mabry, Joint and Shared Parenting: Valuing All Families and All Children in the Adoption Process with an Expanded Notion of Family, 17 Am. U. J. Gender Soc. Pol'y & L. 659 (2009).

4. *Foster parents as adopters.* If the Crumps were deemed qualified to serve as Johnnie's foster parents, why were they not considered suitable adoptive parents for him? Do adoptive parents need different skills and characteristics? In contrast to the strict distinction between foster parents and adoptive parents illustrated by Smith v. OFFER, Chapter 2, section B2, and *Crump*, modern practice reflects a more fluid approach in which many foster placements are expressly designed to serve as pre-adoptive placements (even though TPR might not occur) and permanency planning concurrently pursues both reunification and adoption. See Chapter 3, section A. In some states, foster parents may petition for adoption despite objection by the state agency that has legal custody.[5]

Depictions in Popular Culture: Three Identical Strangers (2018)

When he goes to college at age 19, Bobby Shafran's classmates repeatedly mistake him for someone named Eddy Galland. Bobby and Eddy arrange to meet and, knowing they had each been adopted as infants, conclude they must be twins. Media coverage of their reunion reaches David Kellman, another adoptee whose striking physical resemblance and age prompt him to make contact, allowing all three to determine that they were born as identical triplets. The three bond immediately, discover uncanny similarities, and — trying to make up for all the shared time they missed — decide to live together. Their story attracts widespread attention, making them minor celebrities with television and movie appearances and operation of a New York City restaurant.

Yet all does not go well in this documentary, which intersperses old videos with interviews of many of the major players. Bobby, Eddy, and David all confront mental health challenges, with some speculation that both their separation and undisclosed maternal mental illness could have contributed to their difficulties. Eddy eventually commits suicide. A journalist helps uncover a study of twins in which the triplets and their adoptive families unknowingly participated. The once prominent and highly respected Louise Wise Adoption Agency had chosen the three placements to assist with a "nature versus nurture" experiment that tested the influence of parenting style and class. Accordingly, each triplet had been "matched" with a family that had previously adopted a girl through Louise Wise, so each grew up with an older sister. At the same time, Bobby had an affluent family in which the physician-father had little family time, Eddy a middle-income family in which the father was a

---

[5] See, e.g., In re A.F., 173 Cal. Rptr. 3d 774 (Ct. App. 2014); In re Adoption of A.A.B., 877 N.W.2d 355 (S.D. 2016). See also State in Interest of K.C.C., 188 So. 3d 144 (La. 2016) (holding prospective adopters have standing to petition for TPR).

strict disciplinarian, and David a blue-collar family in which the father was an open, warm, and welcoming man, who treated all three as sons after the initial reunion. In retrospect, the many visits of psychologists to the homes of the boys as they were growing up start to make sense. The results of the study were never published, observers have debated whether nature or nurture prevailed even for the triplets themselves, and other subjects have discovered their inclusion in the experiment and come forward. See Elyse Schein & Paula Bernstein, *Identical Strangers: A Memoir of Twins Separated and Reunited* (2008).

The film raises obvious questions about the ethics of research with human subjects, although research assistants from the study explain that times were different in the 1960s and everyone believed they were doing important, beneficial work. Still, the failure to publish the results and the decision to seal them for decades to come seem to belie confidence in the project's value.

Beyond research ethics, what does the film add to the understanding of the professionalization of placement and the "science" of matching even by the most highly regarded agencies? What momentous consequences rest on the fortuity of placement and the unknowability of the outcome of an alternate history? For example, would Eddy have committed suicide if he had grown up in David's family? Doesn't adoption always raise such questions? And what is the impact on growth and development of separation from one's twin or co-triplets — or siblings or birth parents, for that matter?

5. *Who benefits?* Whom does matching benefit? Standard rhetoric in adoption statutes and cases assert that an adoptive placement must serve the child's best interests.[6] The concern about "over-placement" in *Crump* suggests a belief that matching does so. Might matching also have helped adoptive families "pass" as biological families in a day when infertility had even more stigmatizing effects than it does now? Will matching always achieve equilibrium between supply and demand?

Today, critics challenge attempts to create "the 'as if' family" through adoption, emphasizing the importance of how a family functions, rather than whether it "imitates nature."[7] Some of the most vigorous contemporary debates about matching explore the role of race and cultural heritage in adoption, as the following materials show.

---

[6] E.g., D.C. Code Ann. §16-309(b)(3).
[7] E.g., Mary Lyndon Shanley, Making Babies, Making Families: What Matters Most in an Age of Reproductive Technologies, Surrogacy, Adoption, and Same-Sex and Unwed Parents 15-20 (2001).

ELIZABETH BARTHOLET, WHERE DO BLACK CHILDREN BELONG?
THE POLITICS OF RACE MATCHING IN ADOPTION

139 U. Pa. L. Rev. 1163, 1164-1188, 1237 (1991)

When I first walked into the world of adoption, I was stunned at the dominant role race played. . . . Early in the process of exploring how I might adopt, I discovered that the first order of business for the agencies responsible for matching children waiting for homes with prospective parents is to sort and allocate by race. The public and most of the traditional private adoption agencies would not consider assigning a waiting minority child to me, a white person, except as a last resort, and perhaps not even then. The organizations and individual entrepreneurs that arrange independent adoptions, while more willing to place across racial lines, also sorted children by race. In this part of the adoption world, minority children might actually be easier for the white prospective parent to find than a white child, and they were often available for a lesser fee. . . .

The familiar refrain that there are no children available for adoption is a reflection of the racial policies of many adoption agencies and the racial preferences of many adoptive parents. The reality is that there are very few *white* children by comparison to the large pool of would-be white adopters. But there are many *non-white* children available to this pool, both through independent adoption in this country and through international adoption. And there are many non-white children waiting in foster care who are unavailable solely because of adoption agency insistence that they not be placed transracially.

Racial thinking dominates the world of international adoption as well. [Bartholet, a single mother of one child from an early marriage, adopted two children from Peru.] I discovered during my two adoption trips to Peru something about how children may be rated in racial terms in their own country as well as here. Most of the children available for adoption in Peru are of mixed Indian and Spanish heritage. But there is tremendous variety in ethnic features and skin color. For my second adoption I was offered by the government adoption agency an unusually white, one-month-old baby. My initial reaction upon meeting him was disappointment that he did not look like my first child from Peru. Christopher's brown-skinned face with its Indian features had become the quintessence of what a child — my child — should look like. But I decided that it was foolish to look for another baby Christopher, as I had decided years earlier that it would be foolish to look in adoption for a clone of my biological son. I took this baby home and named him Michael. Within twenty-four hours I found myself tearing through the streets in a taxi, mopping his feverish body with a wet cloth, and terrified, as I saw his eyes lose contact with mine and begin to stare off into the middle distance, that he would die in my arms before we got to the hospital emergency room. . . . Sometime during that taxi ride, or in the hospital room, I became hopelessly attached.

Several weeks later I sat with a blanketed Michael in my arms in the office of one of Lima's fanciest pediatricians. Michael had recovered from the fever but had been suffering from nausea and diarrhea almost ever since. . . . I had been to three different doctors . . . . I told this new doctor the story of Michael's troubles, trying with my words and tone to convey my sense of desperation — to make him understand that if he didn't help us Michael might die. The doctor sat impassively, interrupting me only when my three-year old Christopher wandered over to the bookshelves. Pointing with apparent disgust, as if some small and dirty animal had invaded his office, the doctor asked, "What is he?" I thought the question truly peculiar and the answer rather obvious, but explained that this was my son (perhaps he thought it was the child of the Peruvian nanny who was with me?). At the end of my story the doctor, who had still made no move to look at Michael, assured himself that the nanny spoke no English, and he then proceeded to tell me that he could get me another child, in a way that would avoid all the troublesome procedures of a Peruvian adoption. Women were giving birth in his hospital all the time who would not keep their babies. He could have the birth certificate for one of these babies made out showing me as the mother and the baby would be mine.

When I finally realized that this hospital baby was being suggested as a substitute for the one on my lap, I said in what I hoped was a polite but firm tone that I planned to keep this child and that I was here because I was afraid the child was seriously ill. I asked if the doctor could please now examine the child. . . . I put Michael on the table and started to undress him, and for the first time the doctor looked at him. . . . It was overwhelmingly clear that Michael's value had been transformed in the doctor's eyes by his whiteness. Whiteness made it comprehensible that someone would want to cure and keep this child rather than discard him. . . .

I learned more about my own feelings about race as I puzzled through the process of creating my adoptive family. Adoption compels this kind of learning. You don't just get at the end of one general child line when you're doing adoption. There are a lot of lines, each identified by the race, disabilities, and age of the children available, together with the length of wait and the difficulty and cost of adoption. In choosing which line to join, I had to think about race, and to think on a level that was new to me. I had to try to confront without distortion the reality of parenting someone of another race — since the child and I would have to live that reality. . . . I had to think about whether it would be racist to look for a same-race child or racist to look for a child of another race . . . .

[O]ne day, when he is three and one-half, Christopher says to me across the kitchen table at dinner, "I wish you looked like me." . . . I am left to puzzle at the meaning of this pain. . . . Is it, as the opponents of transracial adoption would have us believe, a piece of a permanent anguish at the sense that he does not truly belong in the place where he should most surely belong — his family? Or should I simply take it as a signal that living as a part of a multi-racial, multi-ethnic, multi-cultural family will force us to confront the meaning of racial and other differences on a regular basis?

This child is as inside my skin as any child could be. It feels entirely right that he should be there. Yet the powers that be in today's adoption world proclaim with near unanimity that race-mixing in the context of adoption should be avoided if at all possible, at least where black or brown-skinned American children are involved. . . .

[C]urrent racial matching policies represent a coming together of powerful and related ideologies — old fashioned white racism, modern-day black nationalism, and what I will call "biologism" — the idea that what is "natural" in the context of the biological family is what is normal and desirable in the context of adoption. Biological families have same-race parents and children. The laws and policies surrounding adoption in this country have generally structured adoption in imitation of biology, giving the adopted child a new birth certificate as if the child had been born to the adoptive parents, sealing off the birth parents as if they had never existed, and attempting to match adoptive parents and children with respect to looks, intellect and religion. The implicit goal has been to create an adoptive family which will resemble as much as possible "the real thing" — the "natural" or biological family that is not. . . .

But the question is . . . whether today's powerful racial matching policies make sense from the viewpoint of either the minority children involved or the larger society. . . . Minority children are pouring, in increasing numbers, into the already overburdened foster care system, and current policies stand in the way of placing these children with available adoptive families. . . .

The controversy over transracial adoption that has arisen in recent decades has primarily involved the placement of children generally identified as black with white families. . . . Through the middle of this century there were near-absolute barriers to transracial adoption posed by adoption agency practice, by social attitudes, and by the law. As adoption agencies gained increasing power in the late nineteenth and early twentieth centuries to screen prospective parents and to assign waiting children to particular homes, they helped to institutionalize the racial barriers. Agencies adopted a powerful "matching" philosophy. Prospective parents were ideally to be matched with children who were physically and mentally as close a match as possible to the biological children they might have produced. This kind of matching was thought to maximize the chances for a successful bonding and nurturing relationship between parent and child. . . .

The 1960s represented a period of relative openness to transracial adoption. Foreign adoptions helped pave the way. In the aftermath of the Korean War, South Korea made many of its abandoned and orphaned children available for adoption. Large numbers of these were mixed race children who had been fathered by black American soldiers stationed in Korea. . . . The civil rights movement in this country brought increasing attention to the plight of the minority children who had languished in the foster care systems over the years. This movement's integrationist ideology made transracial adoption a sympathetic idea to many adoption workers and prospective parents. Transracial adoption also served the needs of the waiting white parents, for whom there were not enough color-matched children available, as well as the interests of the agencies in putting together adoptive families and reducing the foster care population. And so agencies began to place waiting black children with white parents when there were no black parents apparently available. The reported number of transracial placements rose gradually to 733 in 1968, and it more than tripled in the next three years to reach a peak of 2574 in 1971. . . .

In 1972 this brief era of relative openness to transracial adoption came to an abrupt end. That year an organization called the National Association of Black Social Workers (NABSW) issued a position statement against transracial adoption [calling it a form of "genocide"]. It stated:

Black children should be placed only with Black families whether in foster care or for adoption. Black children belong, physically, psychologically and culturally in Black families in order that they receive the total sense of themselves and develop a sound projection of their future. Human beings are products of their environment and develop their sense of values, attitudes and self concept within their family structures. Black children in white homes are cut off from the healthy development of themselves as Black people. . . .

Others joined in the attack on transracial adoption, arguing with the NABSW that transracial adoption constituted an attack upon the black community and that it harmed black children by denying them their black heritage and the survival skills needed for life in a racist society.

The attack on transracial adoption appeared to have an immediate and significant impact. The numbers fell from a peak of 2574 in 1971 [to 831 in 1975]. [The Child Welfare League and adoption] agency bureaucrats moved swiftly to accommodate the position taken by the NABSW. . . . A parallel development occurred with respect to the adoptive placement of Native American children. [My own] investigation has made clear to me that race is used as the basis for official decision-making in adoption in a way that is unparalleled in a society that has generally endorsed an anti-discrimination and pro-integration ideology. . . .

This matching scheme confronts a major problem in the fact that the numbers of children falling into the black and the white pools do not "fit," proportionately, with the number of prospective parents falling into their own black and white pools. In 1987, 37.1% of the children in out-of-home placement were black as compared with 46.1% white. Although no good statistics are available, the general understanding is that a very high percentage of the waiting adoptive parent pool is white. . . .

The matching process surfaces, to a degree, in written rules and documented cases. But it is the unwritten and generally invisible rules that are central to understanding the nature of current policies. . . . The rules generally make race not simply "a factor," but an overwhelmingly important factor in the placement process. . . .

[A]doption is not supposed to be about parent or community rights and interests, but rather about serving the best interests of children. Adoption laws throughout this country provide that agencies are to make children's interests paramount in placement decisions. Arguments can be made that black children in general will benefit from efforts to strengthen the black community, and that racial matching policies represent one such effort. The problem is that . . . racial matching policies seem contrary to the immediate and long-term interests of the specific black children waiting for homes. . . .

DOROTHY ROBERTS, SHATTERED BONDS: THE COLOR OF CHILD WELFARE

165-172 (2002)

The shift in federal policy from family preservation toward adoption [exemplified by the Adoption and Safe Families Act of 1997 (ASFA)] corresponded with the change in the federal position on transracial adoption. The relationship between these two trends was more than a coincidence of timing. The new adoption law was tied to the growing movement to remove barriers to adoption of Black children by white middle-class couples. White adoptive families are seen as a major source for reducing the large numbers of Black children in foster care. At the same time, family preservation policies are seen as a hindrance to white families' ability to adopt them. Although the federal adoption law is racially neutral on its face, its connection to transracial adoption reveals the racial politics that undergirds its popularity. Most of the biological families whose bonds the law disparages are Black, whereas most of the adoptive families whom the law favors are white.

For decades, the federal government permitted public adoption agencies to enforce race-matching policies that sought to place Black children exclusively with Black adoptive families. But in the 1990s, after aggressive lobbying by supporters of transracial adoption, Congress took steps to remove barriers to whites willing to adopt children of other races. Transracial adoption was championed as a critical step in increasing the numbers of adoptions of Black children, the population with the lowest rate of exit from foster care. Advocates argued that race-matching policies forced Black children to languish in foster care awaiting scarce Black adoptive parents when they could have been adopted by whites. . . .

Adoption policy has historically tracked the market for children, serving the interests of adults seeking to adopt more than the interests of children needing stable homes. Foster care and adoption have a supply and demand relationship. While the foster care system provides a source of children for adopters, adoption provides a source of homes for children in foster care. For example, in the early 1900s, child welfare officials softened the child rescue philosophy of the nineteenth century and refrained from terminating parental rights when the supply of newborns available for adoption exceeded demand. In more recent decades, however, the growing demand for adoptable older children as babies became scarce helped to generate policies that free children for adoption by terminating parental rights quickly. . . . Roe v. Wade's protection of women's right to abortion and the diminished social stigma attached to single motherhood have drastically cut the numbers of white women who give up their babies for adoption, creating what has been called the "White Baby Famine." Until recently, the number of adoptions in the United States steadily declined since reaching a peak of 175,000 in 1970.

All of the literature advocating the elimination of racial considerations in child placements focuses on making it easier for white people to adopt Black children. . . . Transracial adoption advocates don't mention the possibility of Blacks adopting white children. Nor do they acknowledge that most race-matching in adoption involves matching white adoptive parents with white children. Child welfare agencies routinely allow whites to choose the white foster children they prefer. . . .

[Congressional and media] rhetoric supporting ASFA praised reforms in federal child welfare policy for removing the twin barriers to adoption — race-matching restrictions and prolonged family preservation efforts. Terminating parents' rights faster and abolishing race-matching policies were linked as a strategy for increasing adoptions of Black children by white families. Connecting these two issues — family preservation and transracial adoption — allowed commentators to claim that the foster care problems could be solved by moving more Black children from their families into white adoptive homes. . . .

Transracial adoption becomes especially explosive in the context of terminating parental rights to free children for adoption. . . . These contests bring to the surface a theme that runs more subtly through some of the discourse supporting transracial adoption — the belief that Black children fare better if raised by white adoptive families than if returned home. Advocates of transracial adoption frequently assert the benefits of racial assimilation that Black children and white parents experience by living together. . . . As in the rhetoric promoting ASFA, the rhetoric promoting transracial adoption supports the dissolution of poor Black families by depicting adoptive homes as superior to children's existing family relationships.

The picture painted by the media and advocates of transracial adoption as a panacea for the foster care crisis bears little connection to the real world adoption market. The transracial adoption issue is a red herring. It diverts attention from the main harms the child welfare system inflicts on Black families. The white couples the public envisions as adoptive parents are typically not interested in the poor Black children who make up the bulk of the foster care population. The vast majority of white adoptive parents are only willing to take a white child. . . .

Even when they adopt outside their race, whites generally prefer non-Black children of Asian or Latin American heritage. . . . The notion that state agencies are turning away thousands of white parents anxious to adopt Black foster children is ludicrous. Yet this mirage is held out as a reason for opposing policies that preserve Black families. . . .

ADOPTIVE COUPLE v. BABY GIRL

570 U.S. 637 (2013)

JUSTICE ALITO delivered the opinion of the Court.

This case is about a little girl (Baby Girl) who is classified as an Indian because she is 1.2% (3/256) Cherokee. Because Baby Girl is classified in this way, the South Carolina Supreme Court held that certain provisions of the federal Indian Child Welfare Act of 1978 required her to be taken, at the age of 27 months, from the only parents she had ever known and handed over to her biological father, who had attempted to relinquish his parental rights and who had no prior contact with the child. The provisions of the federal statute at issue here do not demand this result. . . .

"The Indian Child Welfare Act of 1978 (ICWA), 25 U.S.C. §§1901-1963, was the product of rising concern in the mid-1970's over the consequences to Indian children, Indian families, and Indian tribes of abusive child welfare practices that resulted in the separation of large numbers of Indian children from their families and tribes through adoption or foster care placement, usually in non-Indian homes." Mississippi Band of Choctaw Indians v. Holyfield, 490 U.S. 30, 32 (1989). Congress found that "an alarmingly high percentage of Indian families [were being] broken up by the removal, often unwarranted, of their children from them by nontribal public and private agencies." §1901(4). This "wholesale removal of Indian children from their homes" prompted Congress to enact the ICWA, which establishes federal standards that govern state-court child custody proceedings involving

Indian children [including proceedings for termination of parental rights and adoption].

In this case, Birth Mother (who is predominantly Hispanic) and Biological Father (who is a member of the Cherokee Nation) became engaged in December 2008. One month later, [after] learning of [Birth Mother's] pregnancy, Biological Father asked Birth Mother to move up the date of the wedding. He also refused to provide any financial support until after the two had married. The couple's relationship deteriorated, and Birth Mother broke off the engagement in May 2009. In June, Birth Mother sent Biological Father a text message asking if he would rather pay child support or relinquish his parental rights. Biological Father responded via text message that he relinquished his rights.

Birth Mother then decided to put Baby Girl up for adoption. [Her attorney contacted the Cherokee Nation to determine whether Biological Father was formally enrolled, but misspelled his name and provided an incorrect birth date, so Biological Father's membership in the tribal records could not be verified.]

Working through a private adoption agency, Birth Mother selected Adoptive Couple, non-Indians living in South Carolina, to adopt Baby Girl. Adoptive Couple supported Birth Mother both emotionally and financially throughout her pregnancy. Adoptive Couple was present at Baby Girl's birth in Oklahoma on September 15, 2009, and Adoptive Father even cut the umbilical cord. The next morning, Birth Mother signed forms relinquishing her parental rights and consenting to the adoption. Adoptive Couple initiated adoption proceedings in South Carolina a few days later, and returned there with Baby Girl. After returning to South Carolina, Adoptive Couple allowed Birth Mother to visit and communicate with Baby Girl. . . .

. . . Biological Father [received notice and] signed papers stating that he accepted service and that he was "not contesting the adoption." But [he later testified that] he thought that he was relinquishing his rights to Birth Mother, not to Adoptive Couple. Biological Father contacted a lawyer the day after signing the papers, and subsequently requested a stay of the adoption proceedings. [The Cherokee Nation identified Biological Father as a registered member and intervened in the litigation.] In the adoption proceedings, Biological Father sought custody and stated that he did not consent to Baby Girl's adoption. . . .

[After a trial, the South Carolina Family Court denied the adoption petition on the ground that Adoptive Couple had not shown compliance with applicable ICWA provisions. Biological Father was awarded custody, and Baby Girl, age 27 months, was handed over to him. He terminated contact with Adoptive Couple and has made no attempt to contact Birth Mother. The South Carolina Supreme Court affirmed, and we granted certiorari.] . . . It is undisputed that, had Baby Girl not been 3/256 Cherokee, Biological Father would have had no right to object to her adoption under South Carolina law. . . .

[The Court considers the ICWA provisions applied by the courts below.] Section 1912(f) [of the ICWA] provides that "[n]o termination of parental rights may be ordered in such proceeding in the absence of a determination, supported by evidence beyond a reasonable doubt, . . . that the continued custody of the child by the parent or Indian custodian is likely to result in serious emotional or physical damage to the child." (Emphasis added.) . . . The adjective "continued" plainly refers to a pre-existing state [and does not apply to an Indian parent who never had custody of the child.] [T]he primary mischief the ICWA was designed to counteract was the unwarranted removal of Indian children from Indian families due to the cultural insensitivity and biases of social workers and state courts. . . . [W]hen, as here, the adoption of an Indian child is voluntarily and lawfully initiated by a non-Indian parent with sole custodial rights, the ICWA's primary goal of preventing the unwarranted removal of Indian children and the dissolution of Indian families is not implicated. . . .

Section 1912(d) provides that "[a]ny party" seeking to terminate parental rights to an Indian child under state law "shall satisfy the court that active efforts have been made to provide remedial services and rehabilitative programs designed to prevent the breakup of the Indian family and that these efforts have proved unsuccessful." (Emphasis added.) . . . Section 1912(d) is a sensible requirement when applied to state social workers who might otherwise be too quick to remove Indian children from their Indian families. It would, however, be unusual to apply §1912(d) in the context of an Indian parent who abandoned a child prior to birth and who never had custody of the child. . . .

In the decision below, the South Carolina Supreme Court suggested that if it had terminated Biological Father's rights, then §1915(a)'s preferences for the adoptive placement of an Indian child would have been applicable. . . . Section 1915(a) provides that "[i]n any adoptive placement of an Indian child under State law, a preference shall be given, in the absence of good cause to the contrary, to a placement with (1) a member of the child's extended family; (2) other members of the Indian child's tribe; or (3) other Indian families." Contrary to the South Carolina Supreme Court's suggestion, §1915(a)'s preferences are inapplicable in cases where no alternative party has formally sought to adopt the child. This is because there simply is no "preference" to apply if no alternative party that is eligible to be preferred under §1915(a) has come forward. [No adoption petition was filed by the Biological Father, the paternal grandparents, or other members of the Tribe.]

The Indian Child Welfare Act was enacted to help preserve the cultural identity and heritage of Indian tribes, but under the State Supreme Court's reading, the Act would put certain vulnerable children at a great disadvantage solely because an ancestor — even a remote one — was an Indian. [A] biological Indian father could abandon his child in utero and refuse any support for the birth mother — perhaps contributing to the mother's decision to put the child up for adoption — and then could play his ICWA trump card at the eleventh hour to override the mother's decision and the child's best interests. If this were possible, many prospective adoptive parents would surely pause before adopting any child who might possibly qualify as an Indian under the ICWA. Such an interpretation would raise equal protection concerns, but [the ICWA provisions used below do not apply here.] We therefore reverse the judgment of the South Carolina Supreme Court and remand the case for further proceedings not inconsistent with this opinion. . . .

SCALIA, J., dissenting.

. . . The Court's opinion, it seems to me, needlessly demeans the rights of parenthood. It has been the constant practice of the common law to respect the entitlement of those who bring a child into the world to raise that child. We do not inquire whether leaving a child with his parents is "in the best interest of the child." It sometimes is not; he would be better off raised by someone else. But parents have their rights, no less than children do. This father wants to raise his daughter, and the statute amply protects his right to do so. There is no reason in law or policy to dilute that protection.

SOTOMAYOR, J., with whom GINSBERG and KAGAN, J., join and SCALIA, J., joins in part, dissenting.

A casual reader of the Court's opinion could be forgiven for thinking this an easy case, one in which the text of the applicable statute clearly points the way to the only sensible result. In truth, however, the path from the text of the Indian Child Welfare Act of 1978 (ICWA) to the result the Court reaches is anything but clear, and its result anything but right. . . .

Better to start at the beginning and consider the operation of the statute as a whole. ICWA commences with express findings. Congress recognized that "there is no resource that is more vital to the continued existence and integrity of Indian tribes than their children," 25 U.S.C. §1901(3), and it found that this resource was threatened. State authorities insufficiently sensitive to "the essential tribal relations of Indian people and the cultural and social standards prevailing in Indian communities and families" were breaking up Indian families and moving Indian children to non-Indian homes and institutions. . . . Consistent with these findings, Congress declared its purpose "to protect the best interests of Indian children and to promote the stability and security of Indian tribes and families by the establishment of minimum Federal standards" applicable to child custody proceedings involving Indian children. . . .

First, ICWA defines the term "parent" broadly to mean "any biological parent . . . of an Indian child or any Indian person who has lawfully adopted an Indian child." §1903(9). . . . [I]t is clear that Birth Father has a federally recognized status as Baby Girl's "parent" and that his "parent-child relationship" with her is subject to the protections of the Act [based on the Act's comprehensive definition of "child custody proceeding"]. . . .

The majority . . . asserts baldly that "when an Indian parent abandons an Indian child prior to birth and that child has never been in the Indian parent's legal or physical custody, there is no 'relationship' that would be 'discontinu[ed]' . . . by the termination of the Indian parent's rights." Says who? Certainly not the statute. Section 1903 recognizes Birth Father as Baby Girl's "parent," and, in conjunction with ICWA's other provisions, it further establishes that their "parent-child relationship" is protected under federal law. . . .

The entire foundation of the majority's argument that subsection (f) does not apply is the lonely phrase "continued custody." It simply cannot bear the interpretive weight the majority would place on it. . . . A court applying §1912(f) where the parent does not have pre-existing custody should, as Birth Father argues, determine whether the party seeking termination of parental rights has established that the continuation of the parent-child relationship will result in "serious emotional or physical damage to the child." . . .

The majority's textually strained and illogical reading of the statute might be explicable, if not justified, if there were reason to believe that it avoided anomalous results or furthered a clear congressional policy.... With respect to §1912(d), [there] is nothing "bizarre" about placing on the party seeking to terminate a father's parental rights the burden of showing that the step is necessary as well as justified.... In any event, the question is a non-issue in this case given the family court's finding that Birth Father is "a fit and proper person to have custody of his child" who "has demonstrated [his] ability to parent effectively" and who possesses "unwavering love for this child." Petitioners cannot show that rehabilitative efforts have "proved unsuccessful," 25 U.S.C. §1912(d), because Birth Father is not in need of rehabilitation.[11] ...

On a more general level, the majority intimates that ICWA grants Birth Father an undeserved windfall: in the majority's words, an "ICWA trump card" he can "play ... at the eleventh hour to override the mother's decision and the child's best interests." The implicit argument is that Congress could not possibly have intended to recognize a parent-child relationship between Birth Father and Baby Girl that would have to be legally terminated (either by valid consent or involuntary termination) before the adoption could proceed.

But this supposed anomaly is illusory. In fact, the law of at least 15 States did precisely that at the time ICWA was passed [citations to state statutes omitted]. And the law of a number of States still does so [citing authorities that require notice of adoption to all potential fathers or consent in the absence of termination of parental rights for parental fault].

Without doubt, laws protecting biological fathers' parental rights can lead — even outside the context of ICWA — to outcomes that are painful and distressing for both would-be adoptive families, who lose a much wanted child, and children who must make a difficult transition [citing cases]....

The majority also protests that a contrary result to the one it reaches would interfere with the adoption of Indian children. This claim is the most perplexing of all. A central purpose of ICWA is to "promote the stability and security of Indian ... families," 25 U.S.C. §1902, in part by countering the trend of placing "an alarmingly high percentage of [Indian] children ... in non-Indian foster and adoptive homes and institutions." §1901(4).... ICWA does not interfere with the adoption of Indian children except to the extent that it attempts to avert the necessity of adoptive placement and makes adoptions of Indian children by non-Indian families less likely. The majority may consider this scheme unwise. But no principle of construction licenses a court to interpret a statute with a view to averting the very consequences Congress expressly stated it was trying to bring about....

---

11. The majority's concerns about what might happen if no state or tribal authority stepped in to provide remedial services are therefore irrelevant here. But as a general matter, if a parent has rights that are an obstacle to an adoption, the state- and federal-law safeguards of those rights must be honored, irrespective of prospective adoptive parents' understandable and valid desire to see the adoption finalized. "We must remember that the purpose of an adoption is to provide a home for a child, not a child for a home." In re Petition of Doe, [638 N.E.2d 181, 190 (Ill. 1994)] (Heiple, J., supplemental opinion supporting denial of rehearing).

NOTES AND QUESTIONS

1. *The debate.* What role should race play in choosing an adoptive family? Ethnic and cultural background? Why does a federal statute, the Indian Child Welfare Act (ICWA), prefer the placement of Native American children with Native American families, according to *Adoptive Couple*? Do similar reasons justify race matching in adoption? To what extent can or should the law specify such placement preferences for minority children without doing the same for all children? Whose analysis do you find more persuasive, Professor Bartholet's or Professor Roberts's?[8]

2. *Constitutional limits.*

a. *Race and child custody in the Supreme Court.* In Palmore v. Sidoti, 466 U.S. 429 (1984), the Supreme Court overturned the modification of a child custody arrangement because the modification improperly rested on race, in violation of the Equal Protection Clause of the Fourteenth Amendment. The case arose after a white couple divorced in Florida, the court awarded the mother custody of their three-year-old daughter, and the father successfully got the earlier decree changed (so that custody was awarded to him) once the mother began cohabiting with an African-American man, whom she married two months later.

The court that granted the father's request for modification justified its decision on the best interests of the child. It stated (in language later quoted by the United States Supreme Court):

> The father's evident resentment of the mother's choice of a black partner is not sufficient to wrest custody from the mother. It is of some significance, however, that the mother did see fit to bring a man into her home and carry on a sexual relationship with him without being married to him. Such action tended to place gratification of her own desires ahead of her concern for the child's future welfare. *This Court feels that despite the strides that have been made in bettering relations between the races in this country, it is inevitable that Melanie will, if allowed to remain in her present situation and attains school age and thus more vulnerable to peer pressures, suffer from the social stigmatization that is sure to come.*

Id. at 431 (emphasis in Supreme Court opinion).

In the Supreme Court's view, the lower "court correctly stated that the child's welfare was the controlling factor, [but] made no effort to place its holding on any ground other than race." Id. at 432. Is that a correct reading of the quoted paragraph?

Turning to the Fourteenth Amendment, the Supreme Court identified as a "core purpose" the elimination of "all governmentally imposed

---

[8] See Randall Kennedy, Interracial Intimacies: Sex, Marriage, Identity, and Adoption 402-446, 480-518 (2004) (opposing race matching and the ICWA's preferences); Rachel F. Moran, Interracial Intimacy: The Regulation of Race and Romance 127-153 (2001) (emphasizing complexities of determining the proper role of race and background); Twila L. Perry, The Transracial Adoption Controversy: An Analysis of Discourse and Subordination, 21 N.Y.U. Rev. L. & Soc. Change 33 (1993) (critiquing political agenda underlying transracial adoption and the emotional strains placed on adoptees). See also Black Children and Their Families in the 21st Century: Surviving the American Nightmare or Living the American Dream?, 26 B.C. Third World L.J. 1, 1-129 (2006) (symposium including articles on transracial adoption by Professors Twila L. Perry, Michele Goodwin, and Angela Mae Kupenda).

discrimination based on race." Id. Yet, the Court acknowledged both that racial prejudice exists and that the "goal of granting custody based on the best interests of the child is indisputably a substantial governmental interest for purposes of the Equal Protection Clause." Id. at 433. The Supreme Court concluded with the following effort to balance the competing considerations:

> The question, however, is whether the reality of private biases and the possible injury they might inflict are permissible considerations for removal of an infant child from the custody of its natural mother. We have little difficulty concluding that they are not. The Constitution cannot control such prejudices but neither can it tolerate them. Private biases may be outside the reach of the law, but the law cannot, directly or indirectly, give them effect.... The effects of racial prejudice, however real, cannot justify a racial classification removing an infant child from the custody of its natural mother found to be an appropriate person to have such custody.

Id.

Following the U.S. Supreme Court's decision, the mother filed a petition in Texas (where the father and child had moved) for a writ of habeas corpus to recover the child and, in Florida, a motion to compel the return of the child (that was opposed there by the father). The Florida court declined jurisdiction in favor of the Texas court. When the mother appealed that decision, the Florida Court of Appeals affirmed, stating:

> The Supreme Court's decision [in *Palmore*] was that the modification of custody could not be predicated upon the mother's association with a black man. Its opinion did not direct a reinstatement of the original custody decree and the immediate return of the child. The Supreme Court did not say that a Florida court could not defer to a Texas court.

Palmore v. Sidoti, 472 So. 2d 843, 846 (Fla. Dist. Ct. App. 1985). The court then suggested that it would serve the child's best interests to remain in her father's custody given the passage of time and the already "substantial upheavals" in her life.

How far does *Palmore* extend? Does it bar all considerations of race in child custody decisions? Only in modifications? Only when race provides the sole basis for the custody decision?

b. *Race and adoption.* What implications does *Palmore* have for considerations of race in adoptive placements? What factors differentiate adoption from postdissolution custody adjudications?

Pre-*Palmore*, in challenges to some of the restrictive policies described by Bartholet, usually by white adults seeking to adopt African-American children, courts held unconstitutional absolute prohibitions on transracial adoptions, but allowed race to constitute one factor, given its relevance to the child's identity and best interests.[9] After *Palmore*, courts cited it to invalidate statutory preferences for same-race placement.[10] If *Palmore* applies to

---

[9] Compare Compos v. McKeithen, 341 F. Supp. 264 (E.D. La. 1972), and In re Adoption of Gomez, 424 S.W.2d 656 (Tex. Civ. App. 1967), with In re R.M.G., 454 A.2d 776 (D.C. 1982).
[10] See, e.g., In re D.L., 479 N.W.2d 408 (Minn. Ct. App. 1991).

adoption and strict scrutiny governs, might race matching in some cases still satisfy this most demanding standard?[11]

c. *The ICWA and race. Adoptive Couple*, the principal case, became known as the Baby Veronica case. How do you read the majority's references to the child's heritage — the fact that she is 3/256 Cherokee and thus "classified" as Indian?[12] To what extent does such language recall the oft-criticized "one-drop rule" that long determined the racial classifications of African Americans?[13] Does the ICWA classify on the basis of race? If so, could the classification survive strict scrutiny?

Several foster parents and prospective adopters along with several states charged with applying the ICWA have challenged the statute's constitutionality. Rejecting the reasoning below that the ICWA classifies on the basis of race, requiring strict scrutiny, a panel of the U.S. Court of Appeals for the Fifth Circuit ruled that the "ICWA's definition of Indian child is a political classification," that rational-basis review governs, and that the political classification "is rationally related to the fulfillment of Congress's unique obligation toward Indians." Brackeen v. Bernhardt, 937 F.3d 406, 428, 441 (5th Cir. 2019). The Court of Appeals, however, has vacated that ruling and agreed to rehear the case en banc. 942 F.3d 287 (5th Cir. 2019). How should the en banc court decide?[14]

3. *Relative preferences.* To what extent can states promote race matching, while avoiding constitutional problems, by promulgating preferences for adoptive placements with relatives? Does this approach assume mono-racial families?[15] Would placement preferences for relatives violate equal protection if statutorily applicable only to minority children or Native American children?[16]

What considerations support such preferences? Recall the observation in the Berebitsky excerpt, supra, that social workers initially resisted adoption because they valued family preservation and blood ties. Would adoptive placements with relatives address such concerns? What difficulties do relative preferences pose? Like the ICWA, many states prefer adoptive placement with relatives.[17] Who counts as a relative?[18]

---

[11] See David D. Meyer, *Palmore* Comes of Age: The Place of Race in the Placement of Children, 18 U. Fla. J.L. & Pub. Pol'y 183 (2007) (advocating strict scrutiny and case-by-case analysis).

[12] See Bethany R. Berger, In the Name of the Child: Race, Gender, and Economics in Adoptive Couple v. Baby Girl, 67 Fla. L. Rev. 295, 327-329 (2015).

[13] See, e.g., Kevin Brown, Evolution of the Racial Identity of Children of *Loving*: Has Our Thinking About Race and Racial Issues Become Obsolete?, 86 Fordham L. Rev. 2773, 2774 (2018).

[14] See Restatement (Third) of Law of American Indians §9(a) (Am. Law Inst., Tentative Draft No. 1, 2015) ("Federal laws that treat Indians or Indian tribes differentially from other individuals or groups create political, not racial, classifications and are not subject to strict scrutiny under the equal protection component of the Fifth Amendment."); Carole Goldberg, Descent into Race, 49 UCLA L. Rev. 1373 (2002).

[15] See generally Angela Onwuachi-Willig & Jacob Willig-Onwuachi, A House Divided: The Invisibility of the Multiracial Family, 44 Harv. C.R.-C.L. L. Rev. 231 (2009).

[16] See, e.g., *D.L.*, 479 N.W.2d at 413.

[17] E.g., Cal. Fam. Code §8710(a).

[18] See, e.g., C.J. v. M.S., 572 S.W.3d 492, 498 (Ky. Ct. App. 2019) (treating adopters as "fictive kin," based on child's bond after placement with them, despite absence of preapproval or a licensed agency).

Does the Constitution give relatives a right to adopt over strangers? Do their biological connections to the child require the same analysis applicable to unmarried fathers? Why?[19]

4. *Empirical data.* According to data from the 2010 census, 24 percent of adopted children under 18 differ in race from the householder.[20] Many authorities agree that a same-race placement is ideal but a transracial placement is better than continuous foster care.[21] Empirical studies over the years have supported transracial adoption as a "basically positive" alternative to long-term foster care.[22] More recent investigations have focused on the racial identity and self-esteem of African-American children reared by parents of a different race. For example, one synthesis of past studies concluded that healthy outcomes for such transracial adoptees were correlated with the parents' practice of racial-ethnic socialization, specifically "family agreement on how to talk to one another about racial differences, learning about and educating the child on the history of their race and culture, teaching children about racial discrimination, preparation for bias, and being around people of the same race and culture."[23] A study in Minnesota, which included only a small number of African-American transracial adoptees, found that parents of transracial adoptees communicated more about race and ethnicity than parents of other adopted children, but that same-race white adoptees and transracial adoptees generally had similar scores on measures of adjustment.[24] Others have written about parents' efforts to engage members of the Black community to mentor their children and answer their questions, even if the adoptees had little exposure to upper middle-class African-American youth and families.[25] Finally, the literature also includes memoirs reflecting personal experiences with transracial adoption.[26]

---

[19] See Mullins v. Oregon, 57 F.3d 789 (9th Cir. 1995); Rees v. Off. of Child. & Youth, 744 F. Supp. 2d 434 (E.D. Pa. 2010).

[20] Rose M. Kreider & Daphne A. Lofquist, Adopted Children and Stepchildren: 2010, U.S. Census Bureau 1, 16 (April 2014), https://www.census.gov/prod/2014pubs/p20-572.pdf.

[21] See Colleen Butler-Sweet, "A Healthy Black Identity" Transracial Adoption, Middle-Class Families, and Racial Socialization, 42 J. Comp. Fam. Stud. 193, 196 (2011).

[22] Rita J. Simon et al., The Case for Transracial Adoption 74, 155 (1994) (20-year study of 83 families).

[23] Jordan E. Montgomery & Nickolas A. Jordan, Racial-Ethnic Socialization and Transracial Adoptee Outcomes: A Systematic Research Synthesis, 35 Child & Adolescent Soc. Work J. 439, 457 (2018), https://link.springer.com/content/pdf/10.1007/s10560-018-0541-9.pdf.

[24] Emma R. Hamilton et al., Identity Development in a Transracial Environment: Racial/Ethnic Minority Adoptees in Minnesota, 18 Adoption Q. 217, 224-26, 228 (2015); Femmie Juffer & Marinus H. van IJzendoorn, Adoptees Do Not Lack Self-Esteem: A Meta-Analysis of Studies on Self-Esteem of Transracial, International, and Domestic Adoptees, 133 Psych. Stud. 1067, 1077-1078 (2007), https://pdfs.semanticscholar.org/1854/bd93de8b93b85f9c68651d284b8f3a357518.pdf (finding no differences in self-esteem between adoptees, including transracial adoptees, and nonadopted comparisons).

[25] See Butler-Sweet, supra note [21], at 202.

[26] E.g., Barbara Katz Rothman, Weaving a Family: Untangling Race and Adoption (2005) (adoptive parent's perspective); Susan R. Harris, Race, Search, and My Baby-Self: Reflections of a Transracial Adoptee, 9 Yale J.L. & Feminism 5 (1997); Andrew Morrison, Transracial Adoption: The Pros and Cons and the Parents' Perspective, 20 Harv. BlackLetter L.J. 167 (2004) (adoptive sibling's view). See Kennedy, supra note [8], at 447-479 (summarizing such literature).

What other types of studies would you like to see? Why might studies focused on adoptees' self-esteem fail to assess accurately the success of transracial placements?[27]

5. *Federal statutes.* Federal legislation now shapes the way states approach several different aspects of adoptive placements. As you consider the following laws, evaluate both the benefits and disadvantages of federal intervention in this area traditionally relegated to the states.[28]

a. *"Barriers to interethnic adoption."* As Professor Roberts indicates, supra, Congress has legislated the "removal of barriers to interethnic adoption" by providing that no state nor other entity in a state receiving federal funds can "deny to any individual the opportunity to become an adoptive or a foster parent, on the basis of the race, color, or national origin of the individual, or of the child, involved." 42 U.S.C. §1996b (amending the earlier, and less restrictive, federal Multi-Ethnic Placement Act). Does this statute limit only the practices of adoption agencies, or does it bind judges as well?[29] Does it require complete "colorblindness" in adoption — a goal many of the Justices have suggested in cases about affirmative action?[30] How can a court decide whether an adoptive placement would serve a child's best interests without considering all factors, including race?[31] Evaluate the following observation by Roberts:

> Examining the public-private dichotomy's political significance reveals that courts' views of race in each realm are not really contradictory. Understanding race as a natural category that is salient to families complements, rather than opposes, a view that racism is irrelevant in education, employment, criminal justice, and voting. Both are consistent with a conservative ideology that holds that races exist at the biological level, but that racism does not exist at the social level.[32]

Should courts or Congress require transracial adopters to undergo special training?[33] Can they?

Note that, in removing "barriers to interethnic adoption," Congress explicitly left intact the ICWA's placement preferences based on Native American heritage. 42 U.S.C. §1996b(3). Why shouldn't minority identities, families,

---

[27] See Jessica M. Hadley, Transracial Adoptions in America: An Analysis of the Role of Racial Identity Among Black Adoptees and the Benefits of Reconceptualizing Success Within Adoptions, 26 Wm. & Mary J. Race, Gender & Soc. Just. 689, 692-696 (2020).

[28] See, e.g., Vivek S. Sankaran, Innovation Held Hostage: Has Federal Intervention Stifled Efforts to Reform the Child Welfare System?, 41 U. Mich. J.L. Reform 281 (2007).

[29] See In re Adoption of Vito, 712 N.E.2d 1188, 1196 (Mass. App. Ct. 1999) (federal law does not constrain judges in "crafting an order she determines to be in the child's best interests"), vacated and remanded, 728 N.E.2d 292, 305 n.27 (Mass. 2000) (avoiding this issue).

[30] See generally Katie Eyer, Constitutional Colorblindness and the Family, 162 U. Pa. L. Rev. 537 (2014) (historical analysis).

[31] See Ruth-Arlene W. Howe, Race Matters in Adoption, 42 Fam. L.Q. 465 (2008).

[32] Dorothy E. Roberts, Reconciling Equal Protection Law in the Public and in the Family: The Role of Racial Politics, 162 U. Pa. L. Rev. Online 283, 289 (2014).

[33] Child Welfare Information Gateway, Preparing Families for Transracial/Transcultural Adoption, U.S. Dept. of Health & Human Servs., https://www.childwelfare.gov/topics/adoption/preplacement/culturally-competent/transracial/ [https://perma.cc/Q9LQ-FBTC]; Hadley, supra note [27], at 702-704.

cultures, and traditions merit the same protection granted to those of Indians?[34]

b. *ASFA.* Congress enacted the Adoption and Safe Families Act 1997, decreasing the emphasis on family preservation,[35] in order to promote adoption by, inter alia, requiring states to seek terminations of parental rights after a limited period of foster care (42 U.S.C. §675(5)) and providing financial incentives for states to increase adoptions of children in foster care (id. §673b). See Chapter 2, section B2, & Chapter 3, section A. AFSA today no longer reflects best practices, and critics have pointed out the harm it has caused disproportionately to children of color.[36] To what extent do these measures encourage transfer of African-American children to white families — serving the needs of adopters rather than children, as Roberts contends? What reforms would address these problems?

c. *The ICWA.* The background of the ICWA's enactment includes the forcible removal of Native children from their homes to federally operated boarding schools, where they were required to abandon their language and culture and assimilate to white society.[37] In Mississippi Band of Choctaw Indians v. Holyfield, the Supreme Court explained that Congress enacted the ICWA to respond to such abuses. 490 U.S. 30, 32-36 (1989). Which opinion offers the more persuasive interpretation of the ICWA's provisions in *Adoptive Couple*, the majority's or Justice Sotomayor's dissent?

Who counts as an Indian child under the ICWA? The ICWA defines "Indian child" as "any unmarried person who is under age eighteen and is either (a) a member of an Indian tribe or (b) is eligible for membership in an Indian tribe and is the biological child of a member of an Indian tribe." 25 U.S.C. §1903(4). Does this definition promote the ICWA's goals? Optimize child placements?

What counts as "active efforts" under the ICWA? Does the "active efforts" requirement impose a higher standard than the usual "reasonable efforts" required before TPR? See Chapter 3, section A. Does the ICWA's requirement of "active efforts" to prevent family breakup apply to protect the parental rights of a non-Indian parent of an Indian child?[38]

What constitutes "good cause" for departing from the ICWA's placement preferences? Does a child's bond with a foster family meet the test?[39] A general finding of best interests?[40] What of the placement choice made by the mother in *Adoptive Couple*?[41] Should parental autonomy trump the policies underlying the ICWA? Why?[42] In stating that the ICWA's placement

---

[34] Cf. In re A.W., 741 N.W.2d 793 (Iowa 2007) (including ethnic Indians not eligible for tribal membership within the state ICWA unconstitutionally classifies by race).

[35] See, e.g., In re C.B., 611 N.W.2d 489, 493 (Iowa 2000).

[36] Marcia Zug, ICWA's Irony, 45 Am. Indian L. Rev. (forthcoming 2021).

[37] See, e.g., Maggie Blackhawk, Federal Indian Law as Paradigm within Public Law, 132 Harv. L. Rev. 1787, 1831 (2019).

[38] See In re Adoption of T.A.W., 383 P.3d 492, 496 (Wash. 2016).

[39] See In re Alexandria P., 176 Cal. Rptr. 3d 468, 492-493 (Ct. App. 2014).

[40] See State ex rel. Child., Youth, & Fam. Dept. v. Casey J., 355 P.3d 814, 820-821 (N.M. Ct. App. 2015).

[41] In re T.S.W., 276 P.3d 133 (Kan. 2012).

[42] See Mississippi Band of Choctaw Indians v. Holyfield, 490 U.S. 30 (1989); Cherokee Nation v. Nomura, 160 P.3d 967 (Okla. 2007) (applying Oklahoma's Indian Child Welfare Act). See Twila L. Perry, Transracial and International Adoption: Mothers, Hierarchy, Race, and Feminist

preferences do not apply in the absence of a competing adoption petition, is *Adoptive Couple* treating this situation as "good cause"?[43]

Lower courts have divided on the question whether the ICWA and similar state statutes include an implicit exception, limiting application to cases in which a child is living with "an existing Indian family."[44] As one author describes it: "The 'existing Indian family exception' is an entirely judge-made doctrine that precludes application of the ICWA when neither the child nor the child's parents have maintained a significant social, cultural, or political relationship with his or her tribe."[45] Courts supporting the exception invoke legislative intent, reasoning that the ICWA was designed to prevent the breakup of Indian families, so the statute should not apply when there is no such family to break up. Some have also reasoned that the exception is necessary to prevent applications of special protections based on "Indian blood" alone, which would amount to unconstitutional race-based discrimination.[46] The number of states recognizing the exception has been dwindling, with only six states now using it.[47] Does the *Adoptive Couple* majority's interpretation of §1915(f) effectively approve the exception?

Evaluate the *Adoptive Couple* majority's assertion that, strictly construed, the ICWA would disadvantage children covered by the statute. Does the case portend the demise of the ICWA? According to Professor Marcia Zug, the claim that the ICWA accords special treatment to Indian children fails to appreciate how the statute's approach parallels national child welfare policies, applicable to all children. If critics of the ICWA prevail in dismantling it, she argues, then Indian children will be singled out for harmful treatment.[48]

6. *Biracial children.* To the extent that matching practices persist, what families provide a good "match" for children of mixed race? Consider the observations and questions of Professor Twila Perry:

> Until recently, there has been little focus on the fact that a substantial number of the Black children who have been adopted by Whites in the United States during the past few decades are, in fact, biracial — the progeny of one parent who is Black and one who is White. Historically, Americans considered persons of mixed racial heritage that included Black ancestry to be Black, both socially and legally. There is little data that indicates the race of adoptive families into which biracial children were placed prior to the late 1960s when the number of transracial adoptions began to increase. This is part of a larger problem that, until fairly recently, there were few reliable statistics on adoption. . . .

Legal Theory, 10 Yale J.L. & Feminism 101, 150-151 (1998) (feminists must address the conflict between parental autonomy and the argument for deference to ethnic groups' desires for intra-ethnic placement).

[43] See Native Vill. of Tununak v. State, 334 P.3d 165 (Alaska 2014).

[44] Compare, e.g., In re Adoption of B.B., 417 P.3d 1, 29-30 (Utah 2017) (rejecting exception and distinguishing *Adoptive Couple*), with, e.g., Rye v. Weasel, 934 S.W.2d 257, 261-262 (Ky. 1996) (applying exception).

[45] Barbara Ann Atwood, Flashpoints Under the Indian Child Welfare Act: Toward a New Understanding of State Court Resistance, 51 Emory L.J. 587, 625 (2002).

[46] See, e.g., In re Santos Y., 112 Cal. Rptr. 2d 692, 727-731 (Ct. App. 2001).

[47] Shawn L. Murphy, Comment, The Supreme Court's Revitalization of the Dying "Existing Indian Family" Exception, 46 McGeorge L. Rev. 629, 637 (2014) (describing doctrine as "in decline," with only six states following it).

[48] Zug, supra note [36].

> [W]hat if any role should race play in the adoptive placement of [biracial] children? Is there reason to treat biracial children any differently from Black children who would not be considered to be biracial? How should the "best interest of the child" standard, the law's traditional inquiry for child placement decisions, apply to the adoption of biracial children in the adoption context? Should adults who seek to adopt biracial children be evaluated by adoption professionals to determine whether they are likely to be able to meet any special needs such children might have as a result of their mixed racial heritage?[49]

Professor Ruth-Arlene W. Howe has predicted that eliminating consideration of race, as federal law directs, will actually increase discrimination:

> Elimination of race from all placement decisionmaking sets the stage for reinforcing old prejudices and discriminatory practices toward African Americans and for anachronistic recommodification of *young* African American children, without providing any strong assurance that the needs of such children will be met appropriately. Instead, white adults seeking healthy infants now have an opportunity to "garner the market" on the only expanding "crop" of healthy newborns — voluntarily relinquished biracial nonmarital infants (many with one black and one white parent). Prior to Interethnic Adoption Provisions, these babies would be considered black under the customary "one-drop" rule for determining race.[50]

7. *Religious matching.* New York law includes a preference for placing children with caregivers of the same religion. N.Y. Soc. Serv. Law §373. How should the law classify children for purposes of religious matching? What problems does this practice pose? Suppose the state directs deference to the birth parent's choice of religion in placement.[51] Does that solve the problems?

8. *Thwarted fathers redux?* Does *Adoptive Couple* present a case of a thwarted father?[52] See Chapter 3, section B2. Evaluate Justice Scalia's dissent. What do you make of the birth mother's notification of the father via text message? Would a Facebook message have sufficed?[53] What do you make of the birth father's failure to provide support and his argument that he was willing to surrender his parental rights when he thought the birth mother would be rearing the child herself? Professor Laura Briggs suggests that feminists misunderstand the case if they do not side with the father:

> Here's why feminists should care about this [case]: it's a racist case designed to gut federal Indian law. It's a "states rights" case, which should haunt anyone who thinks slavery was a bad thing. It involves a high-profile cast of right-wing actors, from an evangelical Christian adoption agency to lawyer Paul Clement. Making adoption easy and giving birth parents and unwed parents few rights has been a conservative anti-abortion agenda for a long time. It's time feminists noticed, and opposed it. When unmarried fathers are not really parents,

---

[49] Twila L. Perry, Race, Color, and the Adoption of Biracial Children, 17 J. Gender Race & Just. 73, 74-76 (2014).

[50] Ruth-Arlene W. Howe, Adoption Laws and Practices in 2000: Serving Whose Interests?, 33 Fam. L.Q. 677, 684-685 (1999).

[51] E.g., Ark. Code Ann. §9-9-102; Mass. Gen. Laws Ann. ch. 210, §5B.

[52] See Shreya A. Fadia, Note, Adopting "Biology Plus" in Federal Indian Law: Adoptive Couple v. Baby Girl's Refashioning of ICWA's Framework, 114 Colum. L. Rev. 2007 (2014).

[53] See In re Adoption of K.P.M.A., 341 P.3d 38 (Okla. 2014).

unmarried mothers are vulnerable too, as when Newt Gingrich threatened to take the children of welfare mothers and put them in orphanages. If this case is successful, it would make it much easier for poor people to lose children, including against their will, which mostly affects mothers.[54]

Do you agree?

Consider the following portions of Justice Sotomayor's dissent, in which she recalls the precedents about unmarried fathers, while placing the ICWA's provisions in the context of states' varying approaches to such questions:

> Balancing the legitimate interests of unwed biological fathers against the need for stability in a child's family situation is difficult, to be sure, and States have, over the years, taken different approaches to the problem. Some States, like South Carolina, have opted to hew to the constitutional baseline established by this Court's precedents and do not require a biological father's consent to adoption unless he has provided financial support during pregnancy. Other States, however, have decided to give the rights of biological fathers more robust protection and to afford them consent rights on the basis of their biological link to the child. At the time that ICWA was passed, as noted, over one-fourth of States did so. ICWA, on a straightforward reading of the statute, is consistent with the law of those States that protected, and protect, birth fathers' rights more vigorously....
>
> The majority casts Birth Father as responsible for the painful circumstances in this case, suggesting that he intervened "at the eleventh hour to override the mother's decision and the child's best interests." I have no wish to minimize the trauma of removing a 27-month-old child from her adoptive family. It bears remembering, however, that Birth Father took action to assert his parental rights when Baby Girl was four months old, as soon as he learned of the impending adoption.... Baby Girl has now resided with her father for 18 months. However difficult it must have been for her to leave Adoptive Couple's home when she was just over 2 years old, it will be equally devastating now if, at the age of 3½, she is again removed from her home and sent to live halfway across the country. Such a fate is not foreordained, of course. But it can be said with certainty that the anguish this case has caused will only be compounded by today's decision....

570 U.S. at 686-687, 692 (Sotomayor, J., dissenting).

9. *Epilogue.* After the Supreme Court decision, the Supreme Court of South Carolina ordered the adoption by Matt and Melanie Capobianco, the adoptive couple, finalized. 746 S.E.2d 346 (S.C. 2013). Baby Veronica returned to their custody. Some news reports suggest that her birth father, Dusten Brown, has maintained contact with her.[55]

---

[54] Laura Briggs, Why Feminists Should Care About the Baby Veronica Case, Indian Country Today (Aug. 16, 2013), https://indiancountrytoday.com/archive/why-feminists-should-care-about-the-baby-veronica-case-vRp4N7Q3M0eWjsfmHlG7vg [https://perma.cc/2MDT-4EDK]. See also Laura Briggs, Somebody's Children, 2009 Utah L. Rev. 421 (2009).

[55] See Michael Overall, One Year Later, Baby Veronica Case Still Resonates, Tulsa World (Sept. 21, 2014), https://tulsaworld.com/news/courts/one-year-later-baby-veronica-case-still-resonates/article_2b85eeef-72c5-50cb-b3e8-74f9dfe7355e.html (last updated Feb. 13, 2019); Michael Overall, Dusten Brown Makes First Public Comments Since "Baby Veronica" Custody Battle, Tulsa World (May 15, 2015), https://tulsaworld.com/news/local/dusten-brown-makes-first-public-comments-since-baby-veronica-custody/article_b9da8f5f-7aa1-55d4-a960-39b2fc2add05.html (last updated Feb. 19, 2019).

Depictions in Popular Culture: Losing Isaiah (1985)

After an unmarried and drug-addicted African-American mother, Khalia Richards (Halle Berry), abandons her infant during winter in a garbage dump, hospital-based social worker Margaret Lewin (Jessica Lange) bonds with the child, who had been rescued by garbage collectors when they heard a cry. The child, Isaiah, experiences withdrawal from his own drug addiction acquired during Khalia's pregnancy and comes to live with Margaret, her husband, and teenage daughter, Hannah — an all white family. In the meantime, Khalia, haunted by fears that she must have caused Isaiah's death, is arrested, and she begins a long struggle to rehabilitate herself, through work as a nanny, reading instruction, and counseling. Her counselor, an African-American woman who has overcome her own past substance abuse, investigates Khalia's reluctantly recounted story of Isaiah's abandonment and presumed death only to discover his completed adoption by the Lewin family.

Khalia finds an attorney (Samuel L. Jackson) who will sue to overturn the adoption, based on inadequate notice of the TPR, because the case is "socially relevant." He later explains to Khalia, "This goes way beyond you. Black babies belong with Black mothers." Even the Lewins' African-American attorney remarks on the complexity of transracial adoption: "You might raise a Black child with the best intentions in the world, color-blind, but in the end the world is still out there. He needs to know who he is." To bring the point home, in the next scene the hands of Hannah and Isaiah meet while the two are playing; Hannah asks what is different about their hands; and Isaiah responds: "My hand's smaller."

Having left behind her old life and living arrangement with another addicted mother, a very well-groomed and determined Khalia goes to court, and — after several witnesses take the stand — the judge rules in Khalia's favor, overturning the adoption. Devastated, the Lewins must hand over a screaming Isaiah to a social worker who brings him to Khalia. Isaiah's transition to his new life proves excruciatingly difficult. Finally, Khalia, distraught by his pain and unmistakable longing for Margaret, asks her to help. Because Khalia loves Isaiah, she wants him to live with the Lewins "till he can understand all this." She explains to Margaret, "You might not like me but you're going to have to deal with me."

What stereotypes does this film bring to life? Promotional materials feature the question: "Who Decides What Makes a Mother?" How does the film answer this question? Note that the denouement, entailing a cooperative effort by Khalia and Margaret, resembles the suggestions for postadoption visitation by birth parents proposed by some scholars (see Chapter 3, sections A & B2). What message does the denouement send? Is this resolution a "happy ending"? Why?

Note that another tale of a disputed adoption in popular culture ends in a similar fashion. In Barbara Kingsolver's pair of novels,

The Bean Trees (1988) and *Pigs in Heaven* (1993), a non-Indian woman, Taylor Greer, while traveling across the country finds a child foisted into her care. She rears the child, who becomes attached to her, but subsequent publicity reveals the child's Cherokee identity. Pursuant to the ICWA, the child's Cherokee grandfather is appointed her legal guardian, but he must share custody with Taylor. Is such shared parenting a fairy tale? Or a realistic solution to an otherwise intractable problem? What does the allure of this ending suggest?

PROBLEMS

1. States routinely honor the race-based preferences of adoptive parents. Thus, for example, the state will not place an African-American baby with a white couple who says they want only a white baby. Does such action make the state complicit in discrimination, in violation of the Equal Protection Clause? If so, what remedy would you recommend? Should (must?) the state ignore such preferences when placing children?[56]

2. Many states require that older children, typically those age 14 and above, consent to adoption.[57] Suppose Max, an African-American child who is ten years old and has a history of "acting out" in several foster placements with white families, insists that he wants to be adopted only by a married African-American couple. What weight *may* the state social services agency give to Max's preference?[58] What weight *should* such expressed preferences receive?[59]

b. Sexual Orientation

NEW HOPE FAMILY SERVICES, INC. V. POOLE

966 F.3d 145 (2d Cir. 2020)

REENA RAGGI, Circuit Judge: . . .

I. Background . . .

Private charities — many of them religiously affiliated — have long played an important role in caring for orphans and abandoned children in

---

[56] See R. Richard Banks, The Color of Desire: Fulfilling Adoptive Parents' Racial Preferences through Discriminatory State Action, 107 Yale L.J. 875 (1998); Hawley Fogg-Davis, The Ethics of Transracial Adoption 74-92 (2002); Solangel Maldonado, Discouraging Racial Preferences in Adoptions, 39 U.C. Davis L. Rev. 1415, 1472-1473 (2006).

[57] E.g., Wash. Rev. Code §26.33.160(1)(a); James G. Dwyer, The Relationship Rights of Children 36 (2006).

[58] See Elizabeth Bartholet, Commentary: Cultural Stereotypes Can and Do Die: It's Time to Move on with Transracial Adoption, 34 J. Am. Acad. Psychiatry & L. 315, 319 (2006); Jessica Dixon Weaver, The Changing Tides of Adoption: Why Marriage, Race, and Family Identity Still Matter, 71 SMU L. Rev. 159, 175 (2018). See generally American Bar Association Child Custody and Adoption Pro Bono Project, Hearing Children's Voices and Interests in Adoption and Guardianship Proceedings, 41 Fam. L.Q. 385 (2007).

[59] See Hadley, supra note [27], at 706-709.

New York.[3] Adoption in New York, however, is now "solely the creature of. . .statute," and requires "a judicial proceeding" for a person (or couple) to "take[ ] another person into the relation of child and thereby acquire[ ] the rights and incur[ ] the responsibilities of parent in respect of such other person," N.Y. Dom. Rel. Law §110. Since first enacted in 1873, New York's adoption law has had as its primary purpose ensuring the "best interest[s]" of the child to be adopted. . . .

Adoption services in New York can only be provided by "authorized agencies," *i.e.*, entities incorporated or organized under New York law with corporate or legal authority "to care for, to place out or to board out children." N.Y. Soc. Serv. Law §§371(10)(a), 374(2).[4] More than 130 authorized agencies presently operate in New York. Fifty-eight such agencies are public, each operating as a unit of one of the State's social services districts. More than 70 authorized agencies are private, non-profit organizations that voluntarily provide adoption services. Some do so pursuant to contracts with local social services districts and with government funding; others, such as New Hope, operate independently.

The need for adoption services in New York, whether public or private, is undeniably great. In fiscal year 2017, more than 27,000 children in the State were in foster care. Some 4,400 were awaiting adoption. Nevertheless, only 1,729 were actually adopted that year. . . .

A thicket of regulations applies to an authorized agency's placement of a child for adoption. These regulations detail numerous areas for agency consideration, but they comprise no mere quantitative checklist. Rather, most regulations, by their nature, entrust authorized agencies with considerable discretion in determining the best interests of a child. . . .

Judgment and discretion . . . necessarily inform the "adoption study process" that must precede any placement. *Id.* §421.15. . . . Agency judgment will also have to inform the required assessment of a prospective adoptive parent's [capacities including, for example, the ability] to accept the intrinsic worth of a child, to respect and share his past, to understand the meaning of separation he has experienced, and to have realistic expectations and goals . . . . [I]f, after completion of the required study, an authorized agency decides to approve adoption by a particular applicant or applicants . . . [, the] agency works with the approved prospective parents to identify an adoptive child to be placed with them, "[m]ak[ing] placement decisions on the basis of the best interests of th[at] child." *Id.* §421.18(d). The agency and prospective parents then submit to a court a verified petition for adoption and an adoptive placement agreement, *see* N.Y. Dom. Rel. Law §112(2)-(3), (5), and the court decides whether to accept the agency's approval and to order adoption, *id.* §§113, 114. Generally, "no order of adoption shall be made

---

3. For example, in 1806, a group of New York City women — including Mrs. Alexander Hamilton — founded the Orphan Asylum Society, the city's first private charity devoted to caring for orphaned children who would otherwise have been consigned to public almshouses . . . . New York's two best known institutions devoted to caring for orphaned, abandoned, and otherwise needy children, the Children's Aid Society and the New York Foundling Hospital, were created, respectively, in 1853 by private philanthropists and in 1869 by the Sisters of Charity.

4. Children are "placed out" for adoption; they are "boarded out" for foster care. See N.Y. Soc. Serv. Law §371(12), (14).

until [the adoptive] child has resided with the adoptive parents for at least three months." *Id.* §112(6). . . .

As the New York Court of Appeals has observed, the "pattern of amendments" to New York adoption law over the last 75 years "evidences a successive expansion of the categories of persons entitled to adopt." . . . [T]he New York State legislature, in 2010, amended §110 to state that "[an] adult unmarried person, an adult married couple together, or any two unmarried adult intimate partners together may adopt another person." N.Y. Dom. Rel. Law §110. In a signing statement accompanying his approval of the bill, then-Governor David Paterson observed that the amendment expanded qualified adoption applicants to include same-sex couples, "mak[ing] absolutely clear a principle that has already been established by the courts, and that ensures fairness and equal treatment to families that are ready, willing and able to provide a child with a loving home . . . includ[ing] same-sex couples, regardless of whether they are married." At the same time, however, the Governor stated that "since the statute is permissive, it would allow for such adoptions without compelling any agency to alter its present policies." . . .

[In 2013 the New York State Office of Children and Family Services ("OCFS") promulgated a new regulation, 18 NYCRR §421.3(d), to prohibit discrimination and harassment against applicants for adoption services on the basis of race, creed, color, national origin, age, sex, sexual orientation, gender identity or expression, marital status, religion, or disability, and to take reasonable and appropriate corrective or disciplinary action when such incidents occur.] . . .

New Hope's Christian ministry was conceived by clergyman Clinton H. Tasker who, in 1958, sensed a "call of God" to care for women facing unplanned pregnancies and for their children. Tasker's idea was realized in 1965, when Evangelical Family Service, Inc. — New Hope's predecessor agency — sought and obtained from New York's Board of Social Welfare a two-year certificate of incorporation authorizing it "to accept legal custody and guardianship of children; to provide protective service for children; to provide foster care service to child[ren] and unwed mother[s]; to place children for adoption; and [to] function in complete cooperation with all existing social welfare agencies." . . .

The particular religious belief subscribed to by New Hope and relevant to this appeal is that "[t]he biblical model for the family as set out in the Bible — one man married to one woman for life for their mutual benefit and the benefit of their children — is the ideal and healthiest family structure for mankind and specifically for the upbringing of children." Because of this belief, New Hope asserts that it "will not recommend or place children with unmarried couples or same-sex couples as adoptive parents." It does not believe that such a placement is in a child's best interests.

. . . [M]indful that its religious beliefs are not universal, New Hope does not itself "reject" unmarried or same-sex couples as adoptive parents. Rather, it effectively recuses itself from considering their adoption applications, referring them at the outset to "the appropriate county social services office or another [authorized adoption services] provider." . . .

[OCFS informed New Hope that it must revise its policy or submit a plan for closing out its adoption services. Instead, New Hope brought this challenge. The district court granted OCFS's motion to dismiss and denied as moot New Hope's motion for a preliminary injunction. New Hope appeals.] . . .

II. Discussion . . .

As the Supreme Court reiterated only last term, "[t]he Religion Clauses of the Constitution aim to foster a society in which people of all beliefs can live together harmoniously," not a society devoid of religious beliefs and symbols. American Legion v. Am. Humanist Assoc., 139 S. Ct. 2067, 2074 (2019). The Free Exercise Clause, in particular, guarantees to all Americans the "right to believe and profess whatever religious doctrine [they] desire[ ]," even doctrines out of favor with a majority of fellow citizens. . . . "[The] Constitution commits government itself to religious tolerance, and upon even slight suspicion that proposals for state intervention stem from animosity to religion or distrust of its practices, all officials must pause to remember their own high duty to the Constitution and to the rights it secures." Masterpiece Cakeshop v. Colo. Civil Rights Comm'n, [138 S. Ct. 1719, 1731 (2018)].

These principles are particularly relevant to beliefs about family and marriage, where society's views have sometimes proved more fluid than religion's. As pertinent here, the Supreme Court recently traced how society's view of same-sex marriage has evolved over the last forty years, such that what was once prosecuted as a criminal offense is now recognized as a fundamental right. See Obergefell v. Hodges, [576 U.S. 644, 660-676] (2015). Nevertheless, some religions maintain that same-sex marriage is morally wrong, just as some religions view unmarried co-habitation, remarriage after divorce, or conception without marriage as morally wrong notwithstanding society's general acceptance of such conduct. [The court notes how the Supreme Court recognized potential clashes with religious convictions and presumptive protection for religious expression in *Obergefell, Masterpiece Cakeshop*, and Bostock v. Clayton Cty., 140 S. Ct. 1731, 1753-54 (2020) (construing Title VII to prohibit discrimination on the basis of sexual orientation and transgender identity).] . . . But if some accommodation on this matter is the Court's expectation, delineating constitutional boundaries is challenging. . . .

In confronting those hard questions here, we are mindful that the Supreme Court has recognized that the exercise of religion can involve not only belief and expression, but also "physical acts". . . . But the law has permitted government to avoid showing a compelling interest and narrow tailoring if the challenged ban on a religious practice is required by a valid and neutral law of general applicability. Employment Div., Dept. of Hum. Resources v. Smith, 494 U.S. 872, 879 (1990). . . .

Almost from its pronouncement, *Smith*'s construction of the Free Exercise Clause has prompted criticism. The Supreme Court has recently agreed to revisit its decision in *Smith,* with argument expected some time next term. See Fulton v. City of Philadelphia, 140 S. Ct. 1104 (Feb. 24, 2020) (mem.). We need not delay deciding this case, however, to see if *Fulton* yields a more protective Free Exercise standard than *Smith* because we conclude that New Hope's Free Exercise claim should not have been dismissed even under the *Smith* standard as presently applied. A court construing the pleadings in the light most favorable to New Hope could not conclude as a matter of law that OCFS was simply applying a valid neutral law of general application when it instructed New Hope either to agree to approve unmarried and same-sex couples as adoptive parents or to close its 50-year adoption ministry. . . .

[T]he district court thought that New Hope's pleadings "more closely align with Fulton [v. City of Philadelphia, 922 F.3d 140 (3d Cir. 2019), *cert. granted*, 140 S. Ct. 1104 (2020)], where the Third Circuit found that the plaintiff was unlikely to succeed on its claim because the record demonstrated that the defendant respected the plaintiff's sincerely held beliefs while enforcing the anti-discrimination provision at issue."

We cannot agree. At first glance, *Fulton* may appear similar to this case in that, there, a religious foster care agency, Catholic Social Services ("CSS"), claimed that a government entity, the City of Philadelphia, violated its Free Exercise and Free Speech rights by insisting that CSS not discriminate against same-sex couples as a condition of its continuing to provide foster care services. But, in fact, this case differs from *Fulton* in ways important to our review.

First, the relationship between CSS and Philadelphia was contractual and compensatory. [See *Fulton*, 922 F.3d 147-148.] By contrast, while New Hope is authorized by New York to provide adoption services, it does not do so pursuant to any government contract, nor does it receive any government funding. Thus, whatever authority a government entity might claim to limit the free exercise of religion by those who become its agents or accept its funding, no such authority can be claimed here. Second, in *Fulton*, the issue under review was not the sufficiency of the pleadings, but the denial of CSS's motion for a preliminary injunction. . . .

In any event, New Hope's pleadings easily give rise to the "slight suspicion" of religious animosity that the Supreme Court, in . . . *Masterpiece Cakeshop*, indicated could raise constitutional concern. . . .

First, suspicion is raised by an apparent disconnect between 18 NYCRR §421.3(d) and the law it purports to implement, N.Y. Dom. Rel. Law §110. As New Hope correctly observes, the statutory text is permissive, expanding the persons who "may adopt" to include unmarried and same-sex couples. It contains no mandate requiring adoption agencies to approve adoption by any persons. . . .

Second, a suspicion of religious animosity is further raised here by the fact that for five years after 18 NYCRR §421.3(d) was promulgated — from 2013 until 2018 — OCFS voiced no objection to [New Hope's recusal practice] . . . . To be sure, New Hope's recusal policy meant that unmarried and same-sex couples could not obtain adoption services *from* New Hope. We need not here consider what discrimination concerns this might raise if New Hope qualified as a public accommodation under New York law, because OCFS does not attempt formally to denominate it as such. This is not surprising. New Hope's adoption services are not easily analogized to traditional public accommodations such as barbershops that provide haircuts, accounting firms that offer tax advice, or bakeshops that make wedding cakes. And children awaiting adoption hardly equate to a commodity, even if their "supply" in New York (unfortunately) greatly exceeds "demand." Moreover, it appears that an authorized agency offers adoption services not only for the benefit of a public clientele (prospective parents) but, also, so that the agency itself can render a *judgment*: whether it is in the best interests of a child to be adopted by a particular applicant or applicants. Recusal is a familiar and accepted way for decisionmakers to step aside when they recognize that personal interest, predispositions, or even religious beliefs might unduly influence (or appear to influence) their ability to render impartial judgment....

Third, even before discovery, New Hope points to some statements by OCFS personnel that are similar to statements in *Masterpiece Cakeshop* that the Supreme Court interpreted as arguably evincing religious hostility.... As in *Masterpiece Cakeshop*, these statements are subject to various interpretations, some benign. But on a motion to dismiss, we must draw the inference most favorable to New Hope, *i.e.*, that OCFS did not think New Hope's religious beliefs about family and marriage could "legitimately be carried into the public sphere." ...

Fourth, another matter bearing on religious hostility and making dismissal premature is the severity of OCFS's actions in ordering New Hope's closure. It is plainly a serious step to order an authorized adoption agency such as New Hope — operating without complaint for 50 years, taking no government funding, successfully placing approximately 1,000 children, and with adoptions pending or being supervised — to close all its adoption operations....

[The dismissal below of New Hope's free speech claims was also premature.] The pleadings here, viewed most favorably to New Hope, plausibly charge OCFS with an impermissible direct regulation of speech.... [A]ll New Hope's adoption services — from counseling birthmothers, to instructing and evaluating prospective adoptive parents, to filing its ultimate reports with the court — are laden with speech. But, more to the point, these services are provided so that, at their end, New Hope itself can *speak* on the determinative question for any adoption: whether it would be in the best interests of a child to be adopted by particular applicants....

[Regarding New Hope's claim of "compelled speech," it] is hardly evident from the pleadings that OCFS, in requiring New Hope to conform its policies to 18 NYCRR §421.3(d), would permit New Hope to counsel unmarried and same-sex couples that it is in the best interests of a child to be adopted by a heterosexual married couple and *not* in the best interests of a child to be adopted by an unmarried or same-sex couple....

New Hope asserts that its adoption ministry is an expressive association in that it employs protected speech to "convey[ ] a system of values about life, marriage, family and sexuality to both birthparents and adoptive parents through its comprehensive evaluation, training, and placement programs." ... [W]e need not now conclusively decide whether a claim of compelled association with unmarried and same-sex couples pursuing adoption implicates expressive association.... Rather, the pleadings, viewed most favorably to New Hope, indicate that OCFS is requiring New Hope to associate with unmarried and same-sex couples for the purpose of providing services leading to adoption, an outcome that could tie New Hope, the couple, and an adopted child together for months, or even years....

[B]ecause we reverse the dismissal of New Hope's Free Exercise and Free Speech claims, we also vacate the denial of New Hope's preliminary injunction motion as moot. This court does not order the district court on remand to grant such an injunction. Rather, we leave it to the district court, in the first instance, to weigh the merits of the motion consistent with this opinion....

NOTES AND QUESTIONS

1. *State restrictions on LGBTQ adoptions.* At one time, laws on the book effectively disqualified many LGBTQ adults from adopting. For example, before the 2010 reforms recounted in *New Hope*, New York had a statute that limited adoption eligibility to "an adult unmarried person or an adult husband and his adult wife." Some states took more explicit positions. Upon request from the legislature, the Justices of the New Hampshire Supreme Court opined that a bill expressly disallowing "homosexuals" (defined as "any person who performs or submits to any sexual act involving the sex organs of one person and the mouth or anus of another person of the same gender") did not violate equal protection under either the federal or state Constitution, given its rational relationship to the state's interest in providing "appropriate role models for children." Opinion of the Justices, 530 A.2d 21 (N.H. 1987). This ruling came at a time when the leading authority on LGBTQ matters was Bowers v. Hardwick, 478 U.S. 186 (1986), which upheld Georgia's criminal prohibition on same-sex sodomy, in part because "[n]o connection between family, marriage, or procreation on the one hand and homosexual activity on the other [had] been demonstrated . . . ." Id. at 191.

Even after the Court overturned *Bowers* in Lawrence v. Texas, 539 U.S. 558 (2003), on the ground that state action criminalizing private activities associated with sexual minorities unconstitutionally infringes liberty, Florida's explicit ban on adopting by "practicing homosexuals" withstood constitutional review. In Lofton v. Secretary of the Department of Children and Family Services, 358 F.3d 804 (11th Cir. 2004), a gay couple rearing several medically challenged foster children whom they sought to adopt sued to invalidate the law. The federal court of appeals found no infringement of protected liberty because adoption is statutory, the foster-family relationship does not give rise to a right of family integrity, the decision to adopt is a public (not private) act, and there is no fundamental right to adopt. The court also decided that the ban did not rest on a suspect class. Applying rational-basis review, the court concluded:

> Florida clearly has a legitimate interest in encouraging a stable and nurturing environment for the education and socialization of its adopted children. It is chiefly from parental figures that children learn about the world and their place in it, and the formative influence of parents extends well beyond the years spent under their roof, shaping their children's psychology, character, and personality for years to come. In time, children grow up to become full members of society, which they in turn influence, whether for good or ill. . . .
>
> More importantly for present purposes, the state has a legitimate interest in encouraging [the] optimal family structure by seeking to place adoptive children in homes that have both a mother and father. Florida argues that its preference for adoptive marital families is based on the premise that the marital family structure is more stable than other household arrangements and that children benefit from the presence of both a father and mother in the home. Given that appellants have offered no competent evidence to the contrary, we find this premise to be one of those "unprovable assumptions" that nevertheless can provide a legitimate basis for legislative action. Although social theorists from Plato to Simone de Beauvoir have proposed alternative child-rearing arrangements, none has proven as enduring as the marital family structure, nor has the accumulated wisdom of several

millennia of human experience discovered a superior model. See, e.g., Plato, The Republic, Bk. V, 459d–461e; Simone de Beauvoir, The Second Sex (H.M. Parshley trans., Vintage Books 1989) (1949). Against this "sum of experience," it is rational for Florida to conclude that it is in the best interests of adoptive children, many of whom come from troubled and unstable backgrounds, to be placed in a home anchored by both a father and a mother.

Id. at 819-820 (citations omitted). The fact that Florida allowed those prohibited from adopting to serve as foster parents did not undermine this rational basis, according to the court. Id. at 824. Several years later, a state court of appeals relied on the individualized best-interests evaluation required for every adoption as well as social science evidence adduced in the trial court showing that children reared by LGBTQ parents are as well-adjusted as others to hold that the categorical ban had no rational basis.[60]

After Obergefell v. Hodges, 576 U.S. 644, ushered in nationwide marriage equality, LGBTQ adoption and foster care became a focus in the "culture wars." Does marriage equality necessarily protect access to adoption by same-sex couples? Why?[61] Does any of the reasoning in Lofton, supra, survive Obergefell? Would a state's preference for "dual-gender parenting" violate equal protection because it relies on stereotypes about gender performance?

2. *Religious objections: epilogue. New Hope* and *Fulton*, a foster care case that *New Hope* invokes, exemplify the clash between state antidiscrimination laws and religion-based opposition to same-sex relationships.[62] As *New Hope* states, the Supreme Court has shown interest in such matters, but took a muddled position when faced with a baker who declined to create a wedding cake for a same-sex couple.[63] Now the Court has agreed to review *Fulton.* 140 S. Ct. 1104 (2020). How will the Court decide? Would a ruling against Catholic Social Services in *Fulton* necessarily mean defeat for the agency in *New Hope* as well? Why? Are adoption agencies public accommodations? What does *New Hope* say? What makes a state-licensed agency "private"? How relevant is the agency's role in judicial adoption proceedings? Do private but state-licensed agencies like that in *New Hope* merit different treatment regarding the exclusion of LGBTQ adopters than that accorded to public agencies, as the *New Hope* court describes the one in *Fulton*? Why? What follows from an agency's receipt of public funds? According to the trial court in *Fulton*, the legitimate government objectives supporting the application of nondiscrimination policies to the agency include "ensuring that individuals who pay taxes to fund government contractors are not denied access to those services." Fulton v. City of Philadelphia, 320 F. Supp. 3d 661, 685 (E.D. Pa. 2018).

[60] Florida Dept. of Child. & Fam. v. Adoption of X.X.G., 45 So. 3d 79 (Fla. Dist. Ct. App. 2010).

[61] See Campaign for S. Equal. v. Miss. Dept. of Hum. Servs., 175 F. Supp. 3d 691, 710 (S.D. Miss. 2016) (*Obergefell*'s holding extends "to marriage-related benefits — which includes the right to adopt").

[62] For other cases, see, e.g., Buck v. Gordon, 429 F.Supp.3d 447 (W.D. Mich. 2019); Marouf v. Azar, 391 F. Supp. 3d 23 (D.D.C. 2019); Dumont v. Lyon, 341 F. Supp. 3d 706 (E.D. Mich. 2018).

[63] Masterpiece Cakeshop, Ltd. v. Colo. Civil Rights Comm'n, 138 S. Ct. 1719 (2018). See Marc Spindelman, *Masterpiece Cakeshop's* Homiletics, 68 Clev. St. L. Rev. 347 (2020).

Some states have enacted legislation allowing private, state-licensed agencies to decline to participate that "in any placement of a child for foster care or adoption when the proposed placement would violate the agency's written religious or moral convictions or policies," to the extent permitted by federal law.[64] In late 2019, the Trump administration proposed regulations that would allow child welfare agencies to receive federal funds while excluding LGBTQ families;[65] the proposal, however, would require compliance with federal antidiscrimination laws — which the Supreme Court decided in 2020 bar sexual-orientation and gender-identity discrimination as sex discrimination, at least in the employment context.[66]

Should (must) antidiscrimination measures contain "conscience clauses" for individuals and organizations with religious objections?[67] Alternatively, do such exemptions reflect class-based animus, triggering heightened scrutiny under the Equal Protection Clause?[68] What do such exemptions mean for LGBTQ youth, who are overrepresented in the child welfare system, often because they are pushed out of their homes by family rejection?[69]

3. *"Normative families"?* Many states have laws explicitly *prohibiting discrimination* against LGBTQ adopters and foster parents, as *New Hope* and *Fulton* illustrate. Recall the thesis of Berebitsky, supra, that adoption provides a template for the normative family. How do such antidiscrimination measures shape the normative family? What is the normative family today?

According to Professor Cynthia Godsoe, while marriage equality commanded the limelight,

> LGB foster parenting and adoption in the child protection system, however, has remained largely below the radar. Yet this type of family formation has been occurring for decades, long before same-sex marriage was a possibility, and has served as a meaningful avenue to parenthood for gay men and lesbians.[70]

Indeed, such families helped pave the way for marriage equality, and "[n]ot one state allowed same-sex marriage before permitting adoption and foster parenting by LGB people."[71] One prominent illustration comes from

---

[64] Tenn. Code Ann. §36-1-147(a).

[65] See Veronica Stracqualursi, Trump Administration Proposes Rule that Allows Faith-Based Child Welfare Groups to Exclude LGBTQ Families, CNN (Nov. 2, 2019), https://www.cnn.com/2019/11/02/politics/trump-hhs-lgbtq-families-adoption-foster-care/index.html (discussing proposed change to 45 C.F.R. Pt. 75).

[66] See Bostock v. Clayton Cty., 140 S. Ct. 1731 (2020).

[67] Compare Douglas NeJaime, Marriage Inequality: Same-Sex Relationships, Religious Exemptions, and the Production of Sexual Orientation Discrimination, 100 Calif. L. Rev. 1169 (2012) (criticizing such exemptions, as part of the larger movement for conscience protection in the face of gay rights), with Robin Fretwell Wilson, A Matter of Conviction: Moral Clashes over Same-Sex Adoption, 22 BYU J. Pub. L. 475 (2008) (recommending conscience clauses like those developed in the abortion context to resolve moral clashes over same-sex adoption). See generally The Contested Place of Religion in Family Law (Robin Fretwell Wilson ed., 2018).

[68] See Jessica Troisi Franey, Dependency Is Different: Why Religious Accommodations in Agency Adoptions Violate the Constitutional Rights of Same-Sex Families and Foster Youth, 16 Dukeminier Awards 1 (2017) (so arguing).

[69] See Jordan Blair Woods, Religious Objections and LGBTQ Child Welfare, 103 Minn. L. Rev. 2343 (2019).

[70] Cynthia Godsoe, Adopting the Gay Family, 90 Tul. L. Rev. 311, 330 (2015).

[71] Id. at 334.

Obergefell itself, in which two of the plaintiffs, April DeBoer and Jayne Rowse, sought to marry to provide more legal protection for their family, should an emergency arise; each of the two nurses had individually adopted two "special needs" children from the child welfare system because Michigan law allowed joint adoption only by married couples. 135 S. Ct. at 2595.[72]

4. *Adoption and "queer kinship."* As Professor Michael Boucai has noted, "queer kinship," rather than biological or genetic family ties, has long been a hallmark of LGBTQ culture. He recounts:

> No later than the mid-1970s, and amid considerable controversy, social service agencies began placing sexually active, gay-identified adolescents in households headed by gay men and lesbians. By the late 1980s, and despite the insulting truth that their homes usually were considered a "last resort," gay and lesbian people had demonstrated an unusual willingness to adopt or foster other "hard-to-place children — older children [,]...those with developmental delays, psychological issues, [and] physical disabilities," especially AIDS. To this day, gay and lesbian adopters remain more amenable than heterosexuals to accept children who are "the most difficult to place," and same-sex couples are more likely than different-sex couples to adopt "across racial lines."
>
> Lesbians, gay men, and bisexuals are also more likely than non-LGB people to adopt, more likely to contemplate adopting, and more likely to identify adoption as "their preference from the start." Research comparing LGBT and non-LGBT adopters reveals significant differences in attitudes toward biogenetic parenthood. A 2009 study found that, despite the relative ease of assisted insemination, female same-sex couples who adopted were markedly less likely than their different-sex counterparts to have pursued fertility treatments. Even more tellingly, same-sex couples were far less likely than different-sex couples to feel "a strong desire for biological children" — 40% of lesbians and 34% of gay men, versus 90% of straights. Complementary results were obtained in a 2011 study finding that same-sex adoptive couples were considerably less prone than different-sex couples to "internalize adoption stigma," defined as the "feeling that being an adoptive parent is inferior to being a biological parent."
>
> LGBT people's uncommonly warm embrace of adoption demonstrates the persistence, even in this age of assisted procreation, of the belief that love does not need blood to make a family. This belief is no mere acquiescence to circumstance — a defense against mourning what one cannot easily have. To the contrary,...the particular ethic on which LGBT adoptive parents build their "families of choice" partakes of a rich history of queer resistance, both personal and political, to the ideology of biogenetic kinship.[73]

What does this analysis mean for controversies like those in *New Hope*?

5. *Constitutional protections in adoption.* A number of authorities, like *Lofton*, supra, disclaim the existence of a right to adopt.[74] What consequences follow from this principle? Can state actors reject adoption applications for

---

[72] See Julie Bosman, One Couple's Unanticipated Journey to Center of Landmark Gay Rights Case, N.Y. Times, Jan. 25, 2015, at A14.

[73] Michael Boucai, Is Assisted Procreation an LGBT Right?, 2016 Wis. L. Rev. 1065, 1105-1106 (2016).

[74] See, e.g., Griffith v. Johnston, 899 F.2d 1427, 1437 (5th Cir. 1990); Howe, supra note [50], at 678-679.

any reason? Do applicants have a right to a statement of reasons for rejection or fair procedures? Would the Crumps in Crump v. Montgomery, supra, have a procedural due process argument? Does the reasoning in *Lofton* leave room for race-based matching and other placement criteria designed to find the "best" adoptive home for a particular child?

How would the analysis change if the law recognized a child's fundamental right to adoption?[75] Recall that, as noted by Boucai, supra, LGBTQ adults have long showed greater openness than others to transracial adoption and the parenting of "hard to place" children. Accordingly, without LGBTQ adopters in the pool, some eligible children might not find adoptive homes.[76] What reasons, other than those theorized by Boucai, might explain the phenomenon?

6. *Social science evidence.* What role should social science data play in resolving disputes such as challenges to restrictions on the adoption of children by same-sex couples? Do constitutional values, like equality, suffice to resolve the issue? Or should the constitutional analysis include data showing how children fare when reared by LGBTQ parents, compared to straight parents? Professor Marie-Amélie George has documented how social workers relied on scientific evidence to resist and subvert anti-LGBTQ child placement laws, creating controversy and ultimately law reform.[77]

As noted with respect to Florida's ban, *Lofton*, supra, found the empirical evidence wanting, but a later state court case determined that existing evidence made Florida's law irrational.[78] As the evidence continues to accumulate, suppose the consensus changes. And what does it mean to say that children do well in such families? Must their performance on various metrics be the same as for their counterparts reared by a couple of "dual gender" parents? Suppose, for example, "both boys and girls raised by two mothers [are] somewhat more tolerant of gender nonconformity in peers," as one study found.[79] Would all members of society evaluate that finding in the same way? Further, what weight should evidence of the detrimental impact of "legal status ambiguity" have in evaluating the treatment of LGBTQ parents?[80]

As the question of marriage equality worked its way to the Supreme Court, advocates introduced considerable evidence in the lower courts, both in written submissions and trial testimony. In deciding *Obergefell*, the major-

---

[75] See Barbara Bennett Woodhouse, Waiting for Loving: The Child's Fundamental Right to Adoption, 34 Cap. U. L. Rev. 297 (2005). See also Mark Strasser, Deliberate Indifference, Professional Judgment, and the Constitution: On Liberty Interests in the Child Placement Context, 15 Duke J. Gender L. & Pol'y 223 (2008).

[76] See Allen P. Fisher, Still "Not Quite as Good as Having Your Own"? Toward a Sociology of Adoption, 29 Ann. Rev. Soc. 335, 349 (2003); Tanya M. Washington, Throwing Black Babies Out With the Bathwater: A Child-Centered Challenge to Same-Sex Adoption Bans, 6 Hastings Race & Poverty L.J. 1 (2009).

[77] Marie-Amélie George, Bureaucratic Agency: Administering the Transformation of LGBT Rights, 36 Yale L. & Pol'y Rev. 83 (2017).

[78] See *X.X.G.*, 45 So. 3d 79.

[79] Timothy J. Biblarz & Judith Stacey, How Does the Gender of Parents Matter?, 72 J. of Marriage & Fam. 3, 13 (Feb. 2010).

[80] Alison Gash & Judith Raiskin, Parenting Without Protection: How Legal Status Ambiguity Affects Lesbian and Gay Parenthood, 43 Law & Soc. Inquiry 82 (2018).

ity noted that "hundreds of thousands of children are presently being raised by [LGBTQ] couples," citing an amicus brief prepared by Gary Gates, an expert on the demography and geography of the LGBTQ population and Research Director at the Williams Institute on Sexual Orientation and Gender Identity Law and Public Policy at UCLA School of Law. 135 S. Ct. at 2600. Synthesizing the results of many studies, the Williams Institute reported, inter alia, the following findings in 2014:

Impact on Children of Having LGB Parents

- Researchers have found few differences between children raised by lesbian and heterosexual parents in terms of self-esteem, quality of life, psychological adjustment, or social functioning (research on the psychosocial outcomes of children with gay male parents is limited).

- Several studies, some of which have utilized nationally representative datasets, provide no evidence that children with same-sex parents demonstrate problems with respect to their academic and educational outcomes.

- According to self-, peer-, and parent-report, children and adolescents with same- and different-sex parents do not differ in social competence or relationships with peers.

- There is some evidence that the play behavior of girls and boys in same-sex parent families may be less gender-stereotyped than the play behavior of girls and boys in different-sex-parent families.

- Research on adolescents reared since birth by lesbian mothers found that youth with male role models were similar in psychological adjustment to adolescents without male role models.

- Although adolescents and young adults reared by LGB parents are no more likely to self-identify as exclusively lesbian/gay than those reared by heterosexual parents, having a lesbian mother was associated with a greater likelihood of considering or having a same-sex relationship, and more expansive, less categorical notions of sexuality.

- Adolescents and adults point to potential strengths associated with growing up in LGB-parent households, including resilience and empathy toward diverse and marginalized groups.[81]

To what extent does the preoccupation with the how children fare when reared by LGBTQ parents reveal what Professor Clifford Rosky calls "fear of the queer child" and the value judgment that children should be protected from environments that might increase the likelihood that they will grow up to be LGBTQ adults?[82] Consider the following account by a gay dad.

---

[81] Abbie E. Goldberg et al., Research Report on LGB-Parent Families 3, UCLA School of Law Williams Institute (July 2014), https://williamsinstitute.law.ucla.edu/wp-content/uploads/LGB-Parent-Families-Jul-2014.pdf.

[82] Clifford J. Rosky, Fear of the Queer Child, 61 Buff. L. Rev. 607 (2013).

DAN SAVAGE, THE COMMITMENT: LOVE, SEX,
MARRIAGE, AND MY FAMILY

236-238 (2005)

... D.J. [age 6] woke up in the middle of the night with an earache. ... I got some Children's Tylenol into D.J., and we curled up together on the couch in the living room waiting for the medicine to do its job. It was three in the morning on a Sunday. ...

"I want to be gay with Joshua [the child's best friend] when I grow up," D.J. suddenly said. It was a radical change of topic, but it wasn't a bolt from the blue. ...

It was one of those through-the-looking-glass moments unique to gay parents, like the moment we saw our names on our adopted child's birth certificate on the lines marked "mother" and "father." I didn't want to tell D.J. he *couldn't* be gay when he grew up, but I didn't believe he was going to be gay when he grew up. It would be misleading to present gayness and straightness to him as an "either/or" proposition. Telling him he would be one or the other, gay or straight, would give the false impression that sexual orientation was a coin toss.

But the odds weren't fifty/fifty; the odds were so clearly stacked in favor of D.J. being straight that I almost told him he wouldn't be gay. ... But on the off chance that he wasn't going to be straight, I starting naming all the couples we knew, gay and straight, and D.J. joined in. ...

"Most of the men we know are with...?" I asked.

"Girls," D.J. said.

"That's because most men wind up falling in love with women when they grow up, and most women wind up falling in love with men. Those kind of men are called 'straight.' Men who fall in love with men, like me and Daddy, are called 'gay.'"

"Am I going to be gay?"

"I don't know, but probably not," I said. "Most men aren't gay. You could be gay when you grow up, but it's much more likely that you're going to be straight like Uncle Bill or Uncle Eddie or Tim or Brad or Barak."

"But I want to be gay like you and Daddy."

Ah, I thought, somewhere a fundamentalist Christian's heart is breaking. This is precisely what they worry about, they insist, when they condemn gay parents. Our kids will want to be gay, they will emulate their parents, and adopt their sexuality. If you believe — against all the evidence — that sexuality is a matter of choice, it may be a rational fear. But sexuality isn't a matter of choice, it's an inborn trait, and D.J. could no more choose to be gay, like his parents, than I could choose to be straight, like mine.

"It's not a decision you get to make," I said. "It's not a decision I got to make. It's a decision your heart makes."

"When?"

"When you're older," I said. "One day your heart will let you know whether you're going to be the kind of man who falls in love with a woman or a man." ...

PROBLEMS

1. Megan surrenders her son for adoption. Subsequently, she marries and then two years after the surrender and a series of foster home placements for her son, she learns (through media publicity) about the state agency's placement of her son with a gay couple for prospective adoption. Megan describes this placement as her "worst nightmare." Should the court allow Megan to revoke her consent, now that the couple is petitioning to adopt? If not, should it allow her and her husband also to petition to adopt the child, enabling the court to consider the two available adoptive placements?[83]

2. Christine knowingly surrenders her baby for adoption by a same-sex couple. Under state statutes, the biological parent can select the adoptive parents so long as a court determines the placement serves the child's best interests. During the adoption proceedings, Christine's parents (with whom she and the baby lived for four months after the birth) submit a competing petition to adopt the child. They argue that, despite a favorable home study for the placement Christine chose, adoption by LGBTQ adults is not in the child's best interests. They also attack the constitutionality of the adoption statutes, arguing that (a) the Constitution requires a preference for placement with relatives, particularly those who have established a relationship with the child; (b) the absence of a statutory preference for placement with relatives in the adoption statute violates equal protection, given the relative preference in the foster care statute; and (c) the adoption statutes are unconstitutional because they permit the biological parent to select a placement to the exclusion of other biological relatives, to the detriment of the child. Are these arguments persuasive? Why?[84]

3. Some scholars have proposed that states screen and license *all* parents, not only those who take children into their homes through adoption and foster care. They claim that parenting entails responsibilities at least as significant as operating a motor vehicle, which requires a driver's license. With the development of long-acting reversible contraceptives for women, a means of implementing a parental licensing program exists. The program might include the same sort of home study, investigation, and evaluation required for adoptive parents. Would this program be desirable? Constitutional? If neither, what justifies parental screening and state approval for adoption?[85]

---

[83] See In re Dependency of G.C.B., 870 P.2d 1037 (Wash. Ct. App.), review denied, 881 P.2d 254 (Wash. 1994); Shannon E. Phillips, Note, Preventing Bidding Wars in Washington Adoptions: The Need for Statutory Reform After In re Dependency of G.C.B., 70 Wash. L. Rev. 277 (1995). See also In re C.B.D., 394 P.3d 202 (Mont. 2017). Cf. In re Adoption of B.T., 78 P.3d 634 (Wash. 2003) (limiting *G.C.B.*).

[84] See In re Adoption of M.J.S., 44 S.W.3d 41 (Tenn. Ct. App. 2000). See also In re T.L.A., 677 N.W.2d 428 (Minn. Ct. App. 2004).

[85] See, e.g., Hugh LaFollette, Licensing Parents, 9 Phil. & Pub. Aff. 182 (1980). See also See Carter Dillard, Child Welfare and Future Persons, 43 Ga. L. Rev. 367 (2009); Dwyer, supra note [57], at 36. For additional literature supporting the idea, see Howard B. Eisenberg, A "Modest" Proposal: State Licensing of Parents, 26 Conn. L. Rev. 1415 (1994); Roger W. McIntire, Parenthood Training or Mandatory Birth Control: Take Your Choice, Psychology Today, Oct. 1973, at 34; Claudia Pap Mangel, Licensing Parents: How Feasible?, 22 Fam. L.Q. 17 (1988). For a counterargument, see Lawrence E. Frisch, On Licentious Licensing: A Reply to Hugh LaFollette, 11 Phil. & Pub. Aff. 173 (1982). Cf. Isabel V. Sawhill, Generation Unbound: Drifting into Sex and Parenthood Without Marriage (2014) (urging increased access to contraception to delay procreation until parents are ready).

2. THE ATTORNEY'S ROLE

STARK COUNTY BAR ASSOCIATION v. HARE

791 N.E.2d 966 (Ohio 2003)

PER CURIAM. . . .

In April 2000, respondent [David B. Hare, an attorney since 1989,] attempted to arrange an adoption for the first time. The birth mother, whom respondent had represented in a divorce and who still owed him $2,300 in legal fees, was pregnant with twins. Respondent learned of the pregnancy at a debtor's exam in March 2000, at which time he also learned that the birth mother was unemployed and unmarried and did not intend to marry the biological father. They discussed adoption, and he advised that he would be willing to help with the arrangements.

. . . Although respondent had never done an adoption before, [the birth mother] testified that he said he had handled "a lot" of adoptions. She also testified that respondent offered to pay her for her time off work during pregnancy and for six to eight weeks after the twins' delivery, her medical bills and other expenses, and "anything" else she needed. . . .

The birth mother, who was scheduled to deliver in June 2000, agreed to have respondent arrange the adoption of her unborn children. Between April and June of that year, respondent issued eight checks totaling $2,889 for the birth mother's use [which she applied] to rental payments, a motor vehicle inspection, a daughter's trip to Washington, D.C., and [other] expenses. . . . Respondent disputed the birth mother's testimony, insisting that as far as he knew all of these checks had been issued to the birth mother to pay for medical expenses. . . .

On April 28, 2000, respondent interviewed a couple who wanted to adopt the twins. He demanded a $1,500 nonrefundable retainer to pay for their interview and advised that the twins' adoptions would cost $50,000. Respondent decided to charge this amount because he knew parents who had adopted one child from a foreign country, and they had paid $25,000 in legal fees. The couple agreed to proceed, and respondent interviewed them about their background. Three days later, respondent selected the couple as the prospective adoptive parents.

Respondent told the prospective adoptive parents that in addition to the $50,000 legal fee, they would also have to pay $10,000 for the birth mother's medical expenses before the births. In total, the couple paid respondent $61,500: $1,500 for the interview, $20,000 on May 12, 2000, and $40,000 on June 19, 2000. Respondent picked up the $40,000 check himself at the couple's home, explaining that he needed the money to finish paying the bills for the adoptions.

Between April and June 2000, the birth mother, biological father, and prospective adoptive parents completed preliminary adoption requirements. During those proceedings, respondent assured the adoptive mother that although the court had concerns about her previous divorces, they would be able to complete the adoption because he was a friend of the probate judge. At some point, respondent also told the birth mother that he could no longer represent her in the adoption because of a conflict of interest [and] arranged for her representation by another attorney, telling the other attorney first that his fee would be either $134 or $143 and later that his representation would have to be on a pro bono basis . . . because the birth mother did not have any money.

The birth mother delivered the twins on June 22, 2000. On June 27, 2000, respondent filed preliminary estimated accountings in probate court that were required to disclose any disbursements of value in connection with the adoptions. Respondent, who had paid living expenses to the birth mother and had received over $60,000 from the prospective adoptive parents, represented in those filings that no such disbursements had been made. . . .

Also on June 27, 2000, respondent appeared on the adoptive parents' behalf in probate court, along with the birth mother and her counsel and the birth father, for the initial consent hearing. The court awarded temporary custody of the twins to the adoptive parents subject to a final consent hearing six months later.

Prior to the June 2000 hearing, respondent had permitted the birth mother to use a 1993 Oldsmobile that he said was worth $6,000. In July 2000, after the birth mother gave her initial consent to the adoptions, respondent transferred title of the vehicle to her. Respondent also filed a notice of satisfaction of the $2,300 judgment he had against the birth mother. The birth mother testified that respondent told her, "I let you go" on the judgment amount, which he quoted as $2,700. Respondent denied this and testified that he declared the judgment satisfied because he knew the birth mother had no assets. Thereafter, respondent stopped assisting the birth mother financially [including refusing to pay the medical bills that she submitted].

In anticipation of the final consent hearing, respondent forwarded for the birth parents' signature the final accountings for the twins' adoptions. Again, these documents did not list any disbursements for medical expenses or attorney fees. The adoptive mother asked respondent why he had omitted the $50,000 in legal fees and $10,000 in medical expenses they had paid. Respondent explained that "in a private adoption, the monies involved do not need to be disclosed." . . . The adoptive parents signed the accounts, and respondent filed them with the probate court on November 20, 2000. . . .

On December 28, 2000, at what was to be the final adoption hearing, the birth mother withdrew her consent to the adoption, citing her unpaid medical bills. She testified that she no longer trusted respondent's representations about the twins' placement. At the same hearing, the birth mother's attorney asserted a conflict of interest and withdrew.

Thereafter, the birth mother retained a third attorney, who also eventually represented the birth father. The new attorney arranged for the birth mother to become more familiar with the adoptive parents. At the birth mother's request and with the adoptive parents' consent, respondent subsequently withdrew from representing the adoptive parents. Notwithstanding this withdrawal, respondent advised the adoptive parents prior to a meeting with the birth mother and her new attorney "not to discuss money whatsoever because money in a private adoption is private."

[With a new attorney, the birth parents consented again; the adoptive parents disclosed to the court their payment to Hare; and the twins, who had been removed from the adoptive parents and placed in foster care, were returned to them. They recouped some of their money and completed the adoption requirements again.] The probate court approved the twins' adoptions in July 2002.

The panel found that by charging the adoptive parents a $50,000 legal fee in these adoptions, respondent clearly violated DR 2-106(A) (charging or collecting a clearly excessive fee). The panel cited evidence indicating that local adoption lawyers charged hourly rates of $125 to $150 for customary total fees of $2,000 to $3,000 and the fact that respondent had formally accounted for only a few hours of work.

The panel also found respondent in violation of DR 5-101(A)(1) (accepting employment in a conflict of interest without a client's consent after full disclosure) because he had acquired an interest in these adoptions through improper payments to the birth mother and also had not disclosed these payments to the adoptive parents. The panel further found violations of DR 5-103(A) (acquiring an improper proprietary interest in a client's case) and (B) (providing improper financial assistance to a client) because respondent had paid the birth mother's personal expenses and given her a car, neither of which was a permissible advance of court costs or other litigation expenses.

The panel additionally found respondent in violation of DR 7-102(A)(3) (knowingly failing to disclose that which an attorney is required by law to reveal [i.e., the fees and payments]), (4) (knowingly using perjured or false evidence), (5) (making a false statement of law or fact), (6) (creating or preserving evidence the attorney knows or should know is false), and (7) (counseling a client in conduct the attorney knows is illegal or fraudulent). . . . Finally, the panel found that respondent violated DR 9-102(A) (failing to keep client's funds in a separate and identifiable trust account) by depositing into his personal accounts all the money paid to him by the adoptive parents, which included unearned and unapproved attorney fees as well as funds intended to be used for the birth mother's medical expenses. . . .

. . . The panel concluded that respondent had dishonestly and selfishly attempted to conceal the exorbitant fee he charged for these adoptions. [R]espondent has attempted to evade responsibility for and conceal evidence of his shameful betrayal of his clients' interests and professional oath. Disbarment is the only appropriate sanction. . . .

NOTES AND QUESTIONS

1. *Attorneys in private placements.* Private adoptions present a host of challenges for the attorney. Beyond the ethical violations cited in the principal case, consider the following: On what basis did Hare select the adoptive parents? What obligation, if any, does he have to ensure their suitability as parents? Or is that the court's responsibility? What difficulties does his representation of both the birth mother and the adopters, even temporarily, pose?

2. *"Baby broker" laws.* Statutes in many states impose tight restrictions on child placement. For example, New York prohibits all placements except those by "an authorized agency" or "a parent, legal guardian or relative with the second degree." N.Y. Soc. Serv. Law §374(2). The statute defines the prohibited conduct, "plac[ing] out," as arranging for the child's free care in a family other than that of a relative, "for the purpose of adoption or for the

purpose of providing care." N.Y. Soc. Serv. Law §371(12).[86] Such "baby broker" laws were enacted both to prevent commercial trafficking in babies ("baby selling") and to prevent placement by the untrained.[87] Given the latter goal, what activities do such statutes prohibit? Why do such laws exempt parents and some relatives? (For problems stemming from this statutory exemption, see Chapter 6, section C.) To what extent can attorneys or other third parties serve as intermediaries under the New York statute?[88]

3. *Adoption facilitators.* When only parents and licensed agencies can place children, what services can nonagency intermediaries, including attorneys, provide to assist a parent in selecting a placement? Consider, for example, California's statutory scheme:

Cal. Fam. Code §8801:

(a) The selection of a prospective adoptive parent or parents shall be personally made by the child's birth parent or parents and may not be delegated to an agent. The act of selection by the birth parent or parents shall be based upon personal knowledge of the prospective adoptive parent or parents.

(b) "Personal knowledge" as used in this section includes, but is not limited to, substantially correct knowledge of all of the following regarding the prospective adoptive parents: their full legal names, ages, religion, race or ethnicity, length of current marriage and number of previous marriages, employment, whether other children or adults reside in their home, whether there are other children who do not reside in their home and the child support obligation for these children and any failure to meet these obligations, any health conditions curtailing their normal daily activities or reducing their normal life expectancies, any convictions for crimes other than minor traffic violations, any removals of children from their care due to child abuse or neglect, and their general area of residence or, upon request, their address.

Cal. Fam. Code §8623:

A person or organization is an adoption facilitator if the person or organization is not licensed as an adoption agency by the State of California and engages in either of the following activities:

(a) Advertises for the purpose of soliciting parties to an adoption or locating children for an adoption or acting as an intermediary between the parties to an adoption.

(b) Charges a fee or other valuable consideration for services rendered relating to an adoption.

Cal. Fam. Code §8637:

Notwithstanding the provisions of this chapter, an attorney who provides services specified in Section 8623 related to facilitating an

[86] For other examples, see Ala. Code §26-10A-33; Del. Code Ann. tit. 13, §904; Mass. Gen. Laws ch. 210, §11A.

[87] See In re Carballo, 521 N.Y.S.2d 375 (Fam. Ct. 1987).

[88] For authorities from other states, see, e.g., Galison v. District of Columbia, 402 A.2d 1263 (D.C. 1979); People v. Schwartz, 356 N.E.2d 8 (Ill. 1976); In re Adoption of M.M.H., 981 A.2d 261 (Pa. Super. Ct. 2009).

adoption shall be subject only to those provisions of law regulating the practice of law.

Can attorneys receive fees for "facilitation" or only for their legal services?[89] Can facilitators place advertisements? Notwithstanding California's approach, some states prohibit advertisements other than by authorized agencies.[90] What do such restrictions mean for Internet websites, such as Adoption.com, that post profiles of hopeful adoptive parents and expectant birth parents?[91]

4. *Expenses.* Despite the usual exemption for parents in placement restrictions, even parents, of course, cannot "sell" their children.[92] Further, payment to a birth parent can raise questions about the validity of the surrender.[93] Nonetheless, payment of the birth mother's medical expenses by the adoptive parents has long been permissible. What other costs can be reimbursed? Statutes often list both allowable and prohibited expenses, as illustrated by this Oklahoma provision:

Okla. Stat. Ann. tit. 10 §7505-3.2.B

1. Except as otherwise specifically provided by law, the following list of adoption-related costs and expenses specified in this paragraph may be deemed proper items for a person to pay in connection with an adoption:

a. reasonable attorney fees and court costs,

b. reasonable medical expenses for birth mother and minor to be adopted,

c. reasonable adoption counseling expenses for birth parents before and after the birth of the minor, not to exceed six (6) months from placement of the minor,

d. reasonable fees of a licensed child-placing agency, including social services staff fees provided by agency employees that include:

(1) casework services,

(2) adoptive child and family studies,

(3) placement services,

(4) certification of agency facilities,

(5) admission assessments, and

(6) service planning,

e. (1) reasonable and necessary living expenses of the birth mother that are incurred during the adoption planning process or during the pregnancy, not to exceed two (2) months after the birth of the minor

---

[89] Nev. Rev. Stat. Ann. §127.285 (disallowing compensation for the attorney's work in finding children or prospective parents for adoption).

[90] Id. §127.310.

[91] See https://adoption.com/about (last visited July 21, 2020) ("Adoption.com is not a licensed adoption agency or facilitator and it does not provide professional, legal or medical advice. It does not place children for adoption or match birth parents and adoptive parents."). See also Nev. Rev. Stat. Ann. §127.310(3) ("A periodical, newspaper, radio station, Internet website or other public medium is not subject to any criminal penalty or civil liability for disseminating an advertisement that violates the provisions of this section."); Butler v. Adoption Media, LLC, 486 F. Supp. 2d 1022 (N.D. Cal. 2007), discussed in Chapter 6, section B (Problem 1).

[92] See, e.g., Colo. Rev. Stat. Ann. §19-5-213; N.C. Gen. Stat. Ann. §48-10-102; see also State v. Runkles, 605 A.2d 111 (Md. 1992).

[93] E.g., State ex rel. C.V. v. Adoption Link, Inc., 132 N.E.3d 651, 657 (Ohio 2019).

or after the consent or relinquishment of the birth mother. Reasonable and necessary living expenses include but are not limited to:

(a) housing expenses,

(b) utilities, such as electric, gas, water, or telephone bills,

(c) food for the birth mother and any minor child of the birth mother residing in the home of the birth mother,

(d) travel expenses for transportation to support the pregnancy, such as gasoline, bus fares, or providing for the temporary use of a vehicle during the pregnancy, and

(e) child care or foster care for any minor child of the birth mother associated with pregnancy-related medical care.

(2) Reasonable and necessary living expenses shall not include:

(a) any expenses met by existing resources of the birth mother,

(b) any expenses used for the support of family members who are not minor children of the mother,

(c) any expenses for recreational or leisure activities, and

(d) the purchase or gift of an automobile,

f. reasonable expenses for a home study,

g. reasonable and necessary costs associated with an international adoption,

h. reasonable expenses legally required by any governmental entity related to the adoption of a minor, and

i. a one-time gift to the birth mother from the prospective adoptive parents of no greater value than One Hundred Dollars ($100.00).[94]

Would you support a proposal to ban payment of birth mothers' living expenses? Why?[95] What about a proposal for an overall cap on adoption expenses?[96]

5. *Attorneys' ethical challenges.* May an attorney ethically keep a file of adults interested in adopting and then select one over the others when a birth parent seeks help in placement?[97] Does the birth mother's attorney, who facilitates her plan to surrender her newborn for adoption, have any obligation to the birth father and his parents, who want to rear the child? Does the duty to the birth mother require the attorney to assist in thwarting the father's effort to assert paternity and rear the child himself?[98] In Wyatt v. McDermott, 725 S.E.2d 555 (Va. 2012), a divided Virginia Supreme Court held that a birth father could recover against the mother's attorneys and the

---

[94] See also, e.g., In re Adoption No. 9979, 591 A.2d 468 (Md. 1991) (disallowing maternity clothes); In re Baby Girl D., 517 A.2d 925 (Pa. 1986) (disallowing reimbursement for counseling, housing, medical expenses not directly beneficial to the child, including Lamaze classes and sonograms).

[95] See Andrea B. Carroll, Reregulating the Baby Market: A Call for a Ban on Payment of Birth-Mother Living Expenses, 59 U. Kan. L. Rev. 285 (2011).

[96] See Andrea B. Carroll, Cracks in the Cost Structure of Agency Adoption, 39 Cap. U. L. Rev. 443 (2011).

[97] See In re Petrie, 742 P.2d 796 (Ariz. 1987).

[98] See In re Krigel, 480 S.W.3d 294 (Mo. 2016). See also Malinda L. Seymore, Ethical Blind Spots in Adoption Lawyering, 54 U. Rich. L. Rev. 461, 473-474, 479-484 (2020) (discussing *Krigel*).

adoption agency for common law tortious interference with parental rights, based on their participation in thwarting his effort to rear the child himself.[99]

6. *Multiple clients.* Under what circumstances can one attorney represent both the adoptive parents, whom the attorney has selected, and the birth mother or father? Do such parties always have adverse interests, presenting a conflict of interest for the attorney under the Model Rules of Professional Conduct?[100] How might such dual representation cast doubt on a birth parent's consent to adoption in a later revocation effort?[101] After full disclosure, should parties nonetheless be able to consent to dual representation? Why?[102]

7. *The commodification controversy.* Despite the prohibition on buying and selling children, most authorities agree that today's practice of independent adoption often entails the payment of money, particularly for white infants.[103] Birth parents often have the opportunity to choose from several competing prospective adopters, as dramatized on a prime-time televised broadcast that tracked a young woman's interviews with five couples seeking to adopt her baby and her ultimate selection of one.[104] Sometimes, the birth mother lives temporarily with the prospective adopters to assess personally their parenting styles and interactions with the child. What are the advantages and disadvantages of this selection process? Recall *D.N.T.*, Chapter 3, section B3.

Why not legitimize baby selling, given the existence of a market and controversy about matching and other longstanding placement practices? A provocative article contends that an adopter's willingness to pay ensures the child will be well cared for. The authors attribute discomfort with the idea to concerns about overreaching, racial ranking, and the specter of baby breeding. Nonetheless, citing the current availability of abortion and the decreased stigma of rearing nonmarital children, they ask: "[W]hat social purposes are served by encouraging [existing] alternatives to the baby sale?"[105] How would you answer the question?

---

[99] See also Collins v. Missouri Bar Plan, 157 S.W.3d 726 (Mo. Ct. App. 2005) (reversing summary judgments for attorneys in a malpractice action for negligently advising birth parents that they could revoke their consent, causing their loss of exclusive care of the child).

[100] Model Rules of Prof'l Conduct r. 1.7(a) (Am. Bar Ass'n 2020). See also ABA Comm. on Ethics and Prof'l Responsibility, Informal Op. 1523 (1987) (stating that "a lawyer may not ethically represent both the adoptive and biological parents in a private adoption proceeding," while recognizing that "some authorities have held otherwise"); Restatement (Third) of Law Governing Lawyers §130 (Am. Law Inst. 2000) (requiring consent for multiple representation in nonlitigated matter if there is a substantial risk of material and adverse effect on one client's interests). See also Debra Lyn Bassett, Three's A Crowd: A Proposal to Abolish Joint Representation, 32 Rutgers L.J. 387 (2001).

[101] See K.F. v. B.B., 145 N.E.3d 813 (Ind. Ct. App. 2020).

[102] Compare, e.g., Cal. Fam. Code §8800 (allowing consent when statutory requirements met), with Seymore, supra note [98], at 499-502 (citing problems with such consent).

[103] See Madelyn Freundlich, The Market Forces in Adoption 11-13 (2000); Adam Pertman, Adoption Nation: How the Adoption Revolution Is Transforming America 185-203 (2000); Carroll, supra note [96]. But see Martha M. Ertman, What's Wrong With a Parenthood Market? A New and Improved Theory of Commodification, 82 N.C. L. Rev. 1 (2003); Amanda C. Pustilnik, Note, Private Ordering, Legal Ordering, and the Getting of Children: A Counterhistory of Adoption Law, 20 Yale L. & Pol'y Rev. 263 (2002).

[104] 20/20: Be My Baby (ABC television broadcast Apr. 30, 2004).

[105] Elisabeth M. Landes & Richard A. Posner, The Economics of the Baby Shortage, 7 J. Legal Stud. 323, 346 (1978). See also Richard A. Posner, Sex and Reason 409-416 (1992) (advocating removing the "price ceiling" for independent adoptions, given the decreasing supply of available children). But see Carroll, supra note [95].

NOTE: ADOPTION OF CHILDREN WITH SPECIAL NEEDS

Despite market analyses that suggest a "baby shortage," many children with disabilities, children of color, older children, and children in foster care with histories of abuse and neglect await placement. These children are often called "children with special needs" or "hard to place children" — terms that also include sibling groups and children with HIV infection or other medical problems.[106] What inferences about adoption's objectives arise from the coexistence of an alleged "baby shortage" and the number of children awaiting placement?[107]

To encourage adoptions of children with special needs, state and federal programs provide financial assistance.[108] Tax law offers incentives, including some credits and exclusions.[109] How can you reconcile such financial incentives for adoption of children with special needs and the consensus against commodifying children that the condemnation of "baby selling" and critiques high-priced adoption suggest? To what extent do these incentives encourage white parents to adopt African-American children, in turn reinforcing the problems that critics of transracial adoption have pointed out?[110]

In 2014, adoptions of children with special needs had risen to constitute 88.5 percent of domestic adoptions by nonrelatives.[111] Although many adopters of children with special needs report satisfaction with these placements, some such placements end before the final decree is issued. Most of these disrupted adoptions involve older children, while placements of younger children with disabilities and serious medical problems produce higher success rates. Like age, emotional and behavioral problems (including a past history of physical and sexual abuse) are predictors of disruption.[112]

According to some critics, existing governmental support is inadequate. Adoptive families complain about the state's failure to disclose the full extent of the problems experienced by some children in subsidized adoption programs, preventing appropriate treatment; they also contend that more services, including those that begin before placement and continue after

---

[106] See 42 U.S.C. §673(c)(1)(B) (defining "children with special needs" based on specific factors or conditions, including "ethnic background, age, or membership in a minority or sibling group, or the presence of factors such as medical conditions or physical, mental, or emotional handicaps").

[107] See, e.g., Susan Frelich Appleton, Adoption in the Age of Reproductive Technology, 2004 U. Chi. Legal F. 393, 402-405 (2004). On September 30, 2018, 437,283 children were in foster care, with 125,422 awaiting adoption. U.S. Dept. of Health & Hum. Servs., Admin. for Child. & Fam., The AFCARS Report No. 26: Preliminary FY 2018 Estimates as of Aug. 22, 2019, Child. Bureau 1, 1, https://www.acf.hhs.gov/sites/default/files/cb/afcarsreport26.pdf.

[108] See, e.g., 42 U.S.C. §673; Barbara L. Seaton, Promoting the Adoption of Special Needs Children, 17 Widener L.J. 469 (2008). See also In re SH RG ex rel. Northstar Adoption Assistance, 907 N.W.2d 680 (Minn. Ct. App. 2018) (holding federal law of eligibility for adoption assistance does not preempt state law).

[109] See I.R.C. §§23, 137 (2008).

[110] See Hadley, supra note [27], at 696-698.

[111] Jo Jones & Paul Placek, Adoption by the Numbers: A Comprehensive Report of U.S. Adoption Statistics, National Council for Adoption 1, 28 (2017), https://www.adoptioncouncil.org/files/large/249e5e967173624.

[112] See Child Welfare Information Gateway, Adoption Disruption and Dissolution, Children's Bureau (2012), June 2012, https://www.childwelfare.gov/pubPDFs/s_disrup.pdf; Josh Gupta-Kagan, The New Permanency, 19 U.C. Davis J. Juv. L. & Pol'y 1, 19 (2015) (citing data on increased disruptions, given increased placements of older children and children with special needs).

the adoption, are necessary to make such placements work — because adoption is a process rather than a discrete event.[113] The Uniform Law Commission is considering a possible new model statute that would require the provision of specific information and preparation for "high-risk adoptions," including those of children who had been in foster or institutional care or had been previously adopted.[114]

Other calls for reform reflect the persistent tension between those seeking action that would facilitate permanency in the form of adoption, as embodied in ASFA, and those who seek systemic reform that would support birth families, as suggested by the Family First Prevention Services Act. See supra Chapter 2, section B2. Because children of color are usually included in the definition of children with special needs, the debate about transracial adoption inevitably surfaces in these calls for reform.

B. BEYOND CHILD PLACEMENT: OTHER PATHS TO ADOPTION

Not all adoptions reflect the stereotypical child placement scenario depicted in the foregoing cases and materials. This section examines two important departures from the usual scenario: equitable adoption and adult adoption. Two other significant departures, stepparent adoptions and second-parent adoptions, are covered in Chapter 5 because of the questions they also raise about the legal consequences of adoption.

1. EQUITABLE ADOPTION

ESTATE OF NORTH FORD

200 A.3d 1207 (D.C. 2019)

EASTERLY, ASSOCIATE JUDGE:

In this case, we consider whether an individual who is neither the biological nor legally adopted child of a decedent may equitably claim to be the decedent's "child" and "heir" under the District's intestacy statutes such that he has standing as an "interested person" to probate the decedent's estate. We hold that an individual may claim equitable status as a decedent's child, but only in the strictly limited circumstance where he proves by clear and convincing evidence that the decedent took him in as a minor and, from that time on, objectively and subjectively stood in the shoes of his parent. We endorse a fact-specific, equitable inquiry specific to probate matters. . . .

---

[113] See *Griffith*, 899 F.2d 1427; J. Savannah Lengsfelder, Who Is a "Suitable" Adoptive Parent?, 5 Harv. L. & Pol'y Rev. 433 (2011); Dawn J. Post & Brian Zimmerman, The Revolving Doors of Family Court: Confronting Broken Adoptions, 40 Cap. U. L. Rev. 437 (2012).

[114] See Unregulated Transfers of Adopted Children Act §2-101 (Jan. 31-Feb. 1, 2020), https://www.uniformlaws.org/HigherLogic/System/DownloadDocumentFile.ashx?DocumentFileKey=219526fe-bcda-8051-2524-114584424c4f&forceDialog=0 (draft for discussion only).

Rosa North Ford died intestate in 1998. Her estate was not probated at that time. Ms. North Ford had no biological offspring, but she raised several children in her home, among them: Mr. Raymond North-Bey, [who came to live with her in the mid-1950s when he was only a few months old]. Ms. North Ford obtained a Social Security card for Mr. North-Bey bearing the surname "North" (not his birth surname) and she enrolled him in school. According to Mr. North-Bey's counsel, "[h]e lived his life believing and understanding himself to be the adopted child of Rosa North," and Ms. North Ford held herself out as his mother. In 2006, Mr. North-Bey returned to live in the house he had grown up in, thinking that he had inherited the property.

[Litigation began in 2016, when Dorothy Lenoir, one of the children who grew up in the home, sought to protect the house, the estate's only asset.] Ms. Lenoir subsequently withdrew from the litigation of the probate matter after informing the court that she had reason to believe that Ms. North Ford had not legally adopted her . . . or Mr. North-Bey. In response, Mr. North-Bey . . . asked the court to recognize "his right to inherit as an adopted child of Rosa North Ford" and thus his status as "an Interested Person pursuant to D.C. Code §20-101(d)(1)." After his effort to locate records of his adoption in D.C. Superior Court proved unsuccessful, Mr. North-Bey filed a supplemental motion asking the court to recognize his right "to inherit as an adopted or equitably-adopted child" of Ms. North Ford. . . . [The court held that the jurisdiction does not recognize equitable adoption and North-Bey now appeals.] . . .

Having determined that the term "child" in the intestacy statute is unambiguous and does not apply to Mr. North-Bey if he was not legally adopted, we turn to consider his argument that, as a matter of equity, he should be deemed to stand in the shoes of a "child" under the intestacy statute. In addressing this argument, the trial court's dominant and legitimate concern was that the District's intestacy statutes are the final word on intestate succession and foreclose equitable relief. . . .[12]

We agree with the trial court that the District's intestacy and adoption statutes would seem to bar Mr. North-Bey's claim. But there is one other statute that must be considered: D.C. Code §45-401(a) (2012 Repl.). Section 45-401(a) provides that "the principles of equity . . . remain in force except insofar as the same are inconsistent with . . . some provision of the 1901 Code." Applying the principles of equity is not inconsistent with the District's intestacy statute; to the contrary, such application would seem to enhance its inherently equitable function.

. . . [C]onsistent with the general recognition that "society prefers to keep real property within the family as most broadly defined," the intestacy statute presumes that a decedent — even though she did not take the requisite steps to make her desires legally binding — would have wanted her property to be distributed to her family. The hierarchy of succession set forth in

---

12. As Mr. North-Bey acknowledges, a minority of state courts have considered and rejected as a matter of law that an individual may be deemed a decedent's "child" as a matter of equity in the intestacy context, but the split is close, with twenty-seven in favor and twenty against.

the intestacy statute is meant to approximate the distributional choices we expect most decedents would make within a family structure.

As noted, see supra note 12, other jurisdictions have similarly held that their intestacy statutes do not foreclose equitable relief and have endorsed what some call the "doctrine of equitable adoption." Although we add ourselves to this group, we are wary of recognizing such a "doctrine" for at least two reasons. First, the question before us has nothing to do with adoption, which is a distinct legal event under the D.C. Code, generally concerning the long-term welfare of a minor. Our distinct task in this case is to determine who possesses standing as an interested person to initiate a probate matter, which requires us to identify who possesses the right to inherit from an intestate decedent, i.e., who may materially benefit from an intestate decedent's estate.

Second, we resist elevating our application of equitable principles to "doctrine" where we can discern no widely agreed upon animating principle, much less an established test, and we are unpersuaded of the utility of some of the disparate criteria endorsed by other states. As Mr. North-Bey acknowledges, states that recognize "equitable adoption" in intestate succession cases espouse roughly three different rationales, and the criteria they set out for proving equitable status as the decedent's "child" vary accordingly.

Some states ground their theory of "equitable adoption" in principles of implied contract and specific performance [citing cases from Maryland, Alaska, and Colorado]. These states require an individual claiming "child" status to prove the existence of an unperformed contract or agreement to adopt. But this diverts the inquiry from discerning to whom the decedent would have wanted to distribute her property to examining whether a contract was formed. We are uncertain of the logic underpinning this formalistic focus. Indeed, one could argue that evidence of an unratified agreement to adopt cuts against a claim for equitable status as the decedent's "child," as it could suggest that the decedent at one point intended to make the child a permanent family member, but then changed her mind.

Other states rely on principles of equitable estoppel [citing an Iowa case], which generally requires a showing of detrimental reliance. But it seems unlikely that a putative child, particularly one taken in by the decedent as an infant, would have altered his behavior or performance depending on whether he expected to inherit; and, in any event, absent proof of a promise to devise property to the putative child, the child arguably has no equitable interest in inheriting. Rather, as described, the equitable interest is in ensuring that the decedent's wishes regarding the disposition of her property are realized.

A third group of states more generally seeks to promote fairness and to honor the intent of the decedent to treat a child as if the child were the decedent's own. [See, e.g., In re Ford, 82 P.3d 747, 754 (Cal. 2004); DeHart v. DeHart, 986 N.E.2d 85, 103 (Ill. 2013); Wheeling Dollar Sav. & Tr. Co., 250 S.E.2d 369, 372, 373 (W.Va. 1978).] We align ourselves with these states' focus on the decedent's intent[18] and examination of whether the claimant was functionally

---

18. We acknowledge that even these states provide somewhat mixed messages regarding the nature of the decedent's intent. For example, in [In re Estate of Ford, 82 P.3d 747 (Cal. 2004)], the

the decedent's child. This approach, however, appears to be less the stuff of distinct doctrine and more the traditional practice of considering what is equitable in light of the particular facts of the case.

... [W]e conclude that if an individual seeks to establish that he is an intestate decedent's child and heir as a matter of equity, he must prove that the decedent objectively and subjectively stood in the shoes of his parent. At a minimum, the putative child must prove that, as a minor, the decedent gave him a permanent home. Further, the court should consider the particular facts regarding the nature of the decedent's relationship with the putative child, including but not limited to whether the decedent cared for the putative child (i.e., took charge of his health, education, and general welfare) until he reached the age of majority, as a parent would; whether the putative child was incorporated into the decedent's broader family; whether the decedent gave the putative child her surname; and whether the decedent held herself out to others in the community as a parent to the putative child. The court may also consider whether the putative child continued to maintain a relationship with his biological family and if so, if that relationship was inconsistent with the decedent assuming the role of parent to the putative child.

We intentionally set a high substantive bar — one that we anticipate will be difficult if not impossible for individuals younger than Mr. North-Bey to surpass. Our highly-regulated foster care and adoption systems now leave little room for doubt about the creation — or not — of a parent-child relationship. But we cannot say that this has always been the case in the District of Columbia. Certainly, the facts proffered by Mr. North-Bey to the trial court suggest a very different era, where parent-child relationships could have formed extralegally. And it is these proffered facts that persuade us that the identification of an intestate decedent's child and heir under the District's intestacy statutes may be subject to equitable interpretation.

We further hold that an individual who seeks to establish that he was functionally the decedent's child under the intestacy statute must support his claim by clear and convincing evidence. [Most courts that have faced this issue require such a showing.]

For the reasons set forth above, we reverse the trial court's ruling that Mr. North-Bey did not have standing to initiate a proceeding to probate Ms. North Ford's estate. We remand this case to the trial court for a hearing at which Mr. North-Bey may present evidence in support of his claim that he is Ms. North Ford's child and heir as a matter of equity and thus establish his standing to litigate this probate matter. . . .

California Supreme Court states both that an equitable adoption claimant "must demonstrate the existence of some direct expression, on the decedent's part, of an intent to adopt the claimant" and also that a claimant can carry his burden by presenting "proof of other acts or statements directly showing that the decedent intended the child to be, or to be treated as, a legally adopted child." Id. at 754 (emphasis added); id. at 753 (explaining that "[t]he existence of a mutually affectionate relationship, without any direct expression by the decedent of an intent to adopt the child or to have him or her treated as a legally adopted child, sheds little light on the decedent's likely intent regarding distribution of property"). We endorse the latter articulation of the decedent's intent.

NOTES AND QUESTIONS

1. *Background.* Equitable adoption, sometimes called "virtual adoption," is a judicially created doctrine — although *North Ford* hesitates to call it a "doctrine." The majority of courts (among those that have considered the issue) recognize equitable adoption, as *North Ford* states (footnote 12).[115] Authorities trace its use back to the era when "orphan trains" brought indigent children from urban centers to families in the West.[116] Could it also prove useful in cases of informal but permanent caregiving arrangements such as those long practiced in African-American communities?[117] If so, what criteria and requirements should govern equitable adoption?[118]

2. *Theories. North Ford* outlines three theoretical bases for equitable adoption. Which approach is most persuasive?

Each of the theoretical bases has shortcomings. The implied contract approach suffers because of conceptual difficulties in applying specific performance (e.g., enforcement after the death of a party, a reluctance to enforce personal service contracts, and the lack of a meeting of the minds). Estoppel raises questions about the child's detrimental reliance on the contract, especially a child who is too young to understand the contract and who lacks meaningful alternatives.[119] Under each of these contractual theories, courts often condition relief on a showing of some agreement between those acting as parents and the biological parent(s).[120] In cases like *North Ford*, evidence of such agreement is unlikely to be available. Does that make the third theory, focused on fairness and the decedent's intent, the most sound? Why?

3. *Intent.* Under the third approach, what sort of intent on the part of the decedent does equitable adoption require? What kind of evidence will satisfy the requirement? A leading case in California, Estate of Ford, 82 P.3d 747, 749, 753 (Cal. 2004), cited with approval by *North Ford*, expressly requires clear and convincing evidence of an "intent to adopt," which can be demonstrated "by proof of . . . acts or statements directly showing that the decedent intended the child to be, or to be treated as a legally adopted child." Given that language, does *North Ford* correctly rely on *Ford* as an illustration of the fairness approach that it decides to follow?[121]

4. *Functional approach.* In addition to focusing on intent, *North Ford* emphasizes an examination of "whether the claimant was functionally the

---

[115] But see In re Estate of Scherer, 336 P.3d 129 (Wyo. 2014) (holding Wyoming does not recognize equitable adoption).

[116] See Johnson v. Johnson, 617 N.W.2d 97, 101-102 (N.D. 2000). See also Hendrik Hartog, Someday All This Will Be Yours: Inheritance, Adoption, and Obligation in Capitalist America, 79 Ind. L.J. 345 (2004).

[117] See Carol B. Stack, All Our Kin: Strategies for Survival in a Black Community (1974).

[118] For the description of one such potential scenario, see Michael J. Higdon, When Informal Adoption Meets Intestate Succession: The Cultural Myopia of the Equitable Adoption Doctrine, 43 Wake Forest L. Rev. 223, 224-225 (2008) (describing facts of O'Neal v. Wilkes, 439 S.E.2d 490 (Ga. 1994)). See also Danaya C. Wright, Inheritance Equity: Reforming the Inheritance Penalties Facing Children in Nontraditional Families, 25 Cornell J. L. & Pub. Pol'y 1, 46-53 (2015) (advocating expansion of equitable adoption to include nontraditional families).

[119] See Jan Ellen Rein, Relatives by Blood, Adoption, and Association: Who Should Get What and Why?, 37 Vand. L. Rev. 711, 774-777 (1984) (discussing these and other criticisms).

[120] E.g., Hulsey v. Carter, 588 S.E.2d 717 (Ga. 2003).

[121] See also Smalley v. Parks, 108 S.W.3d 138, 141 (Mo. Ct. App. 2003) (holding "acts, conduct, and admissions of the adopting parent" can supply the necessary evidence of intent or agreement).

decedent's child." What is the relationship between intent and function? In Wheeling Dollar Savs. & Trust Co. v. Singer, West Virginia pioneered a functional or status-based approach, which it explained as follows:

> While the existence of an express contract of adoption is very convincing evidence, an implied contract of adoption is an unnecessary fiction created by courts as a protection from fraudulent claims. We find that if a claimant can, by clear, cogent and convincing evidence, prove sufficient facts to convince the trier of fact that his status is identical to that of a formally adopted child, except only for the absence of a formal order of adoption, a finding of an equitable adoption is proper without proof of an adoption contract.

250 S.E.2d 369, 374 (W. Va. 1978). Accordingly, the court required proof by clear and convincing evidence that the claimant was treated the same, from a young age, as a formally adopted child. Relevant circumstances include love and affection, filial obedience, reliance, representation that the child is a natural or adopted child, an invalid or ineffectual adoption proceeding, and the birth parent's surrender of ties. Id. at 373-374. *North Ford* cites both *Ford* and *Wheeling* for the fairness approach that it approves.

By contrast, in selecting among the available approaches, the Illinois Supreme Court in DeHart v. DeHart, 986 N.E.2d 85 (Ill. 2013), chose to follow California, but not West Virginia:

> We believe that the California Supreme Court struck the proper balance in *Ford*, and therefore adopt its holding here. We do not believe it sufficient merely to prove that a familial relationship existed between the decedent and the plaintiff. Nor do we deem it sufficient to show, as *Wheeling* [in West Virginia] held, that the plaintiff merely demonstrate that from an age of tender years, he held a position exactly equivalent to a statutorily adopted child. Rather, we hold that a plaintiff bringing an equitable adoption claim must prove an intent to adopt along the lines described in *Ford* and, additionally, must show that the decedent acted consistently with that intent by forming with the plaintiff a close and enduring familial relationship.

Id. at 103. Yet, *North Ford* relies on this case as well. Do *Ford*, *Wheeling*, and *DeHart* all exemplify the same approach? Which presents a more accurate reading of the precedents, *DeHart* or *North Ford*?

How do the intent-based and functional approaches here resemble de facto parentage and other doctrines used during an adult's lifetime to determine parentage of a child in the absence of biological relationship or formal adoption? How do they differ? See supra Chapter 1, section C.

Which of these different approaches, if any, would address the criticism of Professor Michael Higdon, who laments how "equitable adoption, although created to make inheritance rights more inclusive, has instead served to reaffirm the preeminence of the nuclear family model as the standard for identifying the 'children' of an intestate decedent" — excluding the many minority children who are reared in extended-family settings?[122]

5. *Equitable adoptee's belief and actions.* Should equitable adoption depend on the adoptee's good faith belief that he or she was a legally adopted

---

[122] See Higdon, supra note [118]. See also Irene D. Johnson, A Suggested Solution to the Problem of Intestate Succession in Nontraditional Family Arrangements: Taking the "Adoption" (and the Inequity) Out of the Doctrine of "Equitable Adoption," 54 St. Louis U. L.J. 271 (2009).

child or a biological child? Is it relevant that North-Bey initially thought he could find his adoption records, then questioned whether records from the 1950s were "entirely reliable," and never conceded that he was not legally adopted (per an omitted part of the opinion)? Suppose a court finds sufficient evidence of an equitable adoption of the claimant by her stepfather but also finds evidence that, as a teenager, she connected with her biological father and later invited him to her wedding. Should such action "undo" the equitable adoption, as you understand it? In Sanders v. Riley, 770 S.E.2d 570 (Ga. 2015), the Georgia Supreme Court answered in the negative, reasoning as follows:

> Just as children, once legally adopted, do not become unadopted by forming a relationship later in life with their biological parents — something that is occurring with increasing frequency — children, once virtually adopted, do not become unadopted by developing a relationship later on with their biological parents.

Id. at 577.

6. *Legal obstacle.* In a common scenario in equitable adoption cases, an impediment prevents the foster parents from finalizing the adoption. What counts as an impediment?[123] Would past agency policies that discouraged foster parents from seeking to adopt foster children and sometimes moved them to another home if they became too attached explain why a wish to adopt might never be pursued? Recall Crump v. Montgomery, supra. Would it count as an impediment? Under several tests, the relationship and/or agreement to adopt must occur during the child's minority.[124] Why?

7. *Scope.* Should the doctrine of equitable adoption apply only to inheritance questions? Traditionally, the doctrine has had this narrow scope. Indeed, most states restrict the doctrine to intestacy cases.[125] Even with such restrictions, some courts recognize the equitably adopted child's right to inherit only *from* (not through) the would-be adopter.[126] What explains this narrow scope? Should the doctrine apply in other contexts? Which ones?

8. *Beyond inheritance.* Although many courts adhere to the traditionally narrow scope of equitable adoption,[127] some courts apply it in additional contexts, such as custody and child support disputes. For example, in Nguyen v. Boynes, 396 P.3d 774 (Nev. 2017), the court relied on equitable adoption to affirm paternity, as well as joint legal and physical custody, for an adoptive father's former partner based on findings of: "(1) intent to adopt,

---

[123] See, e.g., Estate of Wilson, 168 Cal. Rptr. 533 (Ct. App. 1980); Cal. Prob. Code §6454 (codifying holding of *Wilson*).

[124] See, e.g., Samek v. Sanders, 788 So. 2d 872 (Ala. 2000); In re Estate of Bovey, 132 P.3d 510 (Mont. 2006).

[125] E.g., In re Estate of Musil, 965 So. 2d 1157 (Fla. Dist. Ct. App. 2007) (listing elements of virtual adoption). See also Poncho v. Bowdoin, 126 P.3d 1221 (N.M. Ct. App. 2005) (disallowing equitable adoption by mother's husband as a means for biological father to avoid support duties); In re M.L.P.J., 16 S.W.3d 45 (Tex. App. 2000) (doctrine inapplicable to claims for child support and health insurance).

[126] E.g., Estate of Furia, 126 Cal. Rptr. 2d 384 (Ct. App. 2002); see also In re Estate of Seader, 76 P.3d 1236 (Wyo. 2003) (doctrine inapplicable to anti-lapse statute, when would-be adopter dies testate).

[127] E.g., In re Scarlett Z.-D., 28 N.E.3d 776, 792 (Ill. 2015) (ruling that equitable adoption applies in inheritance cases, but not in cases about parentage, custody, or visitation).

(2) promise to adopt, (3) justifiable reliance, and (4) harm resulting from repudiation." Id. at 779. In this case, while the two were a couple, Ken and Rob made plans to adopt a child, but Ken alone took that formal action because the agency, Catholic Charities, disallowed joint adoptions by same-sex couples. Rob testified that they planned for Rob to adopt later, and both men participated in every step of the initial adoption process. Further, Rob participated actively in caregiving. Why is equitable adoption necessary in this case? What other doctrines might have resolved this litigation?

The North Dakota Supreme Court has used equitable adoption in a divorce case to impose on the husband a child support obligation for the wife's granddaughter, whom the couple had been rearing for ten years without any formal adoption.[128] Again, how might that result obtain even without equitable adoption?

2. ADULT ADOPTION

IN RE P.B.

920 A.2d 155 (N.J. Super. Ct. Ch. Div. 2006)

JULIO L. MENDEZ, P.J.F.P.

A married couple, P.B. and S.B., ages fifty and fifty-three, respectively, seek to adopt an unmarried fifty-two-year-old female, L.C. L.C. has resided with the couple for over ten years and wishes to formalize her familial relationship with P.B. and S.B. through adoption and changing her last name to theirs. At the adoption hearing on July 14, 2006, the parties testified as to how they operate as a "team" and desire the adoption in order to make their relationship permanent. L.C. testified that she had been married twice previously, had a troubled relationship with her birth parents and siblings, is currently disabled, and has no valuable personal property. P.B. and S.B. currently rent a two-bedroom mobile home, and testified that they are childless, do not seek to adopt L.C. for inheritance, tax, or other such purposes, but instead seek to make their "family unit" official in the eyes of the law. The parties are assumed to have a platonic relationship, although it should be noted that there was testimony indicating S.B. and L.C. share a bedroom. P.B., S.B., and L.C. presented themselves as a team of three equals.

The issue before the court is whether an adult adoption should be granted when the statutorily-required minimum age difference of ten years between the adopter and adoptee is not satisfied. No case law in this State addresses this issue.

Adoption is solely a creature of statute; it did not exist at common law. In researching adult adoption, this Court has found that there are several common reasons for why one adult would choose to adopt another. The first such reason concerns inheritance. See In re the Adoption of Swanson, 623 A.2d 1095 (Del. 1993). Creating a parent-child relationship through adult adoption allows the adoptee to have legally recognizable inheritance rights. A second main reason for adult adoption is to formalize an existing parent-

---

[128] *Johnson*, 617 N.W.2d 97.

child relationship. For instance, a step-child who has developed a strong relationship with a step-parent may be adopted as an adult by the step-parent. Similarly, a former foster child who had grown close to the foster family, but was not legally available for adoption as a child, could choose to be adopted as an adult. Another common reason for adult adoption is to provide for perpetual care of the adoptee. This allows an adoptee of diminished capacity or abilities some assurance of lifetime care under family insurance and inheritance rights. Finally, in some states adult adoption is used to create a legally binding relationship where marriage is not available.[1]

In New Jersey, there are three statutory sections concerning adult adoption, N.J.S.A. 2A:22-1, -2 and -3. The first section, N.J.S.A. 2A:22-1, provides the standards for adult adoptions, allowing an unmarried adult or a jointly consenting married couple to adopt an adult person if

> [t]he adopting parent or parents are of good moral character and of reputable standing in their community, and . . . the adoption will be to the advantage and benefit of the person to be adopted.

The second section addressing adult adoption, N.J.S.A. 2A:22-2, further stipulates that an adult adoption will not be granted unless: (1) there is an age difference of at least 10 years between adopting parents and the adoptee; and (2) the adoptee has requested the adoption (and change of name, if desired) in writing. The court may waive these requirements if the best interests of adoptee would be promoted by the adoption. Ibid. The third and last section, N.J.S.A. 2A:22-3, deals with inheritance rights of an adopted adult.

Here, the parties arguably do meet many of the above-listed statutory requirements. . . . The statutory terms of N.J.S.A. 2A:22-2 do allow the court to waive the age difference requirement, if the court is "satisfied that the best interests of the person to be adopted would be promoted by granting the adoption." Therefore, this court must next consider whether L.C.'s best interests would be promoted by granting this adoption.

But before [doing so], the court will examine why the New Jersey Legislature chose to enact the age difference requirement. On March 13, 1925, the Legislature first approved "An Act Relating to And Providing for the Adoption of Adults," whose terms in large part remain unchanged today. N.J.S.A. 2:39-2, 3. However, one major difference was the initial requirement that "the person or persons petitioning aforesaid shall be at least fifteen years older than the person sought to be adopted." Ibid. Notably, the 1925 statute did not provide for judicial waiver of this age difference requirement. In 1977, the Legislature reduced the fifteen year age difference requirement to ten years solely to "conform the age differential" of adult adoption with that of minor adoption.[2]

---

1. Gay and lesbian couples routinely use adult adoption as such a vehicle in California and various other states. This is a moot issue in New Jersey because of the newly enacted domestic partnership act, N.J.S.A. 26:8A-1 to -13.

2. The full text of the Assembly Statement No. 541, dated June 20, 1977, reads as follows:

> . . . This bill amends the law concerning adoption of adults. Under present law persons who are adopting a minor must be at least 10 years older than the minor, but persons who are adopting an adult must be at least 15 years older than the adult. This can result in situations whereby a 27-year-old may adopt a 17-year-old, while a 28-year-old may not adopt an 18-year old.

This court believes that the age difference requirement was intended by the New Jersey Legislature as a method of ensuring that at least a semblance of a parent-child relationship existed between the adult parties. In fact, this court cannot conceive of any other reason why the Legislature would mandate such a requirement but to ensure such a parent-child relationship. Indeed, it is widely accepted that adult adoption law in most states derives from the ancient Roman principle of *adoptio naturam imitatur,* i.e., adoption imitates nature. Walter J. Wadlington, Minimum Age Difference as a Requisite for Adoption, 1966 Duke L.J. 392 (1966). This principle has formed the basis of legislative safeguards such as the age difference requirement which disallow adoptions between those persons not old enough to be the adoptee's natural parent. It seems reasonable to surmise then that the New Jersey Legislature enacted this requirement to safeguard against illogical adult adoptions, where there is no semblance of a parent-child relationship....

The limited case law in New Jersey concerning adult adoption has not confronted the age difference requirement, or its waiver.... In [In re Estate of Maria Fenton, 901 A.2d 455 (N.J. Super. Ct. App. Div. 2006),] the validity of the adoption was challenged by appellants, *inter alia,* on the basis that the adoption had been spitefully and improperly undertaken by Maria Fenton for the purpose of diverting the trust fund proceeds. [T]he Appellate Division found no evidence of the alleged spiteful motivation and determined that Ms. Fenton's statement that she desired a "nice, close family" was a sufficient motivation for the adoption. In any event, the Appellate Division found that Ms. Fenton's motivation for the adoption was moot, and emphasized that "New Jersey does not require adoptive parents to indicate their reasons for the adoption," id. at 416, 901 A.2d 455, although it cautioned that courts should always be "mindful of the possibility of fraud."

The Appellate Division in *Fenton* continued to echo the prevailing sentiment of existing New Jersey case law in describing adult adoption as "ordinarily quite simple and almost in the nature of a civil contract." The Appellate Division further found that the adult adoption statute "reflects the State's public policy of allowing 'adoption[s] between consenting persons ... when there is a strong benefit to be gained,'" and a "'mutually beneficial adoptive relationship will result.'"

Due to the Appellate Division's characterization of adult adoption as practically a civil contract requiring little inquiry into the parties' purpose, it might appear that inquiry into the presence of a parent-child relationship would not be proper. This court agrees that existing case law, including *Fenton,* supports limited inquiry into the parties' purpose, and thus, by extension, inquiry into the existence of a parent-child relationship, *as long as the initial statutory requirements are met.* Here, unlike *Fenton* and all other previously-published cases concerning adult adoption, the court is

---

This bill would require a 10 year age differential between the adopter and the adoptee regardless of whether the person to be adopted was a minor or an adult.

Furthermore, the court would be allowed discretion in waiving this 10 year differential if it determined that such waiver would be in the best interest of the person being adopted.

[Assembly Institutions, Health and Welfare Committee Statement to A. 541 (June 20, 1977).]

confronted with a case in which the parties cannot satisfy the statutorily required age difference, and is asked to waive this requirement. Because this court believes that the age difference requirement was enacted by the New Jersey Legislature as a means of ensuring a semblance of a parent-child relationship, it logically follows that, if this age difference cannot be met, the court must examine whether the parties' purpose is to legally solidify their already existing parent-child relationship. If the parties do not have a parent-child relationship and are not separated in age by ten years, the adoption petition must necessarily be denied, as it is contrary to the Legislature's intent. Otherwise, courts would be providing a legal stamp of approval to illogical and on some occasions bizarre relationships without any consideration or weight given to the statutory age difference requirement.

[T]he court turns for further guidance to the case law of other jurisdictions. . . . In New York, the Court of Appeals has held that where the relationship between the adult parties is utterly incompatible with the creation of a parent-child relationship, an adoption should not be granted by the court. In the Matter of the Adoption of Robert Paul P., 471 N.E.2d 424 (N.Y. 1984). In this case, a fifty-seven-year-old male sought to adopt his fifty-year-old male homosexual partner. The Court of Appeals decided that adoption is "plainly not a quasi-matrimonial vehicle to provide non-married partners with a legal imprimatur for their sexual relationship, be it heterosexual or homosexual." The Court found that since adoption was unknown at common law, legislative purposes and mandates must be strictly observed. The Court of Appeals further found that, under New York's statute, an adult adoption must still be in the adoptee's "best interests," and the relevant "familial, social, religious, emotional, and financial circumstances" of the adoptive parents still must be investigated. The Court held that permitting adults to feign a parent and child union through the adoption process could not have been the Legislature's intent.

In sharp contrast, the Supreme Court of Delaware held that evidence of a parent-child relationship between the parties is not a condition to adult adoption. In re the Adoption of James A. Swanson, an adult, 623 A.2d 1095 (Del. 1993). In *Swanson*, a sixty-six-year-old male sought to adopt his fifty-one-year-old male homosexual companion in order to formalize their emotional relationship and to facilitate their estate planning. The Delaware Court explained that most jurisdictions limit judicial inquiry into the motives behind adult adoption, but that adult adoption for the purpose of creating inheritance rights has been expressly approved. . . .

Like New York's statute requiring inquiry into the adoptee's best interests, New Jersey's adoption statute similarly requires the trial court to inquire into the adoptee's best interests if the statutory requirements are not met and the parties seek waiver of these requirements. . . . This court concludes that N.J.S.A. 2A:22-2 supports a similar finding. The New Jersey State Legislature can likewise be presumed to have intended adult adoption to require a preexisting parent-child relationship, especially when the age difference requirement is not met, due to the best interests analysis required before waiver can be granted.

In the instant case, not only is the age difference requirement not met, the adoptee, L.C., is older than one of her potential adoptive parents. Therefore, this court finds that inquiry into L.C.'s best interests — which entails inquiry to the existence of a parent-child relationship — is necessary to determine if this statutory mandate should be waived. The court can discern no reason why the parties desire the adoption other than to obtain legal recognition for their emotional bond. Each party testified that the three operate as a "team" of equals. The court saw no evidence of a parent-child relationship between the parties, and the parties never characterized their relationship as such. Further, the court finds no other compelling evidence as to why it would be in L.C.'s best interests to grant the adoption and waive the age difference requirement. The parties testified that they did not seek the adoption to establish inheritance rights or to address issues of perpetual care, but to solidify their emotional connection as a family.

The court understands that this adoption factored as an important emotional milestone in the parties' relationship, and that the parties appear to want nothing more than to have their relationship made "official" in the eyes of the law. This court's denial of the adoption does not lessen the significance of the parties' relationship. Indeed, "[t]he law does not require or prohibit love or kindness. It deals only with legal rights and duties." In re Adoption of A., 286 A.2d 751 (Cty. Ct. 1972). P.B. and S.B. have the right to treat L.C. as a family member of equal standing without adopting her. They may also provide her with love and affection or provide for her in their wills. If L.C. wants to change her last name to theirs, she may do so without an adoption decree. . . .

NOTES AND QUESTIONS

1. *Reasons for adult adoption.* Adult adoption provides one vehicle for creating a legally recognized relationship for inheritance purposes or to gain decisionmaking authority for a partner in cases of emergency or incapacity, to secure hospital visitation rights, and to obtain benefits under insurance policies or employee benefit packages.

Before the advent of marriage equality, same-sex partners often sought to establish an adoptive relationship, although it provided a problematic marriage substitute. In one famous example, the "late civil rights activist Bayard Rustin adopted his partner, Walter Naegle, in 1982. Though Naegle and Rustin's romantic relationship was well-known, Rustin's obituary cited Naegle as his 'child.' Naegle has since lamented that this erasure of his loving relationship with [Rustin] felt particularly painful."[129] In addition, the adoption required Naegle's mother to disown him and a social worker to determine whether the couple's home was fit.[130] What other difficulties does adult adoption as a marriage substitute present? In the inheritance context, does it always make sense to treat the adopter as the "parent" and the adoptee as the "child"? What is the legal impact of such treatment?[131]

[129] Sarah A. Quarles, Vacating Adult Adoptions Post-*Obergefell*, 106 Ky. L.J. 837, 842-843 (2017-2018).
[130] See Elon Green, The Lost History of Gay Adult Adoption, N.Y. Times Mag. (Oct. 19, 2015), https://www.nytimes.com/2015/10/19/magazine/the-lost-history-of-gay-adult-adoption.html?searchResultPosition=1 [https://perma.cc/7BP3-SHKD].
[131] See Richard C. Ausness, Planned Parenthood: Adult Adoption and the Right of Adoptees to Inherit, 41 ACTEC L.J. 241 (2015).

Although the advent of marriage equality and domestic-partnership and civil-union laws eliminated some need for adult adoption as a marriage substitute, such reforms would not have helped the individuals in the principal case. Why did they seek an adoption decree?

2. *After marriage equality.* Once same-sex couples won the right to marry, the adoptions that some had previously procured became an issue. Must they vacate such adoptions in order to marry? Why? Is the interest in marrying a sufficient basis for vacating an earlier adoption?[132] When the couple's relationship ends, what differences distinguish a dissolution of marriage (divorce) proceeding from a proceeding to vacate an adoption? See Chapter 5, section D & Chapter 6, section C. How might state legislatures remedy the problem?[133]

3. *General rule and exceptions.* Almost all states permit adult adoption by statute or judicial recognition. Adult adoption generally requires only the consent of the parties (unlike the adoption of a child, which is predicated on best interests).[134] However, a few states have particular requirements (i.e., co-residence, consanguinity, or age restrictions) that cause difficulties, as in the principal case. For example, some statutes include requirements that the adoptee be a stepchild, birth child, or close relative.[135] Why? Other states require that the adoptee's relationship commence during the latter's minority.[136] Why? Finally, as the principal case illustrates, some states require that the adoptee be some statutorily specified age younger than the adopter. Why?

Case law on adult adoption as a vehicle for estate-planning purposes remains divided, as the precedents surveyed in principal case show. In one legendary case involving a childless couple, Kentucky upheld the husband's adoption of his wife, undertaken to make her his lawful heir and thereby defeat the claims of cousins and charities to the remainder of an earlier testamentary trust established by the husband's mother.[137] Should all adult adoptees come within inheritance laws applicable to "children," or should different rules govern in quasi-family adoptions versus strategic adoptions, as Professor Richard Ausness recommends?[138]

4. *Challenges to adult adoptions.* Although adoption may be used as an estate-planning tool, it does not ensure inheritance rights because an adoption may still be contested (for example, on grounds of fraud or undue influence) even after the adopter's death.[139] To what extent does expanded access to marriage eliminate that problem?

In a much publicized case, Olive Watson, a granddaughter of the founder of IBM, adopted her same-sex partner of 14 years, Patricia Spado, in 1991,

[132] See Green, supra note [130]; Quarles, supra note [129].
[133] See Robert Keefe, Note, Sweet Child O' Mine: Adult Adoption & Same-Sex Marriage in the Post-*Obergefell* Era, 69 Fla. L. Rev. 1477 (2017).
[134] See generally Ausness, supra note [131].
[135] E.g., Va. Code Ann §63.2-1243.
[136] E.g., Wyo. Stat. Ann. §1-22-102.
[137] Bedinger v. Graybill's Ex'r & Trustee, 302 S.W.2d 594 (Ky. 1957). See generally Rein, supra note [119], at 752-753.
[138] See Ausness, supra note [131].
[139] Jeffrey G. Sherman, Undue Influence and the Homosexual Testator, 42 U. Pitt. L. Rev. 225, 260-261 (1981). See also Ferguson v. Spalding Rehab., LLC, 456 P.3d 59 (Colo. App. 2019) (holding adult adoptee to be heir for purposes of recovery for parent's wrongful death).

when Watson was 43 years old and Spado 44. They broke up a year later. At that time, Watson paid Spado $500,000 and wrote her a letter affirming that "I shall not at any time initiate any action to revoke or annul my adoption of you." The validity of the adoption became an issue upon the 2005 death of Watson's mother, who left millions of dollars in trusts established by her late husband, Thomas, to be divided among 18 grandchildren; Spado claimed that the adoption made her a grandchild too, eligible for a share of the trust funds. Watson family trustees attempted to annul the adoption on public policy grounds, but the Supreme Court of Maine declined to do so, leaving Spado as the legal granddaughter of Thomas Watson. In re Adoption of Patricia S., 976 A.2d 966 (Me. 2009). The probate case then settled in 2011, with recognition of Spado as a beneficiary of Thomas Watson's trust, payment to her of $2,500,000, and her agreement to a distribution of the trust as if she had never been adopted.[140]

5. *Friends as family?* Reconsider the petitioners in the principal case. Why does the court suggest their relationship might be "bizarre"? If local statutes preclude adoption, would some other vehicle achieve their goal? Why does their notion of family defy what the law permits? What would be the implications of extending the legal recognition of family law to groups of close friends or others who choose to live their lives as a "team" of equals rather than as a conjugal couple or parent(s) with children?[141] Or does the court assume conjugality and fear legitimizing polyamory?[142] See Chapter 8, section B.

---

[140] Frank S. Berall, Legal Aspects of Same-Sex Relationships in Connecticut, 85 Conn. B.J. 199, 227-229 (2011). See Pam Belluck & Alison Leigh Cowan, Partner Adopted by an Heiress Stakes Her Claim, N.Y. Times, Mar. 19, 2007, at A1; Gregory D. Kesich, Ex-Lover's Adoption Hinges on Key Point, Portland Press Herald, Apr. 19, 2007, at B1.

[141] Compare Laura A. Rosenbury, Friends with Benefits?, 106 Mich. L. Rev. 189 (2007), with Katherine M. Franke, Longing for *Loving*, 76 Fordham L. Rev. 2685 (2008). See also Brown v. Buhman, 822 F.3d 1151 (10th Cir. 2016) (holding moot challenge to Utah's bigamous cohabitation ban); Elizabeth F. Emens, Compulsory Sexuality, 66 Stan. L. Rev. 303 (2014) (examining assumptions about conjugality embedded in law, including family law). Cf. Law Comm'n of Can., Beyond Conjugality: Recognizing and Supporting Close Personal Adult Relationships (2001), https://ssrn.com/abstract=1720747.

[142] See Elizabeth F. Emens, Monogamy's Law: Compulsory Monogamy and Polyamorous Existence, 29 N.Y.U. Rev. L. & Soc. Change 277 (2004).

CHAPTER 5

CONSEQUENCES OF ADOPTION

If adoption creates a legal fiction, what consequences does this fiction entail? This chapter explores this question, from doctrinal, policy-based, and emotional perspectives.

A. THE "CUTOFF" RULE

IN RE PIEL

884 N.E.2d 1040 (N.Y. 2008)

KAYE, Chief Judge:

[In re Best 485 N.E.2d 1010 (1985)], this Court relied on strong policy considerations to conclude that a child adopted out of the family by strangers does not presumptively share in a class gift to the biological parent's issue established in the biological grandmother's 1973 testamentary trust. This appeal presents the same scenario, but with class gifts created by 1926 and 1963 irrevocable trusts. Despite the time difference, we conclude that the policy considerations that were determinative in *Best* equally determine the case before us, and that the adopted-out child does not share in the trust proceeds.

Background

Florence Woodward created two irrevocable trusts, one in 1926 and a second in 1963, for the lifetime benefit of her daughter, Barbara W. Piel, and upon her death the trusts directed the trustee (successor-in-interest Fleet Bank) to distribute the principal to Barbara's descendants. Specifically, the 1926 trust net income was to be paid "to her descendants, if any, in equal shares, per stirpes. . . ." The 1963 trust principal was to be divided equally for "each then living child of hers. . . ." Barbara Piel died in July 2003, and in October 2004 Fleet Bank instituted two proceedings for judicial settlement of the final account for each trust. This appeal concerns the distribution of approximately $9.7 million in trust principal.

Barbara Piel gave birth to three daughters. Her first daughter, intervenor-respondent Elizabeth McNabb, was born out of wedlock on August 15, 1955 in Portland, Oregon. Within days, Barbara signed a Consent to Adoption, relinquishing her parental rights and agreeing to Elizabeth's adoption by strangers. An Oregon court finalized the adoption in November 1955 and Elizabeth lived her life in Oregon as a member of the Jones family. There is no indication that Florence Woodward knew of Elizabeth's birth or adoption. Barbara's other two daughters, Stobie Piel, born in 1959, and Lila Piel-Ollman, born in 1961, are the children of her marriage to Michael Piel.

Fleet Bank cited Stobie and Lila in the October 2004 proceedings, but failed to include Elizabeth or her children as interested persons. In November 2004 Elizabeth moved for permission to intervene and file objections to the accounts, later joined by her two children. Elizabeth objected to each account because it failed to provide her with a one-third distribution of the principal and income of each trust. [On cross-motions for summary judgment, the Surrogate's Court dismissed Elizabeth's objections, but the intermediate appellate court reversed. Here, the court reverses and reinstates the decision of the Surrogate's Court.]

Analysis

We begin with the fundamental premise that a court must first look within the four corners of a trust instrument to determine the grantor's intent . . . . The question in *Best*, as here, was whether the adopted-out child was an intended beneficiary of the class gift. . . . Before addressing the policy considerations relied upon in *Best*, we outline the significant change in the Domestic Relations Law that distinguishes the present facts, but not the result.

From 1896 through 1963, an adopted child's right "to inheritance and succession" from the biological family "remain[ed] unaffected" by the order of adoption (Domestic Relations Law §64, as codified by L 1896, ch 272). . . . Unclear, however, is whether an adopted-out child was presumptively included in a class gift to a biological parent's issue, descendants or children. In 1963 the Legislature amended Domestic Relations Law §117 by terminating — for the first time since 1896 — an adopted child's rights to inheritance and succession from the biological family. Effective March 1, 1964, the amendments included a savings clause for wills and irrevocable instruments executed prior to that date.

In 1985, when *Best* was decided, Domestic Relations Law §117 provided that the "rights of an adoptive child to inheritance and succession from and through his natural parents shall terminate upon the making of the order of adoption. . . ." Subsection 2 clarified that the termination of rights applied "only to the intestate descent and distribution of real and personal property and *shall not affect the right of any child to distribution of property under the will . . . or under any inter vivos instrument . . .* executed by such natural parent or his or her kindred." Significantly, the Court determined that this statutory provision "does not mandate that [an adopted-out] child receive a gift by implication[,]" but only protects an adopted-out child's right to inherit when specifically identified in the instrument. Thus, section 117(2) merely preserved rights of inheritance expressly intended by the grantor; it did not create additional rights.

As in *Best*, the Domestic Relations Law in effect at the time Florence Woodward executed the trusts does not create rights for an adopted-out child to share in a class gift by implication. *Best* determined that question, concluding that similar statutory language did not create such a right. Nothing in the pre-1964 legislative history or case law, moreover, indicates that an adopted-out child would share in a class gift to a biological parent's issue, descendants or children.

Having determined that the statutory law effective prior to March 1, 1964 does not require a different result, we turn to the strong policy considerations supporting adherence to *Best*. In excluding adopted-out children from class gifts to the biological parent's issue, the Court highlighted the legislative objective of fully assimilating the adopted child into the adoptive family and, relatedly, the importance of keeping adoption records confidential. From the very inception of the adoption law [in 1896] the Legislature has sought to promote assimilation of the adopted child by providing the new family with the "legal relation of parent and child." Additionally, by 1924 the Legislature had explicitly recognized the importance of confidentiality in adoption records, and in 1938 it mandated the sealing of those records. These policy considerations pre-date the execution of both Woodward trusts.

The facts of this case also compellingly demonstrate the importance of the third policy concern identified in *Best*. As the Court noted, the finality of judicial decrees would be compromised if adopted-out children were included in such class gifts "because there would always lurk the possibility, no matter how remote, that a secret out-of-wedlock child had been adopted out of the family by a biological parent or ancestor of a class of beneficiaries." That lurking possibility materialized here. In this case the adopted-out child intervened and relieved the trustee of the duty to identify and cite her. In other cases, neither the family nor the child may be aware of a birth or adoption, thereby placing on a trustee seeking closure the onerous burden of searching out unknown potential beneficiaries.

This case raises additional policy concerns: here we address classes of beneficiaries created in irrevocable instruments prior to 1964. The chances of unearthing adoption decrees potentially dating back to the late 1800s, or of identifying witnesses to recall the details of an adoption, dwindle as time passes. Permitting adopted-out children to participate in a class created by a pre-1964 instrument would pose greater practical problems to the procedural administration of a gift, and — without any legal basis for doing so — would create two classes of beneficiaries, those receiving a gift in an instrument executed before 1964 and those after. The policy interests of finality in court decrees and stability in property titles weigh heavily in favor of consistency with *Best*.

Therefore, we conclude that the *Best* rule of construction also applies to irrevocable trusts executed prior to March 1, 1964. Where, as here, the grantor's intent is indiscernible and the statutory intent at best ambiguous, we conclude that the policy considerations disfavoring inclusion of adopted-out children in such a class determine this case. . . .

NOTES AND QUESTIONS

1. *Adoption and inheritance.* An adoption decree terminates or "cuts off" the legal relationship between the adoptee and all biological relatives and replaces it with ties to the adoptive family. This principle treats the adoptee as if she were a legitimate blood descendant of the adopter for all purposes. It follows, as *Piel* indicates in its discussion of New York's statutes, that

adopted children inherit by intestate succession from their adoptive, but not from their biological, parents.[1] What reasons support this rule? Although the Uniform Law Commission has withdrawn the Uniform Adoption Act (UAA) as obsolete, a comment in the 1969 version offers this rationale for the cutoff rule:

> The termination of relationship of parent and child between the adopted person and his natural parents and the family of the natural parents follows the trend of modern statutes and is desirable for many reasons. It eases the transition from old family to new family by providing for a clean final "cut-off" of legal relationships with the old family. It also preserves the secrecy of adoption proceedings ... by reducing the selfish reasons an individual might have to discover his antecedents.

UAA §14 cmt. (1999).[2] Nonetheless, some states allow for inheritance by adopted children from their biological parents.[3]

At one time, the "stranger-to-the-adoption" doctrine prevailed in construing wills and trusts. Under this doctrine, class-gift language — such as "children," "issue," "descendants," or "heirs" — does not include an adoptee when the testator or settlor was not the adoptive parent. The modern trend has been to abolish this doctrine for adoptees who were adopted as minors, and wills and trusts written today carry a presumption that inclusion of such adoptees is intended, unless the document expressly excludes them.[4]

2. *Other consequences.* The general rule that adoption creates new relationships in place of biological ties raises questions other than inheritance. For example, does the preference for placing siblings together still apply once one sibling has been adopted?[5] Should laws barring marriages between close relatives (incest restrictions) apply to relationships by adoption?[6]

3. *Policy considerations.* To what extent do the policy considerations cited in *Piel* and noted in the UAA comment, supra, remain compelling today? Do the diminution of secrecy in adoptive placements, the rise of open adoption, and the recognition of psychological reasons prompting adoptees to seek out their birth parents (all explored infra) require rethinking the cutoff rule? Are there situations in which cutting off the original parent-child relationship works to the child's detriment?

---

[1] See also Estate of Obata, 238 Cal. Rptr. 3d 545 (Ct. App. 2018) (holding that practice of yōshi-engumi, undertaken in Japan, functions like an adoption, cutting off original relationship for purposes of intestate succession in California).

[2] The Uniform Probate Code (UPC) speaks of an adoptee's "replacement family" and "fresh start." UPC §2-119 cmt. to subsection (b) (2019).

[3] See, e.g., Rogers v. Pratt, 467 P.3d 651, 654 (Okla. 2020); Tex. Fam. Code Ann. §161.206(b); see also Andrea Smith, Blood & Money: A Conflict in Texas Statutes Regarding Adoptees' Inheritance Rights From and Through Biological Parents, 3 Tex. A&M J. Prop. L. 217 (2016).

[4] See Restatement (Third) of Property (Wills & Donative Transfers) §2.5 cmt. d (Am. Law Inst.); UPC §2-705(d) cmt. (2019). Cf. Walters v. Corder, 146 N.E.3d 965, 970 (Ind. Ct. App. 2020).

[5] Compare, e.g., In re Shanee Carol B., 550 S.E.2d 636 (W. Va. 2001), with, e.g., In re Miguel A., 67 Cal. Rptr. 3d 307 (Ct. App. 2007). See Randi Mandelbaum, Delicate Balances: Assessing the Needs and Rights of Siblings in Foster Care to Maintain Their Relationships Post-Adoption, 41 N.M. L. Rev. 1 (2011); Rebecca L. Scharf, Separated at Adoption: Addressing the Challenges of Maintaining Sibling-of-Origin Bonds in Post-Adoption Families, 19 U.C. Davis J. Juv. L. & Pol'y 84 (2015).

[6] Compare Israel v. Allen, 577 P.2d 762 (Colo. 1978), with In re Marriage of MEW, 4 Pa. D. & C.3d 51 (C.P. Allegheny 1977). See also State v. Hall, 48 P.3d 350 (Wash. Ct. App. 2002) (biological father guilty of incest with daughter adopted out of his family).

B. STEPPARENT AND SECOND-PARENT ADOPTIONS

In the stereotypical stepparent adoption, one birth parent terminates his parental rights (or fails to assert them or dies) while the spouse of the second birth parent steps in, assuming parental rights by adoption. How do stepparent adoptions resemble "stranger adoptions"? How do they differ? What underlying assumptions do the two practices share — about the normative family, the optimal number of parents for each child, the gender of those parents, and the relationship between those parents? The following pair of cases challenges traditional assumptions in the legal construction of "family."

ADOPTION OF TAMMY

619 N.E.2d 315 (Mass. 1993)

GREANEY, J.

In this case, two unmarried women, Susan and Helen, filed a joint petition in the Probate and Family Court Department under G.L. c. 210, §1 (1992 ed.) to adopt as their child Tammy, a minor, who is Susan's biological daughter.... Based on [a] finding that Helen and Susan "are each functioning, separately and together, as the custodial and psychological parents of [Tammy]," and that "it is the best interest of said [Tammy] that she be adopted by both," the judge entered a decree allowing the adoption. Simultaneously, the [Probate and Family Court] judge reserved and reported to the Appeals Court the evidence and all questions of law, in an effort to "secure [the] decree from any attack in the future on jurisdictional grounds." We transferred the case to this court on our own motion. We conclude that the adoption was properly allowed under G.L. c. 210.

... Helen and Susan have lived together in a committed relationship, which they consider to be permanent, for more than ten years. In June, 1983, they jointly purchased a house in Cambridge. Both women are physicians specializing in surgery. At the time the petition was filed, Helen maintained a private practice in general surgery at Mount Auburn Hospital and Susan, a nationally recognized expert in the field of breast cancer, was director of the Faulkner Breast Center and a surgical oncologist at the Dana Farber Cancer Institute. Both women also held positions on the faculty of Harvard Medical School.

For several years prior to the birth of Tammy, Helen and Susan planned to have a child, biologically related to both of them, whom they would jointly parent. Helen first attempted to conceive a child through artificial insemination by Susan's brother. When those efforts failed, Susan successfully conceived a child through artificial insemination by Helen's biological cousin, Francis. The women attended childbirth classes together and Helen was present when Susan gave birth to Tammy on April 30, 1988. Although Tammy's birth certificate reflects Francis as her biological father, she was given a hyphenated surname using Susan and Helen's last names.

Since her birth, Tammy has lived with, and been raised and supported by, Helen and Susan. Tammy views both women as her parents, calling Helen "mama" and Susan "mommy." Tammy has strong emotional and psychological bonds with both Helen and Susan. Together, Helen and Susan have provided Tammy with a comfortable home, and have created a warm and stable environment which is supportive of Tammy's growth and over-all well being. Both women jointly and equally participate in parenting Tammy, and both have a strong financial commitment to her.... Francis does not participate in parenting Tammy and does not support her. His intention was to assist Helen and Susan in having a child, and he does not intend to be involved with Tammy, except as a distant relative. Francis signed an adoption surrender and supports the joint adoption by both women.

Helen and Susan, recognizing that the laws of the Commonwealth do not permit them to enter into a legally cognizable marriage, believe that the best interests of Tammy require legal recognition of her identical emotional relationship to both women. Susan expressed her understanding that it may not be in her own long-term interest to permit Helen to adopt Tammy because, in the event that Helen and Susan separate, Helen would have equal rights to primary custody. Susan indicated, however, that she has no reservation about allowing Helen to adopt. Apart from the emotional security and current practical ramifications which legal recognition of the reality of her parental relationships will provide Tammy, Susan indicated that the adoption is important for Tammy in terms of potential inheritance from Helen. Helen and her living issue are the beneficiaries of three irrevocable family trusts. Unless Tammy is adopted, Helen's share of the trusts may pass to others....

Over a dozen witnesses, including mental health professionals, teachers, colleagues, neighbors, blood relatives and a priest and nun, testified to the fact that Helen and Susan participate equally in raising Tammy, that Tammy relates to both women as her parents, and that the three form a healthy, happy, and stable family unit.... [Both extended families unreservedly endorsed the adoption. The home study conducted by the Department of Social Services, the psychiatrist appointed as Tammy's guardian ad litem, and the attorney appointed to represent her interests all supported the adoption for her best interests.]

1. The initial question is whether the Probate Court judge had jurisdiction under G.L. c. 210 to enter a judgment on a joint petition for adoption brought by two unmarried cohabitants in the petitioners' circumstances. We answer this question in the affirmative.

There is nothing on the face of the statute which precludes the joint adoption of a child by two unmarried cohabitants such as the petitioners. Chapter 210, §1, provides that "[a] person of full age may petition the probate court in the county where he resides for leave to adopt as his child another person younger than himself, unless such other person is his or her wife or husband, or brother, sister, uncle or aunt, of the whole or half blood." Other than requiring that a spouse join in the petition, if the petitioner is married and the spouse is competent to join therein, the statute does not expressly prohibit or require joinder by any person. [I]t is apparent from the first sentence of G.L. c. 210, §1, that the Legislature considered and defined those combinations of persons which would lead to adoptions in violation of public policy. Clearly absent is any prohibition of adoption by two unmarried individuals like the petitioners....

In this case all requirements in [the statute] are met, and there is no question that the judge's findings demonstrate that the directives [in the statute,] and in case law, have been satisfied. Adoption will not result in any tangible change in Tammy's daily life; it will, however, serve to provide her with a significant legal relationship which may be important in her future. At the most practical level, adoption will entitle Tammy to inherit from Helen's family trusts and from Helen and her family under the law of intestate succession, to receive support from Helen, who will be legally obligated to provide such support, to be eligible for coverage under Helen's health insurance policies, and to be eligible for social security benefits in the event of Helen's disability or death. Of equal, if not greater significance, adoption will enable Tammy to preserve her unique filial ties to Helen in the event that Helen and Susan separate, or Susan predeceases Helen. . . . The conclusion that the adoption is in the best interests of Tammy is also well warranted.

2. The judge also posed the question whether, pursuant to G.L. c. 210, §6 (1992 ed.), Susan's legal relationship to Tammy must be terminated if Tammy is adopted. Section 6 provides that, on entry of an adoption decree, "all rights, duties and other legal consequences of the natural relation of child and parent shall . . . except as regards marriage, incest or cohabitation, terminate between the child so adopted and his natural parents and kindred." Although G.L. c. 210, §2, clearly permits a child's natural parent to be an adoptive parent, §6 does not contain any express exceptions to its termination provision. The Legislature obviously did not intend that a natural parent's legal relationship to its child be terminated when the natural parent is a party to the adoption petition.

Section 6 clearly is directed to the more usual circumstances of adoption, where the child is adopted by persons who are not the child's natural parents (either because the natural parents have elected to relinquish the child for adoption or their parental rights have been involuntarily terminated). The purpose of the termination provision is to protect the security of the child's newly-created family unit by eliminating involvement with the child's natural parents. . . . Reading the adoption statute as a whole, we conclude that the termination provision contained in §6 was intended to apply only when the natural parents (or parent) are not parties to the adoption petition. . . .

IN RE ADOPTION OF GARRETT

841 N.Y.S.2d 731 (Sur. Ct. 2007)

RANDAL B. CALDWELL, J.

Before this Court is a petition for adoption filed by the natural mother of the child, Pamela V., and the proposed adoptive father, Michael J. The proposed adoptive father is the biological brother of the natural mother and they have resided at the same address only since December 2006.

The background to this adoption proceeding is found in the recent divorce decree of the biological parents of the child, present Petitioner Pamela and her ex-husband, Chad, dated June 13, 2007. The decree incorporates an opting-out agreement between the parties which provides that the father execute an irrevocable consent to the adoption of the child by his ex-wife and an unnamed "another male." In return, the mother agreed that the payment of $4,000 would satisfy the obligation to pay the outstanding child support arrears of $7,628.00 and that his child support obligation would cease. In essence, the father of the child agreed to relinquish all parental rights in exchange for the ending of his future support obligation and a favorable settlement of the past due amount.

It is undeniable that the area of adoption law has undergone a significant transformation in recent years whereby same-sex couples were deemed eligible to adopt (see, Matter of Jacob, [660 N.E.2d 397 (N.Y. 1995)]), and unmarried heterosexual couples were also permitted to adopt (see, Matter of Carl, [709 N.Y.S.2d 905 (Fam. Ct. 2000)]). Indeed this Court was the venue of one of the leading cases in this area, decided by former Surrogate John G. Ringrose, namely Matter of Joseph, [684 N.Y.S.2d 760 (Sur. Ct. 1998)], which held that an unmarried couple, residing together, would be permitted to adopt their foster child even though neither adoptive parent was the child's biological parent. Notably, however, all of these decisions have been predicated on the rationale that the relationship between the proposed adoptive parents is the functional equivalent of the traditional husband-wife relationship, albeit between same-sex couples or unmarried partners. The first case in Matter of Jacob, supra, involved the biological mother of the child and her unmarried heterosexual partner who had been living together for three years, and the second case involved the natural mother of the child and her lesbian partner who had lived together in a relationship for nineteen years. In analyzing the terms of the statute, the Court stated:

> The statute uses the word "together" only to describe married persons and thus does not preclude an unmarried person *in a relationship* with another unmarried person from adopting.

(86 N.Y.2d at p. 660, emphasis added).

The Court also discussed the nature of the changing American family where "at least 1.2 of the 3.5 million American households which consist of an unmarried adult couple have children under 15 years old." Similarly, in Matter of Carl, supra, the Court expressly considered the length of the relationship between the unmarried petitioners in that case and in Matter of Joseph, . . . in contrast to the high rate of divorce for married persons.

As recently noted by the Appellate Division of the Fourth Department, the adoption statute must be strictly construed as adoption is solely the creature of statute (Matter of Zoe D.K., [804 N.Y.S.2d 197 (App. Div. 2005)]). In that case, the Fourth Department would not permit the adoption of a child born out of wedlock by her unmarried biological parent where the effect would be to terminate the rights of the natural father while leaving unchanged the rights and responsibilities of the mother. The Court noted that the adoption did not foster the goals of providing the best possible home for the child or giving legal recognition to an existing family unit.

We are now asked to further expand the prior holdings to virtually unlimited boundaries, namely to authorize the adoption of a child by a natural parent and another member of that parent's family, namely the brother of the natural mother. This Court finds that the reasoning employed in the prior decisions expanding the right to adopt is simply inapplicable to the present case. In absence of direction by a higher Court that the right to adopt should be extended in this fashion, this Court will dismiss the pending petition. . . .

NOTES AND QUESTIONS ON *TAMMY* AND *GARRETT*

1. *Stepparents and stepchildren generally.*

a. *Prevalence.* Census data reveal that 4 percent of all children of householders are stepchildren.[7] The term "stepchildren" traditionally referred only to a relationship by marriage (that is, when one of the child's parents marries a nonparent) but today often includes relationships based on cohabitation without marriage.[8]

b. *Support.* In the absence of adoption, the common law imposed no duty on stepparents to support their stepchildren either during a marriage or following its dissolution.[9] Several states have statutes imposing financial responsibility on a stepparent who receives a child into the family or looking to a stepparent when parental support would be insufficient, so long as the parent's and the stepparent's marriage continues.[10] The ALI Principles do not recognize a general duty of support by stepparents. One who agrees or undertakes to assume a parental support obligation to a child, however, might later be estopped from denying a parental support obligation. American Law Institute, Principles of the Law of Family Dissolution: Analysis and Recommendations §3.03(1)(a) (Am. Law Inst. 2002). Under such circumstances, a court could impose a child support obligation on the stepparent after the dissolution of the relationship with the child's parent. See id. cmt. b. An adult obligated to pay child support is a parent by estoppel for purposes of determining custodial and decisionmaking responsibility. Id. §2.03.[11] See Chapter 1, section C.

c. *Custody and visitation.* Traditionally, if a former stepparent sought postdissolution custody in the face of parental objection, that stepparent had to overcome the legal preference for the biological parent.[12] Even if stepparents had a legally cognizable relationship with the child during the marriage, such recognition ended when the marriage terminated.[13] Courts have become increasingly willing to grant custody and visitation to former stepparents, especially given a long-term relationship with the child, using doctrines like de facto parentage, as spelled out in UPA (2017), and other functional approaches (discussed in Chapter 1, section C). Further, those nonparents covered by the UNCVA's provisions for visitation explicitly include stepparents who meet the statute's criteria. UNCVA §2(7). Such expanded

---

[7] Rose M. Kreider & Daphne A. Lofquist, Adopted Children and Stepchildren: 2010, U.S. Census Bureau 1, 4 (April 2014), https://www.census.gov/prod/2014pubs/p20-572.pdf.

[8] Id. at 19-21.

[9] E.g., Okla. Stat. Ann. tit. 43, §112.4. See generally Margaret M. Mahoney, Stepfamilies and the Law (1994).

[10] Compare, e.g., Vt. Stat. Ann. tit. 15, §296, with, e.g., Wash. Rev. Code §26.16.205.

[11] Mary Ann Mason & Nicole Zayac, Rethinking Stepparent Rights: Has the ALI Found a Better Definition?, 36 Fam. L.Q. 227 (2002).

[12] See David R. Fine & Mark A. Fine, Learning from Social Sciences: A Model for Reformation of the Laws Affecting Stepfamilies, 97 Dick. L. Rev. 49, 56 (1992) (citing survey finding that 38 states have such presumptions).

[13] See June Carbone, The Legal Definition of Parenthood: Uncertainty at the Core of Family Identity, 65 La. L. Rev. 1295, 1312 (2005).

protection of a stepparent's relationship with a child raises constitutional questions when a parent objects, asserting the right to make childrearing decisions. See Troxel v. Granville, reprinted Chapter 2, section B1.

d. *Policy.* Professor David Chambers has observed that empirical studies find stepparents play an important family role:

> Some empirical evidence suggests that when residential stepparents enter children's lives, the children generally see their absent parents less often than they did before. [D]espite the ambiguities of the stepparent relationship, many individual stepparents do form strong emotional bonds with their stepchildren. They are seen by the child as "parent." And, of course, there is ample corresponding evidence that biologic fathers who do not live with their children will not pay child support unless compelled to do so and that they visit their children less and less as time passes, whether or not the mother remarries. In the future, we may come to view residential stepparents as replacing absent parents and assuming some or all of their responsibilities.[14]

e. *Surnames.* Should stepchildren use the same surname as the members of the stepfamily? Or should they retain their original surnames? What values are at stake? What principles should guide courts in deciding such cases?[15]

2. *Stepparent adoptions.* A stepparent who adopts a stepchild becomes the child's legal parent. Census data cannot distinguish children adopted by stepparents, grandparents and other relatives, although earlier studies found 42 percent of all adoptions were by stepparents and other relatives.[16]

a. *Applicable standard.* What standard should a court use to decide whether to decree a stepparent adoption? Even if the child's best interests support formal recognition of the new family unit created when a custodial parent remarries, does that test suffice for terminating the noncustodial parent's rights, the traditional prerequisite of adoption? Does Santosky v. Kramer (reprinted Chapter 3, section A) apply in this context? Should a more permissive substantive standard govern TPR before stepparent adoption than for other adoptions? What weight, if any, does the custodial parent's autonomy carry in such cases?

Courts in the states have taken a range of positions on protecting the interests of the original parent in stepparent adoption cases — from denying involuntary TPR when a mother was absent for more than a year while focusing on recovery from opioid addiction to allowing TPR although the father had maintained regular contact with the child but whose visits were deemed of insufficient "quality."[17] In addition, some states have held

---

[14] David L. Chambers, Stepparents, Biologic Parents, and the Law's Perceptions of "Family" After Divorce, in Divorce Reform at the Crossroads 102, 117 (Stephen D. Sugarman & Herma Hill Kay eds., 1990).

[15] Compare In re Name Change of L.M.G., 738 N.W.2d 71 (S.D. 2007), with Hunter v. Haunert, 270 S.W.3d 339 (Ark. Ct. App. 2007). See generally Merle H. Weiner, "We Are Family": Valuing Associationalism in Disputes Over Children's Surnames, 75 N.C. L. Rev. 1625 (1997).

[16] Kreider & Lofquist, supra note [7], at 2 n.5.

[17] Compare, e.g., E.B.F. v. D.F., 93 N.E.3d 759 (Ind. 2018), with, e.g., S.S.S. v. C.V.S., 529 S.W.3d 811 (Mo. 2017) (en banc). See also, e.g., In re AGD, 933 N.W.2d 751 (Mich. Ct. App. 2019) (holding stepparent adoption statute requires parent petitioning to terminate other parent's rights to have court-ordered custody beforehand).

that indigent parents facing TPR in stepparent adoptions have a right to counsel.[18]

b. *The cutoff rule.* Should stepparent adoption cut off the relationship with the original parent? Why? Referring to an original parent as "a parent before the adoption," the Uniform Probate Code (UPC) recognizes exceptions to the usual rule when the adoption:

> (A) was by the spouse of a parent before the adoption;
> (B) was by a relative or the spouse or surviving spouse of a relative of a parent before the adoption; or
> (C) occurred after the death of a parent before the adoption.

UPC §2-119(b)(2) (2019).[19] Such statutory protections raise the possibility of dual inheritance, affording adoptees an advantage denied to biological children. Why permit dual inheritance in these cases? Might the policy of keeping dependency private provide an explanation? Note that, without such provisions, courts might deny stepparent adoptions because the loss of intestate inheritance from the biological parent would prevent the adoption from serving the child's best (financial) interest.[20]

3. *Second-parent adoption. Tammy* is a classic case showcasing the challenges of securing legal co-parentage by same-sex couples before marriage equality. The case permits a practice called second-parent adoption. How does the practice resemble stepparent adoption? How does it differ?[21]

Before Vermont permitted same-sex couples to enter civil unions, its supreme court allowed second-parent adoptions to come within the statutory exception for stepparents. The legislature later codified this holding.[22] Yet, some courts declined to construe "stepparent" to cover someone like Helen in *Tammy.*[23] Although the term "stepparent" today is increasingly used to refer to a parent's partner, regardless of marriage, some states have insisted on a marital relationship.[24] What does the contemporary "retreat from marriage"[25] mean for stepparent and second-parent adoptions? Should we expect more partner adoptions, whether called "stepparent" or "second-parent"? Or

---

[18] E.g., In re Adoption of L.T.M., 824 N.E.2d 221 (Ill. 2005); In re Adoption of A.W.S., 339 P.3d 414 (Mont. 2014).

[19] See also, e.g., Wyo. Stat. Ann. § 2-4-107(a)(i) ("An adopted person is the child of an adopting parent for inheritance purposes, but the adoption of a child by the spouse of a natural parent has no effect on the relationship between the child and that natural parent for inheritance purposes....").

[20] See, e.g., In re Gerald G.G., 403 N.Y.S.2d 57, 60 (App. Div. 1978). See also, e.g., In re Estate of Dye, 112 Cal. Rptr. 2d 362, 366-367 (Ct. App. 2001) (explaining statutory revision). See generally James T. R. Jones, Intestate Inheritance and Stepparent Adoption: A Reappraisal, 48 Real Prop. Tr. & Est. L.J. 327, 346 (2013) (describing "good reasons" but "mixed results" for modern approach).

[21] See, e.g., Jane S. Schacter, Constructing Families in a Democracy: Courts, Legislatures and Second-Parent Adoption, 75 Chi.-Kent L. Rev. 933 (2000); Peter Wendel, Inheritance Rights and the Step-Partner Adoption Paradigm: Shades of Discrimination Against Illegitimate Children, 34 Hofstra L. Rev. 351 (2005).

[22] In re Adoption of B.L.V.B., 628 A.2d 1271 (Vt. 1993); Vt. Stat. Ann., tit. 15A, §1-102(b).

[23] See S.J.L.S. v. T.L.S., 265 S.W.3d 804, 822-828 (Ky. Ct. App. 2008) (rejecting concept of "'stepparent-like' adoption" as inconsistent with state adoption laws). But see A.H. v. W.R.L., 482 S.W.3d 372 (Ky. 2016) (allowing former partner to intervene in pending stepparent adoption).

[24] See Utah Code Ann. §78B-6-117; see also In re Adoption of Doe, 326 P.3d 347 (Idaho 2014) (reversing court below, which required marriage).

[25] Shelly Lundberg & Robert A. Pollak, Cohabitation and the Uneven Retreat from Marriage in the United States, 1950-2010, in Human Capital in History: The American Record 241 (Leah Platt Boustan et al. eds., 2014).

does the avoidance of formal state procedures like marriage portend fewer formal adoptions? To what extent will functional approaches like de facto parentage or UNCVA fill the gap?

4. *Statutory construction.* On what basis does the majority decide that the Massachusetts adoption statute permits Susan and Helen to adopt Tammy jointly? An omitted dissent rejects this conclusion, despite deciding that Helen can adopt Tammy while Susan retains her parental rights (the majority's second approach). Which presents the more persuasive statutory interpretation regarding joint adoption, the majority or the dissent?[26] If Susan and Helen can jointly adopt Susan's biological child, would they be able to adopt jointly a child not related to either of them?[27]

Alternatively, consider the second approach: reading the statute to permit Helen to adopt while Susan retains parental rights, despite the usual cutoff rule. Courts have divided on this issue, with some saying a mother's partner can adopt the child only if the mother surrenders her parental rights.[28] To what extent is the restrictive approach a relic of the long-held view that a child can have no more than one mother and one father? Some states now have statutes explicitly permitting the second-parent adoption under specified circumstances, as when the adopter is the registered domestic partner of the parent or the child has only one legal parent who wishes the child to be adopted by a particular second adult.[29]

5. *Revocation.* Do the difficulties of statutory construction in states without explicit legislation authorizing second-parent adoption make such adoptions vulnerable to revocation? In several cases, mothers, who earlier had consented to a second-parent adoption, have invoked both limitations of statutory language and public policy in later challenging the adoption, seeking to bar the child's contact with the second parent after the adult relationship dissolves.[30] Why doesn't estoppel preclude such attacks?

6. *Best interests.* *Tammy* highlights the tension between two oft-stated principles: that adoption law is purely statutory and that adoption law should serve a child's best interests.[31] Considering the child's best interests, what are the advantages to Tammy of the second-parent adoption? How important is second-parent adoption today in order to achieve such benefits? How far do marriage equality and functional approaches to parentage go in securing such benefits for children without second-parent adoption?

---

[26] See In re J.W., 213 A.3d 853 (N.H. 2019) (disallowing joint adoption of father's child by father and his nonmarital cohabitant).

[27] See In re Adoption of M.A., 930 A.2d 1088 (Me. 2007) (permitting joint adoption); In re Adoption of Carolyn B., 774 N.Y.S.2d 227 (App. Div. 2004) (same).

[28] Compare In re Adoption of Luke, 640 N.W.2d 374 (Neb. 2002) (finding child ineligible for adoption under statute without surrender by birth mother), with In re Adoption of R.B.F., 803 A.2d 1195 (Pa. 2002) (allowing same-sex partner to adopt parent's child without surrender of parent's rights).

[29] See, e.g., Cal. Fam. Code §9000(b); Colo. Rev. Stat. Ann. §19-5-203(d.5I).

[30] E.g., Sharon S. v. Super. Ct., 73 P.3d 554 (Cal. 2003); In re Adoption of D.P.P., 158 So. 3d 633 (Fla. Dist. Ct. App. 2014). See also V.L. v. E.L., 136 S. Ct. 1017 (2016) (holding that Alabama must accord full faith and credit to a second-parent adoption in Georgia, thus precluding biological mother's challenge); Schott v. Schott, 744 N.W.2d 85 (Iowa 2008) (reversing trial court's attack sua sponte on the validity of previous second-parent adoptions).

[31] See, e.g., Mark Strasser, Courts, Legislatures, and Second-Parent Adoptions: On Judicial Deference, Specious Reasoning, and the Best Interests of the Child, 66 Tenn. L. Rev. 1019 (1999).

Alternatively, does the availability of second-parent adoption weaken the argument for equitable remedies and functional criteria designed to offer relief to nonnormative families?[32]

7. *The road to marriage equality.* Does the ruling in *Tammy* compel access to same-sex marriage?[33] Once a state permits second-parent adoptions, what reason supports restricting marriage to different-sex couples? Are children in second-parent adoptions disadvantaged compared to children of married parents? When Massachusetts became the first state in the nation to hold that same-sex couples have a right to marry (under the state constitution), the court relied on *Tammy* to reject the state's arguments identifying procreation as the essential element of marriage and supporting marriage restrictions as a means to ensure an optimal setting for childrearing.[34] Scholars have noted how LGBTQ adoptions helped pave the way for marriage equality.[35]

8. *Only conjugal couples?* Given the well-established place of stepparent adoptions that follow a parent's remarriage and new variations such as second-parent adoptions for same-sex couples, why does *Garrett* reject the proposed adoption? Why did the various approaches to statutory construction in *Tammy* not apply in *Garrett*? Why does *Garrett* require a conjugal relationship in order for two persons to share legal parenthood of a child? Children are not expected to witness their parents' sexual activities, so why would a sexual relationship constitute a prerequisite for the proposed adoption? Given the number of marriages and nonmarital conjugal relationships that dissolve, wouldn't the mother and her brother, as in the principal case, provide an even more stable family for the child than a traditional stepparent adoption? Given the policy of keeping dependency private and the two-parent norm (see Elisa B. v. Superior Ct., reprinted Chapter 1, section C), why shouldn't two individuals such as the mother and her brother here be eligible to adopt?

The Pennsylvania Supreme Court grappled with similar issues in In re Adoption of M.R.D., 145 A.3d 1117 (Pa. 2016), in which a mother sought to retain her parental rights, terminate the rights of the father, and support an adoption petition by her father (the children's grandfather), who had been helping her care for the children. Adhering to the statute, which would

---

[32] See, e.g., Titchenal v. Dexter, 693 A.2d 682 (Vt. 1997) (disallowing equitable relief, in absence of second-parent adoption); Mabry v. Mabry, 882 N.W.2d 539 (Mich. 2016) (declining to review denial of standing for custody by biological parent's former unmarried partner); McGaw v. McGaw, 468 S.W.3d 435, 438 (Mo. Ct. App. 2015) (declining to adopt equitable parent doctrine and anticipating "that in the wake of *Obergefell,* situations like this one, in which important issues involving children must be decided outside the established legal framework applicable to married couples, will occur less frequently"). See also Julie Shapiro, A Lesbian-Centered Critique of Second-Parent Adoptions, 14 Berkeley Women's L.J. 17, 32-25 (1999) (using *Titchenal,* 693 A.2d 682, to illustrate problems posed for lesbians by second-parent adoptions).

[33] In fact, the couple (who had moved to Los Angeles) married in San Francisco during a pre-*Obergefell* period when same-sex weddings were being performed there and before the judicial invalidation of such marriages. Helen Cooksey, Susan Love, N.Y. Times, Feb. 22, 2004, §9, at 12 (weddings and celebrations).

[34] Goodridge v. Dept. of Pub. Health, 798 N.E.2d 941, 962 n.24, 963, 966 n.30 (Mass. 2003). But see id. at 1000 (Cordy, J., dissenting).

[35] E.g., Cynthia Godsoe, Adopting the Gay Family, 90 Tul. L. Rev. 311 (2015); Douglas NeJaime, Marriage Equality and the New Parenthood, 129 Harv. L. Rev. 1185 (2016).

require the mother to relinquish her rights in order for her father to adopt, the court rejected the adoption petition, with the following explanation:

> In the standard adoption case, termination and relinquishment of parental rights is necessary so that the child may be adopted by, and form new bonds with, his or her new family, unencumbered by the former legal parents. By contrast, in second-parent adoption cases in which the relinquishment of a parent's rights is not required — i.e., stepparent adoptions and adoptions by same-sex couples — relinquishment of the parent's rights is unnecessary, and indeed damaging. In such cases, the parent and the prospective adoptive parent are committed partners — that is, they are involved in a horizontal relationship, are equals as between each other, and are equals with respect to the child. Adoption in such circumstances allows the prospective adoptive parent to create a new parent-child relationship with the legal parent's child and a family unit together with the co-parent to whom he or she is committed. Thus, because the legal parent and prospective parent in second-parent adoption cases are part of the same family unit, the relinquishment requirement undermines, rather than promotes, family stability.
>
> The same cannot be said for the instant case, however, because Mother and Grandfather are not similarly part of an intact family unit. Indeed, rather than being involved in a committed, horizontal relationship such as stepparents or same-sex partners, Mother and Grandfather share a vertical, parent-child relationship. Moreover, in this case, Grandfather will remain married to Grandmother and will continue to live in a separate residence with her after the adoption. Adoption does not foster a family unit under circumstances where, as here, the adopting party is already part of — and will continue to be part of — a family unit that is separate from the unit which he seeks to promote and join through adoption.
>
> Additionally, relinquishment is necessary in this case to avoid a host of unique complications. For example, such an arrangement would create confusing hybrid relationships within the family — Grandfather would be both Children's father and grandfather, Grandmother would be both a grandmother and a stepmother, and, more confusing still, because of Grandmother's status as a stepmother, Mother would be both a mother to Children and, technically, their stepsister. Further complicating matters, if Mother ever seeks to marry, the Act does not require Grandfather to terminate his parental rights in favor of Mother's spouse; thus, he could decide to remain Children's father and prevent Mother's spouse from having legal rights over Children. Grandfather has neither considered, nor explained, how his role with Children might change if Mother married.
>
> Lastly, although the orphans' court rejected the possibility in the instant case, permitting Grandfather to adopt and co-parent Children with mother would nevertheless open the door for misuse of adoption proceedings by spiteful parents as a means to involuntarily terminate the rights of unwanted parents, potentially allowing grandparents, cousins, pastors, coaches, and a litany of other individuals who have a close relationship with a child to stand in as prospective adoptive parents so that termination may be achieved. Given that the "complete and irrevocable termination of parental rights is one of the most serious and severe steps a court can take," we must ensure that we do not open the floodgates to such gamesmanship.

Id. at 1128-1129. How far does this rationale go in justifying the outcome in *Garrett*?

By contrast, a few courts have shown openness to adoptive arrangements that defy the conjugal or co-residential model. After *Garrett*, one New York judge allowed a second-parent adoption by a father's former male partner, although the two were not married and were no longer intimate,[36] and another allowed a close personal friend of the parent to become a second legal parent by adoption.[37] Other courts have allowed a grandfather to adopt his daughter's child while she retains parental rights.[38]

What limits would you support? Why? To what extent should the decision on an adoption petition in such cases depend on the alternative in the absence of the proposed adoption — whether the maintenance of the second biological parent's rights, continuation of single parenthood, or a continued wait for an adoptive placement?

PROBLEM

Felecia becomes pregnant while engaged in a romantic relationship with Patrick. When she gives birth to a daughter, D.H.H., only Felecia's name is listed on the birth certificate. Initially, D.H.H. lives with Patrick and his mother, but moves to Felecia's home once she begins attending school. More than a decade later, Patrick discovers, to his surprise, that he is not D.H.H.'s biological father, but he continues to visit and support her. Now, Patrick and Felecia petition the court to allow Patrick to adopt D.H.H. while Felecia retains her parental rights. D.H.H.'s biological father remains unknown, and Felecia and Patrick are each married to other people.

The adoption statute includes the following relevant sections:

- Any person may be adopted in accordance with the provisions of this chapter . . . by an unmarried adult or by a married person whose spouse joins in the petition.
- The final decree shall adjudicate, in addition to such other provisions as may be found by the court to be proper for the protection of the interests of the child; and its effect, unless otherwise specifically provided, shall be that . . . all parental rights of the natural parent, or parents, shall be terminated, except as to a natural parent who is the spouse of the adopting parent.

Should the court grant the adoption petition, while allowing Felecia to retain her parental rights? Can it? What additional procedural requirements must the petitioners follow?[39]

---

[36] In re Adoption of Chan, 950 N.Y.S.2d 245 (Sur. 2012).

[37] In re Adoption of G., 978 N.Y.S.2d 622 (Sur. 2013). See Jessica R. Feinberg, Friends as Co-Parents, 43 U.S.F. L. Rev. 799 (2009); Angela Mae Kupenda, Two Parents Are Better Than None: Whether Two Single African American Adults — Who Are Not in a Traditional Marriage or a Romantic or Sexual Relationship with Each Other — Should Be Allowed to Jointly Adopt and Co-Parent African American Children, 35 U. Louisville J. Fam. L. 703 (1996). See also In re Y.L., 190 A.3d 1049 (N.H. 2018) (allowing more flexibility in terms of who may adopt an adult).

[38] In re Adoption of A.M., 930 N.E.2d 613 (Ind. Ct. App. 2010). See also In re Adoption of A., 893 N.Y.S.2d 751 (Fam. Ct. 2010) (considering joint adoption petition of child's grandmother and aunt).

[39] See In re Adoption of D.D.H., 268 So. 3d 449 (Miss. 2018).

C. SECRECY VERSUS DISCLOSURE

1. SEALED-RECORD LAWS

IN RE **R.D.**

876 N.W.2d 786 (Iowa 2016)

WATERMAN, Justice...

R.D., now age fifty-one, was born in Iowa in 1965. R.D.'s biological parents consented to her adoption and waived notice of any further proceedings. R.D. was adopted a few days later, and the adoption records were sealed pursuant to Iowa Code section 600.9 (1962), which stated, "The complete record in adoption proceedings, after filing with the clerk of the court, shall be sealed by said clerk, and the record shall not thereafter be opened except on order of the court."...

R.D.'s adoptive family was loving and supportive. When R.D. turned six, her adoptive parents told her she was adopted. As she grew up, R.D. felt the "loss of [her] biological family" and "the loss of [her] own parents not having given birth to [her.]" Most importantly, she "felt like somebody gave [her] up" because they did not love her. She became obsessed with being the "best of everything" to avoid being abandoned again. R.D. achieved academic success, earning advanced degrees and induction into Phi Beta Kappa. Today she is on the faculty teaching at a prestigious university in another state and has been married to a supportive husband for several decades.

R.D.'s "lack of knowledge about her origins increasingly caused anxiety and depression." R.D. began self-medicating with alcohol in her thirties. [She sought professional assistance for anxiety, depression, and substance abuse. She then petitioned the juvenile court to open her adoption records, relying] on Iowa Code section 600.16A(2)(d) (2015), which allows access to adoption records "if opening is shown to be necessary to save the life of or prevent irreparable physical or mental harm to an adopted person or the person's offspring." [R.D. submitted supporting letters and depositions from her doctors, and R.D. testified herself, attributing] her alcohol abuse to her sense of loss from being adopted. [Her attorney conceded that she was not seeking medical information, but only the identity of her parents for therapeutic purposes. The court denied the petition, and R.D. appeals.]

... We must decide whether the medical showing of the predicted therapeutic benefit to R.D. of learning the identity of her biological parents outweighs the statutory command to protect the identity of the biological parents.... [T]he medical showing R.D. made gets her to first base, not across home plate.... We conclude on this record that the balance the legislature struck in favor of confidentiality mandates denial of R.D.'s application.

A. The Evolution of the Confidentiality of Adoption Records.

...

At one point in the past, adoption records were not sealed. "[A]doption only became part of American law in the late nineteenth and early twentieth centuries, and ... adoption procedures initially established by state statutes provided neither for confidentiality with respect to the public nor for secrecy among the parties, but were subsequently amended to protect the parties from public scrutiny." "In the mid-1920s, there were virtually no confidentiality or secrecy provisions in adoption law. ... By the mid-1930s to the early 1940s, there were more state provisions for confidentiality with respect to the general public's access to court records, but still few provisions for secrecy among the participants." However, "[w]ith respect to court records rather than birth records, contemporary evidence indicates that by the late 1940s and early 1950s a significant, if not a dramatic, shift had occurred: court records by that time were apparently closed in many states to all persons."

In re Adoption of Scott W.V., [124 A.3d 1181, 1190-91 (Md. 2015)] (quoting Elizabeth J. Samuels, The Idea of Adoption: An Inquiry Into the History of Adult Adoptee Access to Birth Records, 53 Rutgers L. Rev. 367, 368, 374, 377 (2001) [hereinafter Samuels] (footnotes omitted)).

The evolving confidentiality of Iowa's adoption records has reflected the national trend. Iowa adoption records were originally filed with real estate deeds and, like real estate deeds, were open to the public. [Iowa law changed to sealed records in 1941. In 1976, the legislature amended the statute to provide conditions for unsealing records, the issue in this case. In 1993, legislation created a consent registry, which allows natural parents to put a written consent to reveal the parent's identity on request of the child, and allowed an adult child to place a written consent to reveal the child's identity to the natural parent upon request.]

B. The Importance of Confidentiality of Adoption Records.

"Confidentiality has been and continues to be the touchstone for these adoption statutes." ... Sealing adoption records helps promote the formation of the adoptive family. Adoptive parents have a strong interest in maintaining closed adoption records so "they may raise [the] child without fear of interference from the natural parents and without fear that the birth status of the illegitimate child will be revealed or used as a means of harming the child or themselves." ... Indeed, R.D. enjoyed a strong familial bond with her adoptive parents. ... However, section 600.16A applies to myriad relationships among adoptees of all ages, biological and adoptive parents, siblings, and extended families. Moreover, R.D.'s biological parents have not consented to revelation of their identities.

> The assurance of secrecy regarding the identity of the natural parents enables them to place the child for adoption with a reputable agency, with the knowledge that their actions and motivations will not become public knowledge. Assured of this privacy by the State, the natural parents are free to move on and attempt to rebuild their lives after what must be a traumatic and emotionally tormenting episode in their lives.

... While some biological parents who gave up children for adoption may welcome contact from them, others may desire continued anonymity. ... Birth mothers filed constitutional challenges to statutory amendments when Oregon and Tennessee opened adoption records. See Doe v. Sundquist, 106 F.3d 702, 708 (6th Cir.1997) (dismissing natural mothers' constitutional challenge to Tennessee's law opening adoption records); Does v. State, 164 Or.App. 543, 993 P.2d 822, 825-26 (1999) (rejecting natural mothers' state and federal constitutional challenges to Oregon's law opening adoption records); Brett S. Silverman, The Winds of Change in

Adoption Laws: Should Adoptees Have Access to Adoption Records?, 39 Fam. & Conciliation Cts. Rev. 85, 91-92 (2001) [hereinafter Silverman] (providing personal stories from the Oregon plaintiffs in Sundquist, 106 F.3d 702). A woman who placed her child for adoption opposed unsealing adoption records in Oregon because she did "not want to have to tell a curious adoptee that he or she would have been aborted barring the danger [of an abortion], especially after four decades." Silverman, 39 Fam. & Conciliation Cts. Rev. at 91. Moreover, she said she would "be very angry" if the child tried to contact her because "[t]he idea of adoption was to permanently sever the relationship with the child." Id. at 92. Another Oregon birth mother placed her daughter for adoption because she was conceived as a result of a "terrifying brutal stranger rape" and said that opening adoption records would be committing "emotional rape." Id.

[C]ourts have noted a constitutional dimension to the privacy rights of biological parents who give up children for adoption. Finally, the State has an interest in maintaining confidentiality to protect and encourage the adoption process.... The [South Carolina Supreme Court] cautioned against overreacting to changing attitudes on the confidentiality of adoption records: ...

> No one has yet shown that decades of policy protecting the anonymity of the biological parents and the security from intrusion of the parent-child relationship after adoption have been misguided. Quite the contrary. The overwhelming success of adoption as an institution which has provided millions of children with families, and vice versa, cannot be easily attacked.
>
> The public has a strong interest, too, in preserving the confidential nonpublic nature of the process. Public attitudes toward illegitimacy and parents who neglect or abuse children have not changed sufficiently to warrant careless disclosure of the circumstances leading to adoption.

[Bradey v. Child. Bureau of S.C., 274 S.E.2d 418, 421-22 (S. Car. 1981).].

R.D.'s yearning to identify her birth parents is undoubtedly shared by most adoptees. That yearning alone is insufficient to open sealed adoption records.... Here, the adoption records contain no medical information, and all R.D. wants to know is the names of her biological parents. The juvenile court correctly denied that request. To hold otherwise would substantially undermine the statutory confidentiality assured to parents who make the painful decision to give up a child for adoption.

The level of confidentiality varies from state to state, and some commentators favor giving adult adoptees greater access to adoption records. [The issue belongs to each state's legislature.] We reiterate that while "changed attitudes" may warrant a fresh look at the confidentiality of Iowa's adoption records, "it is not our function 'to redraft or interpret laws differently' from what the legislature intended 'solely to reflect current values or lifestyles.'" In re Adoption of S.J.D., 641 N.W.2d at 802 ....

NOTES AND QUESTIONS

1. *History.* Secrecy has long shrouded the adoption process in most states. To maintain this secrecy, statutes provide for the issuance of a new birth certificate upon adoption, changing the name of the adoptee to that of the

adoptive parents. (The original birth certificate is then sealed.) Professor Elizabeth Samuels, offers the following historical summary:

> [I]n the 1940s and 1950s, a variety of expert voices advised states to seal court and birth records but to recognize in adult adoptees an unrestricted right of access to the birth records. The reason given for the closing of court and birth records to the parties as well as the public was to protect adoptive families from possible interference by birth parents. In contrast, no reason was generally offered in specific support of the closings of birth records to adult adoptees that did occur from the 1930s through the 1960s. It appears that the early closings of birth records to adult adoptees were not the result of articulated reasons, nor merely the result of confusion or happenstance. The early closings may have been, in no small part, the consequence of a contemporary social attitude or understanding, that is, of the social context in which they occurred. Adoption was beginning to be perceived as a means of creating a perfect and complete substitute for a family created by natural childbirth. Over time, as legal rules established a nearly universal regime of secrecy with respect to all persons' access to court records and all persons' except adult adoptees' access to birth records, the regime of secrecy itself inevitably influenced social attitudes and understandings. Actions once thought natural, such as attempts by adoptees to learn information about their birth families, came to be socially disfavored and considered abnormal. Such attempts acquired negative social meanings: they were the psychologically unhealthful product of unsuccessful adoptions that had failed to create perfect substitutes for natural families created by childbirth, and they indicated adoptees' rejection of and ingratitude toward adoptive parents. Eventually, lifelong secrecy would be viewed as an essential feature of adoptions in which birth and adoptive parents did not know one another.[40]

Another account attributes the practice of secrecy to the corrupt efforts of Georgia Tann, who arranged thousands of adoptions in Tennessee between 1924 and 1950 and sought to cover up the kidnapping and baby selling that were frequently part of her placement service.[41]

2. Activism and litigation. Beginning in the 1970s, support and advocacy groups such as the Adoptees' Liberation Movement Association (the ALMA Society) began to press for the opening of sealed records. Courts rejected adult adoptees' constitutional challenges to sealed-record laws, concluding that the right to privacy does not include a fundamental "right to know" one's biological parents and that adoptees do not constitute a suspect class for equal protection purposes. The laws survived rational basis review as protection for the interests of all parties.[42] Notwithstanding these early cases, do more recent authorities expanding the definition of constitutional

---

[40] Elizabeth J. Samuels, The Idea of Adoption: An Inquiry into the History of Adult Adoptee Access to Birth Records, 53 Rutgers L. Rev. 367, 370-371 (2001).

[41] Barbara Bisantz Raymond, The Baby Thief: The Untold Story of Georgia Tann, the Baby Seller Who Corrupted Adoption 188-189, 209 (2007).

[42] See, e.g., In re Roger B., 418 N.E.2d 751 (Ill.), appeal dismissed sub nom. Barth v. Finley, 454 U.S. 806 (1981).

liberty to include, for example, sexual choices and access to same-sex marriage, suggest that, today, even adolescent adoptees should have a right to decisional autonomy and identity development guaranteeing access to birth records?[43]

3. *Good cause.* Most sealed-record statutes permit disclosure on a showing of good cause or special circumstances like the Iowa provision that R.D. unsuccessfully invoked. Courts have been more willing to find good cause for medical (such as for diagnosis of genetic disease) than psychological reasons.[44]

Evaluate the court's analysis in *R.D.'s*. Did R.D.'s situation and supporting medical evidence meet the statutory test? In the balance of interests considered by the court, why shouldn't a psychological "need to know" prevail, at least when experts opine that it produces dysfunction like R.D.'s? According to a judge in one of the early cases rejecting a challenge to sealed records: "All of us need to know our past, not only for a sense of lineage and heritage, but for a fundamental and crucial sense of our very selves: our identity is incomplete and our sense of self retarded without a real personal historical connection. . . ."[45] Does that mean claims like R.D.'s are too unexceptional to satisfy the statutory requirements? Experts in other fields view adoptees' searches as a helpful response to the psychological problems caused by secrecy.[46] Would a better approach shift the burden of proof to the state to show the absence of good cause?[47]

Sealed records can create special problems for adoptive parents of special needs children whose medical histories might yield important information about their current problems. Further, without health information about their birth families, adult adoptees have trouble providing for their children's medical care.[48] Accordingly, states now commonly require the preparation of a medical and social history, including information about birth relatives, for a child to be placed for adoption.[49]

---

[43] See Note, Jessica R. Caterina, Glorious Bastards: The Legal and Civil Birthright of Adoptees to Access Their Medical Records in Search of Genetic Identity, 61 Syracuse L. Rev. 145 (2010); Jessica Colin-Greene, Note, Identity and Personhood: Advocating for the Abolishment of Closed Adoption Records Law, 49 Conn. L. Rev. 1271 (2017); Ya'ir Ronen, Redefining the Child's Right to Identity, 18 Int'l J. L, Pol'y & Fam. 147 (2004).

[44] Compare, e.g., Scriven v. State, 769 S.E.2d 569 (Ga. Ct. App. 2015) (hereditary cancer in biological brother constitutes good cause), with In re Philip S., 881 A.2d 931 (R.I. 2005) (rejecting asserted religious basis for good cause). See also In re G.D.L., 223 A.3d 100 (D.C. 2020) (applying statutory standard for unsealing record). For a critique of the good cause standard, see Christopher G.A. Loriot, Good Cause Is Bad News: How the Good Cause Standard for Records Access Impacts Adult Adoptees Seeking Personal Information and a Proposal for Reform, 11 U. Mass. L. Rev. 100 (2016).

[45] In re Maples, 563 S.W.2d 760, 767 (Mo. 1978).

[46] See, e.g., Robert S. Andersen, Why Adoptees Search: Motives and More, 67 Child Welfare 15, 18 (1988). See also Annette Baran & Reuben Pannor, Open Adoption, in The Psychology of Adoption 316, 318 (David M. Brodzinsky & Marshall D. Schechter eds., 1990).

[47] See Emily Ingall, Note, A Presumption in Favor of Openness: Unsealing Adoption Records, 26 Cardozo J. Equal Rts. & Soc. Just. 305, 324 (2020) (describing New Jersey case).

[48] See Carol Barbieri, Your Mother Would Know, N.Y. Times, Nov. 29, 2005, at A1 (op-ed).

[49] E.g., Okla. Stat. Ann. tit. 10, §7504-1.1.

Depictions in Popular Culture: A.M. Homes, The Mistress's Daughter: A Memoir (2007)

In this memoir, novelist and writer for popular television shows A.M. Homes recounts, with painstaking self-reflection, her feelings and experiences after her birth parents, who surrendered her for adoption as an infant, initiated contact 31 years later, through her adoptive parents. Homes learns that she was conceived during an extramarital affair of her biological father, Norman, with a much younger unmarried woman, Ellen. Ellen dies during the course of the events covered in the book.

At one point, Norman insists that he and Homes have DNA tests. They go to a lab. Homes poignantly describes a moment of recognition:

> As Norman walks up to the counter, I notice that his butt looks familiar; I am watching him and I'm thinking: There goes my ass. That's my ass walking away. His blue sport coat covers it halfway, but I can see it broken into sections, departments of ass, high and low just like mine. I notice his thighs — chubby, thick, not a pretty thing. This is the first time I have seen anyone else in my body.
>
> I stare as he turns and comes back to me. I look down at his shoes, white loafers, country-club shoes, stretched out, fading. Inside the shoe, his feet are wide and short. I look up; his hands are the same as mine, square like paws. He is an exact replica, the male version of me....

Id. at 51. Later, after Ellen's death, Homes has a similar experience when she finds in Ellen's pants pockets a wad of money, just as she keeps in her own pockets: "It creeps me out, this indescribable subtlety of biology. In her pockets I find the same things I find in mine...." Id. at 102. Homes reflects on the resulting "hum of identification, a sense of wholeness and well-being," while later realizing how hard she must work to find information that her birth relatives "have lived with all along — information that is theirs for the asking...." Id. at 149-151.

In bringing to life the emotions of one adopted individual, what implications, if any, does this memoir have for adoption law and policy?

4. *Law reform.* Although two states, Alaska and Kansas, have long allowed adult adoptees to view their birth records,[50] many other states began to depart from strict secrecy more recently, as *R.D.*'s recitation of Iowa law illustrates. The modern wave of legislative reform includes different approaches: (1) As Iowa did in 1993, some states have created voluntary registries that will provide information when both parties, e.g., birth family member and

---

[50] Alaska Stat. §18.50.500; Kan. Stat. Ann. §65-2423.

adoptee, have registered.[51] Voluntary matching over the Internet and self-initiated DNA testing, without state assistance, have made such laws obsolete, however, often affording identifying information even to young adoptees.[52] (2) Some states have enacted statutes under which an intermediary will contact one party to obtain consent to release certain information once the other party has registered.[53] (3) Some states have enacted laws honoring a party's request for identifying information in the absence of a veto registered by the other party.[54] (4) A few states have gone further. For example, Tennessee enacted both a disclosure provision opening adoption records and a "contact veto" registry to be used if one party does not want communication from the other.[55]

A 1998 ballot initiative in Oregon, Measure 58, gave adult adoptees access to their birth records, as did a New Jersey law that became effective in 2017.[56] As *R.D.* recounts, some these more far-reaching reforms faced constitutional challenges. Birth mothers who surrendered children under promises of confidentiality joined with opponents who claimed the reforms would encourage abortion and discourage adoption to argue unsuccessfully that these reforms unconstitutionally impair vested rights and the obligation of contracts and violate rights of reproductive privacy and nondisclosure.[57]

Given the competing interests, which of these reforms achieves the best balance? Why?[58]

Depictions in Popular Culture: Secrets and Lies (1996)

In this classic and well-received film by famed British director Mike Leigh, Cynthia's depressing, anxiety-ridden, and economically stressed existence with her sullen daughter, Roxanne, a street sweeper, is abruptly interrupted when an older daughter she surrendered as an infant finds her. Hortense, a sophisticated young London optometrist whose adoptive parents recently died, locates Cynthia because of "the 1975 Act" opening birth records to adult adoptees. Just as Hortense, who is Black, is shocked to learn that her mother is white, so

---

[51] E.g., Ark. Code Ann. §9-9-503.

[52] See Adam Pertman, Adoption Nation: How the Adoption Revolution Is Transforming America 32 (2000); Mary Kate Kearney & Arrielle Millstein, Meeting the Challenges of Adoption in an Internet Age, 41 Cap. U. L. Rev. 237 (2013); Bryn Baffer, Comment, Closed Adoption: An Illusory Promise to Birth Parents and the Changing Landscape of Sealed Adoption Records, 28 Cath. U. J. L. & Tech. 147 (2020); Lisa Belkin, I found My Mom Through Facebook, N.Y. Times, June 26, 2011, at ST1; Rachel L. Swarns, With DNA Testing, Suddenly They are Family, N.Y. Times, Jan. 24, 2012, at A1.

[53] E.g., Ind. Code Ann. §31-19-24-2; N.Y. Pub. Health Law §4138-c.

[54] E.g., Mich. Comp. Laws Ann. §710.68(7).

[55] Tenn. Code Ann. §§36-1-127; 36-1-128.

[56] Or. Rev. Stat. Ann. §432.240; N.J. Stat. Ann. 2:8-40.33.

[57] See Doe v. Sundquist, 106 F.3d 702 (6th Cir.), cert. denied, 522 U.S. 810 (1997); Does 1-7 v. State, 993 P.2d 822 (Or. Ct. App. 1999), rev. denied, 6 P.3d 1098 (Or.), stay denied, 530 U.S. 1228 (2000); Doe v. Sundquist, 2 S.W.3d 919 (Tenn. 1999).

[58] See Ingall, supra note [47]; Leigh Kelsey O'Donnell, The Constitutional Implications of New Jersey's Open Adoption Records Law (S.873) and State-Sanctioned Infringements on Birth Parents' Privacy Rights, 13 Rutgers J. L. & Pub. Pol'y 110 (2015).

too does Cynthia believe there must be an error in the identity of the daughter whom she refused to see after birth for fear that she would become too emotionally attached to let go. Hortense's arrival adds a new dimension to her own life as well as to the lives of Cynthia and Roxanne. Further, Cynthia's revelations of her own "secrets and lies" spark other family revelations, including the infertility and resulting deep shame of Cynthia's financially successful brother and his wife.

In beginning her search, Hortense is warned that she should not get her hopes up, that her birth mother never expected to see her again, but that the law had changed. Indeed, although Hortense initiates the search and contact and Cynthia initially resists (hanging up the telephone when Hortense first summons the courage to call), it is Cynthia and those around her who are "reborn" as the result of the reunion.[59] By contrast, Hortense's "life was fine before the action starts and will continue on an even keel afterward."[60] What message, if any, does this story have for law reform regarding adoption records?

Despite the uniqueness of each story of an adoption search and reunion, what do the different races of Cynthia and Hortense add to this particular story? According to one reviewer, "this story has more to do with classism — that perennial British obsession — than racism."[61] And another observed: "[R]ace is not really on anyone's mind in this film."[62] In turn, what does the relative insignificance of race in this story reveal — given the historical emphasis on race in adoption in the United States?

2. OPEN ADOPTION

The movement to unseal adoption records has focused on adoptees who have reached adulthood. In addition, the asserted "need to know," changes in the adoption "market," and the belief that secrecy can result in psychological difficulties for all parties have prompted a different approach, open adoption that focuses on young adoptees.[63]

---

[59] Rita Kempley, "Secrets & Lies": Human Right Down to the Heart, Wash. Post, Oct. 11, 1996, at D1.

[60] Roger Ebert, Sharing "Secrets"; Leigh Has Us Rooting for Family, Chi. Sun Times, Oct. 25, 1996, Weekend Plus section, at 40.

[61] Kempley, supra note [59].

[62] Ebert, supra note [60].

[63] Open adoption was introduced in the literature in 1976 in an article noting the absence of secrecy in adoption in traditional Hawaiian culture. Annette Baran et al., Open Adoption, 21 Soc. Work 97 (1976). See Reuben Pannor & Annette Baran, Open Adoption as Standard Practice, 63 Child Welfare 245 (1984).

GROVES V. CLARK

982 P.2d 446 (Mont. 1999)

Justice WILLIAM E. HUNT, SR. delivered the Opinion of the Court....

This is the second appeal filed in this case concerning post-adoption visitation between Groves and L.C. A more detailed account of the facts of this case can be found in Groves v. Clark, 920 P.2d 981 [(Mont. 1996)]. To summarize, in January 1994, when L.C. was three years old, Groves signed a document terminating her parental rights to L.C., relinquishing custody of L.C. to Lutheran Social Services (LSS), and consenting to adoption. Groves and the Clarks signed a written visitation agreement which provided the following: Groves would have unrestricted visitation with L.C. so long as she gave the Clarks two days notice; Groves would have unrestricted telephone contact with L.C.; and Groves would have the right to take L.C. out of school in the event she had to "go to Butte for some emergency." This agreement was drafted by the LSS and neither party consulted an attorney before signing it. In February 1994, the District Court entered an order terminating Groves' parental rights to L.C. and awarding custody of L.C. to LSS. In September 1994, the Clarks legally adopted L.C.

Groves and the Clarks abided by the terms of the visitation agreement until June 5, 1995, when Groves notified the Clarks that she wanted to take L.C. to Butte for the weekend and the Clarks refused. The Clarks told Groves that she was welcome to visit L.C. in their home, but could not take L.C. on extended out-of-town trips. [Groves then sought specific performance of the visitation agreement, and the Clarks objected, moving for summary judgment. The District Court denied Groves' petition for specific performance on the ground that the post-adoption visitation agreement was void and unenforceable. Groves appealed to this Court, which reversed, holding:]

> [B]irth parents and prospective adoptive parents are free to contract for post-adoption visitation and...trial courts must give effect to such contracts when continued visitation is in the best interest of the child.

We remanded the case to the District Court for a hearing on whether enforcement of the parties' visitation agreement would be in the best interest of L.C.

Based on the evidence produced at trial, the [District Court] found that a bond existed between Groves and L.C. and that it was highly likely L.C. would suffer from issues of abandonment, identity, and grieving unless appropriate visitation with Groves was granted. Ultimately, the court found that continued visitation between Groves and L.C. was in L.C.'s best interest.... Specifically, the court granted Groves unsupervised monthly weekend visitation with L.C. and required the parties to share equally in the transportation costs. Additionally, the court granted Groves telephone contact with L.C. at least once per week. The court recommended that the parties seek adoption counseling and attempt to agree upon future visitation modifications that may be appropriate as L.C. matures.

[On appeal,] the Clarks assert that the adoptive parents' wishes are paramount in deciding whether a post-adoption visitation agreement should be enforced. The Clarks cite several cases from other jurisdictions purportedly holding that adoptive parents have the right to determine whether it is in the best interest of the adopted child to maintain contact with the birth mother. [Citations omitted.] The Clarks also cite cases from other jurisdictions purportedly holding that the mere fact that the adoptive parents oppose visitation provides a sufficient basis for finding that visitation is not in the best interest of the child. [Citations omitted.]

We reject the Clarks' assertions . . . . The law in Montana, which also happens to be the law of this case, is clear: whether a post-adoption visitation agreement is enforceable shall be decided by the District Court pursuant to a "best interests" analysis. The adoptive parents' wishes is but one factor among many to be considered by the District Court.

Next, the Clarks argue that the court did not adequately consider and evaluate the evidence when applying the "best interests" standard. [The Clarks] testified that visitation adversely affected L.C. in that afterward she would evidence insecurity about her adoption status, would be moody and difficult to discipline. On the other hand, the court heard the testimony of the [Groves'] experts including Kathy Gerhke [an adoptive parenting instructor] and Debbie O'Brien [a family counselor] which explained this as a normal occurrence. Based on their testimony, this court finds that it is highly likely L.C. will suffer from issues of abandonment, identity, and grieving unless appropriate visitation is granted. L.C. lived with her mother for over three years. The evidence, including from a visitation facilitator, was that visitation was a happy experience for L.C. . . .

[T]he Clarks assert that visitation with Groves is not in L.C.'s best interests because the Clarks do not know the details of the visitation such as where L.C. will be, what L.C. will be doing, and with whom L.C. will be associating. The Clarks have expressed concern over L.C.'s sleeping arrangements at Groves' residence. The Clarks disapprove of L.C. snowmobiling and riding in a car without wearing a seatbelt. . . . These concerns were not presented to the District Court at trial. . . .

[W]e determine that the court's finding that visitation between Groves and L.C. was in the best interest of L.C. was not clearly erroneous. The finding was supported by substantial evidence, the court did not misapprehend the effect of the evidence, and we do not believe a mistake was committed. . . . We [also] agree with the District Court that modification of the parties' original visitation agreement was within its discretion in accordance with determining the best interests of L.C. The policy of this state is that "in matters relating to children, the best interests of the children are paramount." [F]ailure to apply this rule to disputes involving post-adoption visitation agreements could potentially lead to absurd results. It would be incongruous for a court to hold that visitation is in the best interest of a child and then enforce a visitation agreement that was not in the best interest of the child. For these reasons, we determine that the District Court did not abuse its discretion in modifying the parties' post-adoption visitation agreement. . . .

NOTES AND QUESTIONS

1. *Background.* The rise of open or cooperative adoption emerged from several developments: First, an increasing number of older children, with established bonds to their birth families, became available for adoption.

Second, because of the decreased availability of the most sought-after infants for adoption following the legalization of abortion, birth parents can demand enhanced conditions in placement, including open-adoption arrangements.[64] Finally, experts claim that an open system avoids the damaging psychological effects of anonymity for adoptees, birth parents, and adopters.[65] With the prevalence of both adoptions by stepparents and relatives and also adoptions of foster children, most adoptions today are not anonymous.[66] At the time of surrender, should states require notification of all birth parents about the option of maintaining contact?[67]

2. *Enforcement.* Several states allow voluntary open adoption but permit the adoptive parents to determine whether to abide by such agreements. *Groves* cites cases from Arizona, Colorado, Maryland, and Pennsylvania taking this position. Alternatively, some states authorize judicial approval of such agreements upon a finding of best interests and then enforcement of agreements so approved.[68] Even with court approval, however, breach of the agreement by adoptive parents usually does not constitute grounds for setting aside the birth parents' surrender.[69]

3. *Open adoption in practice.* What mechanisms are necessary for open adoption to succeed? Do states need "formal programs to assist parties to reach, and draft, postadoption contact agreements"?[70] Would mediation assist in the formation and execution of open adoption agreements?[71]

4. *Parental rights.* Why does *Groves* go beyond all of the approaches examined above, allowing courts to fashion arrangements that the parties have not chosen? Does *Groves* make adoptive parents "second-class" parents? Should adoptive parents have the same rights as other parents to determine the extent of their children's visitation, if any, with legal strangers? See Troxel v. Granville, Chapter 2, section B1. In *Groves*, who should resolve

---

[64] See Carol Sanger, Bargaining for Motherhood: Postadoption Visitation Agreements, 41 Hofstra L. Rev. 309 (2012).

[65] See, e.g., Annette Ruth Appell, The Move Toward Legally Sanctioned Cooperative Adoption: Can It Survive the Uniform Adoption Act?, 30 Fam. L.Q. 483, 483 (1996). See also Pertman, supra note [52], at 47; David M. Martin et al., Toward a Greater Understanding of Openness: A Report from the Early Growth and Development Study, in Adoption Factbook V 471, 474 (National Council for Adoption 2011).

[66] See Cynthia R. Mabry, The Psychological and Emotional Ties That Bind Biological and Adoptive Families: Whether Court-Ordered Postadoption Contact Is in an Adoptive Child's Best Interest, 42 Cap. U. L. Rev. 285, 286 (2014) ("With private domestic adoptions, 69% involve some degree of openness. Public adoptions involve some degree of openness in 39% of cases. Comparatively, only 6% of intercountry adoptions involve openness.") (footnotes omitted).

[67] See Kirsten Widner, Comment, Continuing the Evolution: Why California Should Amend Family Code 8616.5 to Allow Visitation in All Postadoption Contact Agreements, 44 San Diego L. Rev. 355, 382-384 (2007) (so arguing).

[68] See, e.g., Minn. Stat. Ann. §259.58; Birth Mother v. Adoptive Parents, 59 P.3d 1233, 1236 (Nev. 2002) (rejecting enforcement "if the agreement is not incorporated in the adoption decree"); Fast v. Moore, 135 P.3d 387 (Or. Ct. App. 2006) (enforcement of agreement requires prior court approval).

[69] See Maria T. v. Jeremy S., 915 N.W.2d 441, 453 (Neb. 2018). But see Monty S. v. Jason W., 863 N.W.2d 484 (Neb. 2015) (holding in private adoption, in which birth parents placed child directly with adopters under promise of open adoption, breach of agreement invalidates surrenders).

[70] Annette R. Appell, Survey of State Utilization of Adoption with Contact, 6 Adoption Q. 75, 80 (2003).

[71] See, e.g., Nev. Rev. Stat. Ann. § 432B.5904; Christina M. Irrera, Note, Let's Make a Brand New Start of It in Old New York: Using Mediation to Resolve Open Adoption Disputes, 58 Fam. Ct. Rev. 604 (2020); Sophie Mashburn, Mediating a Family: The Use of Mediation in the Formation and Enforcement of Post-Adoption Contact Agreements, 2015 J. Disp. Resol. 383 (2015).

the asserted disputes about snowmobiling and seatbelts? Does open adoption conflict with the very concept of adoption, as some older cases held?[72] Recall and evaluate Professor Meyer's proposal for nonconsensual open adoptions to solve the legal problem posed by birth parents' flawed consent in cases in which children had already bonded with adoptive parents, noted Chapter 3, section B2.[73] See also Chapter 4, section A1a (Baby Veronica case). What is the legal status of biological parents after an open adoption? Do they remain parents? Are they legal strangers to the child? Do they occupy some intermediate status, retaining some parental rights?[74]

Depictions in Popular Culture: Immediate Family (1989)

After struggling with the stress and disappointment of infertility, Linda (Glenn Close) and Michael (James Woods), an upper-middle-class couple living in a beautiful home with a breathtaking view in Seattle, consult an attorney who recommends the "relatively new procedure" of open adoption. Lucy (Mary Stuart Masterson) and Sam (Kevin Dillon), blue-collar teenagers from Ohio, choose Linda and Michael as adoptive parents for their expected baby. Lucy travels to Seattle to give birth, and Sam joins her there. Lucy, who has lived with a stepfather ever since her mother died when Lucy was only seven, finds in Linda and Michael the parental figures missing from her life; Michael and Linda find themselves negotiating an awkward and unfamiliar role in their developing relationship with Lucy and Sam and their anticipation of adding a baby to their lives. Lucy experiences a period of uncertainty but ultimately completes the surrender — explaining that the child should know that she based her decision on love. Closing scenes depict the next year, when the child celebrates his first birthday, Lucy and Sam seem to have achieved some economic stability, and the presence of a photograph in Lucy's possession shows that communication between the birth parents and the adoptive parents has continued.

Despite the film's trite plot and predictable denouement, it provides a glimpse of the collaborative familial relationships that open adoption creates and that might flourish even without legal supervision. Should Linda and Michael treat Lucy and Sam as their teenage kids? But then what would that mean for their relationship with the baby? Will the connections among these people, from different states and different backgrounds, go beyond the mailing of occasional photographs? What will the open adoption — however it plays

---

[72] E.g., Hill v. Moorman, 525 So. 2d 681 (La. Ct. App. 1988); Cage v. Harrisonburg Dept. of Soc. Servs., 410 S.E.2d 405 (Va. Ct. App. 1991).

[73] See David D. Meyer, Family Ties: Solving the Constitutional Dilemma of the Faultless Father, 41 Ariz. L. Rev. 753, 833-846 (1999).

[74] See, e.g., *Monty S.*, 863 N.W.2d at 491 (referring to "slight" retention of parental rights).

out in the coming years — mean for the child? Will he have the best of both worlds or feel longing and distress? What stance should the law take with respect to open adoption? Why? For a similar story, see journalist Lincoln Caplan's book of the same time period, *An Open Adoption* (1990).

6. *Visitation with other birth relatives.* Some states have special rules protecting post-TPR visitation by grandparents, but others make plain that grandparent visitation rights do not survive an adoption of the child outside the extended birth family.[75] What standard governs in intrafamily adoptions? To what extent does *Troxel* (Chapter 2, section B1) apply to protect the autonomy of the adoptive parents from unwanted visits by other relatives?[76] Can particular circumstances, such as preserving a child's tie with a birth parent's religion, justify an order for visitation with a relative?[77] Do sibling relationships warrant special rules for postadoption contact? Why? Judges have pointed to social science evidence showing "the importance of sibling relationships to a child's emotional well-being," especially for children who have experienced family disruption.[78] Massachusetts, by statute, provides that courts can arrange sibling visitation with adopted children and that adopted children over 12 years of age can themselves request sibling visitation. Mass. Gen. Laws Ann. ch. 119 §26B(b). Some courts have read *Troxel* to allow judges to require such visitation when necessary to avoid harm, but have rejected claims that siblings have a constitutionally protected to maintain their relationship post-adoption.[79] By contrast, some courts have ordered such visitation based on best interests and others have halted it on the same basis.[80] Commentators have contrasted the respect for sibling relationships during foster care with the absence of protection after adoption.[81] Should preservation of a child's relationship with a biological sibling operate as a reason to reject adoption as the best permanency plan

---

[75] Compare, e.g., Tex. Fam. Code §161.206(c), with, e.g., Ind. Code Ann. §31-17-5-9 and S.D. Codified Laws §25-4-54.

[76] Compare Ex Parte D.W., 835 So. 2d 186 (Ala. 2002) (distinguishing *Troxel* to uphold authorization of visitation by "natural grandparents" after intrafamily adoption), with In re P.B., 117 A.3d 711 (N.H. 2015) (applying *Troxel* and denying grandparents' visitation petition after children's adoption by relatives, following parents' deaths), and Visitation of Cathy L.(R.)M. v. Mark Brent R., 617 S.E.2d 866 (W. Va. 2005) (*Troxel* requires giving adoptive parents special weight in deciding whether biological grandparents can visit, even in intrafamily adoptions).

[77] See In re Adoption of Odetta, 32 N.E.3d 1277 (Mass. App. Ct. 2015) (so holding).

[78] In re D.C., 4 A.3d 1004, 1012-1013 (N.J. 2010).

[79] Compare id. (reading *Troxel* to allow court-ordered sibling visitation), with In re Meridian H., 798 N.W.2d 96 (Neb. 2011) (rejecting asserted constitutional right).

[80] Compare, e.g., In re Adoption of Anthony, 448 N.Y.S.2d 377 (Fam. Ct. 1982) (ordering visitation in child's best interests), with In re Adoption of T.J.F., 798 N.E.2d 867 (Ind. Ct. App. 2003) (using adopted child's best interests to halt visitation with biological sibling). See generally Jill Elaine Hasday, Family Law Reimagined 161-194 (2014) (examining how family law has ignored sibling relationships); Anne C. Dailey & Laura A. Rosenbury, The New Law of the Child, 127 Yale L.J. 1448, 1487-1491 (2018) (critiquing law for undervaluing sibling relationships).

[81] See *D.C.*, 4 A.3d 1004; Dawn J. Post et al., Are You Still My Family? Post-Adoption Sibling Visitation, 43 Cap. U. L. Rev. 307, 311 (2015).

for the child?[82] Should the court consider the impact on both siblings or only the child to be adopted?[83]

D. WRONGFUL ADOPTION AND ADOPTION FAILURE

ROSS V. LOUISE WISE SERVICES, INC.

868 N.E.2d 189 (N.Y. 2007)

KAYE, Chief Judge.

In 1960 plaintiffs applied to Louise Wise (the Agency) for assistance in adopting an infant. They told the Agency that they preferred a "healthy infant from a healthy family," and that "it would be nice if the baby's birth family had an artistic background." Mr. Ross was nationally recognized in the advertising field, had won awards and made a good salary, and the couple were engaged in various cultural activities. According to one social worker who had interviewed them, plaintiffs were mature, seemed comfortable about adopting a child and could handle the situation "better than the average couple with whom we place a child."

In the spring of 1961 plaintiffs were offered a boy, born January 11, 1961. In response to plaintiffs' question about the health of the baby and his biological family, the social worker told plaintiffs this was "a demanding baby who likes attention." She described the physical appearance and artistic interests of the birth parents and indicated that they were healthy but the birth father was allergic to penicillin and the maternal grandfather had died of heart disease. The Agency did not, however, disclose that either of the birth parents or members of their families had suffered from emotional disturbance.

According to Agency files, the biological mother never had a "normal" home life. [She had major adjustment problems, her father was hospitalized for schizophrenia, and a psychiatrist classified the biological father as a paranoid schizophrenic.]

Plaintiffs accepted the child, and on March 30, 1961, took home the baby they named Anthony. Although he was an active, difficult infant who could not sleep well, Ms. Ross attended to him and he was a happy baby. The adoption was finalized in 1962, and in 1964 plaintiffs adopted a daughter from the Agency. By the time Anthony was four, his troublesome behavior led plaintiffs to seek professional help. . . .

[Plaintiffs contacted the Barbara Miller at the Agency in 1970 when nine-year-old Anthony] was experiencing "night terrors," cursed at the family, hit his parents and threatened people with objects. Ms. Ross suspected that he was hyperactive and might have brain dysfunction. Plaintiffs asked whether there could have been problems with the birth mother . . . . Miller's letter to [a

[82] In re Fernando M., 41 Cal. Rptr. 3d 511 (Ct. App. 2006) (preserving relationship with siblings can constitute an exceptional circumstance warranting guardianship instead of adoption).
[83] See In re Celine R., 71 P.3d 787 (Cal. 2003).

psychiatrist she recommended, Dr. Anne-Marie Weil] noted that Anthony's birth mother and grandfather "had histories of emotional instability"; however, Miller did not give Weil any specifics of the schizophrenia, and neither Miller nor Weil told plaintiffs of any emotional instability. Weil never saw Anthony himself, and her suggestions for behavior modification were to no avail. [Plaintiffs consulted another psychiatrist, Dr. Stella Chess, who requested a full birth history and background information.] Ms. Ross indicated that she suspected more and more that Anthony's difficulties were organically based and divulged that she was forced to separate herself from her son as much as possible since his violence was getting progressively worse.

When she phoned the Agency in 1981, Ms. Ross told Miller that, fearful of her own and her daughter's physical well-being, she had moved out of her home in 1978 when Anthony had finished a special high school. Plaintiffs divorced in 1979. The daughter then lived with her mother and Anthony with his father. Though Miller stated in her notes that Anthony remained disturbed and undiagnosed, she mentioned nothing to plaintiffs about his biological background.

Anthony continued to live with his father and graduated from college. Over the years, he did see several doctors, none of whom could assist him. He had some odd jobs but could not keep any. Ms. Ross called the Agency in 1994 and told them that she thought Anthony had ADHD. The Agency again did not disclose any information, including that it had received a call in 1984 that Anthony's birth mother had committed suicide in 1973. Anthony's behavior became more erratic, and he started to see a psychiatrist again. In 1995, when Anthony was 34, Mr. Ross woke up to find his son about to hit him with a large flashlight. Anthony was taken to Bellevue, where he was diagnosed as a paranoid schizophrenic....

The New York Times Magazine on March 14, 1999, published an article, *What the Jumans Didn't Know About Michael*, describing a family who adopted a boy from the Agency and learned years later that the birth family's history included schizophrenia. As a result, plaintiffs sought Anthony's medical records. These were sent in April 1999, and plaintiffs filed suit on June 25, 1999. Plaintiffs testified in their depositions that much as they love Anthony, they would not have adopted him before they saw him if they had been told about the schizophrenia in his biological family, and that psychiatrists might have treated him differently had disclosure been made earlier. Further, they claimed that the stresses in their family resulted in both plaintiffs' clinical depression, the dissolution of their marriage and lost employment....

In the 1960s and 1970s, the belief among the social workers and psychiatrists who worked for the Agency was that, in the development of a child, nurture played a far more significant role than nature. For that reason, the policy of the Agency was not to disclose certain information about a birth family's medical history if the doctors were unsure whether the factors were hereditary. [Social workers believed then that mental illness would not be passed on to a child placed in a loving home and that negative information about birth parents could impair bonding within the adoptive family.]...

Miller conceded that she concealed the biological information from all adoptive parents, including plaintiffs, when they called with post-adoptive questions. She followed what the Agency considered normative policy. Generally, the Agency might have told a couple that there was some disturbance in the family background, but more likely the Agency, without divulging aberrant history, would find an adoptive couple who could be accepting of emotional problems.... A "healthy baby" at that time meant a physically healthy child....

It was not until 1983 that the Legislature enacted Social Services Law §373-a (L. 1983, ch. 326, amended by L. 1985, chs. 103, 142), which provides that medical histories should be disclosed to preadoptive parents and adult adoptees. In 1985, the statute was amended to include adoptive parents. The Legislature also enacted Public Health Law §§4138-b, 4138-c and 4138-d, effective December 6, 1983, establishing an Adoption Information Registry in the Department of Health to allow adult adoptees to obtain non-identifying medical information.

[This appeal concerns plaintiffs' claim to recover punitive damages in their suit for wrongful adoption and their claims for negligence and intentional infliction of emotional distress.]

As a threshold matter, the Agency, in failing to challenge the order leaving in place the action for wrongful adoption, acknowledges that plaintiffs have raised a cognizable claim under common-law fraud principles in the adoption setting (see Juman v. Louise Wise Servs., [608 N.Y.S.2d 612 [N.Y. County 1994], affd. 620 N.Y.S.2d 371 [1st Dept.1995]]). The court in *Juman* indicated that the tort concerned not simply an agency's silence but " 'the deliberate act of misinforming' " a couple who were deprived of their right to make informed parenting decisions. To establish a prima facie case for fraud, plaintiffs would have to prove that

> "(1) defendant made a representation as to a material fact; (2) such representation was false; (3) defendant[ ] intended to deceive plaintiff; (4) plaintiff believed and justifiably relied upon the statement and was induced by it to engage in a certain course of conduct; and (5) as a result of such reliance plaintiff sustained pecuniary loss" (608 N.Y.S.2d 612)....

Compensatory damages are intended to have the wrongdoer make the victim whole — to assure that the victim receive fair and just compensation commensurate with the injury sustained. Punitive damages are not to compensate the injured party but rather to punish the tortfeasor and to deter this wrongdoer and others similarly situated from indulging in the same conduct in the future....

In this case, the Agency has conceded that it intentionally misrepresented facts about Anthony's background. We are troubled by such concealment, and sympathetic to the suffering plaintiffs have endured. They have presented sufficient triable facts to proceed on their fraud claim for compensatory damages.

In its motion for summary judgment, however, the Agency has shown that, even if its failure to disclose may have been tortious, its conduct in connection with the adoption did not evince the high degree of moral turpitude required for punitive damages. Nor would punitive damages be warranted against the Agency for deterrence. [The court cites agency policy and professional opinion at the time, which nothing in the record disproves, as well as new statutory duties of disclosure, which make deterrence through punitive damages unnecessary.]

The complaint here includes a single cause of action for wrongful adoption and fraud at the time of the adoption. There are no separate counts of fraud concerning conduct in later years. Thus, even though no justification may exist, for example, for the Agency's failure to disclose information to the doctors plaintiffs consulted for Anthony in the 1970s, the fraud of wrongful adoption must center on the conduct that induced the prospective parents to accept the child. . . .

The second and third causes of action — for negligence and infliction of emotional distress — are barred by the statutes of limitations. . . . [Plaintiffs claim they did not sue earlier because of the Agency's misrepresentations, but they did not contact the Agency until 1970, when] both torts of negligence and infliction of emotional distress were already time-barred. Therefore, even if the Agency made fraudulent misrepresentations, plaintiffs had not been induced to refrain from filing suit, and equitable estoppel is not warranted in this case. . . .

NOTES AND QUESTIONS

1. *A new tort?* Professor Malinda Seymore recounts the history of cause of action in *Ross*:

> Ohio became the first state to recognize the tort of wrongful adoption. It was a small opening: the Ohio Supreme Court warned, "In no way do we imply that adoption agencies are guarantors of their placements. Such a view would be tantamount to imposing an untenable contract of insurance that each child adopted would mature to be healthy and happy. Such matters are solely in the hands of a higher authority." Only in the face of "the deliberate act of misinforming this couple," not mere failure to disclose the inherent risks, could a suit be successful.[84]

Earlier, courts had rejected such claims on public policy grounds, noting that "natural parents, when fortunate enough to bring into the world a healthy child, have no guarantee whatsoever that the child will continue to enjoy good physical and emotional health."[85] What are the public policy reasons in favor of imposing liability?[86]

To what extent do sealed-record laws, supra, facilitate fraud by adoption agencies? Will subsidized adoption of children with special needs reduce the incidence of fraud?

2. *Elements.* Should only deliberate misstatements, not failure to disclose, trigger liability?[87] How does *Ross* answer this question? Evaluate the court's analysis. Why does the opinion say: "the fraud of wrongful adoption must center on the conduct that induced the prospective parents to accept the child," not later conduct? If the purpose of the suit is to win damages to

---

[84] Malinda L. Seymore, Adopting Civil Damages: Wrongful Family Separation in Adoption, 76 Wash. & Lee L. Rev. 895, 918-919 (2019) (summarizing Burr v. Board of Cty. Comm'rs, 491 N.E.2d 1101 (Ohio 1986) (footnotes omitted).

[85] Richard P. v. Vista Del Mar Child Care Serv., 165 Cal. Rptr. 370, 374 (Ct. App. 1980).

[86] See Harshaw v. Bethany Christian Servs., 714 F. Supp. 2d 771, 797-798 (W.D. Mich. 2010).

[87] See id. at 797 (recognizing cause of action for negligent failure to disclose).

support medical and other expenses of the adoptee, why shouldn't later misrepresentations provide a basis for recovery if the delay in treatment caused by the absence of information exacerbated the problem?

3. *Additional issues.* Wrongful adoption raises a host of additional questions. When should the statute of limitations begin to run in wrongful adoption cases?[88] Putting aside the statute of limitations in *Ross*, can plaintiffs in such cases recover for emotional distress?[89] Does the adopted child have a claim?[90] Does Anthony's adopted sister, placed by the same agency, also have a claim, given the upheaval Anthony's problems caused in her life and the agency's duty not to place her in a home with a troubled child?[91] Can plaintiffs sue for breach of contract?[92] Can agencies obtain valid waivers of disclosure?[93]

Should governmental immunity protect state placement agencies from such claims?[94] In the adoptive parents' suit for damages, can a court compel adult adoptees to release their medical treatment records?[95]

4. *Disclosure laws.* As *Ross* notes, state statutes now require full disclosure of the child's medical history to prospective adoptive parents (and adoptive parents). According to the New York statute:

> Such medical histories shall include all available information setting forth conditions or diseases believed to be hereditary, any drugs or medication taken during pregnancy by the child's birth mother and any other information, including any psychological information in the case of a child legally freed for adoption or when such child has been adopted, or in the case of a child to be placed in foster care or placed in foster care which may be a factor influencing the child's present or future health.

N.Y. Soc. Servs. §373-a.[96] What does "available" mean? How readily can the information be obtained?[97] Do biological parents have a duty of full disclosure? Should preadoptive genetic testing become a part of the placement process? Would such tests violate privacy rights?[98]

Should required disclosure include only individualized medical and familial histories or also data gathered from adoptions more generally? If "[d]isproportionate percentages of adopted children have learning disabilities

---

[88] See Roe v. Jewish Child. Bureau of Chicago, 790 N.E.2d 882, 892 (Ill. App. Ct. 2003).

[89] Compare Price v. State, 57 P.3d 639 (Wash. 2002) (permitting recovery), with Rowey v. Child. Friend & Servs., 2003 WL 23196347 (R.I. Super. 2003) (only when supported by medical evidence).

[90] See *Harshaw,* 714 F. Supp. 2d at 792 (applying Virginia law, which would likely recognize a duty to disclose running from the agency to the adoptee); Dresser v. Cradle of Hope Adoption Ctr., Inc., 358 F. Supp. 2d 620, 640-642 (E.D. Mich. 2005) (agency owes duty to child to provide medical information so adopters can obtain proper treatment). But see *Rowey,* 2003 WL 23196347.

[91] See *Roe,* 790 N.E.2d at 896.

[92] Id. at 888-889.

[93] See Ferenc v. World Child, Inc., 977 F. Supp. 56 (D.D.C. 1997), aff'd, 172 F.3d 919 (D.C. Cir. 1998) (permitting waivers).

[94] Compare Young v. Van Duyne, 92 P.3d 1269 (N.M. Ct. App. 2004), with Eischen v. Stark Cty. Bd. of Comm'rs., 2002 WL 31831395 (Ohio Ct. App. 2002).

[95] See Sirca v. Medina County Dep't of Human Servs., 762 N.E.2d 407 (Ohio Ct. App. 2001).

[96] See also, e.g., Ariz. Rev. Stat. Ann. §8-129(A); Cal. Fam. Code §8706.

[97] See Marianne Brower Blair, The Uniform Adoption Act's Health Disclosure Provisions: A Model That Should Not Be Overlooked, 30 Fam. L.Q. 427 (1996).

[98] See Jessica Ann Schlee, Notes & Comments, Genetic Testing: Technology That Is Changing the Adoption Process, 18 N.Y.L. Sch. J. Hum. Rts. 133 (2001).

and/or mental illness," as one commentator (an adoptive parent) asserts, would the disclosure necessary for adopters' informed consent include not only specific information about a particular child's history but also "general adoption information — such as the general rates of disability and mental illness in adopted populations"?[99]

5. *Adoption failure.* Sometimes difficulties like those in *Ross* become so severe in the eyes of the adoptive parents that they seek to end the placement. For more detailed treatment of this topic, see Chapter 6, section C, examining failure in the context of children adopted from abroad.

a. *Incidence.* Adoption failure occurs either when the child is removed before the adoption is final (disruption) or when a final adoption is abrogated or annulled (dissolution).[100] Data remain scant, but authorities say the rate is increasing, probably because of the growing number of placements of special needs children, older children with previous foster care, and international adoptees.[101]

b. *Standards.* Must the adopters have a reasonable basis for a court to vacate an adoption?[102] Does abrogation ever serve the child's best interests?[103] Recall the issue of adult adoptions undertaken as marriage substitutes and the efforts to set them aside once marriage equality arrived, Chapter 4, section B2.

Some states still have statutes, enacted years ago, allowing an adoption to be set aside in particular situations, as when the child manifests a developmental disability or unexpectedly shows "definite traits of ethnological ancestry different from those of the adoptive parents."[104] Such measures were often rationalized as a way to encourage adoption by minimizing the risks. The popular press has featured stories of Rebecca, a child whose white adoptive parents returned her when they realized she was African American and adopted a white daughter, Amy, in her place.[105]

c. *Support after vacation.* When adopters surrender their parental rights after a failed adoption, who is responsible for supporting the child? Consistent with the policy of keeping dependency private, several courts have ruled that the adoptive parents have a continuing obligation to support the child, at least until the child is adopted again.[106] What implications do such

---

[99] Ellen Wertheimer, Of Apples and Trees: Adoption and Informed Consent, 25 Quinnipiac L. Rev. 601, 601-602 (2007).

[100] See Jennifer F. Coakley & Jill D. Berrick, Research Review: In a Rush to Permanency: Preventing Adoption Disruption, 13 Child & Fam. Soc. Work 101, 102 (2007). See also Jenn Morson, When Families Un-Adopt a Child, The Atlantic (Nov. 16, 2018), https://www.theatlantic.com/family/archive/2018/11/children-who-have-second-adoptions/575902/ [https://perma.cc/9GRV-VYWP] (estimating between one and five percent).

[101] See Coakley & Berrick, supra note [100], at 102, 107-263; Andrea B. Carroll, Breaking Forever Families, 76 Ohio St. L.J. 259, 261 (2015). See generally Lita Linzer Schwartz, When Adoption Goes Wrong: Psychological and Legal Issues of Adoption Disruption (2006).

[102] See, e.g., See McAdams v. McAdams, 109 S.W.3d 649 (Ark. 2003); In re J.F., 862 A.2d 1258 (Pa. Super. Ct. 2004); In re Lisa Diane G., 537 A.2d 131 (R.I. 1988).

[103] See In re Adoption of B.J.H., 564 N.W.2d 387, 392-393 (Iowa 1997); In re Adoption of Hemmer, 619 N.W.2d 848 (Neb. 2000); In re Adoption of M., 722 A.2d 615 (N.J. Super. Ct. Ch. Div. 1998).

[104] See, e.g., Cal. Fam. Code §9100; Ky. Rev. Stat. Ann. §199.540(1).

[105] John Eligon, The Adopted Black Baby, and the White One Who Replaced Her, N.Y. Times, Dec. 8, 2017, at A14; Snap Judgment: Finding Rebecca (N.Y. Public Radio broadcast Dec. 7, 2017), https://www.wnycstudios.org/podcasts/snapjudgment/episodes/snap-831-finding-rebecca.

[106] See Greene Cty. Dept. of Soc. Servs. ex rel. Ward v. Ward, 870 N.E.2d 1132 (N.Y. 2007); State ex rel. C.V. v. Visser, 2007 WL 1462235 (Tenn. Ct. App. 2007).

outcomes have for the policy of encouraging adoptions of children with special needs? And for the likelihood of seeking relief informally?

d. *Informal remedies.* Critics have condemned the rise self-help efforts in which adoptive parents themselves "rehome" children they feel they cannot rear.[107] The Uniform Law Commission has begun formulating a model statute to address this problem, to be called either the Unregulated Transfers of Adopted Children Act or the Uniform Child Placement Protection Act.[108] What should such legislation say? See Chapter 6, section C.

PROBLEMS

1. Barbara gives birth to a child and surrenders him to the Children's Home Society (CHS), a state-licensed private adoption agency, which places the baby in an adoptive family. As part of the surrender process, CHS provides counseling for Barbara. It also obtains detailed health and background information from her. Ten years later Barbara marries and has two children, a daughter and a son. When this son dies in infancy, Barbara learns she carries a genetic defect that afflicts male offspring. Barbara contacts CHS to determine the health of her first son and learns from CHS that he, too, suffers from the genetic disease.

Barbara sues CHS for wrongful death, negligent and intentional infliction of emotional distress, and fraud. In essence, she claims CHS had a duty to inform her of the genetic disease of the son she surrendered, to enable her to make informed choices about future childbearing. What result and why?[109] Did Barbara have a duty to inform CHS when she discovered the condition of her second son?[110]

2. Henry and Wilma, a married couple, adopted Denise when she was 15. Sometime thereafter, the marriage of Henry and Wilma failed, and a court ultimately granted Wilma's divorce petition. At age 22, Denise gave birth to a son, Sam. No one contests that Henry is Sam's father and that Sam must have been conceived before the court dissolved Henry's and Wilma's marriage. Denise and Henry now wish to marry to legitimize Sam. State incest laws, however, bar marriages between fathers and daughters, including those whose relationship rests on adoption. As a result, Denise sues to abrogate Henry's adoption of her, while leaving her adoption by Wilma undisturbed; Henry and Wilma both support Denise's petition. What result and why?[111]

---

[107] E.g., Sally Terry Green, The Law Demands Process for Rehomed Children, 69 Ark. L. Rev. 729 (2016); Elizabeth A. Dahl, Re-Homing: The Underground Market for Adopted Children and How Current Laws Fail to Protect the Innocent, 6 Wake Forest J. L. & Pol'y 549 (2016).

[108] See Unregulated Transfers of Adopted Children Act, Jan. 31–Feb. 1, 2020 (draft for discussion only), https://www.uniformlaws.org/HigherLogic/System/DownloadDocumentFile.ashx?DocumentFileKey=219526fe-bcda-8051-2524-114584424c4f&forceDialog=0.

[109] See Olson v. Child. Home Soc'y, 252 Cal. Rptr. 11 (Ct. App. 1988). But cf. Molloy v. Meier, 679 N.W.2d 711 (Minn. 2004).

[110] See R. Scott Smith, Disclosure of Post-Adoption Family Medical Information: A Continuing Birth Parent Duty, 35 Fam. L.Q. 553 (2001).

[111] See *Adoption of M.*, 722 A.2d 615. See also State v. Howard, 598 S.W.3d 146 (Mo. Ct. App. 2020).

CHAPTER 6

ADOPTION ACROSS STATE AND NATIONAL BOUNDARIES

Mobility characterizes contemporary society, and birth parents, adopters, and children often travel among jurisdictions with different legal regimes. This chapter "maps" adoption, exploring the issues posed by cases with connections to more than one state or country.

A. ADOPTION JURISDICTION

IN RE BABY GIRL CLAUSEN

502 N.W.2d 649 (Mich. 1993)

PER CURIAM. . . .

[O]n February 8, 1991, Cara Clausen gave birth to a baby girl in Iowa. . . . On February 10, 1991, Clausen signed a release of custody form, relinquishing her parental rights to the child. Clausen, who was unmarried at the time of the birth, had named Scott Seefeldt as the father. On February 14, 1991, he executed a release of custody form.

[On February 25, 1991, petitioners Roberta and Jan DeBoer, Michigan residents, petitioned a juvenile court in Iowa to adopt the child. At a hearing held the same day,] the parental rights of Cara Clausen and Seefeldt were terminated, and petitioners were granted custody of the child during the pendency of the proceeding. The DeBoers returned to Michigan with the child, and she has lived with them in Michigan continuously since then.

However, the prospective adoption never took place. On March 6, 1991, nine days after the filing of the adoption petition, Cara Clausen filed a motion in the Iowa Juvenile Court to revoke her release of custody. In an affidavit accompanying the request, Clausen stated that she had lied when she named Seefeldt as the father of the child, and that the child's father actually was Daniel Schmidt. Schmidt filed an affidavit of paternity on March 12, 1991, and on March 27, 1991, he filed a petition in the Iowa district court, seeking to intervene in the adoption proceeding initiated by the DeBoers. [He and Clausen married in April 1992.]

[The Iowa district court found that Schmidt was the biological father and that the DeBoers failed to establish either that Schmidt had abandoned the

235

child or that his rights should be terminated. It determined that a best interests of the child analysis becomes appropriate only after a showing of abandonment.] On the basis of these findings, the court concluded that the termination proceeding was void with respect to Schmidt, and that the DeBoers' petition to adopt the child must be denied. Those decisions have been affirmed by the Iowa appellate courts. [In re BGC, 496 N.W.2d 239 (Iowa, 1992). On remand, the Iowa district terminated the DeBoers' rights as temporary guardians and custodians.]

On the same day their rights were terminated in Iowa, the DeBoers filed a petition in Washtenaw Circuit Court [in Michigan], asking the court to assume jurisdiction under the UCCJA. The petition requested that the court enjoin enforcement of the Iowa custody order and find that it was not enforceable, or, in the alternative, to modify it to give custody to the DeBoers. [The Michigan court] entered an ex parte temporary restraining order, which directed that the child remain in the custody of the DeBoers, and ordered Schmidt not to remove the child from Washtenaw County.

[The Michigan court] found that it had jurisdiction to determine the best interests of the child. It denied Schmidt's motion for summary judgment [to dissolve the preliminary injunction and enforce the Iowa judgment], and directed that the child remain with the DeBoers until further order of the court.[9] [The court of appeals reversed, concluding Michigan lacked jurisdiction under the UCCJA and the DeBoers lacked standing. Following a petition for declaratory and injunctive relief by the child's guardian ad litem, the circuit court entered an order temporarily continuing the status quo. This court granted the DeBoers' application to appeal, limited to issues of jurisdiction and standing, and the Schmidts' application to appeal, limited to the question whether the complaint should be dismissed for failure to state a claim.]

Interstate enforcement of child custody orders has long presented vexing problems. This arose principally from uncertainties about the applicability of the Full Faith and Credit Clause of the United States Constitution. Because custody decrees were generally regarded as subject to modification, states had traditionally felt free to modify another state's prior order.

The initial attempt to deal with these jurisdictional problems was the drafting of the Uniform Child Custody Jurisdiction Act, promulgated by the National Conference of Commissioners on Uniform State Laws in 1968. That uniform act has now been enacted, in some form, in all fifty states, the District of Columbia, and the U.S. Virgin Islands. . . . In 1980, Congress [enacted] the Parental Kidnapping Prevention Act, 28 U.S.C. §1738A. The PKPA "imposes a duty on the States to enforce a child custody determination entered by a court of a sister State if the determination is consistent with the provisions of the Act." Thompson v. Thompson, 484 U.S. 174, 175-176 (1988).

---

9. [P]roceedings have continued in Iowa. On January 27, 1993, the Iowa district court held the DeBoers in contempt of court, and issued bench warrants for their arrest. The Iowa juvenile court entered an order on February 17, 1993, restoring Cara (Clausen) Schmidt's parental rights. A best interests of the child determination hearing began in Washtenaw Circuit Court on January 29, 1993, and continued for eight days. In a decision rendered from the bench on February 12, 1993, the Washtenaw Circuit Court found that it was in the best interests of the child for her to remain with the DeBoers. That decision is not at issue in the instant appeal.

The PKPA includes provisions similar to the UCCJA, and emphatically imposes the requirement that sister-state custody orders be given effect....

In its March 29, 1993, opinion, the Court of Appeals agreed with Daniel Schmidt that the Washtenaw Circuit Court lacked jurisdiction to modify the Iowa custody orders and was instead required to enforce them. [It explained that adoption proceedings are custody proceedings under the UCCJA; that the custody matter was still pending in Iowa, where further proceedings had been scheduled; and that Iowa did not fail to conform to the UCCJA when it did not determine the best interests of the child.]

The congressionally declared purpose of the PKPA is to deal with inconsistent and conflicting laws and practices by which courts determine their jurisdiction to decide disputes between persons claiming rights of custody. Inconsistency in the determination by courts of their jurisdiction to decide custody disputes contributes to "the disregard of court orders, excessive relitigation of cases, [and] obtaining of conflicting orders by the courts of various jurisdictions...." For these reasons, among others, Congress declared that the best interests of the child required the establishment of a uniform system for the assumption of jurisdiction....

The [DeBoers' argument] that in this context the best interests purpose of the PKPA mandates a best interests analysis in Iowa, failing which the Iowa decision is not entitled to full faith and credit, would permit the forum state's view of the merits of the case to govern the assumption of jurisdiction to modify the foreign decree....

It has been aptly noted that the vulnerability of a custody decree to an out-of-state modification presented the greatest need of all for the reform effort of the PKPA.... Certainty and stability are given priority under the PKPA, which gives the home state exclusive continuing jurisdiction. Thus, the PKPA expressly provides that if a custody determination is made consistently with its provisions, the appropriate authorities of every State *shall* enforce [it] according to its terms, and *shall not* modify that custody decision. 28 U.S.C. §1738A(a) (emphasis added).... At the time of commencement of both the termination and adoption proceedings, Iowa unquestionably had jurisdiction under its own laws and Iowa was unquestionably the home state of the child....

Where the custody determination is made consistently with the provisions of the PKPA, the jurisdiction of the court that made the decision is exclusive and continuing as long as that state "remains the residence of the child or of any contestant," and it still has jurisdiction under its own laws. 28 U.S.C. §1738A(d). Unquestionably, Daniel Schmidt continues to reside in Iowa. Furthermore, Iowa law provides for continuing jurisdiction in custody matters.... The courts of this state may only modify Iowa's order if Iowa has declined to exercise its jurisdiction to modify it. 28 U.S.C. §1738A(f). Iowa has not declined to exercise its jurisdiction to modify its custody order; it has simply declined to order the relief sought by the DeBoers....

The DeBoers advance a variety of arguments in support of their claim that they have standing to litigate regarding the custody of the child. [Yet] when the temporary custody order was rescinded, they became third parties to the child and no longer had a basis on which to claim a substantive right of custody....

[T]he next friend for the child argues that we should recognize the right of a minor child to bring a Child Custody Act action and obtain a best interests of the child hearing regarding her custody. . . . We do not believe that the Child Custody Act can be read as authorizing such an action. The act's consistent distinction between the "parties" and the "child" makes clear that the act is intended to resolve disputes among adults seeking custody of the child.

It is true that children, as well as their parents, have a due process liberty interest in their family life. However, in our view those interests are not independent of the child's parents. [T]he natural parent's right to custody is not to be disturbed [absent a showing of unfitness], sometimes despite the preferences of the child. [The court rejected the due process and equal protection arguments raised on the child's behalf.] In the Iowa proceedings, a challenge to Daniel Schmidt's fitness was vigorously prosecuted by the DeBoers, and they failed to prove that he was unfit. . . .[48]

We direct the Washtenaw Circuit Court to enter an order enforcing the custody orders entered by the Iowa courts. In consultation with counsel for the Schmidts and the DeBoers, the circuit court shall promptly establish a plan for the transfer of custody [within 31 days]. It is now time for the adults to move beyond saying that their only concern is the welfare of the child and to put those words into action by assuring that the transfer of custody is accomplished promptly with minimum disruption of the life of the child.

LEVIN, J. (dissenting).

I would agree with the majority's analysis if the DeBoers had gone to Iowa, purchased a carload of hay from Cara Clausen, and then found themselves in litigation in Iowa with Daniel Schmidt, who also claimed an interest in the hay. It could then properly be said that the DeBoers "must be taken to have known" that, rightly or wrongly, the Iowa courts might rule against them, and they should, as gracefully as possible, accept an adverse decision of the Iowa courts. Michigan would then have had no interest in the outcome, and would routinely enforce a decree of the Iowa courts against the DeBoers. But this is not a lawsuit concerning the ownership, the legal title, to a bale of hay. . . .

The PKPA was enacted to protect the child. . . . Congress enacted the PKPA, not because of an abstract concern about "interstate controversies over child custody," but rather "in the interest of greater stability of home environment and of secure *family relationships* for the child." . . . Congress identified the "home state" of the child as the "state which can best decide the case in the interest of the child." "Home state" is defined as the "State in which, immediately preceding the time involved, the child lived with his parents, a parent, *or a person acting as a parent, for at least six consecutive months,* and in the case of a child less than six months old, the State in which the child lived from birth with any of such persons." (Emphasis added.) . . .

Michigan is the child's home state because she has lived in Michigan with the DeBoers, persons "acting as a parent," for at least six consecutive months — actually for over two years. Michigan, the home state, would also

---

48. Even if we were to conclude that the child has [constitutional] interests that were not adequately represented in the previous Iowa proceedings, the PKPA would require that any new action on her behalf be brought in Iowa, which has continuing exclusive jurisdiction. . . .

qualify as the state having jurisdiction under the PKPA pursuant to the alternative "significant connection" test for a case where no state is the home state.... There is more substantial evidence concerning the child's present or future care, protection, training and personal relationships in Michigan than in Iowa.... There was no contact between Daniel Schmidt and the child in Iowa, minimum contact between Cara Schmidt and the child in Iowa, and maximum contact between the child and the DeBoers in Michigan.... Assuming that the PKPA applies to adoption proceedings, and that is the assumption on which the majority opinion is predicated, the underlying themes of the act must be observed....

Professor Clark wrote that subject matter jurisdiction in adoption should be given to the home state of the child .... As Professor Clark explains, the only issues in an adoption proceeding with respect to the natural parents, are "whether the consent is genuine, or whether the alleged abandonment or neglect did occur. These resemble *the issues in the ordinary transitory lawsuit*, and there is thus no need for any requirements of domicile or residence on the part of the natural parents."[53]

But, suggests Professor Clark, "since adoption consists of matching a child with a new parent or set of parents," there is a need for a "thorough opportunity to study the child and his background. To give the court this opportunity, the child must be present and available in the jurisdiction."[54] He concludes ... that that subject matter jurisdiction in adoption should be where the adoptive parents reside and the child is physically present....

A decree rendered by a state other than the home state is not a determination made "consistent with the provisions" of the PKPA. A decree rendered without consideration of the child's best interests is not a decree that the Congress intended that all other states must enforce. [Michigan law would require a best interests hearing.]

The sympathetic portrayal of the Schmidts in the majority opinion ignores that it was Cara Schmidt's fraud on the Iowa court and on Daniel Schmidt that is at the root of this controversy.... To fault the DeBoers is unwarranted. [They left Iowa with the child in good faith.] Why should they have believed that Cara Schmidt was telling the truth when she said she had fraudulently named the other man as the father? The DeBoers discovered that Schmidt had a dismal record as a father.... The Iowa courts thought there was sufficient merit in the DeBoers' claims that they maintained custody of the child with the DeBoers until after the Iowa Supreme Court ruled. One [dissenting] justice agreed with the DeBoers....

If the danger confronting this child were physical injury, no one would question her right to invoke judicial process to protect herself against such injury. There is little difference, when viewed from the child's frame of reference, between a physical assault and a psychological assault.... It is only because this child cannot speak for herself that adults can avert their eyes from the pain that she will suffer.

---

53. [2 Clark, Domestic Relations, 2d ed., §21.3,] p. 595. (Emphasis added.)
54. Id., §21.3, p. 596.

NOTES AND QUESTIONS

1. *Epilogue.* The litigation in the principal case, often called the Baby Jessica case, gripped the nation. The United States Supreme Court refused to stay the order entered pursuant to the Michigan Supreme Court's opinion. 509 U.S. 1301 (1993). After the transfer, Baby Jessica became Anna Schmidt. Although Anna's home life was marked by parental unemployment and divorce, she fared well by all accounts, despite the emotional trauma predicted when she left the DeBoers' custody.[1] The DeBoers adopted again, then divorced, but later reconciled and remarried.[2]

2. *Background: child custody jurisdiction.* The statutes examined in *Clausen* originated as responses to particular problems characterizing child custody adjudication: First, courts long regarded jurisdiction to decide child custody matters to exist concurrently in multiple fora — in the state of the child's domicile, any state where the child is physically present, and any state with personal jurisdiction over both parents.[3] Second, courts decide custody cases on the basis of the notoriously indeterminate "best interests of the child" standard.[4] Third, the outcomes of child custody litigation are never final, but always subject to modification upon changed circumstances. Finally, the modifiability of custody decisions left uncertainties about whether such decrees required full faith and credit in other states.[5] The confluence of these features meant that a parent disappointed with an outcome in one state could take the child to another state (or refuse to return a child following visitation in another state) and seek modification, in the hope that the new forum would reach a different decision on the child's best interests. One Supreme Court Justice condemned the law that fostered this practice as "a rule of seize-and-run."[6]

Three legislative initiatives attempted to respond: (1) The Uniform Child Custody Jurisdiction Act (UCCJA), drafted in 1968, adopted by almost every state, and applied in *Clausen*;[7] (2) The Parental Kidnapping Prevention Act, 28 U.S.C. §1738A, initially enacted by Congress in 1980 and applied in *Clausen*; and (3) the Uniform Child Jurisdiction and Enforcement Act (UCCJEA), promulgated in 1997 to supersede the UCCJA, revised in 2013, and adopted in every state except Massachusetts, where it was introduced in 2020.[8]

All three reform measures — the UCCJA, the PKPA, and the UCCJEA — share several important features, which lawmakers became more adept at

---

[1] See Brian Dickerson, A Child's Life Shows Folly of Adults, Media, Detroit Free Press, Feb. 24, 2003, at 1B.

[2] Pair Who Fought for Baby Jessica Plan to Remarry, Atlanta J. & Atlanta Const., Feb. 4, 2001, at A6; Milestones, Time Mag., June 20, 1994, at 23.

[3] See Sampsell v. Super. Court, 197 P.2d 739 (Cal. 1948).

[4] See Robert Mnookin, Child Custody Revisited, 77 L. & Contemp. Probs. 249, 251 (2014) ("The lack of a social consensus about values still plagues best-interests determinations. Determining what is best for a particular child inevitably involves judgments about the hierarchy of and trade-offs between often competing values.").

[5] See generally Leonard G. Ratner, Child Custody in a Federal System, 62 Mich. L. Rev. 795 (1964).

[6] May v. Anderson, 345 U.S. 528, 542 (1953) (Jackson, J., dissenting).

[7] See Uniform Law Commission, Child Custody Jurisdiction Act (1968), https://www.uniformlaws.org/committees/community-home?CommunityKey=020a80d7-902e-412b-9b44-112a1693760c (showing map and listing states).

[8] Id.

articulating with each successive legislative effort and which respond to the particular problems characterizing custody adjudications:

First, these measures limit jurisdiction. Responding to the difficulties posed by concurrent jurisdiction, the PKPA and UCCJEA clearly indicate that only one state at a time should have authority to decide a given child custody matter.

Second, these reforms reflect an understanding of child custody adjudications as intensely fact-specific assessments in which evidence about the child's day-to-day interactions and the availability of witnesses with knowledge of the child and the environment loom large. Hence, the drafters expressly incorporated a preference for a forum with "maximum rather than minimum contact" with the child, specifically the child's "home state."[9] As the PKPA and UCCJEA make clear, only when there is no home state (defined usually as a state where the child lived for at least six consecutive months) may one of the states meeting alternative requirements, such as the child's significant connection with the state, assert jurisdiction. Further, in personam jurisdiction over a parent provides neither a necessary nor a sufficient condition for jurisdiction. In other words, based on the rationale that child custody adjudications resolve issues of status, like divorce (which does not require in personam jurisdiction), a parent need not have minimum contacts with the forum.[10]

Third, the court initially deciding custody retains exclusive, continuing jurisdiction, so that modification proceedings must take place there — unless all the parties and the child have left this state. Finally, under these statutes, other states must respect and enforce custody adjudications made consistent with the legislation's jurisdictional rules; thus, these measures include a statutory requirement of full faith and credit.

The PKPA, invoked in *Baby Girl Clausen*, illustrates these features. In full, the current version of this statute provides:

28 U.S.C. §1738A. Full faith and credit given to child custody determinations

(a) The appropriate authorities of every State shall enforce according to its terms, and shall not modify except as provided in subsections (f), (g), and (h) of this section, any custody determination or visitation determination made consistently with the provisions of this section by a court of another State.

(b) As used in this section, the term —

(1) "child" means a person under the age of eighteen;

(2) "contestant" means a person, including a parent or grandparent, who claims a right to custody or visitation of a child;

(3) "custody determination" means a judgment, decree, or other order of a court providing for the custody of a child, and includes permanent and temporary orders, and initial orders and modifications;

(4) "home State" means the State in which, immediately preceding the time involved, the child lived with his parents, a parent,

---

[9] See UCCJA §3 cmt. (1968).
[10] See UCCJEA §201 cmt. 2 (1997).

or a person acting as parent, for at least six consecutive months, and in the case of a child less than six months old, the State in which the child lived from birth with any of such persons. Periods of temporary absence of any of such persons are counted as part of the six-month or other period;

(5) "modification" and "modify" refer to a custody or visitation determination which modifies, replaces, supersedes, or otherwise is made subsequent to, a prior custody or visitation determination concerning the same child, whether made by the same court or not;

(6) "person acting as a parent" means a person, other than a parent, who has physical custody of a child and who has either been awarded custody by a court or claims a right to custody;

(7) "physical custody" means actual possession and control of a child;

(8) "State" means a State of the United States, the District of Columbia, the Commonwealth of Puerto Rico, or a territory or possession of the United States; and

(9) "visitation determination" means a judgment, decree, or other order of a court providing for the visitation of a child and includes permanent and temporary orders and initial orders and modifications.

(c) A child custody or visitation determination made by a court of a State is consistent with the provisions of this section only if —

(1) such court has jurisdiction under the law of such State; and

(2) one of the following conditions is met:

(A) such State (i) is the home State of the child on the date of the commencement of the proceeding, or (ii) had been the child's home State within six months before the date of the commencement of the proceeding and the child is absent from such State because of his removal or retention by a contestant or for other reasons, and a contestant continues to live in such State;

(B) (i) it appears that no other State would have jurisdiction under subparagraph (A), and (ii) it is in the best interest of the child that a court of such State assume jurisdiction because (I) the child and his parents, or the child and at least one contestant, have a significant connection with such State other than mere physical presence in such State, and (II) there is available in such State substantial evidence concerning the child's present or future care, protection, training, and personal relationships;

(C) the child is physically present in such State and (i) the child has been abandoned, or (ii) it is necessary in an emergency to protect the child because the child, a sibling, or parent of the child has been subjected to or threatened with mistreatment or abuse;

(D) (i) it appears that no other State would have jurisdiction under subparagraph (A), (B), (C), or (E), or another State has declined to exercise jurisdiction on the ground that the State whose jurisdiction is in issue is the more appropriate forum to determine the custody or visitation of the child, and (ii) it is in the best interest of the child that such court assume jurisdiction; or

(E) the court has continuing jurisdiction pursuant to subsection (d) of this section.

(d) The jurisdiction of a court of a State which has made a child custody or visitation determination consistently with the provisions of this section continues as long as the requirement of subsection (c)(1) of this section continues to be met and such State remains the residence of the child or of any contestant.

(e) Before a child custody or visitation determination is made, reasonable notice and opportunity to be heard shall be given to the contestants, any parent whose parental rights have not been previously terminated and any person who has physical custody of a child.

(f) A court of a State may modify a determination of the custody of the same child made by a court of another State, if —

(1) it has jurisdiction to make such a child custody determination; and

(2) the court of the other State no longer has jurisdiction, or it has declined to exercise such jurisdiction to modify such determination.

(g) A court of a State shall not exercise jurisdiction in any proceeding for a custody or visitation determination commenced during the pendency of a proceeding in a court of another State where such court of that other State is exercising jurisdiction consistently with the provisions of this section to make a custody or visitation determination.

(h) A court of a State may not modify a visitation determination made by a court of another State unless the court of the other State no longer has jurisdiction to modify such determination or has declined to exercise jurisdiction to modify such determination.

3. *Applying the statutes.* In *Baby Girl Clausen*, how sound is the majority's premise that the UCCJA and the PKPA control in adoption proceedings? How do such proceedings resemble custody proceedings and how do they differ? Note that adoption decrees, unlike custody adjudications, are final (not modifiable) and require full faith and credit in other states. See infra section B. What does that mean for appropriate jurisdictional rules? Considerable authority supports the view of *Baby Girl Clausen* that adoption proceedings are custody proceedings covered by the federal PKPA.[11]

The applicability of state laws modeled on the UCCJEA is more controversial, even today, because that statute explicitly disclaims application to adoption proceedings. UCCJEA §103 & cmt. (1997). Instead, it says that the Uniform Adoption Act (UAA), promulgated by the ULC in 1994 with a jurisdictional scheme designed specifically for adoptions, should control.[12] Yet, only one state enacted UAA, and ULC no longer includes it in the list of Uniform Laws. With a gap in state laws, then, uncertainty persists about jurisdiction for adoption proceedings. Nonetheless, if a state adoption

---

[11] See In re N.D., 142 N.E.3d 1225, 1227-1228 (Ohio Ct. App. 2019); In re Adoption of Baby E.Z., 266 P.3d 702 (Utah 2011). See also D.B. v. M.A., 975 So. 2d 927, 936 (Ala. Civ. App. 2006) (applying UCCJEA and PKPA because "case involve[s] more than adoption, it involve[s] the custody of the child as well"). But see People ex rel. A.J.C., 88 P.3d 599 (Colo. 2004) (distinguishing adoptions from custody cases, but deciding that custody must be adjudicated after failed adoption).

[12] See Herma Hill Kay, Adoption in the Conflict of Laws: The UAA, Not the UCCJA, Is the Answer, 84 Cal. L. Rev. 703, 712-728 (1996).

proceeding comports with the jurisdictional requirements of the federal PKPA, then other states must respect it.

4. *Home state.* Assuming that the PKPA applies, which analysis in *Baby Girl Clausen* is more convincing, the majority's or the dissent's? Did Iowa satisfy the requirements for "home state" for the child, as defined in §1738A(b)(4)? Note that home-state jurisdiction requires that the child live there for the specified time with "parents, a parent, or a person acting as parent." Does Baby Girl Clausen have a home state?[13] Will the majority's reasoning invite fraudulent identification of a child's father (as the dissent predicts)? Will the dissent's approach encourage prospective adopters to delay returning a child, despite an impediment to adoption in the state where the child was surrendered, in hopes of obtaining in their domicile a more favorable outcome based on a best interests analysis (as the majority fears)? Might the home state nonetheless constitute an inconvenient forum, so that it should abstain from asserting jurisdiction?[14]

5. *Significant connection to the forum.* If a child has no home state, then the PKPA says that jurisdiction belongs in a forum that meets the requirements of §1738A(c)(2)(B), which focuses on connection to the forum and entails a best-interests inquiry.[15] Why did the court reject the DeBoers' argument on a best-interests analysis at the jurisdictional stage? Like Professor Clark, quoted in the dissent, several authorities would locate adoption jurisdiction at the domicile of the child or the adoptive parents, which would have access to most information about the placement and the child's adjustment to it.[16] Does that make more sense? Where is an infant domiciled?[17]

6. *Contested multistate adoptions.* Even if Michigan might have the most evidence about the child's situation and best interests because she had been living there, of what relevance is the fact that adoption proceedings began in Iowa? If the PKPA and similar legislation seek to prevent jurisdictional competition and forum shopping by limiting authority to one state at a time, which approach — the majority's or the dissent's — best achieves the goal?[18]

7. *Interstate compact.* The Interstate Compact on the Placement of Children (ICPC), a statutory agreement enacted in 52 jurisdictions, also

---

[13] Applying the UCCJEA, which tracks the PKPA's definition of "home state," several courts have held that a child born in one state and taken to another within a few days of birth for adoption does not have a home state. See, e.g., In re Baby Girl F., 932 N.E.2d 428, 440 (Ill. App. Ct. 2008); Nevares v. Adoptive Couple, 384 P.3d 213, 218 (Utah 2016); In re A.W., 94 A.3d 1161, 1168 (Vt. 2014).

[14] See In re Adoption of Baby Boy M., 193 P.3d 520 (Kan. Ct. App. 2008).

[15] See, e.g., *A.W.,* 94 A.3d at 1168-1169 (applying UCCJEA to jurisdiction over a child in need of care).

[16] See Restatement (Second) of Conflict of Laws §78 (Am. Law Inst. 1971). See also, e.g., Miss. Code Ann. §93-17-3(1)(b) (allowing adoption jurisdiction when adoptive parents have lived in the state for at least six months immediately before proceeding and substantial evidence is available there).

[17] See Miss. Band of Choctaw Indians v. Holyfield, 490 U.S. 30, 47-48 (1989) (common law assigns nonmarital children their mother's domicile; hence, a child's domicile of origin may be a place where child has never been).

[18] Compare *N.D.,* 142 N.E.3d at 1231, with *A.J.C.,* 88 P.3d 599. See also id. at 614 (Coats, J., dissenting) (lamenting "the jurisdictional free-for-all that will surely result [if multiple states have jurisdiction] and the harm done to children who will be forced to suffer under conflicting custody orders and perpetual jurisdictional disputes"); In re Adoption of Jaelyn B., 883 N.W.2d 22, 32 (Neb. 2016) (noting that the court below failed to determine whether the case pending in another state rested on jurisdiction under PKPA).

governs multistate adoptions.[19] The statute specifies procedural requirements for transferring the custody of a child to adoptive parents from
another state but does not establish jurisdiction.[20]

8. *Other jurisdictional requirements.*

a. *Personal jurisdiction.* Must a court at the child's or adopter's domicile have personal jurisdiction over the child's birth parents, absent a previous TPR?[21] Would this requirement remain controlling if the custody
jurisdiction statutes, such as the PKPA, govern adoptions?

In Division of Youth & Family Services v. M.Y.J.P., 823 A.2d 817 (N.J. Super.
Ct. App. Div. 2003), a mother who remained in Haiti after the father took
their son to live in New Jersey challenged that state's jurisdiction to terminate her parental rights. In New Jersey, the child had been removed from
the father and placed with foster parents, who wished to adopt him.
The lower court decided it had jurisdiction, based on its parens patriae
authority to serve the child's best interests. On appeal, the court affirmed,
invoking both the "status exception" to the minimum-contacts requirement
and the mother's purposeful availment of New Jersey's benefits when she
acceded to the care of her son by state child welfare authorities. Do you agree
with the outcome? Which rationale works best — parens patriae, the status
exception, or purposeful availment? Why?

b. *TPR.* Although it explicitly excludes adoption, UCCJEA defines "child
custody proceeding" expansively as:

> a proceeding in which legal custody, physical custody, or visitation with
> respect to a child is an issue. The term includes a proceeding for divorce,
> separation, neglect, abuse, dependency, guardianship, paternity, termination
> of parental rights, and protection from domestic violence, in which the issue
> may appear.

UCCJEA §102(4). Could the child's home state terminate the rights of a parent
over whom it lacked personal jurisdiction? Can you reconcile that implication with Santosky v. Kramer, Chapter 3, section A.

c. *Consent.* Some states treat parental consent to adoption as a jurisdictional prerequisite for adoption (absent TPR).[22] The absence of a birth

---

[19] See American Public Human Services Association, Association of Administrators of the
Interstate Compact on the Placement of Children, https://www.aphsa.org/AAICPC/default.aspx.

[20] E.g., In re Adoption of Asente, 734 N.E.2d 1224, 1230-1231 (Ohio 2000). See generally, e.g.,
Moore v. Asente, 110 S.W.3d 336 (Ky. 2003); Vivek Sankaran, Perpetuating the Impermanence of
Foster Children: A Critical Analysis of Efforts to Reform the Interstate Compact on the Placement
of Children, 40 Fam. L.Q. 435 (2006); Robert G. Spector & Cara N. Rodriguez, Jurisdiction Over
Children in Interstate Placement: The UCCJEA, Not the ICPC, Is the Answer, 41 Fam. L.Q. 145
(2007). See also Neoshia R. Roemer, Finding Harmony or Swimming in the Void: The Unavoidable
Conflict Between the Interstate Compact on the Placement of Children and the Indian Child
Welfare Act, 94 N.D. L. Rev. 149 (2019) (arguing the ICWA preempts the ICPC). Sometimes courts
apply the compact to the placement of children with an out-of-state parent, prolonging a child's
time in foster care. See, e.g., In re Suhey G., 164 Cal. Rptr. 3d 772 (Ct. App. 2013); Matter of B.H., 456
P.3d 233 (Mont. 2020).

[21] See Armstrong v. Manzo, 380 U.S. 545 (1965) (holding that due process requires notice of
adoption).

[22] E.g., In re Adoption of X.J.A., 166 P.3d 396, 402 (Kan. 2007); *Jaelyn B.*, 883 N.W.2d at 33; In re
Adoption of B.B., 417 P.3d 1, 8 (Utah 2017). But see In re Adoption of L-MHB, 431 P.3d 560, 566 (Wyo.
2018).

father's consent often becomes a crucial issue when a birth mother attempts to thwart his involvement by forum shopping — secretly fleeing to a state with relaxed requirements where she gives birth and surrenders the child. Courts have divided on whether the applicable standard for proceeding without the birth father's consent should be that of the state of surrender, the state where the father thought the mother would give birth, or the state where both had lived previously.[23] Do these situations make the case for a national putative father registry database? Would that solve the problem?[24] Should the Uniform Law Commission try once more to develop a uniform statute on adoption for the states to enact?[25]

d. *Pre-birth jurisdiction.* Most states do not allow jurisdiction to attach before birth. Although such cases have arisen outside the adoption context, their holdings leave a putative father who fears "thwarting" unable to know where adoption proceedings might begin.[26]

e. *Stepparent adoptions.* A stepparent adoption often follows an earlier custody determination made at the time of dissolution of marriage or the end of a relationship. In such situations do the provisions of both the UCCJEA and the PKPA on continuing exclusive jurisdiction govern unless all parties have left the original forum?[27]

PROBLEMS

1. Reconsider the facts of In re Adoption of D.N.T., Chapter 3, section B3. In their effort to regain Diane, Camille and her mother Sally contend that Mississippi lacks jurisdiction over the adoption that Carol and Rick are pursuing there. Who should prevail and why? Should the same jurisdictional rules govern consensual adoptions and contested adoptions, like this one? Why?[28]

---

[23] Compare Frank R. v. Mother Goose Adoptions, 402 P.3d 996 (Ariz. 2017) (putative father's failure to register in Arizona allows adoption without his consent, despite mother's deceptive conduct and father's lack of knowledge of child's birth there), with Nevares v. M.L.S, 345 P.3d 719, 724 (Utah 2015) (holding that father's compliance with requirements of Colorado, mother's last home state, establish his parental rights despite failure to comply with Utah law, when he had no knowledge the birth would take place there). See also In re Adoption of Baby Boy B., 394 S.W.3d 837, 844 (Ark. 2012) (requiring father's consent because mother thwarted his effort to establish the relationship required by Arkansas law and he registered as a putative father in four states and filed paternity actions in two); In re Adoption of H.C.H. 304 P.3d 1271 (Kan. 2013) (applying jurisdictional provision of Kansas statute on surrender and adoption); In re J.W.B., 215 A.3d 602 (Pa. Super. Ct. 2019) (applying law of consent of state of adoption proceeding, not state where father signed consent form).

[24] See Mary Beck, Toward a National Putative Father Registry Database, 25 Harv. J.L. & Pub. Pol'y 1031 (2002).

[25] See Deborah E. Crum, Note, Uniform Adoption Laws: A Public Health Perspective, 7 Pitt. J. Envtl. Pub. Health L. 127 (2012).

[26] See Fleckles v. Diamond, 35 N.E.3d 176 (Ill. App. Ct. 2015); Sara Ashton McK. v. Samuel Bode M., 974 N.Y.S.2d 434 (App. Div. 2013). But see Barwick v. Ceruti, 31 N.E.3d 1008 (Ind. Ct. App. 2015) (allowing Indiana to assert prebirth jurisdiction).

[27] Adoption of K.C., 203 Cal. Rptr. 3d 110 (Ct. App. 2016) (ruling that UCCJEA does not apply to stepparent adoption).

[28] In re Adoption of D.N.T., 843 So. 2d 690, 697-706 (Miss. 2003).

2. Thomaszine moves from Texas to Washington state four months before giving birth to a son. A few weeks after the birth, Carl and Yvonne, a married couple living in Oregon, meet Thomaszine in Washington to discuss adopting the child. Because Thomaszine is not ready to relinquish him permanently, no agreement results. For the next several months, Thomaszine and her son live in a crisis shelter. When forced to move, she places the child in foster care, and the state (Washington) initiates dependency proceedings.

When her son is seven months old, Thomaszine finally decides to place him for adoption. Her physician contacts Carl and Yvonne, who travel to Washington to pick up the child. Thomaszine signs a consent, stating that Carl and Yvonne "will car[e] for the child during the adoptive process, after which they will become his legal parents." Carl and Yvonne return to Oregon with the child. A week later, the dependency proceedings are dismissed. Two months thereafter, Thomaszine informs Carl and Yvonne she wants her child back and no longer consents to adoption. In Oregon, Carl and Yvonne have just completed a home study and have prepared a petition for adoption.

As attorney for Carl and Yvonne, what would you advise? Should they return the child to Thomaszine? What "compromises" might you explore? Alternatively, if they insist on filing their adoption petition, what problems should they anticipate? Which state has jurisdiction? Suppose, instead, the biological father (whom Thomaszine refused to identify) contacts you just before the adoption petition is filed to convey his refusal to consent?[29]

3. Iva Sue becomes pregnant while living in Illinois, where six of her other children were wards of the state. With the date of delivery approaching, Iva Sue asks her caseworker what would happen to her new baby if she gives birth in Illinois. She learns that the Department of Family and Children's Services would investigate and determine whether to take custody of the baby. Fearing the loss of her baby, Iva Sue decides to move to Tennessee, where two of her other children lives with their father. En route, Iva Sue gives birth in Indiana. Where is the baby's home state? Why?[30] Even if Indiana is not otherwise the baby's home state, would it become the home state if Iva Sue surrenders the baby to an adoption agency there? Why?[31] If Illinois has legal custody of Iva Sue's children because they had been adjudicated dependent and neglected there, does Illinois lose jurisdiction after the children and their parents are no longer in the state?[32] Suppose, instead, only the children's father still lives in Illinois but has consented to TPR and disclaims all interest in any proceedings.[33]

[29] See Stubbs v. Weathersby, 892 P.2d 991 (Or. 1995). But see McCulley v. Bone, 979 P.2d 779 (Or. Ct. App. 1999).
[30] See In re D.S., 840 N.E.2d 1216 (Ill. 2005).
[31] See Adoption House, Inc. v. A.R., 820 A.2d 402 (Del. Fam. Ct. 2003).
[32] See In re Z.T.S., 2008 WL 371184 (Tenn. Ct. App. 2008).
[33] See In re Apex R., 577 S.W.3d 181, 202 (Tenn. Ct. App. 2018).

B. RECOGNITION IN OTHER STATES

V.L. v. E.L.

136 S. Ct. 1017 (2016)

PER CURIAM. . . .

V.L. and E.L. are two women who were in a relationship from approximately 1995 until 2011. Through assisted reproductive technology, E.L. gave birth to a child named S.L. in 2002 and to twins named N.L. and H.L. in 2004. After the children were born, V.L. and E.L. raised them together as joint parents.

V.L. and E.L. eventually decided to give legal status to the relationship between V.L. and the children by having V.L. formally adopt them. To facilitate the adoption, the couple rented a house in Alpharetta, Georgia. V.L. then filed an adoption petition in the Superior Court of Fulton County, Georgia. E.L. also appeared in that proceeding. While not relinquishing her own parental rights, she gave her express consent to V.L.'s adoption of the children as a second parent. The Georgia court determined that V.L. had complied with the applicable requirements of Georgia law, and entered a final decree of adoption allowing V.L. to adopt the children and recognizing both V.L. and E.L. as their legal parents.

V.L. and E.L. ended their relationship in 2011, while living in Alabama, and V.L. moved out of the house that the couple had shared. V.L. later filed a petition in the Circuit Court of Jefferson County, Alabama, alleging that E.L. had denied her access to the children and interfered with her ability to exercise her parental rights. She asked the Alabama court to register the Georgia adoption judgment and award her some measure of custody or visitation rights. The matter was transferred to the Family Court of Jefferson County. That court entered an order awarding V.L. scheduled visitation with the children.

E.L. appealed the visitation order . . . . The Alabama Supreme Court . . . held that the Georgia court had no subject-matter jurisdiction under Georgia law to enter a judgment allowing V.L. to adopt the children while still recognizing E.L.'s parental rights. As a consequence, the Alabama Supreme Court held Alabama courts were not required to accord full faith and credit to the Georgia judgment. . . .

The Constitution provides that "Full Faith and Credit shall be given in each State to the public Acts, Records, and judicial Proceedings of every other State." U.S. Const., Art. IV, §1. That Clause requires each State to recognize and give effect to valid judgments rendered by the courts of its sister States. It serves "to alter the status of the several states as independent foreign sovereignties, each free to ignore obligations created under the laws or by the judicial proceedings of the others, and to make them integral parts of a single nation." . . . "A final judgment in one State, if rendered by a court with adjudicatory authority over the subject matter and persons governed by the judgment, qualifies for recognition throughout the land." A State may not disregard the judgment of a sister State because it disagrees with the reasoning underlying the judgment or deems it to be wrong on the merits. On the contrary, "the full faith and credit clause of the Constitution precludes any inquiry into the merits of the cause of action, the logic or consistency of the decision, or the validity of the legal principles on which the judgment is based."

A State is not required, however, to afford full faith and credit to a judgment rendered by a court that "did not have jurisdiction over the subject matter or the relevant parties." "Consequently, before a court is bound by [a] judgment rendered in another State, it may inquire into the jurisdictional basis of the foreign court's decree." That jurisdictional inquiry, however, is a limited one. "[I]f the judgment on its face appears to be a 'record of a court of general jurisdiction, such jurisdiction over the cause and the parties is to be presumed unless disproved by extrinsic evidence, or by the record itself.'"

Those principles resolve this case. Under Georgia law, as relevant here, "[t]he superior courts of the several counties shall have exclusive jurisdiction in all matters of adoption." Ga.Code Ann. §19-8-2(a) (2015). That provision on its face gave the Georgia Superior Court subject-matter jurisdiction to hear and decide the adoption petition at issue here. . . .

The Alabama Supreme Court reached a different result by relying on Ga.Code Ann. §19-8-5(a). That statute states (as relevant here) that "a child who has any living parent or guardian may be adopted by a third party . . . only if each such living parent and each such guardian has voluntarily and in writing surrendered all of his or her rights to such child." The Alabama Supreme Court concluded that this provision prohibited the Georgia Superior Court from allowing V.L. to adopt the children while also allowing E.L. to keep her existing parental rights. It further concluded that this provision went not to the merits but to the Georgia court's subject-matter jurisdiction. In reaching that crucial second conclusion, the Alabama Supreme Court seems to have relied solely on the fact that the right to adoption under Georgia law is purely statutory, and "'[t]he requirements of Georgia's adoptions statutes are mandatory and must be strictly construed in favor of the natural parents.'"

That analysis is not consistent with this Court's controlling precedent. Where a judgment indicates on its face that it was rendered by a court of competent jurisdiction, such jurisdiction "'is to be presumed unless disproved.'" There is nothing here to rebut that presumption. . . .

Section 19-8-5(a) does not become jurisdictional just because it is "'mandatory'" and "'must be strictly construed.'" . . . Indeed, the Alabama Supreme Court's reasoning would give jurisdictional status to every requirement of the Georgia adoption statutes, since Georgia law indicates those requirements are all mandatory and must be strictly construed. That result would comport neither with Georgia law nor with common sense.

As Justice Holmes observed more than a century ago, "it sometimes may be difficult to decide whether certain words in a statute are directed to jurisdiction or to merits." Fauntleroy v. Lum, 210 U.S. 230, 234-235 (1908). In such cases, especially where the Full Faith and Credit Clause is concerned, a court must be "slow to read ambiguous words, as meaning to leave the judgment open to dispute, or as intended to do more than fix the rule by which the court should decide." That time-honored rule controls here. The Georgia judgment appears on its face to have been issued by a court with jurisdiction, and there is no established Georgia law to the contrary. It follows that the

Alabama Supreme Court erred in refusing to grant that judgment full faith and credit. [Reversed and remanded.]

NOTES AND QUESTIONS

1. *Full faith and credit.* V.L. relies on the same principle that compels, for example, recognition of an out-of-state divorce decree issued by a forum with very different divorce grounds, despite the recognizing state's public policy objections.[34] The underlying values of finality and national uniformity also can be found in several statutes enacted by Congress pursuant to its authority to implement the Constitution's Full Faith and Credit Clause. One such statute is the PKPA, 28 U.S.C. §1738A, which played a pivotal role in *Baby Girl Clausen*, supra. Recall also that VAPs meeting federal statutory standards trigger full faith and credit in other states. See Chapter 1, section C.[35] In addition, the ICWA (Chapter 4, section A1a) contains a full faith and credit provision requiring respect for tribal court judgments, when jurisdiction is proper.[36]

Another such enactment codifies more generally the obligation of interstate respect by providing, in pertinent part, that "Acts, records and judicial proceedings or copies thereof . . . shall have the same full faith and credit in every court within the United States and its Territories and Possessions as they have by law or usage in the courts of such State, Territory or Possession from which they are taken." 28 U.S.C. §1738. Although this language, like the Constitution, makes no distinction between "acts" and "records," on the one hand, and "judicial proceedings," on the other, precedents make clear that the obligation to respect another state's judicial judgments and decrees is far more demanding than that owed to "acts" and "records." Why?

Of course, states might choose to honor another state's "acts" and "records," but they have more flexibility to refuse recognition if their law or policy dictates. Because of this greater flexibility, several states had declined to recognize on public policy grounds same-sex marriages lawfully celebrated elsewhere. In Obergefell v. Hodges, the Court held that liberty and equality principles left "no lawful basis for a State to refuse to recognize a lawful same-sex marriage performed in another State on the ground of its same-sex character." 576 U.S. 644, 681 (2015).

2. *"Travel insurance."*[37] Suppose V.L. had not formally adopted the children. On what basis might have she have been able to maintain her relationship with the children over E.L.'s objections? See Chapter 1, section C. Even when functional approaches and equitable doctrines would recognize an individual like V.L. as the children's parent in the state where the family lives, an adoption decree is thought to provide more protection, including "travel insurance" should the family cross state lines, precisely because of

---

[34] See, e.g., Williams v. North Carolina, 317 U.S. 287 (1942).
[35] See *Jaelyn B.*, 883 N.W.2d at 36.
[36] See, e.g., Simmonds v. Parks, 329 P.3d 995, 1007-1008 (Alaska 2014); Matter of C.J., Jr., 108 N.E.3d 677, 696 (Ohio Ct. App. 2018).
[37] Courtney G. Joslin, Travel Insurance: Protecting Lesbian and Gay Parent Families Across State Lines, 4 Harv. L. & Pol'y Rev. 31 (2010).

the more rigorous recognition demanded for "judicial proceedings" over "acts" and "records."[38]

How should doctrines originating in common law, like the presumption of legitimacy, or judge-made rules such as "equitable parent" be classified for this purpose? In a New York case, a court refused to issue a second-parent adoption decree to a woman married to the child's mother on the grounds that the marital presumption made adoption unnecessary and impermissible.[39] What's a risk-averse parent to do?

3. *Discrimination?* May Alabama treat adoption decrees issued out of state differently from the way it treats adoption decrees issued in Alabama? Assume the children in *V.L.* were born in Alabama, which issued birth certificate identifying only E.L. as their parent, and that Alabama routinely issues new birth certificates upon the adoption of children in Alabama showing instead the adoptive parent or parents. Does Alabama deny full faith and credit to the Georgia adoption decrees if it refuses to issue new birth certificates reflecting the addition of V.L. as a second parent? Put differently, can Alabama give less respect to Georgia adoptions than to its own? In Adar v. Smith, a divided U.S. Court of Appeals for the Fifth Circuit decided en banc that Louisiana could refuse to amend birth certificates after New York adoptions by same-sex couples, even though it routinely issued new birth certificates after local adoptions (which did not include any adoptions by same-sex couples). 639 F.3d 146 (5th Cir. 2011) (en banc). The majority distinguished between recognition, which full faith and credit compels for the out-of-state decrees, from enforcement, which it does not — and deemed the issuance of amended birth certificates to be a matter of enforcing the New York decrees. Id. at 160.[40]

Can the result and reasoning in *Adar* survive the Supreme Court's marriage-equality ruling in *Obergefell?* May Alabama treat adoption decrees issued to same-sex couples out of state differently from the way it treats adoption decrees issued to different-sex couples out of state? What are the implications of *Obergefell* and the Supreme Court's later ruling in Pavan v. Smith, 137 S. Ct. 2075 (2017), which held that Arkansas cannot omit the name of a mother's wife as the second parent on child's birth certificate if it routinely includes the name of a mother's husband? *Pavan* said that including a mother's spouse on her child's birth certificate falls within the "constellation of benefits . . . linked to marriage" to which *Obergefell* guarantees equal access. Id. at 2078.

4. *The jurisdiction exception.* As *V.L.* acknowledges, the original forum must have jurisdiction for the full faith and credit obligation to apply.[41] According to the Court, the Georgia adoption statute gave the superior court

---

[38] See id. But see Anna Marie D'Ginto, Comment, The Birth Certificate Solution: Ensuring the Interstate Recognition of Same-Sex Parentage, 167 U. Pa. L. Rev. 975 (2019).

[39] Matter of Seb C-M, Redacted by Court, NYLJ 1202640527093, *1 (Sur., NY, Decided January 06, 2014).

[40] Cf. Estin v. Estin, 334 U.S. 541 (1948) (addressing differential treatment of in-state and out-of-state divorces and support awards). The Supreme Court denied certiorari in *Adar.* 565 U.S. 942 (2011).

[41] See also, e.g., Schott v. Schott, 744 N.W.2d 85 (Iowa 2008).

subject matter jurisdiction. Yet, was the family's connection to Georgia sufficient? The facts suggest that the family lived in Alabama, but rented a house
in Georgia in a forum-shopping effort to establish ties with a state more
hospitable to second-parent adoption. Is that enough? Is the PKPA relevant?
If so, how? Does the Georgia court's determination "that V.L. had complied
with the applicable requirements of Georgia law" insulate the adoption
decree from further challenge on the basis of jurisdiction?

PROBLEMS

1. Michael and Richard registered as domestic partners in California.
Hoping to start a family, they received approval as prospective adoptive
parents in California and then sought to post their profiles on a website operated by an Arizona-based Adoption Media, LLC, which runs the largest, most
active, and most well-known Internet adoption-related business in the
United States. Adoption Media, LLC rejected their request, based on a policy
restricting eligibility to different-sex married couples. California has civil
rights statutes prohibiting discrimination based on sexual orientation and
marital status. Arizona prohibits neither sexual-orientation discrimination
nor marital-status discrimination; it does not have a law on domestic partnerships; and its citizens had rejected a proposed constitutional amendment
that would have prohibited recognizing same-sex relationships akin to marriage before nationwide marriage equality. Michael and Richard sue Adoption Media, LLC in California, seeking damages under California's civil
rights statutes. Adoption Media argues that California lacks jurisdiction and,
even if it has jurisdiction, its statutes do not apply. What result and why?[42]
Suppose Adoption Media objects on the merits, based on religious or moral
opposition to adoptions by same-sex couples.[43]

2. K.M., from Utah, becomes pregnant during a one-week visit to
Oklahoma. Back in Utah, she informs T.C. of Oklahoma of her pregnancy
and her plan to surrender the baby for adoption. Although K.M. communicates with T.C. several times and tells him how to reach her, she does
not name him as the father on the birth certificate when she delivers the
baby, K.J.C., in Utah. After K.M. surrenders the baby to a social services agency
in Utah, the agency and the state conduct paternity searches; finding no
registration of paternity rights, the agency places K.J.C. for adoption
with C.J. and A.J. Three days later, in Oklahoma, T.C. files a petition to determine the baby's paternity. Should (must) the Utah court now decline to
finalize the petition for adoption filed by C.J. and A.J.? Specifically, what
effect does T.C.'s paternity proceeding in Oklahoma have in the Utah
adoption case? Why?[44]

---

[42] See Butler v. Adoption Media, LLC, 486 F. Supp. 2d 1022 (N.D. Cal. 2007).
[43] See New Hope Family Services, Inc. v. Poole, reprinted in Chapter 4, section A1b.
[44] See In re Adoption of K.C.J., 184 P.3d 1239 (Utah Ct. App. 2008). Cf. H.U.F. v. W.P.W., 203
P.3d 943 (Utah 2009).

C. INTERCOUNTRY ADOPTION

In re Adoption of Child A

---

997 N.Y.S.2d 312 (Sur. Ct. 2014)

Edward W. McCarty III, J.

The following constitutes the court's decision and order concerning the issue of Re-Homing in the Nassau County Surrogate's Court, reviewed during the A and C adoption related proceeding. Parent Father (hereinafter ["P1"]) and Parent Mother (hereinafter ["P2"]) reside in Nassau County, New York. They adopted the children, A and C, in Russia in 2008. Child A was born in 2000 and child C was born in 2002. They seek a decree denying recognition of the Russian adoption order or, alternatively, vacating the Russian adoption order.

Before exploring the Re-Homing issue certain observations in regard to this case must be made. Judicial Notice is the rule of law of evidence that allows the fact to be introduced into evidence if the truth of that fact is so notorious or well known, or so authoritatively attested, that it cannot be reasonably doubted. This decision will also take Judicial notice of the many undisputed facts of the Russian/American adoption trade as well as the practice of Re-Homing of children.

1. In the past 30 years, 60,000 Russian children have been adopted by Americans;
2. The estimated payments to private and public Russian sources have been estimated to be one third of a billion dollars;
3. Russia is not a party to the Hague Convention on Protection of Children and Co-Operation in Respect of Inter-Country Adoption. This convention guarantees certain rights to adoptive children and the process of adoption;
4. An estimated 20 percent of Russian children adopted in the United States suffer from developmental disabilities from severe to mild;
5. Since 2001, over 18 adopted Russian children have died through violence of their adoptive parents or supervisors. Seventy-five percent of these children were in the United States for less than 6 months and under the age of two years;
6. In 2013, Russian President Putin publicly stopped the Russian-American adoption trade yet Russian children can still be obtained in the worldwide adoption market through other Eastern European adoption agencies;
7. Adopted Russian children have been returned to Russia without American due process; and
8. Adopted Russian children throughout the United States are currently being exchanged on the Internet through a process called Re-Homing without the benefit of any court or governmental supervision. . . .

If the application for [rescission] of their adoption status by P1 and P2 is denied they may wish to pursue the process called Re-Homing. . . . Re-Homing is the placement or replacement of a child with new care givers who are not related to that child. It is a procedure outside of official government and judicial review in the unofficial and involuntary transfer of children (see, Donovan M. Stelzner, Intercountry Adoption; Toward a Regime That Recognizes the "Best Interest" of Adoptive Parents, 35 Case W.Res.J.Int., L L.113, 132 [2003]). Last year in the United States it has been estimated that between 200 and 300 foreign and American born children were traded in this Internet fashion. Most often the transfers of these children found them to be between the ages of 6 to 14 with some as young as 10 months. The most often cited reason for the rejection by their adoptive/natural parents is a failure to bond (Megan Twohey, The Child Exchange; Inside Americas Underground Market for Adoptive Children, Reuters Investigates [September 9, 2003]). . . . Placement of the to-be Re-Homed child is made through advertising on the Internet or other public media process.

1) There is no prior home study of the accepting person;
2) There is no court approval of the process;
3) There is no court supervision of the process;
4) It is often accomplished with the person placing the child knowing little, if anything, of the person or persons with whom the child is placed.

In 2014 children are still being sent off to receiving person(s) with their original adoption papers or birth certificate and a Power of Attorney from the sending parents to the receiving person(s). Such Re-Homing or any other descriptive phrase to classify this trade is unmistakably "human trafficking in children," even absent any financial element being present. This decision is an attempt to publicize [and regulate] the Re-Homing trade in children. . . .

The Court's original intention was to enact a local rule to forbid [Re-Homing]. However, I am now of the opinion that a local rule will likely be both improper and inadequate.

The Court is aware of the provisions of [New York Social Services Law §374] which appear to authorize this very practice, though that was not and could not have been the intent of the Legislature in enacting this statute. The Court urges the Legislature to amend [§374] to permit the temporary placement of a child where the parent is currently unable to provide sufficient care, but to prohibit the unsavory and unsupervised practice of adoptive parents ridding themselves of the responsibility of caring for their children by placing them with people whose motives and qualifications are, at best, entirely unknown. . . .

This decision is a first step to control Re-Homing and the unofficial adoption process. In the event that P1 and P2's application for the dissolution of their adoption status is denied and they wish to place the children with another person or persons they must make application to do so through this Court. A Guardian Ad Litem will be appointed to determine the best interests of the children and their report will be issued for further action to the Surrogate. . . .

NOTES AND QUESTIONS

1. *Background.*

a. *Numbers and trends.* Only 2,971 children born abroad joined U.S. families in 2019, continuing a recent decline.[45] Consider this brief account of the changing numbers:

> The high point for international adoptions occurred in 2004, with an estimated global total of 45,000 international adoptions, nearly 23,000 of which were completed by parents in the United States. Annual totals decreased after that, so that by 2009, fewer international adoptions occurred than in 1998 — nearly 30,000 globally in 2009, compared with about 32,000 in 1998. By the late 2000s, further changes in the policies of particular countries and the implementation of Hague Convention and Intercountry Adoption Act (IAA) had the overall effect of reducing international adoptions to the United States. . . .
>
> In 2009-2011, 13 percent of adopted children under 18 were internationally adopted. About half (51 percent) of the internationally adopted children were born in Asia, about one-fifth (20 percent) in Latin America, and about one-quarter (25 percent) in Europe . . . . Fifty-seven percent of the children from Asia were born in China, and an additional 23 percent were born in Korea. In contrast, for adopted children 18 and over who were born in Asia and lived with their parents, 71 percent were born in Korea. Although only a small proportion of adults live with their parents, these data reflect the dominance of Korea as a source country for adopted children prior to the 1990s. In 2009-2011, the majority (73 percent) of internationally adopted children under 18 from Europe were adopted from Russia. The majority (71 percent) of those adopted from Latin America were born in Guatemala, for children under 18. China was the largest single-country source of internationally adopted children, comprising about 60,000 children or about 30 percent (29 percent) of all internationally adopted children under 18.[46]

Why do U.S. citizens seek children from abroad? Observers point to the shortage of "highly desirable" adoptees, agency restrictions on adopters, and the increase in domestic adoptions that are open.[47] Further, the highly publicized cases like that of Baby Jessica, supra, which returned children to biological parents after lengthy periods with adoptive families, reportedly sparked increased interest in intercountry adoptions, believed by many to be less vulnerable to such disruptions.[48] Poverty and natural disasters abroad, as well as religious imperatives, also have moved some prospective

---

[45] United States Dept. of State, Annual Report on Intercountry Adoption 6 (2020), https://travel.state.gov/content/dam/NEWadoptionassets/pdfs/FY%202019%20Annual%20Report%20.pdf.

[46] Rose M. Kreider & Daphne A. Lofquist, Adopted Children and Stepchildren: 2010, U.S. Census Bureau 1, 22-24 (Apr. 2014) (footnotes omitted), https://www.census.gov/prod/2014pubs/p20-572.pdf.

[47] See Joan Catherine Bohl, The Future of Children in International Law Inter-Country Adoption: Is International Law Protecting the Best Interests of the Children?, 19 Sw. J. Int'l L. 323, 327-328 (2013).

[48] See, e.g., Alison Fleisher, Note, The Decline of Domestic Adoption: Intercountry Adoption as a Response to Local Adoption Laws and Proposals to Foster Domestic Adoption, 13 S. Cal. Rev. L. & Women's Stud. 171 (2003).

adopters.[49] Reports that China's one-child policy (since rescinded) prompted parents there to abandon daughters because they preferred a son led to the adoption of over 80,000 Chinese girls in the United States.[50]

Newer restrictions on intercountry adoptions might help explain recent declines, and so might the rise of commercial surrogacy, which has emerged as a preferable option for adding a child to a family.[51] In the meantime, the U.S. has become a sending country. Outgoing adoptions have sent U.S. children (usually children of color) to Canada, the Netherlands, and the United Kingdom.[52]

b. *Applicable laws.* Several bodies of law might ordinarily apply to incoming international adoptions: federal immigration laws, state adoption statutes, and the foreign country's surrender requirements. Two adoptions were routinely required: the first in the country of origin to enable the child to travel to the United States, and the second in the adoptive parents' state, given the absence of full faith and credit for decrees from foreign countries.[53]

Significant changes have occurred in recent years. For example, federal law, which limits entry to foreign adoptees who are "orphans," expanded the definition of the term to include not only children whose parents both have died but also those whose parents both have disappeared, abandoned or deserted them, or become separated or lost from them, as well as children for whom the sole surviving parent cannot provide care and has irrevocably released the child for adoption and emigration.[54] In addition, some jurisdictions stopped requiring a full state proceeding if a foreign adoption has been completed.[55] Moreover, federal legislation provides for automatic U.S. citizenship for many children adopted abroad by U.S. citizens, just as children born abroad to U.S. citizens receive.[56]

The Hague Convention on Protection of Children and Cooperation in Respect of Intercountry Adoption has ushered in even more notable reforms. This Convention, which applies only when both countries involved are Convention parties, seeks to regularize international adoptions by requiring a finding that the child is adoptable and a determination that the adoption would serve the child's best interests. For example, the Convention lists the following requirements for intercountry adoptions:

---

[49] See, e.g., John Seabrook, The Last Babylift: Adopting a Child in Haiti, The New Yorker (May 3, 2010), https://www.newyorker.com/magazine/2010/05/10/the-last-babylift; David M. Smolin, Of Orphans and Adoption, Parents and the Poor, Exploitation and Rescue: A Scriptural and Theological Critique of the Evangelical Christian Adoption and Orphan Care Movement, 8 Regent J. Int'l L. 267 (2012).

[50] See Barbara Demick, One Is Chinese. One Is American. How a Journalist Discovered and Reunited Identical Twins, L.A. Times (Aug. 8, 2019), https://www.latimes.com/world-nation/story/2019-08-07/how-a-journalist-discovered-and-reunited-identical-twins. See also Edward Wong, China's Longtime One-Child Rule Is Gone, but Trauma Lingers, N.Y. Times, Oct. 31, 2015, at A8.

[51] See Kerry O'Halloran, Adoption Law and Human Rights: International Perspectives 148 (2018).

[52] Id.; Cynthia R. Mabry-King, Outgoing Adoptions: What Should Happen When Things Go Wrong?, 44 Cap. U. L. Rev. 1 (2016).

[53] See, e.g., Adoption of M.S., 103 Cal. Rptr. 3d 715 (Ct. App. 2010).

[54] 8 U.S.C. §1101(b)(1)(F).

[55] See, e.g., In re Adoption of Doe, 923 N.E.2d 1129 (N.Y. 2010) (according comity to Cambodian adoption).

[56] 8 U.S.C. §1431(b). See also id. §1101(b)(1)(F) (providing immediate relative classification for such children).

Article 4

An adoption within the scope of the Convention shall take place only if the competent authorities of the State of origin —

a) have established that the child is adoptable;

b) have determined, after possibilities for placement of the child within the State of origin have been given due consideration, that an intercountry adoption is in the child's best interests;

c) have ensured that

(1) the persons, institutions and authorities whose consent is necessary for adoption, have been counselled as may be necessary and duly informed of the effects of their consent, in particular whether or not an adoption will result in the termination of the legal relationship between the child and his or her family of origin,

(2) such persons, institutions and authorities have given their consent freely, in the required legal form, and expressed or evidenced in writing,

(3) the consents have not been induced by payment or compensation of any kind and have not been withdrawn, and

(4) the consent of the mother, where required, has been given only after the birth of the child; and

d) have ensured, having regard to the age and degree of maturity of the child, that

(1) he or she has been counselled and duly informed of the effects of the adoption and of his or her consent to the adoption, where such consent is required,

(2) consideration has been given to the child's wishes and opinions,

(3) the child's consent to the adoption, where such consent is required, has been given freely, in the required legal form, and expressed or evidenced in writing, and

(4) such consent has not been induced by payment or compensation of any kind.

Article 5

An adoption within the scope of the Convention shall take place only if the competent authorities of the receiving State —

a) have determined that the prospective adoptive parents are eligible and suited to adopt;

b) have ensured that the prospective adoptive parents have been counselled as may be necessary; and

c) have determined that the child is or will be authorized to enter and reside permanently in that State.

Hague Conference on Private International Law, 33: Convention of 29 May 1993 on Protection of Children and Co-operation in respect of Intercountry Adoption.[57] The Convention also establishes supervisory Central Authorities to impose minimum norms and procedures and mandates recognition in other signatory countries of adoptions that meet the standards.

---

[57] See Hague Conference on Private International Law, Conventions, Protocols and Principles, http://www.hcch.net/index_en.php?act=conventions.pdf&cid=69.

In 2000, the United States enacted implementing legislation, 42 U.S.C. §§14901-14954 (with a few subsequent amendments), but ratification here did not occur until 2007, with the Convention entering into force in this country on April 1, 2008.[58] The Intercountry Adoption Universal Accreditation Act, federal legislation that became effective in 2013, requires adoption service providers facilitating adoptions in non-Convention countries to meet the same requirements and standards as Convention countries. 42 U.S.C. §14925.[59]

The Convention and ancillary legislation have met with both praise and criticism. Observers point out that this regime facilitates U.S. citizens' intercountry adoptions by removing procedural hurdles, such as the need for readoption in the parents' domicile, while also creating new barriers, increasing expenses, and imposing requirements difficult for small agencies to meet.[60] Further, concern persists that the U.S. regulations issued pursuant to the Convention fail to address payments to birth parents and might increase child trafficking.[61]

Depictions in Popular Culture: Anne Tyler, Digging to America (2006)

This novel, a *New York Times* bestseller, tells the story of two families, one Iranian American, the Yazdans, and one with less obvious and less recent immigrant roots, the Donaldsons, who meet at the airport while awaiting the arrival of daughters whom they are adopting from Korea. Although the Donaldsons name their daughter Jin-Ho and affirmatively seek to emphasize her ties to her native country, the assimilated Yazdans rear their daughter, Susan, without explicitly formulating such a cultural agenda. Ordinary family life, with its joys and misfortunes, unfolds as the two families celebrate together, year after year, the date of arrival of Jin-Ho and Susan. All the while, Maryam, Susan's adoptive and widowed grandmother, discovers through her new connections with Susan and the Donaldsons that, even after 35 years in the United States, she still has not fully addressed the meaning of her own "foreignness."

The two families exemplify sharply contrasting approaches to childrearing. Such different choices are protected by parental autonomy and family privacy, Chapter 2, section B1. Nonetheless, what are the merits and disadvantages of each approach, given the background of Jin-Ho and Susan? How do the situations of children who

---

[58] See Anne Laquer Estin, Families Across Borders: The Hague Children's Conventions and the Case for International Family Law in the United States, 62 Fla. L. Rev. 47, 80-84 (2010).
[59] See Zachary C. Myers, Development in the Legislative Branch, The Intercountry Adoption Universal Accreditation Act of 2012, 27 Geo. Immigr. L.J. 243 (2012).
[60] See id. at 85-90.
[61] See Trish Maskew, The Failure of Promise: The U.S. Regulations on Intercountry Adoption Under the Hague Convention, 60 Admin. L. Rev. 487 (2008); Jordan Bunn, Note, Regulating Corruption in Intercountry Adoption, 52 Vand. J. Transnat'l L. 685 (2019).

come to the United States as intercountry adoptees both differ from and also resemble the situation of others who immigrate to the United States, such as Maryam? To what extent can one achieve "belonging" without some loss of cultural distinctiveness and identity?

---

2. *Adoption failure and "rehoming."* What problems and practices does the principal case reveal? Despite scant data, authorities opine that the growing number of placements of special needs children, older children with previous foster care, and international adoptees has increased the rate of adoption failure.[62] What should happen when adoptions fail?

Most of the public reacted with shock and horror when Torry Ann Hansen of Tennessee placed the seven-year-old boy whom she had adopted in Russia on a one-way flight to Moscow alone, with a note pinned to his backpack stating that she could no longer care for him because of behavioral problems and that she wanted to annul the adoption.[63] Adoptive parents of other children with difficulties took a more understanding approach.[64] The Russian Federation Supreme Court annulled the adoption, but ruled that Hansen was obligated to continue paying child support pursuant to an adoption agreement she had signed, and litigation continued as the juvenile court held her in contempt for failing to do so.[65] In the wake of this episode, Russia banned adoptions of Russian children by American citizens, a move that observers attribute in fact to retaliation for U.S. laws protecting human rights.[66]

Evaluate the judge's effort to control rehoming in the principal case. The reference to New York Social Services Law §374 apparently concerns the following language "No person, agency, association, corporation, institution, society or other organization except an authorized agency shall place out or board out any child but the provisions of this section shall not restrict or limit the right of a parent, legal guardian or relative within the second degree to place out or board out a child." (Recall the "baby broker laws"

---

[62] See Jennifer F. Coakley & Jill D. Berrick, Research Review: In a Rush to Permanency: Preventing Adoption Disruption, 13 Child & Fam. Soc. Work 101, 102 (2007). See also Jenn Morson, When Families Un-Adopt a Child, The Atlantic (Nov. 16, 2018), https://www.theatlantic.com/family/archive/2018/11/children-who-have-second-adoptions/575902/ (estimating between one and five percent).

[63] See In re Justin A.H., 2014 WL 3058439 (Tenn. Ct. App. 2014).

[64] See Sarah Kershaw, In Some Adoptions, Love Doesn't Conquer All, N.Y. Times, Apr. 18, 2010, at ST1.

[65] See *Justin A.H.*, 2014 WL 3058439 at *4; In re Justin H., 2015 WL 3455953 (Tenn. Ct. App. 2015).

[66] See Marie A. Failinger, Moving Toward Human Rights Principles for Intercountry Adoption, 39 N.C. J. Int'l L. & Com. Reg. 523, 523-524 (2014). See also Marsha Lipman, What's Behind the Russian Adoption Ban?, The New Yorker (Dec. 21, 2012), https://www.newyorker.com/news/news-desk/whats-behind-the-russian-adoption-ban; All Things Considered: Russian Ban on U.S. Adoptions Becomes Embroiled in Trump Controversy, NPR (July 20, 2017), https://www.npr.org/2017/07/20/538370632/russian-ban-on-u-s-adoptions-becomes-embroiled-in-trump-controversy.

examined in Chapter 4, section A2.) How should the legislature amend the law? The Uniform Law Commission has begun formulating a model statute to address rehoming, to be entitled either the Unregulated Transfers of Adopted Children Act or the Uniform Child Placement Protection Act.[67]

Annulling an intercountry adoption presents procedural complications. For example, if the child was adopted abroad and no local court issued a domestic adoption decree, then there may be no forum with jurisdiction to grant the requested relief.[68] As in additional proceedings in *Adoption of Child A*, issues might arise concerning whether the courtroom should be open or closed and whether government entities constitute necessary parties.[69]

3. *Other remedies.* The parents in *Adoption of Child A* also alleged fraud, including "bait and switch" of children, by American adoption agencies as well as "Russian organized criminal component in the Russian/American adoption process both in Russia and the United States."[70] Should damages for wrongful adoption that some states recognize based on misrepresentations in domestic cases also apply to intercountry adoptions? See Chapter 5, section D. Why? Suppose the adoptive parents signed an agreement as Torry Hansen had, stating that the agency had provided all of the information it had about the child, but could not "guarantee the present or future mental or physical health of the child(ren)" and that the adopter agrees to "remain financially responsible for all costs of care for the child(ren)" in the event of removal from the home.[71]

4. *A controversial practice.* Like transracial adoption, intercountry adoption provokes controversy. Supporters contend that such adoptions represent humanitarian and empathetic responses to the plight of children living in institutions or on the streets in other countries — indeed, a compelling matter of international human rights.[72] Some critics, like Professor Twila Perry, condemn the colonialism reflected in the practice:

> As troubling as it may be for many to admit, a conception of poor, third-world countries as subordinate nations fits very comfortably with the practice of international adoption. This kind of view translates easily into the idea that Western adoptive parents are simply saving unfortunate third-world children by bringing them out of primitive, impoverished and disease-ridden countries into the more affluent life that the West can offer. It permits

---

[67] See Unregulated Transfers of Adopted Children Act, Jan. 31-Feb. 1, 2020 (draft for discussion only), https://www.uniformlaws.org/HigherLogic/System/DownloadDocumentFile.ashx?DocumentFileKey=219526fe-bcda-8051-2524-114584424c4f&forceDialog=0. For calls for action in response to rehoming, see, e.g., Sally Terry Green, The Law Demands Process for Rehomed Children, 69 Ark. L. Rev. 729 (2016); Elizabeth A. Dahl, Re-Homing: The Underground Market for Adopted Children and How Current Laws Fail to Protect the Innocent, 6 Wake Forest J.L. & Pol'y 549 (2016).
[68] *M.S.*, 103 Cal. Rptr. 3d 715.
[69] See In re Adoption of Child A, 994 N.Y.S.2d 832 (Sur. Ct. 2014) (denying application to close courtroom); In re Adoption of Child A, 9 N.Y.S.3d 592 (Sur. Ct. 2015) (holding U.S. Department of State and Russian Federation are not necessary parties).
[70] 994 N.Y.S.2d at 834.
[71] *Justin A.H.*, 2014 WL 3058439 at *1.
[72] See, e.g., Elizabeth Bartholet, International Adoption: A Way Forward, 55 N.Y.L. Sch. L. Rev. 687 (2010); James G. Dwyer, Inter-Country Adoption and the Special Rights Fallacy, 35 U. Pa. J. Int'l L. 189 (2013); Failinger, supra note [66].

a discourse that allows Westerners to take the high ground and portray their international adoptions as simple acts of humanitarianism and altruism.

Admittedly, there is a humanitarian aspect to many international adoptions. Obviously, there are children adopted from poor countries who would face a very bleak life or even death in their homelands. However, a feminist analysis of international adoption should go farther than a simple altruism narrative. Indeed, an appropriate question might not be what Westerners are giving to the children of impoverished countries, but what they are taking from those countries or from the poor women who live in them. "Taking" might appear to be a harsh word in the context of a situation in which women have voluntarily surrendered their children. However, the "voluntariness" of these surrenders must be examined in light of the economic, social, and political circumstances under which the mothers often live. . . . [73]

Others point out the similarity to baby selling, given the predominance of market behavior.[74] Charges of trafficking receive reinforcement from reports both old and new about babies taken without parental consent abroad and placed for adoption in the United States. For example, the successful film *Philomena* (2013) recounts the true story of London resident Philomena Lee and her search for her son, who was forcibly taken from her after she give birth in an Irish convent and was placed with wealthy Americans. Meanwhile, Guatemala, once a popular sending jurisdiction to the U.S., now faces State Department restrictions following evidence of stolen babies and other corruption in adoption.[76] The reunion of teenage identical twins born in China revealed that the birth parents had violated the one-child policy, so one of the girls was seized by officials and ultimately placed for adoption with a U.S. family.[77]

---

[73] Twila L. Perry, Transracial and International Adoption: Mothers, Hierarchy, Race, and Feminist Legal Theory, 10 Yale J.L. & Feminism 101, 135 (1998). See also Rickie Solinger, Beggars and Choosers: How the Politics of Choice Shapes Adoption, Abortion, and Welfare in the United States 67 (2001) ("[T]he incidence of adoption, that is, the transfer of babies from women of one social classification to women in a higher social classification or group (within the same country or transnationally), may be a very accurate index of the vulnerable status of women in the country of the birth mother.").

[74] Patricia Meier, Note, Small Commodities: How Child Traffickers Exploit Children and Families in Intercountry Adoption and What the United States Must Do to Stop Them, 12 J. Gender Race & Just. 185 (2008); David M. Smolin, Child Laundering and the Hague Convention on Intercountry Adoption: The Future and Past of Intercountry Adoption, 48 U. Louisville L. Rev. 441 (2010). See also Sara Corbett, Where Do Babies Come From?, N.Y. Times, June 16, 2002, §6 (Magazine), at 42 (cover story examining "baby laundering" and the "mysterious origins of Cambodian 'orphans' — and the complex ethics for Americans adopting them").

[76] See Nicole Acevedo, A Painful Truth: Guatemalan Adoptees Learn They Were Fraudulently Given Away, NBC News (Dec. 8, 2019), https://www.nbcnews.com/news/latino/painful-truth-guatemalan-adoptees-learn-they-were-fraudulently-given-away-n1095066; Tests Point to Adoption Fraud, L.A. Times (July 24, 2008), https://www.latimes.com/archives/la-xpm-2008-jul-24-fg-briefs24.s2-story.html; FAQ: U.S. Withdrawal of Interest in Participating in Guatemala's Pilot Adoption Program, Travel.State.Gov, U.S. Department of State — Bureau of Consular Affairs, https://travel.state.gov/content/travel/en/Intercountry-Adoption/adopt_ref/adoption-FAQs/us-withdrawal-interest-guatemala-pilot-program.html.

[77] See Demick, supra note [50].

Who benefits from intercountry adoption? Whom does it harm? What impact does it have on the adoption of U.S.-born children? Has the Hague Convention improved the landscape? What law reforms would you suggest?[78] What difference would increased "openness" in intercountry adoption make?[79]

Depictions in Popular Culture: Casa de los Babys (2003)

As this film presenting many perspectives on intercountry adoption by acclaimed director John Sayles opens, one sees a large room with dozens of cribs, each containing a brown-skinned baby, while an attendant softly sings to one baby she holds in her arms. Meanwhile, six women from the United States meet and spend weeks together in an upscale South American hotel, nicknamed "Casa de los Babys," while awaiting the babies they have traveled to adopt. Although each woman has her own story, all of them are white. Juxtaposed with depictions of the women's habits, disappointments, concerns, and dreams — from fitness regimens to tragic losses of biological children to opportunistic behavior to idealized visions of motherhood — are scenes of the abject poverty of many homeless children who live on the streets in the community. In a particularly poignant exchange, one of the women, Eileen, candidly describes her fantasy of spending a snowy day with the young daughter she hopes to rear at her home in Boston; in response, the hotel maid, Asuncion, tells of her own biological daughter, Esmeralda, whose "other mother up there in the North" Asuncion hopes is just like Eileen. Because Eileen speaks only English and Asuncion only Spanish, however, the two women do not understand one another's stories. Yet, perhaps by coincidence, when Eileen is about to meet her baby daughter, she mentions to another prospective adopter that she will name her Esmeralda.

The film raises but does not answer numerous questions. Who benefits from the practices examined here? Do the impoverished lives of the street children justify the corruption of local adoption officials and the "cultural imperialism" that one character perceives in the adopters' quest for children? Or, should we blame the stark class differences within the local community — between the hotel operator and her brother, the adoption attorney, on the one hand, and the hotel workers and the homeless, on the other? Why are the

---

[78] See generally, e.g., Bohl, supra note [47]; Shani M. King, Immigration, Adoption and Our National Identity, 26 Duke J. Gender L. & Pol'y 85 (2019); Operation Babylift: The Lost Children of Vietnam (2009) (documentary).

[79] See Malinda L. Seymore, Openness in International Adoption, 46 Colum. Hum. Rts. L. Rev. 163 (2015) (noting that interest in openness seen in domestic adoptions is just beginning in intercountry adoptions). See also Choe Sang-Hung, Court Backs U.S. Citizen Seeking Korean Relatives, N.Y. Times, June 13, 2020, at A12 (reporting landmark Korean case identifying intercountry adoptee's birth father).

U.S. women adopting internationally? Why are they all white? Could the money spent on their travel, hotel stays, legal expenses, and payoffs address the plight of the poorest members of the community, perhaps making many of the surrenders unnecessary? Are some of these women not fit to be mothers? On what basis? Will the adoptive mothers feel like "real mothers"? And, why have the adoptive fathers all remained in the United States?

PROBLEM

At a family gathering, your cousin and your cousin's spouse approach you for a private conversation after hearing you mention that you have been taking a course on adoption. They want to adopt a child, but they are having difficulty making sense of the conflicting stories and opinions from well-meaning friends and web-based support groups about both the advantages and disadvantages of domestic adoption, on the one hand, and intercountry adoption, on the other. They ask you what considerations you would find important as they try to choose which option to pursue. What would you say? How, if at all, would your statement change if you were an attorney counseling clients who had asked for similar advice?

PART III

ASSISTED REPRODUCTION

7

FROM ALTERNATIVE INSEMINATION TO IN VITRO FERTILIZATION

To the extent that adoption provides a way for adults to construct a family in the face of infertility or the absence of sexual reproduction, medicine and science offer alternatives: assisted reproductive technologies or "ARTs," including alternative insemination and, more recently, in vitro fertilization. In the United States, direct regulation remains largely absent from the practice of ARTs, leaving them in a space that some have described as a "wild west"[1] dominated by the interests of consumers and providers of fertility services or genetic materials. Gender, race, class, and particular visions of family play salient roles in the resulting markets. Further, for ARTs, the participants' own intent is emerging as a principal determinant of parentage, contrasting with the state scrutiny and judicial decree that parentage by adoption requires.

What explains the relatively hands-off approach to ARTs? An understanding of procreative activities as an aspect of liberty? A commitment to a free-market economy? Law's failure to keep pace with medical advances? Conflicting views of morality? The power of repronormativity? What does the absence of direct regulation, the ability to choose genetic components for a child, and intent-based parentage mean not only for ARTs but also for adoption, which the state so closely regulates? How does the legal landscape shape prospective parents' choices? What indirect regulations emerge from the following materials, and what changes in existing law would you recommend?

---

[1] Lori B. Andrews, The Clone Age: Adventures in the New World of Reproductive Technology 219 (2000). An emerging exception to the absence of direct regulation would be surrogacy arrangements, the focus of Chapter 8.

A. INFERTILITY AND PROCREATIVE LIBERTY

1. EMBRYO CONTESTS

IN RE MARRIAGE OF ROOKS

429 P.3d 579 (Colo. 2018) (en banc)

JUSTICE MÁRQUEZ, delivered the Opinion of the Court. . . .

We are asked to decide how a court should determine, in dissolution of marriage proceedings, which spouse should receive remaining cryogenically preserved pre-embryos produced by the couple during their marriage. Although this case fundamentally concerns the disposition of a couple's marital property, it presents difficult issues of procreational autonomy for which there are no easy answers because it pits one spouse's right to procreate directly against the other spouse's equivalently important right to avoid procreation, and because the fundamental liberty and privacy interests at stake are deeply personal and emotionally charged. . . .

Petitioner Ms. Mandy Rooks and Respondent Mr. Drake Rooks married in 2002. They separated in August 2014, and Mr. Rooks filed a petition for dissolution of marriage the following month. When the trial court entered its final orders in the dissolution proceedings in 2015, Mr. and Ms. Rooks had three children, and Ms. Rooks was not pregnant.

Mr. and Ms. Rooks used IVF to have their three children. In 2011, and again in 2013, they entered into agreements with the Colorado Center for Reproductive Medicine ("CCRM") and Fertility Laboratories of Colorado ("FLC") for the IVF services. . . .

IVF is a procedure that helps those facing fertility issues to become pregnant. The technique involves several steps: (1) developing eggs in the contributor's ovaries using hormones to stimulate ovulation, (2) removing the eggs from the contributor's ovaries, (3) placing the eggs and sperm together in a laboratory to allow fertilization to occur, and (4) transferring fertilized pre-embryos into the carrier's uterus.

As described in the agreements with CCRM and FLC, the purpose of cryopreservation is to preserve excess pre-embryos produced in an IVF treatment cycle in order to (1) reduce the risks of multiple gestation, (2) preserve fertility potential in the face of certain medical procedures, and (3) minimize the medical risk and cost to the patient by decreasing the number of hormone stimulation cycles and egg retrievals. . . . Although the couple's agreements with CCRM and FLC use the terms "embryo" and "pre-embryo" interchangeably, we use the term "pre-embryos" in this opinion to refer to eggs that have been fertilized using the IVF process but not implanted in a uterus. . . .

Both the 2011 and 2013 agreements with CCRM and FLC include an "Embryo and Pre-Embryo Cryopreservation/Storage Consent" form with a "Disposition Plan" recording the couple's decisions regarding the disposition of the frozen pre-embryos under certain scenarios. Mr. and Ms. Rooks selected the same options in both the 2011 and 2013 disposition plans. For example, in the event of Mr. Rooks's death, the couple agreed the pre-embryos should be "[t]ransferred to the care of the female partner if she wishes," but in the event of Ms. Rooks's death, the pre-embryos should be "[t]hawed and discarded." In the event they both died, the couple agreed the pre-embryos should be discarded.

The disposition plans further state that in the event of divorce or dissolution of marriage, "the disposition of our embryos will be part of the divorce/dissolution decree paperwork," and that FLC may deal exclusively with the person to whom all rights in the pre-embryos are awarded. The plans also provide that "[i]n the event that the divorce/dissolution decree paperwork does not address the disposition of the embryo(s)," the pre-embryos should be thawed and discarded.

[The disposition of the pre-embryos became a contentious issue in the trial court.] . . . Ms. Rooks appealed from the portion of the permanent orders awarding the pre-embryos to Mr. Rooks . . . . [The court of appeals affirmed. Later, Ms. Rooks became pregnant, but] still wishes to use the cryogenically frozen pre-embryos to have more children. . . .

A. Reproductive Rights and Autonomy . . .

The U.S. Supreme Court has recognized the importance of individual autonomy over decisions involving reproduction. Over seventy-five years ago, the Court recognized that procreation is "one of the basic civil rights" and that marriage and procreation are fundamental to human existence and survival. Skinner v. Oklahoma ex rel. Williamson, 316 U.S. 535, 541 (1942). As the Court considered new questions involving reproductive rights, such as the right to access contraception, it began to articulate those rights as part of a cluster of privacy rights grounded in several fundamental constitutional guarantees. . . . "If the right of privacy means anything, it is the right of the individual, married or single, to be free from unwarranted governmental intrusion into matters so fundamentally affecting a person as the decision whether to bear or beget a child." Eisenstadt v. Baird, 405 U.S. 438, 453 (1972). . . .

We note that the right to procreate or to avoid procreation does not depend on the means by which that right is exercised. An individual may exercise her right to procreate through conventional conception or IVF — or she may exercise her right to avoid procreation through abstinence, contraception, voluntary sterilization, or even abortion — but the nature of the right itself (to procreate or to avoid procreation) remains the same. . . .

[In disputes like this, courts in other jurisdictions] have adhered to or combined aspects of three main approaches: (1) interpreting the parties' contract or agreement regarding disposition of the pre-embryos; (2) balancing the parties' respective interests in receiving the pre-embryos; or (3) requiring the parties' mutual contemporaneous consent regarding disposition of the pre-embryos. . . .

C. Colorado Statutes

. . . Colorado statutes provide that an individual is not obligated to be the legal parent of a child eventually born as a result of their contribution of genetic material where the couple divorces, or where one party withdraws consent. Although these statutes address the resulting legal relationships with any children eventually born using assisted reproductive technology, they do not address how a trial court should resolve disputes over how to allocate remaining cryogenically preserved pre-embryos in a dissolution of marriage proceeding. . . .

Before turning to that task, we note that Colorado law generally provides that pre-embryos are not "persons," as a legal matter. . . . At the same time, we acknowledge that pre-embryos contain the potential for human life and are formed using genetic material from two parties with significant, but potentially competing, interests in their ultimate disposition. Thus, we agree with courts that have categorized pre-embryos as marital property of a special character.

Although Colorado statutes do not address the proper disposition of marital pre-embryos upon divorce, the Uniform Dissolution of Marriage Act ("UMDA") does generally direct a court presiding over dissolution proceedings to "divide the marital property . . . in such proportions as the court deems just." §14-10-113(1), C.R.S. (2018). That the UMDA requires the court to divide the marital property "in such proportions as the court deems just" directs that some sort of balancing is appropriate here.

D. Resolving Pre-Embryo Disputes in Colorado . . .

First, we reject the mutual contemporaneous consent approach. . . . [I]f the parties' mutual contemporaneous consent were required to proceed with implantation, there would be no need to address the legal relationship between a non-consenting party and a resulting child, because that child could not exist. We also agree with those courts that have criticized the mutual contemporaneous consent approach as being "totally unrealistic" because if the parties were capable of reaching an agreement, they would not be in court. . . . And we worry that this de facto veto creates incentives for a party to leverage this issue unfairly in divorce proceedings. Moreover, because it disregards the parties' preexisting agreements, the mutual contemporaneous consent approach injects legal uncertainty into the process and eliminates any incentive for the parties to avoid litigation by agreeing in advance about disposition of remaining pre-embryos in the event of divorce. Finally, the mutual contemporaneous consent approach essentially requires us to abdicate our judicial responsibilities by ignoring the legislature's directive to distribute equitably the parties' marital property in a dissolution proceeding. The parties here have turned to the courts to resolve their dispute. We cannot simply do nothing.

. . . [W]e conclude that a court presiding over dissolution proceedings should strive, where possible, to honor both parties' interests in procreational autonomy when resolving these disputes. Thus, we hold that a court should look first to any existing agreement expressing the spouses' intent regarding disposition of the couple's remaining pre-embryos in the event of divorce. In the absence of such an agreement, a court should seek to balance the parties' respective interests when awarding the pre-embryos . . . .

To begin with [in balancing], courts should consider the intended use of the party seeking to preserve the disputed pre-embryos. A party who seeks to become a genetic parent through implantation of the pre-embryos, for example, has a weightier interest than one who seeks to donate the pre-embryos to another couple. A court should also consider the demonstrated physical ability (or, conversely, inability) of the party seeking to implant the disputed pre-embryos to have biological children through other means.

Relatedly, the court should consider the parties' original reasons for pursuing IVF, which may favor preservation over disposition. For example, the couple may have turned to IVF to preserve a spouse's future ability to have biological children in the face of fertility-implicating medical treatment, such as chemotherapy. The court's analysis should also include consideration of hardship for the person seeking to avoid becoming a genetic parent, including emotional, financial, or logistical considerations. See [Davis v. Davis, 842 S.W.2d 588, 603-04] (Tenn. 1992) (considering ex-husband's opposition to fathering a child who would not live with both parents because of his own childhood experiences involving separation from his parents). In addition, a court should consider either spouse's demonstrated bad faith or attempt to use the pre-embryos as unfair leverage in the divorce proceedings.

Factors other than the ones described above may be relevant on a case-by-case basis. That said, we hold that the following are improper considerations in a dissolution court's allocation of a couple's cryogenically preserved pre-embryos. First, we decline to adopt a test that would allow courts to limit the size of a family based on financial and economic distinctions. Thus, a dissolution court should not assess whether the party seeking to become a genetic parent using the pre-embryos can afford another child. Nor shall the sheer number of a party's existing children, standing alone, be a reason to preclude preservation or use of the pre-embryos. Finally, we note that some courts have mentioned adoption as an alternative to biological or genetic parenthood through conventional or assisted reproduction. See *Davis*, 842 S.W.2d at 604. However, because we conclude the relevant interest at stake is the interest in achieving or avoiding genetic parenthood, courts should not consider whether a spouse seeking to use the pre-embryos to become a genetic parent could instead adopt a child or otherwise parent non-biological children. . . .

[Because the parties had not agreed on disposition in the event of divorce, this court remands for the trial court to balance the parties' interests according to the framework in the majority opinion.]

JUSTICE HOOD, dissenting [joined by Chief Justice Coats and Justice Samour]. . . .

Here, the impediment to Ms. Rooks exercising her right to procreate is not the court, it is Mr. Rooks. In order for a person to exercise his or her right to procreate, obviously a second party is needed. . . . Under the majority's test, the courts are forced to mediate a fundamentally personal decision and, in the process, infringe on a litigant's constitutional rights. In some contexts, this judicial choice may be unavoidable. Not so here. The contemporaneous mutual consent approach appropriately minimizes the government's role in resolving this constitutional dilemma. . . .

Of the approaches outlined by the majority, only the contemporaneous mutual consent approach adequately shields citizens from unwarranted governmental intrusion. . . . Yet what exactly is it that the contemporaneous mutual consent test guards against? True, it keeps the courts from intruding on a donor's constitutional right to not procreate. But to properly understand this right, we must see what types of harms a violation of it would engender. . . .

For the non-consenting donor, there are several harms that may be inflicted, each of which derives "from the unwanted existence of a child to whom one stands in relationship of parent." See I. Glenn Cohen, The Right Not to Be a Genetic Parent?, 81 S. Cal. L. Rev. 1115, 1135 (2008). While Mr. Rooks will not be the legal or (obviously) the gestational parent, he will still have some residual, societal parenthood attached to him by both the nature of his previous relationship with Ms. Rooks and his genetic tie to the child.

First, how is Mr. Rooks to respond when someone tells him how brilliant or troubled his new daughter is growing up to be? See id. at 1136. Should he be required to explain that he is not the child's legal parent and that he only became a genetic parent over his objection? Or must he simply smile and nod? Either one is a constitutional harm against which the right to not procreate protects. But the majority's test may very well require the state to inflict these harms.

Second, Ms. Rooks's resulting child could, quite understandably, perceive Mr. Rooks as her father, irrespective of the legal technicalities we discuss today. See id. Adopted children and children born of sperm donors sometimes seek out their genetic parents. Id. There is no guarantee that the new child will not discover and want to explore her genetic circumstances. Mr. Rooks then must endure another constitutional harm: the potential for pressure to be placed on him by his unwanted genetic child.

Third, Mr. Rooks, himself, may view the resulting child as his own, even though the law does not recognize him as the parent. See id. at 1137. Presumably, a consenting spouse does not view a child born from IVF as his or her own simply because the law bestows legal parentage. Rather, it is more typically the social and genetic tie that causes the spouse to care for and love the child. But both are still present in the case of the non-consenting former spouse. And that former spouse is stuck with the "powerful attendant reverberations of guilt, attachment, or responsibility which . . . knowledge [of the resulting child] can ignite." John A. Robertson, In the Beginning: The Legal Status of Early Embryos, 76 Va. L. Rev. 437, 479 (1990). . . .

As each of these examples demonstrates, the majority's test permits the state to use its power to inflict constitutional harm. Citizens are meant to be "free from unwarranted governmental intrusion" when deciding "whether to bear or beget a child." Eisenstadt, 405 U.S. at 453. But instead of unfettering citizens, the majority's test places the state directly between two people in a decision that "fundamentally affect[s]" their lives. Id. . . . Ms. Rooks has the right to be free from "unwarranted governmental intrusion" in exercising her right to procreate. She does not have the right to compel genetic procreation against another person's will. . . .

[When must both parties consent?] Some proponents of other approaches argue that the parties consent when they allow the sperm and eggs to be harvested and united. . . . Imagine twenty-five eggs are successfully fertilized. Do we really want to say that partners who agree to IVF thereby forever consent to genetically parent all children resulting from successful implantation of any of those pre-embryos? My answer is no. . . .

[With contemporaneous mutual consent,] the court need not enter the fray as to whether a person is capable of genetically reproducing, as the majority's approach requires. That is no small matter. Consider that here Ms. Rooks alleged in the lower courts that she could not procreate without use of these pre-embryos, only to discover during the course of her appearance before us that she could.

Or consider the amorphous requirement to look to the "hardship" of the spouse seeking to avoid becoming a genetic parent, which includes "emotional, financial, or logistical considerations." Which "emotional" factors are relevant? And in which direction should such factors cut? The majority cites favorably *Davis*, which considered the ex-husband's childhood experiences involving divorce. Is the court now to probe the intimate early childhood experiences of non-consenting donors just so they can avoid being compelled to produce genetic offspring? . . .

The decision to have children is one of the most consequential choices people make in life. The considerations that go into it are numerous and personal; it is not a decision that most would leave to their dearest friends, let alone the state. It is difficult, if not impossible, for a court to properly determine whose constitutional rights should prevail in cases like the one before us. [Here,] where the decision is ultimately a private one between two people, the court need not get involved. Only once the court involves itself is there any constitutional violation. Up to and until that point, it is an intimate, personal decision. . . .

Jody Lyneé Madeira, Taking Baby Steps: How Patients and Fertility Clinics Collaborate in Conception

49-56 (2018)

In 1978, the birth of a baby girl named Louise Brown produced a seismic shift in reproductive medicine. Louise was no ordinary baby, but the first child to be born through IVF. No longer was infertility an automatic life sentence to involuntary childlessness, to be negotiated only through adoption or donor sperm and IUI [intrauterine insemination]. For those with resources, like insurance, savings, credit cards, and generous relatives, IVF offered new opportunities to get pregnant. Intervening decades have brought new technological breakthroughs, but fairly stable (and high) prices. But with these reproductive medical advances come the emotional, psychological, and financial realities of unequal access. Others who can afford such treatment might find that it's not successful. For many the dream of a biologically related child still shimmers on the horizon, seemingly just out of reach.

For decades, many have used the term "desperate" to describe individuals caught up in conceiving. . . . Legislators, policymakers, and the entertainment media frequently use a discourse of desperation and emotional extremism to justify proposals for ART regulation. . . . Why are emotion-related rationales necessary for regulating reproductive technologies in the first place, when such call could logically come from IVF's scientific, medical, and ethical risks like multiple births? . . .

. . . Many individuals consider themselves desperate and even describe this emotion in stereotypical ways — but very few report that it interferes with decision making. . . . According to patients' reflections, desperation rarely paralyzes them. It might take over their lives, frustrate them, prompt them to rethink life goals or treatment limits, or make them ever more determined to find a successful treatment. But even in the face of severely constrained options, individuals most often treat these points as decisions that require engagement, not moments to act carelessly. Rather than signaling imperiled decision-making capacity, then, desperation often summons agency or autonomy. . . .

NOTES AND QUESTIONS

1. *Infertility and gender.* According to the Centers for Disease Control and Prevention, "[a]bout 6% of married women aged 15 to 44 years in the United States are unable to get pregnant after one year of trying (infertility). Also, about 12% of women aged 15 to 44 years in the United States have difficulty getting pregnant or carrying a pregnancy to term, regardless of marital status (impaired fecundity)."[2] Why do the infertility rates exclude unmarried women? Why do women provide the reference point, when a male factor causes infertility in 8 percent of the cases?[3] Among women aged 15 to 49, 12.7 percent have used fertility services.[4]

Infertility and impaired fecundity have increased with intentionally delayed childbearing beyond age 35 as women pursue additional education and career establishment.[5] Are women to blame for their own infertility? Pointing to inadequacies in leave policies, childcare, and shared parenting by men, sociologist Barbara Katz Rothman writes:

> Shall we blame the woman for putting off childbearing while she became a lawyer, art historian, physician, set designer, or engineer? Or shall we blame the system that makes it so very difficult for young lawyers, art historians, physicians, set designers, and engineers to have children without wives to care for them? Men did not have to delay entry into parenthood for nearly as many years in the pursuit of their careers as women do now. It is easier to blame the individual woman than to understand the political and economic context in which she must act, but it does not make for good social policy.[6]

Professor Madeira's book compiles and analyzes empirical data from interviews and surveys of 478 IVF participants — both patients and health-care providers — with particular emphasis on the informed consent process.[7] Although Madeira refers to "individuals caught up in conceiving," she also makes clear how attributions of "desperation" often "come from (and reinforce) problematic perceptions about women's 'natural' emotionality and . . . 'hard wir[ing]' for parenthood."[8] Infertility in families of color attracted public

[2] Centers for Disease Control and Prevention (CDC), Reproductive Health, Infertility FAQs (Jan. 16, 2019), https://www.cdc.gov/reproductivehealth/infertility/index.htm [https://perma.cc/PPQ2-CV55].

[3] See id.

[4] Centers for Disease Control and Prevention (CDC), National Center for Health Statistics (July 16, 2016), https://www.cdc.gov/nchs/fastats/infertility.htm [https://perma.cc/P2LD-T3MZ]. See also Centers for Disease Control and Prevention (CDC), National Public Health Action Plan for the Detection, Prevention, and Management of Infertility (June 2014), https://pdfs.semanticscholar.org/82b6/1684ac0f40b4e748e361f7f2927d7875c99a.pdf.

[5] Juan Balasch & Eduard Gratacós, Delayed Childbearing: Effects on Fertility and the Outcome of Pregnancy, 24 Current Op. in Ob. & Gyn. 187 (June 2012).

[6] Barbara Katz Rothman, Recreating Motherhood 98 (2d ed. 2000).

[7] Jody Lyneé Madeira, Taking Baby Steps: How Patients and Fertility Clinics Collaborate in Conception 16 (2018).

[8] Id. at 64.

attention with the publication of First Lady Michelle Obama's memoir, in which she disclosed her use of IVF.[9]

Note that consumers of reproductive interventions include not only patients like those in Madeira's study, but also the "socially infertile," such as same-sex couples and single individuals. Further, the common medical definition of infertility fails to include such populations.[10]

2. *A constitutional right?* Both the majority and dissent in *Rooks* assume that ARTs like IVF are covered by the constitutional right protected in abortion and contraception cases like Eisenstadt v. Baird, Chapter 2, section A. The leading proponent of this position, the late Professor John Robertson, has written that "procreative liberty is a deeply held moral and legal value that deserves a strong measure of respect in all reproductive activities [to be] equally honored when reproduction requires technological assistance."[11] Robertson's book goes on to advocate reproductive autonomy for seven major reproductive technologies, including IVF and forms of collaborative reproduction, that is, procreation that requires contribution from parties other than the intended parents. Dean Kimberly Mutcherson goes further, arguing that reproductive justice may impose affirmative obligations on states to provide access to ARTs services.[12]

Do cases establishing a right to avoid procreation (via contraception and abortion) necessarily imply a right to use available interventions to have children? What might the increasing difficulty to muster a Supreme Court majority to protect abortion access[13] mean for procreative liberty? Why does the *Rooks* dissent conclude that, properly understood, Ms. Rooks's procreative liberty is not at stake in the case at hand? Why does the majority disagree?

3. *Intent and its timing.* Cryopreservation of pre-embryos offers several advantages. It allows successive pregnancy attempts without repeating surgery to remove ova. It also allows for the transfer of pre-embryos during a spontaneous ovulatory cycle and avoids the risk of multi-fetal pregnancy that inheres in the simultaneous use of numerous pre-embryos.[14]

With cryopreservation, then, pre-embryos created at Time A are frozen, to be used later, at Time B. Disputes arise when the parties fail to indicate at Time A what should happen at Time B or when they did so but one party at Time B no longer wants to abide by the agreement or "precommitment" made at Time A. What does the agreement in *Rooks* mean when it says: "in the event of divorce or dissolution of marriage, 'the disposition of our embryos will be part of the divorce/dissolution decree paperwork,' and that FLC may deal exclusively with the person to whom all rights in the pre-

[9] Michelle Obama, Becoming 188 (2018).
[10] See Anna Louie Sussman, The Case for Redefining Infertility, New Yorker (June 18, 2019), https://www.newyorker.com/culture/annals-of-inquiry/the-case-for-social-infertility.
[11] John A. Robertson, Children of Choice: Freedom and The New Reproductive Technologies 4 (1994).
[12] Kimberly M. Mutcherson, Procreative Pluralism, 30 Berkeley J. Gender L. & Just. 22 (2015).
[13] See June Med. Servs., L.L.C. v. Russo, 140 S. Ct. 2103 (2020).
[14] See, e.g., The Ethics Committee of the American Fertility Society, Ethical Considerations of the New Reproductive Technologies, 53 Fertility and Sterility 58S (Supp. 2 1990) (explaining the process).

embryos are awarded"? Does that language contemplate a judicial resolution or at least a divorce settlement approved by a court?

When the *Rooks* majority states that "any existing agreement expressing the spouses' intent regarding disposition of the couple's remaining pre-embryos in the event of divorce" would control, what sort of agreement does it contemplate? If a form agreement made with a clinic, like the document in *Rooks*, had specified a disposition upon divorce, should it bind the progenitors in a dispute inter se?[15] Would an oral agreement or an exchange of emails between the parties suffice?[16] What are the advantages of binding the parties to the intent that they expressed at Time A?[17] What procedural safeguards should be required for enforcing such agreements?[18]

In Bilbao v. Goodwin, 217 A.3d 977 (Conn. 2019), a case of first impression in the state, the court decided to follow the contractual approach. It decided that the storage agreement constitutes a contract between the divorcing progenitors supported by adequate consideration and thus ruled in favor of disposal, over the objection of the husband. The court added, this language at the end of the opinion:

> [O]ur decision applies to contracts that, if enforced, will not result in procreation. We do not decide whether the contractual approach applies in a scenario that would force one party to become a genetic parent against his or her wishes or, if the contractual approach does apply, whether such a contract would be unenforceable for other reasons, including public policy.

Id. at 992. How do you explain the limitation? Is the court really following the contractual approach?

4. *"Forced parenthood"?* In stating that an applicable agreement at Time A to use the pre-embryos at Time B would control, the *Rooks* majority stands at odds with several earlier cases that resolved all disputes in favor of the party wishing to avoid procreation at Time B, regardless of intent at Time A.[19] As the Massachusetts Supreme Court explained in A.Z. v. B.Z., 725 N.E.2d 1051, 1059 (Mass. 2000), citing constitutional cases and authorities rejecting suits for breach of promise to marry: "[P]rior agreements to enter into familial relationships (marriage or parenthood) should not be enforced against individuals who subsequently reconsider their decisions. This enhances the 'freedom of personal choice in matters of marriage and family life.'"

Commentators read such cases to articulate a principle against forcing parenthood on an unwilling party,[20] a theme emphasized by the *Rooks*

---

[15] See, e.g., Fla. Stat. Ann. §742.17 (calling for written agreements between the commissioning couple and the treating physician about embryo disposition in "unforeseen circumstance[s]" and spelling out default rules for particular situations); In re Marriage of Dahl & Angle, 194 P.3d 834 (Or. Ct. App. 2008) (treating an agreement with the storage facility that the former wife would get unused embryos to destroy them as her contractual right, constituting personal property to be allocated to her at dissolution).

[16] See Szafranski v. Dunston, 34 N.E.3d 1132 (Ill. App. Ct. 2015) (holding oral contract should be enforced).

[17] See John A. Robertson, Precommitment Strategies for Disposition of Frozen Embryos, 50 Emory L.J. 989, 1038-1041 (2001).

[18] See Deborah L. Forman, Embryo Disposition, Divorce, & Family Law Contracting: A Model for Enforceability, 24 Colum. J. Gender & L. 378 (2013).

[19] E.g., J.B. v. M.B., 783 A.2d 707 (N.J. 2001); Davis v. Davis, 842 S.W.2d 588, 604 (Tenn. 1992).

[20] See Susan B. Apel, Cryopreserved Embryos: A Response to "Forced Parenthood" and the Role of Intent, 39 Fam. L.Q. 663 (2005).

dissent. What does forced parenthood entail? Why does the dissent conclude that relief from the financial obligations of parentage would not address this problem? How might abortion jurisprudence, including the invalidity of spousal consent and notification requirements, offer insights into disputes over frozen embryos?[21]

Similar to the statute noted in *Rooks*, the UPA provides as follows (with bracketed language to be chosen by the enacting state):

> If a marriage of a woman who gives birth to a child conceived by assisted reproduction is [terminated through divorce or dissolution, subject to legal separation or separate maintenance, declared invalid, or annulled] before transfer of gametes or embryos to the woman, a former spouse of the woman is not a parent of the child unless the former spouse consented in a record that the former spouse would be a parent of the child if assisted reproduction were to occur after a [divorce, dissolution, annulment, declaration of invalidity, legal separation, or separate maintenance], and the former spouse did not withdraw consent. . . .

UPA §706 (2017). Further, the UPA allows any participant to withdraw consent before a transfer that results in pregnancy and provides that one who so withdraws consent is not a parent. Id. §707. As *Rooks* shows, however, the issues presented go beyond official parental status.

5. *Contemporaneous mutual consent.* Allowing parties to reconsider at Time B any precommitments made at Time A yields a requirement of contemporaneous mutual consent, which the *Rooks* dissent embraces. Which approach better advances reproductive autonomy and "freedom of personal choice in matters of marriage and family life" — adherence to precommitments or contemporaneous mutual consent? Why?[22]

6. *Balancing interests.* Evaluate the contrasting positions of the *Rooks* majority and dissent on the propriety of balancing the progenitors' interests. If a court should balance the interests, how sound do you find the majority's list of considerations to include and to exclude? What weight should each party's moral views of discarding embryos carry?[23] What implications for adoption does the majority's emphasis on genetic reproduction convey?

The balancing-of-interests approach first emerged in an Israeli opinion emphasizing that use of the pre-embryos presented the woman's "last

---

[21] See generally Mary Ziegler, Abortion and the Constitutional Right (Not) to Procreate, 48 U. Rich. L. Rev. 1263 (2014).

[22] Compare Carl H. Coleman, Procreative Liberty and Contemporaneous Choice: An Inalienable Rights Approach to Frozen Embryo Disputes, 84 Minn. L. Rev. 55 (1999), and Sarah B. Kirschbaum, Who Gets the Frozen Embryos During a Divorce: A Cases for the Contemporaneous Consent Approach, 21 N.C. J. L. & Tech. 113 (2019), with Deborah Zalesne, The Intersection of Contract Law, Reproductive Technology, and the Market: Families in the Age of ART, 51 U. Rich. L. Rev. 419, 467 (2017) ("Enforcing advanced dispositional agreements when the parties make informed decisions provides donors with the greatest amount of procreative liberty, and ensures that individuals participating in IVF fully understand and consider the consequences of their actions."). See generally Susan Frelich Appleton, Reproduction and Regret, 23 Yale J.L. & Feminism 255 (2011).

[23] See In re Marriage of Fabos & Olsen, 451 P.3d 1218, 1227-1228 (Colo. App. 2019) (applying *Rooks*).

procreative chance."[24] Robertson points out the gendered significance of this consideration because, "[a]lthough there will be few men who will become infertile during the IVF and embryo storage process, many women might," with advancing age.[25] Individuals with female anatomy face another disadvantage here compared to those with male anatomy. When preparing for medical treatment that would impair future fertility, the latter can freeze sperm at Time A for use at Time B; frozen ova, however, offer much less reliable success than frozen pre-embryos — behooving those with female anatomy to find someone to contribute sperm at Time A.[26] This situation, then, can result in subsequent disagreements at Time B.[27] What other gendered considerations might be at play in balancing?[28]

7. *The legal status of pre-embryos.* How does *Rooks* classify pre-embryos? What follows from that classification?

a. *Background.* Courts have struggled with such issues. In Del Zio v. Presbyterian Hospital, 1978 U.S. Dist. LEXIS 14450 (S.D.N.Y. 1978), a couple won $50,000 for the deliberate destruction of a culture containing their eggs and sperm by health care providers who questioned the safety of this then-untried procedure. The jury based its award on plaintiffs' claims for emotional distress, while rejecting their claims for conversion of property. Holding that before implantation an embryo is not a "distinct human entity," an Ohio court rejected a wrongful death claim by plaintiffs after an equipment malfunction destroyed their stored pre-embryos.[29] Some courts have classified pre-embryos as property or "marital property of a special character," while others have deemed them to belong in an intermediate category between "persons" and "property."[30] Should pre-embryos, ova, and sperm all have the same legal status for purposes of property and tort law?[31]

b. *Embryonic "personhood."* Louisiana legislation defines the "in vitro fertilized human ovum" as both a "juridical person" until implanted and a "biological human being" and entitling "such ovum to sue or be sued." The law prohibits intentional destruction of "viable" fertilized ova, explaining that

---

[24] In Nahmani v. Nahmani, F.H. 2401/95, several of the justices noted that the pre-embryos represented the only chance for the estranged wife (who sought to implant them) to become a genetic mother. Daphne Barak-Erez, IVF Battles: Legal Categories and Comparative Tales, 28 Duke J. Comp. & Int'l L. 247, 262-264 (2018) (analyzing *Nahmani* case).

[25] Robertson, supra note [17], at 1014.

[26] Ethics Committee of the American Society for Reproductive Medicine, Planned Oocyte Cryopreservation for Women Seeking to Preserve Future Reproductive Potential: An Ethics Committee Opinion, 110 Fertility & Sterility 1022 (2018), https://www.asrm.org/globalassets/asrm/asrm-content/news-and-publications/ethics-committee-opinions/planned_oocyte_cryopreservation_for_women_seeking_to_preserve-pdfmembers.pdf. See Sarah Elizabeth Richards, What Happened to All the Frozen Eggs, N.Y. Times, Dec. 22, 2019, at SR7 (noting that the principal benefit to date is a feeling of control that egg freezing gives women, regardless of outcome).

[27] See, e.g., *Szafranski*, 34 N.E.3d 1132. See also Estate of Kievernagel, 83 Cal. Rptr. 3d 311, 318 (Ct. App. 2008) (noting how cases with only one gamete donor are easier than those with two).

[28] See Mary Ziegler, Men's Reproductive Rights: A Legal History, 47 Pepp. L. Rev. 665 (2020).

[29] Penniman v. Univ. Hosps. Health Sys., 130 N.E.3d 333 (Ohio Ct. App. 2019).

[30] Compare York v. Jones, 717 F. Supp. 421 (E.D. Va. 1989), and McQueen v. Gadberry, 507 S.W.3d 127, 149 (Mo. Ct. App. 2016), with *Davis*, 842 S.W.2d at 594-597. See also Miller v. Am. Infertility Grp. of Ill., 897 N.E.2d 837 (Ill. App. Ct. 2008) (rejecting wrongful-death claim for an embryo not yet implanted).

[31] See Emma D. McBride, Note, "I'd Like My Eggs Frozen": Negligent Emotional Distress Compensation for Lost Frozen Human Eggs, 61 B.C. L. Rev. 749 (2020).

"[a]n in vitro fertilized human ovum that fails to develop further over a thirty-six hour period except when the embryo is in a state of cryopreservation, is considered non-viable and is not a juridical person." The statute makes available for "adoptive implantation" those fertilized ova for which the IVF patients have renounced their own parental rights. The law precludes inheritance rights for an ovum unless live birth occurs. Louisiana applies the "best interest of the in vitro fertilized ovum" test in any disputes. La. Rev. Stat. Ann. §§9:121-9:133. Does this test mean that the party seeking implantation must prevail?[32] To date, no Louisiana court has cited the statute, which was enacted in 1986.[33] What could "personhood" initiatives designed to halt abortion mean for IVF?[34]

8. *Disposition.* What legal rules should govern the storage of the growing number of unused cryopreserved pre-embryos?[35] Should they be treated as unclaimed abandoned property?[36] Under a model law proposed by the American Bar Association (ABA), absent a contrary agreement, embryos are deemed abandoned after five years and an unsuccessful search to find the interested participants; disposal of abandoned embryos must follow the most recent recorded agreement between the participants and the storage facility, with a court order for disposition required in the absence of such agreement.[37]

Madeira's empirical study determined that patients took seriously embryo disposition forms and found decisions about how to complete them emotionally difficult, if not "weird." Although almost one-third felt they could not make an informed decision about disposition, the vast majority made a choice, felt satisfied with it, and would make the same decision again.[38] On "embryo adoption," see infra section B2.

9. *Paying for IVF.* Is infertility an "illness" and IVF and allied procedures "medically necessary" treatment therefor? The issue arises in determining whether the procedure is covered by medical insurance that reimburses only for treatment of illness or for medically necessary health care.[39] Some

---

[32] See *Davis*, 842 S.W.2d at 594 (stating that the trial court so ruled). See generally Jessica Berg, Of Elephants and Embryos: A Proposed Framework for Legal Personhood, 59 Hastings L.J. 369 (2007).

[33] See Monica Hof Wallace, A Primer on Natural and Juridical Persons in Louisiana, 64 Loy. L. Rev. 407, 419-421 (2018).

[34] See, e.g., Ashley Pittman, Assisted Reproduction Technology and the Status of the Embryo, 81 Supra 99 (2011).

[35] See M.C. Schiewe et al., Comprehensive Assessment of Cryogenic Storage Risk and Quality Management Concerns: Best Practice Guidelines for ART Labs, 36 J. Assist. Reprod. Genetics 5 (Jan. 2019), https://link.springer.com/content/pdf/10.1007/s10815-018-1310-6.pdf.

[36] Beth E. Roxland & Arthur Caplan, Should Unclaimed Frozen Embryos Be Considered Abandoned Property and Donated to Stem Cell Research?, 21 B.U. J. Sci. & Tech. L. 108 (2015).

[37] American Bar Assn., Model Act Governing Assisted Reproduction §504 (2019), https://www.americanbar.org/content/dam/aba/administrative/family_law/committees/art/resolution-111.pdf.

[38] Madeira, supra note [7], at 249. See also Tamar Lewin, Industry's Growth Leads to Leftover Embryos, and Painful Choices, N.Y. Times, June 18, 2015, at A1; Jenni Millbank, Exploring the Ineffable in Women's Experiences of Relationality with Their Stored IVF Embryos, 23 Body & Soc'y 95 (2017). See generally Gregory S. Alexander, Of Buildings, Statues, Art, and Sperm: The Right to Destroy and the Duty to Preserve, 27 Cornell J.L. & Pub. Pol'y 619, 651-660 (2018); June Carbone & Naomi Cahn, Embryo Fundamentalism, 18 Wm. & Mary Bill Rts. J. 1015 (2010).

[39] Compare Egert v. Connecticut Gen. Life Ins., 900 F.2d 1032 (7th Cir. 1990), with Kinzie v. Physician's Liab. Ins., 750 P.2d 1140 (Okla. Ct. App. 1987). The American Medical Association deemed infertility a disease in 2017. See Jenna Casolo et al., Assisted Reproductive Technologies, 20 Geo. J. Gender & L. 313, 345 (2019).

challenges to restrictive insurance coverage under the Americans with Disabilities Act (ADA) have succeeded.[40] Only a minority of states (around 15) have laws mandating coverage or mandating a coverage offer for fertility services, and some include specific limits.[41] For example, a Connecticut statute requires insurance coverage for two cycles of IVF (with no more than two pre-embryos implanted per cycle) but only for women no older than 40 years of age. Conn. Gen. Stat. §38a-509. What reasons explain this particular legislative response?

Without insurance coverage, IVF and allied treatments might well be out of reach because of costs ($12,000 to $22,000 per cycle).[42] Many pay even more because expensive "add-on" treatments claim to offer improved chances of a live birth.[43] Although the Affordable Care Act (ACA) expanded access to medical care, it maintained the status quo on fertility interventions — no required coverage.

What do the ACA's requirement for nondiscrimination in the provision of health care together with marriage equality mean for insurance coverage for same-sex couples who wish to use ARTs, given that they do not meet the traditional medical definition of "infertile"?[44] What does an understanding of the constitutional right to procreate, as embraced in *Rooks*, contribute to the analysis?

Beyond questions of insurance, can patients deduct the costs of infertility treatment as medical expenses on their tax returns?[45] Should Medicaid provide assistance for poor persons seeking fertility treatments? Note that infertility rates are highest in the population of low-income people of color.[46] What consequences follow from the prevailing approach, under which Medicaid benefits do not cover IVF and most private physicians are unwilling to serve Medicaid recipients?[47]

---

[40] See, e.g., Pacourek v. Inland Steel Co., 858 F. Supp. 1393 (N.D. Ill. 1994); 916 F. Supp. 797 (N.D. Ill. 1996). See also Bragdon v. Abbott, 524 U.S. 624 (1998). But see Krauel v. Iowa Methodist Med. Ctr., 95 F.3d 674 (8th Cir. 1996).

[41] See Casolo et al., supra note [39], at 341-342.

[42] See id. at 338; Megan Leonhardt, Women Are Traveling Far and Wide for Affordable IVF — Here's Why It's So Expensive, CNBC Make It (Aug. 13, 2019), https://www.cnbc.com/2019/08/13/women-are-traveling-far-and-wide-for-affordable-ivf.html [https://perma.cc/GD4T-3H8S].

[43] Jack Wilkinson et al., Do à la Carte Menus Serve Infertility Patients? The Ethics and Regulation of In Vitro Fertility Add-Ons, 112 Fertility & Sterility 973 (2019), https://www.fertstert.org/action/showPdf?pii=S0015-0282%2819%2932454-9.

[44] See Casolo et al., supra note [39], at 345-347; Seema Mohapatra, Assisted Reproduction Inequality and Marriage Equality, 92 Chi.-Kent L. Rev. 87 (2017). Cf. Michael Boucai, Is Assisted Procreation an LGBT Right?, 2016 Wis. L. Rev. 1065 (2016).

[45] See Morrissey v. United States, 871 F.3d 1260, 1263 (11th Cir. 2017) (holding that gay male's costs of IVF, egg donation, and surrogacy "were not paid for the purpose of affecting the taxpayer's own reproductive function — and therefore are not deductible"); Katherine Pratt, The Curious State of Tax Deductions for Fertility Treatment Costs, 28 S. Cal. Rev. L. & Soc. Just. 261, 314 (2019) ("If the family formation rights of same-sex intended parents are to be taken seriously, under Obergefell v. Hodges, treating dysfertility the same as medical infertility for purposes of [tax deductions] would further that constitutional goal.").

[46] See Rachel Rebouché, Contracting Pregnancy, 105 Iowa L. Rev. 1591, 1638 n.233 (2020) (citing Emily Galpern, Assisted Reproductive Technologies: Overview and Perspective Using a Reproductive Justice Framework, 7-8 (2007)).

[47] See Naomi R. Cahn, Test Tube Families: Why the Fertility Market Needs Legal Regulation 37 (2009) (noting how some states fund fertility treatment for recipients of public assistance); Dorothy Roberts, Killing the Black Body: Race, Reproduction, and the Meaning of Liberty 253 (1999) (noting that most African Americans are excluded from access).

Depictions in Popular Culture: Private Life (2018)

The film *Private Life* presents the poignant but comedic story of 40-something author Rachel (Kathryn Hahn) and one-time experimental theater director Richard (Paul Giamatti), who for several years have been trying any way they can to have a child. Pursuing both adoption and fertility treatments, they endure a devastating failed adoption, the felt intrusiveness of another home study, and the factory-like approach to IVF that their New York specialists provide and that they cannot really afford — all causing their relationship to fray a little with each new indignity and disappointment. Yet, after some adjustment, they seem to come to terms with every problem and forge ahead. For example, their initial disagreement about the doctor's recommendation that they consider using a younger donor egg exposes the raw emotions at stake and the personal investments in their visions for their family. As one reviewer notes: "*Private Life* is a snapshot of a sensitive time in its central couple's life; every fight they have is touched off by someone saying something innocuous that nonetheless hits deep."[48] Yet, as with other forks in the road Rachel and Richard have faced, they come to accept that their reality requires this compromise, and they begin exploring possibilities from an egg donor website.

The film takes a turn when Rachel and Richard realize that that the solution might lie in their own extended family: Richard's step-niece, Sadie (Kayli Carter), an alienated young writer trying to find herself. Sadie has always said she feels closer to the artistic Rachel and Richard than to her own parents, and just as Rachel and Richard have come to accept that they will use donor eggs, Sadie decides to stay with Rachel and Richard in New York after dropping out of her college writing program. Sadie quickly agrees to help these adults whom she adores, but the family relationship necessarily brings complications. According to one reviewer: "Rachel rattles off a lot of the script's best jokes, but her eyes, especially when she's looking at Sadie, tell an almost unspeakably complex story of affection, envy, reluctance and regret."[49] In the end, the IVF with Sadie's eggs fails too, but everyone moves on, with Rachel and Richard taking Sadie to Yaddo, a writers' colony, where she has won a residency, and Rachel and Richard actively pursuing adoption again.

The film provides an intimate, detailed portrait of infertility, from regular at-home hormone injections to the emotional roller coaster often depicted in the literature. While Richard's masculinity is "temporarily ignored or discarded,"[50] Rachel's fervent pursuit of

---

[48] David Sims, Netflix's *Private Life* Is Brutal, Honest, and Brilliant, The Atlantic (Oct. 4, 2018), https://www.theatlantic.com/entertainment/archive/2018/10/private-life-review/571780/.
[49] A.O. Scott, A Couple Longs to Become Larger, N.Y. Times, Oct. 5, 2018, at C5.
[50] Sims, supra note [48].

motherhood brings nuance to the gendered desperation often described. At the same, the film exposes how adoption, as an alternative to fertility treatment, can also prove risky, with no assurance of success.

What is the relationship, if any, between such portrayals of infertility and the law of ARTs? What might be missing from the film? What legal and ethical questions does it raise?

PROBLEMS

1. Cheryl sues Nalco Company for firing her after she took time off work for IVF, following an infertility diagnosis. She relies on Title VII of the Civil Rights Act of 1964, which prohibits sex discrimination, and the Pregnancy Discrimination Act, which amended Title VII to define pregnancy discrimination as sex discrimination. 42 U.S.C. §2000e(k). The district court grants summary judgment to Nalco on the ground that Cheryl cannot prove sex discrimination because infertility is a gender-neutral condition. Cheryl appeals. What result and why?[51] Could she also sue under the ADA, 42 U.S.C. §§12101 et seq.?[52] If applicable to her employer, would the Family and Medical Leave Act (FMLA), 29 U.S.C. §§2601-2654, provide protection for Cheryl's job? For those who work for covered employers, this statute accords 12 weeks of leave and protects the employee's right to return to work when the employee seeks to care for a child upon birth or adoptive placement; seeks to care for a son, daughter, spouse, or parent who has a serious medical condition; cannot work because of a serious health condition; or is addressing certain exigencies arising out of the military deployment of a spouse, son, daughter, or parent. Id. §2612.[53] What disadvantages should Cheryl consider before proceeding under the FMLA?

2. Mother obtained anonymously donated sperm from Sperm Bank and used it to conceive a daughter through IVF. A few years after her daughter's birth, Mother returned to Sperm Bank to obtain a specimen from the same donor so that she could conceive a second child who would be her daughter's genetic sibling. Sperm Bank declined because the donor had withdrawn his consent, notifying Sperm Bank that he had had a change of heart and no longer wanted to create children with whom he had no formal connection. Mother sues Sperm Bank for release of the donor's sperm. What result and why?[54] What additional information would you need?

---

[51] See Hall v. Nalco Co., 534 F.3d 644 (7th Cir. 2008). But see Saks v. Franklin Covey Co., 316 F.3d 337 (2d Cir. 2003).

[52] See Erickson v. Bd. of Governors, 207 F.3d 945 (7th Cir. 2000); LaPorta v. Wal-Mart Stores, 163 F. Supp. 2d 758 (W.D. Mich. 2001).

[53] See Sinico v. Barry, 2020 WL 528765 (M.D. Pa. 2020), at *8. Cf. Drevaleva v. U.S Dept. of Veterans Affairs, 2019 WL 3037549 (N.D. Cal. 2019).

[54] See Barak-Erez, supra note [24], at 269-270.

3. In response to a highly publicized case in which the court awarded the frozen pre-embryos to another couple, pursuant to the divorcing spouses' earlier agreement,[55] the Arizona legislature enacted the following statute. Would you recommend similar legislation in your state? What changes might you suggest? Why?

Human embryos; disposition; responsibility for resulting child ...

A. If an action [for dissolution of marriage or legal separation] involves the disposition of in vitro human embryos, the court shall:

1. Award the in vitro human embryos to the spouse who intends to allow the in vitro human embryos to develop to birth.

2. If both spouses intend to allow the in vitro human embryos to develop to birth and both spouses provided their gametes for the in vitro human embryos, resolve any dispute on disposition of the in vitro human embryos in a manner that provides the best chance for the in vitro human embryos to develop to birth.

3. If both spouses intend to allow the in vitro human embryos to develop to birth but only one spouse provided gametes for the in vitro human embryos, award the in vitro human embryos to the spouse that provided gametes for the in vitro human embryos.

B. If an agreement between the spouses concerning the disposition of the in vitro human embryos is brought before the court in an action described in §25-318, subsection A [on disposition of community property], the court shall award the in vitro human embryos as prescribed in subsection A of this section.

C. The spouse that is not awarded the in vitro human embryos has no parental responsibilities and no right, obligation or interest with respect to any child resulting from the disputed in vitro human embryos, unless the spouse provided gametes for the in vitro human embryos and consents in writing to be a parent to any resulting child as part of the proceedings concerning the disposition of the in vitro human embryos.

D. If the spouse who is not awarded the in vitro human embryos does not consent to being a parent as provided in subsection C of this section, any resulting child from the disputed in vitro human embryos is not a child of the spouse and has no right, obligation or interest with respect to the spouse.

E. A spouse who provided gametes for the in vitro human embryos and who does not consent to being a parent as provided in subsection C of this section shall provide the spouse awarded the in vitro human embryos as provided in subsection A of this section with detailed written nonidentifying information that includes the health and genetic history of the spouse and the spouse's family in a document that is separate from a document containing identifying information. . . .[56]

Ariz. Rev. Stat. Ann. §25-318.03.

[55] The case ultimately reached the Arizona Supreme Court, Terrell v. Torres, 456 P.3d 13 (Ariz. 2020).

[56] See Catherine Wheatley, Note, Arizona's Torres v. Terrell and Section 318.03: The Wild West of Pre-Embryo Disposition, 95 Ind. L.J. 299 (2020). Cf. Comment, Mary Joy Dingler, Family Law's Coldest War: The Battle for Frozen Embryos and the Need for a Statutory White Flag, 43 Seattle U. L. Rev. 293 (2019).

2. POSTHUMOUS CONCEPTION

ASTRUE v. CAPATO

---

566 U.S. 541 (2012)

Karen and Robert Capato married in 1999. Robert died of cancer less than three years later. With the help of in vitro fertilization, Karen gave birth to twins 18 months after her husband's death [using sperm that he froze before undergoing chemotherapy]. Karen's application for Social Security survivors benefits for the twins, which the Social Security Administration (SSA) denied, prompted this litigation. The technology that made the twins' conception and birth possible, it is safe to say, was not contemplated by Congress when the relevant provisions of the Social Security Act (Act) originated (1939) or were amended to read as they now do (1965).

[The Capatos, who lived in Florida, had a son before Robert died. Robert's will made no provision for children conceived after his death, although the couple had asked their lawyer to place future offspring on a par with existing children. In seeking survivors benefits for the twins,] Karen Capato, respondent here, relies on the Act's initial definition of "child" in 42 U.S.C. §416(e): " '[C]hild' means . . . the child or legally adopted child of an [insured] individual." Robert was an insured individual, and the twins, it is uncontested, are the biological children of Karen and Robert. That satisfies the Act's terms, and no further inquiry is in order, Karen maintains. The SSA, however, identifies subsequent provisions, §§416(h)(2) and (h)(3)(C), as critical, and reads them to entitle biological children to benefits only if they qualify for inheritance from the decedent under state intestacy law, or satisfy one of the statutory alternatives to that requirement.

We conclude that the SSA's reading is better attuned to the statute's text and its design to benefit primarily those supported by the deceased wage earner in his or her lifetime. And even if the SSA's longstanding interpretation is not the only reasonable one, it is at least a permissible construction that garners the Court's respect under [principles of administrative law].

Congress amended the Social Security Act in 1939 to provide a monthly benefit or designated surviving family members of a deceased insured wage earner. "Child's insurance benefits" are among the Act's family-protective measures. [W]e must decide whether the Capato twins rank as "child[ren]" under the Act's definitional provisions. . . . Under the heading "Determination of family status," §416(h)(2)(A) provides: "In determining whether an applicant is the child or parent of [an] insured individual for purposes of this subchapter, the Commissioner of Social Security shall apply [the intestacy law of the insured individual's domiciliary State]." . . .

. . . As the SSA reads the statute, 42 U.S.C. §416(h) governs the meaning of "child" in §416(e)(1). In other words, §416(h) is a gateway through which all applicants for insurance benefits as a "child" must pass. . . . [Citing biology and marriage,] Karen Capato argues, and the Third Circuit held, that §416(h), far from supplying the governing law, is irrelevant in this case. Instead, the Court of Appeals determined, §416(e) alone is dispositive of the controversy. 631 F.3d, at 630-631. . . . Section 416(h) comes into play, the court reasoned, only when "a claimant's status as a deceased wage-earner's child is in doubt." Id., at 631. That limitation, the court suggested, is evident from §416(h)'s caption: "Determination of family status." Here, "there is no family status to determine," the court said, id., at 630, so §416(h) has no role to play. . . .

Nothing in §416(e)'s tautological definition ("'child' means . . . the child . . . of an individual") suggests that Congress understood the word "child" to refer only to the children of married parents. . . . Nor does §416(e) indicate that Congress intended "biological" parentage to be prerequisite to "child" status under that provision. As the SSA points out, "[i]n 1939, there was no such thing as a scientifically proven biological relationship between a child and a father, which is . . . part of the reason that the word 'biological' appears nowhere in the Act." Moreover, laws directly addressing use of today's assisted reproduction technology do not make biological parentage a universally determinative criterion [citing donor insemination statutes from California and Massachusetts]. We note, in addition, that marriage does not ever and always make the parentage of a child certain, nor does the absence of marriage necessarily mean that a child's parentage is uncertain. An unmarried couple can agree that a child is theirs, while the parentage of a child born during a marriage may be uncertain.

Finally, it is far from obvious that Karen Capato's proposed definition — "biological child of married parents," — would cover the posthumously conceived Capato twins. Under Florida law, a marriage ends upon the death of a spouse. If that law applies, rather than a court-declared preemptive federal law, the Capato twins, conceived after the death of their father, would not qualify as "marital" children. . . .

[T]he SSA finds a key textual cue in §416(h)(2)(A)'s opening instruction: "In determining whether an applicant is the child . . . of [an] insured individual for purposes of this subchapter," the Commissioner shall apply state intestacy law. (Emphasis added.) . . . The Act commonly refers to state law [of the domicile] on matters of family status . . . . Time limits also qualify the statutes of several States that accord inheritance rights to posthumously conceived children [citing statutes from various states]. See also Uniform Probate Code §2-120(k), 8 U.L.A. 58 (Supp. 2011) (treating a posthumously conceived child as "in gestation at the individual's death," but only if specified time limits are met). No time constraints attend the Third Circuit's ruling in this case, under which the biological child of married parents is eligible for survivors benefits, no matter the length of time between the father's death and the child's conception and birth.

The paths to receipt of benefits laid out in the Act and regulations, we must not forget, proceed from Congress' perception of the core purpose of the legislation. The aim was not to create a program "generally benefiting needy persons"; it was, more particularly, to "provide . . . dependent members of [a wage earner's] family with protection against the hardship occasioned by [the] loss of [the insured's] earnings." . . .

The SSA's construction of the Act, respondent charges, raises serious constitutional concerns under the equal protection component of the Due Process Clause. She alleges: "Under the government's interpretation . . . , posthumously conceived children are treated as an inferior subset of natural children who are ineligible for government benefits simply because of their date of birth and method of conception."

... We have applied an intermediate level of scrutiny to laws "burden[ing] illegitimate children for the sake of punishing the illicit relations of their parents, because 'visiting this condemnation on the head of an infant is illogical and unjust.'" Clark v. Jeter, 486 U.S. 456, 461, (1988) (quoting Weber v. Aetna Casualty & Surety Co., 406 U.S. 164, 175 (1972)). No showing has been made that posthumously conceived children share the characteristics that prompted our skepticism of classifications disadvantaging children of unwed parents. We therefore need not decide whether heightened scrutiny would be appropriate were that the case.[10] Under rational-basis review, the regime Congress adopted easily passes inspection [because] that regime is "reasonably related to the government's twin interests in [reserving] benefits [for] those children who have lost a parent's support, and in using reasonable presumptions to minimize the administrative burden of proving dependency on a case-by-case basis." ...

Tragic circumstances — Robert Capato's death before he and his wife could raise a family — gave rise to this case. But the law Congress enacted calls for resolution of Karen Capato's application for child's insurance benefits by reference to state intestacy law. We cannot replace that reference by creating a uniform federal rule the statute's text scarcely supports. ...

NOTES AND QUESTIONS

1. *Background.* A posthumous child traditionally was a child conceived before a parent's death but born thereafter. A common law presumption, now codified in many states, legitimates a child born within nine months after the death of the mother's husband. ARTs, including cryopreservation of genetic material, have made possible the birth of children conceived after a parent's death. Frozen semen, for example, can be thawed for insemination or fertilization of ova in vitro, as in the principal case. Embryos and even ova can also be preserved for future use. And physicians can extract semen from men after death.[57]

Posthumous conception raises several intertwined legal issues, including the interests of the deceased gamete providers, the parentage of the resulting children, and the treatment of the latter by inheritance law.[58] To what extent should the resolution of these issues determine eligibility for the federal benefits at stake in *Capato*? Consider the following questions.

2. *Progenitors' and children's interests.* Is posthumous conception a protected right of the deceased? What interests do the children have at stake?[59]

---

10. Ironically, while drawing an analogy to the "illogical and unjust" discrimination [that] children born out of wedlock encounter, see Weber v. Aetna Casualty & Surety Co., 406 U.S. 164, 175-176 (1972), respondent asks us to differentiate between children whose parents were married and children whose parents' liaisons were not blessed by clergy or the State. She would eliminate the intestacy test only for biological children of married parents.

[57] See Andrews, supra note [1], at 222-236 ("the sperminator").

[58] Browne Lewis, Graveside Birthday Parties: The Legal Consequences of Forming Families Posthumously, 60 Case W. Res. L. Rev. 1159 (2010).

[59] See John A. Robertson, Posthumous Reproduction, 69 Ind. L.J. 1027 (1994).

Do the children-to-be have interests at stake justifying state restrictions on access to posthumous reproduction?[60]

Does a surviving spouse have a right to procreate using the deceased's genetic offspring?[61] Or, suppose a parent of a deceased adult child seeks to use the child's genetic material? What weight should a court accord to the prospective grandparents' interests? What evidence of the deceased's wishes should be required? For example, a New York court granted a petition filed by a deceased West Point cadet's parents to use his sperm to create and rear his genetic children, based on what the court found to be his "presumed intent."[62] Should presumed intent suffice? What safeguards would you recommend to ensure respect for a deceased progenitor's right *not* to procreate?[63] What would the "contemporaneous mutual consent" approach, described in *Rooks,* supra, mean for posthumous procreation?

3. *Posthumous parentage.* Why did *Capato* reject the arguments that the twins are Robert's children? Is Robert the twins' father? Do they have no father?[64] To what extent might the policy of keeping dependency private explain the outcome? See Chapter 1, section C.

A model statute proposed by the ABA recognizes the decedent as a parent when ARTs are used after death only if the decedent consented in a record to such parental recognition if the assisted reproduction were to occur after death.[65] By contrast, the UPA provides:

Section 708. Parental Status of Deceased Individual

(a) If an individual who intends to be a parent of a child conceived by assisted reproduction dies during the period between the transfer of a gamete or embryo and the birth of the child, the individual's death does not preclude the establishment of the individual's parentage of the child if the individual otherwise would be a parent of the child under this [act].

(b) If an individual who consented in a record to assisted reproduction by a woman who agreed to give birth to a child dies before a transfer of gametes or embryos, the deceased individual is a parent of a child conceived by the assisted reproduction only if:

---

[60] Compare John A. Robertson, Gay and Lesbian Access to Assisted Reproductive Technology, 55 Case W. Res. L. Rev. 323, 347 (2004) (noting "nonidentity problem" in attempts to justify restrictions to protect children because "the children sought to be protected by banning . . . access to ARTs will not then be born"), with Pamela Laufer-Ukeles, The Lost Children: When the Right to Children Conflicts with the Rights of Children, 8 Law & Ethics Hum. Rts. 219 (2014) (identifying rights of children in ARTs generally, despite nonidentity problem).

[61] See, e.g., *Kievernagel,* 83 Cal. Rptr. 3d at 312 (holding intent of late husband, who directed destruction of frozen semen, must control, regardless of widow's interests).

[62] Compare Matter of Zhu, 103 N.Y.S.3d 775 (Sup. Ct. 2019), with Robertson v. Saadat, 262 Cal. Rptr. 3d 215, 230-231 (Ct. App. 2020). Cf. Speranza v. Repro Lab, Inc., 875 N.Y.S.2d 449 (App. Div. 2009) (denying deceased man's parents his frozen semen as part of his estate, based on his directive for destruction of specimens). See generally Nofar Yakovi Gan-Or, Securing Posterity: The Right to Postmortem Grandparenthood and the Problem for Law, 37 Colum. J. Gender & L. 109 (2019).

[63] See Jean Denise Krebs, Any Man Can Be a Father, but Should a Dead Man Be a Dad?: An Approach to the Formal Legalization of Posthumous Sperm Retrieval and Posthumous Reproduction in the United States, 47 Hofstra L. Rev. 775 (2018); Shelly Simana, Creating Life After Death: Should Posthumous Reproduction Be Legally Permissible without the Deceased's Prior Consent, 5 J.L. & Biosciences 329 (2018).

[64] See Arianne Renan Barzilay, You're on Your Own, Baby: Reflections on *Capato*'s Legacy, 46 Ind. L. Rev. 557 (2013) (reading case and statute to reflect a concept of family dominated by a male breadwinner).

[65] American Bar Assn., supra note [37], §607.

> (1) either:
>> (A) the individual consented in a record that if assisted reproduction were to occur after the death of the individual, the individual would be a parent of the child; or
>> (B) the individual's intent to be a parent of a child conceived by assisted reproduction after the individual's death is established by clear-and-convincing evidence; and
>
> (2) either:
>> (A) the embryo is in utero not later than [36] months after the individual's death; or
>> (B) the child is born not later than [45] months after the individual's death.

UPA §708 (2017). What explains the suggested time limits? Do they provide adequate opportunity for a surviving parent to grieve the other's death and to prepare to rear a child alone?[66]

4. *Inheritance.* By tying survivors benefits to state inheritance law, *Capato* has an "effect [that] is double or nothing: Either the child inherits from the deceased parent and collects Social Security benefits or gets neither . . . ."[67] Some state statutes grant rights to such children if the deceased parent gave consent during his lifetime, while differing on required details.[68] In the absence of state statutes, federal courts have certified such questions to state courts, which in turn have struggled with such issues.[69] If consent to procreate posthumously is necessary, how does one prove it?[70]

Because the Social Security Act looks to state intestacy law, some posthumously conceived children have succeeded in receiving the benefits sought on behalf of the Capato twins. For example, in Gillett-Netting v. Barnhart, 371 F.3d 593 (9th Cir. 2004), the court ruled that, because the twins in that case were "legitimate children under Arizona law, they [were conclusively] deemed dependent under §402(d)(3) and [need] not demonstrate actual dependency nor deemed dependency under the provisions of §416(h)." Id. at 599. Does this analysis remain good law after *Capato*? How would one show "actual dependency" when the child is conceived after the insured's death?[71] The Uniform Probate Code's provisions on intestate succession follow the UPA (2017) on posthumous parentage, supra, but reject the time

---

[66] See Kristen M. Benvenuti Pytel, Left Out No Longer: A Call for Advancement in Legislation for Posthumously Conceived Children, 11 J.L. Soc'y 70, 105-107 (2009/2010).

[67] David Shayne, Posthumously Conceived Child as Heir Depends on Where, 42 Est. Plan. 28, 28 (2015).

[68] Compare La. Rev. Stat. Ann. §9:391.1(A) (requiring deceased's specific, written authorization for spouse to use his gametes), with Tex. Fam. Code Ann. §160.707 (requiring that deceased spouse "consented in a record kept by a licensed physician that if assisted reproduction were to occur after death the deceased spouse would be a parent of the child").

[69] See, e.g., Delzer v. Berryhill, 886 F.3d 1282 (9th Cir. 2018); Woodward v. Commissioner of Soc. Sec., 760 N.E.2d 257, 269 (Mass. 2002). See generally Jennifer Matystik, Posthumously Conceived Children: Why States Should Update Their Intestacy Laws After Astrue v. Capato, 28 Berkeley J. Gender L. & Just. 269 (2013).

[70] Compare *Woodward*, 760 N.E.2d at 269 (requiring proof of the deceased genetic parent's affirmative consent to both posthumous reproduction and support of any resulting child), with Burns v. Astrue, 289 P.3d 551, 553 (Utah 2012) (holding that "an agreement leaving preserved frozen semen to the deceased donor's wife does not, without more, confer on the donor the status of a parent for purposes of social security benefits").

[71] See Jessica Knouse, Liberty, Equality, and Parentage in the Era of Posthumous Conception, 27 J.L. & Health 9 (2014).

limits as "inappropriate." UPC §2-104 cmt. (2019). Why? Should class gifts to "children" include those born of posthumous pregnancies? See id. §2-705 cmt. (construing class gifts to accord with intestate succession rules).[72]

5. *Bequeathing genetic material.* Is genetic material property that one owns? Does one have a right to bequeath gametes or embryos for use in post-humous reproduction? In a famous will contest between the decedent's adult children from a prior marriage and his girlfriend, to whom he had bequeathed frozen sperm before his suicide, the court deemed the decedent's interest in his sperm to be "property" subject to distribution under the pro-bate court's jurisdiction and ruled that the girlfriend's use for insemination would not violate any public policy. The court subsequently ordered release of the sperm to the girlfriend without deciding whether any resulting child could inherit as decedent's heir.[73]

B. IN THE GAMETE MARKET

1. PARENTAGE: THE MEANS OF CONCEPTION

In re M.F.

938 N.E.2d 1256 (Ind. Ct. App. 2010)

FRIEDLANDER, Judge. . . .

[This is an appeal in a suit against W.M. (Father) to establish his paternity of two children, M.F. and C.F., born to J.F. (Mother). The suit arose from the following facts:] [I]n 1996, Mother was cohabiting and in a committed, long-term relationship with a woman we shall refer to henceforth as Life Partner. They wanted a child, so Mother and Father, who was a friend of Mother's, agreed that he would provide sperm with which to impregnate Mother. After [M.F.] was conceived but a few weeks before M.F. was born, the parties signed an agreement (the Donor Agreement) prepared by counsel for Mother [which] contained the following provisions:

> 6. *Waiver and Release by Mother.* Mother hereby waives all rights to child support and financial assistance from Donor . . . .
> 7. *Waiver and Release by Donor.* Donor hereby waives all rights to custody of or visitation with such child . . . .
> 8. *Mutual Covenant Not to Sue.* Mother and Donor mutually agree to forever refrain from initiating, pressing, or in any way aiding or proceeding upon an action to establish legal paternity of the child due to be born on or about September 19, 1996.

[72] See also In re Martin B., 841 N.Y.S.2d 207 (Sur. Ct. 2007) (ruling that the terms "issue" and "descendants" in trust documents include children conceived with cryopreserved semen of the grantor's adult son when the son was alive at the trust's execution).
[73] Hecht v. Super. Ct., 20 Cal. Rptr. 2d 275 (Ct. App. 1993), 59 Cal. Rptr. 2d 222, 228 (Ct. App. 1996). See also *Robertson*, 262 Cal. Rptr. 3d at 227-233 (rejecting widow's negligence claims for tissue bank's loss of husband's sperm because she was not entitled to use sperm for posthu-mous conception); Kurchner v. State Farm Fire & Cas. Co., 858 So. 2d 1220 (Fla. Dist. Ct. App. 2003) (treating frozen semen as personal property, so that its destruction is not covered by insurance policy for bodily injury).

[After conception with help again from Father,] C.F. was born to [M]other seven years later, in 2003. Mother and Life Partner were still together at the time.

Mother and Life Partner's relationship ended sometime around 2008, when the [two] children were approximately twelve and five years old, respectively. [Mother sought public assistance, so the county prosecutor filed, on Mother's behalf, a petition to establish Father's paternity, for purposes of obtaining child support from him. Father cited the Donor Agreement as his defense. Despite DNA evidence of his genetic paternity, the trial court denied the petition to establish paternity, based on contract grounds. This appeal followed.]

[Despite the presence of all elements of an otherwise valid contract, we have here] a specific kind of contract, i.e., one between sperm donor and recipient regarding the conception of a child. . . . Our Supreme Court discussed contracts of this particular variety at some length in Straub v. B.M.T. by Todd, 645 N.E.2d 597 (Ind. 1994). [Straub] noted that other jurisdictions that have addressed support issues arising from situations involving artificial fertilization have done so via the adoption of statutes based on the Uniform Parentage Act (UPA) and the Uniform Status of Children of Assisted Conception Act (USCACA). [Straub also noted] that "[t]he majority of states adopting [similar] legislation . . . hold that the donor of semen . . . provided to a licensed physician for use in the artificial fertilization of a woman, is treated under the law as if he . . . were not the natural parent of the child thereby conceived." [Straub,] 645 N.E.2d at 600 [(citing Jhordan v. Mary K., 224 Cal. Rptr. 530 (Ct. App. 1986)).]

[Although Straub explicitly addressed "the emerging contract principles surrounding reproductive technology," the parties in Straub had not used alternative insemination or other technologies, but rather sexual intercourse. Thus, on] the critical question of the enforceability of assisted conception contracts in Indiana, [Straub] held that the agreement [in that case] failed on several counts, including: (1) insemination was achieved via intercourse ("there is no such thing as 'artificial insemination by intercourse'", [645 N.E.2d] at 601); (2) the agreement appeared "for all the world as a rather traditional attempt to forego this child's right to support from [the donor]", id.; and (3) the agreement contained "none of the formalities and protections which the legislatures and courts of other jurisdictions have thought necessary to address when enabling childless individuals to bear children." Id. Notably, however, the Court in Straub appears to have signaled that assisted conception contracts might be enforceable in Indiana in certain circumstances. . . . Straub may be fairly read as endorsing the view that such contracts may be valid if they comport with [certain legal] requirements. . . .

[B]oth Mother and Father appear to concede that the viability of the Donor Agreement in the instant case depends upon the manner in which insemination occurred. Per Straub, if insemination occurred via intercourse, the Donor Agreement would be unenforceable as against public policy. . . . Thus, an apparently complicated issue can be boiled down to simple legal question — who bore the burden of proof [on the method of conception]?

In this case, the parties entered into a facially valid contract whereby Mother agreed that she would not seek to establish paternity of M.F. in

Father. Mother seeks to invalidate that Donor Agreement on the ground that the manner of insemination renders the Donor Agreement void as against public policy. As such, she seeks to avoid the contract. We conclude that this case is governed by the rule providing that a party that seeks to avoid a contract bears the burden of proof on matters of avoidance. . . . Thus, Mother bore the burden of proving that [conception occurred by intercourse, not alternative insemination, in turn rendering] the Donor Agreement unenforceable.

We . . . can find no indication of the manner in which Mother was inseminated with respect to the first pregnancy. . . . Therefore, Mother failed to prove that insemination [occurred] in such a way as to render the Donor Agreement unenforceable and void as against public policy. [Hence,] the trial court did not err in denying her petition to establish paternity with respect to M.F.

We pause at this point to make several observations about [an] area of concern expressed by the dissent, i.e., the formalities of the contract itself. Specifically, we address our colleague's concern that our holding today might enable parties to easily escape the responsibility of supporting one's biological child [by] concocting an informal, spur-of-the-moment written instrument whereby the biological mother and father agree that the father is absolved of any responsibility in connection with the child. Two aspects of our ruling prevent this possibility. First, . . . we hold today that a physician must be involved in the process of artificial insemination. At a minimum, this involvement includes the requirement that the semen first be provided to the physician. . . .

Second, we do not mean to sanction the view that a writing consisting of a few lines scribbled on the back of a scrap of paper found lying about will suffice in this kind of case. To the contrary, the instrument in question must reflect the parties' careful consideration of the implications of such an agreement and a thorough understanding of its meaning and import. The Donor Agreement in the instant case easily meets these requirements . . . . In fact, Paragraph 21 provides, "Donor specifically acknowledges that the Agreement was drafted by counsel retained by Mother, and that he has been provided full opportunity to review this Agreement with counsel of his own choosing before executing this Agreement." The structure and sophistication of the document leaves little doubt about the veracity of this paragraph.

The Donor Agreement itself is a six-page, twenty-four-paragraph document that covers in detail matters such as acknowledgment of rights and obligations, waiver, mutual consent not to sue, a consent to adopt, a hold-harmless clause, mediation and arbitration, penalties for failure to comply, amending the agreement, severability, a four-corners clause, and a choice-of-laws provision. [Although] we are reluctant to set forth specific requirements with respect to such a contract's form and content, . . . parties who execute a contract less formal and thorough than this one do so at their own peril.

Although we have affirmed the trial court's order with respect to M.F., we address sua sponte an issue not separately presented by the parties, i.e., the correctness of the order denying the petition to establish paternity with respect to the second child, C.F. In its order, the trial court found: "Shortly before the birth of the first child, the mother and Respondent entered into a written agreement stating that the Respondent would not be responsible for the child *and any further children which might result from the Respondent's donated sperm."* The highlighted language reflects the trial court's determination that the Donor Agreement applied to C.F. as well as M.F. We conclude this construction of the Donor Agreement is erroneous.

The Donor Agreement provided as follows:

> 2. Donor has provided his semen to Mother for the purpose of inseminating Mother, and as a result, Mother has become pregnant and is expected to give birth on or about September 19, 1996....

Throughout the remainder of the Donor Agreement, the product of insemination, i.e., the subject of the Donor Agreement, is referred to as either "the child" or "such child".... [The contract] cannot be construed to apply to future children conceived as a result of artificial insemination involving Mother and Father. Therefore, the trial court erred in holding that a valid, enforceable contract existed that would prohibit an action to establish paternity of C.F. in Father. In view of the fact that DNA testing established, and Father concedes, that he is the biological father of C.F., this cause is remanded with instructions to grant Mother's petition to establish paternity with respect to C.F....

Crone, Judge, concurring in part and dissenting in part.

... Because the core of this dispute falls squarely within the province of family law ... and because our default position in Indiana is that a parent is legally obligated to support his biological child, I would hold that Father must bear the burden of proving that the terms of the Donor Agreement are consistent with public policy and/or that the Donor Agreement was performed consistent with public policy. In other words, as the party seeking to avoid his support obligation, Father should bear the burden of proving the validity of an exception to a well-established rule.

I agree with the majority that our supreme court in *Straub* "appears to have signaled that assisted conception contracts might be enforceable in Indiana in certain circumstances." I would hold that those circumstances must be extremely limited.... At the very least, an assisted conception contract should provide that a donor's semen must be given to a licensed physician and that the artificial insemination must be performed by (or at least under the supervision of) the physician. Such a provision would both impress upon the parties the seriousness of their endeavor and safeguard the health of everyone involved. [Physician involvement can also create a formal, documented structure for the donor-recipient relationship, preventing misunderstandings between the parties.] I believe that such prerequisites to finding a valid exception to the general obligation to support would be consistent with *Straub* and a natural extension of its reasoning....

Patton v. Vanterpool

806 S.E.2d 493 (Ga. 2017)

Hunstein, Justice....

In January 2014, after approximately three years of marriage, David Patton ("Appellant") filed a complaint for divorce against Jocelyn Vanterpool, M.D. ("Appellee"). During the pendency of the divorce, the parties consented to Appellee undergoing IVF treatment,[1] which would eventually utilize both donor ova and donor sperm; on November 10, 2014, Appellee traveled to the Czech Republic for the IVF procedure. Four days later, on November 14, 2014, a final judgment and decree of divorce was entered in the divorce action. The divorce decree incorporated the parties' settlement agreement, which reflects that, at the time of the agreement, the parties neither had nor were expecting children produced of the marriage.

Approximately 29 weeks later, on June 6, 2015, Appellee gave birth as a result of the November 2014 IVF procedure. Appellee subsequently moved the superior court to set aside the decree of divorce, seeking to include the minor child in the divorce agreement . . . . [After the court denied this motion, she instituted a paternity action, relying on OCGA §19-7-21, and sought child support.] In response, Appellant argued that he did not meaningfully consent to IVF and that, even if he did, OCGA §19-7-21 is unconstitutional. [Appellee prevailed, and Appellant appeals, arguing the statute does not apply and, if it does, it is unconstitutional.]

OCGA §19-7-21 concerns the parent-child relationship generally, stating as follows: "All children born within wedlock or within the usual period of gestation thereafter who have been conceived by means of artificial insemination are irrebuttably presumed legitimate if both spouses have consented in writing to the use and administration of artificial insemination." At issue here is the term "artificial insemination," which is not defined by statute. Artificial insemination, which has been in use since the late 18th century and has been so named since the early 19th century, see Kara W. Swanson, Adultery By Doctor: Artificial Insemination, 1890-1945, 87 Chi.-Kent L. Rev. 591 (2012), has been consistently defined as the "introduction of semen into the uterus or oviduct by other than natural means . . . in order to increase the probability of conception." Webster's Third International Dictionary 124 (1967). . . . We conclude, given the history and well-established meaning and use of the term "artificial insemination," that the term is not ambiguous as it is used in OCGA §19-7-21.[5] We now must address whether artificial insemination includes IVF.

In vitro fertilization was first described in the 1970s, see Janet L. Dolgin, The Law Debates the Family: Reproductive Transformations, 7 Yale J. L. & Feminisim 37 (1995), and involves "[a] procedure [in] which an egg is fertilized

---

1. The record suggests that Appellee wanted to have a child but could not undergo the procedure without Appellant's consent.

5. Appellee contends that this Court should adopt the reasoning of Maryland's highest court, which has concluded that the phrase "artificial insemination" is "ambiguous" because there are numerous ways in which artificial insemination may be accomplished. See Sieglein v. Schmidt, [136 A.3d 751, 759-761 (Md. 2016)]. The Sieglein decision explains that sperm may be introduced via intrafollicular insemination (injecting semen directly into an ovarian follicle), intraperitoneal insemination (injecting semen into the peritoneal cavity), intratubal/intrafallopian insemination (injecting semen into the fallopian tube) or intrauterine insemination (injecting semen directly into the uterus). Id. at 760, n.13. The Maryland court also noted that artificial insemination could be used with sperm from a spouse (homologous insemination), commonly known as Artificial Insemination by Husband ("AIH"), or from a donor (heterologous insemination), otherwise known as Artificial Insemination by Donor ("AID").

We cannot agree that a decades-old term is rendered ambiguous simply because the procedure may utilize donor sperm or various locations in the female reproductive tract; irrespective of the use of donor sperm or the location of injection, sperm is being introduced to the female reproductive tract for the purpose of encouraging in vivo fertilization.

outside a woman's body and then inserted into the womb for gestation." Black's Law Dictionary 956 (10th ed. 2014). . . . To summarize, while artificial insemination involves the introduction of sperm to the female reproductive tract to encourage fertilization, IVF involves implanting a fertilized egg into a female; though each procedure aims for pregnancy, the procedures are distinct, and we conclude that the term "artificial insemination" does not encompass IVF. . . .

We are unswayed by Appellee's argument that such a plain-language construction of OCGA §19-7-21 is unnecessarily restrictive. While Georgia law favors legitimation, OCGA §19-7-21 creates an *irrebuttable presumption*, which is generally disfavored in the law . . . . Further, the irrebuttable presumption of legitimacy in OCGA §19-7-21 is an exception to the general rule, found in OCGA §19-7-20 (b), that legitimacy may be disputed, and an expansive reading of OCGA §19-7-21 would allow the exception to swallow the rule.[7]

Appellee also contends that when the General Assembly enacted OCGA §19-7-21 in 1964, that body could not have conceived of the advent of IVF (and related medical advancements) . . . . Although OCGA §19-7-21 was enacted over 50 years ago — at a time when IVF and various assisted reproductive technologies were not yet developed — recent amendments to other portions of Title 19 make plain that the General Assembly is now well acquainted with the developments in reproductive medicine. In May 2009, the General Assembly passed the "Domestic Relations — Guardian — Social Services — Options to Adoption Act," which amended Chapter 8 of Title 19 to address, among other things, the custody, relinquishment, and adoption of embryos. See Ga. L. 2009, pp. 800-803. OCGA §19-8-40, which was created by the 2009 Act, defines both embryo and embryo transfer, which "means the medical procedure of physically placing an embryo into the uterus of a female." OCGA §19-8-40 (3). . . . Accordingly, this is not a case in which the General Assembly has failed to anticipate scientific and medical advancements, but, instead, the General Assembly has chosen not to act; we must, therefore, presume that OCGA §19-7-21 remains the will of the legislature. [Reversed.]

McFADDEN, Presiding Judge, dissenting.

OCGA §19-7-21 contains a latent ambiguity. The ambiguity arose because the General Assembly failed to anticipate subsequent advances in medical technology when it described the class of children under the statute's protection. In resolving that ambiguity we are required to apply a rule that is in our current Code, was in our first Code, can be traced back to Blackstone's Commentaries on the Law of England, and so was part of the "common law and statutes of England in force prior to May 14, 1776 [that, in 1784,] were adopted in this [s]tate by statute." Often called the "mischief rule," as Blackstone's Commentaries refer to "the old law, the mischief, and the remedy," that rule is now codified at OCGA §1-3-1 (a): "In all interpretations of statutes, the courts shall look diligently for the intention of the

---

7. Though Appellee may not establish legitimacy through OCGA §19-7-21, we do not speak to whether Appellee may establish legal paternity through other means, such as OCGA §19-7-20.

General Assembly, keeping in view at all times the old law, the evil, and the remedy...."

That rule directs us to the conclusion that the intention of the General Assembly was to protect children like S., the child in this case. So I respectfully dissent....

NOTES AND QUESTIONS ON *M.F.* AND *PATTON*

1. *M.F.'s rationale.* The parties and the court all agree that W.M. is the genetic father of both children. Why does the court conclude he is the legal father only of the younger sibling? The U.S. Supreme Court has emphasized the equal treatment of children, regardless of the circumstances of their birth, in striking down discrimination once aimed at nonmarital children. Such "illegitimacy" cases often emphasize that it is "illogical and unjust" to disadvantage children based on the circumstances of their birth, when they have no say in such matters, as recalled in *Capato*, supra.[74] To what extent does the outcome in *M.F.* depart from these precedents — because one sibling has two parents and sources of child support while the other has only one? (Obviously, children cannot control the circumstances of their conception.)

2. *Sexual conception.* Why should the means of conception matter in determining whether legal parentage follows from genetic parentage? Why is "there is no such thing as 'artificial insemination by intercourse,'" as the court observes?[75] What policies do you see at work?

Consistent with the dominant approach, the *M.F.* court recognizes the genetic father as the legal father of the younger sibling, whom its presumption treats as a child conceived sexually. Many courts justify this approach on the ground that the benefits to the child of additional child support trump a man's interest in avoiding unwanted fatherhood, even when he can establish intentionally false assurances that the woman with whom he engaged sexually was using contraception.[76] Such contraception-fraud cases reveal underlying principles of "personal responsibility" for sexual conduct and assumptions about the private nature of support obligations.[77] Essentially, a man who ejaculates assumes the risk of fatherhood and the financial commitments it entails.[78]

How would you reconcile such cases with constitutional protection for procreative liberty, as elaborated in *Rooks*, supra? To the extent that keeping dependency private guides the analysis, why is W.M. the appropriate candidate for responsibility at least for the second child? What about Life Partner?[79] Recall Elisa B. v. Superior Court, Chapter 1, section C. As late as 2020, Indiana was still fighting in court the obligation to apply its

---

[74] E.g., Gomez v. Perez, 409 U.S. 535, 538 (1973).

[75] But see In re Parental Responsibilities of A.R.L., 318 P.3d 581 (Colo. Ct. App. 2013) (allowing mother's female partner to petition for recognition as child's second parent and excluding "donor" from consideration, despite sexual conception).

[76] See, e.g., Dubay v. Wells, 506 F.3d 422 (6th Cir. 2007); Wallis v. Smith, 22 P.3d 682 (N.M. Ct. App. 2001).

[77] See, e.g., N.E. v. Hedges, 391 F.3d 832 (6th Cir. 2004).

[78] See, e.g., Michael J. Higdon, Fatherhood by Conscription: Nonconsensual Insemination and the Duty of Child Support, 46 Ga. L. Rev. 407 (2012) (critiquing doctrine).

[79] Melissa Murray, Family Law's Doctrines, 163 U. Pa. L. Rev. 1985, 2017 (2015).

presumption of legitimacy equally to children born to mothers married to women.[80]

What explains the exception, applied in *M.F.*, for genetic fathers by non-sexual conception ("artificial insemination" that meets particular requirements)? Don't both children in *M.F.* equally need support, regardless of the means of conception?[81] How might the different treatment of sexual conception versus conception by alternative insemination unfairly disadvantage gay men seeking fatherhood?[82]

3. *Alternative insemination.* Alternative (or "artificial") insemination as a medical response to male infertility using the husband's semen (AIH) reportedly began in the 1790s and using donor semen (AID) in 1884.[83] The popularity of AID grew over the years, especially during the "baby boom" following World War II, a time that also saw a rise in white infant adoptions.[84] In 1987, the number of women using alternative insemination in the United States was 172,000; between 2006-2010 the number rose to about 714,000 who had ever used it (1.7 percent of women aged 25-44).[85]

a. *Married women and AID.* When courts and legislatures first confronted AID, the typical scenario featured a married woman and her infertile husband. Rejecting early analogies to adultery, given the physician's involvement, and using doctrines such as the presumption of legitimacy and equitable estoppel, courts recognized the husband as the legal father.[86] As *Patton* notes, Georgia codified this approach in 1964. To ensure termination of any parental rights of the donor, some courts allowed the husband to adopt the child.[87]

Eighteen jurisdictions followed the original UPA, which recognized as the father a husband who consents in writing to AID performed by a licensed physician and, as noted in *M.F.*, stated that the "donor of semen provided to a licensed physician for artificial insemination of a woman other than the donor's wife is treated in law as if he were not the natural father ...." UPA §5(b) (1973). The latter rule often goes by the name "donor nonpaternity."

---

[80] See Henderson v. Box, 947 F.3d 482 (7th Cir. 2020).

[81] See Susan Frelich Appleton, Illegitimacy and Sex, Old and New, 20 Am U. J. Gender Soc. Pol'y & L. 347, 372 (2012). For another case in which the would-be donor failed to satisfy contractual requirements and thus was declared the child's father, with support duties, see Claudia B. v. Darrin M., 185 A.D. 3d 453 (N.Y. App. Div. 2020).

[82] See Elizabeth J. Levy, Virgin Fathers: Paternity Law, Assisted Reproductive Technology, and the Legal Bias Against Gay Dads, 22 Am. U. J. Gender Soc. Pol'y & L. 893 (2014).

[83] See Lee M. Silver, Remaking Eden: How Genetic Engineering and Cloning Will Transform the American Family 178-179 (1998); Kara W. Swanson, Banking on the Body: The Market in Blood, Milk, and Sperm in Modern America (2014); Gaia Bernstein, The Socio-Legal Acceptance of New Technologies: A Close Look at Artificial Insemination, 77 Wash. L. Rev. 1035 (2002) (tracing history, diffusion into society, and the roles of the medical profession and law).

[84] See Elaine Tyler May, Barren in the Promised Land: Childless Americans and the Pursuit of Happiness 75-78, 147-149 (1997).

[85] Compare Congress of the United States, Office of Technology Assessment, Artificial Insemination in the United States: Summary of a 1987 Survey — Background Paper 3 (1988), with Anjani Chandra et al., Infertility Service Use in the United States: Data From the National Survey of Family Growth, 1982–2010, 73 National Health Statistics Reports 1, 7, 15 (Jan. 22, 2014), https://www.cdc.gov/nchs/data/nhsr/nhsr073.pdf.

[86] See, e.g., In re Adoption of Anonymous, 345 N.Y.S.2d 430 (Sur. Ct. 1973).

[87] Compare Welborn v. Doe, 394 S.E.2d 732 (Va. Ct. App. 1990), with In re Adoption of a Minor, 29 N.E.3d 830 (Mass. 2015).

b. *Unmarried women and AID.* Early on, courts had trouble determining how to apply these principles when unmarried women used AID, with some reading their statutes to apply only to married women and concluding that the donor, if known, must be the second parent.[88] Later, consistent with *M.F.*'s conclusions about the older sibling, several jurisdictions recognized a single mother as the sole legal parent of children conceived by donor insemination. For example, California explicitly departed from the UPA in order to provide for donor nonpaternity when unmarried women use AID.[89] In In re K.M.H., 169 P.3d 1025 (Kan. 2007), the majority rejected the paternity claim of the genetic father, who wanted to exercise visitation and provide support, because his failure to "opt in" to fatherhood via written agreement, required by Kansas statute, made him a donor, with no legal status; the court also upheld the constitutionality of the statute. In Ferguson v. McKiernan, 940 A.2d 1236 (Pa. 2007), the woman unsuccessfully sought child support from the genetic father, notwithstanding an agreement that he would have no parental responsibilities if he would donate sperm to her, with the majority upholding the contract. What interests and policies explain such results?[90] While protecting donors and facilitating reproductive choices, do such results undermine the interests of children and the policy of privatized dependency? Does procreative liberty include the right to be a solo parent?[91]

c. *Parentage by intent: marriage equality and beyond.* Even before marriage equality, courts began applying the parentage principles developed for AID and married women more broadly. *Elisa B.* (Chapter 1, section C) shows how courts can use intent and function to identify the second parent when one woman in an unmarried same-sex couple conceives by AID. With the advent of marriage equality, courts turned to the presumption of legitimacy to recognize a mother's wife as the donor-conceived child's second parent.[92] Revisions to the UPA capture these developments, decentering both gender and marriage and emphasizing intent:

Section 702. Parental Status of Donor.

A donor is not a parent of a child conceived by assisted reproduction.

Section 703. Parentage of Child of Assisted Reproduction.

An individual who consents under Section 704 to assisted reproduction by a woman with the intent to be a parent of a child conceived by the assisted reproduction is a parent of the child.

---

[88] E.g., C.M. v. C.C., 377 A.2d 821 (N.J. Super. Ct. 1977).

[89] See K.M. v. E.G., 117 P.3d 673, 679-680 (Cal. 2005) (recounting legislation's history).

[90] See, e.g., Mary Ziegler, Earned Rights, 44 N.Y.U. Rev. L. & Soc. Change 261, 291 (2020) (theorizing that genetic father had not "earned" right to be recognized because he failed to comply with statute).

[91] See Marsha Garrison, Law Making for Baby Making: An Interpretive Approach to the Determination of Legal Parentage, 113 Harv. L. Rev. 835, 906 (2000) ("our legal system grants no parent, male or female, the right to be a sole parent"). But see Ferguson v. McKiernan, 940 A.2d 1236, 1248 (Pa. 2007) (noting that these children would never have been born, absent agreement).

[92] E.g., McLaughlin v. Jones, 401 P.3d 492 (Ariz. 2017). Cf. Wendy G-M v. Erin G-M, 985 N.Y.S.2d 845 (Sup. Ct. 2014) (relying on common law presumption); In re Madrone, 350 P.3d 495 (Or. Ct. App. 2015) (suggesting that presumption applies only to married same-sex couples or those who would have married if they could).

Section 704. Consent to Assisted Reproduction.

(a) Except as otherwise provided in subsection (b), the consent described in Section 703 must be in a record signed by a woman giving birth to a child conceived by assisted reproduction and an individual who intends to be a parent of the child.

(b) Failure to consent in a record as required by subsection (a), before, on, or after birth of the child, does not preclude the court from finding consent to parentage if:

(1) the woman or the individual proves by clear-and-convincing evidence the existence of an express agreement entered into before conception that the individual and the woman intended they both would be parents of the child; or

(2) the woman and the individual for the first two years of the child's life, including any period of temporary absence, resided together in the same household with the child and both openly held out the child as the individual's child, unless the individual dies or becomes incapacitated before the child attains two years of age or the child dies before the child attains two years of age, in which case the court may find consent under this subsection to parentage if a party proves by clear-and-convincing evidence that the woman and the individual intended to reside together in the same household with the child and both intended the individual would openly hold out the child as the individual's child, but the individual was prevented from carrying out that intent by death or incapacity.

UPA §§702-704 (2017). Note that the absence of written consent does not preclude showing consent by other means. What problems might that approach present?[93]

Note also that the gender-neutral criterion of intent not only determines parentage of children of assisted reproduction but also affects the legal treatment of donors. Accordingly, the rule of "donor nonpaternity" first developed in the case law for AID has become a rule of "donor nonparentage" and governs ova donors too. The court in *Patton* assumes this principle, without analysis.

d. *Physician's participation.* Does the traditional understanding of AID as a medical treatment for infertility explain why *M.F.* requires physician assistance in order to "cut off" the donor's parental status?[94] What purposes does this requirement serve? Although the original UPA (cited in *M.F.*) required physician participation for donor nonparentage to apply, later versions purposely omitted this requirement. UPA §702 cmt. (2002) & UPA Art. 7 cmt. (2017). What explains the change?

e. *Gender implications.* Despite physician-participation requirements, women have long performed alternative insemination themselves, without

---

[93] See, e.g., Matter of W.L., 441 P.3d 495 (Kan. Ct. App. 2019), rev. granted (Kan. Sept. 3, 2019).
[94] See, e.g., Bruce v. Boardwine, 770 S.E.2d 774 (Va. Ct. App. 2015); Jhordan C. v. Mary K., 224 Cal. Rptr. 530 (Ct. App. 1986).

medical assistance. What are the consequences for attempts to restrict and regulate the practice? Evaluate the observations of Judge Posner:

> Artificial insemination . . . is rich with social implications. [A]s a practical matter, it places lesbian custody of children beyond the reach of governmental regulation. Beyond that, it allows women to escape having to share parental rights with men, since the sperm donor, whether provided through the woman's physician or through a sperm bank, is anonymous. It therefore accelerates the shift of economic power from men to women. . . .[95]

4. *Alternative insemination versus IVF.* Why does the *Patton* majority decline to extend Georgia's parentage rules for AID to IVF? The high courts in other states, including Maryland (as noted in the majority's footnote 5) and Massachusetts,[96] have read their alternative insemination statutes broadly to cover IVF. True, IVF requires medical intervention, while AID can be accomplished without such assistance, but do the procedures differ in ways that justify variations in applicable parentage regimes?

Evaluate *Patton's* argument that the AID statute would be unconstitutional if it made him a parent under these facts. What result should a court reach on remand regarding Patton's parentage under the rebuttable presumption of legitimacy (the question left open by the majority in footnote 7)? On remand, the court decided Vanterpool was estopped from claiming Patton's paternity, based on the divorce decree stating there were no children of the marriage. The court of appeals affirmed. Vanterpool v. Patton, 835 S.E.2d 407 (Ga. Ct. App. 2019).[97]

5. *Intent.* What would the UPA's intent-based parentage mean if applied in *Patton?* What role should Patton's consent play in the analysis? Should it estop him from challenging parentage? What weight should his claimed failure to give "meaningful consent" receive? According to the court of appeals, the agreement Patton signed "included standard, preprinted language stating that Patton would accept the newborn child as his own with all parental rights and responsibilities," and he argued that he signed "under duress."[98]

The UPA allows a spouse limited opportunities for disputing parentage of a child of assisted conception, including when there was no consent, no cohabitation since the probable time of the assisted reproduction, and no holding out of the child. UPA §705(b) (2017). In addition, timing becomes critical under the UPA. If the embryo transfer that resulted in pregnancy occurred after November 14, the date of the divorce decree, then husband would not be the legal father of the child unless he consented in a record to parentage of a child from a post-divorce procedure. Id. §706.

---

[95] Richard A. Posner, Sex and Reason 421 (1992). See generally Courtney Megan Cahill, Regulating at the Margins: Non-Traditional Kinship and the Legal Regulation of Intimate and Family Life, 54 Ariz. L. Rev. 43 (2012).

[96] *Adoption of a Minor,* 29 N.E.3d 830.

[97] See generally June Carbone & Naomi Cahn, *Jane the Virgin* and Other Stories of Unintentional Parenthood, 7 U.C. Irvine 511 (2017).

[98] Id. at 408. Cf. In re Marriage of Buzzanca, 72 Cal. Rptr. 2d 280 (Ct. App. 1998) (holding husband's signature on the consent form on the eve of divorce made him the legal father, despite wife's assurances to him of her sole responsibility for the child).

5. *Commodification.* Although the couple in *M.F.* turned to a friend and *Patton*'s facts do not identify the source of the donor ova and sperm, many women and couples who pursue alternative insemination or IVF with donor gametes obtain the materials from a bank or a fertility clinic. Focusing on alternative insemination, Professor Martha Ertman offers the following description:

> . . . AI is a literal market and a relatively free, open market. . . . Markets, by definition, exist where supply and demand determine prices for the transfer of goods and services. Banks and recipients demand sperm, and donors and banks supply it. Suppliers (donors and sperm banks) transfer sperm on the condition of donor anonymity and indemnity for any injury or illness. Buyers (sperm banks and prospective mothers), in turn, demand medical and social information about the donor, further protections against disease transmission, and anonymity. . . . Moreover, lack of regulation and a relatively low price for the gametes means that it is both an open market in which a large number of people can participate, and a free market that flourishes because of its comparative freedom from regulation. . . .
>
> Alternative insemination generally involves at least two separate transactions. The sperm bank first purchases sperm from a donor and subsequently sells the sperm to a woman who uses it to become a mother. . . . While the transactions differ in important respects, both transactions commodify gametes, and in doing so commodify parental rights and responsibilities. . . .[99]

Indeed, prospective parents can shop on websites profiling donors' physical descriptions, interests, available gamete supply, openness to identity release, and the like.[100] For sperm, shipping for at-home insemination in response to COVID-19 is available.[101] What does this state of affairs mean for adoption?[102]

Ertman's analysis proceeds to highlight the negative implications of such commodification as well as its benefits, including facilitation of new family forms. How should law respond? Specifically, what regulations and restrictions may state or federal actors directly impose on this this market and on practitioners of ARTs, consistent with individual rights of procreative liberty?

---

[99] Martha M. Ertman, What's Wrong with a Parenthood Market? A New and Improved Theory of Commodification, 82 N.C. L. Rev. 1, 14-16 (2003). See generally Baby Markets: Money and the New Politics of Creating Families (Michele Bratcher Goodwin ed., 2010).

[100] See, e.g., Rene Almeling, Sex Cells: The Medical Market for Eggs and Sperm (2011); Growing Generations, Find an Egg Donor-How it Works, https://www.growinggenerations.com/egg-donor-program/intended-parents/egg-donation-program-overview/.

[101] See, e.g., California Cryobank by Generate Life Sciences, Donor Search, Start Your Family at Home, https://www.cryobank.com/search/.

[102] Susan Frelich Appleton, Adoption in the Age of Reproductive Technology, 2004 U. Chi. Legal F. 393. See also Richard F. Storrow, Marginalizing Adoption Through the Regulation of Assisted Reproduction, 35 Cap. U. L. Rev. 479 (2006) (including international comparisons).

Depictions in Popular Culture: The Kids Are All Right (2010)

What makes a family? Who belongs, and who is an interloper? *The Kids Are All Right*, one of many films centered on sperm donation, poses such questions in the era of "the new kinship."[103]

Nic (Annette Bening) and Jules (Julianne Moore) seem to be picture-perfect lesbian parents who have it all, including two teenage children, Joni and Laser, a beautiful suburban home, and occasional sex, although one senses that this long marriage has seen much better days. Friction arises from Nic's demanding work as a physician and her habit of putting down Jules, a stay-at-home mom struggling to figure out her "next act" now that the children are grown. With at most lukewarm support from Nic, Jules announces her interest in launching a landscaping business.

During the summer before Joni will leave for college, Laser asks his less curious older sister to contact the sperm bank and obtain information about their up-until-now unknown donor because at age 18 she can do so. Joni agrees, but warns Laser that he might be disappointed.

Joni and Laser connect with Paul (Mark Ruffalo), who explains that he sold his sperm when he was 19 in an effort to help people who wanted children and to make some money. Although he now runs a successful restaurant and grows organic vegetables, Paul never settled down and comes across as sincere, slightly awkward, and commitment-free, suggesting that the 19-year-old who donated sperm is still alive and well inside.

Paul and the children forge meaningful connections — no surprise given that teens routinely appreciate all that adults other than their parents have to offer. At an initial family gathering, Paul hires Jules to work on a landscaping project at his home. Nic acts increasingly stressed, taking it out on both Jules and the children. She confesses to Jules that the problem is Paul, whom she feels is taking over her family. She's more correct than she consciously knows because the landscaping project has provided the opportunity for a sexual relationship between Jules and Paul, with Paul confessing he's falling in love with Jules. Nic feels shattered when she realizes what is happening, and considerable pain ripples through the entire family. When Paul tries to apologize to Joni just before she will depart for college and asks if he can ever see her again, she answers in despair: "I just wish you could have been . . . better." As Nic, Jules, and Laser drive Joni to school, the process of family repair begins.

---

[103] For other films centered on sperm donation, see, e.g., Made in America (1996); The Switch (2010); Starbuck (2011); Delivery Man (2013). See also She Hate Me (2004) (sperm donation by sexual conception). "The new kinship" is Naomi Cahn's term. Naomi Cahn, The New Kinship: Constructing Donor-Conceived Families (2013).

The film, released in 2010, garnered critical acclaim for both its art and its groundbreaking portrait of contemporary family life. As one reviewer wrote:

> [The film] is so canny in its insights and so agile in its negotiation of complex emotions that it deserves to stand on its own. It is outrageously funny without ever exaggerating for comic effect, and heartbreaking with only minimal melodramatic embellishment.
>
> But its originality — the thrilling, vertiginous sense of never having seen anything quite like it before — also arises from the particular circumstances of the family at its heart. There is undeniable novelty to a movie about a lesbian couple whose two teenage children were conceived with the help of an anonymous sperm donor. Families like this are hardly uncommon in the real world. . . .[104]

So, what does make a family? And what meaning(s) do you ascribe to the film's title?

---

2. HEALTH, SAFETY, AND PUBLIC POLICY REGULATION

Norman v. Xytex Corporation

_____ S.E.2d _____ (2020 WL 5752325) (Ga., Sept. 28, 2020)

Peterson, Justice.

"Respect for life and the rights proceeding from it are at the heart of our legal system and, broader still, our civilization." Fulton-DeKalb Hosp. Auth. v. Graves, [314 S.E.2d 653 (Ga. 1984)]. For this reason, this Court has repeatedly refused to allow damages in tort that necessarily presume that life itself can ever be an injury. See, e.g., [Atlanta Obstetrics & Gynecology Group v. Abelson, 398 S.E.2d 557 (Ga. 1990)] . . . . But that rule does not fully resolve this appeal, which is about what sort of damages the rule actually bars.

Wendy and Janet Norman allege that Xytex Corporation, a sperm bank, sold them human sperm under false pretenses about the characteristics of its donor, and that the child conceived with that sperm now suffers from a variety of impairments inherited from the sperm donor. . . . Because we are reviewing an order on a motion to dismiss, we take the allegations in the complaint as true and resolve all doubts in favor of the Normans. In that light, Xytex represented that it carefully screened the personal health, criminal history, and family history of all donors; that donors were put through rigorous physical exams and interviews to confirm the accuracy of the information donors provided; and that because of its thorough screening process, fewer than five percent of candidates became donors. Xytex also represented that it required sperm donors to update their medical history every six months; that the company would update the donors' profiles with any

---

[104] A.O. Scott, Meet the Sperm Donor: Modern Family Ties, N.Y. Times, July 9, 2010, at C1.

new information; and that, if the company received "medically significant" information about a donor, it would notify patients who used that donor's sperm. Xytex promoted Donor #9623 as one of its "best" sperm donors on account of his profile in which he represented that he was a Ph.D. candidate with an IQ of 160 and had no history of mental health issues or criminal activity.

On his Xytex questionnaire, Donor #9623 lied about his mental health. Xytex never asked him to verify his answers, supply his medical records, or sign a release for such records. Xytex also never asked about his criminal history or asked him to provide any identification. At Donor #9623's initial visit, Xytex's employee Mary Hartley told him that intelligent donors with high levels of education were more popular sperm donors and encouraged Donor #9623 to exaggerate his IQ and education. Although he claimed he had advanced degrees, Donor #9623 had no degrees at all when he completed his questionnaire.

During the time Donor #9623 sold sperm to Xytex, from 2000 to 2016, he was arrested for burglary, trespassing, DUI, and disorderly conduct; he pleaded guilty to burglary in 2005. After a lawsuit was filed against Xytex in 2014 concerning Donor #9623, he provided Xytex with forged graduation diplomas that it accepted without question.

Based on the representations that Xytex made regarding its screening procedures and the representations made in Donor #9623's profile, the Normans purchased Donor #9623's sperm. Wendy was inseminated with the sperm, and she gave birth to a son, A.A., in June 2002. Xytex was not involved in the insemination process.

A.A. has been diagnosed with Attention Deficit Hyperactivity Disorder and Thalassemia Minor, an inheritable blood disorder for which Wendy is not a carrier. A.A. regularly has suicidal and homicidal ideations, requiring multiple periods of extended hospitalizations. A.A. regularly sees a therapist for his anger and depression, and he takes ADHD, anti-depressant, and anti-psychotic medications.

In March 2017, A.A. conducted an internet search on Donor #9623, and he and the Normans discovered in publically available documents that the representations Xytex made regarding Donor #9623 were false. In reviewing those documents and through interviewing Donor #9623, the Normans learned that, before Donor #9623 began selling his sperm to Xytex in 2000, he had been hospitalized for mental health treatment and diagnosed with psychotic schizophrenia, narcissistic personality disorder, and significant grandiose delusions.

. . . The Normans [sued Xytex, raising] claims for fraud, negligent misrepresentation, products liability and/or strict liability, products liability and/or negligence, breach of express warranty, breach of implied warranty, battery, negligence, unfair business practices, specific performance, false advertising, promissory estoppel, and unjust enrichment. [Xytex filed a motion to dismiss, which the trial court granted in part,] concluding that all of the Normans' claims for relief, with the exception of the specific performance claim, were claims for "wrongful birth camouflaged as some other tort." [The Court of Appeals affirmed, citing inter alia *Graves* and *Abelson*.] . . .

Graves and *Abelson* both involved medical malpractice claims against physicians for negligence that led to the birth of a child. In *Graves*, we considered whether a mother could maintain an action against a hospital whose staff physician negligently performed a sterilization procedure that left the mother capable of conceiving, which later resulted in the birth of a child. Applying traditional tort principles, we held that such wrongful conception or wrongful pregnancy claims are cognizable because they are "no more than a species of malpractice which allows recovery from a tortfeasor in the presence of an injury caused by intentional or negligent conduct." But we limited the amount of damages the mother could recover. We allowed "recovery of expenses for the unsuccessful medical procedure which led to conception or pregnancy, for pain and suffering, medical complications, costs of delivery, lost wages, and loss of consortium." We did not permit the mother to collect damages for the expenses of raising the child, however, because "a parent cannot be said to have suffered an injury in the birth of a child."

In contrast to wrongful conception claims, which are based on allegations that the parents did not want to conceive a child at all, wrongful birth claims typically arise when parents claim they would have aborted the child had they been fully aware of the child's condition. In *Abelson*, we considered a damages suit against a doctor who failed to inform the plaintiff of a post-conception diagnostic test that could have diagnosed a genetic chromosomal disorder in the plaintiff's child. Again applying traditional tort principles, we concluded in *Abelson* that the claim failed under the injury prong because we were "unwilling to say that life, even life with severe impairments, may ever amount to a legal injury." . . . The plaintiffs' claims also failed under proximate causation, because the plaintiffs came to the doctor after conception, and the doctor could not be said to have caused the genetic impairment in the child. . . .

. . . *Graves* and *Abelson* establish a key principle that affects the viability of the Normans' claims: life can never amount to a legal injury. . . . We made clear in *Abelson* that any change to this prohibition on wrongful birth claims should come from the General Assembly, not the judiciary. . . . Although Georgia law does not recognize life as an injury, there can be injuries that predate a child's birth and are not premised on the child's life as an injury. [The court recounts the history of claims based on both prenatal and preconception injuries, which Georgia has long recognized.] Thus, in both pre- and post-conception cases, Georgia law has recognized that a cognizable claim may exist for pre-birth injuries to a child without deeming the child's existence an injury. Any such claims the Normans have brought are not wrongful birth claims and should not have been dismissed on that ground. . . .

One of the many allegations the Normans made is that they would not have purchased sperm from Donor #9623 had Xytex revealed the true facts about the donor. This is a classic wrongful birth claim because the necessary and direct result of not buying Donor #9623's sperm is that A.A. would not exist. Georgia law does not allow such a claim, and so it is barred. [Likewise, the Normans] cannot recover the costs of pregnancy and raising A.A., such as the medical expenses of child birth and lost wages due to artificial insemination and child birth. [Similarly, because] the Normans wished to conceive a child, allowing them to recover the costs of childbirth or the expenses incurred by raising A.A. would impermissibly transform A.A.'s birth into a legal injury.

But those principles do not create blanket immunity for reproductive service providers and do not preclude all claims relating to the birth of a child. Damages may be recoverable as long as plaintiffs sufficiently prove that the Defendants caused the alleged injuries (other than the life of A.A.). For example, the Normans alleged that they relied on Xytex's representations that it screened the medical and mental health history of its donors. The Normans also allege that Xytex represented that it would notify patients who used Donor #9623's sperm if the company received any "medically significant" information about Donor #9623, and that the company failed to do so even after Donor #9623's mental illness and criminal history came to light. And they allege that, even after a lawsuit was filed against the company concerning Donor #9623 in 2014, the company accepted his forged college graduation diplomas without verifying their authenticity and continued to promote his sperm to other patients.

[T]here is a possibility that the Normans were harmed by their reliance on Xytex's representations that (1) it had screened Donor #9623's medical history when he first started donating his sperm in 2000, or (2) it would update patients with "medically significant" information regarding donors. [T]he Normans also may be able to recover damages for the difference in price between the cost of the sperm they received and the fair market value of the sperm that Xytex told them they were getting. Xytex represented that Donor #9623 was one of its "best" donors, but the allegations regarding his background show otherwise. . . . The Normans also raise at least one consumer claim that is not barred by *Graves* and *Abelson*. [T]he Normans brought a cause of action under the Fair Business Practice Act, OCGA §10-1-390 et seq. ("FBPA"), claiming that Xytex misrepresented the quality of its goods and services. [The FBPA allows punitive damages for intentional violations.]

Given the allegations in the complaint, the Normans have asserted at least some damages that are not necessarily dependent on recognizing A.A.'s life as an injury. . . . Although the Normans' complaint does not identify with specificity every injury they might have suffered, we must construe all doubts in their favor. In this procedural posture, we cannot say with certainty that the Normans cannot prove a state of facts that would entitle them to any relief. To the extent that the Normans have pled claims predicated on injuries that are not predicated on life as an injury, these claims are not barred by *Graves* or *Abelson*. [Affirmed in part, reversed in part, and remanded.]

COLTON WOOTEN, A FATHER'S DAY PLEA TO SPERM DONORS

N.Y. Times, June 19, 2011, at WK9 (op-ed)

When I was 5, my mother revealed to me that I had been conceived through artificial insemination. . . . Because my understanding of conventional conception was so thin, my mom remained vague about the details of my conception — in all its complexity — until I got older.

When that time came, I learned how my mother, closing in on her 40s, found herself unmarried and childless. She had finished graduate school and established a career, but regretted not having a family. And so she decided to take the business of having a baby into her own capable hands [with the help of the University of North Carolina fertility clinic's sperm bank]. Artificial insemination seemed like a smart idea, perhaps the only idea. . . .

My mom's decision intrigued many people. Some saw it as a triumph of female self-sufficiency. But others, particularly her close friends and family, were shocked. "You can't have a baby without a man!" they would gasp.

It turns out, of course, you can, and pretty easily. The harder part, at least for that baby as he grows older, is the mystery of who that man was. Or is.

I didn't think much about that until 2006, when I was in eighth grade and my teacher assigned my class a genealogy project. We were supposed to research our family history and create a family tree to share with the class. In the past, whenever questioned about my father's absence by friends or teachers, I wove intricate alibis: he was a doctor on call; he was away on business in Russia; he had died, prematurely, of a heart attack. In my head, I'd always dismissed him as my "biological father," with that distant, medical phrase.

But the assignment made me think about him in a new way. I decided to call the U.N.C. fertility center, hoping at least to learn my father's name, his age or any minutiae of his existence that the clinic would be willing to divulge. But I was told that no files were saved for anonymous donors, so there was no information they could give me.

In the early days of in vitro fertilization, single women and sterile couples often overlooked a child's eventual desire to know where he came from. Even today, despite recent movies like "The Kids Are All Right," there is too little substantial debate on the subject. The emotional and developmental deficits that stem from an ignorance of one's origins are still largely ignored.

I understand why fertility centers chose to keep sperm donation anonymous. They were attempting to prevent extra chaos, like custody battles, intrusion upon happy families (on either party's side), mothers showing up on donors' doorsteps with homely, misbegotten children with runny noses and untied shoelaces to beg for child support. It's entirely reasonable, and yet the void that many children and young adults born from artificial insemination experience from simply not knowing transcends reason.

I don't resent my mom; she did the best thing she knew how to do at the time, and found a way to make a child under the circumstances. But babies born of the procedure in the future should have the right to know who their donors are, and even have some contact with them. Sperm donors need to realize that they are fathers. When I was doing college interviews, one of the interviewers told me that he didn't have any children, but that he had donated sperm while in college because he needed the money. He didn't realize that he probably is someone's father, regardless of whether he knows his child.

I'm one of those children, and I want to know who my father is. There are some programs like the Donor Sibling Registry that try to connect those conceived through sperm and egg donation with lost half-siblings and sometimes even parents. But I don't have much hope that I'll ever find him.

For my eighth grade project, I settled on fabricating the unknown side of my family tree, and not much has changed since then. I'm 18 now, today is Father's Day, and I still hardly know anything about my biological father, just a few vague details that my mother remembers from reading his profile so many years ago. I know that he was a medical student at U.N.C. the year I was born. I know that he had olive skin and brown hair. I know that his mother was Italian and his father Irish.

I call myself an only child, but I could very well be one of many siblings. I could even be predisposed to some potentially devastating disease. Because I do not know what my father looks like, I could never recognize him in a crowd of people. I am sometimes overwhelmed by the infinite possibilities, by the reality that my father could be anywhere: in the neighboring lane of traffic on a Friday during rush hour, behind me in line at the bank or the pharmacy, or even changing the oil in my car after many weeks of mechanical neglect.

I am sometimes at such a petrifying loss for words or emotions that make sense that I can only feel astonished by the fact that he could be anyone.

NOTES AND QUESTIONS

1. *"Reproductive negligence."*[105]

a. *Background for* Norman. What is the appropriate standard of care in reproductive medicine and fertility services and the legal remedy for failure to meet it? First, how persuasive do you find *Norman's* effort to distinguish permissible claims for wrongful conception, wrongful pregnancy, and prenatal and preconception injuries, on the one hand, from impermissible claims for wrongful birth, on the other? In the latter (which have sometimes been joined with wrongful life claims on behalf of the child), the prenatal testing that underlay many of the lawsuits began to flourish once abortion became legal after Roe v. Wade, 410 U.S. 113 (1973).[106] Yet, in many states with anti-abortion policies, these claims provoked legislative and judicial hostility because plaintiffs often argued that they would have terminated the pregnancy if they had accurate information about fetal health that the provider negligently failed to convey. In addition, defendants often successfully argued that the child, although born with an impairment, is a blessing for the parents (notwithstanding additional medical and other expenses necessitated by the impairment) and that, for the child, courts could not compare nonexistence and existence with impairments for purposes of assessing damages.[107] Causation often proved a sticking point as well, as *Norman* indicates. Should similar considerations bar the claims in *Norman*, as the court of appeals held below?

Second, how persuasive do you find *Norman's* effort to distinguish permissible damages from those precluded by Georgia precedent? If the Normans prove their case, will the recoverable damages make them whole? Which allegations must they prove for punitive damages under the FBPA?

b. *Taxonomy of wrongs.* The proliferation of reproductive technologies has increased the opportunities for care to go awry.[108] Challenging dodges

---

[105] Dov Fox, Reproductive Negligence, 117 Colum. L. Rev. 149 (2017).

[106] See Berman v. Allan, 404 A.2d 8 (N.J. 1979), abrogated by Hummel v. Reiss, 608 A.2d 1341 (N.J. 1992).

[107] For a classic analysis, see Alexander Morgan Capron, Tort Liability in Genetic Counseling, 79 Colum. L. Rev. 618 (1979).

[108] For a similar problem, see Ariana Eunjung Cha, The Children of Donor H898, Wash. Post (Sept. 14, 2019), https://www.washingtonpost.com/health/the-children-of-donor-h898/2019/09/14/dcc191d8-86da-11e9-a491-25df61c78dc4_story.html (recounting another lawsuit, based on autism in donor offspring). See also Sarah Zhang, One Sperm Donor. 36 Children. A Mess of Lawsuits., The Atlantic (Sept. 11, 2020), https://www.theatlantic.com/science/archive/2020/09/sperm-donor-identity-mental-health/616081/.

that courts have used to avoid awarding damages for reproductive negligence,[109] Professor Dov Fox argues for accountability that should address the specific nature of the wrong:

> Different kinds of reproductive wrongs call for different kinds of rights. In some cases, procreation is *deprived*—as when a lab technician drops the tray of embryos that are an infertile couple's last chance to have biological children, or when a doctor leads an eagerly expecting pregnant woman to abort by misinforming her that her healthy fetus would be born with a fatal disease. In other cases, procreation is *imposed*—as when a pharmacist fills a woman's birth control prescription with prenatal vitamins, or when a surgeon botches the sterilization that parents of five had sought because they were already struggling to make ends meet. Procreation is *confounded* when an IVF clinic fertilizes a patient's eggs with sperm from a stranger instead of her spouse, or when a sperm bank neglects to inform prospective parents that the anonymous donor it called "perfect" had actually dropped out of college, been convicted of burglary, and diagnosed with schizophrenia....[110]

The developing case law has confronted a number of ancillary questions. For example, to whom do health professionals performing genetic testing and counseling owe a duty of care? All the members of the patient's family who might carry or pass on the gene or chromosomal abnormality?[111] Is there a cause of action for negligent disruption of family planning?[112] Are there any situations in which the child should have a claim?[113]

c. *"Procreation confounded."* What damages are warranted for what Fox calls procreation confounded? Does *Norman* go far enough? What role should the concept of procreative liberty play in the analysis? Beyond the injuries alleged by the families who chose donor #9623, what of the harms to society, including public health problems?[114] If the availability of more expansive remedies requires legislative action, as Georgia case law states, what statutory reform would you recommend?

What damages should be recoverable in the case of the white lesbian couple in Ohio who chose a Caucasian sperm donor but received instead sperm from an African-American donor because of the alleged negligence of the sperm bank?[115] Or for each of the two couples—one white and one Black—whose embryos were switched and thus gestated by the wrong

---

[109] Fox, supra note [105].

[110] Dov Fox, Birth Rights and Wrongs: How Medicine and Technology Are Remaking Reproduction and the Law 165-166 (2019). For additional analysis of the underlying theories, see Dov Fox, Redressing Future Intangible Losses, 69 DePaul L. Rev. 419 (2020).

[111] See Molloy v. Meier, 679 N.W.2d 711 (Minn. 2004).

[112] See Rye v. Women's Care Cntr. of Memphis, MPLLC, 477 S.W.3d 235, 272-273 (Tenn. 2015) (no).

[113] See Barbara Pfeffer Billauer, Wrongful Life in the Age of CRISPR-CAS: Using the Legal Fiction of "The Conceptual Being" to Redress Wrongful Gamete Manipulation, 124 Penn St. L. Rev. 435 (2020).

[114] See Barbara Pfeffer Billauer, The Sperminator as Public Nuisance: Redressing Wrongful Life and Birth Claims in New Ways (A.K.A. New Tricks for Old Torts), 42 U. Ark. Little Rock L. Rev. 1 (2019) (proposing use of public nuisance tort).

[115] See Cramblett v. Midwest Sperm Bank, LLC, 230 F. Supp. 3d 865 (N.D. Ill. 2017); Camille Gear Rich, Contracting Our Way to Inequality: Race, Reproductive Freedom, and the Quest for the Perfect Child, 104 Minn. L. Rev. 2375 (2020) (examining "packaging of race" in the ARTs market); R.H. Lenhardt, The Color of Kinship, 102 Iowa L. Rev. 2071 (2017) (analyzing *Cramblett* to show how kinship is not race-neutral).

mother?[116] Or for plaintiffs who assert emotional distress from wondering whether the clinic's mistake means that they have genetic children somewhere born to others?[117] Or for the parents of red-haired triplets who selected sperm from a dark-haired donor and had it mixed with the husband's sperm in the hopes of seeing the children as the husband's genetic offspring only to find this "alternative reality" out of reach because the clinic used semen from the wrong donor?[118] Although the majority rejected plaintiffs' claim in this last scenario, the dissenting judge explained the nature of their loss:

> The majority opinion dismisses the Harnichers' desire to believe and represent that any children born as a result of the treatment they received were David Harnicher's biological offspring as a "fiction," which it cannot be tortious to destroy. But Mrs. Harnicher's testimony asserts that she would not have undergone donor sperm in vitro fertilization without the assurance that she, her husband, and any children they had would never need to know whether a biological bond existed. Had it not been for the University's negligence in mixing sperm from the wrong donor with David's, the "fiction" would never have been labeled a fiction; it would simply have been an "alternative reality" for the Harnicher family. In fact, in a sense, it was this alternative that the Harnichers negotiated for in their contract with the University, and that the University destroyed through its negligent act.[119]

Should the plaintiffs have a claim? If so, what is their loss worth in damages?

d. *Insemination fraud.* In several highly publicized cases, fertility patients have learned years later that the physician used his own sperm for insemination rather than that of an anonymous donor as promised.[120] What cause of action might they have? Should this type of misrepresentation be governed by principles stated in *Norman*? Which ones? Why?

2. *Medical regulation.* Despite frequent claims that ARTs remain largely unregulated in the U.S., Professor Glenn Cohen contends that a more accurate description would acknowledge that regulation in this country is fragmented and diffuse, with loci of control in federal law, state law (including tort and family law), and professional self-regulation.[121]

a. *Sperm and oocyte donation.* Given the problem in *Norman*, what role should the state play in screening and checking the medical histories of gamete donors? What records should be kept? Beyond those exemplified

---

[116] See Perry-Rogers v. Fasano, 715 N.Y.S.2d 19 (App. Div. 2000) (determining legal parentage after the embryo mix-up).

[117] See Andrews v. Keltz, 838 N.Y.S.2d 363 (Sup. Ct. 2007).

[118] See Harnicher v. Univ. of Utah Med. Ctr., 962 P.2d 67 (Utah 1998).

[119] Id. at 74 (Durham, Assoc. C.J., dissenting).

[120] See, e.g., United States v. Jacobson, 4 F.3d 987, 1993 WL 343172 (4th Cir. 1993); Ashby v. Mortimer, 2020 WL 572718 (D. Idaho 2020); Jody Lyneé Madeira, Uncommon Misconceptions: Holding Physicians Accountable for Insemination Fraud, 37 Law & Ineq. 45 (2019); Jacqueline Mroz, "Beyond Reprehensible," N.Y. Times, Aug. 27, 2019, at D1; Sarah Zhang, The Fertility Doctor's Secret, The Atlantic (Mar. 18, 2019), https://www.theatlantic.com/magazine/archive/2019/04/fertility-doctor-donald-cline-secret-children/583249/.

[121] I. Glenn Cohen, The Right(s) to Procreate and Assisted Reproductive Technologies in the United States, in The Oxford Handbook of Comparative Health Law (David Orentlicher & Tamara Hervey eds.) (forthcoming 2020), https://www.oxfordhandbooks.com/view/10.1093/oxfordhb/9780190846756.001.0001/oxfordhb-9780190846756-e-35.

by *Norman*, what risks follow from inadequate donor screening and recordkeeping?[122]

The Food and Drug Administration (FDA) first began regulating donated reproductive tissue in 2005. Donor eligibility rules require testing for specific diseases, including HIV and hepatitis.[123] In accompanying guidance, the FDA recommends ineligibility, based on increased risk, for any man who has had sex with men in the preceding five years (and any woman who has had sex with such men).[124]

Although the hormonal stimulation necessary for superovulation might pose medical risks, no registry keeps track of egg donors and their health after retrieval.[125]

b. *IVF.* In one notable exception to the generally laissez-faire approach to assisted reproduction in the United States, federal legislation (designed to develop "informed consumers") requires fertility programs to report their pregnancy rates to the Department of Health and Human Services for annual publication and distribution to the public.[126] What other information should fertility clinics be required to disclose?[127] The ABA's model act includes quality assurance requirements for ARTs providers and storage facilities, including measures on personnel, equipment, and testing, and it also calls for registries for maintaining information.[128]

Hormones used to induce superovulation can produce dangerous multifetal pregnancies, requiring "selective abortion" or creating significant risks of premature birth and neurological problems in offspring, in addition to health dangers for the woman.[129] In IVF, the problem arises from the transfer of multiple embryos in an effort to improve the chances of successful pregnancy and to avoid the cost of additional cycles should the current one fail. The American Society for Reproductive Medicine has guidelines for the number of embryos

---

[122] See Cahn, supra note [47], at 194-200 (discussing, among others, risks of genetic diseases and "inadvertent consanguinity" when one donor provides gametes to many different families). But see Courtney Megan Cahill, The Oedipus Hex: Regulating Family After Marriage Equality, 49 U.C. Davis L. Rev. 183, 238 (2015) (criticizing normative family suggested by fears of accidental incest between donor-conceived offspring).

[123] 21 C.F.R. §§1271.45-1271.90.

[124] See Luke A. Boso, Note, The Unjust Exclusion of Gay Sperm Donors: Litigation Strategies to End Discrimination in the Gene Pool, 110 W.Va. L. Rev. 843 (2008). The Practice Committees of the American Society for Reproductive Medicine (ASRM) and the Society for Assisted Reproductive Medicine (SART) continue to adhere to such guidance. E-mail from Valerie Ratts, M.D., Professor of Obstetrics & Gynecology, Div. of Reproductive Endocrinology, Wash. U. Sch. of Med., to Susan Frelich Appleton, Professor of Law, Wash. U. (July 9, 2020, 07:03pm CDT) (on file with author).

[125] See Jane E. Brody, For Egg Donors, No Easy Long-Term Answers, N.Y. Times, July 11, 2017, at D5.

[126] 42 U.S.C. §§263a-1 to 263a-7.

[127] See Jim Hawkins, Selling ART: An Empirical Assessment of Advertising on Fertility Clinics' Websites, 88 Ind. L.J. 1147, 1174-1177 (2013).

[128] American Bar Assn., supra note [37], §§901-902.

[129] See, e.g., Lars Noah, Assisted Reproductive Technologies and the Pitfalls of Unregulated Biomedical Innovation, 55 Fla. L. Rev. 603 (2003); Urska Velikonja, The Costs of Multiple Gestation Pregnancies in Assisted Reproduction, 32 Harv. J.L. & Gender 463 (2009).

to transfer depending on the stage of development and age of the woman.[130] The issue captured public attention in 2009, when Nadya Suleman (dubbed "Octomom" in popular culture) gave birth to eight premature infants, exposing the inadequacies of self-regulation by fertility professionals.[131]

Could IVF be banned or restricted to protect the health of the children-to-be? How does one consider harm to a not-yet-conceived individual who would not exist without the technology—an issue that has bedeviled courts in tort cases like *Norman*?[132] In addition, some data indicate that children of IVF suffer a disproportionate incidence of birth defects.[133] Particular concerns have been prompted by intracytoplasmic sperm injection (ICSI), which entails the injection of a single sperm into the center of an ovum and allows, for example, a man with a very low sperm count to become a genetic father. The process might allow fertilization (in vitro) with unsuitable sperm and could risk transmission of genetic abnormalities causing the underlying infertility. ICSI has flourished in the absence of any longitudinal studies about its safety, however.[134]

3. *Anonymity versus disclosure.* The original UPA explicitly provided for sealed records concerning donor insemination. UPA §5 (1973). Do the same considerations that prompted access to adoption records apply to collaborative reproduction? See Chapter 5, section C1. Traditionally, one advantage of ARTs over adoption for prospective parents has been the promised ability for the family to "pass" as one created without assistance.[135] How should law balance such parental concerns with the "need to know" asserted by those like Colton Wooten in his op-ed piece?[136] Some foreign countries, including the United Kingdom, now make available both health and identifying information. See Chapter 9, section A. Is it unconstitutional to require preservation of adoption records so that adoptees may have access to information about their origins without doing the same for those conceived by donor insemination?[137] What downsides or risks might follow a

[130] See Criteria for Number of Embryos to Transfer: A Committee Opinion, 99 Fertil. Steril. 44 (2013), https://reader.elsevier.com/reader/sd/pii/S0015028212022571?token=40C75217080E7F9 8B5E8DDD3B9D453C13808860176A658F8263600FF2AA7747C4975D6B66267E6C916814F4FC38ED 266.

[131] See, e.g., Adam Popescu, Octomom Speaks, N.Y. Times, Dec. 16, 2018, at ST1; Radhika Rao, How (Not) to Regulate Assisted Reproductive Technology: Lessons from "Octomom," 49 Fam. L.Q. 135 (2015).

[132] See Philip G. Peters, Jr., How Safe Is Safe Enough?: Obligations to the Children of Reproductive Technology (2004); I. Glenn Cohen, Regulating Reproduction: The Problem with Best Interests, 96 Minn. L. Rev. 423 (2011).

[133] See Robin Fretwell Wilson, Uncovering the Rationale for Requiring Infertility in Surrogacy Arrangements, 29 Am. J.L. & Med. 337, 343-347 (2003). See also Gina Kolata, Picture Emerging on Genetic Risks of IVF, N.Y. Times, Feb. 17, 2009, at D1.

[134] The President's Council on Bioethics, Reproduction and Responsibility: The Regulation of New Biotechnologies 39-40 (2004).

[135] See, e.g., *Harnicher*, 962 P.2d 67.

[136] See also Katrina Clark, Who's Your Daddy? Mine Was an Anonymous Sperm Donor. That Made Me Mad. So I Decided to Find Him., Wash. Post, Dec. 17, 2006, at B1 ("It's hypocritical of parents and medical professionals to assume that biological roots won't matter to the 'products' of the cryobanks' service, when the longing for a biological relationship is what brings customers to the banks in the first place.").

[137] See Pratten v. British Columbia (Attorney General), [2011] B.C.J. No. 931 (so holding by a Canadian provincial court).

system of mandatory disclosure, at least once children of assisted conception reach young adulthood?

A lively debate in the literature, including empirical studies, on such topics[138] has been largely overtaken by on-the-ground developments. First, parents now often openly discuss their children's origins, sperm banks facilitate donor-child meetings when the donor has agreed to such contact, and children can register on a website designed to introduce them to others conceived by the same donor.[139] Second, popular do-it-yourself DNA tests and internet genealogy sites have revealed genetic connections that were never supposed to come to light, making contemporary promises of anonymity borderline fraudulent and unsettling the lives of offspring and donors alike.[140] How should law respond?

In a new addition to the UPA framework, the 2017 version requires collection and recordkeeping of donor information. At the time of donation, donors must provide their medical history and select whether identifying information may be disclosed once the child reaches age 18. Even if the donor selects nondisclosure, the bank or clinic must make a good-faith effort to provide nonidentifying medical history to the child (if 18) or the parents (if the child is a minor). UPA §§901-906 (2017).

4. *Policy, religious, and moral concerns.* A host of reservations about ARTs arise from concerns beyond those rooted in health and safety. Which ones might support restricting access to ARTs?

a. *Family life.* The conversation inspired by Octomom, supra, focused not only on medical risks but also on her status as an economically challenged unmarried woman of color who, thanks to ARTs, would be rearing 14 children (the octuplets plus six from a previous multi-fetal IVF pregnancy).[141] Can government restrict access to ARTs based on economics or family life? Can a private doctor or fertility clinic? Recall how *Rooks*, supra, deemed "the sheer number of a party's existing children" to be an impermissible basis for deciding a dispute over frozen embryos. Suppose a physician has moral or

---

[138] Compare, e.g., Mary Patricia Byrn & Rebecca Ireland, Anonymously Provided Sperm and the Constitution, 23 Colum. J. Gender & L. 1 (2012) (arguing that requiring identifying information about donors infringes the constitutional rights of those who conceive with ARTs), with Naomi Cahn, The New "ART" of Family: Connecting Assisted Reproductive Technologies and Identity Rights, 2018 U. Ill. L. Rev. 1443 (2018), and Elizabeth J. Samuels, An Immodest Proposal for Birth Registration in Donor-Assisted Reproduction in the Interest of Science and Human Rights, 48 N.M. L. Rev. 416 (2018). See Glenn Cohen et al., Sperm Donor Anonymity and Compensation: An Experiment with American Sperm Donors, 3 J. L. & Biosciences 468 (2016) (finding some sperm donors would not donate without anonymity and others would require additional payment); J. Lyn Entrikin, Family Secrets and Relational Privacy: Protecting Not-So-Personal, Sensitive Information from Public Disclosure, 74 U. Miami L. Rev. 781, 878 (2020) (raising question of "*informational* privacy rights" of donor-conceived offspring or third-party contributors).

[139] See Cahn, supra note [103]. Sometimes such registries disclose unexpected information. See Jacqueline Mroz, From One Sperm Donor, 150 Children, N.Y. Times, Sept. 6, 2011, at D1; Pia Peterson, Photographing His Dozens of Siblings, N.Y. Times, June 29, 2019, at A2.

[140] Cahn, supra note [138], at 1446. See, e.g., *Ashby,* 2020 WL 572718; Nofar Yakovi Gan-Or, Reproductive Dreams and Nightmares: Sperm Donation in the Age of At-Home Genetic Testing, 51 Loy. U. Chi. L.J. 791 (2020); Susan Dominus, Epilogue: A Dark Secret No More, N.Y. Times Mag., June 30, 2019, at 52; Kyle Swenson, Nineteen Children and Counting, Wash. Post (Sept. 7, 2020), https://www.washingtonpost.com/national/sperm-donor-father-19-children/2020/09/07/97b6f8de-ba65-11ea-8cf5-9c1b8d7f84c6_story.html?utm_campaign=wp_post_most&utm_medium=email&utm_source=newsletter&wpisrc=nl_most.

[141] See, e.g., Rao, supra note [131].

religious objections to assisting LGBTQ adults to become parents.[142] How do the issues resemble those in cases of adoption agencies asserting objections to placing children with LGBTQ adults? See Chapter 4, section A1b. How do they differ?

b. *Religious tenets.* The Catholic Church has found IVF morally illicit because it deprives the child *"of being the result and fruit of a conjugal act* in which spouses can become 'cooperators with God for giving life to a new person.' "[143] Also, destruction of embryos offends "pro-life" values in and out of the Church.

c. *Race and heritage.* Recall the debate about race-matching in adoption. See Chapter 4, section A1a. Observers have noted that ARTs allow white parents to get white infants, in short supply for adoption, commodifying race, entrenching racial hierarchy, and treating race as a biological variable.[144] What implications, if any, does ICWA have for ARTs?[145]

d. *Eugenics.* The ability to choose the genetic makeup of one's child in the gamete marketplace, the emergence of noninvastive prenatal testing,[146] and the availability of preimplantation genetic diagnosis (PGD, which allows testing of embryos before transfer)[147] necessarily recall early twentieth-century America's progressive eugenics movement, in which mandatory sterilization laws and other coercive interventions deprived marginalized members of society of the opportunity to procreate.[148] What are the similarities? The differences?[149]

In the 1980s, the Repository of Germinal Choice, established by a wealthy Californian, promised to provide the sperm of Nobel Prize winners.[150] Sometimes the quest for a "designer baby" entails choosing,

---

[142] See, e.g., See N. Coast Women's Care Med. Grp., v. Super. Ct., 189 P.3d 959 (Cal. 2008); Douglas NeJaime & Reva Siegel, Religious Exemptions and Antidiscrimination Law in *Masterpiece Cakeshop*, 128 Yale L.J. F. 201, 222-223 (2018).

[143] Congregation for the Doctrine of the Faith, Instruction on Respect for Human Life in its Origin and on the Dignity of Procreation: Replies to Certain Questions of the Day 29-31 (1987). See also Congregation for the Doctrine of the Faith, Instruction Dignitas Personae on Certain Bioethical Questions 8-13 (2008) (condemning IVF, destruction of embryos, and cryopreservation of genetic material).

[144] See generally Appleton, supra note [102]; Dov Fox, Race Sorting in Family Formation, 49 Fam. L.Q. 55 (2015); Rich, supra note [115].

[145] See Adrea Korthase, Seminal Choices: The Definition of "Indian Child" in a Time of Assisted Reproductive Technology, 31 J. Am. Acad. Matrimonial Law. 131 (2018).

[146] See Elizabeth Scotchman et al., Noninvastive Pretnatal Diagnosis of Single-Gene Diseases: The Next Frontier, 66 Clin. Chemistry 53 (2020), https://academic.oup.com/clinchem/article/66/1/53/5688824.

[147] See Fox, supra note [110], at 21.

[148] See id. at 11. See also, e.g., In re House, 813 S.E.2d 230 (N.C. 2016) (seeking compensation for involuntary sterilization under state's Eugenics Asexualization and Sterilization Compensation program), review allowed and remanded, 813 S.E.2d 230 (N.C. 2017); No Más Bebés (2016) (documentary about involuntary sterilizations of immigrant women in Los Angeles who brought unsuccessful class action against hospital).

[149] See id. at 162. See also John A. Robertson, Abortion and Technology: Sonograms, Fetal Pain, Viability, and Early Prenatal Diagnosis, 14 U. Pa. J. Con. L. 327, 380 (2011) (distinguishing public and private eugenics). Cf. Carl H. Coleman, Conceiving Harm: Disability Discrimination in Assisted Reproductive Technologies, 50 UCLA L. Rev. 17, 60-67 (2002) (analyzing whether the Americans with Disabilities Act restricts physicians' discretion to reject ARTs patients with disabilities to prevent the birth of children with disabilities).

[150] For a journalist's investigation and profiles of some of the donors and resulting children, see David Plotz, The Genius Factory: The Curious History of the Nobel Prize Sperm Bank (2005). See generally Sonja Pavlovic et al., Using Genetics for Enhancement (Liberal Eugenics), in Clinical Ethics at the Crossroads of Genetic and Reproductive Technologies 335 (Sorin Hostiuc ed., 2018).

via PGD, a disability such as deafness so that a parent can share deaf culture with the child.[151] Today, the subject of eugenics—specifically opposition thereto—surfaces in state restrictions on abortions sought for reason of race, sex, or disability and judicial responses to such measures.[152]

Despite the perils of eugenics, why shouldn't those using ARTs be informed and demanding consumers? Instead, should medical personnel make the selection? The state?[153]

e. *Age.* In response to pregnancies achieved by postmenopausal women using donor eggs ("granny births"), some countries have enacted age-based restrictions. Would similar legislation in the United States survive constitutional challenge? Does "old" parenthood pose harm to children? Parents? Society? Should similar restrictions apply to alternative insemination to deter old fatherhood? Such questions regularly surface with news reports of births to women in their sixties and seventies using donor eggs.[154]

f. *Feminist critiques.* Some feminists condemn IVF and other interventions, claiming they exploit women.[155] Professor Dorothy Roberts observes that ARTs "function primarily to fulfill men's desires for genetically related offspring."[156] Reports from Egypt substantiate this hypothesis. There, infertile husbands, whose wives could have conceived while young but became too old to bear children, left these wives and remarried women of reproductive age with whom they could use ICSI to father biological children.[157] Others claim the procedures perpetuate a view of women as, first and foremost, mothers. What legal conclusions for IVF follow from these feminist critiques? A ban on these procedures? Mandated warnings to ensure "informed" consent, as some states require for abortions? Suppose some women long to contribute to the stereotype. Could they bring a successful sex discrimination challenge to restrictive laws?

g. *Pricing.* Who should set the price for gametes? What does *Norman* say about the price that plaintiffs paid Xytex for Donor #9623's sperm?

Despite the term "donor," those who provide genetic material usually receive payment. Should egg donors with the most desirable characteristics be able receive whatever the market will bear, or do would-be donors need protection from exploitation? Some fertility clinics have oocyte-sharing

[151] See Sara Weinberger et al., They Choose . . . Poorly: A Novel Cause of Action to Discourage Detrimental Genetic Selection, 43 Am. J.L. & Med. 107 (2017).

[152] See Box v. Planned Parenthood of Ind. & Ky., Inc., 139 S. Ct. 1780, 1782-1793 (2019) (Thomas, J., concurring); Reproductive Health Servs. of Planned Parenthood of the St. Louis Region, Inc. v. Parson, 389 F. Supp. 3d 631, 634, modified, 408 F. Supp. 3d 1049 (W.D. Mo. 2019).

[153] See Rich, supra note [115], at 2435-2436 (describing system in Spain "where donors are pre-matched with consumers based on skin color, hair texture, blood type, ethnicity, and a range of characteristics and then delivered a sample chosen by the state").

[154] See, e.g., Joshua Bote, A 74-Year-Old Woman Reportedly Gave Birth to Twins, May Be the Oldest Ever to Give Birth, USA Today, Sept. 9, 2019, https://www.usatoday.com/story/life/parenting/2019/09/06/oldest-woman-to-ever-give-birth-has-twins-at-74-years-old/2231598001/. See also Terry Wilkinson, Fertility Law Divides Italians, L.A. Times, June 11, 2005, at A3 (attributing support for Italy's restrictions, in part, to past "granny births").

[155] See, e.g., Gena Corea, The Mother Machine: Reproductive Technologies from Artificial Insemination to Artificial Wombs 100-134 (1985). See also Robyn Rowland, Living Laboratories: Women and Reproductive Technologies (1992).

[156] Dorothy E. Roberts, The Genetic Tie, 62 U. Chi. L. Rev. 209, 239 (1995).

[157] Marcia C. Inhorn, Global Infertility and the Globalization of New Reproductive Technologies: Illustrations from Egypt, 56 Soc. Sci. & Med. 1837, 1846 (2003).

programs, allowing patients to receive treatment for reduced fees in exchange for donating some of their eggs or pre-embryos to other patients. What is the proper way to balance autonomy, protection from exploitation and racial ranking, and fair compensation for hormonal therapy and surgery that entail some risks?

Using as a baseline sperm donors, who earn between $60 and $75 per hour, the American Society for Reproductive Medicine published guidelines stating that, for oocyte donors, more than $5,000 requires justification, more than $10,000 is inappropriate, and sharing programs need clear and fair policies.[158] Revealing that they prioritized autonomy over protection, egg donors challenged this price fixing in a class action that ultimately settled.[159] Payments to egg donors constitute taxable income for services rendered.[160]

With respect to rules allowing or prohibiting payments, should law treat sperm, eggs, and embryos alike? Why? While conceding the existing commerce in sperm and eggs, the President's Council on Bioethics called for interim legislation prohibiting the purchase and sale of human embryos. Why do embryos merit different treatment?[161] Nonetheless, some fertility entrepreneurs create and then sell "off the rack" donor embryos in order to lower the cost.[162]

5. *"Embryo adoption."* When families create embryos (from their own genetic material or that donated by others), they often have many left over. Some donate them for research, while others make them available to other families. The choice of terminology for the latter disposition — "embryo adoption" versus "embryo donation" — evokes abortion politics.[163] How does the terminology affect the understanding of adoption, with its traditional emphasis on child welfare? Despite conventional wisdom claiming that facilitating assisted reproduction decreases adoption (by creating children who will take the place of adoptees in families), empirical studies fail to find such effects and, in fact, suggest that increased access to IVF might actually boost adoption.[164] Even if ARTs would have a negative impact on adoption, "why [do] infertile couples alone and not all persons who

---

[158] Kimberly D. Krawiec, Lessons from Law About Incomplete Commodification in the Egg Market, 33 J. Applied Phil. 160, 164-165 (2016), https://onlinelibrary.wiley.com/doi/epdf/10.1111/japp.12144.

[159] See Wynter K. Miller, Assumption of What? Building a Better Market Architecture for Egg Donation, 86 Tenn. L. Rev. 33, 55-57 (2018). See also Kimberly D. Krawiec, Markets, Morals, and Limits in the Exchange of Human Eggs, 13 Geo. J. L. & Pub. Pol'y 349 (2015).

[160] Perez v. Comm'r of Internal Revenue, 144 T,C, 51 (2015).

[161] See The President's Council on Bioethics, supra note [134], at 226-227.

[162] See California IVF Fertility Center, California Conceptions Donor Embryo Program, https://californiaconceptions.com/.

[163] See Jessica R. Hoffman, You Say Adoption, I Say Objection: Why the Word War over Embryo Disposition Is More Than Just Semantics, 46 Fam. L.Q. 397 (2012); Polina M. Dostalik, Note & Case Comment, Embryo "Adoption"?: The Rhetoric, the Law, and the Legal Consequences, 55 N.Y. L. Sch. L. Rev. 867 (2010/2011); Caroline Lester, Embryo "Adoption" Gets Mired in Abortion Debate, N.Y. Times, Feb. 18, 2019, at A14. See also Doe v. Obama, 631 F.3d 157 (4th Cir. 2011) (holding frozen embryos and prospective embryo adopters lack standing to challenge federal funding of embryonic stem cell research).

[164] Compare I. Glenn Cohen & Daniel L. Chen, Trading-Off Reproductive Technology and Adoption: Does Subsidizing IVF Decrease Adoption Rates and Should It Matter?, 95 Minn. L. Rev. 485 (2010), with Susan Frelich Appleton & Robert A. Pollak, Exploring the Connections Between Adoption and IVF: Twibling Analyses, 95 Minn. L. Rev. Headnotes 60 (2011).

reproduce have the obligation to adopt kids in need of parents"?[165] Alternatively, does the use of the term "adoption" in this new context reinforce adoption's stigma, suggesting "there is something deeply suspect" about parenting someone else's child?[166]

6. *New frontiers.* Reproductive research continues to advance, often with controversy in its wake. State and federal bans, moratoria, and funding limits on such research have emerged based on moral, ethical, and religious objections and concerns about unforeseen harm.[167] Yet a technique prohibited as experimentation on an embryo one day might well become routine practice later, leaving some such restrictions unconstitutionally vague.[168]

The specter of human cloning as a means of reproduction ignited enormous debate about the ethics of the procedure and whether bans could survive constitutional challenge.[169] More recently, germline genome editing has become the eye of the storm; this intervention, which could serve therapeutic or other purposes, makes changes in DNA affecting generations to come.[170] Other less contested procedures have begun to gain acceptance. Mitochondrial replacement therapy, permitted in the United Kingdom and designed to avoid passing on genetic diseases, allows what some dub "three-parent IVF."[171] And in vitro gametogenesis (IVG) could enable men without sperm and women (or two men or two women) to procreate without genetic contributions from others by using cells, often skin cells; converting them into pluripotent stem cells; and then programming them to become sperm cells or egg cells.[172]

Like the other interventions examined in this chapter, these new developments raise questions about the scope of procreative liberty (in the face of possible restrictions) and, relatedly, about the parentage of resulting children.[173] By allowing reproduction in once impossible contexts, ARTs can transform understandings of family, sex, and gender.[174]

---

[165] Robertson, supra note [11], at 277 n.27.

[166] Elizabeth Bartholet, Family Bonds: Adoption, Infertility, and the New World of Child Production 69 (rev. ed. 1999).

[167] See Russell A. Spivak et al., Moratoria and Innovation in the Reproductive Sciences: Of Pretext, Permanence, Transparency, and Time Limits, 14 J. Health & Biomed. L. 5 (2018) (cataloguing bans and moratoria on reproductive research).

[168] See Lifchez v. Hartigan, 735 F. Supp. 1361, 1372 (N.D. Ill. 1990).

[169] Compare, e.g., Russell Korobkin, Stem Cell Research and the Cloning Wars, 18 Stan. L. & Pol'y Rev. 161 (2007), with Cass R. Sunstein, Is There a Constitutional Right to Clone?, 53 Hastings L.J. 987 (2002). See also Lori B. Andrews, Is There a Right to Clone? Constitutional Challenges to Bans on Human Cloning, in The Reproductive Rights Reader: Law, Medicine, and the Construction of Motherhood 320 (Nancy Ehrenreich ed., 2008); Bonnie Steinbock, Reproductive Cloning: Another Look, 2006 U. Chi. Legal F. 87 (reviewing debate and concluding that the only real problems are safety based — a situation that might change).

[170] See Paul Enriquez, Editing Humanity: On the Precise Manipulation of DNA in Human Embryos, 97 N.C. L. Rev. 1147 (2019).

[171] See I. Glenn Cohen et al., Transatlantic Lessons in Regulation of Mitochondrial Replacement Therapy, 348 Science, Apr. 2015, at 178; Daniel Green, Note & Comment, Assessing Parental Rights for Children with Genetic Material from Three Parents, 19 Minn. J.L. Sci. & Tech. 251 (2018).

[172] See Brian Esser, IVG: The New IVF?, 41 Fam. Advoc. 37 (Winter 2019); Debora L. Spar, The Poly-Parents Are Coming, N.Y. Times, Aug. 16, 2020, at SR9.

[173] See generally, e.g., Courtney Megan Cahill, The New Maternity, 133 Harv. L. Rev. 2221 (2020); Douglas NeJaime, The Constitution of Parenthood, 72 Stan. L. Rev. 261 (2020).

[174] See Kimberly M. Mutcherson, Transformative Reproduction, 16 J. Gender Race & Just. 187 (2013). But see Courtney Megan Cahill, After Sex, 97 Neb. L. Rev. 1 (2018) (predicting persistence of sexual norms and ideals even with nonsexual procreation).

Depictions in Popular Culture: Kazuo Ishiguro, Never Let Me Go (2005)

In this haunting dystopian novel, Kathy H., the narrator, reminisces in rich detail about her pleasant-enough years at Hailsham, a British boarding school that seems to lack the opportunities and facilities that surely would be available at an institution reputed to be the best, as Hailsham is. Yet everyone seems to accept not only the absence of the privileges one would expect but also other apparent absences. Why do Kathy and her classmates never mention their parents or other family members? How do they know they will never have children? And what does it mean to become, after leaving Hailsham, a "carer" and then a "donor"? While depicting familiar experiences of childhood, Ishiguro subtly communicates that something here is eerily unfamiliar. Slowly, the reader begins to decipher the role of Kathy and her friends in a world in which therapeutic cloning has become an established practice, offering valuable medical treatment to some — but not all — segments of the population.

One reviewer asks whether, in selecting the theme of cloning, Ishiguro is "issuing a warning about the ethics of reproductive science."[175] She answers her own question as follows:

> I suspect Ishiguro's intention is both more personal and more literary. The theme of cloning lets him push to the limit ideas he's nurtured in earlier fiction about memory and the human self . . . .
>
> So the dare Ishiguro has taken on might be this: to capture what is unmistakably human, what survives and insists on subtly expressing itself after you subtract the big stuff — the specific baggage, the parents, orientation toward a culture, a past and possible futures — that shapes people into individuals. . . . At times uncomfortably, for a work that aims to give us a distilled and persevering human essence, we can sense the controlling care with which Ishiguro invents and organizes [Kathy's] memories. Yet if the novel feels a bit too distant to move us to outright heartbreak, it delivers images of odd beauty and a mounting existential distress that hangs around long after we read it.[176]

To the extent the reviewer is correct about Ishiguro's objectives and accomplishments, the novel might still have some relevance to "the ethics of reproductive science." How would you articulate this relevance? Are therapeutic and reproductive cloning distinguishable as a matter of ethics? As a matter of law? What legal implications does the novel have?[177]

---

[175] Sarah Kerr, When They Were Orphans, N.Y. Times, Apr. 17, 2005, §7, at 16 (book review).
[176] Id.
[177] See, e.g., Dorothy Franks, The Rumor on Adopting Children for Their Organs: A Compelling Reason to Address a Thriving Organ Black Market and the Prevalence of Children Being Trafficked into Adoption, 14 J. Health & Biomedical L. 169 (2018).

PROBLEMS

1. A "free sperm" movement challenges the FDA's health-based regulatory regime (see supra). Seeking to legitimize the practice of using informal arrangements between donors and recipients (often initiated online) without government oversight, a California woman sues the FDA, contending that its screening requirements for donor insemination are expensive and burdensome and unconstitutionally interfere with privacy, sexual liberty, and procreative autonomy. She also asserts equal protection violations because the FDA regulates alternative insemination but not sexual insemination, in turn driving some donors and recipients simply to use sexual insemination instead. How should the court decide the case? Why?[178]

2. Danielle and Jason have an on-again-off-again relationship. After Danielle moves out of Jason's home, she purchases sperm from an anonymous donor from a sperm bank with the plan to become a single mother. Jason then gives Danielle a letter stating that he is not ready to be a father but, if Danielle wants to use his sperm to conceive, she has his blessing as long as she does not tell others. Danielle decides to use Jason's sperm rather than the anonymous donor's sperm she had purchased. After baby Gus is born, Danielle and Gus spend time with Jason, and Gus begins to call him "Dada." When Danielle terminates Jason's contact with Gus, Jason claims to be Gus's father and sues Danielle, seeking joint custody. Danielle defends by asserting the state statute that codifies the rule of donor nonparentage. What result and why? How should the court decide Jason's argument that, if the donor nonparentage statute precludes him from establishing parentage, then it violates his constitutional rights as a biological parent.[179]

3. How would you answer the writer of the following letter seeking ethical advice?

> I am an American woman, of Ashkenazi Jewish ancestry, and I strive to live my life as an active agent against racism and white supremacy. I am beginning to consider having children and am open to bearing a child as a single mother. It is possible to sort through sperm donors by race, eye color, education level and so on. If I choose a donor of color, am I condemning my child to be born into a system designed not to serve them? Or can I use my white privilege to help them fight that system? Would my future child of color feel separated from their heritage with me as their mother? If I choose a white donor, am I succumbing to racist ideas of what traits are "desirable," or taking the "easy road" in knowing my child will look more like me? What do you think? Name Withheld[180]

What legal reforms, if any, would you recommend to address such situations?

---

[178] See Doe v. Hamburg, 2013 WL 3783749 (N.D. Cal. 2013); Susan Frelich Appleton, Between the Binaries: Exploring the Legal Boundaries of Nonanonymous Sperm Donation, 49 Fam. L.Q. 93, 109-115 (2015); Courtney Megan Cahill, Reproduction Reconceived, 101 Minn. L. Rev. 617 (2016).

[179] See Jason P. v. Danielle S., 171 Cal. Rptr. 3d 789 (Ct. App. 2014), 215 Cal. Rptr. 3d 542 (Ct. App. 2017); L.F. v. Breit, 736 S.E.2d 711 (Va. 2013).

[180] See Kwame Anthony Appiah, I'm Considering a Sperm Donor. How Should I Choose the Race of My Child?, The Ethicist, N.Y Times Mag., June 21, 2020, at 12.

CHAPTER 8

COLLABORATIVE REPRODUCTION: GENES, GESTATION, AND INTENT

A. THE EVOLUTION OF SURROGACY

With alternative insemination and IVF, reproduction can become a collaborative project, with separate contributors supplying gametes, gestation, and (after birth) childrearing. The outsourcing of gestation — surrogacy arrangements — has generated extensive public conversation about such collaborations, in both law and culture. This section explores how surrogacy and the legal responses to it have evolved.

1. TRADITIONAL (GENETIC) SURROGACY ARRANGEMENTS

IN RE BABY M

537 A.2d 1227 (N.J. 1988)

WILENTZ, C.J. . . .

In February 1985, William Stern and Mary Beth Whitehead entered into a surrogacy contract. It recited that Stern's wife, Elizabeth, was infertile, that they wanted a child, and that Mrs. Whitehead was willing to provide that child as the mother with Mr. Stern as the father.

The contract provided that through artificial insemination using Mr. Stern's sperm, Mrs. Whitehead would become pregnant, carry the child to term, bear it, deliver it to the Sterns, and thereafter do whatever was necessary to terminate her maternal rights so that Mrs. Stern could thereafter adopt the child. Mrs. Whitehead's husband, Richard, was also a party to the contract; Mrs. Stern was not. Mr. Whitehead promised to do all acts necessary to rebut the presumption of paternity under the Parentage Act. N.J.S.A. 9:17-43a(l), -44a. Although Mrs. Stern was not a party to the surrogacy agreement, the contract gave her sole custody of the child in the event of Mr. Stern's death. . . .

Mr. Stern, on his part, agreed to attempt the artificial insemination and to pay Mrs. Whitehead $10,000 after the child's birth, on its delivery to him. In a separate contract, Mr. Stern agreed to pay $7,500 to the Infertility Center of New York ("ICNY"). The Center's advertising campaigns solicit surrogate mothers and encourage infertile couples to consider surrogacy. ICNY arranged for the surrogacy contract by bringing the parties together, explaining the process to them, furnishing the contractual form, and providing legal counsel.

The history of the parties' involvement in this arrangement suggests their good faith. William and Elizabeth Stern were married in July 1974, having met at the University of Michigan, where both were Ph.D. candidates. Due to financial considerations and Mrs. Stern's pursuit of a medical degree and residency, they decided to defer starting a family until 1981. . . . Based on the perceived risk [of Mrs. Stern's possible multiple sclerosis,] the Sterns decided to forego having their own children. The decision had special significance for Mr. Stern. Most of his family had been destroyed in the Holocaust. As the family's only survivor, he very much wanted to continue his bloodline.

Initially the Sterns considered adoption, but were discouraged by the substantial delay apparently involved and by the potential problem they saw arising from their age and their differing religious backgrounds. . . .

The paths of Mrs. Whitehead and the Sterns to surrogacy were similar. Both responded to advertising by ICNY. . . . Mrs. Whitehead's response apparently resulted from her sympathy with family members and others who could have no children (she stated that she wanted to give another couple the "gift of life"); she also wanted the $10,000 to help her family. . . . On February 6, 1985, Mr. Stern and Mr. and Mrs. Whitehead executed the surrogate parenting agreement. After several artificial inseminations over a period of months, Mrs. Whitehead became pregnant. The pregnancy was uneventful and on March 27, 1986, Baby M was born. . . .

Mrs. Whitehead realized, almost from the moment of birth, that she could not part with this child. . . . Nonetheless, Mrs. Whitehead was, for the moment, true to her word. Despite powerful inclinations to the contrary, she turned her child over to the Sterns on March 30 at the Whiteheads' home.

The Sterns were thrilled with their new child [whom they named Melissa]. They had planned extensively for its arrival . . . . Later in the evening of March 30, Mrs. Whitehead became deeply disturbed, disconsolate, stricken with unbearable sadness. She had to have her child. . . . The Sterns, concerned that Mrs. Whitehead might indeed commit suicide, not wanting under any circumstances to risk that, and in any event believing that Mrs. Whitehead would keep her word [that she would return her in a week], turned the child over to her. . . .

The struggle over Baby M began when it became apparent that Mrs. Whitehead could not return the child to Mr. Stern. Due to Mrs. Whitehead's refusal to relinquish the baby, Mr. Stern filed a complaint seeking enforcement of the surrogacy contract. . . . After the order [in favor of Stern] was entered, ex parte, the process server, aided by the police, in the presence of the Sterns, entered Mrs. Whitehead's home to execute the order. Mr. Whitehead fled with the child, who had been handed to him through a window while those who came to enforce the order were thrown off balance by a dispute over the child's current name.

The Whiteheads immediately fled to Florida with Baby M. . . . Police in Florida enforced [a court order obtained by Mr. Stern], forcibly removing the child from her grandparents' home. She was soon thereafter brought to New Jersey and turned over to the Sterns. [The *ex parte* order awarding custody to the Sterns *pendente lite* was affirmed.] Pending final judgment, Mrs. Whitehead was awarded limited visitation with Baby M. . . .

The trial took thirty-two days over a period of more than two months. [The trial court] held that the surrogacy contract was valid; ordered that Mrs. Whitehead's parental rights be terminated and that sole custody of the child be granted to Mr. Stern; and, after hearing brief testimony from Mrs. Stern, immediately entered an order allowing the adoption of Melissa by Mrs. Stern, all in accordance with the surrogacy contract. Pending the outcome of the appeal, we granted a continuation of visitation to Mrs. Whitehead, although slightly more limited than the visitation allowed during the trial.

Although clearly expressing its view that the surrogacy contract was valid, the trial court devoted the major portion of its opinion to the question of the baby's best interests. . . . Its rationalization . . . was that while the surrogacy contract was valid, specific performance would not be granted unless that remedy was in the best interests of the child. The factual issues confronted and decided by the trial court were the same as if Mr. Stern and Mrs. Whitehead had had the child out of wedlock, intended or unintended, and then disagreed about custody. . . .

On the question of best interests [raised in this appeal by Mrs. Whitehead, we] agree substantially with both [the trial court's] analysis and conclusions on the matter of custody. The court's review and analysis of the surrogacy contract, however, is not at all in accord with ours. . . .

Invalidity and Unenforceability of Surrogacy Contract . . .

A. Conflict with Statutory Provisions

The surrogacy contract conflicts with: (1) laws prohibiting the use of money in connection with adoptions; (2) laws requiring proof of parental unfitness or abandonment before termination of parental rights is ordered or an adoption is granted; and (3) laws that make surrender of custody and consent to adoption revocable in private placement adoptions. . . .

(1) . . . Considerable care was taken in this case to structure the surrogacy arrangement so as not to violate [the prohibition on payment in connection with adoption]. The arrangement was structured as follows: the adopting parent, Mrs. Stern, was not a party to the surrogacy contract; the money paid to Mrs. Whitehead was stated to be for her services — not for the adoption; the sole purpose of the contract was stated as being that "of giving a child to William Stern, its natural and biological father"; the money was purported to be "compensation for services and expenses and in no way . . . a fee for termination of parental rights or a payment in exchange for consent to surrender a child for adoption"; the fee to the Infertility Center ($7,500) was stated to be for legal representation, advice, administrative work, and other "services." Nevertheless, it seems clear that the money was paid and accepted in connection with an adoption [in violation of criminal law]. As for the contention that the Sterns are paying only for services and not for an adoption,

we need note only that they would pay nothing in the event the child died before the fourth month of pregnancy, and only $1,000 if the child were still-born, even though the "services" had been fully rendered....

The prohibition of our statute is strong. Violation constitutes a high misdemeanor, N.J.S.A. 9:3-54c, a third-degree crime, N.J.S.A. 2C:43-lb, carrying a penalty of three to five years imprisonment. N.J.S.A. 2C:43-6a(3). The evils inherent in baby-bartering are loathsome for a myriad of reasons. The child is sold without regard for whether the purchasers will be suitable parents. The natural mother does not receive the benefit of counseling and guidance to assist her in making a decision that may affect her for a lifetime. In fact, the monetary incentive to sell her child may, depending on her financial circumstances, make her decision less voluntary.... Baby-selling potentially results in the exploitation of all parties involved....

(2) The termination of Mrs. Whitehead's parental rights, called for by the surrogacy contract and actually ordered by the court fails to comply with the stringent requirements of New Jersey law. Our law, recognizing the finality of any termination of parental rights, provides for such termination only where there has been a voluntary surrender of a child to an approved agency or to the Division of Youth and Family Services ("DYFS"), accompanied by a formal document acknowledging termination of parental rights, N.J.S.A. 9:2-16, -17; N.J.S.A. 9:3-41; N.J.S.A. 30:4C-23, or where there has been a showing of parental abandonment or unfitness. A termination may ordinarily take one of three forms: an action by an approved agency, an action by DYFS, or an action in connection with a private placement adoption....

In this case a termination of parental rights was obtained not by proving the statutory prerequisites but by claiming the benefit of contractual provisions.... Since the termination was invalid, it follows, as noted above, that adoption of Melissa by Mrs. Stern could not properly be granted.

(3) The provision in the surrogacy contract stating that Mary Beth Whitehead agrees to "surrender custody ... and terminate all parental rights" contains no clause giving her a right to rescind. It is intended to be an irrevocable consent to surrender the child for adoption ....

It is clear that the Legislature so carefully circumscribed all aspects of a consent to surrender custody — its form and substance, its manner of execution, and the agency or agencies to which it may be made — in order to provide the basis for irrevocability.... There is only one irrevocable consent, and that is the one explicitly provided for by statute: a consent to surrender of custody and a placement with an approved agency or with DYFS. The provision in the surrogacy contract, agreed to before conception, requiring the natural mother to surrender custody of the child without any right of revocation is one more indication of the essential nature of this transaction: the creation of a contractual system of termination and adoption designed to circumvent our statutes.

B. Public Policy Considerations ...

The surrogacy contract guarantees permanent separation of the child from one of its natural parents. Our policy, however, has long been that to the extent possible, children should remain with and be brought up by both of their natural parents. ...

The surrogacy contract violates the policy of this State that the rights of natural parents are equal concerning their child, the father's right no greater than the mother's. . . . The whole purpose and effect of the surrogacy contract was to give the father the exclusive right to the child by destroying the rights of the mother.

The policies expressed in our comprehensive laws governing consent to the surrender of a child . . . stand in stark contrast to the surrogacy contract and what it implies. Here there is no counseling, independent or otherwise, of the natural mother, no evaluation, no warning. . . .

Worst of all, however, is the contract's total disregard of the best interests of the child. There is not the slightest suggestion that any inquiry will be made at any time to determine the fitness of the Sterns as custodial parents, of Mrs. Stern as an adoptive parent, their superiority to Mrs. Whitehead, or the effect on the child of not living with her natural mother.

This is the sale of a child, or, at the very least, the sale of a mother's right to her child, the only mitigating factor being that one of the purchasers is the father. Almost every evil that prompted the prohibition on the payment of money in connection with adoptions exists here. . . .

The differences between adoption and a surrogacy contract should be noted, since it is asserted that the use of money in connection with surrogacy does not pose the risks found where money buys adoption. First, and perhaps most important, all parties concede that it is unlikely that surrogacy will survive without money. . . . That conclusion contrasts with adoption; for obvious reasons, there remains a steady supply, albeit insufficient, despite the prohibitions against payment. The adoption itself, relieving the natural mother of the financial burden of supporting an infant, is in some sense the equivalent of payment.

Second, the use of money in adoptions does not produce the problem — conception occurs, and usually the birth itself, before illicit funds are offered. With surrogacy, the "problem," if one views it as such, consisting of the purchase of a woman's procreative capacity, at the risk of her life, is caused by and originates with the offer of money.

Third, with the law prohibiting the use of money in connection with adoptions, the built-in financial pressure of the unwanted pregnancy and the consequent support obligation do not lead the mother to the highest paying, ill-suited, adoptive parents. She is just as well-off surrendering the child to an approved agency. In surrogacy, the highest bidders will presumably become the adoptive parents regardless of suitability, so long as payment of money is permitted. . . .

The main difference, that the unwanted pregnancy is unintended while the situation of the surrogate mother is voluntary and intended, is really not significant. [T]he essential evil is the same, taking advantage of a woman's circumstances (the unwanted pregnancy or the need for money) in order to take away her child . . . . Intimated, but disputed, is the assertion that surrogacy will be used for the benefit of the rich at the expense of the poor. . . . The point is made that Mrs. Whitehead agreed to the surrogacy arrangement, supposedly fully understanding the consequences. Putting aside the issue of how compelling her need for money may have been, and how significant her understanding of the consequences, we suggest that her consent is irrelevant. There are, in a civilized society, some things that money cannot buy. . . .

The long-term effects of surrogacy contracts are not known, but feared —
the impact on the child who learns her life was bought, that she is the offspring of someone who gave birth to her only to obtain money; the impact
on the natural mother as the full weight of her isolation is felt along with
the full reality of the sale of her body and her child; the impact on the natural father and adoptive mother once they realize the consequences of their
conduct.... In New Jersey the surrogate mother's agreement to sell her child
is void.

Termination . . .

Although the question of best interests of the child is dispositive of the
custody issue in a dispute between natural parents, it does not govern the
question of termination. It has long been decided that the mere fact that a
child would be better off with one set of parents than with another is an
insufficient basis for terminating the natural parent's rights.... There is simply no basis ... to warrant termination of Mrs. Whitehead's parental rights....

Constitutional Issues . . .

The right to procreate, as protected by the Constitution, has been ruled
on directly only once by the United States Supreme Court. See Skinner v.
Oklahoma, 316 U.S. 535 (forced sterilization of habitual criminals violates
equal protection clause of fourteenth amendment). Although Griswold v.
Connecticut, 381 U.S. 479, is obviously of a similar class, strictly speaking
it involves the right not to procreate. The right to procreate very simply is
the right to have natural children, whether through sexual intercourse or
artificial insemination. It is no more than that. Mr. Stern has not been
deprived of that right. Through artificial insemination of Mrs. Whitehead,
Baby M is his child.... To assert that Mr. Stern's right of procreation gives
him the right to the custody of Baby M ... would be to assert that the constitutional right of procreation includes within it a constitutionally protected
contractual right to destroy someone else's right of procreation....

Mr. Stern also contends that he has been denied equal protection of the
laws by the State's statute granting full parental rights to a husband in relation to the child produced, with his consent, by the union of his wife with
a sperm donor. N.J.S.A. 9:17-44. The claim really is that of Mrs. Stern. It is that
she is in precisely the same position as the husband in the statute: she is presumably infertile, as is the husband in the statute; her spouse by agreement
with a third party procreates with the understanding that the child will be
the couple's child....

... The State has more than a sufficient basis to distinguish the two
situations — even if the only difference is between the time it takes to
provide sperm for artificial insemination and the time invested in a nine-
month pregnancy — so as to justify automatically divesting the sperm donor
of his parental rights without automatically divesting a surrogate mother.
Some basis for an equal protection argument might exist if Mary Beth
Whitehead had contributed her egg to be implanted, fertilized or otherwise,
in Mrs. Stern, resulting in the latter's pregnancy. That is not the case here,
however.

Mrs. Whitehead, on the other hand, ... claims the right to the companionship of her child. This is a fundamental interest, constitutionally protected.

Furthermore, it was taken away from her by the action of the court below.... Having held the contract invalid and having found no other grounds for the termination of Mrs. Whitehead's parental rights, we find that nothing remains of her constitutional claim. We express no opinion on whether a prolonged suspension of visitation would constitute a termination of parental rights, or whether, assuming it would, a showing of unfitness would be required....

Custody

... With the surrogacy contract disposed of, the legal framework becomes a dispute between two couples over the custody of a child produced by the artificial insemination of one couple's wife by the other's husband. Under the Parentage Act the claims of the natural father and the natural mother are entitled to equal weight, i.e., one is not preferred over the other solely because he or she is the father or the mother.[3] [T]he child's best interests determine custody....

... The Whiteheads claim that even if the child's best interests would be served by our awarding custody to the Sterns, we should not do so, since that will encourage surrogacy contracts.... We disagree. Our declaration that this surrogacy contract is unenforceable and illegal is sufficient to deter similar agreements. We need not sacrifice the child's interests in order to make that point sharper....

The Whiteheads also contend that the award of custody to the Sterns *pendente lite* was erroneous and that the error should not be allowed to affect the final custody decision. [They argue that] one of the most important factors, whether mentioned or not, in favor of custody in the Sterns is their continuing custody during the litigation, now having lasted for one-and-a-half years.... We disagree with the premise, however, that in determining custody a court should decide what the child's best interests would be if some hypothetical state of facts had existed. Rather, we must look to what those best interests are, today, even if some of the facts may have resulted in part from legal error....

[Eleven experts testified on the child's best interests.] Our reading of the record persuades us that the trial court's decision awarding custody to the Sterns (technically to Mr. Stern) should be affirmed....

Our custody conclusion is based on strongly persuasive testimony contrasting both the family life of the Whiteheads and the Sterns and the personalities and characters of the individuals. The stability of the Whitehead family life was doubtful at the time of trial. Their finances were in serious trouble (foreclosure by Mrs. Whitehead's sister on a second mortgage was in process). Mr. Whitehead's employment, though relatively steady, was always at risk because of his alcoholism, a condition that he seems not to have been able to confront effectively. Mrs. Whitehead had not worked for quite some

---

3. ...This does not mean that a mother who has had custody of her child for three, four, or five months does not have a particularly strong claim arising out of the unquestionable bond that exists at that point between the child and its mother; in other words, equality does not mean that all of the considerations underlying the [sex-based] "tender years" doctrine have been abolished.

time, her last two employments having been part-time. One of the White-heads' positive attributes was their ability to bring up two children, and apparently well, even in so vulnerable a household. Yet substantial question was raised even about that aspect of their home life. The expert testimony contained criticism of Mrs. Whitehead's handling of her son's educational difficulties. Certain of the experts noted that Mrs. Whitehead perceived herself as omnipotent and omniscient concerning her children.... Her inconsistent stories about various things engendered grave doubts about her ability to explain honestly and sensitively to Baby M — and at the right time — the nature of her origin. Although faith in professional counseling is not a *sine qua non* of parenting, several experts believed that Mrs. Whitehead's contempt for professional help, especially professional psychological help, coincided with her feelings of omnipotence in a way that could be devastating to a child who most likely will need such help.... The prospects for wholesome, independent psychological growth and development would be at serious risk. [Mrs. Whitehead subsequently divorced, became pregnant by another man and remarried, developments that the court said had no effect on its decision.]

The Sterns have no other children, but all indications are that their household and their personalities promise a much more likely foundation for Melissa to grow and thrive. There is a track record of sorts — during the one-and-a-half years of custody Baby M has done very well, and the relationship between both Mr. and Mrs. Stern and the baby has become very strong. The household is stable, and likely to remain so. Their finances are more than adequate, their circle of friends supportive, and their marriage happy. Most important, they are loving, giving, nurturing, and open-minded people. They have demonstrated the wish and ability to nurture and protect Melissa, yet at the same time to encourage her independence. Their lack of experience is more than made up for by a willingness to learn and to listen, a willingness that is enhanced by their professional training, especially Mrs. Stern's experience as a pediatrician. They are honest; they can recognize error, deal with it, and learn from it. They will try to determine rationally the best way to cope with problems in their relationship with Melissa. When the time comes to tell her about her origins, they will probably have found a means of doing so that accords with the best interests of Baby M. All in all, Melissa's future appears solid, happy, and promising with them. Based on all of this we have concluded ... that Melissa's best interests call for custody in the Sterns [an outcome favored by the expert witnesses].

Some comment is required on the initial *ex parte* order awarding custody *pendente lite* to the Sterns (and the continuation of that order after a plenary hearing). The issue, although irrelevant to our disposition of this case, may recur; and when it does, it can be of crucial importance. When father and mother are separated and disagree, at birth, on custody, only in an extreme, truly rare, case should the child be taken from its mother *pendente lite* .... The probable bond between mother and child, and the child's need, not just the mother's, to strengthen that bond, along with the likelihood, in most cases, of a significantly lesser, if any, bond with the father — all counsel against temporary custody in the father [absent the mother's unfitness or danger to the child.]

Even [the mother's] threats to flee should not suffice to warrant any other relief unless her unfitness is clearly shown. At most, it should result in an order enjoining such flight. The erroneous transfer of custody, as we view it, represents a greater risk to the child than removal to a foreign jurisdiction . . . .

Visitation

. . . Our reversal of the trial court's order. . . requires delineation of Mrs. Whitehead's rights to visitation. [The experts called by Melissa's court-appointed guardian] were concerned that, given Mrs. Whitehead's determination to have custody, visitation might be used to undermine the Sterns' parental authority and thereby jeopardize the stability and security so badly needed by this child. Two of the experts recommended suspension of visitation for five years and the other suspension for an undefined period. [The guardian ad litem] now argues that instead of five years, visitation should be suspended until Melissa reaches majority. . . .

We also note the following for the trial court's consideration: First, this is not a divorce case where visitation is almost invariably granted to the non-custodial spouse. To some extent the facts here resemble cases where the non-custodial spouse has had practically no relationship with the child, but it only "resembles" those cases. In the instant case, Mrs. Whitehead spent the first four months of this child's life as her mother and has regularly visited the child since then. Second, she is not only the natural mother, but also the legal mother, and is not to be penalized one iota because of the surrogacy contract. [A touchstone of visitation is] that it is desirable for the child to have contact with both parents . . . .

We have decided that Mrs. Whitehead is entitled to visitation at some point, and that question is not open to the trial court on this remand. [T]he guardian's recommendation of a five-year delay is most unusual — one might argue that it begins to border on termination. Nevertheless, if the circumstances as further developed by appropriate proofs or as reconsidered on remand clearly call for that suspension under applicable legal principles of visitation, it should be so ordered. . . .

Conclusion

This case affords some insight into a new reproductive arrangement: the artificial insemination of a surrogate mother. The unfortunate events that have unfolded illustrate that its unregulated use can bring suffering to all involved. . . .

We have found that our present laws do not permit the surrogacy contract used in this case. Nowhere, however, do we find any legal prohibition against surrogacy when the surrogate mother volunteers, without any payment, to act as a surrogate and is given the right to change her mind and to assert her parental rights. Moreover, the Legislature remains free to deal with this most sensitive issue as it sees fit, subject only to constitutional constraints. . . .

The judgment is affirmed in part, reversed in part, and remanded for further proceedings consistent with this opinion.

LORI B. ANDREWS, BETWEEN STRANGERS: SURROGATE MOTHERS,
EXPECTANT FATHERS, AND BRAVE NEW BABIES

11-24 (1989)

... Carol Pavek knew exactly why she was different from the people of Amarillo. She was adopted. She came, at least prenatally, from somewhere else.... Carol felt no need to seek out her birth parents. She loved the couple who raised her, and felt she could get from them any help and advice she needed. But when she got pregnant with her own child, her link to her biological mother became crucially important....

[After her child's birth, Carol began training as a midwife. She and her husband Rick were disappointed they could not experience the home birth they had planned for their son.] "We felt unfulfilled," says Carol. "We teased each other that we would keep giving birth until we got it right, only we would have to find families to give the children to."

When their son, Chris, was eighteen months old, their joking took a serious turn. That's when they first heard about the possibility of surrogate motherhood on a television show. The guest on the show was Noel Keane, the Dearborn, Michigan, attorney.... As Noel Keane and an infertile couple described surrogate motherhood to the television audience, Carol Pavek recognized how she could connect her dream of a home birth with a couple's dream of a baby.... "This was a way for Carol to express herself and do something for others," Rick said later. "There was a lot of altruism. . . ." ...

It took six months' reflection before Carol actually began to fashion a letter to Noel expressing her interest. "It wasn't actually a letter," she says. "It was more like a book." ... Carol was candid in her portrait of herself, mentioning her receding chin, heavy hips, and nearsightedness. She was equally blunt about what she was looking for in a couple. They would have to agree, of course, to a home birth and the adoptive mother would have to be present. If possible, the father and any other children in the family should be present as well. Carol would breast-feed the baby for three to five days to pass on her immunities.

At the time Carol contacted Noel, in 1980, surrogate mothers were not being paid. It hadn't even occurred to Carol to ask for any money. Her main concern was the quality of the relationship she would have with the couple....

Noel received the letter the same day he received a desperate call from a couple of modest means who lived in a rural section of northern California. Nancy's first husband had died when she was pregnant with their second child. She raised their two daughters alone through childhood, then required a hysterectomy. When she later married Andy, it was clear that she would not be able to bear children. But now, in part because of his attachment to Nancy's two daughters, they were wishing they could have another child [one with Andy's traits].

By sundown, Andy and Nancy had called Carol. Within a week, they had taken the tiresome three-and-a-half-day bus ride to the Texas panhandle to meet Carol and Rick face-to-face.... Carol and Rick immediately took to the couple.... Their conversations over the next few days were not at all like a business negotiation; they were getting to know each other like new neighbors. Surrogacy is not like a merger of corporations. It is the creation of a relationship — and, as with any intimate relationship, it takes a certain level of compatibility to allow the relationship to flower....

The first insemination [at Carol's house] did not result in a pregnancy, so the following month, May of 1980, Carol flew out to their home in the California mountains. They lived out in the country in a cabin with a dog and horses, about four miles from an old mining town. Carol was immediately enchanted by the area as the perfect place to raise a child. [E]very other day for a week, Carol artificially inseminated herself. [She became pregnant.]

Four days before the scheduled due date, Andy, Nancy, and the two teen-aged daughters drove down to Amarillo in a motor home. The four of them rushed to Carol's house once her labor began. By this time, Carol had helped with thirty-five successful home births; she hoped her own would be the thirty-sixth. But, again, there was a problem with Carol's delivery and by midnight she was giving birth in a local hospital.... Andy and Nancy stayed with Carol through the labor, but once delivery began, they had to leave because no advance arrangements had been made for their presence. Rick was left to coach Carol through and oversee the birth of a ten-pound boy....

The baby was gently lowered onto Carol's abdomen. She slowly opened her eyes, and was relieved to find that she didn't have any feeling of possession. Her only thought was "What a gorgeous baby."

Two hours later, Andy and Nancy wanted to give Carol the baby to breast-feed. A nurse took Nancy aside, saying "Oh you must not let her breast-feed the baby, she will bond."

"I've trusted her this far, I'm going to trust her again," Nancy replied.

Carol fed the baby, then spent a peaceful hour watching Nancy hold her son. Carol thought of how, in traditional adoptions, the hospital staff did everything they could to keep the biological mother and the baby apart. It wasn't right to rip a baby away, Carol thought as she drifted off to sleep; the mother must have a chance to say good-bye.

The next day, back at home, Rick turned to Carol before she fell asleep. "You're already thinking of trying again, aren't you?" he asked. [Carol twice subsequently served as a "surrogate."]

MARY BETH WHITEHEAD WITH LORETTA SCHWARTZ-NOBEL,
A MOTHER'S STORY: THE TRUTH ABOUT THE *BABY M* CASE

25-27 (1989)

Rick [the then husband of Mary Beth Whitehead] tried to comfort me. He tried everything he knew. Nothing worked.... You don't comfort somebody who is giving away her child.

Everybody said, "You have two other children." It wasn't as if my baby were dead. My child was alive, and I had given her to two strangers....

The Sterns and the Infertility Center had told me I was doing a beautiful thing, but I wasn't. All the way through my pregnancy, I had tried to believe it. I had suppressed the reality; I had denied my feelings. I had not allowed myself to deal with it. But now I couldn't pretend anymore. I just didn't want to be a party to it, no matter how much it was going to disappoint them. I couldn't bear to be a woman who gave away her child....

I began to feel angry and defensive. My body, my soul, my heart, my breathing, my everything had gone into making this baby. What had Bill

Stern done? Put some sperm in cup. What had Betsy done? Bought some clothes, a box of diapers, and a case of formula. . . .

. . . I just couldn't stop crying. It just kept coming, and the emptiness that I felt was something I never want to feel again.

Eventually I fell asleep. Suddenly I opened my eyes. The room was dark, and I was lying in a pool of milk. The sheets were full of milk. I knew it was time to feed my baby. I knew she was hungry, but I could not hear her crying. The room was quiet as I sat up in the bed, alone in the darkness, with the milk running down my chest and soaking my nightgown. I held out my empty arms and screamed at the top of my lungs, "Oh, God, what have I done—I want my baby!" . . .

NOTES AND QUESTIONS

1. *"Traditional surrogacy."* Baby M illustrates what came to be known as "traditional surrogacy," an arrangement pioneered by Michigan attorney Noel Keane, who drafted the first such formal agreement in 1976. Traditional surrogacy entails the same process as AID (Chapter 7, section B1), albeit with a mirror-image purpose: A woman is inseminated with the sperm of a man who (with his spouse, if he is married) intends to serve as the child's parent. Thus, the "surrogate" provides both gestation and genes — or is the mother, as some would argue. Accordingly, some contemporary authorities call this type "genetic surrogacy" or "full surrogacy."[1] In part because of the outcome of Baby M and the argument that a genetic surrogate is the child's mother, today traditional surrogacy has largely given way to "gestational surrogacy," made possible by IVF.[2] See infra section A2.

2. Baby M's *context and legacy.* Baby M garnered extensive publicity during the legal proceedings that culminated in the principal case, introducing the public to surrogacy arrangements and sparking considerable controversy. Despite the impression left by Baby M, contemporaneous studies of the practice indicated that, in the vast majority of surrogacy arrangements, the parties perform their agreements without resort to judicial intervention.[3]

Nonetheless, Baby M raised two primary questions about surrogacy: First, what legal restrictions ought to apply to consensual arrangements in which all parties are willing to perform? For example, Baby M holds that surrogacy for pay constitutes an illegal sale of a child, regardless of the parties' wishes. Second, what rules ought to govern "failed" surrogacy arrangements such as that in Baby M? Note that failure also can occur when the intended parents

---

[1] UPA Art. 8, Pt. 3 (2017) ("special rules for genetic surrogacy agreement"); Carla Spivack, The Law of Surrogate Motherhood in the United States, 58 Am. J. Comp. L. 97, 98 (2010).

[2] See also, e.g., In re F.T.R., 833 N.W.2d 634 (Wis. 2013) (holding TPR provisions of genetic surrogacy contract are unenforceable, but other provisions can be enforced unless contrary to the child's best interests); In re Baby, 447 S.W.3d 807 (Tenn. 2014) (denying full enforcement to traditional surrogacy agreement).

[3] See John A. Robertson, Children of Choice: Freedom and the New Reproductive Technologies 131 (1994). See also Susan Fischer & Irene Gillman, Surrogate Motherhood: Attachment, Attitudes and Social Support, 54 Psychiatry 13, 19 (1991) (describing Whitehead as an "anomaly"); Rachel Rebouché, Contracting Pregnancy, 105 Iowa L. Rev. 1591, 1635 (2020) (noting that "most surrogacy arrangements appear to be 'carried out without a hitch'").

repudiate the agreement, as when they reject the child because of disabilities.[4] Both questions ask about the appropriate limits on private ordering in what *Baby M* calls "a new way of bringing children into a family."

3. *Surrogacy analogies.* The apparent novelty of the issues posed by *Baby M* and collaborative reproduction more generally prompted a search for rules to borrow from analogous areas of law, including adoption and the traditional law of parentage.[5]

a. *Adoption.* How does surrogacy resemble adoption? *Baby M* looks to adoption law to rule the contract void. Yet, how can the court ignore the contract when, without it, this particular child would not exist? Thus, isn't surrogacy distinguishable from adoption?

What are the advantages and disadvantages of surrogacy over adoption? For prospective parents? Birth mothers (surrogates)? Children? Society?

Had the arrangement not failed, adoption by Elizabeth Stern would have followed termination of Mary Beth Whitehead's parental rights. Should the adoption be treated as a stepparent adoption, in which there is typically little screening of adopters, or as an adoption of an unrelated child, in which the state usually intervenes more extensively? See also infra (preconception adoption).

b. *AID.* Alternatively, does the law of donor insemination provide a more appropriate framework than adoption for surrogacy? Could the two be understood as physically dictated responses to different kinds of infertility that individuals and couples experience? Consider the reasoning of Judge Sorkow, the trial judge in *Baby M*. He reasoned that surrogates must be allowed to sell their services and the intended mother must be recognized as a legal parent because these rules apply to AID: "To rule otherwise denies equal protection of the law to the childless couple, the surrogate, whether male or female, and the unborn child." 525 A.2d 1128, 1165 (N.J. Super. Ct. Ch. Div. 1987).[6] What is the biological father's legal status with respect to the child if the surrogate conceives while married, as did Whitehead? Is he just a sperm donor with no legal status under AID law?[7] If so, then how could the resulting adoption be classified as a stepparent adoption? If it must be treated as an adoption by a nonrelative, why should the state have more opportunities for intervention in, and thus more control over, surrogacy than AID?

4. *"Gender neutrality."* Given his physical limitations, what more could William Stern — or any man — have done to show his interest in his anticipated child? Or do sex-specific contributions to reproduction compel

---

[4] Cf., e.g., Stiver v. Parker, 975 F.2d 261 (6th Cir. 1992); Caitlin Keating, Surrogate Mom Gives Birth to Baby Girl with Serious Birth Defects Despite Parents' Order to Abort: "She Is Everything I Believed She Would Be," People (Mar. 3, 2016), https://people.com/parents/surrogate-crystal-kelley-baby-with-birth-defects-parents-order-to-abort.

[5] Marsha Garrison, Law Making for Baby Making: An Interpretive Approach to the Determination of Legal Parentage, 113 Harv. L. Rev. 835 (2000) (calling this approach "interpretative").

[6] See also Carmel Shalev, Birth Power: The Case for Surrogacy 87 (1989) ("surrogacy presents a mirror situation to that of artificial insemination of a married woman with donor sperm").

[7] See, e.g., R.R. v. M.H., 689 N.E.2d 790, 795-796 (Mass. 1998).

different treatment of mothers and fathers? According to Professor Marjorie Shultz, the *Baby M* court missed an opportunity for equal treatment:

> To say that the factual issues are "the same" as if Whitehead and William Stern had simply had a child out of wedlock, ignores the centrally important fact that modern reproductive techniques allow the separation of personal and sexual intimacy from procreation.... It ignores that the father here differs in important ways from stereotypical unwed fathers. In particular, it ignores that the child in question exists only because of its progenitors' individual intentions, their reciprocal decisions, and their behavior and expectations in the wake of such decisions....
>
> ... Unlike biologically-based variables, the capacity to form and express intentions is gender-neutral. [H]aving rejected any role for intention, the court fell back on gender stereotypes to resolve the issues.... The court's decision reinforced stereotypes regarding the desirability of segregating women from the market, the unpredictability of women's intentions and decisions, and the givenness of women's biological destiny. Perhaps worst of all, it acted to lock in existing gender-based spheres of influence in our society, refusing to recognize fragile, emergent male efforts to claim a meaningful role in access to and nurture of children....[8]

5. *Feminist debate. Baby M* sparked sharp divisions among feminists. Some submitted briefs supporting Whitehead, others for the Sterns.[9] In the wake of this case, some feminists advocated the prohibition of surrogacy agreements, even those women willingly make.[10] These scholars condemned surrogacy as a practice that commodifies and exploits women and children.[11] From this perspective, surrogacy reduces women to "baby machines"[12] and resembles slavery[13] and prostitution.[14] Surrogacy also

---

[8] Marjorie Maguire Shultz, Reproductive Technology and Intent-Based Parenthood: An Opportunity for Gender Neutrality, 1990 Wis. L. Rev. 297, 376-379. But see Pamela Laufer-Ukeles, Essay, Approaching Surrogate Motherhood: Reconsidering Difference, 26 Vt. L. Rev. 407, 436 (2002) (arguing surrogacy reveals the need for "an asymmetrical notion of [gender] equality").

[9] Lori B. Andrews, Between Strangers: Surrogate Mothers, Expectant Fathers, and Brave New Babies 171-182 (1989).

[10] See, e.g., Margaret Jane Radin, Market-Inalienability, 100 Harv. L. Rev. 1849 (1987); Robin L. West, Taking Preferences Seriously, 64 Tul. L. Rev. 659 (1990).

[11] See, e.g., Anita L. Allen, Privacy, Surrogacy, and the *Baby M* Case, 76 Geo. L.J. 1759, 1783, 1791 (1988) (rejecting linkage of freedom-of-contract theory and the privacy jurisprudence of reproductive liberty because of the unique harms risked by surrogates); Cass R. Sunstein, Neutrality in Constitutional Law (With Special Reference to Pornography, Abortion, and Surrogacy), 92 Colum. L. Rev. 1, 47 (1992) ("[A] world in which female sexual and reproductive services are freely traded on markets would legitimate and reinforce a pervasive form of inequality — one that sees the social role of women as that of breeders, and that uses that role to create second-class citizenship.").

[12] See, e.g., Gena Corea, Junk Liberty, in Reconstructing Babylon: Essays on Women and Technology 142, 153-156 (H. Patricia Hynes ed., 1991). See also Robyn Rowland, Living Laboratories: Women and Reproductive Technologies 198 (1992) (use of brain-dead "surrogates" as "female incubators").

[13] Anita L. Allen, Surrogacy, Slavery and the Ownership of Life, 13 Harv. J.L. & Pub. Pol'y 139, 140 (1990) (observing that slavery "had the effect of causing black women to become surrogate mothers on behalf of slave owners"). See also Dov Fox, Thirteenth Amendment Reflections on Abortion, Surrogacy, and Race Selection, 104 Cornell L. Rev. Online 114, 112-124 (2019); Patricia J. Williams, On Being the Object of Property, 14 Signs 5 (1988).

[14] E.g., Carole Pateman, The Sexual Contract 209-218 (1988); Margaret Jane Radin, Contested Commodities 131-153 (1996).

reflects patriarchal, racist, and eugenic motivations, at the expense of existing children who need homes.[15]

Would banning consensual surrogacy, however, suggest that women need protection from their own decisions? Some feminists thus condemned efforts to outlaw surrogacy as an unwarranted intrusion on reproductive autonomy, reflecting gender stereotypes and paternalism.[16] This position supports legality for surrogacy, including compensated surrogacy, on the ground that it respects freedom of contract and offers women new employment opportunities.[17]

Still other feminists took an intermediate position, recommending that the law permit surrogacy but allow the birth mother to renounce the contract.[18] Which of these positions is most consistent with the notion of procreative liberty, which enjoys some constitutional protection? The increasing importance of gender equality in family law? The best interests of children? How do the stories of Carol Pavek and Mary Beth Whitehead influence your answers?

Finally, how might the idea of surrogacy suggest a more basic challenge to the family and its place in contemporary (capitalist) society?[19] What would it take to create "the conditions of possibility for open-source, fully collaborative gestation" in which "every pregnancy [would] be for everyone"?[20]

Depictions in Popular Culture: Margaret Atwood, The Handmaid's Tale (1985)

This frightening novel portrays a dystopia in which humans have poisoned the earth's environment, threatening the future of the species, and religious fundamentalists have conscripted women of childbearing age, Handmaids, to carry pregnancies for those in positions of power, namely Commanders and their Wives, whose authority receives reinforcement from women performing supportive functions — from the Aunts (who control thought) to the Marthas (who perform housework). The Handmaids' status is signified by their appellations: In place of their own names, they must go by words that

---

[15] Barbara Katz Rothman, Recreating Motherhood (2d ed. 2000); Elizabeth S. Anderson, Is Women's Labor a Commodity?, 19 Phil. & Pub. Affairs 71, 91 (1990): Dorothy E. Roberts, The Genetic Tie, 62 U. Chi. L. Rev. 209 (1995).

[16] See, e.g., Debra Satz, Markets in Women's Reproductive Labor, 21 Phil. & Pub. Affairs 107, 117 (1992) (noting the "dilemma for those who wish to use the mother-fetus bond to condemn [surrogacy] contracts while endorsing [privacy] right to choose abortion"); Shalev, supra note [6], at 9-10 ("[A]mid the serious debate on the morality of [all varieties of] medical reproduction, only surrogacy has been addressed in terms of criminal norms. It occurred to me that the reason for this was the untraditional role that women play in these arrangements."); Shultz, supra note [8].

[17] See, e.g., Shalev, supra note [6], at 160-166 (reviewing how public-private dichotomy excluded women from market and concluding that "exclusion of domestic reproductive labor from the public economy is the ultimate manifestation of a patriarchal double standard").

[18] Martha A. Field, Surrogate Motherhood (1988). See also Lawrence O. Gostin, Surrogacy from the Perspectives of Economic and Civil Liberties, 17 J. Contemp. Health L. & Pol'y 429 (2001).

[19] See Sophie Lewis, Full Surrogacy Now: Feminism Against Family 22 (2019). Cf. Alice Ristroph & Melissa Murray, Disestablishing the Family, 119 Yale L.J. 1236 (2010.)

[20] Lewis, supra note [19], at 26.

indicate the men whom they serve, "Offred," "Ofwarren," and "Ofglen," for example. The reader experiences this world through the words of Offred, who endures her circumstances and the forced rituals designed to induce compliance, all the while mourning a life that we would take for granted in the world as it existed beforehand.

A political allegory, Atwood's novel has been hailed as "a cautionary tale of postfeminist future shock."[21] In an interview over two decades later, Atwood observes, "You will see that no woman ruler has been successful if she has been an advocate for women at large. Not one, ever."[22] To what extent does this comment pertain to issues raised by the fictional *The Handmaid's Tale* and by real-life surrogacy arrangements?

The book has had multiple afterlives. It became the basis of a popular television series (with Elisabeth Moss as Offred) beginning in 2017, the handmaids' red garb and enveloping hats have appeared frequently in state legislatures and Congress as a way for protestors to dramatize their objections to proposed restrictions on reproductive freedom, and Margaret Atwood released a sequel, *The Testaments*, in 2019.[23]

6. *Failed surrogacy agreements.* When an arrangement fails (because it is illegal or a court refuses enforcement), numerous questions arise. Using *Baby M* as an example, if Mary Beth Whitehead is the mother, what is Elizabeth Stern's legal status? Note how modern functional approaches that allow more than two parents might apply in this situation, especially once the child has lived principally in the Sterns' home.[24] See Chapter 1, section C. Should William Stern and Mary Beth Whitehead share parenting of the child, through joint custody or a custody-visitation arrangement?[25] Even if such arrangements routinely follow divorce or the dissolution of an intimate nonmarital relationship, do they make sense when the parents have only a contractual relationship? What do the best interests of the child dictate in *Baby M*? Does the Constitution permit termination of Mary Beth Whitehead's parental rights on grounds of the child's best interests? See Chapter 3, section A. When "Baby M," Melissa Stern, turned 18, she initiated proceedings to terminate Mary Beth Whitehead's parental rights, and

[21] See Christmas Books: Editor's Choice: The Best Books of 1986, N.Y. Times, Dec. 7, 1986, §7, at 3.

[22] Deborah Solomon, Questions for Margaret Atwood: In the Red, N.Y. Times, Sept. 26, 2008, §M (Magazine), at 21.

[23] Alexandra Alter, A Return to Gilead 15 Years Later, N.Y. Times, Sept. 7, 2019, at C1. See Margaret Atwood, The Testaments (2019).

[24] See Nancy D. Polikoff, This Child Does Have Two Mothers: Redefining Parenthood to Meet the Needs of Children in Lesbian-Mother and Other Nontraditional Families, 78 Geo. L.J. 459, 474-477 (1990).

[25] On remand, the court granted Mary Beth Whitehead unsupervised visitation for one eight-hour period per week, increasing to two days every other week beginning in September 1988; overnight visits followed after one year as well as a two-week visit in summer, 1989. Surrogacy — Baby M — Mother's Visitation Rights, 14 Fam. L. Rep. (BNA) 1276 (Apr. 12, 1988).

Elizabeth Stern then adopted her.[26] Does a termination initiated by the now-adult child avoid the constitutional problems arguably posed if the court had taken such action soon after birth? Why?

7. *Legislative responses.* Should legislatures regulate surrogacy? If so, how? What policy considerations should they consider? Should participants face criminal penalties? Which participants? Should the law distinguish commercial surrogacy from unpaid arrangements? What rules should govern in the event of breach?

According to a detailed survey by Professor Courtney Joslin, about half the jurisdictions in the United States (27) address surrogacy by statute. Although most focus on gestational surrogacy (see infra), five authorize genetic surrogacy, as in *Baby M*: Arkansas, Florida, Virginia, Washington, and the District of Columbia, with Maine and Vermont also allowing it but for family members only; most of these statutes are silent on compensation, beyond reasonable expenses and "ancillary costs," although both Washington and the District of Columbia explicitly permit more.[27]

Like earlier efforts to create a model for states, including the now repealed Uniform Status of Children of Assisted Conception Act (1988) (USCACA),[28] the UPA (2017) recognizes the absence of consensus and therefore offers legislative options on surrogacy. Article 8 is designed for states opting for statutory recognition of surrogacy agreements and includes provisions for both gestational and genetic surrogacy. UPA Art. 8 cmt. (2017). Although many of the eligibility and process requirements are the same for both, special rules for genetic surrogacy include a proceeding for judicial validation of the agreement before the assisted reproduction takes place to recognize the intended parents and a provision allowing withdrawal of the surrogate's consent any time before 72 hours after birth. Id. §§813-815. Note how the judicial validation resembles an adoption decree (albeit prepregnancy) and how the time period for revoking consent parallels an approach found in adoption law. See Chapter 3, section B1. Additional provisions address nonvalidated agreements, deceased intended parents, and remedies for breach of contract. Id. §§816-818.

8. *The attorney's role.* What role should attorneys play in surrogacy arrangements? What payments to attorneys are appropriate? In the *Baby M* era, attorneys often operated as matchmakers or intermediaries, bringing the parties together and shaping the market.[29] Recall the material on the

---

[26] See Suzanne A. Kim, In the Matter of Baby M (1988): Reining in Surrogate Parenting and Defining Children's Best Interests, in Courting Justice: 10 New Jersey Cases that Shook the Nation 139, 149 (Paul Tractenberg ed., 2013).

[27] Courtney G. Joslin, (Not) Just Surrogacy, 109 Calif. L. Rev. (forthcoming 2021) (manuscript at 14, 18, Appendix A) (on file with author). See Wash. Rev. Code §26.26A.715(2)(a) (allowing consideration); D.C. Code Ann. §16-401 (defining "ancillary expenses" to included "compensation for risk, inconvenience, forbearance, or restriction of usual activities").

[28] See UPA §1005 (2017).

[29] See Joan Heifetz Hollinger, *Baby M*, Lawyers, and Legal Education, 37 Buff. L. Rev. 675 (1988); Carol Sanger, Developing Markets in Baby-Making: In the Matter of Baby M, 30 Harv. J.L. & Gender 67 (2007). See also, e.g., *Stiver*, 975 F.2d 261 (broker and physicians owed affirmative duty of protection to mother, her husband, and intended father); Huddleston v. Infertility Ctr. of Am., 700 A.2d 453 (Pa. Super. Ct. 1997) (ruling that the broker can be liable to the surrogate for failing to screen the intended father who fatally abused child).

attorney's role in adoptive placements, Chapter 4, section A2. Should similar limitations apply?

Today, most states with legislation permitting surrogacy require independent counsel for the parties, according to Joslin's survey.[30] Likewise, the UPA requires independent legal representation, identified in the agreement itself, for the surrogate and intended parent(s) for consultation throughout the surrogacy arrangement regarding the agreement's terms; it also requires the intended parent(s) to pay for the surrogate's counsel. UPA §803(7) & (8) (2017). Today, fertility lawyers tend to help diffuse disputes that arise between intended parents and surrogates, especially over contract terms about behavior and health care during pregnancy, including prenatal testing and abortion.[31]

PROBLEM

Suppose, after recognizing Mary Beth Whitehead as the child's mother, the *Baby M* court awards custody to her. Should it now order William Stern to pay child support? What precedents would compel this result? Alternatively, what risks would such support duties create? What, if anything, should the legislature say on this subject?[32]

2. THE RISE OF GESTATIONAL SURROGACY

a. Splitting Maternity: Two Mothers

St. Mary v. Damon

309 P.3d 1027 (Nev. 2013) (en banc)

By the Court, Saitta, J.

Approximately one year after entering into a romantic relationship with each other, [Sha'Kayla] St. Mary and [Veronica Lynn] Damon moved in together. They planned to have a child, deciding that Damon would have her egg fertilized by a sperm donor, and St. Mary would carry the fertilized egg and give birth to the child. In October 2007, Damon's eggs were implanted into St. Mary. Around the same time, Damon drafted a co-parenting agreement, which she and St. Mary signed. The agreement indicated that Damon and St. Mary sought to "jointly and equally share parental responsibility, with both of [them] providing support and guidance." In it, they stated that they would "make every effort to jointly share the responsibilities of raising [their] child," including paying for expenses and making major child-related

---

[30] Joslin, supra note [27] (manuscript at 30-31).

[31] See Hillary L. Berk, The Legalization of Emotion: Managing Risk by Managing Feelings in Contracts for Surrogate Labor, 49 Law & Soc'y Rev. 143 (2015); Rebouché, supra note [3], at 1629-1634.

[32] See Field, supra note [18], at 98-101 (1988); Mark Strasser, The Updating of *Baby M*: A Confused Jurisprudence Becomes More Confusing, 78 U. Pitt. L. Rev. 181, 190 (2016). Cf. J.F. v. D.B., 941 A.2d 718 (Pa. Super. Ct. 2008); J.F. v. D.B., 848 N.E.2d 873, 879-881 (Ohio Ct. App. 2006), aff'd in part & rev'd in part, 879 N.E.2d 740 (Ohio 2007).

decisions. The agreement provided that if their relationship ended, they would each work to ensure that the other maintained a close relationship with the child, share the duties of raising the child, and make a "good-faith effort to jointly make all major decisions affecting" the child.

St. Mary gave birth to a child in June 2008. The hospital birth confirmation report and certificate of live birth listed only St. Mary as the child's mother. The child was given both parties' last names, however, in the hyphenated form of St. Mary-Damon.

For several months, St. Mary primarily stayed home caring for the child during the day while Damon worked. But, nearly one year after the child's birth, their romantic relationship ended, St. Mary moved out of the home, and St. Mary and Damon disagreed about how to share their time with the child. St. Mary signed an affidavit declaring that Damon was the biological mother of the child, and in 2009, Damon filed an ex parte petition with the district court to establish maternity, seeking to have the child's birth certificate amended to add Damon as a mother. The district court issued an order stating that St. Mary gave birth to the child and that Damon "is the biological and legal mother of said child." The 2009 order also directed that the birth certificate be amended to add Damon's name as a mother.

Thereafter, St. Mary instituted the underlying case by filing a complaint and motion, in a separate district court case, to establish custody, visitation, and child support. In response, Damon contended that, due to her biological connection, she was entitled to sole custody of the child. Damon attached the 2009 order to her opposition....

[Based on] the 2009 birth certificate order and believing that Damon's status as the sole legal and biological mother had already been determined, the [district] court decided that it would only consider the issue of third-party visitation [and] barred consideration of St. Mary's assertion of custody rights.... [After a hearing,] the district court issued an order providing that St. Mary was entitled to third-party visitation but not custody. The court reiterated that the scope of the evidentiary hearing had been limited to the issue of third-party visitation and noted that St. Mary could not be awarded custody of the child because previous orders determined that she "has no biological or legal rights whatsoever under Nevada law." Relying on NRS 126.045, which was repealed by the 2013 Legislature, the court also concluded that the co-parenting agreement was null and void because under that statute "a surrogate agreement is only for married couples, which only include one man and one woman." See Nev. Stat., ch. 213, §36, at 813 (repealing NRS 126.045). The 2011 order further provided that although St. Mary gave birth to the child, she "was simply a carrier for [the child]," and that she must "realize that [Damon] is the mother." As a result, St. Mary was granted third-party visitation rights and denied any rights as a legal mother. This appeal from the 2011 order followed....

St. Mary may be the child's legal mother

To determine parentage in Nevada, courts must look to the Nevada Parentage Act, which is modeled after the Uniform Parentage Act (UPA).... In Nevada, all of the "rights, privileges, duties and obligations" accompanying parenthood are conferred on those persons who are deemed to have a parent-child relationship with the child, regardless of the parents' marital status. Surrogates who bear a child conceived through assisted conception for another, on the other hand, are often not entitled to claim parental rights. See NRS 126.045 (2009) (defining "[s]urrogate" as "an adult woman who enters into an agreement to bear a child conceived through assisted conception for the intended parents," who are treated as the natural parents); 2013 Nev. Stat., ch. 213, §§10, 23, 27 at 807-08, 810-11 (replacing the term "surrogate" with "[g]estational carrier" and defining such as a woman "who is not an intended parent and who enters into a gestational agreement," wherein she gives up "legal and physical custody" of the child to the intended parent or parents and may "relinquish all rights and duties as the parent[ ] of a child conceived through assisted reproduction"); Black's Law Dictionary 1036 (8th ed.2004) (defining surrogate as "[a] woman who carries out the gestational function and gives birth to a child for another"). Accordingly, whether St. Mary is treated as someone other than a legal mother, such as a surrogate, is of the upmost significance.

The multiple ways to prove maternity

[T]he Nevada Parentage Act provides several ways to determine a child's legal mother [including proof of a woman's giving birth and through application of paternity statutes] "[i]nsofar as practicable." Paternity may be established in a variety of ways, including through presumptions based on marriage and cohabitation, NRS 126.051(1)(a)-(c), presumptions based on receiving the child into the home and openly holding oneself out as a parent, NRS 126.051(1)(d), genetic testing, NRS 126.051(2), and voluntary acknowledgment, NRS 126.053. Hence, a determination of parentage rests upon a wide array of considerations rather than genetics alone.

This case presents a situation where two women proffered evidence that could establish or generate a conclusive presumption of maternity to either woman. . . . By dividing the reproductive roles of conceiving a child, St. Mary and Damon each assumed functions traditionally used to evidence a legal maternal relationship. Hence, this matter raises the issue of whether the Nevada Parentage Act and its policies preclude a child from having two legal mothers where two women split the genetic and physical functions of creating a child.

The law does not preclude a child from having two legal mothers

[In relying on the 2009 birth certificate order and refusing to consider St. Mary's assertions of maternity or custody, the district court] impliedly operated on the premise that a child, created by artificial insemination through an anonymous sperm donor, may not have two mothers under the law. However, contrary to this premise, the Nevada Parentage Act and its policies do not preclude such a child from having two legal mothers.

Although NRS 126.051(3) contains procedures for rebutting paternity presumptions by clear and convincing evidence or "a court decree establishing *paternity* . . . by another *man*" (emphases added), and while NRS 126.051(3) arguably applies in maternity cases, we decline to read this provision of the statute as conveying clear legislative intent to deprive a child conceived by artificial insemination of the emotional, financial, and physical support of an intended mother who "actively assisted in the decision and process of bringing [the child] into this world." In Nevada, as in other states, the best interest of the child is the paramount concern in determining the custody and care of children. Both the Legislature and this court have acknowledged that, generally, a child's best interest is served by maintaining two actively involved parents. . . .

Of the jurisdictions that have addressed the issue of maternity between two women who created a child through assisted reproduction, California is highly instructive. California, like Nevada, enacted statutes modeled after the UPA. The California Supreme Court has determined that its laws do not preclude two women from being the legal mothers of a child. See Elisa B. v. Superior Court, [117 P.3d 660, 666 (Cal. 2005)] (providing that, under the California UPA, there is "no reason why both parents of a child cannot be women"). In [K.M. v. E.G., 117 P.3d 673 (Cal. 2005),] the California Supreme Court dealt with a maternity case that presented facts analogous to the instant case. There, K.M.'s eggs were implanted in E.G., her lesbian partner who gave birth to twins. Thereafter, K.M. and E.G.'s relationship ended, and K.M. sought custody and visitation of the twins, but the trial court denied her request, determining that she had relinquished her parental rights. On appeal, the California Supreme Court agreed with K.M.'s contention that she was the twins' legal mother because her eggs were used for the twins' birth. It concluded that because "K.M.'s genetic relationship with the twins constitutes evidence of a mother and child relationship under the UPA," and "[t]he circumstance that E.G. gave birth to the twins also constitutes evidence of a mother and child relationship[,] . . . both K.M. and E.G. are mothers of the twins under the UPA." Id. at 680-81. The court held that when a woman provides her eggs to her lesbian partner so that the partner can bear children by in vitro fertilization, both women are the child's legal mothers.

California's precedent is highly persuasive because it pertains to a statutory scheme that is substantially similar to Nevada's and advances the policies that underlie the Nevada Parentage Act — preventing children from "becom[ing] wards of the state," minding a child's best interest, and serving a child's best interest with the support of two parents. . . . Hence, there is no legal or policy-based barrier to the establishment under NRS Chapter 126, as it existed at the time of the district court's determinations and as it exists now, of a legal parent and child relationship with both St. Mary and Damon. . . .

. . . Although St. Mary's parentage can be established by virtue of her having given birth to the child, the parties dispute whether they intended for St. Mary to be the child's parent or simply a surrogate or gestational carrier who lacked a legal parent-child relationship to the child. Therefore, upon remand, the district court must hold an evidentiary hearing to determine whether St. Mary is the child's legal mother or if she is someone without a legal relationship to the child, during which the court may consider any relevant evidence for establishing maternity under the Nevada Parentage Act.

The co-parenting agreement was not a surrogacy agreement and was consistent with Nevada's public policy

St. Mary asserts that the co-parenting agreement demonstrates the parties' intent regarding parentage and custody of the child and that the district court erred in determining that the co-parenting agreement was an unenforceable surrogacy agreement under NRS 126.045. Damon responds that, because the agreement was between an unmarried intended parent and a surrogate and purported to resolve issues of parentage and child custody, the district court correctly deemed that the co-parenting agreement was prohibited by NRS 126.045 (2009).

. . . Here, St. Mary and Damon's co-parenting agreement was not within the scope of NRS 126.045. The agreement lacked any language intimating that St. Mary acted as a surrogate, such as language indicating that she surrendered custody of the child or relinquished her rights as a mother to the child. Rather, the agreement expressed that St. Mary would share the parental duties of raising the child and would jointly make major parenting decisions with Damon.

"Parties are free to contract, and the courts will enforce their contracts if they are not unconscionable, illegal, or in violation of public policy." It is presumed that fit parents act in the best interest of their children. Troxel v. Granville, 530 U.S. 57, 68 (2000). Thus, public policy favors fit parents entering agreements to resolve issues pertaining to their minor child's "custody, care, and visitation."

When a child has the opportunity to be supported by two loving and fit parents pursuant to a co-parenting agreement, this opportunity is to be given due consideration and must not be foreclosed on account of the parents being of the same sex. . . . St. Mary and Damon's co-parenting agreement was aligned with Nevada's policy of allowing parents to agree on how to best provide for their child. Within their co-parenting agreement, St. Mary and Damon sought to provide for their child's best interest by agreeing to share the responsibilities of raising the child, even if the relationship between St. Mary and Damon ended. The agreement's language provides the indicia of an effort by St. Mary and Damon to make the child's best interest their priority. Thus, in the event that St. Mary is found to be a legal mother, the district court must consider the parties' co-parenting agreement in making its child custody determination. [Reversed and remanded.]

NOTES AND QUESTIONS

1. *Gestational surrogacy and other collaborations.* IVF permits splitting the genetic and gestational contributions that were traditionally provided by one woman. For example, intended parents can hire a gestational surrogate after creating a preembryo with their own genetic material.[33] Or, an intended mother can gestate a fetus conceived with a donor's egg and the sperm of her husband/partner or a donor, as in *Patton* (Chapter 7, section B1). Or, sometimes, a gestational surrogate carries donated genetic material (a donated embryo or an embryo created with a donor egg or donor sperm or both) so that the intended parent or parents have no biological tie to the resulting child.[34] And, as in *St. Mary* and *K.M.* (discussed in *St. Mary*), lesbian couples can divide genetic and gestational contributions (sometimes called reciprocal IVF), giving each woman a biological tie to the child. Finally,

---

[33] See, e.g., Johnson v. Calvert, 851 P.2d 776 (Cal. 1993); Culliton v. Beth Israel Deaconess Med. Ctr., 756 N.E.2d 1133 (Mass. 2001).

[34] See, e.g., In re Marriage of Buzzanca, 72 Cal. Rptr. 2d 280 (Ct. App. 1998); Litowitz v. Litowitz, 48 P.3d 261 (Wash. 2002).

a trans or nonbinary father can supply genetic material (ova) to create embryos gestated by his partner or a surrogate.[35]

2. *Intent-based parentage.* The same procedure occurs in all of the scenarios described above: the extraction of ova, their fertilization in vitro, and the transfer of resulting preembryos for gestation. How can one distinguish in any given case a gestational surrogacy arrangement from an egg or an embryo donation? Why did the *St. Mary* court reject Damon's argument that the parties had entered into a surrogacy arrangement?

The California Supreme Court first applied an intent test in Johnson v. Calvert, 851 P.2d 776 (Cal. 1993), to recognize as parents the commissioning couple who provided the genetic material and who intended to rear the child, rather than the gestational surrogate who decided during the pregnancy not to abide by the agreement. Given the conflicting indicia of maternity under California parentage statutes (gestation versus genetics), the court broke the "tie" based on the parties' intent and causation (but for the agreement, the child would not exist). Thereafter, in In re Marriage of Buzzanca, 72 Cal. Rptr. 2d 280 (Ct. App. 1998), a court invoked intent to rule that divorcing spouses were both legal parents of a child who was created from a frozen embryo that they obtained from a fertility clinic and who was born to a gestational surrogate whom they hired; as a result, John Buzzanca could not avoid paying child support. Despite these precedents, California courts have not used intent to resolve disputes in traditional surrogacy cases (in which the gestational surrogate bears her genetic child, as in *Baby M*), and its current statutes authorize gestational surrogacy but not traditional surrogacy.[36] What are the advantages of intent-based parentage? The disadvantages? In embracing an intent test, *Buzzanca* explicitly rejected an "adoption default" model for most collaborative reproductive arrangements. 72 Cal. Rptr. 2d at 289. On what basis should couples like the Buzzancas be able to avoid adoption procedures in order to become the parents of a child with no genetic or gestational tie to either of them?[37]

How should a court determine the parties' intent when they offer conflicting testimony, as in *St. Mary*? K.M., which *St. Mary* invokes, was another case of conflicting testimony; dissenting in that case, Justice Werdegar explained how the majority's recognition of K.M. as a mother departed from intent-based parentage. Relying on undisputed evidence that at the time of the procedure the parties intended only for E.G., not K.M., to become the mother, the dissent contrasted "preconception manifestations of intent" with what she described as a new rule based on rearing the children in the parties' joint home. 117 P.3d at 686 (Werdegar, J., dissenting). If the parties' intent controls, when should it be determined? At the time of the procedure or after the children are born, based on the relationships that might develop?[38] To the extent that subsequent conduct counts, does intent

---

[35] See S.U. v. C.J., No. 18-0566, 2019 WL 5692550 (W. Va. 2019).

[36] See In re Marriage of Moschetta, 30 Cal. Rptr. 2d 893 (Ct. App. 1994); Cook v. Harding, 190 F. Supp. 3d 921, 927 (C.D. Cal. 2016) (interpreting Cal. Fam. Code §§7960, 7962), aff'd, 879 F.3d 1035 (9th Cir. 2018).

[37] Elizabeth Bartholet, Family Bonds: Adoption and the Politics of Parenting 219 (2d ed. 1999) (calling such arrangements "technological adoptions").

[38] See Jason P. v. Danielle S., 171 Cal. Rptr. 3d 789 (Ct. App. 2014), 215 Cal. Rptr. 3d 542 (Ct. App. 2017).

merge into a functional approach? See Chapter 1, section C. What role, if any, does gestation itself play in a functional approach to parentage?[39]

3. *Dual maternity.* In recognizing the "multiple ways to prove maternity," *St. Mary,* among other cases, challenges the longstanding principle of maternal certainty that courts, including the U.S. Supreme Court, often use as a foil to analyze the constitutional rights of fathers, according to Professor Courtney Cahill.[40] She continues, noting how "co-maternity law has simultaneously *relied* on the unwed-father doctrine [from the Supreme Court] . . . and *unsettled* that doctrine."[41] How so? See Chapter 1, section B. Why did *St. Mary* decide that both parties can be the child's mother? Is the rationale the same as that in *Elisa B.* (Chapter 1, section C)? What would it mean for the new approach to maternity exemplified by state family law cases like *St. Mary* and *Elisa B.* to "trickle up" to federal constitutional jurisprudence?[42]

4. *Legality.* Nevada's then-applicable surrogacy statute required the intended parents to be a married couple. Should Damon be estopped from arguing that the parties' agreement was a surrogacy agreement, which she concedes would be prohibited and unenforceable in this case? Why does the court simultaneously remand the case for determination whether St. Mary lacks a legal relationship with the child (as a gestational surrogate would) and conclude that the agreement was not a surrogacy agreement?

Consistent with the evolution of states' positions on surrogacy, Nevada is one of 22 states that now statutorily authorize gestational surrogacy and one of 19 that now permit compensation therefor.[43] New Jersey, the site of *Baby M*, has enacted a gestational surrogacy statute.[44] What accounts for the changing legal treatment of surrogacy? What is the impact of an increasingly common approach that makes gestational surrogacy agreements enforceable, but not genetic surrogacy agreements?[45]

After several failed legislative efforts, in 2020 New York switched from a state prohibiting all surrogacy to one legalizing gestational surrogacy, with a statutory scheme effective in February 2021. N.Y. Fam. Ct. Act §§581-401-581-402. LGBTQ activists had long pressed for such law reform, with support from Governor Andrew Cuomo, who launched the "Love Makes a Family" campaign to advocate for legalized gestational surrogacy.[46]

---

[39] Compare Susan Frelich Appleton, Presuming Women: Revisiting the Presumption of Legitimacy in the Same-Sex Couples Era, 86 B.U. L. Rev. 227, 282-285 (2006), with Jennifer S. Hendricks, Essentially a Mother, 13 Wm. & Mary J. Women & L. 429 (2007). See also, e.g., Lewis, supra note [19]; Lauren Springett, Why the Intent Test Falls Short: Examining the Ways in Which the Legal System Devalues Gestation to Promote Nuclear Families, 52 Colum. J.L. & Soc. Probs. 391 (2019).

[40] Courtney Megan Cahill, The New Maternity, 133 Harv. L. Rev. 2221, 2278 (2020).

[41] Id. at 2279.

[42] See id. at 2289-2297. See D.M.T. v. T.M.H., 129 So. 3d 320 (Fla. 2013); Douglas NeJaime, The Constitution of Parenthood, 72 Stan. L. Rev. 261 (2020).

[43] Nev. Rev. Stat. Ann. §§126.580; 126.750; Joslin, supra note [27] (manuscript at 18).

[44] See Courtney Crosby, Keeping Up with Gestational Carrier Agreements: Considerations Regarding the Regulation of Surrogacy, 17 Rutgers J.L. & Pub. Pol'y 357 (2020).

[45] See also Barry E. Adler & Alexis A. Alvarez, Property Rights in Children, 95 Notre Dame L. Rev. 1629, 1631 (2020) (arguing that "an acceptance of property rights in children — however disguised — is the reason reproductive technology may have motivated" the transformation in the law of surrogacy).

[46] "Love Makes a Family" Campaign Advocates for Legalized Surrogacy in New York, CNYCentral (Feb. 11, 2020), https://cnycentral.com/news/local/love-makes-a-family-campaign-advocates-for-legalized-surrogacy-in-new-york.

5. *A right to "fertility equality"?* One impetus for law reform in New York was the movement for "fertility equality." "Still in its infancy, this movement envisions a future when the ability to create a family is no longer determined by one's wealth, sexuality, gender or biology."[47] Proponents thus press for insurance coverage to make ARTs affordable for all and legal support for compensated gestational surrogacy to make parenthood possible for gay male couples,[48] such as the couple in the following case.

b. Splitting Maternity: No Mother

IN RE GESTATIONAL AGREEMENT

449 P.3d 69 (Utah 2019)

CHIEF JUSTICE DURRANT, opinion of the Court. . . .

Petitioners N.T.B. and J.G.M. (Intended Parents) are a married same-sex male couple. Petitioners D.B. and G.M. are an opposite-sex married couple who entered into a written gestational surrogacy agreement with the Intended Parents. The four individuals filed a joint petition requesting that the district court validate their agreement, in accordance with the statutory scheme contained in Utah Code sections 78B-15-801 through 809, the provisions of the Utah Uniform Parentage Act dealing with gestational agreements. . . .

In its order [denying the petition], the district court expressed "concern[ ] about the language of" Utah Code section 78B-15-803(2)(b), which requires, as a prerequisite to court approval, the court to find that "medical evidence shows that the intended mother is unable to bear a child or is unable to do so without unreasonable risk to her physical or mental health or to the unborn child." The district court . . . concluded that "the word[s] mother and her plainly refer to a woman," and, accordingly, found itself "bound to apply the statute as written." . . . The Petitioners appealed, again unopposed [and the court of appeals certified the question to this court]. . . .

I. We Have Jurisdiction to Hear This Case

Before reviewing Petitioners' arguments, we must first address the question of jurisdiction. . . . Utah Code expressly states that the court may issue an order validating a gestational agreement only on a finding that, among other things, "all parties have voluntarily entered into the agreement and understand its terms." . . .

. . . [W]hile the gestational agreement statute certainly does not fit the traditional principles of the "judicial power" — in that it precludes a controversy between adverse parties — adversariness does not completely define the

---

[47] David Kaufman, The Right to a Baby?, N.Y. Times, July 23, 2020, at D1.

[48] See id.; Marie-Amélie George, Queering Reproductive Justice, 54 U. Rich. L. Rev. 671, 677-680 (2020) (reviewing LGBTQ family formation arguments); Peter Nicolas, Straddling the Columbia: A Constitutional Law Professor's Musings on Circumventing Washington State's Criminal Prohibition on Compensated Surrogacy, 89 Wash. L. Rev. 1235 (2014) (critiquing prior Washington ban). But see, e.g., Morrissey v. United States, 871 F.3d 1260, 1270 (11th Cir. 2017) (rejecting taxpayer's argument that he has a fundamental right to assisted reproduction).

scope of our constitutional power. Certain functions that our courts perform may be both entirely non-adversarial and still appropriately fall within the "judicial power," by virtue of the fact that these functions were intended by the framers of our constitution to be included in the constitutional grant to the judiciary. . . .

A review of the history of Utah adoption statutes around the time of the framing reveals that early adoption proceedings, like gestational agreement proceedings today, generally required the joint consent of both the adoptive parents and the biological parents before a court could create a legally enforceable adoption. . . . [I]n 1898, shortly after the Utah Constitution was adopted, the Utah legislature codified a new adoption statute establishing a non-adversarial statutory scheme for adoption cases. The statute provided that

> [t]he person adopting a child and the child adopted and the other persons whose consent is necessary, must appear before the judge of the district court of the county where the person adopting resides, and the necessary consent must thereupon be signed and *an agreement be executed* by the person adopting to the effect that the child shall be adopted and treated in all respects as his own lawful child.[18] . . .

Because the validation of a gestational agreement involves the termination and creation of parental rights — a substantive power intended to be included in the constitutional grant of judicial power to the courts — it is appropriate for our courts to participate in their validation, despite the lack of adversariness in gestational agreement proceedings. . . .

II. The Legislature Intended "Mother" to Mean "Female Parent" in Utah Code Section 78B-15-803

"When interpreting a statute, it is axiomatic that this court's primary goal is to give effect to the legislature's intent in light of the purpose that the statute was meant to achieve." . . .

Petitioners and the State . . . point to the Utah Code section 68-3-12, which provides the following specific instructions for construing terms that are phrased in only one gender or phrased in singular terms: "unless the construction would be . . . inconsistent with the manifest intent of the Legislature; or . . . repugnant to the context of the statute," a word used in "[t]he singular includes the plural, and the plural includes the singular" and "[a] word used in one gender includes the other gender."[30] The State urges us to apply the latter rule of construction and read the word "mother" as including the "other gender," so that, in effect, "mother" means "parent." . . .

Under the State's proposed reading, the statute would provide that a court could validate a gestational agreement where "medical evidence shows that the intended [parent] is unable to bear a child." Under such a construction, an opposite-sex couple could obtain court validation merely by demonstrating that an intended father — who is an "intended parent" — is incapable of bearing a child. Because every opposite-sex couple could make this showing automatically (every opposite-sex couple contains a male member and

---

18. REVISED STATUTES OF UTAH, tit. 1, §6 (1898) (emphasis added).
30. UTAH CODE §68-3-12(1).

obviously a male cannot bear a child), this interpretation would write the intended mother requirement out of the statute. It would therefore be "inconsistent with the manifest intent of the Legislature" and "repugnant to the context of the statute" to read "mother" to mean "parent."

Even were we to employ both codified rules of construction noted above — first, that the word "mother" be construed to include the other gender, and second, that the singular be construed to include the plural — the problem remains. . . . [We could use a reading that] would require that the intended parents as a unit be incapable of safely bearing a child. While this interpretation does not eviscerate the intended mother requirement of section 78B-15-803(2)(b) in the same way as the State's proposed reading, it nevertheless contradicts the plain language of the statute, which clearly limits the meaning of the word "mother" to female parent. . . .

In addition to the clear language of the statute, it seems highly unlikely the legislature intended Petitioners' proposed interpretation, given the legal landscape at the time the law was passed. As noted by the Petitioners, "[t]he statute was . . . written with gender specific language at a time when marriage in Utah could only be between a man and a woman." Section 78B-15-803 was adopted in 2005 — ten years before the United States Supreme Court's decision extending the constitutional right to marry to same-sex couples. At the time the law went into effect, Utah's constitutional provision prohibiting same-sex marriage was operative and legally enforceable. The legislature therefore likely did not contemplate a reading of the statute that would allow same-sex couples to enter valid gestational agreements — a benefit the legislature expressly conditioned on marriage.

Accordingly, the district court was correct in holding the word "mother" under section 78B-15-803 unambiguously refers to woman and that it was bound to apply the statute as written. [The court decides that the canon of constitutional avoidance does not apply.] . . .

IV. Utah Code Section 78B-15-803(2)(b) is Unconstitutional Under *Obergefell* and *Pavan*

Petitioners alternatively argue that the intended mother requirement in section 78B-15-803(2)(b) violates the Utah and federal constitution. . . .

[By effectively conditioning] the validation of a gestational agreement on at least one of the two intended parents being a female parent [the statute] squarely violates [Obergefell v. Hodges, 576 U.S. 644 (2015),] in that it deprives married same-sex male couples of the ability to obtain a valid gestational agreement — a marital benefit freely provided to opposite-sex couples. . . . In *Obergefell*, the United States Supreme Court held as follows: "the right to marry is a fundamental right inherent in the liberty of the person, and under the Due Process and Equal Protection Clauses of the Fourteenth Amendment couples of the same-sex may not be deprived of that right and that liberty." The Court noted, however, that this right may include not only "symbolic recognition," but also "material benefits to protect and nourish the union." . . . The Court further held that because the "States have contributed to the fundamental character of the marriage right by placing that institution at the center of so many facets of the legal and social order," there should be "no difference between same- and opposite-sex couples with respect to [these rights]." . . .

The United States Supreme Court recently affirmed this notion. In Pavan v. Smith [137 S.Ct. 2075 (2017)], the Court reviewed an Arkansas statute that required the name of a mother's male spouse to appear on her child's birth certificate, even when the mother conceived the child by means of artificial insemination through an anonymous sperm donation, but made no such requirement when the mother's spouse was female under the same circumstance. . . . Two married same-sex couples brought suit seeking a declaration that the state's law violated the Constitution under *Obergefell*. On appeal, a divided Arkansas Supreme Court ultimately sided with the state, holding that the statute did "not run afoul of *Obergefell*" because the state law was centered on the biological relationship of the mother or father to the child and not the marital relationship of the husband and wife.

The United States Supreme Court summarily reversed the Arkansas Supreme Court's decision, holding that the law's "differential treatment infringes on *Obergefell*'s commitment to provide same-sex couples 'the constellation of benefits that the States have linked to marriage.'" The Court made clear that the state chose "to make its birth certificates more than a mere marker of biological relationships." Instead, the "State uses those certificates to give married parents a form of legal recognition that is not available to unmarried parents." Accordingly, the Court held that "Arkansas may not, consistent with *Obergefell*, deny married same-sex couples that recognition." . . .

A valid gestational agreement is undoubtedly a benefit linked to marriage. Obtaining a valid gestational agreement is, in many cases, one of the most important benefits afforded to couples who may not be medically capable of having a biological child. Such an agreement works to secure parental rights to an unborn child and bestows rights and benefits upon the intended parents. The State has explicitly conditioned this benefit on a petitioner's marital status; no unmarried couple may obtain one.[69] It is therefore unquestionably linked to marriage.

Application of section 78B-15-803(2)(b) results in disparate treatment of similarly situated same-sex male marriages. The statute requires that medical evidence be presented to the court, showing that the intended mother is medically incapable of bearing a child or to do so would otherwise harm her or the child. It is impossible for married same-sex male couples to meet this requirement since neither member is a "mother" under the statute. Requiring one of the two intended parents to be female precludes married same-sex male couples from entering into a valid gestational agreement[70] — a benefit explicitly conditioned on marriage. The statute therefore treats married same-sex male couples differently than married opposite-sex couples. Under *Obergefell* and *Pavan*, the Constitution proscribes such disparate treatment.

[The court decides that the intended mother provision is severable from the rest of the statute and reverses and remands for further proceedings consistent with the opinion.]

---

69. UTAH CODE §78B-15-801(3) ("The intended parents shall be married, and both spouses must be parties to the gestational agreement.").

70. See id. §78B-15-801(4) ("A gestational agreement is enforceable only if validated as provided in Section 78B-15-803.").

NOTES AND QUESTIONS

1. *Motherless children?* Commentators contend that "even in an age of sex and sexual-orientation equality, courts and legislatures continue to treat biological mothers as the parents from whom the legal family necessarily springs"[49] and that "the law is unable to envision a family without a certain and obvious mother."[50]

How does the principal case challenge these claims? In fact, earlier cases reached compatible results. In Raftopol v. Ramey, 12 A.3d 783 (Conn. 2011), the Supreme Court of Connecticut relied on a presumably valid gestational agreement to hold that a child's birth certificate should list as parents the biological father and his male domestic partner, not the surrogate or the anonymous egg donor. Similarly, in In re Roberto d.B., 923 A.2d 115 (Md. 2007), the highest court in Maryland ruled that a child's birth certificate could list only the name of a man, the sole intended parent, given the use of anonymously donated ova and the gestational carrier's wish not to be listed as the mother. The majority used a sex-discrimination rationale, reasoning that the state's Equal Rights Amendment required that females be permitted to challenge parentage on the basis of genetics, given that paternity statutes allow males to do so. Id. at 124-125. The court also observed that "mother" is legally and socially constructed:

> [I]n this case, the gestational carrier who actually gave birth to the children is not genetically related to the children in any way, but might be considered the birth mother. And the person who is, in fact, genetically related to the children, and might be considered the mother of the children under a genetic definition of the term, is not listed anywhere. So, who actually belongs on the birth certificate as mother depends entirely on the definition accorded to the term.

Id. at 125 n.14. How would you define "mother"? Note, historically, the legally determinative role played the status of a child's mother, from the presumption of legitimacy (see Chapter 1, section B) to the antebellum rule that made the offspring of enslaved mothers the property of the enslaver.[51]

One of the dissenting judges in *Roberto* used the opportunity to take aim at assisted reproduction more generally, at least when used by men:

> This case illustrates that the process of manufacturing children can lead to unusual situations that would have been virtually inconceivable decades ago when the relevant statutory scheme was enacted. . . .
>
> It is important to note what this case is not. It is not about a woman, married or otherwise, wanting to be a mother, who has difficulty in conceiving through sexual intercourse or who does not want to conceive through sexual intercourse or direct artificial insemination, and thus wants to have her egg fertilized outside her body and then implanted back into her womb where

---

[49] Douglas NeJaime, The Nature of Parenthood, 126 Yale L.J. 2260, 2314 (2017). See Appleton, supra note [39].

[50] Cahill, supra note [40], at 2250. See, e.g., J.F. v. D.B., 879 N.E.2d 740, 743 (Ohio 2007) (Cupp, J., dissenting) (the gestational surrogacy contract violates public policy because "it would be necessary to legally declare that the children do not have a mother").

[51] See Camille A. Nelson, American Husbandry: Legal Norms Impacting the Production of (Re)Productivity, 19 Yale J.L. & Feminism 1, 17-20 (2007).

she will, hopefully, be able to give natural birth to a child she will raise as the mother. This case has nothing to do with attempts to cope with female fertility problems of any kind. In this case (so far as the record reflects), there is no woman, genetic mother, birth mother, or otherwise, who wants to mother the resulting child or who wants her name on the birth certificate.

This is simply the case, apparently, of a man who wants to be a father and, recognizing that he could not do it by himself, went out and arranged for (perhaps hired) two different women and an assembler to help him manufacture a child — one woman to donate (or sell) the egg (a genetic mother), a technician (apparently paid) to fertilize the egg in a dish, and another woman (the birth mother) to carry the fetus through the gestation period and then to eject the child in what would normally be considered the birthing process. At the end of this manufacturing process, the result is a child who, according to the majority, is to have no mother at birth . . . — a concept thought impossible for tens of thousands of years.

One supposes that under the aegis of what is occurring in this case, that if a source of sperm does not intend to be a father, he could assert that he was not the father, and under the theories of the majority, a child could come into the world with neither a mother nor a father at birth. . . .

Id. at 132-133 (Cathell, J., dissenting).

Does sex discrimination explain the reasoning in *Gestational Agreement*? Illinois's statute requires, with respect to the intended parent or parents, that "he, she, or they have a medical need for the gestational surrogacy as evidenced by a qualified physician's affidavit. . . ." Chap. 750 Ill. Comp. Stat. §47/20(b)(2). Does this provision avoid the constitutional problem found in *Gestational Agreement*?[52]

Anecdotal evidence indicates that many surrogates prefer to work with male couples, like the one in the principal case.[53] What reasons might explain this preference?

2. *Birth certificates and parentage.* As the principal case explains, *Pavan* concerned the entry of names on a child's birth certificate. How does *Pavan* advance sex equality? How does it reinforce maternal primacy?[54] Dissenting in *Pavan*, Justice Gorsuch opined that a rule naming only biological parents on birth certificates would be reasonable and constitutional. Pavan v. Smith, 137 S.Ct. 2075, 2079-2080 (2017) (Gorsuch, J., dissenting). What problems do you see in this approach?

How far does *Pavan's* holding extend? Does it govern all marriage-related parentage rules? Some courts read it broadly so that, for example, the traditional presumption of legitimacy must apply to a mother's female spouse.[55] Under a narrower reading, however, "parentage rules that make distinctions based on sex or sexual orientation *may* infringe on the fundamental right to marry in violation of the Due Process Clause, or *may* constitute impermissible discrimination in violation of the Equal Protection

---

[52] See Amanda Grau, Comment, A Well-Rounded Argument: How *Skinner* and *Obergefell* Make Medical Requirements for Surrogacy Contracts Unconstitutional, 28 Am. U. J. Gender Soc. Pol'y & L. 441 (2020).

[53] See, e.g., Ginia Bellafante, Surrogate Mothers' New Niche: Bearing Babies for Gay Couples, N.Y. Times, May 27, 2005, at A1.

[54] See Libby Adler, Inconceivable: Status, Contract, and the Search for a Legal Basis for Gay & Lesbian Parenthood, 123 Penn St. L. Rev. 1, 10-11 (2018).

[55] E.g., McLaughlin v. Jones, 401 P.3d 492 (Ariz. 2017).

Clause, or both."[56] Further, "*Pavan* concerned only birth certificates, not the presumption of parentage itself, and generally 'a birth certificate is merely prima facie evidence of the information stated within.'"[57] How do you read *Pavan*, as you consider the quoted language used in *Gestational Agreement*? Would it require entering on the birth certificate the names of both intended parents in *Gestational Agreement* without the judicial proceeding contemplated by the Utah statute — following the practice used for different-sex married couples and now lesbian couples? Can similar marriage-triggered birth certificate practices apply when both intended parents are male spouses?[58]

3. *Surrogacy and adoption.* The agreement in *Baby M*, supra, assumed that Elizabeth Stern would adopt the child after termination of Mary Beth Whitehead's parental rights. *Gestational Agreement* invokes adoption law to support jurisdiction to validate surrogacy arrangements despite the absence of adversariness. What is the relationship between surrogacy proceedings and adoption proceedings? Aside from the absence of adversariness, how do surrogacy arrangements resemble adoption? How do they differ? Should the same adoption-like rules and procedures apply to both genetic and gestational surrogacy? Do gay couples like those in the principal case require some sort judicial proceeding to secure parentage even if different-sex and lesbian couples do not?[59]

4. *Gestational surrogacy statutes.* Among the 22 states that now statutorily permit gestational surrogacy, one can find several different details, including provisions about legal representation, mental health counseling, general eligibility, state residency, genetic relationship to one intended parent (or both), marital status, medical decisionmaking during pregnancy, compensation, and procedures for recognition of the intended parents as legal parents.[60] As Professor Courtney Joslin points out, the contrasts in state approaches go well beyond a "permissive" versus "restrictive" binary, with the variations among permissive states inviting more fine-grained analysis.[61] Using UPA (2017) as a point of departure, consider the following illustrative contrasts:

a. *Eligibility.*

Section 802. Eligibility to Enter Gestational or Genetic Surrogacy Agreement.

(a) To execute an agreement to act as a gestational or genetic surrogate, a woman must:
    (1) have attained 21 years of age;
    (2) previously have given birth to at least one child;

[56] Courtney G. Joslin, Nurturing Parenthood Through the UPA (2017), 127 Yale L.J. F. 589, 596 (2018) (emphasis added).
[57] Jessica Feinberg, Restructuring Rebuttal of the Marital Presumption for the Modern Era, 104 Minn. L. Rev. 243, 255 n.55 (2019) (quoting Courtney G. Joslin et al., Lesbian, Gay, Bisexual & Transgender Family Law §5:25 (2018)).
[58] Jessica Feinberg, After Marriage Equality: Dual Fatherhood for Married Male Same-Sex Couples, 54 U.C. Davis L. Rev. (forthcoming 2021).
[59] See id.
[60] See generally Joslin, supra note [27]; Rebouché, supra note [3].
[61] See generally Joslin, supra note [27].

(3) complete a medical evaluation related to the surrogacy arrangement by a licensed medical doctor;

(4) complete a mental-health consultation by a licensed mental-health professional; and

(5) have independent legal representation of her choice throughout the surrogacy arrangement regarding the terms of the surrogacy agreement and the potential legal consequences of the agreement.

(b) To execute a surrogacy agreement, each intended parent, whether or not genetically related to the child, must:

(1) have attained 21 years of age;

(2) complete a medical evaluation related to the surrogacy arrangement by a licensed medical doctor;

(3) complete a mental-health consultation by a licensed mental health professional; and

(4) have independent legal representation of the intended parent's choice throughout the surrogacy arrangement regarding the terms of the surrogacy agreement and the potential legal consequences of the agreement.

UPA §802 (2017). In addition, the intended parents must pay for the surrogate's legal representation. Id. §803(8). By contrast, for example, Illinois requires the intended parent or parents to contribute at least one of the gametes (ch. 750 Ill. Comp. Stat. §47/20(b)(1)); the Utah statute in *Gestational Agreement* requires the intended parents to be married (using language from the now withdrawn USCACA); and Louisiana requires intended parents to be "a married couple who each exclusively contributes their own gametes" (La. Stat. Ann. §2718.1(6)). What are such requirements' rationales and implications?[62] Why does Louisiana require gametes from both intended parents for surrogacy, while allowing donor insemination in cases of male infertility (La. Civ. Code Art. 188)?

b. *Agreement content.*

Section 804. Requirements of Gestational or Genetic Surrogacy Agreement: Content.

(a) A surrogacy agreement must comply with the following requirements:

(1) A surrogate agrees to attempt to become pregnant by means of assisted reproduction.

(2) Except as otherwise provided . . . , the surrogate and the surrogate's spouse or former spouse, if any, have no claim to parentage of a child conceived by assisted reproduction under the agreement.

(3) The surrogate's spouse, if any, must acknowledge and agree to comply with the obligations imposed on the surrogate by the agreement.

(4) Except as otherwise provided in Sections 811, 814, and 815, the intended parent or, if there are two intended parents, each one jointly and severally, immediately on birth will be the exclusive

---

[62] See, e.g., Linda S. Anderson, Legislative Oppression: Restricting Gestational Surrogacy to Married Couples Is an Attempt to Legislate Morality, 42 U. Balt. L. Rev. 611 (2013).

parent or parents of the child, regardless of number of children born or gender or mental or physical condition of each child.

(5) Except as otherwise provided in Sections 811, 814, and 815, the intended parent or, if there are two intended parents, each parent jointly and severally, immediately on birth will assume responsibility for the financial support of the child, regardless of number of children born or gender or mental or physical condition of each child.

(6) The agreement must include information disclosing how each intended parent will cover the surrogacy-related expenses of the surrogate and the medical expenses of the child. If health-care coverage is used to cover the medical expenses, the disclosure must include a summary of the health-care policy provisions related to coverage for surrogate pregnancy, including any possible liability of the surrogate, third-party-liability liens, other insurance coverage, and any notice requirement that could affect coverage or liability of the surrogate. Unless the agreement expressly provides otherwise, the review and disclosure do not constitute legal advice. If the extent of coverage is uncertain, a statement of that fact is sufficient to comply with this paragraph.

(7) The agreement must permit the surrogate to make all health and welfare decisions regarding herself and her pregnancy. This [act] does not enlarge or diminish the surrogate's right to terminate her pregnancy.

(8) The agreement must include information about each party's right under this [article] to terminate the surrogacy agreement.

(b) A surrogacy agreement may provide for:

(1) payment of consideration and reasonable expenses; and

(2) reimbursement of specific expenses if the agreement is terminated under this [article].

(c) A right created under a surrogacy agreement is not assignable and there is no third party beneficiary of the agreement other than the child.

UPA §804 (2017). Joslin's taxonomy reveals a range of different approaches to such matters, from requirements that the surrogate choose the physician only after consultation with the intended parents to provisions permitting "contract clauses that *limit* or *override* the medical decision-making authority of the person acting as a surrogate with respect to her own body."[63] Illinois's statute lists as an eligibility requirement for the surrogate health insurance coverage, although the intended parents may pay for it. 750 Ill. Comp. Stat. §47/20(a)(6). In 2020, surrogacy contracts began to include restrictions on the surrogate's travel and other activities to avoid exposure to COVID-19. Are such contractual limitations on autonomy enforceable?[64] Constitutional? Professor Rachel Rebouché shows how lawyers mediate

---

[63] Joslin, supra note [27] (manuscript at 35) (emphasis in original).

[64] See Ellen Trachman, The COVID Clause: Adding a Term to Surrogacy Contracts, Above the Law (Apr. 20, 2020), https://abovethelaw.com/2020/04/the-covid-clause-adding-a-term-to-surrogacy-contracts/.

and diffuse disputes over these clauses,[65] while such disagreements can cause relationships between the parties to break down.[66]

   c. *Parentage.*

Section 809. Parentage Under Gestational Surrogacy Agreement.

    (a) Except as otherwise provided . . . , on birth of a child conceived by assisted reproduction under a gestational surrogacy agreement, each intended parent is, by operation of law, a parent of the child.

    (b) Except as otherwise provided . . . , neither a gestational surrogate nor the surrogate's spouse or former spouse, if any, is a parent of the child.

    (c) If a child is alleged to be a genetic child of the woman who agreed to be a gestational surrogate, the court shall order genetic testing of the child. If the child is a genetic child of the woman who agreed to be a gestational surrogate, parentage must be determined based on [other parentage provisions].

    (d) Except as otherwise provided . . . , if, due to a clinical or laboratory error, a child conceived by assisted reproduction under a gestational surrogacy agreement is not genetically related to an intended parent or a donor who donated to the intended parent or parents, each intended parent, and not the gestational surrogate and the surrogate's spouse or former spouse, if any, is a parent of the child, subject to any other claim of parentage.

UPA §809 (2017). A party may terminate the agreement any time before embryo transfer or pregnancy. Id. at §810.

Section 811. Gestational Surrogacy Agreement: Order of Parentage.

    (a) Except as otherwise provided in Sections 809(c) or 812, before, on, or after the birth of a child conceived by assisted reproduction under a gestational surrogacy agreement, a party to the agreement may commence a proceeding in the [appropriate court] for an order or judgment:

    (1) declaring that each intended parent is a parent of the child and ordering that parental rights and duties vest immediately on the birth of the child exclusively in each intended parent;

    (2) declaring that the gestational surrogate and the surrogate's spouse or former spouse, if any, are not the parents of the child;

    (3) designating the content of the birth record in accordance with [cite applicable law of this state other than this [act]] and directing the [state agency maintaining birth records] to designate each intended parent as a parent of the child;

    (4) to protect the privacy of the child and the parties, declaring that the court record is not open to inspection . . . ;

    (5) if necessary, that the child be surrendered to the intended parent or parents; and

    (6) for other relief the court determines necessary and proper.

    (b) The court may issue an order or judgment under subsection (a) before the birth of the child. The court shall stay enforcement of the order or judgment until the birth of the child.

---

[65] Rebouché, supra note [3].
[66] See, e.g., P.M. v. T.B., 907 N.W.2d 522 (Iowa 2018).

(c) Neither this state nor the [state agency maintaining birth records] is a necessary party to a proceeding under subsection (a)....

Id. at §811.

Section 812. Effect of Gestational Surrogacy Agreement.

(a) A gestational surrogacy agreement that complies with Sections 802, 803, and 804 is enforceable.

(b) If a child was conceived by assisted reproduction under a gestational surrogacy agreement that does not comply with [eligibility, process, and content requirements], the court shall determine the rights and duties of the parties to the agreement consistent with the intent of the parties at the time of execution of the agreement. Each party to the agreement and any individual who at the time of the execution of the agreement was a spouse of a party to the agreement has standing to maintain a proceeding to adjudicate an issue related to the enforcement of the agreement.

(c) Except as expressly provided in a gestational surrogacy agreement or subsection (d) or (e), if the agreement is breached by the gestational surrogate or one or more intended parents, the non-breaching party is entitled to the remedies available at law or in equity.

(d) Specific performance is not a remedy available for breach by a gestational surrogate of a provision in the agreement that the gestational surrogate be impregnated, terminate or not terminate a pregnancy, or submit to medical procedures.

(e) Except as otherwise provided in subsection (d), if an intended parent is determined to be a parent of the child, specific performance is a remedy available for:

(1) breach of the agreement by a gestational surrogate which prevents the intended parent from exercising immediately on birth of the child the full rights of parentage; or

(2) breach by the intended parent which prevents the intended parent's acceptance, immediately on birth of the child conceived by assisted reproduction under the agreement, of the duties of parentage.

Id. at §812. These provisions, like those in many states, depart from default parentage rules that govern in the absence of affirmative steps by the parties. When parties comply with the requirements for a valid surrogacy agreement, the default rule recognizing the woman who gives birth as the mother and her spouse as the presumptive second parent does not apply.

Assess the degree of court involvement the UPA requires to depart from the default. Compare this approach with, for example, Utah's (as in *Gestational Agreement*) in which the judicial validation must occur before the pregnancy begins and, unless waived by the court, must be preceded by a home study of the intended parents, who must meet the standards of fitness for adoptive parents (Utah Code Ann. §§75B-15-803(2)(b) & 78B-15-806(1)). Does Utah, in effect, require a prepregnancy adoption — which UPA requires for genetic surrogacy but not gestational surrogacy (see UPA §813 (2017))? According to Joslin (the Reporter for UPA (2017)), "[h]alf of the permissive jurisdictions — 13 of the 22 — clearly provide for automatic determinations that the intended parents are parents of children conceived pursuant to a compliant gestational surrogacy agreement."[67] Is that UPA (2017)'s approach?

Joslin also notes "a trend in favor of statutes that permit courts to issue parentage orders prior to the birth of the child,"[68] a practice same-sex couples had been using for years.[69] Fixing parental status before or at the time of birth (either through a default rule or a prebirth order) not only can allow the intended parents' names to appear on the birth certificate,[70] it can also give them authority to consent to the infant's medical care, provide their insurance coverage for neonatal intensive care,[71] and determine benefit and inheritance rights should an intended parent die before the child is born.[72]

5. *Contested cases in the absence of statutes.* Beyond the 22 states statutorily authorizing gestational surrogacy, another 25 permit it by case law.[73] In the many states without surrogacy legislation, courts must use common law to resolve disputes, including those about parentage. What principles from contract law and its remedies in the event of breach should apply to such agreements?[74]

In P.M. v. T.B., 907 N.W.2d 522 (Iowa 2018),[75] the intended parents (the Ms) and the surrogate (T.B.) and her husband met via Craigslist. The latter were seeking to acquire $13,000 needed for their own IVF, with surrogacy as a means to do so. They used donor eggs and the intended father's (P.M.'s) sperm, but the relationship broke down during the pregnancy, as the intended parents asserted increasing control over the surrogate's medical care and the surrogate sought more money. Name calling ensued. Ultimately, the surrogate gave birth to premature twins without informing the intended parents and refused to relinquish the surviving child, Baby H, after one twin died.

The intended parents prevailed in their suit to enforce the agreement. In holding the agreement enforceable and not against public policy or Iowa precedents on embryo disposition agreements, the court referred to intent but emphasized genetics:

> This is not a situation in which T.B. is choosing to give up her own genetically related child in order to avoid the consequences of an unwanted

---

[67] Joslin, supra note [27] (manuscript at 27).

[68] Id. at 28.

[69] See, e.g., Kristine H. v. Lisa R., 117 P.3d 690, 692 (Cal. 2005); Howard Fink & June Carbone, Between Private Ordering and Public Fiat: A New Paradigm for Family Law Decision-making, 5 J.L. Fam. Stud. 1 (2003). See also Katherine Farese, The Bun's in the Oven, Now What?: How Pre-Birth Orders Promote Clarity in Surrogacy Law, 23 U.C. Davis J. Juv. L. & Pol'y 25, 63 (2019); Steven H. Snyder & Mary Patricia Byrn, The Use of Prebirth Parentage Orders in Surrogacy Proceedings, 39 Fam. L.Q. 633 (2005).

[70] Cf. Culliton v. Beth Israel Deaconess Med. Ctr., 756 N.E.2d 1133 (Mass. 2001).

[71] See Mid-South Ins. Co. v. Doe, 274 F. Supp. 2d 757 (D.S.C. 2003).

[72] See Dara E. Purvis, Intended Parents and the Problem of Perspective, 24 Yale J.L. & Feminism 210, 248 (2012).

[73] See Rebouché, supra note [3], at 1603 (listing a total of 46 states permitting surrogacy by statute or case law before 2020 legalization in New York).

[74] See Yehezkel Margalit, In Defense of Surrogacy Agreements: A Modern Contract Law Perpective, 20 Wm. & Mary J. Women & L. 423 (2014); Deborah S. Mazer, Born Breach: The Challenge of Remedies in Surrogacy Contracts, 28 Yale J.L. & Feminism 211 (2016).

[75] The court noted that Iowa has a statute allowing genetic surrogacy, so it did not intend to prohibit gestational surrogacy, and it also has administrative regulations governing the issuance of new birth certificates for a child born to a gestational surrogate. 907 N.W.2d at 535-536.

pregnancy or the burdens of childrearing. Instead, T.B. agreed to carry a child for the Ms after responding to their advertisement on Craigslist. But for the acted-on intention of the Ms, Baby H would not exist. The Ms would not have entrusted their embryos fertilized with P.M.'s sperm to T.B. if they thought she would attempt to raise the resulting child herself.

We hold that the adoption statute is inapplicable and the Surrogacy Agreement is not inconsistent with Iowa statutes on termination of parental rights. . . .

We see important differences between an embryo disposition agreement signed by the egg and sperm donor during their marriage and the gestational surrogacy agreement at issue here. The former addresses disposition of the parties' own genetic material and assumed the marriage will continue. . . .

We hold the statutory definition of "biological parent" of Baby H does not include a surrogate birth mother who is not the genetic parent. The ordinary meaning of "biological parent" is a person who is the genetic father or mother of the child. That is also the established legal meaning of "biological parent." It makes sense that the legislature and department of health used the term "biological parent" in the commonly understood and established legal meaning of those terms.

Id. at 537-538, 541. Evaluate the reasoning and result. What implications does the focus on genetics have for the law of parentage more generally? How would the case have played out in a jurisdiction with UPA (2017)?

6. *Race and class.* In Johnson v. Calvert, 851 P.2d 776 (Cal. 1993) (discussed supra), the gestational surrogate was part African-American; the genetic, intended mother was Filipina; and the genetic, intended father was white. In *T.B.*, evidence that the white intended mother called T.B. "the 'N' word," leading T.B. to conclude that the Ms were racist, strongly suggests that the surrogate was a person of color. See 907 N.W.2d 527. How might race have influenced the courts' decisions to recognize the intended parents as the legal parents? Does the emphasis on genetics in such cases reflect an unfounded notion of biological race?[76] Will gestational surrogacy produce a new class of poor and minority women who provide care for the children of wealthy whites — prenatally? As sociologist Barbara Katz Rothman long ago observed: "You have only to look at the poor women of color tending their white affluent charges in the playgrounds of every American city to understand which women will be carrying valued white babies in their bellies as a cheap service."[77]

Some analyses dispute such conclusions, noting, for example, that surrogacy is popular among "military wives," who have generous health care plans and can earn money while rearing young children, despite frequent moves from base to base.[78] Of what relevance is T.B.'s motive for becoming a surrogate — to acquire funds to pay for her own IVF?[79] Given the comparative costs

---

[76] See Camille Gear Rich, Contracting Our Way to Inequality: Race, Reproductive Freedom, and the Quest for the Perfect Child, 104 Minn. L. Rev. 2375, 2407 (2020).

[77] Barbara Katz Rothman, Daddy Plants a Seed: Personhood Under Patriarchy: 47 Hastings L.J. 1241, 1246 (1996). See April L. Cherry, Nurturing in the Service of White Culture: Racial Subordination, Gestational Surrogacy, and the Ideology of Motherhood, 10 Tex. J. Women & L. 83 (2001). See also Dorothy E. Roberts, Spiritual and Menial Housework, 9 Yale J.L. & Feminism 51 (1997).

[78] Pamela Laufer-Ukeles, Mothering for Money: Regulating Commercial Intimacy, 88 Ind. L.J. 1223, 1234-1235 (2013).

[79] See Rebouché, supra note [3], at 1638.

of the procedures, what are the class implications of the emerging legal consensus that gestational surrogacy agreements are more likely to be enforced than traditional (genetic) surrogacy agreements?

7. *Compensation.* Under UPA §804(b)(1) (2017), supra, surrogates may receive "payment of consideration and reasonable expenses." Nineteen of the 22 states that permit gestational surrogacy by statute allow compensation,[80] while Louisiana and Nebraska allow uncompensated surrogacy only.[81] What is fair consideration for undergoing embryo transfer, nine months of pregnancy (sometimes with twins or more), and labor and delivery, along with all attendant risks? One study quoted costs in the U.S. as falling between $80,000 and $150,000, figures that include roughly $30,000 to $50,000 for the gestational surrogate (in addition to $20,000 for agency fees, $15,000 to $30,000 for health insurance, $20,000 for legal and counseling fees, and $20,000 for the IVF procedure).[82] Another study found that the average compensation for the surrogate is $23,000.[83]

How do gendered stereotypes of altruism affect the market value of surrogates' services? Is surrogacy simply a job?[84] Does the amount influence the perception of surrogacy payments as exploitation versus well-earned employment compensation? What do you think of the approach followed by some attorneys who advise their clients working as gestational surrogates to treat the payments as child support, which does not constitute taxable income under the Internal Revenue Code?

Suppose a paid gestational surrogate works for an employer covered by the Family and Medical Leave Act (29 U.S.C. §§2601-2654), so that she would otherwise be entitled to twelve weeks of leave and a return to her job (either because of her own incapacity during pregnancy and delivery or in order to care for the child after birth). Does the fact that she has contracted to serve as a paid gestational surrogate change the employer's obligations under the law? Should it?

Depictions in Popular Culture:
Baby Mama (2008)

In this comedic portrayal of surrogacy, Kate, a high-powered, unmarried, fertility-challenged businesswoman (Tina Fey), hires the scheming, working-class Angie (Amy Poehler) to carry her fertilized eggs. When Angie moves in with Kate, their different backgrounds and perspectives stand out distinctly — and invite viewers to laugh. The story line presents a number of unexpected twists, but, throughout, the film assumes without questioning that women long for both

---

[80] Joslin, supra note [27] (manuscript at 18).

[81] La. Stat. Ann. §9:2720(c); Neb. Rev. Stat. Ann. §25-21,200.

[82] See Peter R. Brinsden, Surrogacy's Past, Present, and Future, in Handbook of Gestational Surrogacy: International Clinical Practice and Policy Issues 1, 6 (E. Scott Sills ed., 2016).

[83] Hillary L. Berk, Savvy Surrogates and Rock Star Parents: Compensation Provisions, Contracting Practices, and the Value of Womb Work, 45 Law & Soc. Inquiry 398, 409 (2020).

[84] Id. at 403-405.

motherhood and marriage and that the best sort of parenthood rests on biological connection. Reviews were less than enthusiastic.[85]

Soon after the release of *Baby Mama*, journalist Alex Kuczynski published a lengthy account of her own experience of producing a genetic son by means of gestational surrogacy.[86] Accompanying photographs highlighted apparent class differences between the two women, prompting many critiques of the underlying elitism and the absence of thoughtful exploration of both economic issues and the feelings of the surrogate.[87]

Given the shortcomings of *Baby Mama* and Kuczynski's account, what aspects of gestational surrogacy would you deem important to include in a portrayal aimed at the general public? Aimed at law-makers? Or, given the trend of statutory legalization, are existing por-trayals, however flawed, effective — if the goal is social and legal acceptance?

PROBLEMS

1. Robert and his wife, Denise, arrange to have a Denise bear a child con-ceived from embryos created for them with Robert's sperm and eggs from an anonymous donor. Clinic doctors transfer some of the embryos not only to Denise but, by mistake, also to Susan, a woman who arranged to become a single mother with an embryo from anonymous donors. Denise gives birth to a girl and Susan a boy — genetic siblings. After the clinic discloses the error, Robert and Denise sue for parental rights to the boy while Susan asserts that she is his sole legal parent. Whom should the court recognize as the parents? Why? Can intent-based parentage resolve this dispute? Should the court give both families some access to the child?[88]

Would Susan's claim be stronger or weaker if, instead of giving birth to the child herself, a gestational surrogate had done so pursuant to an agree-ment that complied with the requirements for enforceability under the UPA (2017) — assuming the case unfolded in a jurisdiction that had enacted its pro-visions? Suppose that before discovery of the mix-up Susan had obtained an order of parentage under the UPA §811 (2017). How might the UPA §809(d) (2017), supra, affect the case?

2. C.M. files a petition to be declared the sole legal parent of triplets con-ceived with his sperm and donor ova and gestated by M.C., pursuant to a

---

[85] See, e.g., Manohla Dargis, Learning on the Job About Birthing Babies, N.Y. Times, Apr. 25, 2008, at E1; Anthony Lane, Switching Places, The New Yorker, Apr. 28, 2008, at 86 (from column on "The Critics: The Current Cinema").

[86] Alex Kuczynski, Her Body, My Baby, N.Y. Times, Nov. 30, 2008, §MM, at 42.

[87] See Clark Hoyt, The Privileged and Their Children, N.Y. Times, Dec. 7, 2008, §WK, at 9 (public editor's column); Letters, Her Body, My Baby, N.Y. Times, Dec. 14, 2008, §MM, at 16.

[88] See Robert B. v. Susan B., 135 Cal. Rptr. 2d 785 (Ct. App. 2003); Marjorie M. Shultz, Taking Account of ARTs in Determining Parenthood: A Troubling Dispute in California, 19 Wash. U. J.L. & Pol'y 77 (2005). Cf. *Litowitz*, 48 P.3d 261; Lainie M. C. Dillon, Comment, Conundrums with Penum-bras: The Right to Privacy Encompasses Non-Gamete Providers Who Create Embryos with the Intent to Become Parents, 78 Wash. L. Rev. 625 (2003).

surrogacy agreement that said C.M. would be the sole parent and M.C. would have no parental rights. M.C. opposes the petition and seeks to be declared the triplets' mother. M.C. decided to pursue this course of action on the grounds that, during the pregnancy, (a) C.M. asked her to use selective reduction[89] because at most he could afford to raise twins, not triplets, and M.C. opposes abortion, and (b) she learned that C.M. is single, 50 years old, deaf, employed as a postal worker in Georgia, and responsible for caring for his elderly parents, with whom he lives. What result on the competing petitions and why? Could the court recognize them both as legal parents? Should the court reach the same result for all three children? What constitutional arguments, if any, might either party have?[90]

B. COLLABORATION WITHOUT ARTS

DAWN M. v. MICHAEL M.

47 N.Y.S.3d 898 (Sup. Ct. 2017)

H. PATRICK LEIS, III, J. . . .

Plaintiff [Dawn M.] and defendant [Michael M.] were married on July 9, 1994. After being unsuccessful at attempts to have a child, the parties went to a fertility doctor. The plaintiff was artificially inseminated with defendant's sperm and conceived a child. Unfortunately, that child was miscarried at ten weeks gestation.

In April of 2001, plaintiff met Audria G. (hereinafter referred to as "Audria") and they became close friends. Audria and her boyfriend moved into an apartment downstairs from plaintiff and defendant. When Audria's boyfriend moved out, Audria moved upstairs with plaintiff and defendant. Sometime in 2004, the relationship between plaintiff, defendant and Audria changed and the three began to engage in intimate relations.

As time went on, Audria, plaintiff and defendant began to consider themselves a "family" and decided to have a child together. The parties and Audria went to the fertility doctor previously utilized by plaintiff and defendant with the hope that Audria could be artificially inseminated with defendant's sperm. The fertility doctor, however, refused to artificially inseminate Audria because she was not married to defendant. Thereafter, the parties and Audria decided they would try to conceive a child naturally by defendant and Audria engaging in unprotected sexual relations. The credible

---

[89] Selective reduction is a medical procedure usually undertaken for health purposes in a multifetal pregnancy, resulting in the death in utero of one or more fetuses. See American College of Obstetrics and Gynecology, Multifetal Pregnancy Reduction, ACOG Committee Opinion No. 719 (Sept. 2017), https://www.acog.org/-/media/project/acog/acogorg/clinical/files/committee-opinion/articles/2017/09/multifetal-pregnancy-reduction.pdf.

[90] See C.M. v. M.C., 213 Cal. Rptr. 3d 351 (Ct. App. 2017); Michelle Goldberg, Is a Surrogate a Mother?, Slate (Feb. 15, 2016), http://www.slate.com/articles/double_x/doublex/2016/02/custody_case_over_triplets_in_california_raises_questions_about_surrogacy.html; Holly Jones, Note, Contracts for Children: Constitutional Challenges to Surrogacy Contracts and Selective Reduction Clauses, 70 Hastings L.J. 595 (2019); Vanessa Nahigian, Note, Procreative Autonomy in Gestational Surrogacy Contracts, 53 Loy. L.A. L. Rev. 235 (2019).

evidence establishes that it was agreed, before a child was conceived, that plaintiff, Audria and defendant would all raise the child together as parents.

Audria became pregnant and J.M. was born on January 25, 2007. The evidence establishes that plaintiff's medical insurance was used to cover Audria's pregnancy and delivery, and that plaintiff accompanied Audria to most of her doctor appointments. For more than eighteen months after J.M.'s birth, defendant, plaintiff and Audria continued to live together. Audria and plaintiff shared duties as J.M.'s mother including taking turns getting up during the night to feed J.M. and taking him to doctor visits.

As time went on, however, the relationship between defendant and plaintiff became strained. In October of 2008, Audria and plaintiff moved out of the marital residence with J.M. A divorce action was commenced by plaintiff against defendant in 2011. Plaintiff testified credibly that after the divorce action was commenced, defendant no longer considered her to be J.M.'s parent. Prior to this divorce, a custody case was commenced by defendant against Audria. Defendant and Audria settled their custody proceeding by agreeing to joint custody; residential custody with Audria and liberal visitation accorded to defendant. The plaintiff still resides with Audria and J.M., and sees J.M. on a daily basis. She testified that she brought this action to assure continued visitation and to secure custody rights for J.M. because she fears that without court-ordered visitation and shared custody, her ability to remain in J.M.'s life would be solely dependent upon obtaining the consent of either Audria or the defendant.

The Court finds plaintiff's love for J.M. evident from her actions, testimony and demeanor on the stand. Indeed, during her testimony, plaintiff beamed whenever she spoke of J.M., including her earliest involvement in his life during Audria's pregnancy. The court finds credible the testimony of Audria and plaintiff that J.M. was raised with two mothers and that he continues to the present day to call both "mommy." The court does not find credible defendant's claim that he called plaintiff by her first name and never referred to her as "mommy" in front of J.M. The court finds that in all respects, during the first eighteen months of J.M.'s life when defendant, plaintiff and Audria all lived together, and thereafter, plaintiff acted as a joint mother with Audria and that they all taught the child that he has two mothers. In fact, the credible evidence establishes that when J.M. had an ear operation at age two, the defendant told the nurse that both plaintiff and Audria were J.M.'s mother so that both could be with him in the recovery room.

Moreover, the in camera interview conducted by the court with J.M. clearly establishes that J.M. considers both plaintiff and Audria his mothers. When asked to distinguish them, he refers to Audria as "mommy with the orange truck" and to plaintiff as "mommy with the grey truck." He makes no distinction based on biology. J.M. is a well adjusted ten-year-old boy who loves his father and his two mothers. He knows nothing about this action. He has no idea that his father opposes tri-custody and court-ordered visitation with plaintiff. The in camera with J.M. leaves no doubt that J.M. considers both plaintiff and Audria to be equal "mommies" and that he would be devastated if he were not able to see plaintiff. The interview with J.M. also clearly shows that he enjoys his present living situation and would not want it altered in any way.

... Plaintiff asserts that the best interest of J.M. dictates that she be given shared legal custody of J.M. and visitation with him. J.M.'s biological mother Audria strongly agrees. Plaintiff argues, along with the child's attorney, that defendant should be estopped from opposing this application because he has created and fostered this situation by voluntarily agreeing, before the child was conceived, to raise him with three parents. And, further, that the defendant has acted consistent with this agreement by allowing the child to understand that he has two mothers.

Pursuant to DRL [Domestic Relations Law] §70, a parent may apply to the court for custody based solely upon what is for the best interest of the child .... The Court of Appeals in [Brooke S.B. v. Elizabeth A.C.C., 61 N.E.3d 488 (N.Y. 2016)], stressed that its decision only addressed the ability of a person who was not a biological or adoptive parent to establish standing as a parent to petition for custody and visitation, and that the ultimate determination of whether to grant those rights rests in the sound discretion of trial courts in determining the best interests of the child (28 N.Y.3d at 28, 39 N.Y.S.3d 89, 61 N.E.3d 488).[6] ...

Based on the evidence adduced at trial, including the demeanor and credibility of all three witnesses, the in camera interview and the factual findings made by this court, it is clear that the best interests of J.M. will be served by granting plaintiff's application for shared legal custody with defendant.... Such joint legal custody will actually be a tri-custodial arrangement as Audria and defendant already share joint legal custody. As it appears from Audria's testimony that she whole-heartedly supports such an arrangement, this Court finds no issue with regards to Audria's rights in granting this relief. Indeed, tri-custody is the logical evolution of the Court of Appeals' decision in *Brooke S.B.*, and the passage of the Marriage Equality Act and DRL §10-a which permits same-sex couples to marry in New York.

Regarding visitation, plaintiff requests that she be given one weekend a month and that such weekend can be carved out of defendant's time with J.M. (he presently sees J.M. from Saturday afternoon to Sunday late afternoon, three times a month). To grant plaintiff's request at defendant's expense, however, would be inappropriate as plaintiff presently lives with J.M. and sees him regularly when defendant does not have visitation. Additionally, J.M. enjoys his time with his father. Taking one of defendant's three weekends each month would significantly limit J.M.'s visitation with defendant and could have a detrimental impact on his relationship with his father. The Court does recognize plaintiff's need and right to time alone with J.M. and, accordingly, will grant plaintiff Wednesday night visitation with J.M. for dinner pursuant to a schedule to be established by plaintiff with input from Audria whose time with J.M. will be impacted by this court-ordered visitation. Lastly, plaintiff also requests one week-long school recess visitation each year and two weeks of visitation each summer. The court grants this relief and directs that all parties cooperate to determine which

---

6. Under [*Brooke S.B.*], relying heavily on the dissent written by Chief Judge Judith Kaye in Alison D. [v. Virginia M., 572 N.E.2d 27 (N.Y. 1991)], the law states "where a partner shows by clear & convincing evidence that the parties agreed to conceive a child and to raise the child together, the non-biological, non-adoptive parent has standing to seek visitation and custody under DRL 70." This case represents the logical next step.

school recess and which two weeks out of the summer will belong to plaintiff.

In sum, plaintiff, defendant and Audria created this unconventional family dynamic by agreeing to have a child together and by raising J.M. with two mothers. The Court therefore finds that J.M.'s best interests cry out for an assurance that he will be allowed a continued relationship with plaintiff. No one told these three people to create this unique relationship. Nor did anyone tell defendant to conceive a child with his wife's best friend or to raise that child knowing two women as his mother. Defendant's assertion that plaintiff should not have legal visitation with J.M. is unconscionable given J.M.'s bond with plaintiff and defendant's role in creating this bond. A person simply is responsible for the natural and foreseeable consequences of his or her actions especially when the best interest of a child is involved. Reason and justice dictate that defendant should be estopped from arguing that this woman, whom he has fostered and orchestrated to be his child's mother, be denied legal visitation and custody. As a result of the choices made by all three parents, this ten-year-old child to this day considers both plaintiff and Audria his mothers. To order anything other than joint custody could potentially facilitate plaintiff's removal from J.M.'s life and that would have a devastating consequence to this child. Accordingly, plaintiff is granted shared legal tri-custody and visitation as outlined above.

This Court retains jurisdiction and therefore should circumstances change, either party or Audria may make an application to modify this decision and judgment of the court.

NOTES AND QUESTIONS

1. *"Poly-parentage."*[91] If a child can have two mothers (as in *St. Mary,* supra) or two fathers (as in *Gestational Agreement,* supra), is there any reason why such children can't have still more — of either gender? Would such departures from the traditional two-parent model benefit children? Parents? Society? Or would this change present risks of harm? What are the advantages and disadvantages?[92]

Cases have begun to recognize as parents a same-sex couple and a third person who helped conceive (or conceive and gestate) the child using ARTs.[93] Often, the family harmoniously functions as a poly-parent family by agreement or implicit assent, with legal recognition of the third parent arising as an issue for courts to address when the adults' relationships break down.

---

[91] See Cahill, supra note [40], at 2283. Cf. Lewis, supra note [19], passim (referring to "polymaternalism").

[92] See generally Susan Frelich Appleton, Parents by the Numbers, 37 Hofstra L. Rev. 11 (2008); Melanie B. Jacobs, Why Just Two?: Disaggregating Parental Rights and Responsibilities to Recognize Multiple Parents, 9 J.L. & Fam. Stud. 309 (2007). Cf. Katharine K. Baker, Bionormativity and the Construction of Parenthood, 42 Ga. L. Rev. 649 (2008). But see Tomeka N.H. v. Jesus R., 122 N.Y.S.3d 461 (App. Div. 2020) (denying the mother's former partner standing to petition for tri-custodial arrangement).

[93] E.g., Jacob v. Shultz-Jacob, 923 A.2d 473 (Pa. Super. Ct. 2007) (lesbian couple and known sperm donor); A.A. v. B.B. [2007] 278 D.L.R. (4th) 519 (Can.), leave to appeal denied sub nom. Alliance for Marriage and Family v. A.A., [2007] 3 S.C.R. 124 (same); Raymond T. v. Samantha G., 74 N.Y.S.3d 730 (Fam. Ct. 2018) (gay couple and woman who self-inseminated with the sperm of both).

A few states now have statutes authorizing recognition of more than two legal parents.[94] The UPA also allows for this possibility. UPA §613 (2017). Don't functional and intent-based tests for parentage necessarily invite departures from the two-parent norm? California's statute specifies the following conditions:

> In an appropriate action, a court may find that more than two persons with a claim to parentage under this division are parents if the court finds that recognizing only two parents would be detrimental to the child. In determining detriment to the child, the court shall consider all relevant factors, including, but not limited to, the harm of removing the child from a stable placement with a parent who has fulfilled the child's physical needs and the child's psychological needs for care and affection, and who has assumed that role for a substantial period of time. A finding of detriment to the child does not require a finding of unfitness of any of the parents or persons with a claim to parentage.

Cal. Fam. Code §7612(c). The provision has been interpreted to require a weighing process, and its application to recognize a putative biological father has survived constitutional challenge by the mother and her husband.[95] Does "stable placement" require that the child reside with the candidate as a prerequisite for third-parent status? Might poly-parentage have a beneficial role to play when children are removed from foster families to whom they have become attached? See Chapter 2, section B2.

2. *Tiered parentage.* Does the desire of children born from collaborative reproduction for knowledge about their progenitors (whether gamete donors or gestational surrogates) suggest the need to develop a hierarchy of parents — including some vested with full rights and responsibilities and others having very limited roles, for example, providing information about medical history or identity and participating in an occasional visit, even over the full parent's objection? Could we conceptualize their legal status as analogous to that of birth parents under some open adoption statutes or grandparents under some state visitation statutes?[96] See Chapter 2, section B1; Chapter 5, section C2.

3. *Poly-parenting agreements.* Professor Melanie Jacobs argues that advance agreements about the division of parental rights and responsibilities can facilitate multiparty parenting while avoiding pitfalls, such as future disputes.[97] Are such agreements enforceable while the adults' relationship remains intact? After the adults' relationship dissolves?

---

[94] Me. Rev. Stat. tit. 19-a, §1853(2) (allowing court to determine that a child has more than two parents).

[95] C.A. v. C.P., 240 Cal. Rptr. 3d 38 (Ct. App. 2018) (recognizing putative biological father as third parent over objections of mother and husband).

[96] See Susan Frelich Appleton, Between the Binaries: Exploring the Legal Boundaries of Nonanonymous Sperm Donation, 49 Fam. L.Q. 93, 112 (2015) (suggesting intermediate status instead of all-or-nothing parentage). But see Ayelet Blecher-Prigat, Conceiving Parents, 41 Harv. J. L. & Gender 119, 132-133 (2018) (advocating "all-or-nothing" parentage). Compare Jacobs, supra note [92], at 333, with Baker, supra note [92], at 711-712. Cf. Annette R. Appell, The Endurance of Biological Connection: Heteronormativity, Same-Sex Parenting and the Lessons of Adoption, 22 BYU J. Pub. L. 289 (2008); Caroline Jones, Why Donor Insemination Requires Developments in Family Law: The Need for New Definitions of Parents (2007).

[97] See Jacobs, supra note [92].

4. *Challenging marriage, challenging gender.* How does *Dawn M.* challenge the marital family? Why would the court in *Dawn M.* order a specific time-sharing arrangement between Dawn and Audria, while their relationship remains intact — violating longstanding policies of family privacy and noninterference with ongoing family relationships? Could it be that despite the judge's openness to nontraditional arrangements, including "throuples," he does not see Dawn and Audria as a "real family"?[98] What implications do poly-parenting and cases like *Dawn M.* have for polygamy or polyamorous relationships?[99]

Professor Laura Kessler contends that "community parenting," as she calls the recognition of more than two parents, would advance family law by helping to "deconstruct traditional gender and sexuality norms."[100] For example, collaborative childrearing practices among some gay men and lesbians demonstrate how "disconnecting family formation and reproduction from heterosexual relations . . . reveal[s] heterosexuality and biology to be mere symbols of a privileged relationship."[101] Do you agree? Note that in many of the poly-parentage cases about same-sex couples and assisted reproduction, the third parent supplies a "missing gender," perhaps reinforcing gender norms rather than disrupting them. On this count, *Dawn M.* should offer a more compelling illustration of Kessler's vision.

5. *Sexual conception redux?* Statutes and case law recognizing more than two parents do not distinguish among children based on the method of conception. Thus, they might apply to children of assisted reproduction, to include a donor or surrogate in the family, or to sexually conceived children, for example, to include a long-term stepparent or a married mother's husband and paramour.[102] Note that despite an initial effort to use alternative insemination, the adults in *Dawn M.* relied on sexual conception.[103]

Yet, some modern departures from traditional parentage rules explicitly govern only in cases of assisted reproduction. Thus, the sections on assisted reproduction in the UPA (2017) explicitly have no application to a child conceived by sexual intercourse. Why? Should a single rule apply to all cases of "collaborative reproduction," regardless of the means of conception? Recall *M.F.*, Chapter 7, Section B1.

---

[98] Cf. *C.A.*, 240 Cal. Rptr. 3d 38 (recognizing a putative biological father as a third parent over objections of mother and husband).

[99] See Stu Marvel, The Evolution of Plural Parentage: Applying Vulnerability Theory to Polygamy and Same-Sex Marriage, 64 Emory L.J. 2047 (2015). See also William P. LaPiana, Married Is as Married Does(?), 45 ACTEC L.J. 271 (2020); Edward Stein, How U.S. Family Law Might Deal with Spousal Relationships of Three (or More) People, 51 Ariz. St. L.J. 1395, 1412-1413 (2019).

[100] Laura T. Kessler, Community Parenting, 24 Wash. U. J.L. & Pol'y 47, 50 (2007).

[101] Id. at 73. See also Laura T. Kessler, Transgressive Caregiving, 33 Fla. St. U.L. Rev. 1 (2005).

[102] E.g., *C.A.*, 240 Cal. Rptr. 3d 38. Cf. Sinicropi v. Mazurek, 760 N.W.2d 520 (Mich. Ct. App. 2008).

[103] See also In re Parental Responsibilities of A.R.L., 318 P.3d 581 (Colo. Ct. App. 2013).

CHAPTER 9

ARTS ACROSS STATE AND NATIONAL BOUNDARIES

Variations in ARTs regulation, including divergent approaches for determining the parentage of children born from these interventions, reveal both an absence of consensus and law in flux. In addition to inviting a comparative perspective, such differences often prompt participants to travel to the most hospitable regime, in turn raising questions of choice of law, jurisdiction, and enforcement.

A. "THE REGULATORY MAP"[1]

EVANS v. UNITED KINGDOM

(App. no. 6339/05), 1 FLR 1990 (Eur. Ct. H.R. Grand Chamber 2007)

[The applicant and her partner, J, began treatment for IVF at a clinic in Bath, in England. Preliminary tests revealed pre-cancerous tumors that would require the removal of the applicant's ovaries. Ova could be extracted first, but preservation of unfertilized ova for future use has a much lower rate of success than the preservation of fertilized ova. Accordingly, the applicant's eggs were extracted and were used to create with J's sperm six embryos, which were frozen for future use. Both parties were informed that either could withdraw consent for the use of the embryos at any time. Shortly thereafter, surgeons removed the applicant's ovaries. While the embryos were in storage, the couple's relationship broke down, and J notified the clinic of his lack of further consent for the embryos' use, thus obligating the clinic to destroy them under British law, the Human Fertilisation and Embryology Act of 1990 (1990 Act). The applicant sought an injunction requiring J to restore his consent to the embryos' use and storage and a declaration that he could not withdraw his consent. She also sought a declaration that the relevant provisions of the 1990 Act breached her rights under articles (art) 8, 12 and 14 of the Human Rights Act of 1998, and she pleaded that the embryos were entitled to protection under arts 2 and 8 of the Human

---

[1] The phrase comes from Debora Spar, Perspective: Reproductive Tourism and the Regulatory Map, 352 New Eng. J. Med. 531 (2005).

Rights Act. After a five-day trial, the judge dismissed the applicant's claims. The court of appeal dismissed her appeal, and the House of Lords also refused her leave to appeal. The case then went to a seven-court Chamber of the European Court of Human Rights and ultimately reached that court's Grand Chamber, with 17 judges. The majority of the Grand Chamber reviewed British law and also the law, inter alia, of the Member States of the Council of Europe:]

39. On the basis of the material available to the Court, ... it would appear that IVF treatment is regulated by primary or secondary legislation in Austria, Azerbaijan, Bulgaria, Croatia, Denmark, Estonia, France, Georgia, Germany, Greece, Hungary, Iceland, Italy, Latvia, the Netherlands, Norway, the Russian Federation, Slovenia, Spain, Sweden, Switzerland, Turkey, Ukraine and the United Kingdom; while in Belgium, the Czech Republic, Finland, Ireland, Malta, Lithuania, Poland, Serbia and Slovakia such treatment is governed by clinical practice, professional guidelines, royal or administrative decree or general constitutional principles.

40. The storage of embryos, for varying lengths of time, appears to be permitted in all the above States where IVF is regulated by primary or secondary legislation, except Germany and Switzerland, where in one cycle of treatment no more than three embryos may be created which are, in principle, to be implanted together immediately, and Italy, where the law permits the freezing of embryos only on exceptional, unforeseen medical grounds.

41. In Denmark, France, Greece, the Netherlands and Switzerland, the right of either party freely to withdraw his or her consent at any stage up to the moment of implantation of the embryo in the woman is expressly provided for in primary legislation. It appears that, as a matter of law or practice, in Belgium, Finland and Iceland there is a similar freedom for either gamete provider to withdraw consent before implantation.

42. A number of countries have, however, regulated the consent issue differently. In Hungary, for example, in the absence of a specific contrary agreement by the couple, the woman is entitled to proceed with the treatment notwithstanding the death of her partner or the divorce of the couple. In Austria and Estonia the man's consent can be revoked only up to the point of fertilisation, beyond which it is the woman alone who decides if and when to proceed. In Spain, the man's right to revoke his consent is recognised only where he is married to and living with the woman. In Germany and Italy, neither party can normally withdraw consent after the eggs have been fertilised. In Iceland, the embryos must be destroyed if the gamete providers separate or divorce before the expiry of the maximum storage period. ...

[Relevant international texts, such as the Council of Europe Convention on Human Rights and Biomedicine and the Universal Declaration on Bioethics and Human Rights, emphasize the need for consent.]

The Law

I. Alleged violation of art 2 of the convention

53. In her original application and in her observations before the Chamber, the applicant complained that the provisions of English law requiring the embryos to be destroyed once J withdrew his consent to their continued storage violated the embryos' right to life, contrary to art 2 of

the Convention, which reads as follows: "1. Everyone's right to life shall be protected by law. . . ."

54. In its judgment of 7 March 2006, the Chamber recalled that in Vo v France [2004] ECHR 53924/00 at para 82, the Grand Chamber had held that, in the absence of any European consensus on the scientific and legal definition of the beginning of life, the issue of when the right to life begins comes within the margin of appreciation which the Court generally considers that States should enjoy in this sphere. Under English law, as was made clear by the domestic courts in the present applicant's case, an embryo does not have independent rights or interests and cannot claim — or have claimed on its behalf — a right to life under art 2. There had not, accordingly, been a violation of that provision. . . .

56. The Grand Chamber, for the reasons given by the Chamber, finds that the embryos created by the applicant and J do not have a right to life within the meaning of art 2, and that there has not, therefore, been a violation of that provision.

II. Alleged Violation of Art 8 of the Convention

57. The applicant contended that the provisions of [Schedule] 3 to the 1990 Act, which permitted J to withdraw his consent after the fertilisation of her eggs with his sperm, violated her rights to respect for private and family life under art 8 of the Convention, which states:

"1. Everyone has the right to respect for his private and family life . . .
2. There shall be no interference by a public authority with the exercise of this right except such as is in accordance with the law and is necessary in a democratic society in the interests of national security, public safety or the economic well-being of the country, for the prevention of disorder or crime, for the protection of health or morals, or for the protection of the rights and freedoms of others."

A. The Chamber Judgment

58. In its judgment of 7 March 2006 the Chamber held, in summary, that art 8 was applicable, since the notion of "private life" incorporated the right to respect for both the decisions to become and not to become a parent. The question which arose under art 8 was "whether there exists a positive obligation on the State to ensure that a woman who has embarked on treatment for the specific purpose of giving birth to a genetically related child should be permitted to proceed to implantation of the embryo notwithstanding the withdrawal of consent by her former partner, the male gamete provider."

59. Given that there was no international or European consensus with regard to the regulation of IVF treatment, the use of embryos created by such treatment, or the point at which consent to the use of genetic material provided as part of IVF treatment might be withdrawn; and since the use of IVF treatment gave rise to sensitive moral and ethical issues against a background of fast-moving medical and scientific developments, the margin of appreciation to be afforded to the respondent State must be a wide one.

60. The 1990 Act was the culmination of an exceptionally detailed examination of the social, ethical and legal implications of developments in the field of human fertilisation and embryology. Its policy was to ensure continuing consent from the commencement of treatment to the point of

implantation in the woman. While the pressing nature of the applicant's medical condition required that she and J reach a decision about the fertilisation of her eggs without as much time for reflection and advice as might ordinarily be desired, it was undisputed that it was explained to them both that either was free to withdraw consent at any time before the resulting embryo was implanted in the applicant's uterus. [S]trong policy considerations underlay the decision of the legislature to favour a clear or "bright-line" rule which would serve both to produce legal certainty and to maintain public confidence in the law in a sensitive field. Like the national courts, the Chamber did not find, therefore, that the absence of a power to override a genetic parent's withdrawal of consent, even in the exceptional circumstances of the applicant's case, was such as to upset the fair balance required by art 8 or to exceed the wide margin of appreciation afforded to the State. . . .

[The applicant argues that the woman's role in IVF is much more extensive and "emotionally involving" than the male's and that a woman in her position would have no way to secure her future prospects of bearing a child if the man can unilaterally withdraw his consent.]

B. The Court's Assessment

1. The nature of the rights at issue under art 8

71. It is not disputed between the parties that art 8 is applicable and that the case concerns the applicant's right to respect for her private life. The Grand Chamber agrees with the Chamber that "private life," which is a broad term encompassing, inter alia, aspects of an individual's physical and social identity including the right to personal autonomy, personal development and to establish and develop relationships with other human beings and the outside world, incorporates the right to respect for both the decisions to become and not to become a parent.

72. It must be noted, however, that the applicant does not complain that she is in any way prevented from becoming a mother in a social, legal, or even physical sense, since there is no rule of domestic law or practice to stop her from adopting a child or even giving birth to a child originally created in vitro from donated gametes. The applicant's complaint is, more precisely, that the consent provisions of the 1990 Act prevent her from using the embryos she and J created together, and thus, given her particular circumstances, from ever having a child to whom she is genetically related. The Grand Chamber considers that this more limited issue, concerning the right to respect for the decision to become a parent in the genetic sense, also falls within the scope of art 8.

73. The dilemma central to the present case is that it involves a conflict between the art 8 rights of two private individuals: the applicant and J. Moreover, each person's interest is entirely irreconcilable with the other's, since if the applicant is permitted to use the embryos, J will be forced to become a father, whereas if J's refusal or withdrawal of consent is upheld, the applicant will be denied the opportunity of becoming a genetic parent. . . .

74. In addition, the Grand Chamber, like the Chamber, accepts the Government's submission that the case does not involve simply a conflict between individuals; the legislation in question also served a number of

wider, public interests, in upholding the principle of the primacy of consent and promoting legal clarity and certainty, for example. . . .

3. The margin of appreciation

77. A number of factors must be taken into account when determining the breadth of the margin of appreciation to be enjoyed by the State in any case under art 8. Where a particularly important facet of an individual's existence or identity is at stake, the margin allowed to the State will be restricted [citations omitted]. Where, however, there is no consensus within the Member States of the Council of Europe, either as to the relative importance of the interest at stake or as to the best means of protecting it, particularly where the case raises sensitive moral or ethical issues, the margin will be wider [citations omitted]. There will also usually be a wide margin if the State is required to strike a balance between competing private and public interests or Convention rights [citations omitted].

78. The issues raised by the present case are undoubtedly of a morally and ethically delicate nature. . . .

79. In addition, while the Court is mindful of the applicant's submission to treat the comparative law data with caution, it is at least clear, and the applicant does not contend otherwise, that there is no uniform European approach in this field. . . . While the United Kingdom is not alone in permitting storage of embryos and in providing both gamete providers with the power freely and effectively to withdraw consent up until the moment of implantation, different rules and practices are applied elsewhere in Europe. It cannot be said that there is any consensus as to the stage in IVF treatment when the gamete providers' consent becomes irrevocable.

80. While the applicant contends that her greater physical and emotional expenditure during the IVF process, and her subsequent infertility, entail that her art 8 rights should take precedence over J's, it does not appear to the Court that there is any clear consensus on this point either. . . .

81. In conclusion, therefore, since the use of IVF treatment gives rise to sensitive moral and ethical issues against a background of fast-moving medical and scientific developments, and since the questions raised by the case touch on areas where there is no clear common ground amongst the Member States, the Court considers that the margin of appreciation to be afforded to the respondent State must be a wide one.

82. The Grand Chamber, like the Chamber, considers that the above margin must in principle extend both to the State's decision whether or not to enact legislation governing the use of IVF treatment and, once having intervened, to the detailed rules it lays down in order to achieve a balance between the competing public and private interests.

4. Compliance with art 8

83. It remains for the Court to determine whether, in the special circumstances of the case, the application of a law which permitted J effectively to withdraw or withhold his consent to the implantation in the applicant's uterus of the embryos created jointly by them struck a fair balance between the competing interests. . . .

90. As regards the balance struck between the conflicting art 8 rights of the parties to the IVF treatment, the Grand Chamber, in common with every

other court which has examined this case, has great sympathy for the applicant, who clearly desires a genetically related child above all else. However, given the above considerations, including the lack of any European consensus on this point, it does not consider that the applicant's right to respect for the decision to become a parent in the genetic sense should be accorded greater weight than J's right to respect for his decision not to have a genetically-related child with her.

91. The Court accepts that it would have been possible for Parliament to regulate the situation differently. However, as the Chamber observed, the central question under art 8 is not whether different rules might have been adopted by the legislature, but whether, in striking the balance at the point at which it did, Parliament exceeded the margin of appreciation afforded to it under that article.

92. The Grand Chamber considers that, given the lack of European consensus on this point, the fact that the domestic rules were clear and brought to the attention of the applicant and that they struck a fair balance between the competing interests, there has been no violation of art 8 of the Convention.

III. Alleged Violation of Art 14 of the Convention Taken in Conjunction with Art 8

93. In her application and in the proceedings before the Chamber, the applicant complained of discrimination contrary to art 14 taken in conjunction with art 8, reasoning that a woman who was able to conceive without assistance was subject to no control or influence over how the embryos developed from the moment of fertilisation, whereas a woman such as herself who could conceive only with IVF was, under the 1990 Act, subject to the will of the sperm donor. . . .

95. The Grand Chamber agrees with the Chamber and the parties that it is not required to decide in the present case whether the applicant could properly complain of a difference of treatment as compared to another woman in an analogous position, because the reasons given for finding that there was no violation of art 8 also afford a reasonable and objective justification under art 14.

96. Consequently, there has been no violation of art 14 of the Convention.

For These Reasons, The Court

1. Holds, unanimously, that there has been no violation of art 2 of the Convention;

2. Holds, by thirteen votes to four, that there has been no violation of art 8 of the Convention;

3. Holds, by thirteen votes to four, that there has been no violation of art 14 of the Convention, taken in conjunction with art 8.

[In a joint opinion, the four dissenting judges explained that they would find a violation of article 8 because the interference with the applicant's right to respect for the decision to become a genetically related parent was not necessary or proportionate, under the special circumstances of the case. Invoking for purposes of comparison an infertile man, they would also find a violation of article 14 because the law treats men and women the same even though a "woman is in a different situation as concerns the birth of a child, including where the legislation allows for artificial fertilisation methods."]

NOTES AND QUESTIONS

1. *Regulatory variation.* As *Evans* demonstrates,[2] European nations have taken different approaches to the question of "precommitment strategies versus contemporaneous consent" (see Chapter 7, section A1). The United Kingdom's detailed statutory approach contrasts with what one finds in most of the United States: judicial resolution as courts encounter disputes or silence on the issue. The British statute indirectly controls individual conduct in fertility treatment "by exercising direct control over the clinics providing that treatment."[3]

England, the site of the birth of Louise Brown, the first IVF baby, has actively engaged in investigation, debate, and regulation of ARTs. The U.K.'s Parliament enacted the Surrogacy Arrangements Act in 1985, which was amended in 1990 in the more comprehensive Human Fertilisation and Embryology Act (HFEA), after the careful study of ARTs by a commission often called the Warnock Commission.[4] Additional revisions followed in 2008. *Evans* applied the 1990 version of the HFEA.

Early on in the U.S., a handful of states convened commissions to advise on appropriate legislative responses to the issues presented by ARTs.[5] The President's Council on Bioethics, established by President George W. Bush but now disbanded, weighed in as well, publishing detailed reports on ARTs.[6] Over the years, the Uniform Law Commission has provided several templates for enactment, but they have always contemplated variation among the states because they designate some provisions, such as those on surrogacy, as optional.[7] Critics have called for more public discourse in the United States on the ethical and political issues raised by ARTs innovation.[8]

---

[2] Although *Evans* predates Brexit, the British withdrawal from the European Union has no direct effect on its adherence to the European Convention on Human Rights (ECHR). See Johanna Dawson, How Might Brexit Affect Human Rights in the UK?, House of Commons Library (Dec. 17, 2019), https://commonslibrary.parliament.uk/brexit/how-might-brexit-affect-human-rights-in-the-uk/. But see The Observer View on Dropping the UK's Commitment to Human Rights Law, The Guardian (Mar. 8, 2020), https://www.theguardian.com/commentisfree/2020/mar/08/observer-view-dropping-uk-commitment-to-european-convention-human-rights (editorial) (expressing concern that UK might not follow ECHR after Brexit).

[3] Katharine Wright, Competing Interests in Reproduction: The Case of Natallie Evans, 19 King's L.J. 135 (2008).

[4] See Department of Health & Social Security, Report of the Committee of Inquiry into Human Fertilisation and Embryology (Chairman: Dame Mary Warnock DBE) (Presented to Parliament by Command of Her Majesty, July 1984).

[5] See, e.g., Robert Hanley, Jersey Panel Backs Limits on Unpaid Surrogacy Pacts, N.Y. Times, Mar. 12, 1989, §1, at 38; Lawrence K. Altman, Health Panel Seeks Sweeping Changes in Fertility Therapy, N.Y. Times, Apr. 29, 1998, at A1.

[6] See, e.g., The President's Council on Bioethics, Reproduction and Responsibility: The Regulation of New Biotechnologies (2004).

[7] E.g., USCACA (1988); UPA (2002); UPA (2017). See also American Bar Assn., Model Act Governing Assisted Reproduction (2008), and American Bar Assn., Model Act Governing Assisted Reproduction (2019), https://www.americanbar.org/content/dam/aba/administrative/family_law/committees/art/resolution-111.pdf.

[8] Myrisha S. Lewis, The American Democratic Deficit in Assisted Reproductive Technology Innovation, 45 Am. J.L. & Med. 130 (2019).

2. Experimentation versus a unitary standard?

a. *The United States.* What are the advantages and disadvantages of the variation among legal approaches? Do ARTs pose problems particularly well suited to local responses? Problems whose solution must emerge from the "'laboratory' of the States," such that experimentation constitutes a valuable contribution to development of the law?[9] Alternatively, do ARTs call for a more uniform approach? For example, within the United States, should Congress establish uniform standards by allocating conditional federal funds to the states to incentivize their enactment of particular legislation, as with foster care (see Chapter 2, section B2); by regulating ARTs directly as interstate commerce;[10] or by legislating under the Constitution's Full Faith and Credit Clause, as with the PKPA's efforts to control child custody litigation (see Chapter 6, section A)? Or, should uniformity emerge through constitutional adjudication, as it did for some reproductive rights and marriage equality (see Chapter 2, section A)?[11]

b. *The European Union.* Just as in the United States where a federal law or a constitutional ruling can trump a state's approach to ARTs (thus imposing a unitary standard), parallel questions arise in the European Union.[12] Illustrating such questions, *Evans* explores whether specific provisions in the Convention for the Protection of Human Rights and Fundamental Freedoms, drawn up by the Council of Europe and made effective in the United Kingdom by the Human Rights Act of 1998, require departing from the rules spelled out in the United Kingdom's HFEA of 1990. To what extent does article 8's "right to respect for . . . private and family life" resemble the constitutional rights to privacy, reproductive autonomy, and family autonomy recognized in the United States? (See Chapter 2, sections A & B1 & Chapter 7, section A.) To what extent does article 14's protection against discrimination resemble the Fourteenth Amendment's Equal Protection Clause? What is the basis of the alleged discrimination in *Evans*: women versus men, those with fertility problems versus those who can reproduce without assistance, or prospective parents who procreate versus those who adopt?[13]

Do you find the *Evans* majority's approach persuasive? Why? How does it compare to *Rooks*, Chapter 7, section A1. To what extent does the "margin of appreciation" invoked in *Evans* reflect a useful and pragmatic middle ground, allowing deference to a country or state's own approach, while still leaving room for imposition of an outer limit?

---

[9] See Cruzan v. Mo. Dept. of Health, 497 U.S. 261, 292 (1990) (O'Connor, J., concurring).

[10] See, e.g., Rachel I. Gewurz, Note, My Genetic Child May Not Be My Legal Child? A Functionalist Perspective on the Need for Surrogacy Equality in the United States, 12 Wash. U. Jurisprudence Rev. 295 (2020); Victoria R. Guzman, A Comparison of Surrogacy Laws of the U.S. to Other Countries: Should There Be a Uniform Federal Law Permitting Commercial Surrogacy?, 38 Hous. J. Int'l L. 619 (2016).

[11] See generally I. Glenn Cohen, The Right(s) to Procreate and Assisted Reproductive Technologies in the United States, in The Oxford Handbook of Comparative Health Law (David Orentlicher & Tamara Hervey eds.) (forthcoming 2020), https://www.oxfordhandbooks.com/view/10.1093/oxfordhb/9780190846756.001.0001/oxfordhb-9780190846756-e-35 (noting fragmented regulation of ARTs in U.S.).

[12] See, e.g., Elizabeth Ferrari Morris, Reproductive Tourism and the Role of the European Union, 8 Chi. J. Int'l L. 701 (2008); Richard F. Storrow, International Surrogacy in the European Court of Human Rights, 43 N.C. J. Int'l L. 38 (2018).

[13] See Anne Donchin, Toward a Gender-Sensitive Assisted Reproduction Policy, 23 Bioethics 28 (2009); Wright, supra note [3], at 148-150.

In a well-publicized earlier (pre-Brexit) controversy in the United Kingdom,[14] at the request of a woman, physicians extracted sperm from her husband while he was comatose and just before he died. Later, she sued the Human Fertilisation and Embryology Authority, which refused to let her use the semen because her late husband had not consented to such use. Although she unsuccessfully argued that she should be able to proceed without consent in the United Kingdom, she also argued that she should be allowed to export the semen to another nation in the European Community (EC), pursuant to EC Treaty provisions that protect the rights of EC citizens to receive treatment in another member state. The British court directed the Authority to reconsider its position in light of these provisions, and the Authority then granted permission to export the semen for treatment in a Belgian fertility clinic, enabling the widow to give birth to two sons.[15] Should the use of the frozen semen be governed by the United Kingdom's strict requirements or Belgium's more permissive approach?

3. *Comparative perspectives.* The following snapshots highlight distinctive features of other countries' regulation of ARTs.

a. *HFEA: subsequent amendments.* Parliament enacted a new version of the U.K.'s HFEA in 2008. Note that the British National Health Service makes clinics and providers "public," with health care services administered by the government. Thus, one finds direct regulation of fertility clinics and services. Regarding IVF, for example, the 2008 Act partially addresses the "designer baby" issue by conditioning a clinic's treatment license on its not preferring embryos known to have abnormalities over unaffected embryos. HFEA, (2008) ch. 22, §14(4).[16] Nonetheless, the legislation authorizes regulations to allow the use of eggs or embryos with altered mitochondrial DNA. Id. §26 (adding §35A). As another license condition, the 1990 version explicitly said that service providers must consider "the need of a child for a father" before treating a woman, while the 2008 amendments substitute "supportive parenting" for "a father." Id. §14(2)(b).[17] Departing from the earlier five-year limit on embryo storage and requiring destruction at that time, the 2008 version extends the potential storage time to ten years, followed by destruction. Id. §15.[18]

Another important change in the 2008 amendments permits individuals conceived by donor gametes to obtain, when they turn 16, nonidentifying information about their genetic parents and their donor-conceived genetic siblings and then identifying information, once they turn 18. Id. §24 (§31ZA, amending §31 of the 1990 Act). The amendments also provide for the release of information about genetic parentage to those seeking to marry or to enter

---

[14] See supra note [2].

[15] See R. v. Human Fertilisation and Embryology Authority, ex parte Blood, [1997] 2 All E.R. 687 (Ct. of Appeal, Civ. Div.); Jeremy Laurance, Woman Gives Birth to Husband's Baby 30 Months After His Death, The Independent (London), Oct. 4, 2004, News section, at 19 (updating this case and reviewing new case).

[16] See Human Fertilisation and Embryology Act 2008, c.22, Explanatory Notes ¶ 114 (UK), https://www.legislation.gov.uk/ukpga/2008/22/notes.

[17] See id. ¶ ¶ 115-117.

[18] See id. ¶ 127. See also Youssef M. Ibrahim, Ethical Furor Erupts in Britain: Should Embryos Be Destroyed?, N.Y. Times, Aug. 1, 1996, at A1 (reporting destruction of 6,000 to 10,000 embryos pursuant to 1990 law).

an intimate physical relationship (§31ZB), the release of information about resulting children to gamete donors (§31ZD), and — upon mutual consent — the release of identifying information about donor-conceived genetic siblings (§31ZE). Some of these provisions become effective under a schedule designed to avoid surprise to past donors who expected anonymity (§31ZC).[19] In addition, treatment services using donated gametes must be accompanied by counseling, including information about the importance of apprising resulting children of the facts of their conception. Id. §14 (amending §13 with new subsection 6C).[20]

Despite an earlier ban on commercial surrogacy, the 2008 legislation allows the issuance of parental orders pursuant to surrogacy arrangements for one or two intended parents, but only when the gamete of an intended parent and a method of nonsexual conception have been used. In cases of two applicants, intended parents must be "husband and wife," civil partners, or "two persons who are living as partners in an enduring family relationship and are not within prohibited degrees of relationship in relations to each other." Id. §54(2). Without the transfer of parenthood through a parental order or an adoption, the woman who gestates and gives birth is the mother regardless of location at the time of the treatment. Id. §33.

b. *Other European countries.* Once a country famous for reproductive innovation, Italy initiated a much more restrictive approach to IVF in 2004, adopting prohibitions on donor insemination and on the freezing and testing of embryos, while limiting the number of harvested eggs to three. A referendum to repeal the law failed because 50 percent of the eligible voters declined to participate after the Vatican urged a boycott.[21] While the Constitutional Court invalidated many of the provisions, the restrictions that remain deny ARTs access to same-sex couples, single women (and presumably single men), and persons of advanced reproductive age.[22]

A survey of 43 of 44 European countries[23] reveals that most have specific ARTs legislation, with 11 countries allowing access to different-sex couples only and five countries allowing access by both single women and same-sex couples; in all, a total of 30 countries allow access to treatment for single women and 18 to female couples. Almost all permit the use of donor sperm, but Bosnia and Herzegovina and Turkey do not. Several additional countries do not permit egg donation (Germany, Norway, and Switzerland). Other restrictions in effect in various countries apply to PGD, and embryo sex selection is prohibited in all the countries unless it is used in connection with sex-linked diseases.[24] Although anonymity prevails in 18 countries, five

---

[19] See Human Fertilisation and Embryology Act 2008, c.22, Explanatory Notes ¶ 152 (UK), https://www.legislation.gov.uk/ukpga/2008/22/notes.

[20] See id. ¶ 124. See also R. v. Secretary of State for Health, (2002) EWHC 1593 (Q.B. Admin.) Eng. 28 (recognizing right to personal identity in family life, which allows children of donor insemination to seek information and requires balancing against other interests).

[21] See Ian Fisher, Italian Vote to Ease Fertility Law Fails for Want of Voters, N.Y. Times, June 14, 2005, at A11.

[22] See Irene Riezzo et al., Italian Law on Medically Assisted Reproduction: Do Women's Autonomy and Health Matter?, 16 BMC Women's Health 44 (2016).

[23] C. Calhaz-Jorge et al., Survey on ART and IUI: Legislation, Regulation, Funding, and Registries in European Countries, 2020 Hum. Reprod. Open 1, 3 (2020).

[24] Id.

(including the U.K., supra) allow access to donor identity after the children reach a certain age, and 13 countries have a system that includes both anonymity and nonanonymity.[25] Several of the countries provide public support for ARTs treatments, and some condition such support on the transfer of a limited number of pre-embryos, depending on the patient's age.[26] Fifteen of the countries either allow surrogacy or have no relevant legislation.[27] Surrogacy remains illegal in France,[28] and reports of proposed legislation in the Netherlands say it would make paid surrogacy involving Dutch citizens a crime even if the arrangement takes place in a jurisdiction that permits such arrangements.[29]

c. *Israel*. Israel stands out as a leader in fertility medicine, based on its family-oriented culture and commitment to increasing Jewish population. It guarantees access to treatments and provides public support.[30] Israel legalized surrogacy in 1996 with legislation that permits only gestational surrogacy, limits intended parents to different-sex couples, and requires a government committee to approve all agreements. The surrogate must be unmarried, have children of her own, and must share the intended mother's religion, but they cannot be relatives. Her payment ranges from $45,000 to $65,000.[31] Jews from other countries often seek ARTs services in Israel because they know the procedures comply with Jewish law.[32]

d. *United Arab Emirates (UAE)*. In 2019, the UAE promulgated draft laws outlawing surrogacy, egg donation, and sperm donation, with violations punishable by incarceration and steep fines.[33]

4. *Models*. Which of the approaches to ARTs, whether from jurisdictions in the United States or abroad, do you find most sound, given the personal, medical, societal, and ethical issues presented?[34] Which of the models below offers the best way to conceptualize "the baby business"?

---

[25] Id. at 9.

[26] Id. at 9, 12 (e.g., "single embryo transfer . . . in the first two ART cycles in women up to 35 years").

[27] Id. at 9.

[28] See Storrow, supra note [12], at 44.

[29] See Ellen Trachman, The Netherlands' Surrogacy Laws Are Troubling and Dangerous, Above the Law (July 29, 2020), https://abovethelaw.com/2020/07/the-netherlands-surrogacy-laws-are-troubling-and-dangerous/. See generally Vincent van Woerden, Note, "Lost Identities": Surrogacy and the Rights of the Child in the United States and the Netherlands, 24 Tex. J. C.L. & C.R. 271 (2019) (examining the Netherlands's restrictive surrogacy laws).

[30] See Daphne Barak-Erez, IVF Battles: Legal Categories and Comparative Tales, 28 Duke J. Comp. & Int'l L. 247, 249 (2018). Other countries have also provided support for ARTs in order to encourage population growth in the face of declining fertility rates. See, e.g., Anna Louie Sussman, The End of Babies, N.Y. Times, Nov. 16, 2019 (op-ed citing Denmark).

[31] See D. Kelly Weisberg, The Birth of Surrogacy in Israel 197-200 (2005); Ruth Zafran & Daphna Hacker, Who Will Safeguard Transnational Surrogates' Interests? Lessons from the Israeli Case Study, 44 Law & Soc. Inquiry 1141, 1144 (2019).

[32] Lisa C. Ikemoto, Reproductive Tourism: Equality Concerns in the Global Market for Fertility Services, 27 Law & Ineq. 277, 286 (2009).

[33] See Ellen Trachman, Dramatic Case Results in the First United Arab Emirates Surrogacy Ruling, Above the Law (Nov. 27, 2019), https://abovethelaw.com/2019/11/dramatic-case-results-in-the-first-united-arab-emirates-surrogacy-ruling.

[34] See generally International Surrogacy Arrangements: Legal Regulation at the International Level (Katarina Trimmings & Paul Beaumont eds., 2013) (including descriptions of laws in 25 different countries); Regulating Reproductive Donation (Susan Golumbok ed., 2016) (exploring regulatory frameworks across the globe).

DEBORA L. SPAR, THE BABY BUSINESS: HOW MONEY, SCIENCE, AND POLITICS DRIVE THE COMMERCE OF CONCEPTION

217-221 (2006)

The Luxury Model

One possibility would be to treat the acquisition of children like the purchase of fine jewelry. Children are precious, one could argue just like jewels, and acquiring them entails a certain degree of luxury.... We could ensure that property rights are well-defined and the legal environment ensures the enforcement of baby-making contracts. We could posit, for example, that the presumption of parenthood rests with the intended parents.... And then we could extend this framework to include all forms of assisted reproduction, from IVF to surrogacy, sperm donation and adoption.

Few observers would want to classify any of these transactions as constructing a luxury market. But they effectively function, and could well be regulated, along those lines. Under this approach, access to the market would not be a cause for public concern, nor would equity among the various participants. This is exactly what one would expect in a high-priced luxury market.

The Cocaine Model

Alternatively, we could think of regulating reproduction as we regulate cocaine or heroin. In other words, we could decide that both assisted reproduction and adoption constitute unnatural interventions in the course of human affairs. We could therefore decide to ban them or push whatever transactions might still occur into an explicitly black market....

The Kidney Model

A third option would be to treat babies, and the components of babies, the way we treat kidneys. In the United States, as in most industrialized nations, it is explicitly illegal to sell a kidney, a liver, or a heart. Indeed, under the terms of the National Organ Transplant Act (NOTA), it is illegal for any person to "acquire, receive, or otherwise transfer any human organ for valuable consideration." People can donate their organs posthumously. They can even donate kidneys while they're still alive. But they cannot sell their organs, because doing so would constitute a federal crime.

There are several advantages to this kind of regulatory model. First, by removing the organ trade from any vestiges of the commercial market, it eliminates any concerns over commodification of the "sale of human flesh." ... Second, this regime still allows for organ exchange.... A final virtue of the organ donor model is its tilt toward order and safety. Organs are not exchanged in any open market; instead, the transaction is mediated by the nonprofit National Organ Procurement and Transplantation Network in the United States, and by similar organizations abroad....

The Hip Replacement Model

... Hips (like fertility treatments) are expensive, and the need for their replacement is distributed more or less randomly: some people have perfectly fine hips that work for the duration of their lives, but others do not. When hips deteriorate, replacements are rarely critical, because people can live without them. Yet forgoing replacement hips would arguably place those who need them at a distinct and tragic disadvantage: like those who suffer from infertility, they would be forced, through no fault of their own, to live a distinctly less pleasant life. If we left hip replacements to the free market, therefore, the pain of bad hips would be distributed along economic lines....

In most of the industrialized world, however, we have chosen to treat hips quite differently. [W]e treat their provision as some form of a social good.... In Europe and Canada, provision comes generally through a state-sponsored system of national health care. In the United States, it comes through a combination of private insurance and government programs such as Medicaid and Medicare. The results in both cases are largely the same: after enduring waits, completing paperwork, and clearing administrative hurdles, most people who need replacement hips get them for free....[35]

B. ARTS AND THE CONFLICT OF LAWS

1. PARENTAGE AND CITIZENSHIP

UNITED STATES v. ZODHIATES

901 F.3d 137 (2d Cir. 2018)

BARRINGTON D. PARKER, Circuit Judge:

Defendant-Appellant Philip Zodhiates appeals from a judgment of conviction ... of conspiring with and aiding and abetting parent Lisa Miller to remove her seven-year-old child from the United States to Nicaragua in order to obstruct the lawful exercise of parental rights by Miller's civil union partner, Janet Jenkins, in violation of the International Parental Kidnapping Crime Act ("IPKCA"). See 18 U.S.C. §§371, 1204, and 2....

... Lisa Miller and Janet Jenkins entered into a civil union in Vermont in 2000. In 2002, Miller gave birth to a daughter, "IMJ" [conceived by donor insemination]. About a year later, Miller and Jenkins separated, and Miller took IMJ to Virginia while Jenkins remained in Vermont. In 2003, Miller petitioned a Vermont family court to dissolve the civil union and the court awarded custody to Miller and visitation rights to Jenkins. After Miller repeatedly refused to respect Jenkins' visitation rights, Jenkins sought to enforce them in Virginia and, ultimately, the Virginia Court of Appeals held that Vermont, not Virginia, had jurisdiction over the dispute and ordered its courts to "grant full faith and credit to the custody and visitation orders of the Vermont court." Miller-Jenkins v. Miller-Jenkins, 637 S.E.2d 330, 332 [(Va. Ct. App. 2006)].

In 2007, the Vermont court warned Miller that "[c]ontinued interference with the relationship between IMJ and [Jenkins] could lead to a change of

[35] Reprinted by permission of Harvard Business School Press. From The Baby Business: How Money, Science, and Politics Drive the Commerce of Conception by Deborah L. Spar. Boston, MA 2006, pp. 217-221. Copyright © 2006 by the Harvard Business School Publishing Corporation; all rights reserved.

circumstances and outweigh the disruption that would occur if a change of custody were ordered." Miller refused to comply with the order and, following several contempt citations of Miller, Jenkins returned to court in Vermont. In November 2009, the Vermont family court awarded sole custody of IMJ to Jenkins and visitation rights to Miller.

In September 2009, while the Vermont litigation was pending, Philip Zodhiates, a businessman with strong ties to the Mennonite community, along with Kenneth Miller, a Mennonite pastor living in Virginia, and Timothy Miller, a Mennonite pastor living in Nicaragua, helped Miller to kidnap IMJ and flee to Nicaragua. [Kenneth Miller and Timothy Miller are not related to Lisa Miller.] As confirmed by Zodhiates' cell phone and email records, which were introduced at trial, Zodhiates drove Miller and IMJ from Virginia to Buffalo, and then Miller and IMJ crossed into Ontario. From Ontario, Miller and IMJ traveled to Nicaragua where Miller remains a fugitive and IMJ resides. Email records also show that, following the kidnapping, Zodhiates helped Miller and her daughter settle in Nicaragua. Zodhiates coordinated with others to remove a number of personal items from Miller's Virginia apartment, and, in November 2009, Zodhiates arranged for an acquaintance who was traveling to Nicaragua to bring various personal possessions to Miller. At the time of the kidnapping, Virginia law made same-sex marriages entered into outside of Virginia void there in all respects and such marriages could not be used to establish familial or step-parent rights in Virginia. . . .

. . . Zodhiates, Miller, and Timothy Miller were indicted for violating the IPKCA. . . . Near the end of [Zodhiates's criminal trial], the District Court shared with the parties its proposed jury charge—to which no objection was lodged—which read, in part, as follows:

> In this case, the term "parental rights" means Janet Jenkins' right to visit IMJ, as that right was defined by the law and courts of Vermont at the time IMJ was removed from the United States. . . . To find that Zodhiates acted with the intent to obstruct the lawful exercise of parental rights, you must find that he acted deliberately with the purpose of interfering with Janet Jenkins' parental rights. You may consider all of the evidence of Zodhiates' other acts in determining whether the government has proven beyond a reasonable doubt that Zodhiates acted with this intent.

Relying on the intended charge, the prosecutor stated in his rebuttal summation that "[i]t doesn't matter what [Zodhiates] understands about Virginia litigation," and that the Virginia litigation "should have no bearing on the intent issues." That evening, following closing arguments, the defense concluded that this remark by the prosecutor had been improper and requested that the District Court include in its charge a "curative instruction regarding the relevance of Virginia law," reading in part that:

> Parental rights for purposes of this case are defined by reference to the law of the state where the child, [IMJ], lived before leaving the United States. Prior to this case, there were a series of court proceedings in Vermont and Virginia about the parental rights of Lisa Miller and Janet Jenkins. One legal issue in the proceedings was whether Vermont or Virginia law governed the parental rights of Lisa Miller and Janet Jenkins. In its summation, the Government suggested that Virginia law is irrelevant to this case. That is incorrect.

> If, as Lisa Miller requested, Virginia had found that Janet Jenkins had no parental rights, it would have been impossible for Lisa Miller to obstruct parental rights for purposes of the international parental kidnapping statute because Janet Jenkins would have had no parental rights that could be obstructed. I will instruct you shortly that as a matter of law, Vermont law was found to control. I will also instruct you about what parental rights Janet Jenkins had and when.
>
> By instructing you as to the law, I am not instructing you on what the defendant knew or intended with regard to parental rights. That is a question of fact which you must decide, and which the government must prove beyond a reasonable doubt. In doing so, you may consider evidence about the litigation in both Vermont and Virginia for the purpose of considering whether the prosecution has proven beyond a reasonable doubt that Mr. Zodhiates knew Janet Jenkins had parental rights, understood those rights, and intended to obstruct those rights.

The District Court denied the request. It concluded that "[n]othing in the Court's current charge precludes the jury from considering both the Virginia and the Vermont litigation when it decides whether the defendant knew about and intended to obstruct Vermont rights." It also concluded that "the Court's intended charge gives the jury a properly balanced instruction on what evidence it may consider with regard to the issue of intent" and that "[t]he Court also believes that expressly instructing the jury that it may consider a Virginia litigation . . . runs the risk of unnecessarily confusing the jury." At the conclusion of the trial, the District Court instructed the jury consistent with the proposed instruction it had shared with the parties earlier. . . .

The jury found Zodhiates guilty on both counts of the indictment and the District Court sentenced him principally to 36 months of incarceration. [In this appeal, Zodhiates contends] that the District Court erred in failing to instruct the jury, as he requested . . . .

Zodhiates' challenge fails because, as the District Court correctly noted, "[i]t is clear in this case that, as a matter of state family law, Vermont family law . . . defined parental rights, regardless of where [the child] resided." . . . The IPKCA defines "parental rights" as "the right to physical custody of the child . . . whether arising by operation of law, court order, or legally binding agreement of the parties." Here, a Vermont court order afforded Jenkins parental rights. See Miller-Jenkins v. Miller-Jenkins, 912 A.2d 951, 956 [(Vt. 2006)]. Moreover, at the time IMJ was taken from Virginia, an order from a court of that state had also recognized that the Vermont courts had jurisdiction over the custody dispute and required Virginia courts to give full faith and credit to the Vermont orders. See Miller-Jenkins v. Miller-Jenkins, 637 S.E.2d 330, 337-38 [Va. Ct. App. (2006)]; Miller-Jenkins v. Miller-Jenkins, 661 S.E.2d 822, 827 [(Va. 2008)] (recognizing Vermont's jurisdiction in reliance on law-of-the-case doctrine). Because Virginia itself recognized that the Vermont court order was controlling, the District Court was correct when it instructed the jury that Vermont law defined parental rights. We agree with the District Court that to instruct otherwise would have been misleading and confusing. . . .

Finally, . . . [the] District Court correctly denied the request [for a curative instruction] because the prosecutor's statements, in context, were unobjectionable. The District Court recognized them for what they were: factual interpretations of the evidence and not statements of legal principles. As the District Court observed in denying Zodhiates' motion for a new trial: "[T]he AUSA's comment simply told the jury that, in the Government's view, Zodhiates's interpretation of the evidence was wrong — not that Zodhiates's understanding of the Virginia litigation was legally irrelevant." United States v. Zodhiates, 235 F.Supp.3d 439, 457 (W.D.N.Y. 2017). . . . As the District Court correctly observed, nothing in the charge or the summation precluded the jury from considering both the Virginia and Vermont litigation when it decided whether Zodhiates knew about and intended to obstruct Jenkins' rights. For these reasons, we see no error in the prosecutor's remarks or in the District Court's response to them. . . . [Affirmed.]

April Witt, About Isabella

Washington Post, Feb. 4, 2007, at W14

. . . As with other couples who have split, [the truths of Janet and Lisa] have diverged; through the lens of loss, each views their time together differently. Unlike most warring couples, however, the once hopeful and happy Miller-Jenkinses are at the center of a high-stakes, ideologically charged legal dispute waged across several courtrooms in two states. On one side are lawyers who are leading gay-rights activists; on the other are legal combatants for a conservative Christian foundation associated with Jerry Falwell.

These lawyers are sifting through every detail of the Miller-Jenkinses' lives — from how Isabella was conceived to who burped the baby. They are not fighting over the mundane detritus of love lost: Who gets the house? Who gets stuck with the old car? Who is on the hook for braces should Isabella require them? They are debating questions so profound that the answers have the power to affect legions of families gay and straight: Who is a parent? Who has the legal rights of a parent?

In the *Miller-Jenkins* case, those questions have been raised in Vermont, where state statutes explicitly recognize parental rights for same-sex couples in civil unions, and in Virginia, where they don't. That discrepancy has left Isabella — and a growing number of children like her nationwide — on the legal battlefield of what one judge in the case called civil war. . . .

[After Lisa moved from Vermont to Virginia with Isabella in 2003,] Lisa began attending a conservative Christian church. "All those years of going to church, going to Christian schools, all that started to come back to me," Lisa said. She began to wonder, she said, if she really was gay or merely sexually confused as a result of childhood trauma. . . . Lisa was determined to "leave the lifestyle," she said. "It wasn't a struggle," she recalled. "I felt peace." . . .

In early 2004, seven weeks after Lisa asked the court to dissolve their union, Janet filed a counterclaim seeking custody of Isabella for herself and visitation for Lisa. She felt like Isabella was as much her daughter as she was Lisa's, she said. . . .

Lisa didn't doubt that Janet and Isabella loved each other, and that it was in Isabella's best interests for them to see each other regularly, she later testified. She just didn't think that Janet was a legal parent with rights equal to hers. "To me, it was more like Isabella and Janet had a deep friendship," rather than a mother-daughter bond, Lisa said. Janet scoffed: "Friends don't pay child support for other people's kids."

[Lisa's first attorney, Linda Reis, notified the trial judge in Vermont, William Cohen] that they planned to argue that Janet was not Isabella's legal parent. . . . After a few months, Lisa, frustrated by the case's slow pace, decided to change lawyers. [Eventually, she hired Deborah Lashman, a Vermont law firm's expert in civil union law.]

Lashman is a central figure in the history of legal rights for gay parents in Vermont. [She had pioneered second-parent adoption in Vermont.] Lashman later became an outspoken board member of the Vermont Freedom to Marry Task Force, which supports same-sex marriage.

Lisa didn't know any of that when she hired Lashman, she later said. She maxed out new credit cards and borrowed money from her father to send Lashman the $3,000 retainer she requested. [Thirty minutes before the next court hearing, she met Lashman for the first time.] Lisa's new lawyer "told me that she felt that this was a custody case and that we needed to proceed as such," Lisa later testified. "I said, 'No. I don't even feel that she's a parent, so why should she even have visitation or custody.' She said, 'The judge isn't going to go for that,' and I needed . . . to come up with some kind of [visitation] schedule. I said, 'No, I don't agree with it.' And she said, 'You have to get used to the fact that Janet is a parent.' And I said, 'No, I don't.' And then we were called into the courtroom."

According to a transcript of the hearing, Judge Cohen began by saying, "The last time we were in court, when Ms. Reis was representing the plaintiff, there was an issue at that time involving, I believe it was parentage and civil unions and who the parent would be. I understand that there's been a change in tactics, or a change in course, I guess, is a better word."

"Well, I have a different interpretation of the law than Ms. Reis," Lashman told the judge. "My reading of Vermont law is . . . both these folks are legal parents of Isabella."

"Presumed," the judge said.

"Presumed because she was born during the course of the civil union," Lashman said.

"Right," the judge said.

"So I don't think that's an issue at this point," Lashman said.

"That was an issue she raised," the judge noted. "Your client's waiving that issue now?"

"She is, your honor," Lashman said.

Lashman later said in an interview that Lisa knowingly waived her right that day to contest that Janet was [Isabella's] mom. Lisa, however, disputes that [saying that she was nervous and confused and Lashman declined to discuss the matter with her. Later,] Lisa's attorney told her that if she was going to insist that Janet was not Isabella's parent, then Lashman was going to withdraw from the case. Lisa insisted. Lashman withdrew. . . .

Lisa and Janet's breakup had exposed a fundamental flaw in Vermont law, [Lisa's next attorney, Judy Barone] suggested. Vermont's civil union statute made it a rebuttable presumption that Janet was Isabella's parent, yet spelled out no specific grounds for rebuttal. Other Vermont statutes, which predated the civil union law, detailed two routes to establishing legal parental rights: having a biological connection to a child, or adopting. Janet would not meet either of those standards, Barone said. "I think this case is really about the standard in Vermont that we have to be able to establish parentage," Barone told the judge. "What can be more basic and important?" . . .

[On July 1, 2004, Virginia's Marriage Affirmation Act became law.] The new law prohibited civil unions or other contracts "between persons of the same sex purporting to bestow the privileges or obligations of marriage." Furthermore, the law said, same-sex unions performed in other states "shall be void in all respects in Virginia, and any contractual rights created thereby shall be void and unenforceable." . . .

"I believe that no matter what this court does here," Barone told [Judge Cohen in court], "in the long run, it will not be enforceable against Virginia residents, because Virginia has a statute that says that any matter involving civil unions . . . will not be given any credence in the state of Virginia." . . . [Barone called Lashman to testify.]

"Do you agree with me," Barone asked Lashman, that under Vermont law the concept that Janet is Isabella's parent is "a rebuttable presumption?"

"Yes," Lashman said.

"But did you tell her about the rebuttal that she could have to that presumption under the statute?" Barone asked. [Lashman said they did not have that conversation, that she explained to Lisa why Janet was a parent under Vermont's law treating civil unions just like marriages, and that Lisa agreed to waive any argument that Janet was not a parent.]

[Despite losing in the Vermont proceedings, Lisa continued to resist the visitation ordered for Janet.] "I don't see Janet as a parent, first and foremost," Lisa said. "Secondly, I don't want to expose Isabella to Janet's lifestyle. It goes against all my beliefs. I am raising Isabella to pattern herself after Christ. That's my job as a Christian mom. Homosexuality is a sin.

"I didn't give visitation, and God's protected me for two years," Lisa said. "He's protected Isabella, more importantly."

Just a few days earlier, Cohen had held a contempt hearing in Vermont at which he fined Lisa $25 for each day she refused to let Janet see Isabella. The fines were retroactive and mounting. At that point, Lisa owed Janet more than $9,000. Lisa, who, having closed her home-based day-care center and who now earns a modest annual salary teaching at a preschool, already owed legal bills nearing $100,000 and had no way to pay. She said she wasn't worried. . . .[36]

NOTES AND QUESTIONS

1. *Custody versus parentage.* The principal case presents a snapshot of a controversy spanning 15 years, two states, and three countries. The accompanying news story from the early days of the dispute shows how it became a combat zone in the culture war over LGBTQ families.

The courts in both Vermont and Virginia treated the litigation as a dispute about child custody and visitation. Thus, they found controlling the special statutes governing child custody cases, the Uniform Child Custody

Jurisdiction Act (UCCJA) and the Parental Kidnapping Prevention Act (PKPA) (examined in Chapter 6, section A). These statutes reflect the fact-intensive nature of custody and visitation adjudications and the modifiability of such decrees.

Do you agree that the crux of the litigation in *Miller-Jenkins* is a custody/visitation dispute? What of Lisa's argument that Janet is not a legal parent at all to Isabella and thus is not a candidate for any parental prerogatives? To what extent does Lisa's waiver of the issue, as elaborated in the news story, satisfactorily explain the judicial focus on custody, rather than parentage?

How might the finality of the outcome of the Vermont proceedings and the respect for that outcome in other states change, depending on whether the dispute concerns custody (as the case was actually decided in Vermont) or parentage (which Lisa claimed she wanted to litigate in Vermont)?

2. *Criteria for parentage: jurisdictional implications.* If, in fact, *Miller-Jenkins* concerns a dispute about whether Janet is Isabella's parent, what jurisdictional rules govern? Does the answer depend upon whether the parentage rule in question rests on a single event or datum, such as the presumption of legitimacy or DNA testing, or on more functional criteria, such as holding out behavior or other conduct that might make one a de facto parent? See Chapter 1. Why? According to the news story, Lisa's attorney viewed Isabella's birth during the civil union as determinative — triggering the same sort of presumption that marriage would. The opinion of the Vermont Supreme Court, however, considered such factors as the parties' expectations and intent, Janet's active participation in prenatal care and Isabella's birth, and Janet's performance of a parental role as well as Lisa's explicit treatment of her as a parent. Miller-Jenkins v. Miller-Jenkins, 912 A.2d 951, 970 (Vt. 2006). What difference should that make for purposes of jurisdiction?

In the principal case, evaluate both the initial jury instruction and rejected curative instruction. How accurate is the statement of law? How pertinent is it to the necessary finding of defendant's intent?

3. *A rebuttable presumption?* Suppose that Lisa's attorney had been able to pursue the issue of rebuttal of the presumption of parentage based on the couple's civil union. What sort of evidence would suffice to rebut the presumption? For different-sex married couples, courts are increasingly relying on genetic evidence. See Chapter 1, section B. What would this approach mean for same-sex couples, like Janet and Lisa?[37]

4. *Parental kidnapping.* Laws limiting child custody jurisdiction and requiring respect for custody adjudications in other states, including the federal PKPA (Chapter 6, section A), stemmed from frequent violations of custody orders, in which parents might take a child to another state or fail to return a child after visitation elsewhere. Yet, the same problems play out across international borders as well. The Hague Convention on the Civil Aspects of International Child Abduction, promulgated in 1980 and joined

---

[37] See Jessica Feinberg, Restructuring Rebuttal of the Marital Presumption for the Modern Era, 104 Minn. L. Rev. 243 (2019).

by 101 countries as contracting parties,[38] provides civil remedies for such cases, including a remedy of return to the habitual residence for children wrongfully removed to or retained in another country in violation of a parent's "right of custody."[39] The United States, a contracting party, implemented the Convention by enacting the International Child Abduction Remedies Act (ICARA), 22 U.S.C. §§9001 et seq.

Although the Convention drafters who crafted the remedy of return originally believed that most abductors would be noncustodial parents, the prevalence of domestic violence aimed at custodial parents and the rise of joint custody have complicated that approach.[40] Because Janet was awarded custody in 2009 after Lisa's repeated intransigence in complying with court-ordered visitation, the remedy of return would have been available. (Although Nicaragua is a party to the Convention, it is not a U.S. Treaty Partner under the Convention.[41]) Beyond such civil remedies, federal law criminalizes international parental kidnapping in the International Parental Kidnapping Crime Act ("IPKCA"), 18 U.S.C. §1204, as shown by the principal case.

Complementing these statutes, the Uniform Child Abduction Prevention Act (UCAPA), promulgated in 2006, identifies risk factors and authorizes remedies to prevent abduction, whether intrastate, interstate, or international. Fifteen U.S. jurisdictions have enacted such legislation.[42]

5. *Epilogue.* Isabella, who would turn 16 in 2018, and Lisa remain missing, presumably living in Nicaragua under new names.[43] The Hague Convention applies to children under 16.[44]

PROBLEM

Hollywood star Sofia Vergara and then-partner Nick Loeb create embryos with their own genetic material in California and freeze them there. After their relationship ends, Loeb wants to move forward with the original plan to use the embryos, assisted by a surrogate if necessary, but Vergara refuses. Loeb creates a trust for the children-to-be in Louisiana and sues for custody there in the name of the embryos, relying on Louisiana's statute

---

[38] Status Table, 28: Convention of 25 October 1980 on the Civil Aspects of International Child Abduction, Hague Conference on Private International Law, https://www.hcch.net/en/instruments/conventions/status-table/?cid=24.

[39] See, e.g., Abbott v. Abbott, 560 U.S. 1 (2010).

[40] See id.

[41] U.S Department of State, Bureau of Consular Affairs, https://travel.state.gov/content/travel/en/International-Parental-Child-Abduction/International-Parental-Child-Abduction-Country-Information/Nicaragua.html#:~:text=Nicaragua%20is%20a%20signatory%20to,with%20Nicaragua%20under%20the%20Convention (last updated June 18, 2018).

[42] See Child Abduction Prevention Act, Uniform Law Commission (2006), https://www.uniformlaws.org/committees/community-home?CommunityKey=c8a53ebd-d5aa-4805-95b2-5d6f2a648b2a#:~:text=The%20Uniform%20Child%20Abduction%20Prevention,prevent%20the%20abduction%20of%20children.

[43] See, e.g., Phil Fairbanks, Nation Casts its Eye on an International Kidnapping Case on Trial in Buffalo, Buffalo News (Sept. 22, 2016), https://buffalonews.com/news/local/nation-casts-its-eyes-on-an-international-kidnapping-case-on-trial-in-buffalo/article_406335c8-c6b1-54bf-ae5a-6b1245497ad0.html; Isabella Ruth Miller-Jenkins, The Charley Project, http://charleyproject.org/case/isabella-ruth-miller-jenkins (missing children's site).

[44] See *Abbott*, 560 U.S. at 9.

recognizing embryonic personhood. See Chapter 7, section A1. Does the UCCJEA apply to this controversy? If so, would subject matter jurisdiction lie in Louisiana? Is personal jurisdiction also an issue?[45]

KIVITI V. POMPEO

467 F. Supp. 3d 293 (D. Md. 2020)

THEODORE D. CHUANG, United States District Judge . . .

[Roee Kiviti was born in Israel, moved to the U.S. four years later in 1982, and became a U.S. citizen in 2001. In 2013 in California, at age 41, he married Adiel Kiviti, an Israeli citizen. They two men settled in the U.S. in 2015, and Adiel was naturalized as a U.S. citizen in 2019. The Kivitis had two children, L.R.K., a son, in 2016 and K.R.K., a daughter, in 2019, both born in Canada, with the help of a Canadian gestational surrogate and donated ova. The son was conceived using Roee's sperm, and the daughter with Adiel's. For both children, a Canadian court entered an order that the Kivitis were the only parents, and each child got a birth certificate showing the Kivitis as parents. L.R.K. was granted a U.S. passport with no questions asked about biological relationship. Although the parties agree that the Kivitis are K.R.K.'s legal parents, K.R.K. was not granted a U.S. passport.]

. . . [B]ecause it was determined that Roee Kiviti did not have a biological relationship with K.R.K., the State Department evaluated K.R.K.'s passport application under 8 U.S.C. §1409, the statutory provision that applies to children born out of wedlock and cross-references 8 U.S.C. §1401(g), which applies when a child is born to one U.S. citizen parent and one non-U.S. citizen parent. Because it determined that Adiel Kiviti had not satisfied the requirement of 8 U.S.C. §1401(g) that he had resided in the United States for five years prior to K.R.K.'s birth, the State Department concluded that K.R.K. was not a U.S. citizen by birth and denied K.R.K.'s application for a U.S. passport.

. . . [In this court, plaintiffs] assert that a State Department policy requiring that both parents be biologically related to a child in order to consider that child born in wedlock, and the application of that policy to deny K.R.K.'s passport application, (1) was contrary to the text of the [Immigration and Nationality Act (INA)]; (2) infringed on the substantive due process rights under the Fifth Amendment to the Constitution of the Kivitis to marry, procreate, and raise their children, and of K.R.K. to obtain United States citizenship at birth; (3) discriminated against the Kivitis as a same-sex couple and against K.R.K. based on the circumstances of her birth and parentage, in violation of the equal protection component of the Fifth Amendment's Due Process Clause; and (4) constituted arbitrary and capricious agency action that is contrary to law, in violation of the APA. As relief, Plaintiffs seek (1) a declaratory judgment pursuant to 8 U.S.C. §1503 that K.R.K. acquired U.S. citizenship at birth; (2) an order requiring the State Department to issue her a

---

[45] See Loeb v. Vergara, 326 F. Supp. 3d 295 (E.D. La. 2018); 2018 WL 2985319 (E.D. La. 2018) (denying motion to stay); Nick Loeb, Sofía Vergara's Ex-Fiancé: Our Frozen Embryos Have a Right to Live, N.Y. Times, Apr. 30, 2015, at A31; Monica Hof Wallace, A Primer on Natural and Juridical Persons in Louisiana, 64 Loy. L. Rev. 407, 421 n.111 (2018).

passport; (3) a judgment declaring the State Department's policy unconstitutional and in violation of the INA; (4) a permanent injunction against the State Department treating the children of same-sex couples as born out of wedlock and thereby denying them U.S. citizenship at birth; and (5) attorney's fees and costs. [The State Department filed a motion to dismiss.] . . .

II. Citizenship at Birth . . .

A. The Statutory Framework

Congress has generally provided that under certain circumstances, a child "born . . . of" at least one U.S. citizen parent receives U.S. citizenship at birth even if that child is born outside the United States. 8 U.S.C. §1401. For such children, Congress has set forth different requirements for the acquisition of citizenship at birth depending on whether the child in question was born in or out of wedlock. . . .

[The parents of children born out of wedlock must meet additional residency requirements not applicable to the parents of children born in wedlock, per the statutory scheme.] Although the statute uses gender-specific language and in fact includes another subsection providing that a child born out of wedlock to a U.S. citizen mother receives U.S. citizenship at birth if the mother had been continuously present in the United States for a period of one year, the United States Supreme Court struck down that relaxed residency requirement as violative of equal protection of the law. See 8 U.S.C. §1409(c); Sessions v. Morales-Santana, 137 S.Ct. 1678, 1700-1701 (2017). Thus, the residency requirements of §1401(g) apply to a child born out of wedlock who has either a U.S. citizen father or a U.S. citizen mother. [Section 1401(g) provides: "a person born outside the geographical limits of the United States and its outlying possessions of parents one of whom is an alien, and the other a citizen of the United States who, prior to the birth of such person, was physically present in the United States or its outlying possessions for a period or periods totaling not less than five years, at least two of which were after attaining the age of fourteen years."]

B. The Foreign Affairs Manual . . .

The State Department has provided written guidance for its officials adjudicating passport applications, set forth in the Foreign Affairs Manual ("FAM") . . . . Although the FAM reflects State Department policy, it has been neither approved by Congress nor subjected to notice-and-comment rulemaking.

. . . In general, the FAM states that "[a]bsent a blood relationship between the child and the parent on whose citizenship the child's own claim is based, U.S. citizenship is not acquired." 8 FAM §301.4(D)(1)(a). The FAM also applies a blood relationship requirement to the question of whether a child is born in wedlock or out of wedlock. The FAM states that "[t]o say a child was born 'in wedlock' means that the child's biological parents were married to each other at the time of the birth of the child." 8 FAM §304.1-2(c). . . .

The FAM further states that a male parent has "a biological relationship" with a child, or a "blood relationship" with a child as the term is used in 8 U.S.C. §1409(a) in relation to children born out of wedlock, when he has a "genetic parental relationship to the child." 8 FAM §301.4(D)(1)(c). While the FAM previously included an identical requirement for female parents, in 2014 the State Department altered the FAM to provide that "[a] woman may establish a biological relationship with her child either by virtue of being the genetic mother (the woman whose egg was used in conception) or the gestational mother (the woman who carried and delivered the baby)." Id. There was no amendment to the INA that triggered this change in interpretation.

The FAM contains other provisions clarifying the application of this biological relationship requirement when ART was used in the birth of a child. The FAM provides that a surrogate who gives birth to the child but "who is not the legal parent of the child at the time of the child's birth in the location of the birth" is not relevant to the citizenship analysis. See 8 FAM §304.3-2(a) ("[T]he surrogate's citizenship is irrelevant to the child's citizenship analysis."). Likewise, an anonymous sperm or egg donor is also a nullity in the citizenship analysis. 8 FAM §304.3-3 ("U.S. citizenship cannot be transmitted by an anonymous sperm or egg donor.").

Further, the FAM identifies certain scenarios involving ART in which the child is deemed to be born in wedlock to two U.S. citizen parents. It provides that a child born abroad to a surrogate gestational mother who is not the child's legal parent at birth, but whose legal and biological parents are a U.S. citizen mother and a U.S. citizen father, is considered to have been born in wedlock to two U.S. citizen parents. 8 FAM §304.3-2(b). It also states that where a child is born abroad to a married U.S. citizen gestational mother who is the legal parent of the child at the time of the birth and a U.S. citizen biological father, the child is considered to have been born in wedlock to two U.S. citizen parents, even where an anonymous egg donor was used. 8 FAM §304.3-1(a). Similarly, a child born abroad is deemed to be born in wedlock to two U.S. citizen parents where the gestational mother "is the legal parent of the child at the time of birth in the location of birth" and the "genetic parents are an anonymous sperm donor and the U.S. citizen wife of the gestational legal mother." 8 FAM §304.3-1(b).

However, where a child is born to two married fathers by way of a surrogate who was implanted with an egg from an anonymous donor that was fertilized by one of the father's genetic material, the State Department does not consider that child to have been born in wedlock. According to the deposition testimony of Paul Peek, an official of the State Department's Bureau of Consular Affairs, two married men can never have a child that the State Department considers to have been born in wedlock. Instead, the children of such marriages are always deemed to have been born out of wedlock. . . .

III. INA

Plaintiffs first argue that the State Department, both in policy and practice, has misinterpreted the relevant provisions of the INA, which they contend establish that K.R.K. was a U.S. citizen at birth. [The court discusses various precedents.] . . .

One federal court has addressed this issue in the context of a same-sex couple . . . . In Dvash-Banks v. Pompeo, No. 18-523-JFW(JCX), 2019 WL 911799

[(C.D. Cal. Feb. 21, 2019)], the court considered an application by a same-sex, married couple, one of whom was a U.S. citizen and one of whom was not, for U.S. citizenship for their twins born from a gestational surrogate in Canada though donor eggs, one of whom had the genetic material of the U.S. citizen father and the other of whom had the genetic material of the non-citizen father. Id. at *1-2. . . . [T]he court held that both twins were U.S. citizens under §1401(g) where their parents were married at their birth and one parent was a U.S. citizen, because "the word 'parents' as used in Section [1401(g)] is not limited to biological parents and . . . the presumption of legitimacy that applies when a child is born to married parents — as codified in the INA — cannot be rebutted by evidence that the child does not have a biological tie to a U.S. citizen parent." Id. at *7.

A. Statutory Interpretation

Upon review of the text of §1401 and the surrounding provisions of the INA, the Court agrees with [precedents from] the Second and Ninth Circuits that the term "born . . . of parents" does not limit the provision's application to those children who have biological relationships with both of their married parents. The Court first considers the specific text of the statute.

1. "Parents"

The use of the term "parents" does not necessarily establish that a biological relationship is required with each parent. Nowhere in the INA is the term "parent" defined to include only those with a biological relationship to a child. . . .

In the absence of a specifically applicable definition of a key term, the Court looks to whether the term has an established common law meaning. . . . At common law, the term "parent" does not refer only to those with a biological relationship with a child. The common law presumption of legitimacy, which assumes that where a child is born to a married couple, both married individuals are parents of the child, is a "fundamental principle of the common law." Michael H. v. Gerald D., 491 U.S. 110, 113, 124 (1989) (plurality) . . . . Elsewhere, the Supreme Court has recognized that "[t]he institution of marriage has played a critical role . . . in defining the legal entitlements of family members" and that "the mere existence of a biological link does not merit" constitutional protections relating to parental rights. Lehr v. Robertson, 463 U.S. 248, 256-57, 261 (1983).

Based on these longstanding principles, multiple state laws "generally require[ ] the name of the mother's male spouse to appear on the child's birth certificate — regardless of his biological relationship to the child." See Pavan v. Smith, 137 S. Ct. 2075, 2077 (2017) (per curiam). . . . In turn, certain courts have extended the presumption that a person is the legal parent of a child based on marriage to a biological parent at the time of birth to same-sex marriages, even though it is undisputed that one of the married individuals is not the biological parent of the child. See, e.g., McLaughlin v. Jones ex rel. Cty. of Pima, 401 P.3d 492, 494 (Ariz. 2017) . . . . Thus, the term "parents," on its own, does not impose a requirement that both putative parents have a biological relationship with the child.

2. "Born . . . of"

In the face of this common law principle, the State Department argues that what matters in the phrase "born . . . of parents" is not the word "parents," but rather the words "born of." . . . This argument is unpersuasive for two reasons. First, the phrase "born . . . of parents" must still be viewed against the backdrop of the common law presumption of parentage, which effectively considered a child to be born of parents consisting of a biological parent and that parent's spouse at the time of the birth, without requiring proof that the spouse had a genetic relationship with the child. . . .

Second, even under the State Department's approach, the term "born. . . of" is susceptible to a range of interpretations. A child could fairly be deemed to originate from parents other than through a genetic relationship, such as where two married parents both play a fundamental and instrumental role in the creation of the child, for example by, as here, together planning and supporting the use of surrogacy and ART to bring about the birth of a child to whom they have both committed in advance to be a parent. Indeed, the elasticity of the term "born . . . of" is evident from the State Department's recent change in policy, untethered to any change in the statute, to include within this term gestational mothers with no genetic relationship to the children they bear. Thus, the Court finds no biological requirement inherent in the phrase "born . . . of parents." 8 U.S.C. §1401(c).

3. "Blood Relationship"

In addition to considering the plain text of §1401(c), the Court must also examine the relevant context of the remainder of the statutory scheme in question, including §1409. Critically, while §1401(c) includes no explicit biological requirement alongside its use of the term "born . . . of parents," §1409 uses the term "a blood relationship" to describe a requirement to permit a father to a child born out of wedlock to confer U.S. citizenship upon the child. . . . [Despite the State Department's arguments, the court] finds the failure to use the term "blood relationship" or "natural parent" in §1401 to be convincing evidence that the term "born . . . of parents" does not require a biological relationship with both married parents.

4. Section 1401(g)

. . . Upon consideration of the common law understanding of parentage alongside the text of both §1401(c) specifically and the statutory scheme as a whole, the Court finds that the statute is clear and unambiguous that the phrase "born . . . of parents" in 8 U.S.C. §1401(c) does not require a biological relationship with both parents.

B. Extra-Statutory Arguments

[The court finds unpersuasive the State Department's extra-statutory arguments, including adherence to] the principle of jus sanguinis, the concept that citizenship should be conferred based on "blood" irrespective of place of birth, and the Supreme Court's prior references to "the importance of the government's interest in 'assuring that a biological . . . relationship exists' between a child and a parent through whom the child claims citizenship." . . . [A]lthough the State Department invokes the concept of jus sanguinis, it identifies no place in the Constitution, the INA, or another federal statute where that principle has been explicitly adopted by the United States. . . .

C. Constitutional Avoidance

For their part, Plaintiffs argue that the principle of constitutional avoidance favors adoption of its interpretation of §1401(c) so as to avoid constitutional problems created by the State Department's alternative reading. . . .

Drawing on the Supreme Court's decisions in United States v. Windsor, 570 U.S. 744 (2013), Obergefell [v. Hodges, 576 U.S. 644 (2015)], and *Pavan*, Plaintiffs' constitutional arguments are best understood as asserting three highly related claims. First, they argue that the State Department's policy violates the Kivitis' substantive due process rights by infringing on their fundamental liberty interests in marriage and in forming a family. Second, they argue that the policy violates the Kivitis' equal protection rights by treating their "marriage, as well as the marriages of other same sex couples, as second-class" because under the State Department's policy, a married male, same-sex couple will never be able to have their child considered to have been born in wedlock. Third, they argue that K.R.K.'s equal protection rights are violated because the policy "penalizes children for the circumstances of their birth." Plaintiffs assert both facial and as-applied challenges to the policy. In their Motion, Plaintiffs seek summary judgment only on their facial challenges. . . .

[A]lthough a determination of the constitutionality of the State Department's policy cannot be made without additional analysis, Plaintiffs have, at a minimum, established that the State Department's interpretation of the statute would raise "serious constitutional doubts" warranting application of the canon of constitutional avoidance. If the canon were applied, it would favor Plaintiffs' interpretation, which avoids a likely conflict with constitutional principles by more easily permitting equal treatment of same-sex male couples, particularly by allowing them to have a child in wedlock. Thus, although not necessary to the Court's conclusion, the canon of constitutional avoidance would provide an additional basis to support it.

Accordingly, the Court concludes that the State Department's application of §1409 and §1401(g) to K.R.K.'s application was incorrect. Under the correct provision, §1401(c), K.R.K. was born of married parents who were both U.S. citizens who had resided in the United States before her birth. K.R.K. is thus a U.S. citizen by birth. The Court will therefore grant summary judgment to Plaintiffs based on their claim under 8 U.S.C. §1503. As acknowledged by Plaintiffs at the hearing on the Motions, having granted Plaintiffs' Motion on this basis, the Court need not address and resolve the constitutional claims on the merits.

IV.   APA [Administrative Procedure Act]

In addition to their claim under 8 U.S.C. §1503, Plaintiffs have asserted an APA claim, arguing that the State Department's conduct was "arbitrary and capricious," "contrary to law and in excess of its authority delegated by Congress." . . . [They seek an injunction.] [T]he Court recognizes that a broader injunction would provide a different and likely justifiable form of relief to prevent the State Department from continuing to force individual, similarly situated plaintiffs to expend the time and financial resources to file suit in order to secure citizenship for their child. Such relief, however, would address the interests of other potential plaintiffs, not these Plaintiffs, and "the general rule" is "that injunctive relief should be no more burdensome to the defendant than necessary to provide complete relief to the plaintiffs." Where the declaratory judgment available under 8 U.S.C. §1503 will provide the relief that Plaintiffs seek, they may not use the APA to seek broader injunctions. . . .

For the foregoing reasons, the State Department's Motion to Dismiss will be GRANTED IN PART and DENIED IN PART. It will be granted as to the APA claim and otherwise denied. Plaintiffs' Partial Motion for Summary Judgment will be GRANTED, and a declaratory judgment that K.R.K. is a U.S. citizen by birth will be entered in favor of Plaintiffs. . . .

NOTES AND QUESTIONS

1. *Derivative citizenship.* Derivative citizenship refers to citizenship status that a child acquires from a parent. Yet, as *Kiviti* reveals, federal immigration law and policies do not always track local parentage principles. In the principal case, K.R.K. was the daughter of two legally married parents identified on her birth certificate. What is the State Department's rationale for treating her as a child born out of wedlock? For treating her as lacking a parent-child relationship with Roee Kiviti? Under the State Department's approach, what is K.R.K.'s relationship with Roee?

2. *Applying the statutes.* Section 1401 governs children born abroad of married parents, and §1409 applies to children born abroad out of wedlock; the latter says that §1401(g) applies to a person born out of wedlock if a blood relationship between the person and the father is established by clear and convincing evidence. What relevance do these provisions have in the principal case or Dvash-Banks v. Pompeo, discussed in the opinion and subsequently affirmed on appeal?[46] How do the cases differ?

3. *Jus sanguinis.* Why should citizenship transmission depend on biology rather than legal parentage? The court asserts that the sway of "jus sanguinis" or "the law of blood" is often overstated. Historically, biology has not been a necessary condition of citizenship transmission because children often derived their status from U.S. citizens who were married to their mothers despite the absence of genetic connection, thanks to the traditional presumption of legitimacy.[47] Nor has biology been a sufficient condition, given that nonmarital children could gain citizenship automatically from their American mothers but only under limited circumstances from their American fathers, consistent with common law.[48]

---

[46] E.J. D.-B. v. Pompeo, 2020 WL 5991163 (9th Cir. 2020). See Lena K. Bruce, Note, How to Explain to Your Twins Why Only One Can Be American: The Right to Citizenship of Children Born to Same-Sex Couples Through Assisted Reproductive Technology, 88 Fordham L. Rev. 999, 1008 (2019) ("Despite painstakingly outlining the rules on how to transmit citizenship from parent to child, the [statute] is unclear on what actually constitutes a parent-child relationship.").

[47] See Kerry Abrams & R. Kent Piacenti, Immigration's Family Values, 100 Va. L. Rev. 629, 658 (2014).

[48] See Nguyen v. INS, 533 U.S. 53 (2001); Sessions v. Morales-Santana, 137 S.Ct. 1678 (2017); Kristin A. Collins, Illegitimate Borders: Jus Sanguinis Citizenship and the Legal Construction of Family, Race, and Nation, 123 Yale L.J. 2134 (2014).

Indeed, like traditional parentage rules, citizenship transmission long rested on gender and marriage. Professor Kristin Collins exposes the role of race as well. She explains how citizenship transmission laws, although facially race-neutral, relied on domestic relations doctrines rooted in slavery, which in turn helped to shape "racially nativist and gender-based nationality laws."[49]

> These basic principles of domestic relations law — that within marriage the status of children followed that of the father, while outside marriage the status of children followed that of the mother — were deeply embedded in the logic and practice of slavery and were a fundamental component of the laws that constructed race as a sociolegal category in the antebellum South.[50]

Now, family law embraces considerable gender-neutrality and recognizes same-sex marriage. Have citizenship and nationality laws failed to keep up? Should it be enough that the intended parents of a child born abroad are U.S. citizens, even if they have no genetic or gestational connection to the child?[51]

4. *Discrimination.* On what bases does the State Department's application of the statutes discriminate? Why does State Department policy say that "two married men can never have a child that the State Department considers to have been born in wedlock"? Similar problems have surfaced in cases of married lesbian couples.[52] If the court had reached the constitutional issues, how should it have resolved them? Which constitutional challenge is most compelling?[53] Of what weight is the usual deference accorded to federal authorities in immigration matters?[54] The conclusion that the statutes do not compel the State Department policy here? Why didn't the court offer the broader relief that plaintiffs requested to unburden other similarly situated families from litigating these issues?

5. *Stateless children.* Some international surrogacy arrangements produce children with no citizenship at all. In the famous "Baby Manji case," a Japanese (different-sex) couple used the husband's sperm, an anonymously donated egg, and a gestational surrogate in India, but the couple divorced just before the child's birth. The ex-husband alone sought custody, but the Japanese embassy refused to grant either a passport or a visa, and India declined to grant a birth certificate because of maternal uncertainty and the failure of the egg donor, gestational surrogate, or intended mother to claim parentage. The ex-husband could not adopt the child because of his status as a single man. After the case went to the Indian Supreme Court,

---

[49] Collins, supra note [48], at 2154.

[50] Id. at 2152. See also Gillian R. Chadwick, Legitimating the Transnational Family, 42 Harv. J. L. & Gender 257 (2019).

[51] See Jenna Casolo et al., Assisted Reproductive Technologies, 20 Geo. J. Gender & L. 313, 326-327 (2019).

[52] See Leticia Saucedo & Rose Cuison Villazor, Illegitimate Citizenship Rules, 97 Wash. U. L. Rev. 1179, 1224-1228 (2020).

[53] See Michael J. Higdon, Biological Citizenship and the Children of Same-Sex Marriage, 87 Geo. Wash. L. Rev. 124 (2019).

[54] See, e.g., Fiallo v. Bell, 430 U.S. 787 (1977) (deferring to Congress despite discrimination against nonmarital child and his father).

the Indian government issued an identity certificate, and then the Japanese embassy issued a temporary visa for travel to Japan.[55]

Opposition to surrogacy by European legislatures portend increasing numbers of stateless children.[56] Examples come from cases in which the child's intended citizenship was to be German, Israeli, British, French, and Irish.[57] Which country's law of citizenship and parentage applies in cases when intended parents use donated genetic material and gestational surrogates in other countries?

6. *Stranded children.* Sometimes children of ARTs are stranded in the country of birth. A gay couple from Spain prevailed after 15 months of litigation in Bangkok, where a Thai gestational surrogate delivered their daughter and refused to surrender her.[58] Travel restrictions prompted by the COVID-19 pandemic have kept intended parents from retrieving their babies in Ukraine and even in the U.S.[59] Who is responsible for caring for such children? This is one of many questions posed by reproductive tourism, explored below.

2. REPRODUCTIVE TOURISM

HODAS V. MORIN

814 N.E.2d 320 (Mass. 2004)

MARSHALL, C.J.

Does a Probate and Family Court judge have authority pursuant to G. L. c. 215, §6, to issue prebirth judgments of parentage and to order the issuance of a prebirth record of birth, see Culliton v. Beth Israel Deaconess Med. Ctr., 756 N.E.2d 1133 (Mass. 2001), where neither the genetic parents nor the gestational carrier with whom they contracted to bear a child reside in Massachusetts, but where the contract specifies that the birth occur at a Massachusetts hospital? . . . We conclude that, in the circumstances here, the plaintiffs are entitled to the relief they seek: judgments of paternity and maternity and a prebirth order establishing their legal parentage.

---

[55] Kristine S. Knaplund, Baby Without a Country: Determining Citizenship for Assisted Reproduction Children Born Overseas, 91 Denv. U. L. Rev. 335, 355-356 (2014); Kari Points, Commercial Surrogacy and Fertility Tourism in India: The Case of Baby Manji, Kenan Institute for Ethics, Duke U. (2009), https://kenan.ethics.duke.edu/wp-content/uploads/2018/01/BabyManji_Case2015.pdf.

[56] See Storrow, supra note [12], at 65-67.

[57] Charles P. Kindregan & Danielle White, International Fertility Tourism: The Potential for Stateless Children in Cross-Border Commercial Surrogacy Arrangements, 36 Suffolk Transnat'l L. Rev. 527, 551-578 (2013).

[58] Gay Couple Wins Case; Gains Custody of Baby Born to Thai Surrogate, Morning Edition, NPR (May 2, 2016), https://www.npr.org/2016/05/02/476419507/gay-couple-wins-legal-battle-gains-custody-of-baby-born-to-thai-surrogate.

[59] David Dodge, How Coronavirus Is Affecting Surrogacy, Foster Care and Adoption, N.Y. Times (Apr. 1, 2020), https://www.nytimes.com/2020/04/01/parenting/coronavirus-adoption-surrogacy-foster-care.html?searchResultPosition=1; Mary Ilyushina, Dozens of Surrogacy Babies Stranded by Coronavirus Lockdown in Ukraine, Lawmaker Says, CNN (May 16, 2020), https://www.cnn.com/2020/05/15/europe/ukraine-surrogacy-babies-lockdown-intl/index.html.

1. *Facts.* The plaintiffs, who are married, reside in Connecticut. The gestational carrier and her husband, both nominal defendants, reside in New York. The hospital, the other nominal defendant, is a licensed Massachusetts hospital whose statutory duties include, among others, reporting information concerning births at the hospital to the city or town clerk where the birth occurred.

In April, 2003, the plaintiffs, the gestational carrier, and the gestational carrier's husband entered into a fifteen-page "Contract Between a Genetic Father, a Genetic Mother, a Gestational Carrier and Her Husband" (gestational carrier agreement). . . . Among other things, the gestational carrier agreement provided that any child resulting from the agreement would be delivered at the hospital, if at all possible, and that in any event the gestational carrier would "take all reasonable steps to give birth to any child carried pursuant to this Agreement at a Hospital located in the State of Massachusetts." It is undisputed that the parties chose Massachusetts as the site of the birth in part to facilitate obtaining a prebirth order. [Plaintiffs' counsel further represented that the gestational carrier's insurance would not cover a delivery at a Connecticut hospital.] The parties' preference for Massachusetts was further expressed in the following choice of law provision:

> "The Gestational Carrier and [her] husband agree that they are entering into this Agreement with the intention that in accordance with the laws of the State of Massachusetts, they will take whatever steps are necessary to have the Genetic Father and the Genetic Mother named as the natural, legal and genetic parents, to have the Genetic Father and the Genetic Mother named as the father and mother, respectively, of [the] child on the child's birth certificate, and to permit the Genetic Father and the Genetic Mother to obtain physical custody of any child born as the result of this Agreement. . . . The parties further agree that this Agreement shall be governed by Massachusetts law."

Approximately six months after the parties entered into the gestational carrier agreement, the gestational carrier was successfully implanted with an embryo produced from the male plaintiff's sperm and the female plaintiff's egg. The implantation took place in Connecticut. The gestational carrier received at least some prenatal care at the hospital. At oral argument on June 30, 2004, counsel informed the court that an induced delivery was planned at the hospital the following week.

2. *Jurisdiction.* [The court decides that the Probate and Family Court has jurisdiction to grant the relief requested.] [W]e held in Culliton v. Beth Israel Deaconess Med. Ctr., 756 N.E.2d 1133 (Mass. 2001), a Probate and Family Court judge has [statutory] authority to consider a request for a prebirth order where, as here, "(a) the plaintiffs are the sole genetic sources of the [child]; (b) the gestational carrier agrees with the orders sought; (c) no one, including the hospital, has contested the complaint or petition; and (d) by filing the complaint and stipulation for judgment the plaintiffs agree that they have waived any contradictory provisions in the [gestational carrier] contract (assuming those provisions could be enforced in the first place)." That the gestational carrier, her husband, and the plaintiffs all reside outside of Massachusetts does

not bar the Probate and Family Court's subject matter jurisdiction . . . , because the equity statute poses no residency requirement.[6]

Second, personal jurisdiction is also proper. The Probate and Family Court, of course, has personal jurisdiction over the hospital, a Massachusetts corporation. Indeed, it is doubtful that any other State could grant the plaintiffs the injunction they seek requiring the hospital to report certain information about the child's parentage to Massachusetts officials. The Probate and Family Court's personal jurisdiction over the gestational carrier and her husband derives from their stipulation for entry of judgment in favor of the plaintiffs. . . .

3. *Choice of law.* The driving issue in this case, rather, concerns choice of law. The interested couples come from different States; the chosen hospital from yet a third. None of the individual parties resides in the Commonwealth, yet they have contracted that Massachusetts law govern the gestational carrier agreement and, by extension, the petition for judgments of parentage and for a prebirth order. We must consider whether to respect their choice.

The gestational carrier agreement implicates the policies of multiple States in important questions of individual safety, health, and general welfare. Complicating matters is the fact that the laws of Connecticut, New York, and Massachusetts, the three States that potentially could govern the agreement, are not in accord. In Connecticut, where the genetic parents reside, gestational carrier agreements are not expressly prohibited by, and perhaps may be contemplated by, the recently amended statute governing the issuance of birth certificates. See Conn. Gen. Stat. c. 93, §7-48a, 2004 Conn. Legis Serv. P.A. 04-255 (West 2004) ("On and after January 1, 2002, each birth certificate shall contain the name of the birth mother, except by the order of a court of competent jurisdiction . . ."). The gestational carrier resides in New York, a State that has expressed a strong public policy against all gestational carrier agreements. See N.Y. Dom. Rel. Law §122 (McKinney 1999) ("Surrogate parenting contracts are hereby declared contrary to the public policy of this state, and are void and unenforceable").[8] Massachusetts, as we have noted, recognizes gestational carrier agreements in some circumstances. See Culliton v. Beth Israel Deaconess Med. Ctr., supra; R.R. v. M.H., 689 N.E.2d 790 (Mass. 1998).

In light of these differing State policies and the parties' declared intent to follow Massachusetts law, we look to our established "functional" choice of law principles and to the Restatement (Second) of Conflict of Laws, with which those principles generally are in accord. . . . The Restatement . . .

---

6. No statutory directive limits the court's jurisdiction in actions relating to gestational agreements to Massachusetts residents. Cf. Uniform Parentage Act §802, 9B U.L.A. 363 (Master ed. 2001 & 2004 Supp.) ("A proceeding to validate a gestational agreement may not be maintained unless: the [gestational carrier] or the intended parents have been residents of this State for at least 90 days") and comment (noting that the ninety-day residency requirement is to "discourage forum shopping"). Moreover, the statutory scheme for the recording of births in Massachusetts makes no distinction between resident and nonresident parents . . . .

8. Under New York law, a surrogate parenting contract includes an agreement where "a woman agrees . . . to be impregnated with an embryo that is the product of an ovum fertilized with the sperm of a man who is not her husband." N. Y. Dom. Rel. Law §121 (4) (McKinney 1999).

presumes that the law the parties have chosen applies,[10] unless "(a) the chosen state has no substantial relationship to the parties or the transaction and there is no other reasonable basis for the parties' choice, or (b) application of the law of the chosen state would be contrary to a fundamental policy of a state which has a materially greater interest than the chosen state" and is the State whose law would apply under §188 of the Restatement "in the absence of an effective choice of law by the parties." Restatement (Second) of Conflict of Laws, supra at §187 (2).

Under the two-tiered analysis of §187 (2), we readily conclude that Massachusetts has a "substantial relationship" to the transaction. See §187 (2) (a). That substantial relationship is anchored in the parties' negotiated agreement for the birth to occur at a Massachusetts hospital and for a Massachusetts birth certificate to issue, and bolstered by the gestational carrier's receipt of prenatal care at a Massachusetts hospital in anticipation of delivery at that hospital. See §187 comment f, supra at 566-567 (place of partial performance considered to be sufficient to establish a reasonable basis for the parties' choice of law).

Turning to the second prong of §187 (2), it is a close question whether applying the parties' choice of law would be "contrary to a fundamental policy" of another State with a "materially greater interest." See §187 (2) (b). Certainly the interests of New York and Connecticut are material and significant, for the contracting parties reside in these States. Nevertheless, the interests of New York and Connecticut may be at cross purposes here. New York, the home of the gestational carrier and her husband, expressly prohibits gestational carrier agreements in order to protect women against exploitation as gestational carriers and to protect the gestational carrier's potential parental rights. See N.Y. Dom. Rel. Law §122.[11] New York has thus expressed a "fundamental policy" on a matter in which it has a great interest. Connecticut, the plaintiffs' home State, is silent on the question of gestational carrier agreements, but in any event does not expressly prohibit the plaintiffs from entering into such an arrangement. Massachusetts also has interests here, including interests in "establishing the rights and responsibilities of parents [of children born in Massachusetts] as soon as is practically possible" and "furnishing a measure of stability and protection to children born through such gestational surrogacy arrangements."[12] Culliton v. Beth Israel Deaconess Med. Ctr., supra.

---

10. R.R. v. M.H., 689 N.E.2d 790 (Mass. 1998), is not to the contrary. That case concerned a surrogacy agreement where the genetic mother (not married to the father) carried the child, was required to consent to the father's custody of the child prior to birth, and was to be paid $10,000 for being a gestational carrier. The gestational carrier was a Massachusetts resident, the child was born in Massachusetts, and the genetic father and his wife were residents of Rhode Island. Although the gestational carrier contract provided that "Rhode Island Law shall govern the interpretation of this agreement," we applied Massachusetts law to invalidate the contract as contrary to Massachusetts public policy as expressed through G. L. c. 210, §11A.

11. Massachusetts also seeks to prevent the exploitation of women by prohibiting gestational carrier agreements that compensate the gestational carrier beyond pregnancy-related expenses. Such agreements "raise the concern that, under financial pressure, a woman will permit her body to be used and her child to be given away." R.R. v. M.H., supra.

12. While it is true that Massachusetts interests are contingent on the actual birth of a child in the Commonwealth, any order of a Massachusetts court concerning Massachusetts birth records of course will have minimal, if any, significance if the birth occurs outside the Commonwealth. No party argues otherwise.

However, even if we were to decide that New York had a "materially greater interest" than both Connecticut and Massachusetts, New York's policy would not operate to overrule the parties' choice of law unless New York would have been the applicable law in the absence of any articulated choice by the parties. [Given uncertainties about the place of contracting and the place of negotiation and Massachusetts's role as the planned place of performance,] whatever New York's interest in protecting the gestational carrier and her husband, it is doubtful that the principles of §188 would result in application of New York law to this particular contact. . . .

We conclude, then, that the judge should have applied the parties' choice of law, the law of Massachusetts, to resolve the plaintiffs' complaint. Although the judge in her decision prudently raised the issue of forum shopping in declining to consider the complaint, we are satisfied that, in the circumstances of this case, the parties' choice of law, is one we should respect. We are also satisfied that our established conflict of laws analysis will work to prevent misuse of our courts and our laws. . . .

NOTES AND QUESTIONS

1. *Shopping for ARTs.* With the varied responses to surrogacy and other ARTs among states and foreign countries, consumers often procure fertility services in a permissive jurisdiction or at least, as in *Hodas*, try to establish a connection there. Salient factors also include comparative costs as well as openness to serving nontraditional families. Recall *Kiviti*, supra. Given their connections with Israel and the United States, why did the Kivitis engage a Canadian surrogate, who gave birth in Canada?

In disagreeing with a majority of the Ohio Supreme Court, which ruled that gestational surrogacy arrangements do not violate public policy, one dissenting judge lamented that Ohio will become "an interstate, and perhaps international, marketplace for gestational surrogacy," given the more restrictive approaches in other jurisdictions.[60] Is this consequence one that a jurisdiction would necessarily seek to avoid?

2. *Choice of law.* Such forum shopping results in legal questions parallel to those posed at one time or another by out-of-state abortions, "marriage evasion" (including for same-sex marriage), migratory divorce, and interstate (and international) child custody battles. Can residents of states with restrictive laws evade them elsewhere? How should the restrictive states respond?[61] Although New York legalized gestational surrogacy in 2020 (see Chapter 8, section A2), at the time of *Hodas* it had one of the most restrictive laws in the country. What good is a law like New York's antisurrogacy statute, in light of the court's choice of law analysis?

3. *Enforcing restrictions.* Restrictions might target intended parents or, alternatively, surrogates or donors. What can jurisdictions with restrictive laws of either type do to enforce them?

---

[60] J.F. v. D.B., 879 N.E.2d 740, 744 (Ohio 2007) (Cupp, J., dissenting).
[61] See Susan Frelich Appleton, Surrogacy Arrangements and the Conflict of Laws, 1990 Wis. L. Rev. 399 (1990); Anastasia Grammaticaki-Alexiou, Artificial Reproduction Technologies and Conflict of Laws: An Initial Approach, 60 La. L. Rev. 1113 (2000). See generally Jeffrey A. Parness, Faithful Parents: Choice of Childcare Parentage Laws, 70 Mercer L. Rev. 325 (2019).

If New York's surrogacy ban was designed to protect surrogates, how can it stop an arrangement like that in *Hodas*? Must a state recognize the information on the birth certificate issued elsewhere? Do cases like *Kiviti*, supra, and *Pavan*, on which *Kiviti* relies, provide answers — or do those cases turn on discrimination against same-sex couples, which would not occur when a jurisdiction treats all ARTs consumers alike?[62] Would a birth certificate issued in one U.S. state be entitled to full faith and credit in another?[63] What about a pre-birth order of parentage?[64] If an intended mother travels to a permissive state and becomes pregnant there with a donated embryo, how can her home state, even if more restrictive, enforce its laws?

Do these questions implicate the procreative liberty of intended parents, donors, and surrogates alike? See Chapter 7, section A. Within the United States, does the constitutional right to travel protect the freedom of those who would participate in assisted reproduction in other states?[65]

Consider an alternative approach that would ask lawyers to assume greater responsibilities. As Professor June Carbone and Christina Miller argue:

> [I]t is difficult for any single jurisdiction to control the options available to its citizens. . . . [A]s the fertility business matures, the opportunities to address ethically questionable practices may come more from the oversight of professionals than from regulation of the process through traditional jurisdiction-based regulations. In the surrogacy context, in particular, lawyers are essential to establishing parenthood and overseeing the agency-client, intended parent-gestational carrier relationships. Professional associations and licensing units can and should establish standards for responsible practices.[66]

What should such standards for attorneys say?

4. *Public policy and failed surrogacy agreements.* Would New York's express antisurrogacy policy have received more weight in *Hodas* if a party had refused to perform? For example, if the gestational carrier decided not to surrender the child, would New York's public policy become more important in the resulting dispute? Should it? On what basis does *Hodas* distinguish *R.R. v. M.H.*, discussed in footnote 10? Is it pertinent that *R.R.* concerned an agreement that the surrogate refused to perform? (The court held the contract void and unenforceable.)

In In re Paternity and Custody of Baby Boy A., 2007 WL 4304448 (Minn. Ct. App. 2007), a New York man, P.G.M., and his niece, J.M.A., who lived in Minnesota, entered a gestational surrogacy agreement with a clause stating

---

[62] See, e.g., Martha A. Field, Compensated Surrogacy, 89 Wash. L. Rev. 1155, 1169-1170 (2014) (noting that some people needed surrogacy for procreation before marriage equality, "there is no necessary connection between marriage and surrogacy," and "there are legitimate policy reasons on both sides of the surrogacy issue").

[63] See In re Estate of Gardiner, 42 P.3d 120 (Kan. 2002) (declining full faith and credit to revised birth certificate showing individual's gender identity). But see Anna Marie D'Ginto, Comment, The Birth Certificate Solution: Ensuring the Interstate Recognition of Same-Sex Parentage, 167 U. Pa. L. Rev. 975 (2019).

[64] See Katherine Farese, The Bun's in the Oven, Now What?: How Pre-Birth Orders Promote Clarity in Surrogacy Law, 23 U.C. Davis J. Juv. L. & Pol'y 25, 62-63 (2019).

[65] See generally, e.g., Saenz v. Roe, 526 U.S. 489 (1999). See also Kindregan & White, supra note [57], at 538-540 (2013) (raising question of constitutional right to use cross-border surrogacy).

[66] June Carbone & Christina O. Miller, Surrogacy Professionalism, 31 J. Am. Acad. Matrim. Law. 1, 2 (2018).

that Illinois law would control. The two subsequently traveled to Illinois, where clinic technicians fertilized an anonymously donated egg with P.G.M.'s sperm and transferred the preembryo for gestation in J.M.A. J.M.A. stayed with P.G.M. in New York for two months during the pregnancy, when their relationship deteriorated and J.M.A. demanded money. After J.M.A. returned to Minnesota and gave birth there, she refused to surrender the child to P.G.M., who filed a paternity action in Minnesota. Following the contractual choice of law clause and applying Illinois law, which recognizes surrogacy agreements that meet specified conditions, the Minnesota court held the contract enforceable. The court rejected J.M.A.'s argument that the contract violated Minnesota's public policy because Minnesota had no statute or case law prohibiting gestational surrogacy (nor any authority expressly supporting it). Should J.M.A. have invoked New York's then public policy instead?

5. *Law reform.* Law reform includes several efforts to curb forum shopping. According to the UPA, a gestational or genetic surrogacy agreement requires that "[a]t least one party must be a resident of this state or, if no party is a resident of this state, at least one medical evaluation or procedure or mental-health consultation under the agreement must occur in this state." UPA §803(1) (2017). What would that provision have meant in *Hodas*? Would a stricter residency requirement for either intended parents or surrogates be preferable? Proposed law reform in India, a popular and highly publicized destination for gestational surrogacy consumers in the absence of regulation, would prohibit commercial surrogacy and limit intended parents to Indian married couples, married couples of Indian origin, and Indian single women.[67]

The American Law Institute has begun drafting a new Restatement of Conflict of Laws, designed to have more tailored and predictable rules applicable to particular types of cases. Although it largely defers to choice-of-law clauses, as the Restatement (Second) does in §187, it also contains default rules for particular categories of contacts. For example, it provides: "Conflict-of-laws issues relating to contracts for the rendition of services are governed by the internal law of the place where a major part of the services are to be performed." Restatement (Third) of Conflict of Laws §8.09 (Am. Law Inst., Prelim. Draft No. 3, 2017). Should this provision govern surrogacy arrangements? What result would it have required in *Hodas*? Should the Restatement Reporters include an even more specific rule for surrogacy contracts?[68] How much deference should choice-of-law clauses in surrogacy contracts receive?

Alternatively, should law reformers strive for a unitary standard — such as a federal law regulating surrogacy as interstate commerce[74] or an international instrument? What would it say? For several years, the Hague Conference on Private International Law has been exploring a convention on surrogacy, similar to the Convention on Intercountry Adoption (Chapter 6,

---

[74] See TNN, Surrogacy Bill to Benefit Widows & Divorces Too, Times of India (Feb. 27, 2020), https://timesofindia.indiatimes.com/india/surrogacy-bill-to-benefit-widows-divorcees-too/articleshow/74327003.cms.

[68] See generally Sharon Shakargy, Choice of Law for Surrogacy Agreements: In the In-Between of Status and Contract, 16 J. Private Int'l L. 138 (2020).

[74] See supra note [10] and accompanying text.

section C). The project has proven difficult, with divisions about whether to permit commercial surrogacy or to ban surrogacy altogether.[70] Yet, Professor Seema Mohapatra contends that "an international convention on surrogacy does not have to and should not have a normative position on surrogacy," while also concluding that "[e]ven a weak surrogacy convention is better than none at all." Yet, she also points out the absence of an "international body or document that can even be considered a starting point for any resolution of international surrogacy disputes."[71]

Does the intercountry adoption Convention provide an apt analogy for an international instrument regulating global surrogacy? Mohapatra and others generally answer in the affirmative, while recognizing differences between adoption and surrogacy.[72] A 2016 resolution of the American Bar Association, however, rejects the analogy and urges the U.S. Department of State to negotiate for the following elements:

> a. That any Convention should focus on the conflict of laws and comity problems inherent in international citizenship and parentage proceedings and that any such collective international approach should allow for cross-border recognition of parentage judgments so that the parental relationship and citizenship status of all children, no matter the circumstances of their birth, will be certain; and
>
> b. That any such collective international approach allows individual member countries to regulate surrogacy within their own borders as deemed appropriate by that country without imposing new international restrictions on surrogacy arrangements; and
>
> c. That a Central Authority model to regulate surrogacy arrangements is not an appropriate model for any collective international approach regarding surrogacy; and
>
> d. That any Convention should recognize the clear distinctions between adoption and surrogacy; and
>
> e. That the Hague Convention on the Protection of Children and Co-Operation in Respect of Intercountry Adoption (1993) is not an appropriate model for any Convention regarding surrogacy; and
>
> f. That rather than requiring a genetic link, an intent-based parentage analysis is the most appropriate parentage doctrine for surrogacy; and
>
> g. That human rights abuses are not necessarily inherent in or exclusive to surrogacy arrangement; and, therefore should be addressed separately.[73]

How do adoption and surrogacy resemble one another for purposes of an international convention? How do they differ? Would you support the

---

[70] See Alex Sidwell, Comment, Protect All Parties: Opposing the American Bar Association's Position Statement on Regulation of International Surrogacy Arrangements, 49 Cumb. L. Rev. 125, 128 (2019).

[71] Seema Mohapatra, Adopting an International Convention on Surrogacy — A Lesson from Intercountry Adoption, 13 Loy. U. Chi. Int'l L. Rev. 25, 26, 47 (2015). But see Sharon Bassan, Different but Same: A Call for a Joint Pro-Active Regulation of Cross-Border Egg and Surrogacy Markets, 28 Health Matrix 323 (2018).

[72] See Mohapatra, supra note [71]; Carolyn McLeod & Andrew Botterell, A Hague Convention on Contract Pregnancy (or "Surrogacy"): Avoiding Ethical Inconsistencies with the Convention on Adoption, 7 Int'l J. Fem. Approaches to Bioethics 219 (2014).

[73] Sidwell, supra note [70], at 137-138.

ABA's position? Beyond surrogacy, what other reproductive interventions and technologies might merit transnational regulation?[74]

6. *An international market.* Based on traditional definitions of infertility (Chapter 7, section A1), the condition affects 15 percent of reproductive-aged couples globally, and the rate is higher in some countries, for example, 25 percent in China.[75] This population constitutes the potential "demand side" of the international ARTs market. The following excerpt explains the other components of the market, the phenomenon of international reproductive tourism, and the inequalities[76] that constitute a feature, not a bug, in the system.

LISA C. IKEMOTO, REPRODUCTIVE TOURISM: EQUALITY CONCERNS
IN THE GLOBAL MARKET FOR FERTILITY SERVICES

27 Law & Ineq. 277, 277-278, 282-283, 302-308 (2009)

Assisted reproductive technology (ART) lures people across borders.... Prospective fertility patients leave their home jurisdictions to use ART for a complex mix of reasons. For example, laws or social rules might restrict access at home, or the cost of ART use in other countries may be lower. Some travel to bypass a local dearth of technology, and others seek to use the fruits of third parties' bodies — eggs, sperm, or wombs. Some may simply want secrecy. The supply side of reproductive tourism has formed to satisfy these needs in a sprawling commercial enterprise that is sophisticated in some respects and crude in others....

The most troubling aspects of reproductive tourism arise from the use of third parties who furnish gametes and from surrogates who gestate babies for others. In fact, the strongest critics of these practices use the term "trafficking" rather than "tourism."...

The ART available in the overall global market matches that offered in the most well-supplied jurisdictions such as California, where the fertility industry remains substantially unregulated. Some jurisdictions have become niches for particular ART. Spain, for example, has cultivated a reputation for high success rates of in vitro fertilization (IVF). The media has highlighted India's surrogacy business. Other jurisdictions are emerging markets, formed by a combination of the technologies that they offer and other factors such as cost and national law. The list of specific ART, like the markets in which they operate, changes frequently....

[74] Melanie Hess, Note, A Call for an International Governance Framework for Human Germline Gene Editing, 95 Notre Dame L. Rev. 1369 (2020).

[75] Hui Sun et al., Global, Regional, and National Prevalence and Disability-Adjusted Life-Years for Infertility in 195 Countries and Territories, 1990-2017: Results from a Global Burden of Disease Study, 2017, 11 Aging 10952, 10952 (2019), https://www.ncbi.nlm.nih.gov/pmc/articles/PMC6932903/#:~:text=Infertility%20DALYs,0.552)%20(Figure%207). See also Leslie Tai, My American Surrogate, N.Y. Times (Sept. 24, 2019), https://www.nytimes.com/2019/09/24/opinion/china-america-surrogacy.html?searchResultPosition=1 ("op-doc" showing how a Chinese business-woman in California matches Chinese intended parents with California surrogates).

[76] See David M. Smolin, The One Hundred Thousand Dollar Baby: The Ideological Roots of a New American Export, 49 Cumb. L. Rev. 1,1 (2019) (citing surrogacy to posit that the "United States of America, as represented by the United States government, some states, and leading legal institutions, is actively building worldwide markets in children").

[In between the demand side and the supply side are various commercial enterprises, including clinics and hospitals, cross-border clinic affiliations and partnerships, transnational clinics, service agencies, and donor and surrogate brokers.]

Given that fertility travelers often go to less-developed countries, . . . [o]ne question is whether the effort and resources that are put into fertility clinics and hospitals, in order to attract foreign patients, divert resources to private facilities that provide care for the elite. In many countries, this could reinforce a pre-existing two-tiered health care system. One could argue that the extra revenue generated by reproductive tourism can be used to expand health services for people who are dependent on public health care. There is, however, no evidence that this is occurring.

A closely related question is whether a focus on ART use resets health care priorities without regard to domestic health care needs. . . . A third question is whether reproductive tourism lures physicians to private clinics in a well-paying field of practice and away from public hospitals, creating a shortage where health care is most needed. . . .

. . . ART is gendered technology. As such, it allocates most of the health risks to women. Some of the highest risks arise from egg retrieval and surrogacy. Both require the administration of pharmaceutical hormones, which creates short-term risks, and for which there is little data on long-term risks. Both require invasive procedures that produce real, but low, levels of risk. Surrogacy also places women at risk. The majority of women who give birth experience no adverse health effects. Pregnancy, however, does present significant risk of a wide range of adverse health consequences. In addition, most women who carry children for others do so as gestational surrogates. Typically, a woman undergoing IVF as a gestational carrier takes hormones in order to coordinate her cycle with the embryo transfer, thus increasing the chances that the embryo transfer results in a pregnancy. While these drugs do not prompt multiple egg production, they may produce side effects and pose long term health risks.

The health risks of egg donation and surrogacy may be greater in the context of less developed countries. The well-established corollary is that lack of wealth correlates with lower health status. That is a statistical fact, and is not true for every person in need. But, among even young low-income women in developed countries, morbidity and mortality rates from pregnancy and childbirth are higher than they are for middle class women. Women who provide eggs or become surrogates are usually from lower income groups, and are therefore subject to higher risk.

A more subtle dynamic may also increase risk to egg donors and surrogates. Egg donors and surrogates provide the valuable raw materials of a for-profit industry. Women can provide eggs and gestational services precisely because of their sex. In addition, while egg donors and surrogates are undergoing medical procedures, they are not the patients undergoing fertility treatment. They are the means to fertility treatment. The resulting interplay between biological essentialism and commodification of the women who are the means to the end may permit a laxness in minimizing risk to those women. It may also foster a willingness to violate good medical practice in order to get results for foreign patients. For egg brokers, clinics, and fertility tourists, the more eggs retrieved per cycle, the better. Higher dosages of ovarian stimulation drugs increase the chances of multiple egg production in women. But higher dosages also increase the risk of ovarian hyperstimulation stress syndrome, which includes nausea, vomiting, accumulation of fluid in the abdomen, kidney and liver dysfunction, and even kidney failure among its symptoms. This normative dynamic creates an inverse relation between the egg donor's intrinsic worth and her extrinsic value in the fertility industry....

Reproductive tourism for two high-demand fertility services — IVF with third-party eggs, and surrogacy — depends heavily on a lack of comparable economic alternatives for the women who provide eggs and surrogacy, and significant wealth disparity between those women and fertility travelers. But for those inequalities, fewer women would become egg donors and surrogates. In the current economic recession, in fact, clinics have reported that notably more women are applying to become egg donors and surrogates. In addition, but for those inequalities, the fees for third-party eggs and surrogacy might be too high to justify travel for all but a few individuals.

The causal links between these inequalities and fertility services would seem to indicate that egg procurement and surrogacy are exploitative practices. While some academics assert that exploitation is serious enough to justify regulation of these practices, two other responses have so far prevailed. One argument locates egg procurement and surrogacy in the intimate sphere of family.... [A] dominant explanatory narrative of ART use situates the technology use and all that accompanies it as a means of family formation. The narrative's main characters are the infertile couples who desperately want children. Within the narrative, their ability and willingness to pay for ART use evidences both their suitability and deservedness as parents. Closely examined, the narrative reveals a market-based test for parental suitability, but the narrative's trick is to shift the gaze to the yearning and need — the story's emotional content. That content is compelling because it is real. Infertility is not simply a medical condition for many. It causes emotional pain, loss of self-esteem, and breaks up relationships. Yet, centering the yearning for family also elides the commercial nature of the practices that enable family formation through ART use. Hence, women who provide eggs for others' use are called "donors," even though they receive thousands of dollars for doing so. They provide a "gift" that is priceless, and yet has been carefully priced.

The second response simply accepts the inequalities on which reproductive tourism depends as natural features of a market economy. After all, these inequalities pre-exist reproductive tourism and would persist without reproductive tourism. The free market narrative directly counters the claim of exploitation in a way that the family formation narrative does not. In the free market narrative, women who provide eggs and bear children for others are free agents. The women who participate opt into the market. Yet volunteers can be exploited. Perhaps more telling is the way that some fertility buyers use this narrative to position themselves as the means of eliminating inequality. In a New York Times story, a surrogacy client explained the decision to travel from the United Kingdom to India: "You cannot ignore the discrepancies between Indian poverty and Western wealth.... We try our best not to abuse this power. Part of our choice to come here was the idea that there was an opportunity to help someone in India." This explanation reveals the sense of noblesse oblige at the core of the market narrative.

Both narratives express a sense of entitlement. Purchaser's power may account for some of that. Yet the claim to purchaser's power here is not based solely on greater wealth. The use of women for their biological capacity to reproduce, in a context in which geopolitical differences between departure points and destination spots often account for the wealth disparities, supports a sense of entitlement. . . .

Racial identity figures significantly in ART use. . . . In the gamete market, racial preferences seem natural and unobjectionable because they enable the resulting family to look like a biologically-related family. The goal of a racially matched family in a commercial context may have two problematic effects. First, it makes race a commodity in the gamete market. Second, the naturalizing effect of the racial preference is elastic. It makes other genetic preferences seem both natural and acceptable, thus clouding what might otherwise seem to be obvious eugenic preferences. . . .

When gestational surrogacy is used, the intended parents or third parties provide the gametes. As a result, . . . [r]ace matching plays a smaller role in the preferences of fertility travelers who seek surrogates. Hence, racial differences between fertility travelers and surrogates are more common than they are in the egg market. This enables sites such as India to flourish as destination spots for White fertility travelers from Western Europe and the United States.

The racial difference might even make a destination spot more attractive. The character of the mainstream media's attention to India's surrogacy industry illustrates the reasons for this point. The media stories represent the surrogacy business in India as exotic because of racial, cultural, and economic differences between the fertility tourists from the United Kingdom and United States and the Indian surrogates. At the same time, the stories make India's role in reproductive tourism seem like a predictable aspect of India's success in positioning itself as the destination spot for outsourcing the service economy. What these stories express is the persistence of a form of racial distancing that may make hiring a woman to gestate, give birth to, and give up a child psychologically comfortable. It is a post-industrial form of master-servant privilege. In effect, it makes the non-White woman in the non-White country a marketable source of surrogacy. . . .

Depictions in Popular Culture: Made in India (2010)

This documentary follows Lisa and Brian from San Antonio, Texas, to Mumbai, India, where they undergo IVF, producing embryos that a local surrogate will gestate. Along the way, viewers meet various intermediaries and clinicians as well as the surrogate, Aasia, who can neither read nor write and, despite embarrassment, has agreed to participate "because of my poverty," with the hope she will have money to save for her three children. Lisa and Brian are candid that they have chosen India because they cannot afford to pay for surrogacy at U.S. prices. At the same time, they convince themselves that the $7,000 that they believe Aasia will receive will allow her to "have a better life."

When seven months pregnant, Aasia moves to a "surrogacy house," where others like her are staying. Complications cause her to be rushed to a hospital other than the one arranged for delivery, where twin girls arrive early. This hospital resists identifying Lisa and Brian as the babies' parents on their birth certificates, preventing them from getting U.S. passports for travel back to San Antonio, requiring the U.S. Consulate to intervene, and adding drama to the story. These difficulties parallel problems on Aasia's side of the bargain, as we learn of a discrepancy between the $7,000 that Lisa and Brian thought she was promised and the much lower sum she is told she will receive — a discrepancy that is not clearly resolved by the end of the film.

Lisa and Brian are determined to have a baby, and Aasia is charming, with her frequent giggles, and clearly devoted to her own family. They all evoke sympathy in one way or another. If there are villains in this piece, they are the intermediaries. Activists trying to impose more restrictions on India's surrogacy industry recognize the challenges. What would you recommend? What would your proposal mean not only for Aasia and her counterparts but for those like Lisa and Brian as well?

PROBLEMS

1. Samantha, an unmarried attorney, asked her friend Daryl if he would provide semen so that she could conceive a child by alternative insemination. Daryl agreed, Samantha conceived and gave birth to twins, and then a disagreement erupted. Daryl sought recognition as the twins' father, with all parental rights and responsibilities.

He sues in Kansas on behalf of himself and the children after Samantha refuses to include him in the children's lives. Daryl contends that Samantha assured him he would be the child's father and that he need not put that understanding in writing. The parties do not dispute the following: Both Samantha and Daryl lived in Kansas at all relevant times, but they could not find a local physician who would inseminate an unmarried woman. As a result, the insemination took place in Missouri. The twins were born in Kansas. Kansas has a statute that says a man who provides semen for artificial insemination is "not the birth father" absent a written agreement with the woman. Missouri has no such statute. The parties never entered any written agreement.

What result and why in Daryl's suit in Kansas? Could Daryl have sued in Missouri? Should he have done so? Why? See In re K.M.H., 169 P.3d 1025, 1030 (Kan. 2007), *cert. denied sub nom.* Hendrix v. Harrington, 555 U.S. 937 (2008) (discussed in Chapter 7, section B1).

2. Shannon, a nurse who works in the high-risk obstetrics and delivery department of a major metropolitan hospital, has decided that she wants to serve as a gestational surrogate. She states that her own children, ages seven

and nine, and her work have persuaded her of the value of helping adults who cannot procreate without assistance. Her husband supports her interest. She submits an application to a surrogacy "matchmaker" whom she finds online; after a couple, intended parents who live in another state, select Shannon, the matchmaker — who is a licensed attorney — mails her a contract and encourages Shannon to review the contract with her own attorney before any medical procedures take place. (The intended parents have several frozen embryos, made from donor eggs and the husband's semen.)

Shannon has made an appointment with you, her local attorney, to review the contract, which you have not yet seen. She has already informed you that, although the contract states that the birth and delivery of the child will take place in the intended parents' home state (which uses intent to determine parentage and issues prebirth judgments of parentage), she wants to deliver in her home state, at the hospital where she works and where she trusts the obstetrical facilities and staff. Her home state, however, has no statute governing surrogacy and no appellate judicial opinions on the subject. In preparing to meet with Shannon and review the contract, what specific issues will you put on your "check list" to make certain that the contract covers in a way that will avoid possible problems for your client? How would you counsel Shannon more generally about her plan to become a gestational surrogate?[77]

---

[77] See generally Kelly A. Anderson, Certainty in an Uncertain World: The Ethics of Drafting Surrogacy Contracts, 21 Geo. J. Legal Ethics 615 (2008); Carbone & Miller, supra note [66].

TABLE OF CASES

Principal cases are indicated by italics.

INDEX